WAR HORSE

WAR HORSE

A History of the Military Horse and Rider

LOUIS A. DIMARCO

WESTHOLME
Yardley

Frontis: "The military seat as it is. A plummet line from the shoulder should fall an inch behind the heel. [Cavalry Regulations, Page 11] Saddling. The saddle is to be placed on the middle of the Horses back; the front of it the breadth of a hand behind the play of the shoulder. [Cavalry Regulations, Page 5.]" From *Cavalry: Its History and Tactics* (1853) by Louis Edward Nolan, reprinted by Westholme Publishing, 2007.

First Westholme paperback September 2012.

Westholme Publishing, LLC
904 Edgewood Road
Yardley, Pennsylvania 19067
Visit our Web site at www.westholmepublishing.com

ISBN: 978-1-59416-172-8
Also available as an eBook.

Produced in the United States of America.

To my wife, Colonel Joyce P. DiMarco, whose love of soldiers and horses is the real inspiration for this work, and to my daughters Cara and Gina whose efforts maintaining our barn and small herd of equine partners permitted the completion of this project.

CONTENTS

INTRODUCTION

The war horse and rider were one of history's most enduring military fighting systems. They were a key to the success of Alexander the Great in the fourth century BC, and, likewise, were integral to British General Edmund Allenby's successful Palestine campaign in the same part of the world 2,200 years later. The similarities between Alexander's lance-armed companion cavalry and the Indian lancers of Allenby's cavalry divisions were far greater than the differences. The war horse and rider was a viable military weapons system for more than 3,000 years, far longer than any other military system. There were many reasons for this phenomenal endurance. One was that man-made technology could not outperform the horse as a means of transporting soldiers in battle until the middle of the twentieth century. Also, the horse is a large and powerful animal. As long as physical size and strength were a critical component of close combat fighting, the horse was an important contributor to combat power. The horse was not only a weapon that had a material effect on the battlefield, but also was a psychological weapon that by its mere presence could effect the morale of friendly and enemy troops. The physical presence of horses could inspire courage or instill uncontrollable fear. Even after technology gave soldiers firearms that provided protection from horses, it still took another half a century before the capabilities of technology were sufficient to erase the psychological impact of the horse in battle. The intent of this work is to study the long and fascinating history of the war horse and rider as a military weapons system—possibly the most important and least understood martial arm in military history.

This work examines the horse and rider as a weapons system used in battle—it is not a battle history of cavalry. It reveals the slow and logical evolution of the horse's employment in warfare. The chapters examine how horses were organized within the important armies of history, what type of arms were used in conjunction with horses, and what type of tactics directed the war horse and rider on the battlefield. However, weapons and tactics were only part of the success of mounted forces. The horse itself was also important. The physical characteristics of the horses, breeding programs, and training for military operations were all important. Horsemanship was also a critical component of effective mounted operations. The utility of the horse was greatly dependent on the rider's skill under the stressful conditions of combat. Horse mastership–the science of managing the health and welfare of horses–was also an important aspect of the success of mounted operations. An army's ability to manage its horses could be the difference between battles and campaigns won or lost.

The type of horse used for military operations is an important and much neglected aspect of military history. Much military history assumes generically that all military horses were the same. Such an assumption is akin to assuming all rifles were the same. For most of history, horses were described broadly as types. Horses within a type are common to a geographic area and broadly share some physical characteristics. Breeds are more specific than types. Specific breed identification requires not just careful management to achieve desired physical characteristics, but also detailed record keeping to document that management. Breed organization in its modern form does not appear until the seventeenth century, but even after that period important and recognizable types continued to influence military operations until the end of large-scale mounted military operations. The distinction between type and breed is important, but less so in military history because both terms are sufficient to identify and highlight the characteristics of the important war horses used by various armies over the ages.

The first chapters of this work set the tone for those that follow, establishing the fact that early mounted forces were certainly as equal in importance to infantry–if not the premier military arm. Even without saddles and stirrups, mounted forces were a critical component of ancient warfare. The mounted military power of the Middle East was a force to which Europe's only effective response was Alexander the Great. Rome, despite all its great achievements, was not a state that fielded particularly effective mounted forces, and this characteristic of the Roman military helped define the limits of the Empire.

During the Medieval period, mounted forces became unquestionably the most important military forces in Asia and Europe. But the European knight was a somewhat limited military tool that was only dominant in Europe because of the unique social and political conditions on the continent. The Eastern mounted forces, in contrast, were a true comprehensive military force. The Crusades provide evidence that the Eastern approach to employing the war horse was far superior to that of the knights of the West. The Central Asian steppe horse archers also demonstrated the superiority of the well-trained versatile horseman, using the horse as a firing platform as well as for shock action.

The seventeenth and eighteenth centuries witnessed the rise of military professionalism and resulted in the formation of very competent mounted military organizations in Western Europe for the first time since the Romans. Advances in riding techniques, training, and horse breeding were part of the overall advance of military professionalism. Scientific riding and horse training principles date from this period. Among horses, some of the first recognizable modern breeds, including the hot-blooded Andalusians of Spain and the various warmbloods of Germany, appear in military organizations during this period.

It was during this period that controlled mass cavalry charges against infantry were first deployed. Infantry began to develop the tactics and technology to defend against this kind of cavalry attack; however, the psychological impact of mounted formations on battlefields remained considerable. Fear was an important–possibly the most important–aspect of employing war horses. Speed and timing were also keys to success. Despite infantry firearms and protective formations, charges by mounted forces were both common and had decisive effects.

During the Napoleonic period mass conscript armies, accompanied by large cavalry formations, dominated the battlefields of Europe. Mounted units made up in size and enthusiasm for what they lacked in professional riding skills, making the point that professional armies had their limitations and that expert horsemanship was not always necessary for effective battlefield results. However, declining horsemanship and horse mastership had important negative operational consequences in several important campaigns and battles.

The Industrial Revolution's impact on mounted forces was primarily in the development of firearms that finally achieved longer range, higher rates of fire, and greater accuracy. These new weapons, used by both infantry and mounted troops, had a great effect on the role of horses on the battlefield. American cavalry of the Civil War demonstrated that modern carbine-armed cavalry gave commanders a highly mobile and lethal force that could attack mounted with shock action or dismounted with firepower. Small numbers of American Indians and South African Boers who used the mobility of their war horses to wage very successful guerrilla campaigns against nations far larger and with much greater resources in the closing decades of the nineteenth century further demonstrated the effectiveness of horse mobility combined with firepower. However, the combination of firepower and horse mobility was largely ignored by the major military powers of Europe. The Franco-Prussian War of 1870 reinforced the traditional shock-focused employment of cavalry and set the conditions for generally ineffective cavalry tactics by the French and Germans in World War I.

World War I and World War II demonstrated that a general purpose cavalry well armed with rifles still had utility on the battlefield, but the challenges of increasingly lethal firepower made the successful employment of horse-mounted units more difficult. As infantry weapons became easier to use and more deadly, the cavalry charge became more difficult to accomplish successfully because infantry no longer feared the charging war horse and rider. Improving automotive technology erased the advantage of mobility of horse-mounted forces in World War II. Only Russia fielded large mounted forces that had a major effect on operations. After World War II, continued improvements in automotive technology ensured the end of large-scale military horse operations.

The thousands of years from the ancient Egyptians to World War II is a great expanse of history. Covering such a vast period of time in one volume requires deliberate steps to limit the discussion of the topic. Thus, this work does not include much discussion of the war horse in the Far East or in South America. Another topic not addressed is the role and contribution of logistics and artillery horses, though these horses were critical to military success and often outnumbered the horses of the cavalry. Space constraints also require the omission of many important battles involving horses and cavalry including the famous charge of the light brigade at Balaclava, the destruction of Custer's command at the Little Bighorn River, and the charge of the light horsemen at Beersheba. Enough battle descriptions have been included, it is hoped, to illustrate the combat environment in which horses were placed and the complex factors which influenced the success or failure of mounted operations. Finally, some horse breeds and types that have played a role in military operations are not mentioned. Again, limitations of space have constrained the selection to some of the most important and famous types and breeds that are generally representative of the war horse.

This work was only possible because of the research of many talented historians and horse experts, the written narratives of commanders and cavalrymen, and the surviving records of armies and units. These are recorded in the notes and references. The initiative of Westholme Publishing, who specifically wanted a discussion of the horse as a weapon, served as an inspiration for this project. The talents of excellent editors, and the interest of the knowledgeable members of the Society of the Military Horse, also contributed to the merits of the project. Though all efforts have been made to be accurate throughout, any failures in fact or analysis are completely the responsibility of the author.

Chapter One

THE ANCIENTS

Far back, far back in our dark soul the horse prances.... The horse, the horse! The symbol of surging potency and power of movement, of action.
–D. H. Lawrence, *Apocalypse*

In the fall of 2001 television audiences were surprised to see via satellite video the modern-day use of one of the oldest weapons of war. Most viewers thought this weapon was as obsolete as the smoothbore musket. Ridden by American special operations forces and their northern Afghanistan tribesmen allies, the Americans integrated the war horse into a combat system that combined laser designators, global positioning systems, wireless communications, and sophisticated precision ordinance delivered by U.S. Air Force bombers. What audiences around the world witnessed was a weapons system–rider, war horse, and associated equipment–which has been part of warfare for more than 3,000 years.

Evolution and Domestication of the Horse

To understand the war horse first requires an understanding of the horse's origin and its evolved relationship with man. Horses are an old and hardy survivor of literally millions of years. The horse is a member of the mammal order Perissodactyla, which represents mammals of the odd-toe variety. Three families are members of this order: Equidae, Tapiridae, and Rhinocerotidae. The latter two, represented in modern form by the tapir and the rhinoceros, are much closer to the original species than the Equidae. The horse's ancient predecessor was a small fox-size animal called the Hyracotherium that existed approximately 65 million years ago. Like all Perissodactyla at the time, the Hyracotherium was comfortable living in a relatively wet and forested environment. Over the next several million years, a shifting environment brought about changes in the Equidae.

Climate and geography changed as ice ages came and went, tectonic plates shifted, and untold diseases and natural calamities ravaged the planet. The Northern Hemisphere, once very wet, became dry grassland in many places. The Equidae adapted physically by breeding for speed that enabled survival. They became taller, and the original five toes became three, and eventually one. Nine different species of Equidae evolved over this period representing donkeys, zebras, and horses. Of the nine varieties, the two most relevant to the history of war and horses are *Equus caballus* and *Equus przewalskii*. *Equus caballus* is the modern domesticated horse in all its variety of breeds. *Equus przewalskii* is similar to the domestic horse in many respects, and in fact the two species can interbreed and produce nonsterile offspring–a characteristic that none of the others in the Equidae family share. Popularly known as the Przewalski horse, *Equus przewalskii*, became extinct in the wild in the twentieth century. Today preserves and zoos carefully manage the species.[1]

The domestic horse, *Equus caballus*, descends from a variety of wild equids that ranged over the whole Northern Hemisphere and South America as early as the end of the last ice age–approximately 8000 BC.[2] Scientists have identified four major types of postglacial ancestors of the modern horse: (1) a Celtic pony that resembles the modern breeds of Exmoor and Icelandic ponies; (2) a Norse horse resembling the modern breeds of the Norwegian Fjord pony and the Noriker heavy horse; (3) a Central Asian horse resembling the Akhal-Teke of Central Asia; and (4) a small horse of western Asia resembling the modern breed of Caspian horse.[3] Evidence retrieved from the steppe regions of eastern Europe and central Asia indicates domestication occurred in about 4000 BC among nomadic tribes living in the central Asian steppes north of the Black Sea and Caucasus Mountains.[4] There are also hypotheses that domestication occurred independently at different points from central Europe through western and central Asia to eastern Siberia.[5] By 2000 BC, domesticated horses were widespread throughout the ancient world from Europe to Asia and into the Middle East.[6]

The first domestic use of horses was as a food source. One theory for the first experiments in riding is that at some point herders achieved the ability to ride the animals as a means of facilitating control over them. Another theory, advanced by Marsha A. Levine, is that the domestication of the horse came about through the taming and adoption of the foals of mares kept for food. These youngsters, much easier to handle and more comfortable around humans, gradually were broken for riding and became a useful means of transport and work. Close scientific analysis of horse bits found in archeological digs in Dereivka, Ukraine, combined with carbon dating techniques indicates that the earliest evidence of ridden horses dates to about 4000 BC–which means that the art of riding horses predates the invention of the wheel.[7]

Chariot Warfare

Almost as soon as man discovered the horse's utility as transportation he incorporated the animal into his war-making capability. The first military use of horses was as

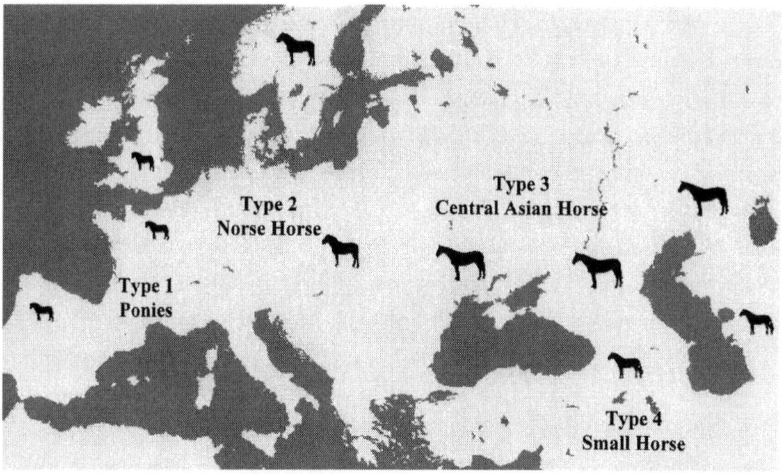

The four major original "types" of domestic horses and their general locations in Europe and Asia. The Przewalski horse is not depicted because it is not genetically of the same species as the domestic horse. (*Author*)

part of a chariot system in the third millennium BC. The battle standard of the ancient Mesopotamian city of Ur, circa 2600 BC, depicts war chariots. Most theories reason that the early use of the horse as part of a chariot system, as opposed to riding, was a function of the small size of the early breeds in central and southwest Asia.

The earliest indicators of horse-drawn wagons date from clay tablets found in Uruk in southern Mesopotamia—within the borders of modern-day Iraq. These small, simple diagrams show both wheeled and sled-mounted boxes with what appears to be a tongue for harnessing oxen or horses. The pictographs date from approximately 3200–3100 BC, although no clear association with horses can be drawn.[8] However, the depiction of "battle wagons" on the wooden box known as the standard of Ur offers much clearer evidence. These illustrations of vehicles may represent the earliest war chariots and show that they were relatively large. In addition to their box shape, the chariots had four solid wood wheels and were pulled by a team of two or four draught animals—either small horses or asses. A fixed center pole harnessed the animals to the wagon but made it very unstable when turning. Traces joined the inner two animals; the outer animals set a pace rather than pulling the load. The vehicle was low to the ground, and large enough for two individuals to stand one behind the other. The forward person drove the animals while the rear person was responsible for engaging the enemy with javelins. A noseband controlled the speed of the horses. Voice commands or the use of a whip controlled direction.[9] A yoke system attached the horses' harnesses to the center pole. Recent scholarship indicates that a variety of different strap arrangements existed. In some cases a neck yoke transmitted strain to the shoulders but inhibited the horses' breathing; in other cases a dorsal yoke system transmitted the point of effort to the chest. The former system appears, at least from illustrations, to be the most common with Bronze Age chariots, although the latter system is optimal for control and endurance.[10]

Javelins were stowed in quivers mounted on the vehicle. The use of javelins indicates that the battle wagons had to close within a relatively short range of the enemy to be effective. In fact, ancient depictions show vehicles riding over fallen enemy warriors. There was undoubtedly a psychological component to their employment–setting a precedent for mounted forces for centuries to come. The vehicles were an elite element of the army manned by members of the royal household. No evidence of these battle wagons exists in the last three centuries of the third millennium BC, which may indicate that over time infantry recognized their weaknesses and became accustomed to their presence, and this reduced their effectiveness.[11]

The heavy four-wheeled chariot had obvious battlefield limitations: it was difficult to maneuver, it was expensive, it required training of both drivers and animals, and it was not very stable. However, it established the precedent that a horse-centric weapons system had advantages over standard dismounted infantry forces. The advantages included speed, firepower (the number of javelins carried was greater than those of the dismounted individual), and some protection. These advantages further encouraged design improvements of the wheeled vehicle to reduce many of the limitations of the four-wheeled battle wagon and resulted in a new two-wheeled war chariot that would prove effective in combat operations during the second millennium BC.

The central Middle Eastern regions of the Mitanni kingdom and Canaan–a loose confederation of city states–sometimes united, sometimes not–improved upon the battle wagons of Mesopotamia in the middle of the sixteenth century BC. A two-wheel design became standard, as did a two-man crew: driver and a warrior. The warrior was an archer. The vehicle was sturdy and had a solid-wood body with a center-mounted axle. A four-spoke wheel that was lighter and larger, thus providing more ground clearance, replaced the solid wheel. The technology for the two-wheeled war chariot migrated in all directions, reaching the Egyptians via the Hyksos conquerors by 1650 BC. By 1400 BC the founders of the Sheng dynasty arrived with chariots in northern China.[12] Within 300 years the horse-drawn war chariot was the standard of advanced military technology throughout the civilized world. It would remain the preeminent weapon of war for about 600 years.

The chariot was an expensive weapon of war. It took time, skilled craftsmanship, and money to build; then it required constant maintenance. In addition, it required breeding or importing horses, and training them to pull it. These significant invest-

The battle standard of Ur. The standard clearly depicts the Ur four wheeled battle wagons from about 2,600 B.C. (*Author*)

ments of time and money spawned the rise of an aristocratic warrior class who specialized in chariot warfare and its associated skills. They managed an entire economic and social segment of society that designed, built, and maintained the vehicles, as well as providing and caring for the horses. The Mariyannu were the chariot warrior class within the Mitanni Kingdom.

The Mariyannu were professional warriors and, more specifically, professional charioteers. A fascinating training document for chariot horses is evidence of their sophistication. This training document comes from a Mitanni charioteer named Kikkuli who was enticed into the service of Mitanni's western neighbor and rival, the Hittite king Suppililiuma. Kikkuli's task was to improve the quality of the Hittite chariot arm. The document, called the "Kikkuli Texts," dates from approximately 1345 BC.[13]

Kikkuli's instructions were comprehensive. He described the evaluation and selection of horses, including techniques for determining any tendency toward respiratory ailments. He also carefully explained horse feeding and diet. The horses were gently broken to the task of chariot driving. They were first trained by hand, then with an empty chariot, and finally with a loaded chariot and driver. In 1991 Ann Hyland, a doctoral student at New England University in Australia, replicated the Kikkuli seven-month training method with a herd of 10 modern Arabian horses. She found that by following the methods described by Kikkuli she was able to keep the entire herd sound and significantly increase their endurance–vital elements in chariot horse training. A horse's endurance gave an army operational and tactical mobility.[14] A horse had to get to the battle (operational mobility) and fight effectively when it got there (tactical mobility). For example, Hittite charioteers in one instance were required to march 48 miles overnight and fight the next morning.[15]

Chariot culture migrated from Mesopotamia through the Mitanni to the Hittites who controlled the dominant kingdom of central Anatolia. The Hittites generally adopted the Mariyannu approach to chariot warfare but placed a greater emphasis on close combat rather than archery. The Hittite tactical concept for the employment of heavy chariots was similar to that depicted in older battle wagon drawings—charging over helpless infantry. The heavy chariot was an offensive weapon. It was designed to physically break infantry formations, and once the formations were broken, to ride down the disorganized opposition and dispatch them, using spears and javelins, as well as horses' hooves and chariot wheels. In this role, it was the army's offensive centerpiece. The focus of army tactics was to bring the heavy chariots to bear in the decisive action of the battle.[16]

The Hittite approach to chariot warfare increasingly included armoring the chariot crew and the horses. Scale armor cloaks were characteristic of both Mitannian and Hittite chariot crews. The cloaks covered the shoulders and were typically calve-length. A wide bronze collar protected the neck, and a scale or bronze helmet provided head cover. The horses were the most vulnerable component of the system and also required armor. The horse's armor typically consisted of a scale mail "coat" covering the back of the horse and may also have included a neck-protecting mail collar.[17]

While most of the information on the Mesopotamian battle wagons comes from interpretations of crude drawings, specific and detailed knowledge of early two-wheeled war chariots is based on archeological research and evidence from ancient Egypt. This includes the discovery of numerous well-preserved and conclusively dated vehicles. In 1922 archeologist Howard Carter discovered the incredibly well-preserved chariots of the Egyptian pharaoh Tutankhamen. These chariots, dated to the year 1323 BC, illustrate the technological changes that had occurred in the 1300 years since the battle wagons of Ur. Also discovered among the royal treasures in the tombs were the pharaoh's weapons of war—composite bows and bits of horse harness.

The Hyksos, foreigners who ruled Egypt from 1674 to 1565 BC, introduced the war chariot to the Egyptians. However, the heavy war chariot of the central Middle East did not perfectly meet the needs of the Egyptians. Therefore the Egyptian chariot evolved unique characteristics that complemented and improved the Egyptian way of war. One reason the heavy war chariot did not work for the Egyptians was the nature of the Egyptian army. The Egyptians were a culture that made a virtue of the organization of their population, and their army correspondingly was infantry based, as opposed to the Hittites and Mitanni where the horse and the aristocratic chariot warrior were central to the culture. After the eviction of the Hyksos, Egyptians discovered that under some conditions Egyptian infantry were at a great disadvantage when facing chariot warriors. The solution to this threat was to develop an Egyptian chariot arm. The purpose of the Egyptian chariot force, unlike the Hittite's, was to counter the adversary's chariots. This required a more maneuverable chariot that could accelerate quickly. The other factor that influenced Egyptian chariot design was terrain. The Egyptian chariots often had to contend with deep sand and other desert conditions, which necessitated a lighter, more versatile model.

The Egyptians gradually adapted the chariot to their needs. They mounted the wheel to the rear of the center of gravity, which created a more stable vehicle after loading and attaching it to animals. It also decreased its turning radius, making the vehicle much more maneuverable. The number of spokes increased, as did the wheel size, giving the vehicle greater strength, higher ground clearance, and improved mobility over rough terrain. Improvements in carpentry techniques also allowed the design of a relatively high curved forward surface that tapered to the rear. Hardwood used to build the vehicle offered greater strength with less weight. In addition, a major weight-saving feature was the construction of a woven wickerlike floor. This floor also had some flexibility, which further increased the stability of the crew when faced with rough terrain or rapid maneuvering. The new war chariot, as employed by the Egyptians, was an extremely light vehicle, weighing approximately 75 pounds, was quite maneuverable, had a tight-turning radius, accelerated very fast, and was easily handled by a single warrior.[18]

The composite bow was also an essential component of the Egyptian war chariot. Javelins carried by the early battle wagons had significant limitations. They had very limited range when thrown from a vehicle–and were particularly ineffective if the vehicle was moving. In fact, the weapon was only effective when the thrower dismounted. Also, javelins were of limited use against enemy infantry and even less effective against other chariots. The composite bow was the weapon of choice for the Egyptian charioteer. Unlike the Hittites, the Egyptians did not employ the war chariot was as a weapon for shock action. Instead, they used it as a highly mobile firing platform.

Conclusively tracing the origin of the composite bow is impossible. However, the available evidence suggests that the bow evolved over time, much like the chariot. People discovered, tested, and adopted each facet of its complex construction independently, and then disseminated the design information through the ancient world by word of mouth, commerce, and warfare. Most likely it originated in the familiar areas of the southern steppes where lands occupied by skilled barbarian hunters touched upon those of emerging urban civilizations and their craftsman. By the second millennium BC, the composite bow was available in essentially the form known today. The composite bow differed from other bows in its construction. Bowyers used several different types of wood, bone, and glue to create a bow with far greater power than bows fashioned from a single stock of wood. Modern tests indicate that a second-millennium composite bow was likely to have about 100 yards greater range than the standard stick bow of the period. This special construction, however, made the composite bow extremely expensive and time-consuming to manufacture. These characteristics made it an impractical arm for standard infantry bowmen. However, it was a weapon ideally suited to specially selected, highly skilled, and elite warriors associated with the royal household: charioteers.

In the several hundred years between the use of the Ur battle wagon and the documented employment of the war chariot by the Egyptians, horses had evolved. During the period of the Ur battle wagon, horses were still a relatively rare and exotic phenomena in southwest Asia. Donkeys or onagers were more likely to draw battle wagons than were horses. By the second millennium, horses were more common, and humans had developed a greater understanding of their training and control. All the great empires established their own stud farm systems to provide mounts and retrain captured stock; horses were among the most prized war booty. In addition, merchants established a lively horse trade between the fringes of the European and Asian steppes and the heart of the Middle East. The horse was also larger (though still generally the size of a large modern pony), faster, and had a more refined appearance–a function of selective breeding by humans.

Horsemen developed more efficient means of controlling horses. The skeletal evidence from archeological digs in Egypt dated to 1675 BC indicates that horse bits were in use by this period. This evidence comes in the form of unnatural wear observed in the horse skeleton's rear teeth. This wearing on the teeth is consistent with the presence and pressure of a bone or bronze bit.[19] The archaeologists also discovered fragments likely to have been bits. These indicate the invention of simple snaffle bits consisting of a single or joined bar with connections for reins on either end. The invention of the bit permitted the chariot driver to control speed and direction simultaneously. Applying or releasing even pressure on the horse's mouth through the bit controlled speed. Increasing pressure on one side of the bit or the other controlled direction. Unlike the earlier noseband, which could constrict respiration, the mouth bit gave control without limiting the horse's performance.

Three critical components combined to create the war chariot, the first effective horse-based weapons system: lethality with the composite bow, speed and endurance in the trained modern horse, and a stable and maneuverable two-wheeled platform with improved harness. This system revolutionized the nature of warfare. Chariot-based armies dominated the centers of the civilized world in the Middle East from around 1800 BC to approximately 900 BC. The composite bow and a large ammuni-

A tapestry of an Egyptian war chariot piloted by the pharaoh on display at the U.S. Army Command and Staff College. The pharaoh is often depicted alone in the chariot though for practical purposes the vehicle required a driver and an archer. (*Author*)

tion supply permitted chariot warriors to decimate infantry formations from outside the range of most dismounted weapons. The speed and maneuverability of the war chariot permitted the charioteers to rapidly break contact and reposition if the slower infantry moved against them. The devastating fire killed enemy infantry, disrupted the integrity of their formations, and created opportunities for allied infantry attacks.

Egyptian drawings show pharaohs riding alone in the chariot with the reins wrapped around their waist as they simultaneously fired their bows. This is an idealized view of the pharaoh's prowess as a charioteer. The bowman did have the reins wrapped around his waist, permitting him to work his bow, but the reins' purpose was to assist the bowman in maintaining his balance. A charioteer drove into battle with the reins in one hand; the other arm wielded a shield. Egyptian charioteers also wore helmets and bronze scale armor. They also used armor and leather on the chariot to add protection, although it was always limited because of weight. Heavy cloth and occasionally armor was used to protect the horses.[20]

Under the right conditions, bow-armed charioteers in battle could destroy an enemy army without ever physically coming into contact with it. The most effective defense against enemy chariots was other chariot formations. Chariot against chariot warfare was often the decisive opening phase of battle. The adversaries had to drive off the chariots of their opponent in order to engage the unprotected infantry. After establishing favorable conditions, long-range effective chariot archery or a chariot charge by heavy chariots set the conditions for close infantry combat. Sometimes infantry combat never occurred because successful chariot skirmishing forced the bulk of the opposition's infantry to withdraw without offering battle.

Chariot combat pitted the Egyptians' speed and maneuverability against the Hittites' armored heavy chariot. In such an engagement, the goal of the Egyptians was to prevent the heavy chariots from closing on their infantry. They did this by closing the range in a countercharge, avoiding physical contact, disrupting the formation of heavy chariots, and most importantly, killing charioteers and horses with deadly and accurate archery. If the enemy charioteers chose to attack the Egyptian chariots, then the Egyptians accomplished their mission. Delaying the adversary's chariots sufficiently so that the Egyptian infantry had time to prepare to withstand the heavy chariot charge also accomplished the mission. After dealing with the enemy's chariots, the Egyptian chariots turned their attention to the enemy's infantry.

A component of the Egyptian chariot weapons system that is not well understood or well documented is the chariot runners. Chariot runners were lightly armed infantry who followed closely behind the chariots. From this vantage, they executed a variety of actions in support of the chariot operation: They could rescue dismounted chariot crews whose horses had been wounded or killed in action; they could use their bows and javelins to attack the enemy charioteers; they could kill or capture dismounted enemy charioteers; and they could replace Egyptian charioteer casualties, as well as claim and fight from unmanned chariots. The chariot runners gave added versatility to the Egyptian chariot arm and reduced its vulnerability in a wide variety of situations.[21]

Trained and conditioned horses permitted charioteers to move 30 to 40 miles in a day, which allowed commanders to send messages long distances and also allowed maneuver on an operational scale. The ability to quickly move across long distances allowed commanders to capitalize on tactical victory by pursuit and destruction of the enemy. This capability made tactical victory both operationally and strategically significant. It also allowed them to control ground beyond the immediate presence of the army–facilitating the consolidation of conquests.

Chariots in Battle: Kadesh, 1275 BC

Most of the major characteristics of chariot warfare are represented in the great chariot battle of Kadesh in 1275 BC.[22] This battle not only demonstrated the decisive role of chariots but also highlighted the two competing tactical concepts of chariot warfare. The battle for Kadesh also holds a unique place in military history as it is the first engagement from which the surviving records are complete enough to permit a general reconstruction of events.

Kadesh was a confrontation between the Egyptian army under Pharaoh Ramses II and the Hittite army led by its king, Muwatallish. The battle occurred in May 1275 BC on the flat plain west of the strategically critical city of Kadesh. Although the detailed interpretations of the battle by historians vary greatly, the Egyptians documented the battle well, and enough uncontested material remains to demonstrate the nature of chariot warfare in the Bronze Age. The following description of the battle highlights the generally accepted course of events.[23]

Kadesh was located astride one of the key valley approaches from the Mediterranean Sea to the interior plains of northern Syria. During the time of Ramses II, Kadesh had been a vassal of Egypt, but the ruler of Kadesh wanted to test the political expediency of changing allegiances. Ramses decided to use military force to prevent an alliance between Kadesh and the Hittite Kingdom. In April, he marched his assembled army from Egypt through Canaan and on to Kadesh. By mid-May the Egyptians were within a day's march of the city.

The Egyptian army marched in five divisions. Four marched under the direct command of the pharaoh and organized in march units separated by about 6 miles—less than half a day's march. The Egyptians named the four divisions for Egyptian gods, in order of the march: Amun, P'Re, Ptah, and Sutekh. Each division's strength was about 5,000 soldiers, of which about 4,500 were infantry. Each march unit had its own integral chariot force. This force likely consisted of five 50-chariot squadrons. The chariot force deployed in a screen to the flanks, forward, and to the rear of the infantry main body. The division baggage section trailed the main formation within the chariot screen. Pharaoh Ramses and his entourage traveled with the lead division.

The fifth march unit was the Ne'arin. Historians are uncertain exactly in which way the Ne'arin differed from the main army. Ne'arin literally translates into "young men," and some believe that the unit consisted of relatively new recruits. Other historians believe the unit contained veterans who had remained in the region as garrisons after previous campaigns. Whatever the specific connotation, the unit was certainly the equal of the other Egyptian divisions as it included its own infantry and chariot force. The Ne'arin marched to Kadesh by a different route and carefully timed their arrival to coincide with that of the main body.

As the Egyptian lead element approached Kadesh, two alleged deserters came to the Egyptian camp and provided information that the Hittite army was far to the north and not a threat to the Egyptians. The next day the Amun division crossed the

Orontes River at a ford and moved approximately 3 miles north and encamped within sight of (and west of) Kadesh. The Egyptians set up a light fortification around their camp using shields. As the Egyptian division made camp, they captured two Hittite scouts. Upon harsh interrogation they revealed the location of the Hittite army–only a few kilometers east of the Egyptian camp, shielded from sight by high ground, the city, and the citadel of Kadesh. The pharaoh immediately dispatched his chief military adviser, the vizier, to contact each of the other three division commanders and order them to rapidly reinforce the pharaoh at Kadesh.

On the day after the pharaoh's arrival at Kadesh, the P'Re division forded the Orontes River and began the last leg of their quick march to reinforce the pharaoh before the Hittites could mass against him. As the division crossed the plain west of Kadesh, almost in sight of the pharaoh's camp, the march column of the P'Re division was struck by a charging formation of Hittite chariots. The Egyptian sources put the number of enemy chariots at 2,500. Most analysts believe it was much smaller. Still, it had to be a sizable force, possibly as many as 1,000, because the Hittites quickly penetrated the Egyptian chariot screen, and the heavy chariots were in and among the surprised Egyptian infantry. The P'Re division broke. The charging charioteers ran down, trampled, or speared the infantrymen in the path of the charge, a zone likely 1,000 to 1,600 yards wide. The shock of the attack caused the rest of the column to turn and retreat–many northward to the perceived safety of the pharaoh and his Amun division encampment.

The Hittite chariots charged through the Egyptians, then wheeled north and attacked the encampment of Amun. Elements of the P'Re fleeing north were caught up in the continuing battle, but the division baggage at the trail of the column, a lucrative target, was not attacked. The action to the south of the Amun camp did not go unnoticed. The division scrambled to affix harnesses, man chariots, and form the infantry. In the midst of this frantic preparation, the Hittite heavy chariots crashed into the southern and western perimeter of the camp.

As the Hittites broke into the Egyptian camp, the Egyptian infantry panicked. The focus of the Hittite chariot crews, however, was not on the Egyptian warriors but on plunder. This slowed the Hittite attack, allowing the pharaoh the opportunity to mount his Amun chariot force, along with his personal bodyguard, and rally a counterattack. Unlike the Hittite attack, the Egyptians based their technique on maneuverability and firepower. Using the speed and swiftness of their chariots, the Egyptians, led by Ramses II wearing his gold mail coat, avoided close combat and charged and darted through their own camp pouring a withering fire of arrows into the vulnerable Hittite force. At first the Hittites, focused on the riches of the camp and the remnants of the Amun infantry, were unaware of the silent deadly fire decimating charioteers and horses. By the time they knew what was happening, the positions of the Egyptians and Hittites were reversed. Panic spread through the Hittites as they realized they were outnumbered, dismounted, and alone deep in the midst of the revitalized Egyptians.

Under devastatingly accurate fire from the circling Egyptian chariots, the Hittites remounted and fought to extricate themselves from what had become a trap. Without archers they could not fire back, and their slower, less maneuverable chariots could not close on the Egyptian vehicles. More importantly, their horse teams were physically spent after charging through the P'Re division and then the Amun encampment. So, with men and horses exhausted, the Hittite charioteers attempted to retreat to the crossing point of the Orontes River. Whipping their tired mounts into a frenzy the Hittites were punished heavily as the retreating force raced for survival. They left behind a trail of dead and injured horses and men along with broken chariots. Egyptian chariot runners followed closely behind the pharaoh and quickly dispatched the disabled. The Egyptians destroyed the bulk of the Hittite chariot force before it could escape.

King Muwatallish observed the advance of his chariots with see-sawing emotions: he saw their early success, but then dust obscured the battlefield; however, glimpses through the swirling air revealed that the tide of battle had turned. To attempt to save his retreating chariots, Muwatallish ordered his available forces (consisting of his personal guard, the allied leaders, and their guards) in a direct attack against the Egyptian camp. Egyptian records indicate that this force numbered 1,000 chariots, but this estimate is also likely exaggerated. Possibly it was half that number. Still, it was a powerful force, and if this counterattack was successful it would take the unprepared Egyptian camp by surprise and divert the Egyptian chariots away from their pursuit of the fleeing Hittite chariots. The assembled elite around King Muwatallish moved quickly to a ford north of the city of Kadesh. The crossing of the Orontes River was disorganized and time-consuming, but as the chariot force emerged from the ford and reorganized, the Egyptian camp appeared to be unguarded since the Egyptian chariots had departed to the south in pursuit of the first group of Hittites.

As soon as the Hittite force was organized, it attacked the Egyptian camp. As they closed the distance, a line of chariots suddenly rode out to meet them. This was the chariot element of the Ne'arin force arriving to support the main Egyptian army. The Ne'arin deployed to meet the new Hittite attack. The Egyptian chariots, supported by their chariot runners and the following main body of infantry, completely disrupted the new Hittite attack. The hastily assembled Hittite composite force did not have the cohesion of a formal unit, and the Ne'arin chariots broke it apart. The heavy Hittite chariots turned and raced back to the river under a rain of deadly fire from the Egyptian composite bows. The Hittites lost numerous leaders to the chariot archers as well as to the fast flowing waters of the river. The King of Kadesh was among the attacking force; he barely managed to avoid drowning in the scramble to get back across the river.

As the broken remnants of the Hittite chariot force dragged themselves back across the Orontes River, the Egyptians regrouped at their camp. Late in the afternoon the Ptah division arrived to reinforce the Egyptians. Both sides declined to initiate additional operations. The Orontes River, positioned as it was between the two forces, would have put any attacking force at a significant disadvantage. The tactical results of the battle were inconclusive. At the end of the day, the relative position of the two forces had not changed. However both forces were significantly weakened and unable to resume offensive action. The Egyptians had suffered a major setback with the destruction the P'Re division and the assault on the Amun division camp. On the other hand, the cost to the Hittite forces was significant as Ramses' counterattack, combined with the counterattack of the Ne'arin formation, resulted in the complete rout of the bulk of the Hittite chariot force. Ultimately, however, the battle was a strategic defeat for the Egyptians because they did not achieve their objective–regaining control over the important city of Kadesh.

The battle of Kadesh demonstrates the two most important ways chariots fought in the ancient world and provides a comparison of two different approaches to chariot operations. The Hittite tactic was to use the chariot as a close combat weapon relying on mass, speed, and shock-action to achieve decisive effects. The Egyptian approach was more sophisticated. Egyptian chariots relied on speed and maneuverability to avoid close combat while simultaneously using composite bows to inflict casualties and disrupt formations from secure stand-off distances. The Hittite chariots were particularly vulnerable to this fire because the horses were a much easier and, in many ways, more lucrative target than the crews or infantry. A downed Hittite horse effectively stopped the entire chariot system including the three-man crew. One arrow would not have nearly the same effect when fired at an infantry formation or even at a chariot crewman. Once the chariot system stopped, chariot runners or infantry easily dealt with the crew. The battle clearly shows that Egyptian chariots had little difficulty dispatching a superior number of heavy chariots, despite the Hittite's initial advantage of surprise. Firepower was clearly superior to shock action.

The battle of Kadesh eventually resulted in compromise: a mutually agreed sphere of influence for the Egyptian and Hittite kingdoms. This balance of power remained stable for about a hundred years, until around 1200 BC, when the entire region was threatened by an invasion of a group called by scholars the Sea People. The Sea People forced Egypt out of Palestine, and the Levant, and back to Egypt

King Assurbanipal hunting from his chariot, 668 BC. The Assyrians were the last of the war charioteers. As a means of keeping the mobility and firepower of the archer/chariot at a reduced cost, the Assyrians eliminated the vehicle and developed the ability to ride and fight purely from horseback. (*Cavalry Journal* [U.S.])

proper. The Hittite army, built around the offensive chariot, was not able to resist invasion. The Sea People swept away the chariot empire of the Hittites, although they did not replace it. The power vacuum in the central Middle East was filled by a new empire that, like the Hittite, was backed by a horse-centric army.[24]

The Assyrians

The Assyrians acquired a chariot tradition directly from the Mitanni, of whom they were a vassal kingdom. Around 1250 BC they successfully defeated the Mitanni, and with the demise of the Hittites, the Assyrians became the dominant power in the central Middle East. The chariot was vital to their army, and they adopted the Egyptian chariot battle tactics. The Assyrians are particularly important in the history of the war horse because it was during their dominance of the Middle East that the transition from chariot to cavalry took place.

Assyrian charioteers, like their Hittite and Egyptian counterparts, were the elite of the army, the favored arm of the nobility, and the decisive arm of battle. The Assyrian king went to battle in his war chariot. The Assyrians were an infantry-based army with chariots serving as an elite arm that was carefully employed to achieve victory. As in previous times, the chariot was an expensive vehicle to build and operate, and it had limitations that could be exploited by the enemy.

The transition from chariot to horse and rider was a function of two factors: cost and maneuverability. Cost may have been particularly important to the Assyrians who in the early period of the kingdom relied entirely on an agricultural economy. The kingdom did not possess a wealth of natural resources such as iron and wood. As these materials had to be imported, they were expensive and difficult to obtain rapidly, thus increasing the costs and difficulty of building and maintaining chariots.

With regard to maneuverability, Assyrian chariots more closely resembled the heavy chariots of the Hittites, rather than the light, nimble chariots of the Egyptians. They were more durable, but less maneuverable. Assyria's heartland was the upper Tigris River, and the kingdom's borders offered no significant natural barriers to potential invading forces. The terrain beyond the borders to the North and East was mountainous, thus affording sanctuary to raiders. For this reason the Assyrian army frequently campaigned in rough terrain north against the Urartu Kingdom and east against the Elam. Campaigning in difficult terrain damaged and restricted the maneuverability of the Assyrian chariots.

Because of the limitations on the chariot, the Assyrians were forced to consider a cost-effective substitute. They gradually adopted the idea of a chariotless chariot system–that is, the chariot itself was eliminated, but the crew and the horses were retained. By the early ninth century BC, the Assyrians had formed the first formally organized cavalry force. The Assyrian cavalry first relegated chariots to a supporting arm, then to transport vehicles, and ultimately to a military anachronism used exclusively in military ceremonies.

Assyrian cavalry operated in teams of two men. The leader was the archer and his partner the shield man. In combat they rode side by side, the archer firing his composite bow, while the shield man held both horses' reins and protected the riders. This system, though somewhat awkward in combat, was less expensive, more mobile, faster, and offered similar firepower capability to the chariot system. Other Middle Eastern kingdoms soon followed the Assyrian example, and chariots rapidly disappeared from the ancient battlefield.

The early Assyrian cavalry, under the reign of Ashurnasipal II (884–859 BC), was not a perfect weapons system, however. Horsemanship was in its infancy and the accepted riding technique was a carry-over from generations of riding donkeys. The position of the rider was to the rear of the horse, over his loins–the accepted position for riding donkeys because of their low withers and the low carriage of their head and neck.[25] The horse was controlled by reins connected to a snaffle bit. The rider rode bareback and barefooted. He maintained his position on the horse primarily through gripping the horse's back with his knees. This awkward position was unstable for the rider, made cantering impractical, and hindered using the bow.

By the reign of Tiglath-Pilser III (744–727 BC), the Assyrian cavalry had made tremendous strides in its horsemanship, and consequently, cavalry's utility as a military force. Assyrian reliefs from the time illustrate the rider sitting forward on the horse, with the leg position dropped in order to grip the belly of the horse with the lower leg, while the upper leg grips with the thigh. Improved horsemanship permitted more accurate use of the bow and the addition of a short sword and a lance to the horseman's arsenal, making him a more versatile threat on the battlefield. His position on the horse also permitted comfortable and secure riding at the canter. During this period, the cavalryman also began to wear scale armor. Stone reliefs of Assyrian horsemen from the reign of Ashurbanipal (668–627 BC) show leggings on the rider's lower leg and scale armor on the horse. Assyrian cavalry began to represent the embodiment of all-purpose cavalry as it would appear in most tribes and empires of the ancient world: a horse and rider lightly armored, equipped with bow, sword, and lance, positioned forward on the horse, riding bareback or with just a cloth or skin between the rider and horse, and controlling the horse through a snaffle bit.[26]

The Assyrian empire fell toward the end of the seventh century BC as it was pressured by the Medes and the Scythians in the north and from Babylonia to the south. Nineveh, the capital of Assyria, was captured and destroyed in 612 BC essentially bringing the kingdom to an end.[27] The Scythians, who were influential in the downfall of the Assyrians, rose to prominence in their place. In fact, they became the first of the steppe nomadic horse peoples to organize their significant military skills to undertake offensive operations against the sedentary empires of Europe, the Middle East, and Asia. Though they were the first, they would not be the last.

With the fall of the Assyrians, in the middle of the first millennia BC, the ancient world was left with three major power centers. The Persian Empire rose in the Tigris and Euphrates valley and eventually encompassed all the land that had once been Babylonia, Assyria, Mitanni, and Hittite. The Greek city-states expanded and became the most influential power on the Aegean and the Mediterranean coasts. From the European steppes, the Scythians pushed down on both sides of the Black Sea into Anatolia. Inevitably, these powers would clash. Two of these empires relied heavily on the horse in their military systems. Thus the cavalry would prove to be a crucial element in these historic confrontations.

Chapter Two

CAVALRY ARMIES

A great horse, in a sense, becomes a king. It is not surprising that kings were made by the first great horses.–JOHN KEEGAN, *A History of Warfare*

The Assyrians demonstrated that powerful cavalry forces were an important component of an effective military system that could not only win battles but also conquer territory. The Persians, who came to dominate the Middle East and built their army around an even more powerful cavalry force, inherited that precedent. Their main opponents, the Greeks, had an effective military system also but built around the heavily armored infantry soldier–the hoplite. The Greeks, however, were not conquerors. Their military system focused on winning battles, not waging campaigns. This changed when Macedonia, with its very capable cavalry arm, became the dominant Greek state. The Macedonians added effective cavalry to the already proven hoplite tradition. This addition created an army that was capable of winning both battles and campaigns and was perhaps the most capable military of the ancient world.

PERSIAN CAVALRY

The Persians rose as a power as several Persian and Iranian groups, in what is today south central Iran, were united under Cyrus II–also known as Cyrus the Great. Cyrus began a series of conquests that ultimately established the kings of Persia as uncontested rulers of what is today the greater Middle East. In 550 BC he conquered the Medes and displaced them as the heirs of the Assyrians. Babylonia, Lydia, and Egypt all fell to Cyrus and his son, Cambyses. A general, Darius I, replaced Cambyses who died while traveling from Egypt to Persia in 522 BC. After consolidating his rule in 516 BC, Darius launched an expedition against the Scythians as part of an overall strategy to deny grain to the Greek city-states that were supporting revolt in Anatolia. Though Darius's expedition failed, the Persians retained the bridgehead in Europe for future operations against the Greeks.[1]

Cavalry was the center of the Persian army, a tradition inherited from the Assyrians and the steppe horsemen from across the Caucasus Mountains. The proportion and numbers of cavalry in the army clearly reflected that it was the dominant arm within the Persian military system. At the battle of Plataea the Persian army, under Mardonius, numbered 50,000 infantry and 10,000 cavalry.[2] Later Persian armies fighting Alexander also fielded large cavalry formations: At Issus, the Persians fielded 30,000 cavalry; at Guagamela, the Persian cavalry numbered over 40,000.[3] In its battles with the Greeks and Macedonians, the Persian cavalry showed itself to be a competent and dangerous foe.

The Persian cavalry was a major factor in the army's ability to rapidly conquer its adversaries in the Middle East. All-purpose cavalry–equipped with bow, javelin, and light armor–were ideally suited not only for campaigning across the vast open spaces of the Middle East but also for maintaining control over the various cities, lands, and peoples once conquered. Relatively small cavalry detachments were capable of controlling large swathes of ground. They were an ideal garrison and police force for the empire. They were fast, allowing them to concentrate rapidly at hot spots within the empire's interior, and they were capable of fighting with some effect dismounted. However, as the Persians attempted to expand into Europe to gain control of the Greek city-states, the Persian military system and its cavalry failed.

Two factors stymied Persian bow- and spear-armed cavalry as the Persians advanced into Greece. The first was the terrain. The rocky, mountainous lands of Greece diminished the ability of cavalry to maneuver at the operational and at the tactical level. At the operational level, the terrain limited the avenues of advance for the large cavalry forces of the Persian army toward any particular Greek city. The Greeks could accurately predict the approach route of the Persians and position an army to intercept. At the lower tactical levels of war, the rough terrain allowed the Greek armies to fight at locations where their flanks were tied in to natural obstacles–typically rivers or steep mountain sides. By completely covering these vulnerable areas, the Greeks eliminated the possibility of cavalry flanking maneuvers that were lethal to infantry battling in more open terrain.

The other factor that frustrated the Persian cavalry was the Greek foot soldier. The hoplite, a disciplined, heavily armored, infantryman, wore a full, face-covering helmet, body armor, greaves on his legs, and carried a large shield. They fought in a phalanx: soldiers stood shoulder to shoulder in deep ranks, each man's shielded left arm protecting not only him but also the right side of the man to his left. The two areas of vulnerability to the phalanx were its rear and flanks, but an experienced commander would ensure that the battle terrain minimized attack from these angles. One shortcoming of the hoplite phalanx was that it was not very maneuverable–

especially over rough or broken terrain–and it was slow. Despite this, the armor, protective formation, and discipline of the hoplites enabled the Greek infantry to withstand a prolonged attack by archers and made them virtually impervious to attack from the front by cavalry or from less well protected and disciplined infantry.[4]

Persian Horses

The Persians ran a relatively efficient military system. Integral to this system was their ability to mount tens of thousands of cavalry and keep them supplied in the field for months of campaigning. This required an effective remount supply network. A by-product of the Persian logistics system was the emergence of a systematic horse breeding and procurement program that established at least three identifiable horse types, two of which relate to modern-day breeds.

There were several sources of remounts for the Persian army, and the remount system of the Persians was a model for all armies of the ancient world. The vassal and allied lands were the first source of horses. These kingdoms and domains, Media (Iraq and Iran), Egypt, Bactria (Afghanistan), and Urartu (Armenia), not only provided mounted contingents to the Persian army but also provided an allocation of remount horses. They inherited this traditional tribute relationship from the Assyrians. Horses, particularly well bred and broken ones, were an extremely valuable commodity in the ancient world; the subject territory paid a portion of its annual tribute, or tax, in the medium of horseflesh. This levy was particularly important when the territory could produce horses of equal or finer quality than the Persians.[5]

A second, although less reliable, source for horses was the battlefield. The victorious side in most ancient battles retained control of the field, holding dominion over discarded weapons and loose mounts. Given that the cavalrymen rode without saddles it was common for riders to become unhorsed during combat. Thus the winning side stood to gain a significant bounty in trained cavalry horses. The lure of this type of valuable plunder was a major incentive for the individual warrior. Rounding up, sorting, and distributing captured horses was a regular task after a battle.

Another means of obtaining horses was through trade. Horse traders often worked as middlemen between kingdoms that had, at least temporarily, good relations. Officials would specify their horse requirements and negotiate a price. The horse trader, with his assistants, would travel to an area such as Scythia or Bactria and procure the animals. This system was, by its nature, relatively small scale and could in no way meet the needs of the large horse armies of the Persians.[6]

A final and important source of horses was indigenous breeding–specifically for military purposes. Stud farms could operate either as private enterprises or as royal farms operated by the kingdom. A private stud farm owned by the satrap of Babylon contained 16,000 mares and 800 stallions. A private stud farm was a large business which essentially produced war material for the army. The stud farms of the satrap of Armenia annually sent 20,000 foals to the Persian king, as well as equipping his own cavalry force.[7]

The Persian army, drawing on the resources of the entire empire to equip its forces, included several distinct horse types within its cavalry. These types included a light Armenian horse, a general purpose medium horse from Scythia, and a heavy battle horse from the central Persian Empire.

The Armenian horse was the smallest of the three types and by modern standards was a very small horse. It is the type 4 of the ancient types that are the root of all modern breeds. Xenophon described it as "smaller than the Persian horses, but much more finely bred." It appears on the famous Persian palace of Persepolis's staircase frieze pulling Darius's hunting chariot. This horse may be the ancestor of the modern, extremely rare, Caspian horse. The modern Caspian was discovered in the wild along the southern shores of the Caspian Sea in northern Iran in 1965. A survey revealed that only 50 of the horses existed. Since then, the horses have been the subject of a carefully managed and controlled breeding program that appears to have successfully saved the breed from extinction. Although the Caspian is quite small–10 to 13 hands–it is not a pony. Physically, the Caspian is attractive and very athletic.[8] By modern standards the size of the Caspian horse would disqualify it for military service, but in the ancient world this was not necessarily so. Mongol horses fall into a similar size range, and they have a well-documented history of military use. Adult male riders in the ancient world were significantly smaller and lighter than modern riders. A modern Caspian horse has no problem managing a rider weighing around 140 pounds and has phenomenal endurance. When rediscovered the local rural population used it as a beast of burden.[9] In the Persian army light cavalry scouts and horse archers with minimal armor and little in the way of equipment used the small Caspian type.

A second important horse found in the Persian army was the Scythian horse. This horse would have come into Persian possession through levies in the satraps of Bactria and Urartu and in battle and trading with the Scythians. The horse is the type 3–the central Asian horse originating on the Turan Flats (located between the Caspian Sea and the Arial Sea encompassing parts of modern-day Iran, Russia, Turkmenistan, and Afghanistan). Well-preserved remains of these horses dating from about 300 BC have been found in Scythian burial tombs in Pazyryk, approximately where China, Mongolia, Russia, and Kazakhstan meet on the western edge of the Sayan mountains– the easternmost border of the Turan Flats.

The most perfectly preserved of these Scythian burial horses may be representative of the type: it was a 12- to 15-year-old mare of average height, measuring about 13 hands. She was dun, with the glow typical of today's Turkoman strains, and saddled with highly ornamented bone, wood, leather, and felt tack–including a "stag mask" with large stylized antlers and a single long strap to tie her tail.[10] Apart from her size, she was virtually identical to the modern Akhal-Teke, also known as the Turkoman horse. The modern breed is medium size and likely larger than the ancient precedent represented by the Pazyryk horses, standing on average between 14.3 and 16 hands.[11] An Akhal-Teke type horse may have been the standard general cavalry horse of the Persians. Its medium size, athleticism, and endurance made it ideal for the general purpose cavalry that made up the bulk of the Persian cavalry forces.

One other significant horse in the Persian cavalry was the Nisaean type, the horse of the Persian elite, discussed by all the ancient writers. Herodotus refers to "the sacred horses called Nisaean, all daintily caparisoned. (Now these horses are called Nisaean, because they come from the Nisaean plain, a vast flat in Media, producing horses of unusual size)." He specifically identifies the breed as pulling the war chariot of Xerxes during his invasion of Greece and as the mount of Masistius, the Persian cavalry commander at Plataea: "a Nisaean charger with a golden bit, and otherwise magnificently caparisoned."[12]

Historians have been unable to specifically locate the "Nisaean plain" because of the numerous ancient sites that use similar names. Alexander the Great marched through the area in 324 BC and observed 50,000 Nisaean horses in the royal stud farm located there. This number represented only a fraction of what was present during the height of the Persian Empire. The Nisaean was likely on average 15 hands tall. However, archaeologists have reported remains as large as 16 hands. Though average by modern standards, its size was notable relative to the other horses of the period. Despite challenges in identifying the actual location of the Nisaean plain, some suggest that it was located near Ecbatana, the capital of Media (west-central Iran). In modern times a species of high protein clover, known as Median grass, grows in this region. This type of diet, if it existed in the region in ancient times, would explain the unusual size of the animals. Depictions of the horse in ancient friezes also indicate a well-muscled and stout horse with a pronounced roman nose.[13]

The Nisaean horse was the mount of the elite of the Persian cavalry. In fact, ancient historians documented the fact that commanders typically rode this mount. None of the modern breeds appear to have a direct link to the most famous and well documented of the ancient cavalry mounts. Some claim that the Nisaean was a variation of the Akhal-Teke, but it seems, from the descriptions, that the breeding of the Nisaean emphasized characteristics quite different from those found in the modern Turkoman breed. Likely, the Nisaean was a unique horse that was a product of specif-

The Caspian horse (top) represents the type 4 small horse. Texanas Adam, the Caspian stallion pictured here, is typical in size for the breed at 12.1 hands. Its proportionate strength, fine features, and endurance were important traits that were passed on to all the breeds originating in Central Asia. (*Victoria Tollman, courtesy of Tachara Caspians*) The Akhal-Teke breed of Central Asia (bottom) represents the type 3 horse, perhaps the most important war horse of the ancient world. Pictured here is Rosanna, a 3-year-old mare who stands 15.2 hands. She perfectly represents the size, athleticism, fine lean features, and sleek profile that made it the primary foundation type for future war horses. (*Tom Keith and Jessica Eile-Keith, Karakum Akhal-Tekes*)

ic breeding in the geographic region of the Nisaean plain, and had both Caspian and Akhal-Teke influences, but its unique physical characteristics did not survive history.

For horse equipment the Persians used only reins, a bit, and a saddle blanket or pad. The bit was a variant of the snaffle bit, a single or joined bar with connections for reins on either end. The simple pad, along with a trousered uniform, allowed the rider to grip the horse directly with his legs.

The Basics of Horsemanship

When riding a horse there are two broad categories of control techniques (known as the aids): natural and artificial. For the Persians, as for all horsemen and cavalrymen since ancient times, the aids were the means by which the rider communicated with the horse. They are still the basic fundamentals of horsemanship. The natural aids are the rider's voice, legs, hands, and body. Artificial aids include spurs, whips, bits, harnesses, and reins. All the natural aids were known and used in ancient times, as confirmed by Xenophon. In fact, they were more important then because before the invention of the saddle the rider was less secure in his seat, making communication with the horse vital when riding swiftly or over dangerous terrain. The Persian cavalry, learning from the horse cultures of the steppes, were adept at applying the aids. The aids, used by a skilled horseman subtly and in sophisticated combinations, are often invisible to an untrained observer.

The aids rely on the natural sensitivity of the horse for effect. A horse is sensitive enough that it can feel a fly land on any part of its body. This sensitivity allows the horse to feel the actions of the rider's body, hands, and legs and to discriminate between subtle differences in those actions. This ability, combined with the horse's good memory, makes it a highly trainable animal.

The rider's legs are used primarily to indicate forward motion. A slight squeeze of the lower legs tells the horse to move forward. Additional pressure moves the horse to the next higher speed. The horse has four speeds: walk, trot, canter, and full gallop. The legs are also used for direction. Pressure from one leg pushes the horse sideways as it is moving forward, causing the horse to move at a diagonal. This is called leg yielding. Pressure from both legs, applied in different places, can cause the horse to bend around the rider's inside leg, in effect turning the horse.

The rider's body is also an effective communications device. The rider can shift his center of gravity lower or higher, forward or back. The horse is very aware of these different body positions. Shifting the center of gravity forward and up tells the horse to move forward. It may also warn the horse to be prepared to jump. Shifting the center of gravity to the rear and down tells the horse to slow down. Purposely positioning the body against the motion of the horse also indicates to the horse to slow down and eventually stop.

The use of leg and body aids to communicate with the horse was essential for mounted archers. A skilled Persian archer, using a combination of body and leg aids, could bring his horse from the walk to the gallop, turn him, slow him down, and stop him, without every using his hands. An expert such as a Persian horse archer could ride in this manner without any more conscious thought than a modern individual would give to the daily mechanics of driving a car—no experienced driver actually "thinks" about stopping, turning, or accelerating. The horse and the skilled archer were a single unit, with the horse an extension of the archer's will. This left the horse archer free to focus on fighting: to work his bow, observe the terrain, pay attention to the enemy, and listen for commands.

Audible commands were another aid for which the horse was trained to respond. In its simplest form, a voice command was associated with slowing down and another with speeding up. In the ancient world, military horns likely communicated some basic unit commands such as charge and rally. However, there is no significant discussion of this in the literature. If such commands were used—as is likely—trained cavalry horses would respond to them with little or no prompting from their riders, as they did in later centuries.

Persian horse archer. The horse archer controlled his horse with his body as he fired his bow. The Greeks had no answer to the Persian horse archers, but if the infantry's discipline held, their armor and shields were effective protection against the Persian arrows. (*Author*)

The Bit

The aid that even most nonriders are familiar with is the hands. The hands are not a purely natural aid because they communicate with the horse through two pieces of equipment: the reins and the bit. The reins are leather straps that connect to rings set into the bit at one end and are held in the hand—or hands—of the rider at the other end. The rider uses them to apply pressure to the bit or to touch the sides of the horse's neck. There are two primary types of bits: snaffle and curb. Both can be dated to at least the time of Darius's Persian Empire and are likely much older. These are still the two main types of horse bits used today. Bitting a horse is an art in which there are literally unlimited variations of technique. The advantages and disadvantages of different bit types, and their relative effectiveness in different situations, have been a source of debate and discussion among horsemen since the origin of the concept of controlling a horse through his mouth. Regardless of the type of bit used, training horses to take the bit and to understand what actions are correct in response to different signals transmitted by the hands through the reins and bit is essential. The following discussion of bits is intentionally basic and generic.

The simplest bit is the snaffle. The snaffle bit influences both direction and speed. The main parts of the simple snaffle are joined pieces of metal, called a bar, which sits in the horse's mouth. The bar has a cheek ring on each end to attach the reins and to prevent the bar from passing through the mouth. The snaffle sends signals to the horse through a technique called direct rein. The rider applies direct pressure from his hands to the bit. In its very simplest use, applying pressure on the left or right rein causes the bit to pull through the horse's mouth and the cheek ring presses on the horse's lips on the opposite side. The horse also feels pressure on the inside bars of the mouth (a sensitive gap between his back teeth). Such action causes the horse's head to move away from the pressure. When the horse is moving, the pressure causes it to change direction. Putting pressure on both reins simultaneously forces the horse's head down and tells the horse to slow. Easing pressure on both reins tells the horse to speed up. Even rearward pressure (applied in pulses) causes the horse to stop. In this reining technique the bit provides no mechanical advantage; the pull on the bit is exactly that applied by the rider's hand. For this reason simple snaffle bits are comfortable for the horse. The major disadvantage of this technique is that it requires constant light contact between both of the rider's hands and the horse's mouth through the reins and bit. For a cavalryman, expected to wield weapons while mounted, this is often impossible. The advantage of this technique is that it allows for precise control over where and how the horse is going.

The other major type of bit used during the ancient period was the curb bit. The curb bit is designed around a solid bar that is placed through the horse's mouth. Its design applies pressure vertically, not laterally like the snaffle. The main parts of the bit are the bar through the horse's mouth; the shanks that extend down from the bar and are the attachment point for the reins; a curb chain that attaches on both ends of the bar and runs under the horse's chin; and the port, which is a break in the bar that relieves pressure on the horse's tongue. The curb bit is primarily a breaking mechanism on the horse. Pulling the reins together to the rear puts pressure on the tongue and bars of the mouth, forcing the horse's head down to slow or stop the animal. In the hands of an unskilled rider, the curb bit can be a severe means of controlling the horse. Under emergency conditions, the curb allows the rider to quickly and efficiently cause the horse to react. Since curb bits are not very effective in getting lateral action from the horse, and because they can be severe, riders use them most often in combination with indirect, or neck reining. The neck rein technique gives instruction to the horse by laying the rein on a side of the horse's neck to indicate desired direction. The horse moves away from the side that it feels the rein on and thus changes direction. The major advantage of the curb bit and neck reining is that they only require one hand, thus allowing the other hand to hold a weapon. The disadvantage is that precise control of direction and speed is not as easy as with a snaffle bit.

The bits described above are simple and generally do not cause significant discomfort to the horse when used properly. Many working bits, both ancient and mod-

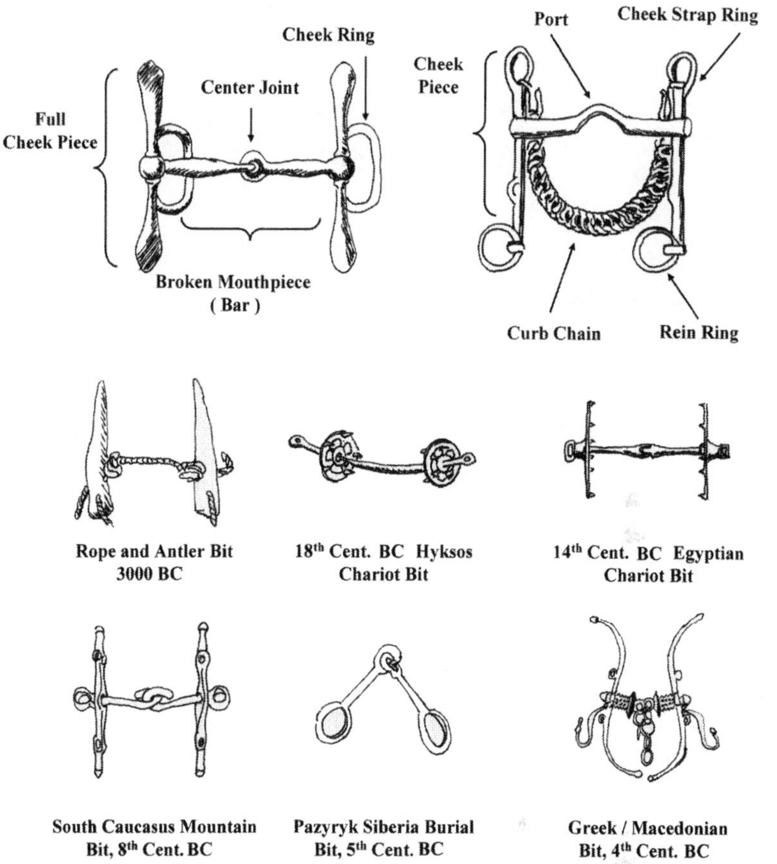

The two basic bits (top) used to control the horse through the reins. Left: A broken (with a joint in the middle) snaffle bit. Right: A curb bit. A collection of ancient horse bits (bottom). The bits are easily identifiable as to type and function and are indicative of the sophisticated level of horsemanship in the ancient world. All the bits are variations of the snaffle design. Note the severity of the 4th Century Greek bit though the basic design is a broken snaffle. (*Author*)

ern, are designed to get very specific, and dramatic, reactions from the horse by inflicting discomfort and pain. Protrusions on the bit, sharp points and edges, and thinness all make the bit more severe. On curb bits, the length of the shank is an important indicator of severity. The type of bitting used by an army can be an indicator of the quality and type of horsemanship practiced by that army and its cavalrymen. It is often easier to get a particular reaction from a horse by increasing the severity of the bit than by training the horse and rider. Still, a severe bit in the hands of a skillful horseman with "soft hands" can be quite comfortable for the horse.

The Greeks often used very severe versions of the snaffle bit. Xenophon, an exceptional horseman, understood the subtleties of bits and commented on it.

> But if a rough [severe] bit is put in, it must be made as easy as a smooth by lightness of hand. . . . Whatever the kind of bit, it must be used according to the following rules, which are in every case the same. . . .The horse's mouth must not be checked too harshly, so that he will toss his head, nor too gently for him to feel it. The moment he acknowledges it and begins to raise his neck, give him the bit. And in everything else, as I have insisted over and over again, the horse should be rewarded as long as he behaves well.[14]

Xenophon wrote his treatise on horsemanship in the early fourth century. Clearly, the ancient cavalrymen understood well the intricacies of horse control through the bit.

The ancient cavalrymen understood the aids and understood that effective riding required that all the techniques be used in combination. Thus a simple command such as moving from a walk to a trot would involve squeezing with the legs, shifting the center of gravity slightly up and forward, clicking with the tongue, and easing pressure on the reins. A well-trained horse would respond to the smallest application of any one of the aids, but when time and conditions permitted, the well-schooled cavalryman would use them all as part of a continuous training process. Different types of cavalry would emphasize different training techniques. Leg and body aids would be important to the horse archers. Heavy cavalry using lance and sword would emphasize neck reining and possibly more advanced turns and kicks. Experts in later centuries estimated that it took at least two years to train a basic proficient cavalryman, and much longer to produce an expert horse and rider combination.

Cavalry in the Greek–Persian Wars

Compared to the tens of thousands of cavalry employed by the Persians, the Greek contemporaries of Darius I did not have much of a cavalry force. Though the Greeks considered the horse a symbol of status and wealth, they focused the bulk of their martial resources and attention on their infantry forces. The tradition of mounted warfare, which had influenced armies in the Middle East for two millennia, was not part of Greek city-state warfare. As noted earlier, much of Greece was steep and rocky terrain. And what remaining land was suitable to agriculture was intensively cultivated. Pasture for non-food-producing animals, such as the horse, was a luxury in Greece. Only wealthy private citizens could afford to buy and maintain horses. Most city-state governments were democratic or inspired by democratic conventions.[15] The horse's association with an elite, wealthy element reduced the horse's popularity and discouraged the Greeks from emphasizing mounted warfare. The

Greeks viewed the hoplite, on the other hand, as a citizen soldier, a concept compatible with the Greek ideals of democracy.

In addition, the nature of Greek warfare, built as it was around the phalanx, was not conducive to mounted combat. The ideal warrior in most of the Greek city-states was a critical component of classical Greek culture. The mounted warrior was not a part of the Greek warrior icon, which contributed to the lack of emphasis on cavalry up to the time of the Greek–Persian wars.

Those wars mark the first meeting between highly disciplined infantry and cavalry formations. Between 499 BC and 449 BC the Persian Empire, firmly in control of all of what is today the Middle East, made numerous attempts to subjugate the Greek city-states that controlled the sea commerce of the Mediterranean and consistently agitated for revolt against Persian rule. The famous battles of Marathon (490 BC), Thermopylae (480 BC), Salamis (480 BC), and Plataea (479 BC) are representative of the military confrontation between Greece and Persia, and the frustration of the Persian plans. In these confrontations the Greek infantrymen and seamen, though badly outnumbered, ultimately prevailed over the army and navy of the Persian rulers Darius I and Xerxes I. The battle of Plataea, where the cavalry army of Persia met the Greek hoplite army, is particularly illustrative of the dynamics of battle between the two armies.

The Persians under Xerxes I invaded Greece in 480 BC with the specific purpose of establishing Persian rule over the independent-minded Greek city-states. Estimates of the size of the army vary greatly, but it was undoubtedly huge. The Greek historian Herodotus puts the total at over 2 million fighting men—clearly an exaggeration. Modern historians place the size of the combat forces at between 50,000 and 200,000 men. Thus, a reasonable estimate might be approximately 125,000 combatants. The army represented not only the military power of Persia but also the administrative proficiency of the Persian Empire. It was a significant accomplishment to support the massive army as it marched hundreds of miles through unfriendly territory. About 75,000 animals of all types, but primarily horses, supported the cavalry forces of the army and the logistics trains. Modern historians believe that the cavalry component of the army numbered about 10,000. Xerxes's generals probably intentionally reduced the size of the cavalry force due to the logistical requirements of the army's animals (daily water and fodder) and the limited ability of the terrain to sustain the herds.[16]

The invading Persian army, advancing along the Greek coast, overawed local rulers, cities, and small kingdoms and encountered no significant resistance. Macedonia and Thessaly both offered earth and water gifts, the symbols of submission, and contributed symbolic contingents to the Persian army. As the Persians advanced, the majority of the Greeks ended internal conflicts and formed the Hellenic League in opposition to the invaders. Mobilizing and assembling the various Greek city-state armies took time. As a delay tactic, a small contingent of Greeks, under the leadership of the Spartan king Leonidas, blocked the Persian advance along the coast at Thermopylae. Leonidas's force of 8,000 infantry delayed the Persians for three days and cost the Persians 20,000 casualties. Despite the valor of the Spartan king, the Persian army was unstoppable after their victory at Thermopylae and quickly moved to overrun southern Greece. The mobilization of the Greek armies was incomplete, and Athens was abandoned in the face of the Persian advance. The only force able to oppose the invading Persian army was the Greek fleet. As Athens burned, the two great fleets met near Athens in the narrow straits of Salamis. Through superior seamanship and tactics the Greek fleet won a decisive victory, crippling the Persians. With control of the sea contested, if not lost, and winter coming on, Xerxes withdrew the bulk of his army from its exposed position in southern Greece to a more secure base in Thessaly where there was sufficient fodder for the army's animals. Xerxes himself, with a small portion of the army, returned to Persia.

Xerxes placed the Persian army in Thessaly under the command of his cousin and son-in-law, Mardonius. It was a formidable force–likely over 100,000 combatants, including the bulk of the cavalry force. After much internal debate, the Greeks united and fielded an army of about the same size to contest the Persians' inevitable resumption of the campaign. Though similar in size, the composition of the two armies was vastly different. The composite Persian army consisted of Persian and allied infantry, and cavalry. The Greek army was much more homogenous–essentially light infantry and hoplites–all from the various member states of the Hellenic League. The Greeks numbered approximately 38,000 hoplites and 70,000 light infantry armed primarily with slings and javelins.[17]

The Battle of Plataea, 479 BC

Mardonius began the spring campaign of 479 BC with the objective of forcing the submission of Athens. He planned to accomplish this through a combination of force and diplomacy: Mardonius threatened to destroy Athens while simultaneously using the Macedonian king, Alexander I, to negotiate with the Athenians for a peaceful surrender. If this maneuver did not work, he planned to engage the Greeks in a decisive battle and win their submission through force of arms. The possibility of Athens surrendering to the Persians forced the Hellenic League to mobilize its forces and give Mardonius the decisive battle he desired.

As the Greek army moved from its defensive positions in Corinth, the Persians withdrew from Attica, into Boeotia, where the open terrain would allow them to use

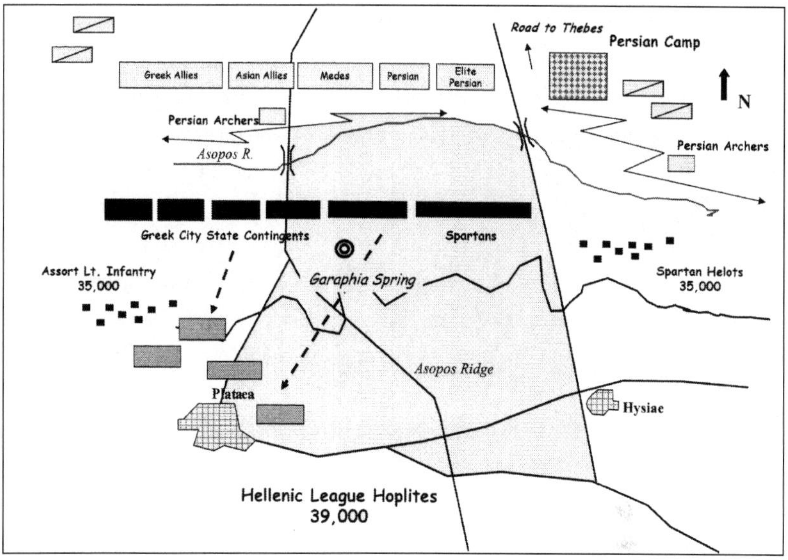

The battle of Plataea, 479 BC.

their cavalry to its best advantage. This also shortened the Persians' logistics line to their forward base at Thebes while forcing the Greeks to extend their logistics from their base in Peloponnesus. Mardonius picked the valley of the Asopus River for the battle.

As the Greek army moved into the Asopus River valley, the Persian army, already encamped on the north side of the river, harassed them with long-range archery. The Greeks employed their light infantry and Spartan helots, armed with javelins and slings, to keep the mounted bowmen out of range of their columns. The Greeks were able to occupy their first positions well east of the town of Plataea without much difficulty. The light infantry deployed to protect both the vulnerable flanks of the phalanx formations and the Greek supply lines.

The Persian horsemen continued their harassing tactics. The steady shower of arrows required the hoplites to remain in formation, using their shields to reduce the impact of the Persian archers. The Greeks placed light infantry among the phalanxes to respond to the Persian cavalry, but the light infantry could not match the mobility of the cavalry. The Persians were able to direct archery fire throughout the Greek ranks. The Persian cavalry commander, Masistius, personally directed the cavalry attacks against the 3,000 hoplites from Megara. The Megarians requested assistance from the Athenians who sent 300 hoplites and dismounted archers to a position forward of the Megarians to disrupt the Persian attacks and return fire. Masistius personally led the cavalry against the Athenians in an attempt to eliminate the exposed infantry. During the action, an arrow took down Masistius's horse, and before the Persian commander could rise the Athenian hoplites killed him. The Persian cavalry attacked ferociously to recover the body of their popular leader. The Megarians moved forward to support the Athenians, and in the close combat between horseman and hoplite the cavalry, casualties mounted rapidly. When the lightly armed and armored cavalry realized the futility of close combat with the heavy Greek infantry they broke off the attack.

Following the successful counterattack against the Persian cavalry, the Greeks moved their entire army farther west to a position between Plataea and the main road between Thebes and Athens. The Greeks took their positions on the high ground, the Asopus Ridge, south of the river to protect the Gargaphia spring that supplied the army's water. The Persian army mirrored the Greek move and took up new positions west of their permanent camp, along the north side of the Asopus River. Persian archers positioned on the north bank prevented the Greeks from using the river as a water supply.

For eight days the two opposing armies observed each other across the river. Despite the fact that the river was easily fordable, the only action during this period consisted of forays by the Persian cavalry to harass, with fire, the nearly 4-mile-long line of hoplites. The Persian commander Mardonius finally broke the standoff. On the eighth day, he launched a cavalry raid around, and behind, the Greek left flank, capturing a pass though the mountains south of Plataea. The Persian cavalrymen captured 500 pack animals laden with grain for the Greek army. More importantly, the Persian cavalry gained control of the critical supply line back to Peloponnesus.

For three more days the Persian cavalry continued to harass the Greeks. On the eleventh day, as the Greeks adjusted their line, Mardonius launched an all-out cavalry attack. The form of the attack was typical of Persian cavalry charges: squadrons charged in formation to a firing position, halted, and fired. As the squadrons became disorganized, were threatened with counterattack, or had expended their arrows, a new squadron moved up. The old unit rode to the rear to reorganize. Some Persian squadrons rode in very close to the phalanxes and fired while moving. This attack caused some material losses to the Greeks but was not decisive. However, it was psychologically frustrating. The Greek light infantry was unable to disrupt the fire of the Persian archers. In the confusion and dust of the Persian mounted attack, a group of Persian cavalry managed to slip inside the Greek lines and foul the Gargaphia spring. At the end of the eleventh day the Greek commanders held a council of war. Their supply line was cut; the soldiers were frustrated; their primarily water supply was fouled; and after eleven days, they had been unable to engage the Persians in battle. The Greek generals decided to withdraw.

The withdrawal was not to be a retreat but rather a tactical repositioning of the army to reestablish a water supply and clear out the Persian cavalry disrupting the supply line. The Greeks withdrew at night. A night withdrawal, while in contact with the enemy, is a difficult and potentially dangerous operation. The Greeks discovered this at dawn the next day when they realized that their center had withdrawn in the wrong direction and that the Spartans had delayed their withdrawal because one of their commanders thought it was dishonorable. The result was a broken Greek battle line with the Spartan and Tegeans in the east, isolated from the Athenians and others positioned around Plataea. More importantly, the sun was up, and Mardonius could easily observe the disordered state of the Greek line.

Mardonius took advantage of the Greeks' disarray. He immediately ordered his cavalry forward against both Greek contingents. The infantry soon followed. Mardonius's intent was to focus his best troops, his Persian forces, against the best Greek troops, the Spartans, knowing that if he destroyed them he would also destroy the Greek army. As the Persian cavalry caught up to the Spartans' retreating columns, the Spartans turned and under a hail of fire formed their phalanx. The Tegeans, moving with the Spartans, did likewise. The Persian cavalry fire held the Spartans at bay until the Persian infantry caught up with the pinned-down Spartans. However, rather than close with the phalanx, the Persian infantry employed their archers, javelin throwers, and slingers to continue the bombardment of the Spartans. Meanwhile, the Athenians, attempting to link up with the Spartans, were stopped and engaged by the Persian allies and right wing cavalry.

The nerve of the Tegeans broke under the bombardment, at about the same time the Spartans realized that the Athenians would not be coming to their aid. The reaction of Greek infantry when discipline broke down was not what one might predict: the Tegeans did not retreat. They attacked. As the Tegean phalanx charged, the Spartan officers ordered the Spartan phalanx to attack in support. The armored Greek infantry were overpowering in close combat, and they slowly, but inexorably, thrust and cut their way through the lightly clad Persians. Mardonius and his elite 1,000-man personal guard could not repel the tide. He and most of his entourage were caught in the melee and killed in the Greek assault. As the Persian leader fell, the Persian infantry broke and began to stream back to their fortified camp. The panic spread quickly through the ranks. Soon the Persian allies also broke before the Athenians and began to stream back toward the camp or down the road toward Thebes. The Persian cavalry were largely immune to the power of the phalanx as long as they kept their distance. The cavalry's discipline held and they were effective covering the retreat of the army. With unbroken cavalry formations still on the field, the Greeks had to maintain control and cohesion, which slowed their pursuit of the

Persians. This lesson was brought home to the Megarians who, in the haste of their pursuit, were caught in open formation by Theban cavalry allied with Persians. The Megarians lost 600 men before they could drive the horsemen off.[18]

With the rout of their army at Plataea, Persian designs on the Greek mainland were extinguished. The Greeks have historically been given great credit for their ability to repeatedly defeat the invading Persians, but in reality they owe their success more to chance than any other factor. One historian summed up the war this way: "The Greek resistance to Persia from Marathon onwards is a catalogue of bad planning, gross inefficiency and selfishness punctuated with occasional acts of brilliance and heroism. It is incredible that they could possibly have won. The Persians, on the other hand, displayed excellent strategy, a great deal of energy and considerable bravery but suffered from appalling bad luck. In the final campaign they completely outmaneuvered the Greeks, and then made one miscalculation which cost them the war."[19] The Persians' unity of command and their resources were superior to the Greeks', and they were certainly at least equal in tactical command ability. The Persians completely outclassed the Greeks in cavalry. Had the Persians prevailed at Plataea, their victory undoubtedly would be attributed to the dominance of their cavalry arm.

Greek military men were not blind to the lessons of the Greek–Persian wars; they understood the limitations of their one-dimensional military system. However, it is not easy to overcome culture and history. It would require a hundred years, and the pain of the Peloponnesian War, for the mounted warrior to earn a place within the Greek military system. When the Greek cavalry finally asserted itself, it did so in a manner that was a reflection of their philosophy of war; they did not create a European copy of the Asian cavalry tradition represented by the Persians at Plataea, but rather a unique mounted version of the hoplite.

Greek Cavalry

The Peloponnesian War, and subsequent city-state wars, pitted the various Greek states against one another in increasingly sophisticated warfare from 458 BC until 362 BC. The cavalry component of the Greek military evolved throughout this period, taking on increasing importance. The cavalry's new role and value changed partly because of the lessons learned from the Persians, and partly as a natural evolution of tactics. Similar Greek hoplite-centric armies sought any means to achieve an advantage over the enemy; and cavalry became one way to achieve an edge and secure victory.

The Greek cavalry developed a fighting style distinctly different from that of the Persians. The Greeks were not particularly superior to the Persians in a number of important areas. However, the Greeks were clearly dominant in the area of close combat. In this arena the factors of victory were morale, unit cohesion, armor, discipline, and individual skill. In all of these, the average Greek hoplite was superior to even the most elite of the Persian infantry. The hoplite was the centerpiece of the Greek way of war; and therefore it was natural that the hoplites had a significant influence on the development of the Greek cavalry.

Although the early Greeks had developed small elite cavalry organizations called Hippeis, these units, used almost exclusively to carry messages and for scouting, had all but disappeared by the time of the Persian wars. The two most dominant Greek states–Athens and Sparta–did not field any cavalry during the Persian wars. Cavalry contingents existed in several other city-states and participated in the Persian wars, but mostly allied with the Persians. Thessalian and Boeotian cavalry were both present at Plataea on the Persian side. Riding and fighting skills needed for an effective cavalry were not unknown in Greece, many of the wealthier hoplites rode to war but fought as part of the phalanx while grooms minded their mounts during battle. Surviving Greek pottery clearly shows Greek warriors in hoplite armor sitting astride horses. Scholars believe these images represent hoplites traveling to battle rather than cavalry because the hoplite armor, particularly the Corinthian helmet, was totally impractical for mounted combat.

Over the almost 100 years of war that ravaged Greece after the defeat of the Persian invasion, true Greek cavalry developed. In Thessaly, unlike other Greek states, the cavalry arm of the military had always been dominant. Thessaly was located north of the main centers of Greek culture. Therefore, rather than looking toward Athens and Sparta, Thessaly was influenced by the Middle East–Assyria and then Persia–and the steppe horse tribes–Scythians and Thracians–on its northeast border. Thessaly was also topographically different from most of Greece. Ample pasture land permitted a large number of horses to be maintained. Finally, Thessalian culture developed a feudal structure where the wealthy and powerful owned land and horses and determined the structure of the army. An indicator of the feudal nature of Thessaly, as well as the importance of horse culture, is that a typical levy for military service on an aristocratic overseer and a section of land was 80 infantrymen and 40 cavalrymen. Cavalry could make up as much as half of the Thessalian army. One source puts the composition of the Thessalian army at the end of the seventh century BC at 10,000 infantry and 6,000 cavalry. The Thessalian cavalry reached its largest size when they fielded a force of 8,000, including their allies, early in the fourth century.[20]

The Thessalians were outstanding horsemen, and the horse was integral to their culture. One of the national sports was *tauroxathapsia*, or bull throwing. This sport was quite similar to modern American rodeo bulldogging: the mounted Thessalian chased down a bull and then leaped from the horse to wrestle the bull to the ground. The Thessalians were also avid horse racers and in fact won the horse race competition in the first Olympic games.[21]

As regional warfare engulfed Greece, the Thessalians were in great demand as mercenaries. By acquiring their service, or the service of other Greeks who also had equestrian skills (such as the Boeotians), a particular side could quickly acquire an advantage over an opposing phalanx. However, it became obvious that a function as important as mounted combat could not be trusted to mercenaries. In 457 BC, during the battle for control of central Greece at Tanagra, 1,000 Thessalian mercenary cavalry deserted the Athenian army and joined Sparta, costing Athens the battle. Events such as these illustrated with blood and defeat the fact that each Greek state required its own competent and reliable cavalry arm.[22]

Cavalry quickly became an integral part of Greek warfare. The primary offensive purpose of the cavalry was to threaten the flanks and rear of an enemy phalanx. An additional task for the cavalry was to isolate a phalanx from its logistics base. Defending cavalry covered the phalanx from enemy cavalry attack. To gain an offensive advantage, light infantry, using javelins and slings, mixed with attacking cavalry, adding weight and dimension to the assault on the defending cavalry. Defending cavalry, in response, added light infantry to create an integrated force to protect the phalanx which, if successful, could free up the defending cavalry to then attempt to threaten the enemy's phalanx. The phalanx was still the center of Greek warfare, but as the fourth century BC entered its second half, winning battles became more complex; no longer was the superior discipline and push of the hoplites in the phalanx enough to secure victory. The superior hoplite force could be defeated if its supporting cavalry and light infantry were not equally superior. Victory in fourth-century Greece required the deft coordination of a combined force of three arms: cavalry, light infantry, and hoplite heavy infantry.

Greek cavalry tactics, as they evolved over the course of the Peloponnesian and subsequent wars, put equal emphasis on attack and defense. The first issue that the cavalry had to address was the opposing force's cavalry. A Persian cavalry force attacked the enemy through a series of archery assaults. Because of the hoplite influence, Greek cavalry had little respect for missile weapons–particularly bows. The main means of destroying or routing the enemy, whether he was cavalry or a hoplite phalanx, was through close combat with lance and sword. Cavalry could be attacked directly, whereas the phalanx had to be attacked in its rear and flanks. Greek cavalry, like the hoplite phalanx, relied on discipline, morale, training, and physical ability to beat their enemy: knee to knee and horse to horse. Fighting from a distance using missile weapons was not honorable.[23] A fast cavalry charge was the Greek solution to a missile attack.

Much of the equipment and technique of the Greek cavalry was similar to that of the Persians. Individual troopers were armed with a lance that may have been a dual-purpose weapon, used in hand-to-hand combat or thrown. An open-faced helmet and a light corselet of armor, boots or lower leg wrappings, and a sword would have completed the standard accoutrements of the Greek cavalryman. Notably absent as a standard and important piece of equipment of the Greek cavalryman was the bow. Instead, two javelins were standard in addition to a spear. Over time the javelins were discarded. A rather severe snaffle-type bit controlled the horse. A body covering armored the horse providing some protection from glancing blows. This light armor was made of either heavy padded cloth or leather. They also may have had bronze armor protecting the horse's neck and thighs.[24]

Alexander's Cavalry

The Thessalians were, without a doubt, the finest Greek cavalry. However, skillful integration of all arms won battles. By the middle of the fourth century, all the Greek states had some sort of cavalry force. To have the best army one had to be superior in all arms, and cavalry was essential to victory. The best Greek army emerged in 342 BC out of the northernmost of the Greek lands: Macedonia.

Over a 36-year period, from 359 to 323 BC, Macedonia fielded one of the greatest armies the world has ever seen. The formula for Macedonian military success was the adroit combination of highly proficient infantry, cavalry, and light forces combined with exceptional tactical command, strategic vision, and unmatched personal leadership and bravery. Among all these attributes, the cavalry was the arm upon which the Macedonian leaders Philip II and his successor and son, Alexander III (Alexander the Great), relied to achieve victory.

Macedonia was on the fringes of the various wars that plagued Greece through the fifth and fourth centuries. They contributed a small force to the battle of Plataea–on the Persian side.[25] Macedonia's peripheral involvement appears to have been a function of its somewhat isolated location as the northernmost of the Greek states. Many of the southern Greeks looked upon the Macedonians as semibarbarian and only marginally Greek. Macedonia did, however, come in conflict with the northern Greek port city of Chalkidike. Chalkidike had easy access to the sea–something that was sorely needed in mostly landlocked Macedonia. Chalkidike and Athens were allies in the Athenian League and this alliance became a source of conflict between Macedonia and the southern Greek power. While skirmishing with its Greek neighbors, Macedonian's primary concern in the fourth century was its non-Greek neighbors: Illyria (modern-day Balkans) to the northwest and Thrace (modern-day northwest Turkey) to the east. Throughout the first half of the fourth century Macedonia was being invaded by, or invading, one or more of these adversaries.

In 359 BC King Perdiccas of Macedonia and 4,000 of his men died in a losing battle with the Illyrians. The morale of the Macedonian army was shattered, and Perdiccas's brother, Philip II, took the throne. Philip immediately set about rebuilding the army as a matter of national survival. His focus was the infantry because he judged Macedonian cavalry to be generally competent. Philip introduced the *sarissa* thrusting spear into the infantry's arsenal. The sarissa was considerably longer than the standard Greek fighting spear and, if well handled, gave Macedonian infantry a distinct advantage in close combat. Philip also emphasized training and drill, thus instilling superb unit cohesion and discipline within the ranks. Philip's reforms had an immediate effect. One year after their defeat, the Macedonians, under Philip, crushed the Illyrian army under Bardylis in a battle in which two characteristics of Macedonian warfare emerged: a vigorous cavalry attack and a punishing pursuit after the battle. The Illyrians lost 7,000 men.[26]

Its location and its aristocratic society contributed to the development of a mounted tradition in Macedonia. Areas of eastern Macedonia, bordering on Thrace and Chalkidike, were suitable for horse pasturing.[27] An aristocratic tradition led to a concentration of wealth, which was necessary to breed, maintain, and train horses. These conditions, combined with an enemy in Thrace that was often mounted, resulted in a competent cavalry arm. Frequently changing and indifferent leadership, however, prevented the Macedonian cavalry from being exceptional, and in the same class as their southern neighbors, the Thessalians. However, this changed under the discipline and leadership of Philip II, who now applied the same strict training regime he developed for his infantry to his cavalry. Training honed the skills of the cavalry force and brought them to a level equal to the Thessalians.

Macedonian cavalry also benefited from the esteem Macedonian culture placed on the horse and horsemanship. The relationship of Philip's son Alexander and his horse Bucephalas exemplifies the place of the horse within Macedonian culture. The prince acquired the horse at a young age, and he was his war mount through all Alexander's most famous battles. At age 30 the horse died while on campaign in India. Alexander's relationship with his horse, as both master and companion, and the manner in which Bucephalas is described in the ancient histories reflects the regard with which individual mounts were viewed within the Macedonian culture.[28]

Macedonian horse equipment had not changed significantly from what the Persians and the Assyrians had used. Cavalrymen rode bareback, with only a horse blanket, often an animal skin, between them and the horse. A leather bridle and a snaffle bit, as well as the rider's position, controlled the horse. The Macedonians used horse armor, but in the existing evidence of Macedonian cavalry in action it is often absent. There were two primary components of Macedonian horse armor, both recommended by the Greek cavalry expert Xenophon: the peytral and the chamfron. The peytral was a metal chest protector that extended from the horse blanket forward and wrapped around the horse's chest similar to a breast plate. The chamfron was a head covering that covered the horse's poll and extended down the forehead to his nose. The peytral might also include a decorative crest.[29]

In the Greek tradition, the composite bow was not a standard part of the heavy cavalry's equipment. Though armored, Macedonian cavalry were not as heavily armored as cavalry in southern Greece where the hoplite influence was stronger. Macedonian cavalry do not appear to have worn armored breastplates as a matter of course. Instead, a padded corselet was sometimes used. Macedonian cavalry usually wore an open face helmet of the Boeotian type, although some illustrations also indicate a Thracian type in use.[30]

The most important Macedonian weapon, and also the most controversial as far as the cavalry is concerned, was the sarissa. The Macedonian infantry became renowned for the exceptionally long sarissa that they employed with deadly force. This two-handed weapon was over 14 feet long and gave the infantry phalanx significant standoff distance when engaging other infantry. However, controversy remains as to whether the cavalry carried this same, unusually long weapon, or a shorter more standard cavalry lance of about 9 feet in length. Despite the controversy, the evidence indicates that whichever the cavalry carried it was longer than the combination javelin/lance of about 7 feet common among the Persian cavalry. The reason for the controversy is that the difference between a 9-foot and a 14-foot lance is significant in terms of weight and the influence the lance had in combat. It is not possible to analyze the close fighting tactics of Macedonian cavalry unless the size of the weapon is first determined. Several well-regarded experts on ancient cavalry stand on different sides of the argument. M. M. Markle, in a 1982 article titled "Macedonian Arms and Tactics under Alexander the Great," makes the case for the longer weapon. Conversely, Robert E. Gaebel makes the argument for the shorter version of the weapon. He bases his argument on the ease of handling a shorter weapon while riding bareback and engaged in hand-to-hand combat. Gaebel maintains that the longer weapon was just too heavy to handle with one hand and that the warrior would not risk being in the midst of combat and have to drop the reins of his horse to handle a two-handed weapon.[31] The more compelling argument, based on horsemanship, is for the shorter lance. A butt point on the opposite end permitted the cavalryman to rapidly change from an underhanded grip to an overhanded grip and thrust by simply reversing the weapon. It also permitted the cavalryman to wield the weapon even if the head was broken off.

Philip inherited a cavalry force of about 600 horsemen from his brother Perdiccas. This force, in the Hippeis tradition, consisted of the loyal noble and wealthy families of Macedonia, but no matter how well trained, it was insufficient in number for the infantry-cavalry army that Philip envisioned. Philip granted land in conquered territory to entice cavalry recruits. As Philip consolidated and expanded his kingdom, more land, and consequently more horsemen, were available. Cavalry recruitment and retention was also encouraged by compensation. A Macedonian cavalryman's pay was three times that of a Macedonian infantryman. Thessalonian cavalry, now allied to Macedonia, were paid two and a half times infantry wages. In six years, Philip expanded his cavalry force from 600 horsemen to 3,000, of which 2,000 were Macedonian natives. By the time of the battle of Chaeronea in 338 BC, the Macedonian native cavalry numbered about 3,000. Later, when Alexander prepared to invade Asia in 334 BC, the total was up to 3,300 heavy cavalry and an additional 400 light cavalry, excluding allied cavalry.[32]

The first obligation of these land-owning cavalrymen was service to their king. This allegiance was their livelihood. In that sense they were professional cavalrymen. As their numbers increased so did their proficiency at riding and fighting. Riding, to a large extent, is an art, and although training can impart the rudiments quickly, acquiring true proficiency requires years of experience. Philip kept his army almost continuously at war, and therefore his professional cavalry became exceptionally experienced both as individuals and as units.

Another indicator of increasing professionalism within the Macedonian cavalry was the growing formality of the organization. When the cavalry reached what was essentially its final form under Alexander, it was composed of two broad types: heavy cavalry, known as the companion cavalry; and light cavalry, called the *prodromoi* or *sarissophoroi*. The companion cavalry were the most numerous and the most important. They were recruited from the major cities and regions of Macedonia and organized into 14 territorial squadrons plus an additional royal squadron. Each squadron consisted of approximately 200 troopers further divided into four, 50-man troops. The 14 squadrons were further organized into two, 7-squadron regiments each with its own commander: one regiment combining the squadrons of upper Macedonia and the other comprising the 7 squadrons of lower Macedonia.[33]

Macedonian cavalry positioned themselves in the traditional locale of cavalry—to either flank of the infantry. Alexander had a preference for his companion heavy cavalry, usually commanding it himself, on the right flank, and positioning his equally competent allied Thessalian cavalry on the left flank. Light cavalry were capable of a

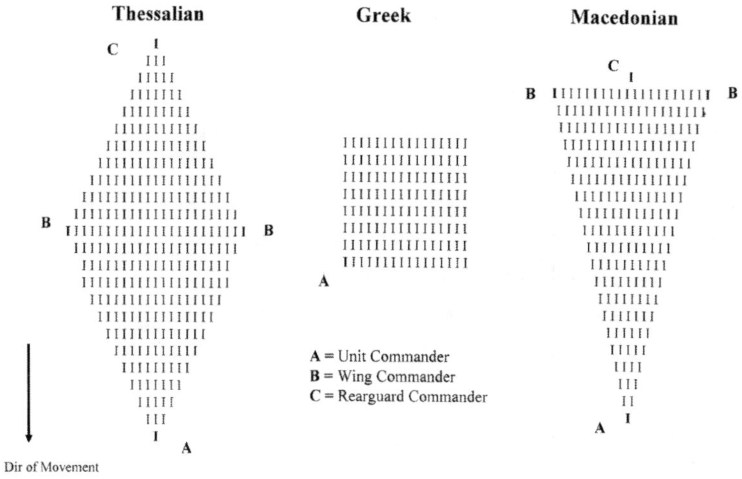

Cavalry formations. Alexander's cavalry was mostly Macedonians and Thessalonians. The Thessalonians were considered the finest horsemen among the Greeks. The complexity of the formations is a reflection of the degree of horsemanship among the troops. The Greek square formation is the simplest formation to maneuver. (*Author*)

variety of tasks independent of the main battle, and they, therefore, could be found virtually anywhere on the battlefield. In a reconnaissance role they might be well forward, making initial contact with the enemy and keeping their commander informed. In a security role, they might be to the flanks of the defending or attacking main body of infantry and cavalry. In this capacity they concealed the movement and dispositions of the main body of soldiers.

Macedonian cavalry preferred the wedge formation. The Thessalians and the Persians likely influenced this choice by the Macedonians. The Thessalians used a diamond-shaped formation while the Persians used the similar but simpler wedge. The broad characteristics of the formations were the same. The squadron commander positioned himself at the apex of the Macedonian wedge formation. This formation was preferred for several reasons. The leader of the wedge was very visible at the apex and the remaining formation was thus able to maintain position and direction within the rapidly moving unit. It also facilitated the leader's ability to concentrate the combat power of the formation on a single point in the enemy formation, which the leader could select during the approach to the charge. Success at the impact point allowed deep penetration into the enemy formation. Such a deep and calculated breach of the enemy line allowed the cavalry to destroy the enemy formation from the inside out.

Macedonian cavalry won their battles through close combat and were trained to attack both infantry and cavalry formations. Macedonian commanders understood that infantry had to be approached judiciously and attacked from the flank or the rear. Upon engagement of the formations, individual combat dominated. Arrian described it thus: "It was a cavalry battle with, as it were, infantry tactics: horse against horse, man against man, locked together."[34] Plutarch wrote, "For the enemy pressed upon them with loud shouts, and matching horse with horse, plied their lances, and their swords when their lances were shattered."[35] The Persians tried to adjust to this new manner of cavalry warfare. After the battle of Granikos, the Persian leader Darius attempted to reequip some of his cavalry with long lances. However, the adoption of new techniques and armaments did not make much of a difference later at the battle of Issos because the Macedonians had greater experience and superior skill.[36]

Macedonian Cavalry in Battle

The Macedonian cavalry was not markedly different from the Greek cavalry. In particular, the Thessalians were comparable in individual and unit capability. The employment of the Macedonian cavalry was what made it superior to anything seen prior, or for a millennium afterward. Boldness, vision, and exquisite timing, derived from the inspired and personal leadership of Alexander, were the characteristics of Macedonian cavalry success. Several battles illustrate the distinctive employment of Macedonian cavalry: Philip II's decisive victory at Chaeronea, and Alexander III's string of victories at Granikos, Issus, and Gaugamela. These battles became the model for the employment of cavalry that other armies tried to emulate into the twentieth century.

One of the few battles that Philip II waged, and of which some detail is known, is perhaps his most important–Chaeronea in 338 BC. This battle established firm Macedonian control over the Greek city-states. Philip arrived on the field with a well-trained Macedonian army of about 30,000, including at least 2,000 cavalry.[37] A Greek army of about the same size, consisting mostly of Athenian and Theban forces, opposed him. The two relatively evenly matched sides brought to the battlefield different tactical approaches. Two main differences existed between the armies. The first was the nature of their infantry. The Macedonian infantry carried the much longer sarrisa spear but did not wear as much armor as the traditional Greek hoplites. The second major difference was in the number and quality of cavalry. The Macedonians fielded an elite force of approximately 2,000 cavalry. This force was the companion cavalry, commanded by Philip's 18-year-old son, Alexander III.

The two armies deployed facing each other in the valley of Chaeronea. Both armies anchored their flanks on the high terrain to the south, and on the river bank

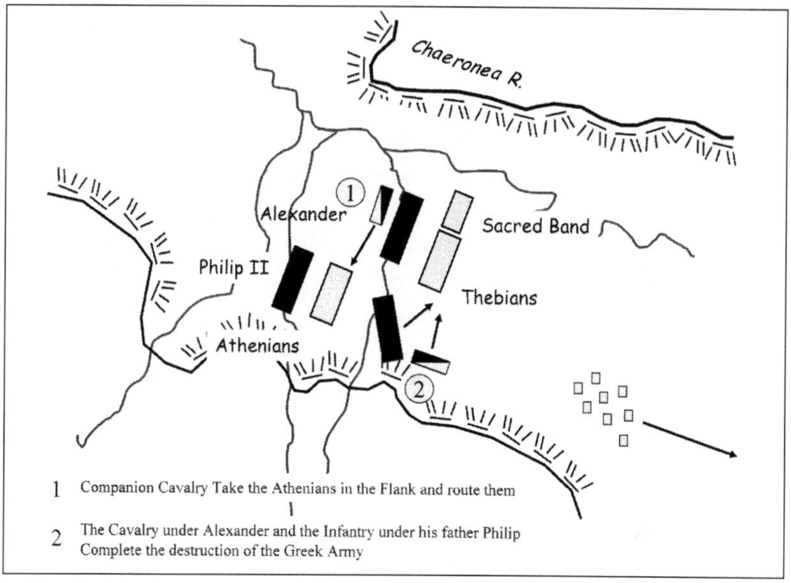

The battle of Chaeronae, 388 BC.

to the north. The southern Greeks deployed with the Athenians on the left and the Thebans on the right. The elite "Sacred Band" of the Theban army occupied the extreme right flank. Philip II positioned himself with his right flank infantry. Alexander commanded the Macedonian left, and positioned himself with the 2,000-strong companion cavalry.

The battle began with infantry phalanxes locked in combat. The infantry of both armies were equally skilled although a slight advantage in numbers favored the Macedonians. As a bloody standoff developed, Philip intentionally withdrew his right flank infantry. As the Athenians advanced against this flank, the flank of their phalanx became exposed. Alexander then led the Macedonian cavalry against this flank as Philip stopped withdrawing and began to advance. The combination of Macedonian infantry in the front and cavalry attacking the flank broke the Athenian phalanx. As the Athenians fled the field, the Macedonian cavalry and right flank turned on the exposed phalanxes of Thebes. Without a solid line, a combination of cavalry and infantry cut the Thebans apart. The Athenians suffered over 2,000 casualties in the battle, and the Theban contingent suffered much worse. Some estimates put Theban casualties as high as 6,000. The entire 300-strong elite "Sacred Band" infantry was destroyed.

The battle established Macedonian hegemony over the Greek city-states. It also demonstrated the superiority of the Macedonian combined arms battle tactics over

Greek hoplite warfare. With Greece a secure Macedonian base, Philip turned his attention to expanding Macedonian dominance east, into Anatolia.

Although he sent an advance army across the Hellespont, Philip never realized his vision of conquering Persia. He was assassinated in 334 BC. It remained for his son, Alexander the Great, to carry out Philip's ambition of avenging the Persian invasion of Greece. The first step in Alexander's campaign to conquer Persia was to establish the Macedonian army in Asia Minor. The battle of Granikos secured the Macedonian beachhead in Anatolia.

Alexander's crossing of the Hellespont was unopposed. However, various satraps united to form a formidable army and challenge Alexander's presence in Anatolia. This Persian force numbered approximately 100,000, including 20,000 Greek mercenaries and 20,000 cavalry. Alexander's army numbered about 40,000; only about 5,000 were cavalry. His cavalry divided into two main contingents: the Macedonian companion cavalry of approximately 2,500, and the Thessalian cavalry of approximately 2,000. The Macedonian infantry had approximately 20,000 men. The balance of the Macedonian force consisted of about 12,000 allied or mercenary infantry. [38]

Possibly because of their inferiority in heavy infantry, the Persian satraps decided to pick a strong defensive position in hopes of destroying Alexander as he attacked.

Alexander immediately recognized the strength of the Persian position and opted for a swift attack to overcome it. Alexander's strategy required a rapid crossing of the river under the fire of Persian archers. The light cavalry led the way across the river. They encountered showers of arrows and javelins, and Persian cavalry who came down to the edge of the riverbank to contest the crossing in close combat. Realizing that the light cavalry might falter, Alexander crossed with the royal squadron to stiffen their attack. As Alexander made his presence felt on the far side of the river, the bulk of the companion cavalry also crossed. With the arrival of the companions the tide of the melee quickly turned in favor of the armored and skilled Macedonian fighters. The sarissa lances of the Macedonians also gave them an advantage. The Persian cavalry broke and began to stream to the rear. This permitted the Macedonian cavalry to gain the far side of the river and fall onto the left flank, and the rear, of the Persian infantry. At the same time the Macedonian infantry began crossing. Without their cavalry and pressed from front and flank, the Persian infantry quickly retreated. The only unbroken Persian forces on the field were the 20,000 Greek mercenaries. These professionals recognized the disaster around them and attempted to surrender. Alexander, thinking in nationalistic terms, considered the mercenaries traitors to the Greek cause and ordered the attack to continue. The phalanx of the Greeks was attacked on all sides, and they were eventually overrun. The Macedonians massacred the Greeks and 2,000 who surrendered became slaves.[39]

The Persian army in Anatolia was broken, and Alexander was free to establish control of the Aegean port cities and to advance south along the Mediterranean coast.

Alexander consolidated his hold on Anatolia in 333 BC. Meanwhile, Darius II, the king of Persia, responded to the disaster at Granikos by raising and personally leading an army out of Mesopotamia with the objective of destroying Alexander once and for all. Darius managed to maneuver his huge army of over 300,000 to a position north of Alexander and astride his land line of communications. Alexander had the option of avoiding Darius and continuing his campaign south along the Mediterranean coast, or of turning back north to eliminate the threat in his rear. He chose the latter option. The two armies met at the town of Issos. Again, the Macedonian cavalry, personally led by Alexander, decisively defeated the Persians. A pursuit ensued in which Darius only escaped capture by abandoning his chariot. His survival was bittersweet as Alexander captured Darius's family along with the Persian baggage train and treasury in Damascus. According to the Greek historian Arrian, 100,000 Persian infantry and 10,000 cavalry were killed in the battle.[40]

Victory at Issus ensured Macedonian control of Anatolia. Rather than turn east, directly into the heart of Persia, Alexander resumed his southward advance, eventually conquering Egypt. In the summer of 331 BC, with the Mediterranean firmly under control, Alexander turned east and advanced into Persia.

Alexander led his army from Egypt, north into Syria, and then east crossing the Euphrates River at Thapsacus. From there he continued along an indirect route north and east toward Babylon. He crossed the Tigris and marched toward Arbela. This more circuitous route protected the left flank of his march and allowed his army to operate in a slightly cooler climate, and in an area with better forage. Four days after crossing the Tigris, the Macedonians encountered the Persian advanced guard. From prisoners, Alexander learned that Darius was encamped near the town of Gaugamela. The Persians were positioned on ground of their choosing, in an area Darius had groomed for battle–a terrain free of any obstacles that could impede his equestrian forces.[41]

Darius planned to employ a significant chariot force as well as elephants, in addition to his cavalry. The Persian army at Gaugamela, despite its losses in previous campaigns, was still a highly formidable force, easily outnumbering the Macedonians. The ancient sources vary considerably but all comment on its large size. A conservative estimate is that the Persian infantry numbered 200,000 and the cavalry 45,000. In addition, the Persian force contained 200 scythed chariots and a contingent of war elephants. The Macedonian force consisted of 40,000 infantry and 7,000 cavalry.[42]

The Macedonians deployed in their usual fashion: Thessalian cavalry on the left, infantry in the center, and Alexander and the Macedonian cavalry on the right.

Allied and mercenary cavalry augmented the Macedonian cavalry. The Macedonian infantry were in a deep, tight, two-tiered formation, with the second line of infantry prepared to face to the rear in anticipation of a successful Persian envelopment.

Although the details and sequencing of the battle are impossible to determine, the essential actions are not. The Persian strategy was fairly simple. The Persians planned to use their large cavalry advantage to envelop both flanks of the Macedonians. Simultaneously, the scythed chariots would rip holes in the center of the Macedonian infantry. Alexander's plan was equally simple: prevent envelopment while locating an opportunity to charge with the companion cavalry against a gap in the Persian line. Then, the combination of companion cavalry and the Macedonian phalanx would destroy the enemy.

Unlike earlier encounters between the Persians and Macedonians, the Persians took the initiative. The Persian right flank cavalry, including 50 scythed chariots, pushed forward against the Thessalians on the Macedonian left flank. The Persian left flank moved to outflank the Macedonians, but the Macedonian allied cavalry matched their move forcing the Persian cavalry to move farther and farther to the flank. Eventually, the Persian left separated from the main body as it sought a flank. In the center, the Persians launched 100 scythed chariots at the Macedonian infantry front.

The Persian attacks achieved mixed results. The Thessalians on the left flank were under extreme pressure. The left wing of the army under Alexander's ablest subordinate, Parmenio, was vastly outnumbered and outflanked. Persian cavalry bypassed the engaged Thessalians and captured the Macedonian baggage train. However, things did not go as well for the Persians in the center. The massed chariot attack failed as light infantry killed many of the chariot horses and then made short work of the crews. The Macedonians then trapped and dispatched those few chariots that made it through the light infantry screen.

On the Macedonian right flank, a pitched cavalry battle developed. Participants included contingents of Macedonian, allied, and mercenary cavalry, facing the Persian cavalry from Scythia, Bactria, and other provinces under the command of Bessus. As this pitched battle drifted ever farther to the Macedonian right, it exposed the left flank of the Persian center. As this gap developed, Alexander led the companion cavalry against it. The charge of the companions hit the gap in the Persian line and quickly blew it open. This put the companions in position to wheel left into the exposed flank of the Persian infantry center. The charge of the companions was the signal for the advance of the Macedonian infantry (minus two left flank units who remained to support Parmenio and the left wing). As the companions crashed into the flank of the Persian center and the infantry phalanx began its assault, panic began to ripple across the Persian ranks. Darius, from his position in the center on his tall chariot, probably observed the units beginning to disintegrate. The Persian center quickly crumbled. With defeat imminent, Darius fled the field, which hastened the destruction of the Persian formations.

From his position on the left flank the Persian cavalry commander Bessus saw the defeat of the Persian center. Recognizing that the battle was lost, he disengaged his cavalry and withdrew in good order. On the right flank, the Persians maintained their pressure until word of Darius's departure reached their ranks. With the news of their leader's retreat, the Persian attack faltered, and in that brief pause the Thessalian cavalry counterattacked, sending the last of the Persian army into retreat.

The charge of the companion cavalry at Granikos. This illustration by Charles Le Brun depicts Alexander leading the companions up the bank of river against Persian cavalry. (*Author*)

The collapse of the Persian center invited a vigorous and immediate pursuit. Alexander, however, remained cautious as he wanted to ensure the integrity of the left wing, still threatened as the Persian center collapsed. Once assured of Parmenio's success, he turned his cavalry to the pursuit of Darius and the Persians. At dusk the cavalry rested, but only long enough to refresh their horses. At midnight the pursuit resumed. The companions captured the Persian camp and baggage train including Darius's chariot. Once again Darius escaped with his life. The pursuit ended at Arbela, 75 miles from the battlefield.[43]

Casualties at Gaugamela were heavier for the Macedonians than in previous battles. The Macedonians suffered because of the outstanding performance of the Persian cavalry on both flanks. Many of the Persian cavalry wore mail and other protective garments and were thus better protected than the Macedonians and their allies. Open terrain around the battlefield permitted the Persians to scatter and avoid pursuit. The Greek historian Arrian's estimate of Macedonian losses in the battle at between 100 and 500 dead and many wounded appears dramatically low; it is more likely to be closer to 4,000. Arrian states that the Macedonians also lost over 1,000 horses, which seems probable. Nearly half the horse losses, the result of wounds or exhaustion, were within the companion cavalry. Persian casualties were very high, but estimates vary considerably between 40,000 and 300,000.[44]

Smashing the Persian army at Gaugamela was not the last of Alexander's victories. Many more would follow as he conquered the remote portions of modern-day Afghanistan, Iran, Pakistan, and India. His subsequent victories did not vary much in the tactics he employed for success. The Macedonian way of war was a watershed in the employment of cavalry. Macedonia's military demonstrated that cavalry, working in conjunction with other arms, increased the capabilities of the total force. They also showed that cavalry could have decisive effects in close combat. Finally, the Macedonians demonstrated that cavalry, executing a vigorous pursuit, could annihilate an enemy force. Successful pursuit by cavalry became an essential component in operational warfare and campaigning.

Chapter Three

THE ROMANS

Charges of cavalry are equally useful at the beginning, the middle, and the end of battle. They should be made always, if possible, on the flanks of the infantry, especially when this last is engaged in front.–NAPOLEON BONAPARTE

Alexander the Great, for all his phenomenal accomplishments, did not establish a definitive procedure for identifying his successor. Because of this, his empire disintegrated soon after his death in 323 BC. Following this collapse, a number of his generals established themselves as the regional rulers in major portions of the short-lived empire. As Alexander's empire disintegrated, the last of the great ancient civilizations was rising in the Mediterranean–beginning in the Italian city-state of Rome.

The foundation of Roman dominance was its military. And like Rome itself, the army as an institution evolved over the more than 800 years of Roman rule. To understand the Roman army, it is helpful to study the military system in its three major incarnations: the republic army, the principate period imperial army, and the army of the late empire. Each army had its own organization, equipment, and style of warfare. The cavalry forces of Rome evolved in parallel with the army.

REPUBLIC CAVALRY

During the early republican period, the Roman army was composed of civilian militia who were not full-time soldiers but rather citizen soldiers of Rome. Although they were not professionals, they were required to serve for the duration of a campaign. This could last several years and in extreme cases, decades. The republic army's performance was usually weak at the beginning of a campaign and improved with experience. At the end of the war or campaign, the army disbanded and recruited a new group when the need arose.

The Romans recruited cavalrymen, known as the *equites* (horsemen), in the same manner as the army except that the cavalry recruits came from the elite of Roman society. Significant property and wealth, as well as Roman citizenship, were required to join the equites. Distinguished service in the cavalry was an effective way for a young ambitious Roman from a good family to make contacts with other upwardly mobile young men and hopefully attract the eye of a politically well-positioned mentor.[1]

The often short service of Roman republic cavalryman is only one of many explanations for the cavalry's generally poor battle performance. The selection of cavalrymen based on wealth rather than ability is another possible explanation. Unlike in the northern Greek states of Thessaly and Macedonia, the wealthy aristocratic class of Rome did not prize the horse and horsemanship as part of its social and cultural tradition. Rome's geographic distance from the horsemen of the steppe and the nature of the local terrain helped ensured no such tradition developed. And, the republic did not often face enemies who mounted significant cavalry forces and thus the need for a competent cavalry force was not compelling. For these reasons, the Roman republic did not produce high-quality cavalry.[2] Nonetheless, the cavalry, because of its social status, were considered the elite of the republican army; and that was reflected in their pay, which was three times that of the infantry legionnaire and half again that of an infantry centurion.[3]

A cavalryman provided his own mount with the understanding that it would be replaced by the state if it were lost in battle. The cavalry was organized into the standard Roman legion of the time, which consisted of five parts: three types of heavy infantry, light infantry, and cavalry. The legion totaled 4,200 infantrymen and occasionally on campaign could number 6,000. To this total the cavalry only added 300 horses and riders. The cavalry of the legion organized into 10, 30-man cavalry troops called *turmae.* Each turmae was further divided into three 10-man squads commanded by a *decurion* (literally, leader of 10). The senior decurion commanded the turmae.[4]

The republic cavalryman was equipped in a manner very similar to the Macedonian heavy cavalry. A lance with a butt spike was the main weapon. The cavalryman's equipment also included the *gladius*, the short sword of the legionnaire. One distinguishing characteristic of Roman cavalry was that a round, 30-inch diameter shield was standard equipment and carried on the left arm. The Roman cavalry wore a mail shirt or bronze cuirass and a helmet. The horse of the republic cavalryman was not armored.[5]

Principate Cavalry

Caius Marius is credited with the professionalization of the Roman army in 107 BC. Due to restrictions on recruiting, he solicited volunteers for military service from citizens who had not, in the past, met the property qualifications for service. These soldiers, drawn from the lower echelons of society, looked at service in the army as a means of social ascent, and many preferred to remain in the service indefinitely.

Marius's actions were precedent setting. From that point on, the only requirement for service in the legions was citizenship. This practice eventually produced a professional army of long-serving volunteer citizens who improved the quality of the army. Unlike the republican army, which disbanded after each major campaign or war, the principate army served continuously. These changes led to the reorganization of the legion and the elimination of class distinctions among the rank and file of the army.[6]

The reorganization of the legion removed almost all cavalry and light infantry. During this time Rome relied increasingly on foreign troops to supplement the combat power of the Roman legions. These units, called *auxilia*, or auxiliaries, replaced the Roman citizen cavalry. These foreign cavalry units organized into discreet units and they reported, through their officers, directly to the army commander. The cavalry auxilia organized into cohorts called *alae*. *Ala*, the Latin word for wing, referred to the cavalry's traditional position in the battle line on the wings of the infantry center. There were two sizes of alae: the *quingeniary alae*, consisting of 512 men divided into 16 turmae of 32 men each; and the *milliary alae*, which fielded a force of 768 men divided into 24 turmae. The alae commander held the rank of prefect. The decurion who led each turmae held the equivalent rank of *centurion* in the infantry. Expectations of the decurion were high: "In like manner the decurion is to be preferred to the command of a troop for his activity and address in mounting his horse completely armed; for his skill in riding and in the use of the lance and bow; for his attention in forming his men to all the evolutions of the cavalry; and for his care in obliging them to keep their cuirasses, lances and helmets always bright and in good order. The splendor of the arms has no inconsiderable effect in striking terror into an enemy."[7] There was no official relationship between particular alae and legions, but commanders often attached alae to legions for specific operations. Over time, some of these relationships became habitual. The alae purchased their horses in the region where they were organized, but were equipped with Roman weapons and supplies, and organized, paid, and trained according to the Roman standards. The official language for duty was Latin.

At the beginning of the imperial period, the Romans recruited the troopers of the alae in mass by tribe. They then served their entire 25-year service within their alae. The veteran and his family received Roman citizenship at the end of his term of service. As time went by, the number of alae members who already had their citizenship steadily increased. This partly reflected the number of second-generation family members enlisting for service. In some cases the trooper could receive his citizenship before the end of his service. Units that performed with particular distinction in battle might receive their citizenship as a reward–in that case the title *civium Romanorum* was added to the unit name. Merit was the usual basis for advancement in the alae. Battle experience, time in service, as well as personal connections were also important for advancement.

Once formed, the alae structure was very durable and scores of alae remained in continuous service from the first century AD into the beginning of the third century.[8] In the first century, Gallic forces (provinces of Lugdunensis, Britannia, and Belgica) made up the vast majority of Roman cavalry: 18,000 of a total *alae* force of 40,500. Other provinces providing significant components were Tarraconenis (Spain), 6,000; Thrace, 4,500; and Pannonia (Hungary), 4,000.[9] The alae gave the imperial Roman army a larger number of cavalry who were united, well trained, and could be trusted to conduct more difficult, independent, and technically challenging missions, such as reconnaissance.[10] Although the alae were an improvement over republic cavalry, and individually the troopers were very good, their performance in battle was mixed. This was due to sometimes wavering allegiances to Rome, but most often to poor tactical employment by Roman officers and generals.

The reorganization in the imperial period did not entirely eliminate the legion cavalry. A small group of 120 cavalrymen remained as part of the legion organization, which had grown to 5,500. These men were no longer recruited specifically from the elite of Roman society, but rather based on either duty performance or prior experience with horses from within the infantry ranks of the legion itself. It also appears from the legion records that these men remained assigned to their original legion cohort. They were then detached for service with the legion cavalry. The legion cavalry all but disappear from the written record because their small numbers precluded them from being a significant combat force. Their missions were reduced to dispatch carrying and scouting. It is likely that in small police actions, conducted separately from a major campaign, their role in the legion was still critical.[11]

In many ways, Julius Caesar represented the ideal Roman cavalry commander. Suetonius, writing in AD 110, describes Caesar as "highly skilled in arms and horsemanship, and of incredible powers of endurance." Plutarch relates that "he had been an expert rider from boyhood. He had trained himself to put his hands behind his back and then, keeping them tightly clasped, to put his horse to its full gallop. And in the Gallic campaigns he got himself into the habit of dictating letters on horseback, keeping two secretaries busy at once, or even more, according to Oppius." He had a great affinity for horses and his personal mount was special: "He rode a remarkable horse, too, with feet that were almost human; for its hoofs were cloven in such a way as to look like toes. This horse was foaled on his own place, and since the soothsayers had declared that it foretold the rule of the world for its master, he reared it with the greatest care, and was the first to mount it, for it would endure no other rider. Afterwards, too, he dedicated a statue of it before the temple of Venus Genetrix."[12]

A first century Roman cavalryman (left) depicted by Roman Cavalry specialist Nigel Apperley of Newmarket, Suffok, England. The cavalryman is equipped with helmet, leather armor, a spatha sword, lance, and shield. A second century alae cavalryman (right). Note his horse, Trajan, is a Connemara pony which is representative of the pony types that were the most common mounts of the early Imperial Roman cavalry. Chain mail armor was standard for Roman cavalry by this period. A replica of the four-horn Roman military saddle is well displayed in this photo. (*Nigel and Tracey Apperley*)

Caesar was unique among Roman generals in both his understanding of the importance of cavalry and its skillful employment. Caesar's use of large numbers of allied Germanic and Gallic cavalry during his campaigns in Gaul was the inspiration for the institutionalization of the imperial alae cavalry formations.

Armor of the imperial period cavalryman did not change much from the republic cavalry. The standard empire cavalryman wore an open-faced helmet with cheek pieces. A mail armor shirt, reinforced at the shoulders, protected him to mid-thigh. Roman cavalryman at this time began to wear leather breeches to protect their legs and to improve their security in the saddle. The cavalryman was armed with a long (36-inch) straight sword called a *spatha*–replacing the short sword of the republic cavalry. Light, dual-purpose javelins were also part of the individual's arsenal, and a man would carry several. These weapons were relatively short, approximately 6 feet long, included a butt spike, and could be thrown or used in close combat. Shields were made of wood with a leather covering and could be round, rectangular, or oval. Oval was the most common shape in the imperial cavalry, and the shields were quite large, approximately 4 feet high and 2 feet wide.[13]

The imperial Romans did not make any formal distinctions between cavalry types, but battle descriptions mention heavy cavalry and archers. There is no documentation that these units existed formally within the principate Roman system, but it is likely that army and alae commanders adapted individual alae to particular weapons as needed. For example, if a particular *alae* was made up primarily of men from a region where archery was imbedded within the culture, it would be reasonable for the alae to have all or a portion of the unit equipped with bows. An example of this is the Thracian and Syrian *auxilia* who were carefully dispersed throughout the empire because they were the best archers in Roman service and this skill was in limited supply. Units could also be trained to a new system. For example, some lightly armored cavalry changed to heavier armor in the late first century after coming into contact with the eastern *cataphractii* heavy cavalry.[14]

During the second and third centuries, heavily armored and armed cavalry were increasingly in evidence. A knee-length mail cloak covered the neck and arms, and there was an increased use of scale armor. Some cavalrymen carried a heavy, two-handed lance called a *contus*, which was 12 feet long. Horse protection included scale armor barding that protected most of the horse's body and neck, as well as leather and bronze chamfrons, which included intricate metal eye protection.[15]

Late Empire Cavalry

The character of warfare changed in the late imperial period. The Roman army adjusted to low-level warfare–warfare that was decentralized and on a much smaller scale. This new type of combat was to stop raids rather than armies. Cavalry, with its speed and mobility, was ideal for challenging marauding barbarian raiders; and therefore the proportion of cavalry in Roman service increased. Analysis of the early fifth-century AD document *Notitia Dignitatum* suggests that there existed one cavalry unit for every two infantry units–making cavalry one-third of the army's complement of units if not total numbers. In addition, the role of cavalry in battle had become much more important: "The strength of the sixth-century army was undoubtedly its cavalry." By that time the Roman army was transformed into a cavalry-heavy force that anticipated the type of warfare that would dominate the Middle Ages.[16]

The late Roman period–beginning in the mid third century and lasting until the fall of the western Roman Empire toward the end of the sixth century–was a time of incredible turmoil and the gradually diminishing influence and control of the central Roman government. This turmoil negatively affected every aspect of Roman society, including the army and the cavalry. Rome's borders were under almost constant attack, and during this period the strategy of the empire, to the extent that a strategy existed, was decidedly defensive. Various Germanic tribes threatened the western and central provinces, and the eastern provinces were under threat by the powerful Sassanian Empire. At the same time, civil war sapped the strength of the empire.

Late Roman cavalry, fourth or fifth century, archer. Archers were not the most common type of cavalry in the Roman forces but become more prominent in the late period. They were usually recruited from parts of the empire where horse archery was a native skill. This archer carries a "Draco" standard which represents a dragon's head and is said to have made a hissing noise when carried at a gallop. (*Nigel and Tracey Apperley*)

The policy of joint rule evolved in this period with an eastern and western Caesar sharing control of the empire and focusing on regional protection. But dual governorship inhibited standardization of army organization, training, and equipment. It also made it more difficult to concentrate all the resources of the empire at a single decisive point.

The army reflected the divided, defensive, and regionally focused nature of the empire. The total number of troops in the army during this period may have increased slightly, but the size of the legion decreased significantly. By the end of the third century the number of legions had risen to approximately 60, but each had only about a thousand legionnaires. In 212 AD Rome extended citizenship to the greater part of the empire, removing much of the ethnic distinction between the legion and the auxilia. Breaking the infantry into smaller units allowed posting these groups as defensive forces around the perimeter of the empire. In the middle of the third century Emperor Gallienus created all-cavalry reserve forces in Greece, northern Italy, and the Balkans. These new cavalry units used the 120-man legion cavalry and light infantry forces for their initial manpower. They eventually formed 500- to 600-man cavalry reaction forces called *vexillationes* that were able to move quickly and reinforce any part of the empire's borders. They were very effective in this role and were successful in restoring calm on countless occasions. Ironically, because of their rapid action and consistent success, the government failed to appreciate the potential threats that had been averted and eventually lost interest in maintaining the defensive forces. The Romans dispersed the frontier armies by the end of the century.[17]

As the fourth century progressed, the empire became increasingly dysfunctional. The army divided into two major components: the *comitatus*, which was the standing field army, and the static forces of the frontier. Emperor Constantine formed a *comitatus* of five *vexillationes* and five legions. However, a single central army was not flexible enough to deal with the expanses of the empire, and Constantine's successors increased and divided the comitatus to provide field armies on a regional basis. Ultimately, field armies divided between the eastern and western portions of the empire. This probably happened in 365 AD under the emperors Valentinian and Valens.

As the army divided, and then divided again, standardization among subordinate units completely eroded. The *Notitia Dignitatum* records the names of all the major units of the Roman armies in the west at the end of the fourth century, and the east at the beginning of the fifth century. This document indicates that virtually no standardized cavalry organization existed. Dozens of different-named units break down into three general types of cavalry: light cavalry and archers, general purpose cavalry lightly armored and armed with javelins, and heavy cavalry. These units were probably smaller, less armored, and less well trained than their predecessors in the imperial period. The number of cavalry armed with the bow as a primary or secondary weapon had increased significantly because of Persian and Hun influence, and by the sixth century they were the dominant type of cavalry in the eastern empire. To the extent that the emperor could afford, the fully armored *cataphractii* heavy cavalry became the most effective type. They were completely armored in calf-length, long-sleeve mail suits with a hood. Conical helmets with a nose guard replaced the legionary-style helmet. The long heavy lance was their main weapon. Though the cataphratii were in many ways operationally superior to other types of cavalry, the expense of buying and maintaining their armor relegated them to a specialized minority among the mounted forces. Late Roman armies could also include a super-heavy cavalry called *clibanarii*, who wore scale and plate armor and whose horses were also heavily armored. This type of super-heavy cavalry was not particularly useful on the battlefield. When clibanarii were used in 312 AD against the army of Constantine, his infantry surrounded the immobile cavalrymen and clubbed them to death.[18]

Major defeats at the hands of the Persians and Goths in 363 and 378 not only hastened the declining efficiency of the army in general, but illustrated the cavalry's lack of discipline. The taxation system within the empire also broke down and the administration of the army faltered. Units were not paid and local commanders had to equip their soldiers. Often commanders required the individual soldier to provide his own equipment and mounts. Increasingly, commanders and wealthy individuals purchased bands of private warriors, mostly cavalry, called *bucellarii*, to supplement the capabilities of the army. In many, if not most, cases the bucellarii were better equipped and trained than the army's forces.[19] In 476 the mostly Germanic troops of the Roman army in Italy disposed of the last Roman emperor in the west, Romulus

Augustulus. The western empire broke apart into independent provinces and kingdoms, each with its own army–many of which retained some of the practices and traditions of the empire. The empire itself would continue for hundreds of years in the east under the banner of Byzantium and centered in the eastern capital of Constantinople.

Roman Cavalry Horses

As might be expected in a diverse empire such as Rome, over the course of several hundred years, no one specific horse type was ever associated with the empire. Instead, the Roman Empire pulled horses from every corner of the empire and used a variety of techniques to acquire them. Based on the evidence in Roman art and the comments of Roman historians, the ideal horse was large, well muscled, and had a slightly convex head.[20] Though the Romans had an image of a good cavalry mount, the Roman cavalry used virtually all serviceable mounts regardless of the particulars of their general appearance.

Rome became the melting pot of the world's horse markets. The ancient writings record over 50 breeds by name. Rome itself, and the Italian peninsula in general, was not known for quality horses in the ancient world–although horses were well established in those areas where natural pasturing was available. Asian horses, or at least the characteristics of the Asian breeds, arrived in Roman service from two directions. The Asian types, known by the Romans as Persian, Parthian, Thracian, or Thessalian, were probably similar to the modern Akhal-Teke and passed from the Middle East into Greece during the reign of Alexander and his successors. These horses entered Roman service from Greece. The primary characteristic of these breeds, which averaged slightly more than 15 hands, with the largest approaching 16 hands, was their size. The lighter Middle Eastern types, predecessors of the Caspian breed, influenced the chariot horses of the pharaohs and came to Rome from North Africa. The Romans knew them as the Libyan breed. Carthaginians and Numidians brought the light, refined characteristics of this breed to Iberia where they mixed with European stock and became known as the Spanish breed. The Libyan breed was probably closely associated with the modern Arab and Barb. Though the Romans considered the Spanish horse "small and ugly," they still used it and considered it an excellent cavalry mount.[21]

The Roman cavalry got their mounts from various sources. In the republican period, when the equites came from the upper class, a recruit arrived with his own horse. During the imperial period and the late empire when many of the cavalry came from northern empire conquests, they brought their own regional mounts to the force in most cases; therefore, their horses were of a totally different type. As long as alae remained based in or near their home regions, they almost certainly replenished with indigenous horses bred by or for the army in the region. Two of the four original ancient horse types were common in northern Europe: type 1, a Celtic pony type; and type 2, a Norse horse type (a coldblood or draught type horse). These two types are likely to have had strong influences on the horses that came into the Roman Empire through its conquests in central and northern Europe. Together, they may have produced a composite type that was larger than a pony but still small (by modern standards), heavy boned, and not very attractive. Short, shaggy, and stout horses were the likely mounts of Caesar's Gallic and Germanic enemies and allies, and came to be the mounts of the early Gallic alae. During and after the Roman conquest, the Gauls were interested in improving their horse stock. They imported Italian horses and took advantage of Spanish and Libyan horses coming from the south.[22] By the late imperial period, three or four hundred years after Caesar's conquest of Gaul, the horses of central Europe had changed significantly. They were still not very refined, but by then the Asian influence combined with selective breeding would have produced a larger horse that made a substantial cavalry mount.

The Romans preferred stallions for military service because of their aggressiveness. The steppe tribes, along with some European tribes, favored geldings. Gelded horses were less aggressive and thus were easier to train and control. Mixing the types would have caused problems on campaign, so units probably were equipped with either all stallions or all mares and geldings.

Roman Riding Techniques and Equipment

The capabilities of cavalry in action took a major step forward at the beginning of the Roman imperial period. Following the Gallic wars, the Roman cavalry adopted the most important new piece of cavalry equipment since the Assyrians began fielding warriors mounted on horseback: the solid frame saddle.

Though likely of Celtic origin, and possibly adopted by the Romans during campaigns in Spain and Gaul, the Romans standardized the design and use of the solid frame saddle. All cavalry of the empire were equipped with it. Awareness of the saddle–its design, use, and advantages–spread throughout the empire and across its borders. Parthian and Sassanian heavy cavalry used a similar design. It is unknown if they developed it independently or picked up the design from the Celts or from the Romans.

Prior to the adoption of the framed saddle, unframed saddles were in use by many different horse cultures. A rider in an unframed saddle was still very unstable and also sat directly on the back of the horse, putting pressure directly on the horse's spine. The framed saddle addressed both of these issues. The Roman saddle consist-

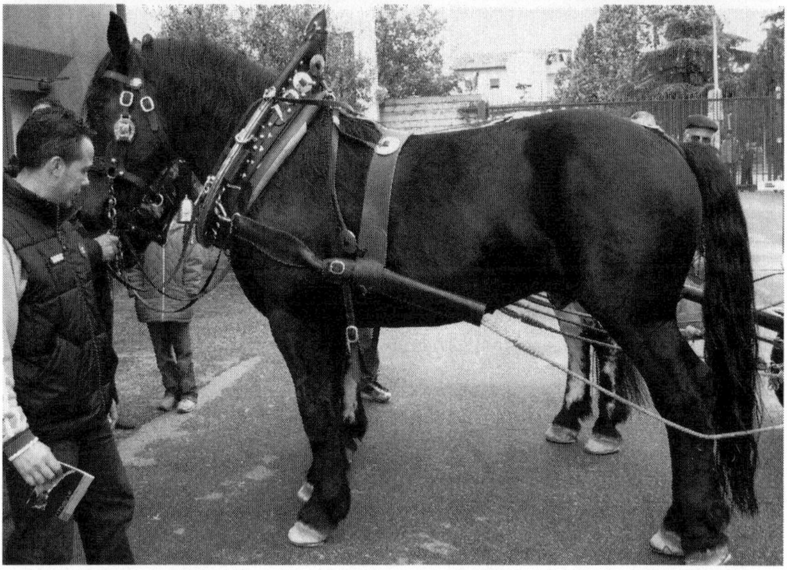

Icelandic horse (top). This breed is representative of the type 1 Northern European pony types common in the ancient world. Austrian Noriker draft horse (bottom). This breed is representative of the type 2 coldblooded heavy horses found in Northern Europe. These two types represent the kinds of horses of the early Imperial Roman alae cavalry. (*Paula Jantunen*)

ed of horns positioned in the four corners of the saddle. A wooden frame covered by leather connected the horns. Key places, where the rider's body came into contact with the frame, and the frame contacted the horse, were padded. The four horns, bracing the rider's upper thighs in the front and his hips in the rear, provided a secure seat. Additionally, the frame arched over the horse's spine, avoiding this sensitive point and resting against the strong back muscles.

Unfortunately, no complete Roman saddles are extant. However, historians and archaeologists working with horse experts, and through experimentation, have managed to infer, with reasonable accuracy, the construction and working of the saddle. Leather saddle covers and metal horn braces have been found at various Roman archeological sites. Using these artifacts as a pattern and by examining Roman statuary of horses and cavalry figures, historian Peter Connolly built a model of a Roman saddle. Stitching holes and stress marks on the original leather and surviving metal parts gave some indication of how the pieces must have fit together and how the internal framing was constructed. Further examination of archeological findings also indicated to Connolly and his colleagues that there were likely two versions of the four horned Roman saddle: a short horn version that was comfortable and useful for general cavalry operations; and a long horn version that was less comfortable, but literally "locked" the rider into the saddle. Connolly surmises that heavy cavalry employing the heavy contus lance used the long horn saddle.[23]

After the replica saddle was complete, a variety of riders tested it including the equestrian historian and competitive endurance riding champion Ann Hyland. Hyland found that the short horn saddle provided incomparable security compared to riding bareback.[24] She also found that the saddle greatly improved the rider's ability to negotiate obstacles of all types, including riding up and down steep hills and jumping. Her conclusions regarding the long horn saddle were equally illuminating. "Similar in concept to the first saddle, it has far more pronounced horns that sweep back from the pommel and forward to form the cantle and to lock the rider in with even greater security. Indeed, a cavalryman receiving a shocking blow would be very hard to dislodge, and a wounded trooper would also be able to remain mounted until he could retire and be assisted to dismount for medical care."[25]

The four-horned Roman saddle came into use around the beginning of the imperial period. It provided the cavalryman the security needed to fight more effectively from horseback, giving him the power and authority to better strike at the enemy with lance or sword. It also removed the threat of being easily dismounted. Further, it greatly improved the tactical mobility of cavalry by allowing them to maneuver at a trot, canter, or gallop easily without fear of the disrupting effects of intervening rough terrain. The advent of the framed saddle permitted teaching basic riding skills more quickly and allowed more time for weapons and collective unit training. It decreased the importance of recruiting troopers who were "born to the horse." Essentially, all aspects of individual horsemanship became easier to manage, which had a positive impact on the combat effectiveness of individual troopers and the cavalry arm as a whole.

Headstones of Roman cavalrymen, a superb source for information and details of Roman cavalry. The stone on the left depicts a charging cavalryman with spatha sword, lance, and shield. The horse wears a curb bit. The inscription reads "Titus Flavius Bassus, son of Mucala, from Dansala, trooper of the Ala Noricorum, from the turma of Fabus Pudens, aged 46 years, served 26 years. His heir had this erected by testament." Headstone of Caius Romanius Capito, on the right, from the first century AD. The inscription reads "Caius Romanus Capito, trooper of the Ala Noricorum, from Celeia, of the voting tribe Claudia, 19 years of service, lies here. His heir had (this) built according to his testament." Note the detail of the four horn saddle. The crupper and breastplate to keep the saddle in position are clearly displayed. (*Jasper Oorthuys*)

Though a great advance over anything previously seen, the Roman horn saddle was still relatively primitive. The fit was not comparable with the comfortable and secure styling of a modern saddle. Just how the Roman saddle was girthed to the horse is not known, but some type of strap, perhaps more than one, had to be used. The Romans used breast straps to prevent the saddle from sliding to the rear and breeching straps to prevent it sliding forward. In addition, a thick pad under the saddle protected the horse from abrasion.[26]

In the area of equitation the Romans were not innovators, but during the imperial period the efficiency of their military system improved as they copied and institutionalized effective techniques, systems, and knowledge from all over the known world and disseminated the information to Roman forces throughout the empire. This made their cavalry much more capable than it otherwise would have been. Standardized practices such as veterinary care for the horses and stabling design and procedures reflected the cutting edge of equine knowledge. The Romans took to heart the training of cavalry as described by the Greek general Xenophon. In fact,

Roman sources describe a school for troopers and horses that included mounting and dismounting drills, jumping exercises, swimming drills, weapons drills, and thrice monthly 20-mile training marches.[27]

The Romans used various types of snaffles and curbs to control their horses. Most of the Roman bits were rather severe and would have quickly gotten the horse's attention.[28] The curb bit had the advantage of lending itself to one-handed usage and was more compatible with the Roman's routine use of a shield which he carried in his left hand. In combat, he also carried both reins in that hand. Through experiments, Ann Hyland found that the shield pressed against the horse's neck on the left side could substitute for the left rein when attempting to make the horse turn to the right. Thus the shield did not drastically affect the rider's ability to control the horse using a neck reining technique.

The Romans also used a type of horseshoe. It was a clamp or tie type designed for temporary use. It could be used when marching on particularly hard surfaces, perhaps on paved Roman roads (although the cavalry is reported to have typically ridden to the side of the road) or on rocky ground. It could also have been used to protect an injured or damaged hoof.[29]

Enemies of Rome

Like the Roman army, the enemies of Rome varied greatly over the long life of the empire. The Carthaginian armies best represent Rome's African adversaries, who were active in the early period of the republic. Carthage based its cavalry on the Macedonian model and did not vary much from the Roman cavalry in equipment or appearance. The other important cavalry closely associated with Carthage were the Numidian cavalry. They rode without saddle or bridle, controlling the horse through natural aids as well as a short stick, through which they transmitted commands to the horse by tapping on various parts of the horse's body. Numidian cavalry, probably because of their unique riding style, avoided close combat. They excelled as skirmishers and scouts. Their sole armament was usually several throwing javelins.[30]

Rome's early primary western European enemies were the Celtic tribes of Germany, Spain, and Gaul. Rome stationed legions in Spain after the Second Punic War to prevent its use as a base for future European invasions by the Carthaginians. Spanish warriors had previously fought Rome as part of Hannibal's army. Hannibal made great use of light Spanish cavalry. During Roman occupation, the indigenous tribes of Spain waged a brutal guerrilla war against Rome that lasted from 201 BC to 133 BC. Cavalry were an important part of the hit-and-run tactics of the Spanish insurgents. Strabo described the level of horsemanship among the Spanish: "And intermingled with their forces of infantry was a force of cavalry, for their horses were trained to climb mountains, and, whenever there was need for it, to kneel down promptly at the word of command."[31] Spanish horsemanship was superior to that of the Roman cavalry and during the fighting in Spain, the Romans regularly hired tribal mercenaries to meet their cavalry needs. These same warriors, when not in Roman employ, would be Rome's enemies. After its complete incorporation into the empire, Spain supplied significant numbers of cavalry to imperial service.

The Gauls, operating in what is today northern and central France, Belgium, and Luxemburg, fielded superior cavalry who were solid horsemen and fierce warriors. Their small horses were adequate to their needs. The senior class of warriors associated with the tribal nobility manned the Gallic cavalry forces. Gallic cavalry tactics were very simple: a volley of javelins followed by a mounted charge using lance and sword. The Gauls prided themselves on their swordsmanship, and the sword was their preferred weapon in close fighting.[32]

The Celtic tribes found in Gaul and Britain still used chariots, which were ineffective in a major battle. British chariots usually transported noted warriors to the battlefield, where the warriors would dismount and retainers would then take the chariots to the rear. Celts reportedly engaged Romans with spears from the chariots in isolated skirmishes. Much of their impact was psychological. Caesar described their employment in Britain:

> Their mode of fighting with their chariots is this: firstly, they drive about in all directions and throw their weapons and generally break the ranks of the enemy with the very dread of their horses and the noise of their wheels; and when they have worked themselves in between the troops of horse, leap from their chariots and engage on foot. The charioteers in the mean time withdrew some little distance from the battle, and so place themselves with the chariots that, if their masters are overpowered by the number of the enemy, they may have a ready retreat to their own troops. Thus they display in battle the speed of horse, [together with] the firmness of infantry; and by daily practice and exercise attain to such expertness that they are accustomed, even on a declining and steep place, to check their horses at full speed, and manage and turn them in an instant and run along the pole, and stand on the yoke, and thence betake themselves with the greatest celerity to their chariots again.[33]

Caesar relied heavily on allied southern Gallic cavalry in his wars against the Gauls from 58 to 50 BC. In the imperial period, the Gallic cavalry became the major component of the Roman cavalry force. Strabo described them as "fighters by nature, they are better as cavalry than as infantry; and the best cavalry force the Romans have comes from these people."

Several other tribal powers challenged Rome, including the Goths and the Huns. The Goths were a Germanic people made up of a variety of tribes who were a constant menace to the late empire's frontiers. Caesar commented on Germanic cavalry and their horses: "But those [are] poor and ill-shaped animals, which belong to their country; these, however, they render capable of the greatest labor by daily exercise. In cavalry actions they frequently leap from their horses and fight on foot; and train their horses to stand still in the very spot on which they leave them." In the late empire the Goths raided deep into Gaul, Spain, Italy, and Greece, and decisively defeated the Roman army in the east and killed Emperor Valens at the battle of Adrianople in 378 AD (see below) and successfully sacked Rome in 410 AD.[34] Like the Gauls, they revered the mounted warrior; their leaders and senior warriors fought as cavalry. In weapons, armor, and horses they often used captured or outdated Roman equipment. Their effectiveness and success in battle was a function of their skill as individual warriors and the declining effectiveness of the Roman military.

The eastern frontiers of the empire posed the most serious military challenges to Rome. Here the legions came into contact with kingdoms derived from the Persian kingdom of Darius and Alexander the Great's eastern empire. These kingdoms were heirs to the combined cavalry traditions of the Persians and the Macedonians.

The Romans first came into contact with the Parthians in 54 BC, and for the next three hundred years they were Rome's most dangerous opponent. After the death of Alexander the Great, Seleucus, one of Alexander's ablest generals, won control of Babylon and eventually expanded his governance throughout most of Alexander's Asian holdings. By 185 BC his Seleucid kingdom included all of modern-day Palestine, Syria, southern Turkey, Iraq, Iran, and Afghanistan. With the exception of Egypt, Armenia, and northern Anatolia, he controlled most of the lands of the great Persian kings. Gradually, the Seleucid kingdom broke apart as regional rulers tested the strength and reach of the capital in Mesopotamia, and powerful enemies encroached on the kingdom from east and west. The Parthian kings led a coalition of smaller provinces and principalities in a successful series of campaigns against the Seleucians, and by 129 BC they had won control of all the old Persian lands from Mesopotamia east.[35] Like the Persians before them, cavalry dominated the organization of the Parthian armies. The Parthian armies contained infantry, but they were not the striking power of the army. The Romans had no fear of Parthian infantry. What gave the Romans pause were the two types of cavalry deployed by the Parthians.

The first and most numerous type of cavalry was the traditional Asian horse archer. Parthian tactics were similar to those employed by the Persians at Plataea, or even the charioteers of Egypt: the Parthian archers moved fast, refused decisive engagement, intimidated the enemy both physically and psychologically from a distance, and only engaged in close combat under favorable conditions.

The Parthians also brought to the battlefield heavily armored cavalrymen, known to the Romans as *cataphractii*. In the Parthian military system the ratio of mounted archers to heavy cavalry was generally 10 to 1. The cataphractii evolved as a response to the steppe bowman. Each cataphract was armed with sword and lance, and he and his horse were heavily armored. The armor techniques used by the cataphractii emerged in central Asia (modern-day Uzbekistan) and were soon adopted by the Persians after the Greek–Persian wars demonstrated the shortcomings of lightly armored cavalry against hoplites. In theory a heavily armored cavalryman and horse could close with both light cavalry and heavy infantry and defeat them. The Persians never developed heavy cavalry in great numbers nor integrated them tactically with infantry and light cavalry. Thus, though they were present on the battlefield against Alexander, they were not exceptionally effective. However, once the concept of heavy cavalry was established, it evolved to become an important part of the Parthian war machine and later the centerpiece of the Sassanian armies.[36]

Parthia and Rome exchanged invasions and raids for three hundred years. The Parthians achieved some notable successes, most dramatically in the victory at Carrhae in northern Syria in 53 BC. The Romans, however, were persistent in their eastern ambitions. The Romans sacked the Parthian capital, Ctesiphon, in 165 AD. This, combined with economic stress and political fragmentation, weakened the Parthian coalition sufficiently that the Sassanians could usurp its dominance.[37]

The Sassanians established themselves as a power in the greater Middle East in 226 AD when the Sassanian king Ardashir defeated the Parthian ruler Artabanus V. Ardashir's son, Shapur I, expanded the kingdom to include all of modern Iran and parts of Pakistan, Afghanistan, both sides of the Caspian, the Euphrates valley, and the Gulf Coast of the Arabian peninsula. Shapur's expansion brought the kingdom into contact with Rome and established the Sassanians as Rome's new eastern threat. Armenia was the prize both empires sought. The Sassasians inflicted a succession of defeats on the Romans, destroying Emperor Gordian III and his army in 244 AD, capturing Emperor Valerian and routing his army in 260, and repelling the invasion of Emperor Julian the Apostate and killing him as his army retreated in 363.[38]

Much of the success of the Sassanian army was a function of elite heavy cavalrymen. These armored warriors, known as *Savaran*, wore long chain mail cloaks; their horses similarly wore armor to the hoof. Both Parthian and Sassanian cavalry wore iron helmets. The Sassanian cavalry favored a conical helmet, often with a nose guard. Riders typically wore a combination of armor: lamellar, laminated, scale, and mail. Mail was the preferred armor because of its all-round protection, flexibility, and comfort–it was made of open links and was much cooler. Mail could be worn over virtually the entire body. It was not, however, very effective against missile weapons such as arrows or javelins. Lamellar were small rectangular plates made of iron, bronze, or leather laced together vertically and horizontally. It covered large exposed areas such as the chest and back. Laminated armor consisted of metal strips, curved to match the body, overlapping and sewn to a leather sleeve. It was most useful for protecting exposed portions of the upper arms and legs. Scale armor consisted of small metal scales laced to a leather garment in an overlapping fashion. The scales were very small, allowing some flexibility in movement. Mail coats were the preferred armor of the Savaran, but often they wore additional armor over the mail. This was particularly true under Shapur II, when his super-heavy cavalry wore a long mail cloak under laminated and lamellar armor. When fully equipped the Sassanian super-heavy cavalryman could not mount his horse by himself.[39]

The lance was the primary weapon of the Sassanian heavy cavalry. It was a long, heavy weapon that required two hands to wield effectively. Long straight swords with a broad guard were the secondary close-combat weapon of the heavy cavalry. The sword hung by a belt slide. All Sassanian cavalrymen carried a composite bow, which was an auxiliary weapon for the heavy cavalry. Sassanian cavalry carried a quiver of 30 arrows on the right hip and a bow case on the left hip. The heavy cavalry did not use shields, though some evidence suggests that shields may have appeared at the end of the period in the sixth and seventh centuries.[40]

The Parthians used their mix of horse archers and heavy cavalry in an integrated manner that placed the role of the mounted archer first. The Parthians used heavy cavalry to keep the enemy infantry bunched up and disordered. This clustered group of infantry became the target of the bowmen. The Parthian bowmen also sought to draw out portions of the enemy line by feigning retreat. Pursuing enemy were led into a trap of massed mounted archers or surprised by heavy cavalry counterattacking. Numerous works of art depict the execution of this tactic. A Parthian bowman firing his bow to the rear as his horse gallops in the opposite direction gave rise to the phrase "Parthian shot."

Sassanian tactics initially were similar to Parthian–emphasizing the mounted archer, but over time the cataphractii came to be the most important cavalry type, and the two types of cavalry reversed roles. The heavy cavalry began the engagement by charging the enemy infantry with lances. This charge could either break the enemy's line and be followed up by additional heavy cavalry or infantry, or, if unsuccessful, by a concentrated attack by horse archers, which in turn was followed by another heavy cavalry charge. As the Romans learned to form a tight infantry formation to repel the cataphractii, the Sassanians could break off the cavalry charge and surprise the Romans with a follow-up attack by heavy infantry. Bowmen were always in proximity of the cataphractii, providing harassing fire in support of the heavy cavalry.[41]

Horses used by the Parthians and Sassanians are not likely to have varied much from those used by the Persians before them. Generally these would have fallen into three main types: a small Caspian type horse for archers and scouts, a medium-build Akhal-Teke type for general purpose cavalry, and a heavier Nisaean type horse for the heavy cavalry. Archeological evidence indicates that a coat of scale armor on a leather backing protected the Parthian heavy cavalry horses. Sassanian horses had their forward parts heavily armored, including chamfrons to protect the head and lamellar armor to protect the neck, shoulders, and chest. The Sassanians also used a saddle similar to the Roman horn saddle to provide stability to the cavalryman, particularly the Savaran, in close combat.[42]

Roman Cavalry Tactics

Roman cavalry performed a variety of tasks for the army. These included reconnaissance, security missions, and combat. All these missions were absolutely essential to battlefield success.

Reconnaissance

Vegetius warned that "the general, before he puts his troops in motion, should send out detachments of trusty and experienced soldiers well mounted, to reconnoiter the places through which he is to march, in front, in rear, and on the right and left, lest he should fall into ambuscades." In the early Roman period there was not enough cavalry, and no cavalry independent of the legion, to carry out such a mission. This left the critical task of reconnoitering to the allies. During his campaign in Gaul, Julius Caesar relied heavily on Gallic and German cavalry. They located the enemy army and then probed for weaknesses. Caesar describes this role of cavalry: "daily . . . in cavalry actions, he strove to ascertain by frequent trials, what the enemy could effect by their prowess and what our men would dare." These allied cavalry were individually superior to Roman cavalry, but because they lacked the formal training and structure of the Roman army they were often not reliable; reconnaissance, a noncombat task, was not part of their warrior culture.[43] Once the foreign cavalry were formally incorporated into the Roman military system in the imperial period, the alae could be relied on to perform this mission competently. However, on numerous occasions, Roman armies suffered reverses because the enemy surprised them. Often this was due to poor generalship rather than an inability of the cavalry to perform their missions.

Security

From the earliest republican armies, Roman commanders understood that security of the main body of the army was a critical function and one that was ideally suited to cavalry. The republic's army organized a special force for this purpose called the *extraordinarii*. Made up of one-third of the army's allied cavalry and one-fifth of the allied infantry, it performed special missions for the army commander, which allowed the core of the army–the infantry Roman legions–to remain intact. One of the most important of these missions was protecting the army on the march. Caesar indicates in his commentaries that they were also responsible for protecting the army's foragers.[44]

Roman armies required elaborate preparations prior to formal battle. Because it could take hours for the legions to properly deploy into formation, one important cavalry mission was to screen and protect this deployment. In the early republic period, when the cavalry was actually part of the legion, the legion's own cavalry performed this mission under legion control. During the middle imperial period, the army commander used the cavalry alae to do the same.[45]

Combat

Roman cavalry engaged in combat as part of the main battle in the tradition of Alexander's companion cavalry. Their role was to protect the flanks of the legions, destroy the enemy cavalry, and ideally, attack the enemy's infantry flanks and rear. Vegetius emphasized that "the best and heaviest horse are to cover the flanks of the foot, and the light horse are posted to surround and disorder the enemy's wings."[46] Javelin throws began the battle, followed by a charge to close with the enemy. Once in close combat, the cavalryman attacked with the lance, and used the spatha straight sword as the backup weapon. Fighting techniques among the alae varied. The early Gallic *alae* preferred the sword to the lance in accordance with tribal traditions. Late Roman heavy cavalry used the heavy contus lance as their primary weapon, while the eastern *alae* used the bow. As the enemy army was broken in the main battle, competent Roman commanders understood the devastating effect cavalry could have in pursuit and employed them in this role to the limit of their endurance.

For most of the Roman period, the legion infantry were the center of the army in the minds of Roman commanders. Although Roman commanders seemed to grasp the critical importance of the cavalry, they were consistently unable to make a firm commitment to that arm. The Romans esteemed cavalry commanders but manned the force with foreigners, and for most of the history of the empire kept its size small. The military commentator Flavius Vegetius Renatus reflected the prejudice of Roman commanders toward foreigners in general and the cavalry alae in particular when he wrote, "Little can be expected from forces so dissimilar in every respect, since it is one of the most essential points in military undertakings that the whole army should be put in motion and governed by one and the same order. . . . And though the legions do not place their principle dependence on them, yet they look on them as a very considerable addition to their strength."[47]

Roman Cavalry in Battle

Most of the important examples of Roman cavalry in battle are examples of their misuse or poor performance. Conversely, the cavalry opponents of the Romans, particularly the eastern enemies, were most often successful because of the superiority of their cavalry arms. Thus, though Roman cavalry of the imperial period and later were competent, they were often outclassed by the premier cavalry opponents of the period.

Carrhae, 53 BC

In the imperial period, gifted Roman commanders such as Julius Caesar understood and employed cavalry effectively, but they were the exceptions. The Roman army was generally successful in Europe fighting unorganized enemies such as the various Celtic and Germanic tribes, but as the empire moved east, it ran into civilizations that predated the Romans by hundreds of years which had effective military systems of their own. The terrain was open and the distances great. It was ideal for the employment of cavalry armies. Rome's military record against the cavalry armies of Parthia and Sassania was undistinguished, and the border with these empires marked the limit of Rome's ability to advance.[48]

The limitations of the professional Roman army were demonstrated when it encountered the Parthians at Carrhae in 53 BC. Rome was in a transitional period between republic and empire. A triumvirate consisting of Marcus Licinius Crassius, Pompey, and Julius Caesar ruled unofficially. Political success in Rome required a combination of political acumen and wealth, which were related to military reputation and success. Caesar had achieved military victory in Spain and was in the midst of an even more successful campaign against the Gallic tribes. Pompey had recently conquered Syria and Palestine. Crassius, at age 60 and reputed to be the wealthiest man in the empire, needed a military victory to buttress his position within the triumvirate. He determined to achieve that notoriety on Rome's eastern frontier against the Parthians.

Rome had a neutrality treaty with the Parthians, but that was no obstacle to Crassius as he marched his army across the Euphrates River in 54 BC. A quick march and the capture of several Mesopotamian cities seemed to get the campaign off to a good start, but then things began to go awry. Crassius and his army were unfamiliar with the area. They originally relied on their ally, the Armenian king Artavasdes and his 6,000 cavalry, for support and advice. The king promised 10,000 more cavalry as well as 30,000 infantry. Advisors recommended that Crassius use Armenia as the invasion route. This would ensure a friendly base of operations, and the rough terrain would inhibit the Parthian cavalry. Crassius ignored this advice and invaded via the Euphrates river valley. Early in the campaign a Parthian invasion of Armenia caused the departure of the Armenian allies and a complete change in the tenor of the operation. With the departure of the Armenians, Crassius's force consisted of seven legions–more than 30,000 infantry, 1,000 Gallic cavalry, 4,000 auxiliary infantry, and 3,000 auxiliary cavalry. The Gallic cavalry, detached from Caesar's force in Gaul, were considered elite. However, they were not formally trained and equipped as an alae of the Roman army. As the Armenians departed, desert Arabs took their place as local expert advisers. Unfortunately for Crassius, the Arabs were more loyal to Parthia than to Rome.

The Arab allies convinced Crassius, against the advice of Gaius Cassius Longinus, his senior lieutenant, that speed was critical and he should march his army on a more direct route through the desert, away from the security of the river. This route, which took the army into the open desert, exhausted the infantry, strained the army's water supply, and was bereft of any natural protection against cavalry. Crassius hurried his force through the desert until his scouts returned to the main body reporting that they had made contact with a significant Parthian force prepared for battle.

The appearance of the Parthians took the Romans completely by surprise. Cassius recommended deploying the army in battle line; instead, Crassius formed the army in a large hollow square. He divided most of his auxiliary cavalry evenly among the four sides to provide local protection. The square formation provided all-around protection from attack. However, it was an unwieldy formation for maneuvering or offensive action. The army advanced in this formation to a small stream. Here, the officers recommended stopping for the night to evaluate the situation. They still had not made contact with the Parthians and only had the vague reports of the scouts. The Romans did not send out any additional reconnaissance force. Crassius gave the order to move forward rapidly, before the army had completed watering at the stream.

The Romans soon made contact with a body of Parthian horse archers but were not initially concerned because the Parthian force did not appear too large. However, as the Romans came under fire, the Parthians unveiled parts of their army previously hidden–including 1,000 cataphracts in full armor. The Parthians, for their part, had planned to begin the battle with a charge by the heavy cavalry, but they changed their plan when they observed the numbers and discipline of the Roman infantry. Instead, the Parthians opened the battle with a hail of arrows. The mounted archers soon surrounded the Roman square and poured a withering fire into the densely packed formation. Sorties by Roman light infantry to drive off the archers were unsuccessful.

The Romans now realized that they were in contact with a substantial Parthian force but probably didn't realize that they actually outnumbered the Parthians almost four to one. The Parthians, under the command of Surena, had about 10,000 archers and 1,000 cataphracts. But because of their mobility, this force was almost invulnerable to the Romans, who lacked sufficient cavalry to drive them off. The Roman shields and armor were of only limited protection against the continuous barrage of arrows. As the afternoon wore on, Roman casualties mounted. The Romans hoped that the Parthian supply of arrows would run low. When they realized that the Parthians had a camel train that continually resupplied the archers, the army became demoralized.

At this point Crassius tried to change the dynamics of the battle and regain the initiative. He dispatched his son Publius with 1,300 cavalry–including all the Gallic cavalry, 500 dismounted archers, and seven cohorts of infantry (about 3,000 infantry)–to drive off the Parthians. The mounted archers quickly retreated in the face of this threat. Publius and his detachment, viewing the Parthians ride away, gave pursuit. After a short chase, the Roman detachment was out of sight of the main body. At this point, the Parthians ambushed the Romans with even more archers supported by the Parthian cataphract heavy cavalry. The Parthians killed most of the messengers dispatched to the army for support–but some got through. Slowly, Crassius reformed the army in a conventional battle formation and began to advance. But he was too late. The detachment under Publius, despite a spirited defense by the unarmored Gallic cavalry, was no match for the armored cataphract cavalry and was quickly overwhelmed. The Roman leaders in the detachment took their own lives. Before Crassius had advanced very far, Parthian horsemen paraded across the front of the Roman lines displaying the head of Publius on a spear. The Roman army halted and their morale plummeted further. While they remained stationary, archers fired a hail of arrows that inflicted more casualties. The cataphracts probed the Roman lines, pushing the Roman infantry into even denser formations and making them more vulnerable to the mounted archers.

As night fell the Parthians broke off their attack. The dispirited Roman infantry were left to their own devices as the officers conferred. The Roman officers did not issue any orders for security, preparations to move, or even to care for the dead and wounded. Crassius himself went to sleep while his commanders discussed breaking contact and retreating to the fortified garrison at Carrhae. But they faced a dilemma: if they abandoned the injured soldiers, the complaints of the wounded might alert the Parthians. If they tried to transport the wounded, the army might not reach the city walls before daylight. They decided to leave the injured soldiers behind.

Although a horse's night vision is superior to that of a human, limited visibility conditions increase the horse's propensity to be startled or spooked. This is particularly true in large groups of horses. This, combined with the human commander's increased difficulty commanding and controlling the formation in darkness, created significant tactical challenges for mounted cavalry operations at night. Thus, for most of the history of the military horse, mounted units have limited operations at night to traveling where contact with the enemy is unlikely. Because of this the Parthian cavalry could not follow the Romans closely at night. The retreat to Carrhae was successful, although at daylight the Parthians destroyed several cohorts that got lost. The Parthians also killed the wounded left in the Roman camp. The next day the Parthian commander sent messengers to the city walls to invite Crassius to parlay. When Crassius declined, Surena knew the Roman army was inside the city, and he surrounded the town. That night, native guides betrayed the continued retreat of the Romans. Instead of guiding the legions to safety, the guides led the army into marshes where the Parthians caught up with them the next morning. Several Roman detachments, including the remaining cavalry under Cassius, broke away from the main body and made their way to the safety of more mountainous terrain.

Crassius found himself in an exposed position with about 9,000 infantry. Surena again offered to parley with Crassius for the safe retreat of his army. As Crassius and a party of officers met with Surena a fight broke out, probably because the Parthians had planned to make Crassius a prisoner. Crassius died in the skirmish, and those of his party who survived retreated to join the remnants of the army. Surena demanded their surrender. While some capitulated, the rest fought a futile battle against the Parthian cavalry. The survivors attempted to escape during the night. Only a few were successful. The Romans lost 20,000 men; another 10,000 became prisoner over the course of the three-day battle.

Carrhae was the first large-scale encounter between the Parthians and the Romans. Two factors account for the Roman defeat. First was the incompetent leadership of Crassius. He made poor tactical decisions, demonstrating a total lack of understanding of combined arms battle and a particular lack of appreciation for cavalry. Second, the Roman army was extremely unbalanced in terms of arms. The army did not have enough cavalry nor enough missile weapons (dismounted archers and slingers) to keep the Parthian archers at a distance. Dismounted archers, in particular, could outrange the smaller bows of mounted archers and were effective at keeping them at a distance where their arrows were useless against shields and armor. In future years, Roman encounters with the Parthians would not be so one-sided, and overconfident Parthian cataphracts were defeated by Roman infantry several times.[49] As the imperial army developed alae cavalry who were disciplined and well equipped, they were able to chase off horse archers and were armored enough to break up a cataphract charge.[50] The key to dealing with the Parthians, and later the Sassanians, was discipline and careful control of the army. Light infantry, archers, and cavalry had to be used to negate the effects of horse archers while not becoming exposed to a cataphract charge. The Roman heavy infantry learned to form a defensive shield against the charge of the cataphracts. But mastering the necessary complex employment of forces was not always within the capabilities of all Roman generals. Even when they achieved tactical success, Roman armies had great difficulty fixing cavalry forces and decisively defeating the Parthian armies. The Sassanians, who followed Parthia, proved even more challenging.

In the second century AD, the Sassanians replaced the Parthians as the major power in the Middle East. The Sassanians were a much more politically cohesive power and, therefore, much more dangerous to Rome. They were able to field large, though inferior, infantry forces, as well as horse archers and cataphracts. In 241 AD, Shapur I became king of the Sassanians. Almost immediately following his ascent to the throne, a Roman army, under Emperor Gordian III, attacked. The Romans invaded the Sassanian western lands (modern-day Iraq) with the objective of capturing the capital, Ctesiphon, on the Tigris River. In 244, Shapur defeated Gordian's army at Misiche and the Romans retreated. In 253, Sharpur went on the offensive and defeated a large Roman army of 60,000 to 70,000 troops at Barbalissos, in Mesopotamia. Shapur continued the offensive deep into Roman Syria and captured Antioch and Dura Europos in 256. A new Roman emperor, Valerian, counterattacked and pushed Shapur out of Syria. But in a second battle at Carrhae in 260 AD, Valerian and a Roman army of 70,000 were decisively defeated. The Sassanians captured Valerian alive–the only emperor ever taken prisoner–along with tens of thousands of his men.[51] The Roman defeats at the hands of the Sassanian cavalry armies between 244 and 260 AD probably cost the empire more than 150,000 soldiers. By some accounts, this represented one-third of the total military strength of the empire. Historians know little about the tactical details of these Roman defeats; however, based on what is known of Roman and Sassanian fighting techniques and equipment, it is likely that the Roman cavalry simply were not equal to the Sassanians, and once the Roman cavalry were defeated, the Sassanians would have been able to wear down the Roman infantry in the great open spaces of the eastern frontier.

The most successful Roman emperor against the Sassanians was Julian the Apostate who invaded the Sassanian Empire in 363 AD. He successfully defeated the Sassanian army several times. His legions resisted Sassanian cavalry attacks and drove their cavalry from the field. However, Julian could not achieve a decisive victory against the Sassanians, and after each defeat the Sassanian army was able to withdraw intact.[52] Julian's operations highlight the inability of the Roman cavalry to press home a pursuit. Julian's cavalry were likely unable to match the Sassanian cavalry tactically, though Julian was able to compensate with his other arms in battle. In this regard he was far superior to his predecessors, Gordian III and Valerian, who were not as tactically skillful. In the end, however, the inability of Roman cavalry alae to match Sassanian cavalry prevented Julian from turning tactical victory into operational and strategic success. Ultimately, Julian's army had to retreat from Persia harassed by the Sassanian cavalry and strategically defeated. The fact that the Romans did not lose a single battle was irrelevant.

Adrianople, 378 AD

Throughout the first and second centuries AD, the Roman imperial armies were effective at protecting the frontiers of the empire. One reason for their effectiveness was the relatively competent, though not numerous, alae. Another was the overall efficiency of the Roman military system, which recruited and equipped competent military formations–in particular exceptionally disciplined heavy infantry legions. However, beginning in the middle of the third century, the quality of Rome's army relative to its enemies began to erode. The defeat of some of the best troops in the battles against the Sassanian Empire contributed to this decline. Various emperors attempted to reverse this trend with varying degrees of success. The military problems were symptomatic of the internal political instability of the empire. Emperor Julian's failed invasion of Persia established Rome's inability to intimidate the empire's enemies and the decisive defeat of Emperor Valens by the Goths at Adrianople in 378 AD cemented the impression. The battle of Adrianople was part of the Roman effort to control the Gothic tribes crossing the Danube into the empire, and illustrates the changed nature of war and the continued inability of the Roman army's mounted forces to provide the type of cavalry support necessary for victory.[53]

In 376 AD, the Huns were pushing the Goths south and west, and some Goth tribal leaders requested permission of the emperor to enter the empire. This was granted, but by 377 additional unauthorized crossings had occurred, and the tribes–both the legal and illegal–were starving. The Romans failed to provide farming land as promised in agreements. The tribal leaders, led by Fritigern, broke out of reservation areas south of the Danube and streamed south into Thrace in search of food and land. They hoped, at a minimum, to force the emperor to grant them their promised land.

In 376 and 377 the Goths, though not formally organized except as tribal warrior bands, defeated Roman frontier forces and the Roman army of Thrace. Roman control was lost except in the fortified cities where Roman garrisons and citizens were secure because the Goths lacked siege skills. In 378 Emperor Flavius Iulius Valens assembled

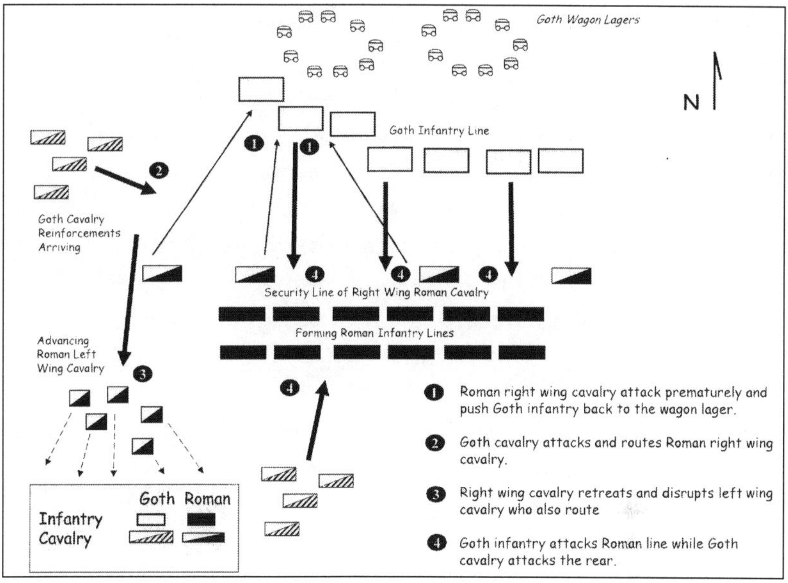

The battle of Adrianople, 378 AD.

the imperial army of the eastern empire to restore Roman authority. Because the Romans judged that a single army was insufficient to subdue the Goths, the western imperial army, under Emperor Gratian, marched east to support Valens' troops. The Roman plan was simple: join the two imperial armies, locate the major Goth force under Fritigern, destroy it in battle, and restore Roman control over Thrace.

Valens's scouts located the Goths' main force and reported 10,000 Goths moving south to the rear of Valens's army, which was moving northwest to link up with Gratian's forces. Valens turned his army around to meet the Goths. The two armies met about eight miles southeast of Adrianople in rough, hilly terrain. Valens's army probably numbered about 15,000 to Fritigern's 10,000, but unknown to the Romans, Fritigern summoned several other Goth tribal bands to join him. Fritigern opened negotiations with the Romans to gain time for his reinforcements to arrive.

As the two leaders negotiated, the armies deployed. The Romans moved from their march order into their battle line with the leading cavalry moving forward to provide security. The lead cavalry covered the infantry deploying to form the Roman center while the trail cavalry force moved forward into the left wing position. Standard procedure then called for the cavalry screen to withdraw and occupy its place as the right wing of the battle line. The Goths, typically much less structured than the Romans, massed their forces on high ground, forward of their fortified laager of baggage wagons. Within the laager were the women and children of the tribe. The majority of the Goth soldiers were on foot, but wealthier warriors were mounted.

The leaders had completed initial negotiations, where they agreed to talk further, when the battle started. Despite the fact that the whole of the Roman army was not yet deployed, the impetuous charge of the lead Roman cavalry against the Goths' left flank began the battle. This charge drew all the Roman right wing cavalry into the attack. The Romans successfully penetrated almost to the Goth baggage train before the Goth infantry rallied. At that point, mounted Goth reinforcements arrived on the Roman's left flank and countercharged the tired Roman cavalry. Under this assault the Roman right wing cavalry was disordered and routed to the rear. As the right wing cavalry ran to the rear, they collided with their own left wing still moving forward into position. The left wing cavalry was disrupted, so that when the Goth mounted forces hit them they were unable to withstand the charge. As a result, they too disintegrated and fled the battlefield. As the Goth cavalry drove off the Roman cavalry, the Goth infantry, inspired by the Goth cavalry success, charged down from their elevated position into the partially formed Roman infantry ranks. The infantry battle became a push of shields and spears; neither side could gain the advantage. Roman infantry had better weapons, armor, and training while the Goths had the benefit of individual warrior skills–and the knowledge that they were fighting for their families nearby. The battle turned when the victorious Goth cavalry attacked the Roman infantry in the flank and rear. The battle took on the classic form of other decisive victories in the ancient world: the Goths gradually and systematically pressed the Roman infantry from all directions and they either died in their formations or were killed as they attempted to flee. The Roman officer and historian Ammianus described the confusion of the last minutes of the Roman eastern army:

> Dust rose in such clouds as to hide the sky, which rang with fearful shouts. In consequence it was impossible to see the enemy's missiles in flight and dodge them; all found their mark and dealt death on every side. The barbarians poured on in huge columns, trampling down horse and man and crushing our ranks so as to make orderly retreat impossible. . . . In this scene of total confusion the infantry, worn out by toil and danger, had no strength left to form a plan. Most had their spears shattered in the constant collisions. . . . The ground was so drenched with blood that they slipped and fell . . . some perished at the hands of their own comrades. . . . The sun, which was high in the sky scorched the Romans, who were weak from hunger, parched with thirst, and weighed down by the burden of their armour. Finally our line gave way under the overpowering pressure of the barbarians, and as a last resort our men took to their heels in a general rout.[54]

Emperor Valens died during this battle. According to one report the emperor died from an arrow wound while on the battlefield among the lines of the legions that did not flee. The Romans lost at least two-thirds of their force–about 10,000 men. The loss of the imperial field army left all of Roman Thrace at the mercy of the Goths. The Goths, however, were able to accomplish little except to plunder the countryside as Roman garrisons and cities were impregnable to their assaults. Eventually a new eastern emperor, Theodosius, reformed the army. The war continued for four years with neither side gaining a decisive advantage. In AD 382 a negotiated peace gave the Goths the rights to land within Thrace originally agreed upon in AD 376.

In the battle at Adrianople Roman cavalry, for once, were not outnumbered. The Roman cavalry is likely to have been between 3,000 and 4,000 men. The Goths, because of the near-starvation conditions under which the tribes existed, did not have an abundance of horses. It is doubtful that they outnumbered the Romans, and it is likely that they had fewer cavalry than the Roman army. However, numbers did not decide the battle; the quality of command, timing, and the psychology of battle were the determining issues. The mistake that cost the lives of the entire army was the Roman cavalry commander's inability to control his forces in the forward screen of the army's deployment. This lack of command and control exposed the Romans to the Goth cavalry charge which established psychological dominance over the Romans, even though the Goths were not as well mounted, armed, or armored–and probably were outnumbered as well.

In cavalry actions, the analysis of battle must take into account both the psychology of the rider and the horse. The two are closely linked. Horses sense and react to the emotional state of the rider. Confident riders can embolden their mounts. Likewise, riders who are surprised or fearful communicate this. Horses also sense the state of mind of the other horses in the herd. This is a natural protective mechanism of herd animals, and combined with the horse's natural instinct to take flight from danger, can have important consequences in the midst of a cavalry battle.

When the Goth cavalry charged they surprised the tired riders and mounts of the Roman cavalry. The Roman cavalrymen instantly transmitted their instinct to flee to their horses and reinforced the horses' own instinct. Humans can recognize and control their instinctual reaction to events, but horses are much less likely to. No amount of riding skill or command orders could stop the flight impulse of the Roman horses. The Roman cavalry mounts galloping to the rear transmitted their fear to the horses of the Roman left wing cavalry moving forward, and most of that cavalry lost control of its horses and joined the herd stampeding to the rear. Controlling a cavalry force once horses sense panic is a severe test of a cavalry unit's horsemanship and leadership. At Adrianople most of the Roman cavalry failed this test, with disastrous consequences.

During the centuries of warfare dominated by the armies of Rome, the employment of cavalry at both the tactical and operational levels of war did not change significantly from that of the campaigns of Alexander. Cavalry was the most economical and decisive means of attacking infantry, as well as the most effective means of protecting it. In an infantry versus infantry battle, both sides invariably suffered significant casualties. Combining cavalry with infantry achieved victory at much less cost. At the operational level of war–that which connects battles to strategic objectives–cavalry were absolutely essential to pursue and destroy a fleeing enemy. An army that could not be completely destroyed on the battlefield had to be fought again. Cavalry were also essential to prevent surprise, to protect logistics lines and bases, and to locate the enemy. Failure of cavalry forces to accomplish any one of these tasks could result in tactical defeat in battle as well as the failure of a campaign–even if an army won all its battles.

The Romans had an important influence on tactical cavalry combat, primarily through disseminating information about the framed saddle. This piece of equipment permitted the cavalryman to become a more reliable and effective close-combat weapon. This invention, combined with increased armor technology, resulted in the appearance of the cataphract heavy cavalry, who although they did not dominate the Roman battlefield set the stage for the increased influence of the heavily armored mounted warrior that occurred later in the Medieval period. The other important specialized cavalry whose importance would last beyond the Roman period was the mounted archer. Rome suffered in battle with cavalry armies and with mounted archers precisely because it could not match, and often could not withstand, the threat of horseman armed with bows. But the Romans demonstrated that it was also important for the bulk of the cavalry to be a multipurpose force. The cavalry of the Roman alae perfectly met this ideal. They had enough armor to participate in the main battle but were mobile enough to operate in the reconnaissance, security, or pursuit roles. When used well by Roman generals, they were an important part of the solution to mounted archers and cataphracts.

Rome was one of the most successful and longest lasting empires in history. This success was due in no small part to the Roman army. The strength of the Roman military was in its infantry. But as the Persians and Alexander the Great demonstrated, consistently successful large-scale campaigning required an effective balance of arms. When adversaries stopped the Roman army, it was often because they did not achieve an effective balance. Because cavalry was not historically central to the

Roman army—or the horse to Roman culture and tradition—the Romans struggled to win their empire and protect it with a small, often poorly handled, cavalry force. Just as the expansion of the empire was associated with the prowess of the infantry legions, the limits of the empire was closely associated with the limits of Rome's relatively small cavalry force.

Chapter Four

THE KNIGHT AND HIS MOUNT

He who has stayed at school till the age of twelve and never ridden a horse is fit only to be a priest.–Carolingian Proverb

Medieval military historian Sir Charles Oman described the art of war in the Middle Ages as the story of "the rise, supremacy, and decline of heavy cavalry as the chief power in war."[1] Oman cites the beginning of the rise of cavalry as the battle of Adrianople where mounted horsemen asserted their domination over infantry. The causes of the Roman defeat at Adrianople were more complex than the superiority of cavalry over infantry. Like the battle of Adrianople, warfare in the Middle Ages was not simply the supremacy of heavy cavalry over infantry formations. Nonetheless, Adrianople does represent the start of the period when cavalry becomes increasingly numerous on the battlefield and military operations make growing use of mounted formations. This phenomenon was unique to Europe, however. In the Middle East the horse had always been the center of military operations and remained so throughout the Medieval period.

Warfare in the Middle Ages

The massive societal shift following the fall of Rome occurred around the heart of the eastern Roman Empire and its center in Constantinople. The eastern empire evolved into the Byzantine Empire and in that form, though constantly assailed and occasionally losing or gaining territories along its edges, remained politically stable well into the Middle Ages. It finally succumbed to Muslim invasion in the fifteenth century. In contrast to the relative stability of Byzantium, western Europe suffered a confusing serious of invasions, temporary kingdoms, and further invasions until a series of Frankish kings–Charles Martel, Pepin, and finally Charlemagne–systematically established control of most of central western Europe. After Charlemagne's death in 814 AD, the Carolingian Empire was divided among his heirs. In addition to territory, they also inherited the armies to maintain political control and a social and political system (feudalism) designed to maintain those armies. The Empire of the

Carolingians continued to fragment in the tenth and eleventh centuries, but despite increased political division, the effectiveness of the military system, based on heavily armored cavalry, increased. Thus, after a period of protecting their newly created kingdoms from Muslim (from the Mediterranean), Viking (from Scandinavia), and Magyar (from western Russia) raiders, in the eleventh century, the Frankish kingdoms of western Europe that evolved out of the Carolingian Empire were ready to expand. Muslim historian Ibn-al-Atihir, writing in Mosul in the thirteenth century, saw this period as the "rise of the empire of the Franks," and recorded the key dates as 1085, the capture of Toledo (Spain), and 1091, the Norman conquest of Sicily. Another success was perhaps the most dramatic example of this expansion: the Norman invasion and conquest of Saxon England in 1066. Expansion continued in a series of religiously justified and materially motivated Crusades. Crusaders expanded European control east across the Elbe River, southwest into the Iberian Peninsula, and southeast into the Holy Lands.[2]

Castles

Although the mounted armored warrior was the dominant military system in battle, he was not the central player in Medieval warfare. Fortifications, including castles. dominated warfare throughout the Middle Ages. Two of the most decisive military campaigns of the period, the campaign to conquer Saxon England and the First Crusade to Palestine, were notable successes for the aggressors because neither region was fortified to a great extent (relative to the density of keeps and castles in western Europe). This situation changed quickly as the Normans and Crusaders consolidated their conquests, partly through an aggressive castle-building program. After the crusader defeat at Hattin in 1187, the extensive and impressive fortifications built by the Crusaders "almost alone resisted Saladin's victorious progress." Fortifications allowed the Crusaders to maintain a viable military and political presence in the Middle East for 200 years—despite their general inability to achieve battlefield success against Muslim armies. Battle was not essential to Medieval warfare, but sieges were.[3] Effective siege operations were critical to the success of any campaign. Cavalry operations were only a minor aspect of siege warfare.

The Chevauchée

The siege was the major large-scale military tactic of Medieval warfare, but the most common was the *chevauchée*, or raid. A few men or an entire army could conduct this important mounted operation. The chevauchée was a feature of warfare in all regions throughout the period. The English were perhaps the most notorious and successful practitioners of the tactic. One of the most common uses of the tactic, which had many purposes, was to subjugate an area to extract tribute and taxes—generally to support local military forces. A chevauchée could also terrorize and pillage a region in order to deny the region's resources, including the inhabitants, to the adversary, or could be used to force an enemy army into an open battle. Finally, it was a means of filling the coffers of the chevauchée itself.

It was not unusual during chevauchée missions to put entire villages to the sword. Small mounted groups systematically hunted down peasants and then tortured them for information about any concealed valuables. Raping women was routine, as was murdering women and children. The English did not spare churches, priests, or nuns during numerous large-scale operations launched in the course of the Hundred Years War. During the Hundred Years War, raids had a major political and military impact on both England and France and were extremely profitable to the English. The potential of a lucrative chevauchée was a major recruiting tool of English kings throughout the war and were a general incentive for military service throughout the Medieval period.

The chevauchée was a mission ideally suited to cavalry forces. A few mounted warriors were much more capable of intimidating and, if necessary, fighting a larger peasant rabble than unmounted men-at-arms. Mounted forces were capable of approaching and assaulting a village or town quickly before the inhabitants could seek refuge or the landowner could mobilize defensive forces. Chevauchée permitted a relatively small army to have operational and strategic effects out of all proportion to its size.[4] Because speed was important, raiding forces avoided engagement with prepared enemy forces, holding ground, and lengthy siege operations. As executed by the English in the Hundred Years War, the raiding force often started out very fast but slowed down as fatigue and accumulated loot weighed down the raiders. It was during the slow return to its sanctuary that the chevauchée was most vulnerable. French armies confronting English chevauchée missions resulted in the famous battles of Crécy, Poitiers, and Agincourt. The devastating effectiveness of and the fear engendered by the chevauchée throughout a region probably contributed as much to the perception of military dominance of cavalry as the performance of mounted men-at-arms in battle.

The Mounted Charge

Once open battle was inevitable, the tactical focus of battle was on the employment of mounted forces. The focus of mounted warfare in Medieval Europe was the successful execution of the premier cavalry tactic: the mounted charge. This was the decisive point of all mounted combat as visualized by the Medieval knight. A detailed description of the tactics of the cavalry charge does not exist in the literature.

Furthermore, it is likely that many Medieval men-at-arms and commanders did not understand the tactical complexity of charging with hundreds, or even thousands, of armored cavalry. Since unit training was nonexistent, the only time a large-scale mounted charge was likely to be attempted was under battlefield conditions.

The mounted cavalry charge was a complicated tactic. Ideally, the charge began at the walk (3–7 mph), moved to the trot (8–10 mph), and transitioned to the canter (10–17 mph) or gallop (20+ mph) as it closed with the enemy (within missile weapon range). While the rider had several options for carrying and employing the light lance, the rider could only hold the heavy lance upright and then level it as the formation neared the target. The primary task of the men-at-arms was to keep a tight formation, stirrup to stirrup, called a *conrois*.[5] However, the disparities in horsemanship, lack of discipline, and almost complete lack of collective training among the knights made forming a conrois difficult at best. Medieval knights never trained together, except in tournaments where small teams organized to represent a particular household or region. Aligning a large group of mounted men in a tightly controlled formation, and retaining that formation while moving under fire at high speed, required a level of training that simply did not exist in the armies of Medieval Europe.

Statuette of a knight of the fourteenth century. The knight is wearing full chain mail armor and a spangenhelm style helmet. The horse is accurately depicted without armor. Though the war horse typically was only armored just before battle, there were many circumstances, such as at the battles of Hattin and Crecy, where it is likely that it was impractical to armor the horses. (*Cavalry Journal* [British], April 1907, No. 6).

Medieval European armies had no standing units; the tactical organizations were useless beyond broad grouping into a battle; and there was virtually no standard system of command and control. In the gallop of the charge, the knight's ability to control his horse was limited to stopping him, spurring him on, or nudging him slightly left or right. The requirements of handling shield and lance would likely cause him to give the horse his head—and the transition in gaits and the speed of individual horses not under firm control would have resulted in a staggered, strungout charge. Under these conditions, maintaining the cohesion of the attack was unlikely, even if it existed at the start of the forward movement. Once the leader gave the order to charge, each knight and mount became an individual bullet aimed generally in the direction of enemy; often success or failure was a matter of chance. The best a commander could hope for was that small banners of knights, perhaps a few dozen horsemen who had a relationship of some type (feudal, family, or regional association), could retain a tight formation and that these units could achieve a breakthrough.

If the charge failed, however, it did not mean the battle was lost. Under the right conditions, and with good leadership, a commander could rally the mounted force to charge repeatedly until they achieved a breakthrough. Trumpets and banners served the purpose of identifying rally points. If the attacking force could not be disengaged, or was routed, the charge could be reinforced or a new charge executed by a reserve force. The order to charge could be one step in the execution of a broader tactical plan.

Western European Cavalry

The rise of cavalry on the European battlefield was in direct proportion to the decline of central state authority. Cavalry became more effective because of lessons learned from Middle Eastern adversaries and a marked decline in the quality of infantry. As the control and administration of the Western Roman Empire began to break down, the infantry forces felt most heavily the effects of decentralization. The strength of the Roman legions, and all good infantry in the ancient world, was dependent on cohesion and discipline. It became increasingly difficult to build either of these as central authority declined. Although the breakdown of central authority also adversely affected the cavalry's capabilities, the effects on cavalry were less debilitating because the core competencies of cavalry were maneuver, shock, and individual skill. The elements of battlefield success returned to balance when military, political, and social conditions permitted the reappearance of disciplined professional infantry forces in the last years of the Middle Ages.[6]

Organization

Charlemagne developed the concept of building a European army around the heavily armored horseman and horse. The senior men-at-arms were knights, who were also minor nobles. Armies of the Middle Ages were relatively small, and the number of men-at-arms, and more specifically knights, was correspondingly small. This was primarily because the states that raised the armies were themselves not very large. In 1300 the population of England was approximately 3 million. The number of knights was as few as 7,000.[7]

The ratio of infantry to cavalry in Medieval armies was an important indicator of the relative importance of the arms. Ratios of infantry to cavalry in the English armies were 2 to 1 in the fourteenth century, 3 to 1 in the early fifteenth century, then climbing steeply to 10 to 1 in the 1440s. The French were slower to incorporate increasing numbers of infantry into their force. At the beginning of the fifteenth century, French armies typically had a ratio of infantry to men-at-arms of 1 to 2, but by the middle of the century the ratio was 5 or 6 to 1.[8] Overall analysis of the composition of the force supports the idea that heavy cavalry was the dominant force on the battlefield during most of the Middle Ages, and this did not change significantly until the middle of the fifteenth century.

The *battle* was the major subunit of armies, and there were normally three of them. The armies typically marched in column of battles and then deployed in line in preparation for fighting. In deploying, the lead battle, known as the *vaward*, wheeled to become the right of the line. The *main battle* turned to become the center of the battle line. The king or the senior nobleman who commanded the entire force typically commanded this battle personally. The *rearward battle* proceeded to its place on the left of the line. In order of prestige, the main battle was foremost, followed by the vaward, and then the rearward battle.[9] *Banners* were the major subunit of battles. These units were of no particular size but could consist of several dozen to several hundred men-at-arms. Banners further divided into smaller units of 25 to 80 men-at-arms. A bannerette knight, who was an experienced soldier and usually of relatively high noble stature, led a banner, which usually consisted of the knight's retinue and independent knights and men-at-arms whom he hired. [10]

The smallest unit was the *lance*. The lance was a small self-contained tactical unit that consisted of the knight and his immediate personal retinue. The tradition of a retinue to support the mounted warrior in an informal form existed in the earliest cavalry. In ancient times it may have been merely a single servant or slave to assist with equipment and care for the horse. The lance became a semiformal military organization across Europe by the middle of the fourteenth century. More important, it had combat capability. This group might consist of only a couple of squires, but it could also include a sergeant and, among English knights, two mounted archers.[11] In some cases, lances could number up to a dozen or so men and might even include infantrymen. However, there was never more than one knight, and he commanded the lance.

Weapons

At the beginning of the Middle Ages the lance was, as it had been in the Macedonian and Roman cavalry, the primary weapon of the mounted warrior. However, the Middle Ages saw the rise of the sword as the weapon of choice of many, if not most, mounted warriors.

The technique for the use of the lance did not differ significantly from the employment of the weapon since antiquity. Until the eleventh century, knights could still throw the lance like a javelin. The preferred grip was overhand, and the weapon was used to thrust at an opponent. Most lances in the Middle Ages did not have a butt point, and so it was not easy to reverse the overhand grip to an underhand balance. It was equally effective against a mounted enemy and infantry. The Bayeux Tapestry, an extensive contemporary illustration of the Battle of Hastings in 1066, clearly shows lances employed in both the overhand grip (prepared to be thrown or thrust), an underhanded grip, and couched under the arm. These early light lances were probably made from ash and measured between 6.5 and 7.5 feet in length.[12] The lance heads were specifically designed to pierce chain mail.

During the fourteenth century the lance began to change. It became much longer–up to 14 feet in length. It could weigh as much as 30 or 40 pounds.[13] A vamplate–a disc guard that protected the hand gripping the lance–prevented it from sliding through the grip. This lance was designed specifically to be used in the underarm, or couched, position. Designers built supports into the knight's armor to assist balancing the weight of the large lance and allowed it to brace tight to the rider's body. The early lances were a practical weapon useful in individual combat; the later heavy lance was an unwieldy weapon that was only useful in the charge. Using the heavy lance correctly took years of practice. Accuracy was extremely important because it was a one-time use weapon. An accurate thrust with the heavy lance could be fatal to both mounted and dismounted adversaries, even if the armor of the enemy was not penetrated. At the battle of Fornovo in 1495, a Venetian observer who was a curious medical doctor determined that very precise lance blows to the neck area killed many of the men-at-arms. The power of the accurate lance attack defeated contemporary armor protection.[14]

There were a variety of types of swords to Medieval men-at-arms. Most knights carried the double-edged, flat-bladed broadsword. These swords varied between 30 and 45 inches in length.[15] They were heavy, weighing about two and half pounds, but careful balancing made the weapons relatively easy to wield. In the thirteenth century the preference changed to a pointed sword with diamond-shaped cross-section designed for thrusting through chain mail. Some mounted knights carried both types.

Armor

Because he traveled on horseback, the mounted soldier could carry more armor than the dismounted soldier. Equipping the mounted warrior with effective armor, however, was extremely expensive. Cost, more than any other consideration, was the limiting factor regarding how much, and what type, of armor the horseman wore. Armor was relatively unchanged from the late Roman Empire to the beginning of

The Bayeux Tapestry is one of the most important sources for early medieval cavalry equipment and tactics. The tapestry's extensive and detailed depiction of the Norman operations in 1066 culminating in the battle of Hastings were done soon after the battle and accurately reflect combat of the period. (*Author*)

the Middle Ages. The mounted warrior's main armor was a thigh-length ring mail coat combined with a kite-shaped shield and iron helmet. Few men-at-arms wore more than this minimum equipment through the eleventh century. In the twelfth and thirteenth centuries, the men-at-arms wore full mail armor, including leggings, arms and mittens, and a hood to fit under the helmet. By the end of the Middle Ages full suits of plate armor, supplemented by mail, were necessary. The typical cost for equipping a mounted warrior with armor in the eighth century was 48 solidi. In comparison, an average mare cost 3 solidi and an ox with horns was worth 2 solidi. The costs of equipment steadily increased throughout the period as horses and armor became even better adapted to the requirements of the mounted men-at-arms. Given these costs, not all men-at-arms were always completely equipped. [16] These costs also limited the number of vassals a nobleman could support and, by extension, the size of the mounted portion of any army.

Chain mail remained the standard armor of the mounted warrior until the Hundred Years War. Chain mail was usually worn as a long thigh-length coat called a hauberk. A hood, gloves, and leggings supplemented the coat. The warrior wore a padded tunic called a gambeson under the hauberk. It cushioned the impact of blows and protected the knight from the coarseness of the mail.[17] The techniques of manufacturing chain mail were similar to those used to make mail for the cataphracti in the Roman period. Plate armor existed, but it was prohibitively expensive. A general change to plate armor did not occur until after the battle of Crécy, where combat revealed the vulnerability of mail to the longbow.

Helmets in the early Middle Ages were conical and not too different from those worn by the last of the Roman cavalry. The only face protection on these helmets, called spangenhelm, was a nasal to protect the nose. Spangenhelm figure prominently in the Bayeux Tapestry's detailed depiction of the battle of Hastings. By the twelfth-century, iron helmets, called great helms, replaced the spangenhelm type. Great Helms gave complete protection to the head but severely restricted vision and were very heavy. A round bacinet helmet—which was lighter, provided full head protection, and often had a visor that raised to improve one's vision—replaced the early simple design. The general adoption of the bacinet helmet during the fourteenth century relegated the great helm to specialized tournament equipment.[18]

Plate armor augmented chain mail beginning in the mid-fourteenth century as a direct response to the employment of the English longbow and the ease with which its arrows penetrated mail. The impact of this weapon on armor development was profound. The destruction of the French army at Crécy in 1346 announced the arrival of the longbow on the battlefield. Within ten years, plate armor, considered 75 percent effective at turning or stopping the arrow of the longbow, replaced mail.[19]

Under plate armor knights wore an arming doublet with patches of mail interwoven at vulnerable points and included laces for attaching plate armor. A fully armored knight at the end of the Middle Ages wore 45 to 55 pounds of armor. The armor was hot, but the weight was evenly distributed over the entire body. A fully armored knight could run, lie down, and even turn cartwheels in his armor. Athletic knights boasted of vaulting directly into the saddle and climbing up the underside of scaling ladders while fully armored. Heat was the knight's primary enemy—especially since the best campaign season was usually in the middle of summer. The armorers of Milan, who were considered the best in Europe, perfected plate armor production by the late fifteenth century. The quality of the metal they used, their technical craftsmanship, and the sheer artistry of their work was never equaled.[20]

Men-at-arms also carried a shield on the left arm. Early in the period these were large kite-shaped "Norman" shields. Armor improvements throughout the Medieval period allowed reducing the size of shield. By the fourteenth century, knights could maneuver their small shields to ward off blows rather than simply providing static protection. By the end of the fourteenth century, warriors discarded the shield altogether in favor of plate armor.

Training

Knights understood that training was the key to the success of the mounted warrior. Training took many forms. Basic training included practice and apprenticeship. Sports and competitions were a key component of advanced training. Incessant local warfare provided an opportunity for men-at-arms to hone their skills while gaining practical combat experience.

The enemies of the European knights, the Saracens and occasionally the Byzantines, considered the knights ferocious individual warriors. Anna Comnena, daughter of the Byzantine emperor Alexius I Comnenus, observed that the knights of the first crusade "have no military discipline nor strategic skills but as soon as they have to fight and do battle, a raging fury seizes their hearts and they become irresistible, common soldiers and leaders alike. They hurl themselves with invincible impetus into the midst of the enemy ranks as soon as the latter give a little ground." Saracen emir Ousama ibn Munquidh made similar comments regarding the fighting prowess of western European knights in his autobiography: "Anyone who knows anything about the Franks has looked on them as beasts, outdoing all others in courage and warlike spirit, just as animals are our superiors when it comes to strength and aggression."[21]

European Horses and Horsemanship

The horse was the knight's most valuable military possession. War horses were extremely expensive. The cost of a war horse in the eighth century was approximately four times the cost of a standard mare. The costs continued to rise, and in 1297 the seven horses of Gerard de Moor, Lord of Wessegem, were worth 1,200 livres tournois. The other 21 horses of Gerard's retinue had a total value of 1,307 livres tournois. The average cost of a war horse was around 89 livres tournois. An average march horse during this period cost 12 livres tournois meaning that the lord's 7 mounts were worth the equivalent of 100 march horses, and the 28 mounts of his retinue were worth as much as 209 march horses.[22] Gerard's household was not unusual. The cost of mounts was part of the overall expense of waging war and contributed to the factors that limited the total number of men-at-arms. The value of the horse could also affect tactics. Men-at-arms and their leaders considered the horse's protection as they developed their tactics. In the Crusades, it was not unusual for knights to disobey orders and not charge Saracen mounted archers because of the toll the arrows could take on the valuable mounts.

Horses

One result of the fall of the Roman Empire was the disintegration of controlled horse breeding in central Europe. Without controlled and systematic breeding programs the overall quality of European horses deteriorated rapidly. By the time the Franks began to raise armies centered on heavy cavalry, finding European horses of sufficient quality was a challenge. Controlled breeding from quality stock was a necessity for building a capable cavalry force. Reestablishing the European stock necessitated importing quality horses. The best source known to Europeans was the Islamic city-states of Spain.[23]

The battle of Poitiers in 778 put the Frankish cavalry of Charles Martel in direct contact with the Muslim cavalry of Spain. During the clash, the quality of the Islamic horses was immediately recognized by the Frankish leadership. The preferred horse of the early Medieval period in Europe quickly became the Spanish horse.[24] The generic Spanish horse at this time would have been an amalgamation of central Asian breeds brought to Spain by the Visigoths, indigenous Spanish horses that were small mountain pony types, and Barbs brought to Spain by the Moors as part of the Islamic invasion of the eighth century.

Using Spanish horses as the model, Europeans reestablished horse breeding by the eleventh century. By the thirteenth century, European breeders had institutionalized systems for strictly controlling all breeding between stallions and mares. In this period, most significant nobles and all European royalty had full-time stud operations that were supervised and carefully managed by long-term professionals whose reputations depended on their skill in producing superior war horses.[25] Manning and maintaining this complex system, however, came at a significant price–a cost that was invariably transferred to the price of a mount.

The weight the horse was required to carry–rider, weapons, and armor–was not significantly different from Roman cavalry. So the horse types that existed were of sufficient size to be good cavalry mounts. Horses that were healthy, and between 14 and 15 hands tall, were the type commonly drafted into military service. The horses indicated on the Bayeux Tapestry appear to be just that–medium-size animals of 14 to 15 hands. Breeding to specific physical characteristics began in Europe in the eleventh and twelfth centuries. Even as breeding for characteristics developed, the evidence suggests that the optimum military characteristics of the twelfth and thirteenth centuries required a horse that weighed approximately a thousand pounds and stood no taller than about 15 hands. Exceptional size was not considered a valuable trait. By the end of the Medieval period, breeders could produce war horses that stood 16 hands and weighed about 1,250 pounds, but they were still the exception. From 1000 to 1500 AD the average size of the war horse probably increased by 0.2 hands to reach an average size of 15.2 hands.[26]

European cavalry of the Middle Ages rode stallions exclusively. This was a matter of chivalric pride. The stallion is a natural fighter who, in nature, has two purposes: cover the mares of his herd and protect his herd from all enemies, including other stallions. To protect their mares, herd stallions will fight to the death. Medieval training sought to incorporate these attributes in battle, and to this end war horses were encouraged and trained to bite, kick, and stomp on their opponents. Their training also had to prepare them for the battlefield environment. As such, they were "schooled to crowds, banners, arrows, noise, and blows." Tournaments were an opportunity not only to train knights but also to test their horses. In a tournament, the knight's horse demonstrated its agility, quickness, and response to both the leg and bit.[27]

Classification of Medieval European military horses was by type and function. The most important was the pure war horse, known as the destrier. Exclusively used for tournament and combat, the destrier was the most expensive of the military types. The warrior mounted the destrier just before going into action. Another expensive horse was the hunting horse, called the courser, which was also large and fast. Some historians maintain that the destrier was so valuable that most owners only used the horse in tournaments and that the courser was the primary battle horse. The major difference between the destrier and the courser may have been training. The man-at-arms' primary mount for transportation was known as a rouncy. This horse was usually smaller and calmer, provided a more comfortable ride, and had greater endurance than the other horses. The rouncy cost about a tenth of a destrier, making it a cost-effective mount. In fact, a poor man-at-arms may have owned only one steed, a rouncy, which he used as transport and combat horse. A palfrey was another riding horse, selected purely for its elegant looks. The palfrey, which cost about the same as a rouncy, was chosen for his appearance, and was the knight's mount only on occasions, such as parades, when the rider wanted to stress an elegant appearance over all other factors.[28]

Armor and Horse Equipment

A significant number of military historians have suggested that the primary reason for the dominance of cavalry in the Middle Ages was directly due to two technological innovations: the stirrup and the framed saddle.[29]

As indicated in previous chapters, new evidence indicates that the framed saddle appeared in the Roman period. The exact origins of the stirrup are unclear. It almost certainly came to Europe by way of the steppe. There are reports of early leather loop stirrups existing among the steppe Sarmatians around 300 BC, probably attached to padded blankets. Definitive evidence of stirrups attached to a framed saddle dates to AD 600. The theory that the stirrup combined with the saddle was the key to the rise of the cavalry and the dominance of the Medieval knight inaccurately assumes the ineffectiveness of ancient cavalry riding without stirrups. It also discounts the important decline in disciplined infantry. The stirrup improved the rider's stability and thus increased his ability to wield his weapons. However, this improvement was incremental not revolutionary. The stirrup improved the overall combat capability of the mounted warrior, but it did not fundamentally alter the nature of cavalry combat.

The saddle evolved in the Middle Ages. Based on contemporary art, Carolingian cavalry of the late ninth and tenth century rode a saddle that was about the same size as the Roman horned saddle. However, instead of "horns" the saddle's forward rise was a continuous pommel and the rear rise was a continuous cantle. The saddles included stirrups. The saddles depicted in the Bayeux Tapestry are not significantly different, other than they clearly show that the cantle of the saddle is higher than the pommel. A twelfth-century design with a higher pummel and cantle replaced this style. The intent of this later Medieval saddle was to lock the rider into position so that he was not easily unhorsed when using the large lance. It had the disadvantage of decreasing the contact of the rider's body with the horse and thus decreasing the rider's ability to control his mount. In its extreme form it included a cantle that literally wrapped partly over the rider's hips. It also included rolls behind the rider's thighs to push his legs forward into the characteristic "chair" seat of the Medieval knight. The significantly raised pommel of the saddle could extend across the bow to just above the rider's knees. The armored exterior (forward facing) portions of the pommel could provide significant protection to the lower body and upper legs. The exterior (rear facing) part of the cantle was also armored.[30]

Curb bits were the dominant type used on military mounts in Europe. Because the horses were exclusively stallions, and because the saddle, armor, and shield all decreased the rider's ability to use his other aids, the Medieval horseman needed a very severe bit that would guarantee him a quick and effective reaction from his horse. Because the horse felt even the slightest adjustment of the rein, the rider had to travel with a very loose rein. The war stallion in action was essentially either responding to an abrupt and severe command or following his instinct and training. Combat horsemanship in Medieval Europe was not subtle. In the course of the melee, the reins could become the target of an opposing cavalryman leading some European cavalrymen to protect the leather reins with hinged metal plates. These were cumbersome and were soon replaced by lightweight bit chains.[31]

An important Medieval addition to horse equipment was the nailed on horseshoe. Although some archaeologists suggest the existence of nailed horseshoes in the Roman period, the conclusive physical evidence places the use of the iron shoe attached with nails in Europe in the tenth century. The iron horseshoe, designed to protect the horse's hoof, greatly increased the horse's utility. In addition to the horseshoe's other merits, a metal-shod hoof was much more dangerous to an infantryman than an unshod hoof. In nature, hoof growth compensates for the natural wear on the hoof. Horses carrying a load wear their hooves more quickly. Riding a horse (especially on hard surfaces) increases wear on the hoof beyond what normal growth can replace. Before the advent of the shoe, ridden horses often went lame early in life. In damp and cold climates, like central Europe, the hoof becomes softer and wears out even faster.

Before the advent of horseshoes, military campaigning had to consider how far the army could travel before the wear of the horse's foot precluded continued operations (and a successful return). It also inclined the military to favor smaller horses,

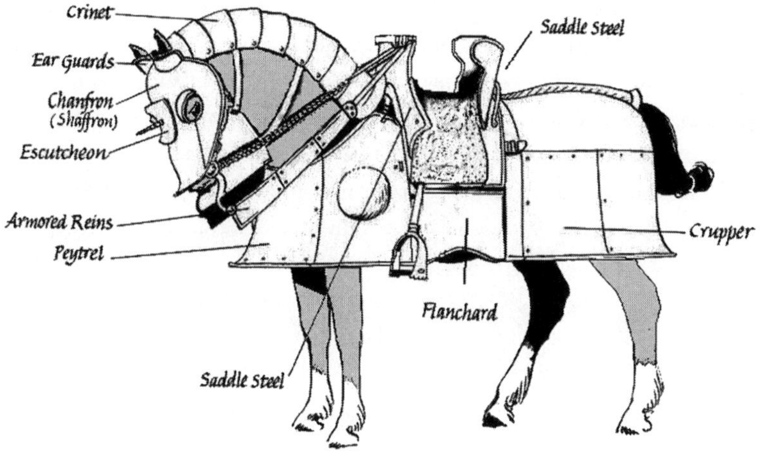

Horse in plate armor, late fifteenth century. (*Author*)

which typically had hardier feet. Development of the horseshoe greatly mitigated these considerations; it also added the trained farrier to the support train of cavalry forces.[32] Horseshoes were not in general use in the Medieval Middle East, probably because the dry climate encouraged a hard, healthy hoof.

Horse armor, a regular feature of ancient cavalry forces, was lost in Europe with the fall of Rome. Unarmored cavalry horses were the norm at the beginning of the Medieval period. The concept of armoring the horse likely came from Spain and probably was associated with encounters with Islamic cavalry during the twelfth and thirteenth centuries. Early armor took the form of a chain mail trapping that draped over the body of the horse and tied around the lower neck to enclose the chest area. The trapping would extend to the knee on the front legs and the hocks of the back legs. The trapper fit around the saddle. A quilted pad, placed under the mail, prevented abrasion and added another layer of protection. A leather chamfron supplemented the mail to add protection to the head. By the thirteenth century a mail crinet might also encircle the neck. In the late twelfth century large cloth caparisons, possibly quilted, covered the horse's armor. Embroidered heraldic colors of the rider's coat of arms often decorated the caparison. In period depictions of men-at-arms, the caparison usually hides the details of the horse's armor. This may have been intentional: with the caparison covering the armor an adversary could not easily identify unarmored aspects of the horse.

The fourteenth century saw the replacement of mail armor with solid plate armor on horse and man. A plate metal chamfron replaced the leather chamfron. The plate chamfron was larger and more encompassing, extending over the poll, and protecting the ears, cheeks, and muzzle. A set of plates were linked together to form a crinet to protect the neck. Plate armor in particularly vulnerable areas like the chest augmented mail trappings. In some cases a plate peytral augmented the mail. Armorers adapted full plate armor to the horse by the fifteenth century. This included, in addition to the chamfron and crinet, a plated peytral designed to conform to the horse's chest and shoulders, and a plate crupper to cover his croup and stifle. A plate called a flanchard covered the exposed belly directly under the saddle between the peytral and the crupper. Use of mail trappings ceased after the second decade of the fifteenth century although use of mail supplements to plate armor continued until the sixteenth century. A full set of horse plate armor weighed about 66 pounds.[33]

Because of its weight and the heat generated under the armor, horses marched without armor. Prior to battle, the squire prepared the mount for combat by adding its armor. Spontaneous combat often required the man-at-arms to fight without full armored protection.

Horsemanship

With the advent of the Medieval saddle and stirrups–and the development of the type of mounted fighting expected of men-at-arms–European horsemanship took a step back from where it had been in Roman times. Despite the formal training knights received, Europeans were far behind the Middle East in equestrian knowledge.[34] The Roman four-horned saddle without stirrups kept the rider in close contact with the horse and required the rider to be a knowledgeable master of his mount. The armored knight required significantly less refined horsemanship.

Ann Hyland described the seat of the European knight throughout the Middle Ages: "The European rode stiff-legged, locked rigidly in his saddle which was raised so far off the horse's back that no muscle or back movement of the horse could have been felt." From a horsemanship point of view, this was not practical. What drove this seat was military necessity. The primary focus of mounted combat among European cavalry became the initial engagement with the lance. As the preferred lance technique became the couched, underarm technique, the knight trained to brace himself for the shock of engagement. To assist him in withstanding that shock he used a saddle with a high cantle. Upon contact with the target, the horse could react in a number of different and unpredictable ways. It might, for instance, stop suddenly. This would force the rider forward out of the saddle and over the horse's neck unless he were braced with his feet forward and firmly in the stirrups. A high pommel on the saddle also helped the rider stay in position atop the horse. The supportive combat saddle and stirrups also kept the rider in position if the horse should turn suddenly. The cost to the rider of a secure position was less contact with and therefore less control of the horse.

Spurs were an important tool for transmitting the rider's intention for movement and increased speed. Because of the saddle and armor, Medieval war horses could not detect more subtle aids. Knights used prick spurs, a riding aid in use since Roman times. Rowled spurs appeared in the early fourteenth century although prick spurs continued in use during that period as well.[35] These spurs were extremely long in order to reach the horse despite the distance between the placement of the rider's leg and the horse's flank. They also had to be able to reach under the horse's trapping.

Islamic Cavalry

The Islamic armies were multiethnic and consisted of three distinct types of Middle Eastern mounted soldiers. The first type is probably the most famous–the Turkish mounted archers. The most important and professional of these were the Mamluks. The two other types were Arab and Persian/Kurdish general purpose cavalrymen. These three major types of cavalry made up the collected mounted group known as the Saracen Faris.

Training

Though different groups excelled in particular skills, the cavalrymen of the Middle East all shared some general regional styles and characteristics. The training of all Middle Eastern cavalry included three primary weapons: lance, sword, and bow. They wore chain mail armor though not to the extent as European knights. Typically their mail was limited to a hauberk reinforced with a scale mail or lamellar cuirass. Most wore an armored helmet supplemented by a mail coif to protect the neck and face. Most Islamic cavalry also carried an iron-reinforced round wooden shield. Though lighter in armor than European knights, the professional cavalry of the Muslim armies were not light cavalry.[36] In response to the European presence, particular units increased their armor to the point of being heavy cavalry, including mail leggings and visored helmets. From a distance it was often impossible to distinguish Muslim from Christian cavalry.

Though Muslim cavalrymen were capable with the lance and sword, Europeans associated them with the bow, which gave them an asymmetric advantage over the crusaders. The Europeans did not have an effective response to mounted archers, whereas they were equal to, or superior to, the Islamic cavalry in lance and sword combat. Thus Muslims emphasized the bow in warfare with Europeans. Though some tribal units used the central Asian hit-and-run technique, professional Islamic cavalry trained to fire their bows from within formations, in controlled volleys, often at the halt, while aiming at a designated target. The emphasis was on volume of fire over accuracy. At the gallop, a horse archer held the arrows in his hand and charged toward the enemy. When the distance closed to 30 yards, he dropped his reins. He then launched five arrows at a distance of 5 to 30 yards. Upon expending his in-hand arrows, he wheeled his horse and galloped back to a rally point.[37] These tactics were similar to those used by the Persian horse archers against the Greek phalanxes at Plataea in 479 BC.

Mamluks

The Turkish Mamluks were the most important of the Medieval Islamic cavalry types. The mainstay of the Egyptian Fatimid caliphate, they were integrated into the Ayyubid armies in the twelfth century. In the Ayyubid army of Saladin, the ex-slave Mamluks were the elite of the army and made up Saladin's personal guard. In 1250 the Mamluk regiments in Egypt revolted against the last of the Ayyubid caliphates and established the Mamluk sultanate with its center in Cairo. They quickly conquered and unified modern-day Syria and Palestine under their rule. In 1260 they defeated an invading Mongol army at the battle of Ayn Jalut ensuring their preeminence in the region for the next 300 years. Mamluks were slave-trained warriors who gained their freedom upon completion of their military training. The Mamluk's primary weapons were the spear and the bow. The sword was strictly a secondary weapon for them. In the Turkish tradition, archery was their preferred method of fighting. Their composite bows had greater range and penetration than all but the most powerful crossbow but with a much greater rate of fire. Mamluk's were equally capable of wielding their bows at the halt and while galloping.[38]

Islamic Horses

The Islamic armies of the Middle East had a direct historical relationship with the ancient kingdoms of the Persia and Alexander. They also had frequent contact with the tribes of the steppe. Thus, they rode superb horses and had a well-developed concept of horse breeding. They formalized the unstructured riding techniques learned from the ancients and imported from the steppe.

Most cavalrymen owned one war horse. The horse was the greatest expense of the cavalryman. Besides his war horse, the cavalryman would own several baggage horses or camels. Frequently, Islamic cavalry rode camels while leading their war horses. An ordinary horse in twelfth-century Egypt was worth about 3 camels while a top-quality war horse was worth approximately 200. Middle Eastern cavalry preferred to ride mares and occasionally geldings. Stallions, though not prohibited from military use, were not common, and their use was strictly controlled.[39]

Because of a lack of pasture, Middle Eastern armies had to import much of their horse herds, which consisted of three primary horse types. The first were the medium-size Akhal-Teke type horses that had been prevalent among the steppe tribes since the days of the Persian Empire. These were the primary mounts of Turkish cavalry from Anatolia. A second type was the classic Arabian that began to appear as a breed during the period of the Arab conquest. The Arab was the mount of the Bedouin tribes of the Arabian Peninsula. A third type was the Barb horse imported into the region from the conquered territories of North Africa and an import type among the Mamluks of Egypt.

The Arab Horse

Apart from Islam, arguably one of the most enduring legacies of Medieval Middle Eastern culture is the Arabian horse. The horse came to the Arabian Peninsula relatively late, probably not until Roman times. The Greek Herodotus and the Roman Strabo both report that the Arabian Peninsula was the home of camels, sheep, and donkeys, but not horses. Arabian horses appear in the literature at the time of Muhammad; and, in fact, they feature prominently in the writing of and about the Prophet. Muhammad made numerous references to horses, their importance to living a good life, their role in warfare, and their care. One story relates that Muhammad wiped the face of his horse with his cloak. When questioned about this strange practice, the Prophet stated that Allah had reproached him for not taking care of his horse. Muhammad is central to the legend of the careful breeding of the pure Arabian. Another story relates that Muhammad ordered a herd of horses to be left without water for seven days. Upon release at the end of the period, the horses raced to water. However, before they could drink Muhammad had a war horn sounded calling the horses to battle. Five mares ignored the water and answered the call. The legend holds that all pure blood Arabs descend from these five most obedient and loyal Arabian mares.[40]

The lack of grazing in the Middle East required strict control of horse herds. The emphasis was on quality over quantity and breeding was strictly controlled. Breeders judged stallions for their excellence and destroyed those that did not meet exacting standards.[41] Breeders managed horses through the line of the mare. This type of control, combined with geographic remoteness, permitted the Arab tribes over generations to maintain and improve the quality of their breed. Under these circumstances the Bedouin were able to produce the first pure-blooded horse breed.

The original stock for the Arab breed is likely to have come to the Arabian Peninsula from Mesopotamia during the Parthian or Sassanid Empire. It may have been this stock that combined the traits of the original type 3 horse–the central Asian horse resembling the Akhal-Teke–and the type 4 horse–resembling the Caspian breed. This would account for the two most notable breed features of the Arabian: its physical endurance and its fine conformation. The remoteness of the Bedouins and the high status they placed on ownership of fine horses provided ideal conditions for careful breeding. The conversion of the region to Islam perpetuated and emphasized the esteem of the horse in Bedouin culture. Thus, when the Islamic armies poured out of Arabia they rode the most carefully bred horses to that point in history.

The Arabian horses of the Medieval armies were the mount of the Bedouin tribal warriors and the favored mount of Islamic military leaders. These horses represented the major features that are still characteristic of the modern Arab breed:

> Even though centuries have passed, today's Arabian cannot be mistaken for any other breed. The Arabian's head has a characteristic dished profile with a prominent eye, large nostrils, and small teacup muzzle. His gracefully arched neck rises out of a long sloping shoulder and broad chest. A short, strong back and high trail carriage complete the picture. Arabians come in grey, chestnut, bay and roan and an occasional solid black. Although some individuals will vary, most are between 14.2 and 15.2 hands in height and weigh between 800 and 1,000 pounds.[42]

Traders prized Arabs because of their bloodlines. For example, Arabians brought to North Africa with the invading Arab armies strongly influenced the breeding of the Medieval Barb horse.

The Barb Horse

The Barb horse was the primary mount of the Moorish tribes of North Africa. The Mamluk cavalry of Egypt knew the Barb horse well and preferred it as their favorite war horse. The Barb horse is likely related to the horse known in Roman times as the Libyan. The Muslim conquest brought the horse to Spain, where they were bred with the indigenous Iberian horses and eventually evolved into the modern Andalusia breed. The name Barb derives from the Berber tribes of North Africa, who also gave their name to the North African Barbary coast. When Medieval Europeans spoke of fine Spanish horses they were referring to horses that were Barbs, or strongly influenced by the Barb horse. The Spanish conquistadors eventually brought the Barb blood to America.

Horse Equipment

The horse equipment of Islamic armies reflected their diverse ethnic influences and utilized a combination of Bedouin, Mediterranean, and Sassanian Iranian styles. Riding bits included both snaffle and curb bits. The saddle was the most interesting feature of Medieval Islamic horse equipment. Saddles varied in detail among the

The Arab horse had developed into a breed by the Middle Ages and was the mount of officers and Bedouin scouts in medieval Islamic armies. In the Middle Ages the Arabian horse was arguably the finest bred horse in the world. The horses were prized by the Crusaders who began the practice of trading for them and shipping them to Europe to improve European stock. The picture, left, represents a Hedjaz Arabian taken in 1929. The Barb horse, right, developed in North Africa with strong influences from the Arab. It was the primary mount of the Moors who invaded Spain and the Mamluk cavalry of Egypt, the only force that withstood the Mongol cavalry in the Middle Ages. Like the Arab, the Barb strongly influenced the development of Iberian horses. (*Cavalry Journal* [U.S.])

Arabs, Turks, and Kurds, but the basic construction was similar. A wooden tree was the basis of saddle construction. The curved tree conformed to the shape of the horse's body. A saddle blanket lay between the saddle and the horse's body. A slight rise in the center of the tree prevented applying weight directly to the horse's spine. This design distributed the weight of the rider to the large muscles on each side of the spine. Stirrup leathers attached to the tree, as did a leather or woven girth strap. Leather and cloth covered the seat of the tree and a leather skirt draped down both sides of the tree to provide protection between the horse and the rider's legs. The stirrup straps fed from the tree, through slots, to the outside of the leather saddle skirt. Iron stirrups attached to the stirrup leathers. A thick woven pad covered the seat of the saddle. The Medieval Islamic cavalry saddle had virtually all the attributes of a modern cavalry saddle. This saddle offered rider security sufficient to negotiate rough terrain and engage in close combat with a variety of weapons while permitting a high degree of contact between the rider's body and legs with the horse. Thus the rider was secure and retained enough body contact to use the natural aids to control the horse. The saddle was also very comfortable for both rider and horse and reduced the potential of saddle sores developing.[43]

Horsemanship

The Arab style of riding was scientific and closer to that of Romans than that of central Asian Turks. Known as the "high Islamic school of riding," it reached its peak in the twelfth and thirteenth centuries. A combination of Persian and Andalusian methods, it was more sophisticated than techniques practiced by the European nobility and emphasized the use of the seat in the saddle. Horsemanship was part of the Islamic military system. Instructors taught young horsemen to ride bareback and develop a stable balanced seat before allowing them to ride in a saddle. The Islamic riding school set stirrups farther back than the Europeans did. Compared to Europeans, the Islamic equestrian used a short stirrup. In the saddle, he rode with stirrups that would touch his ankles when his leg hung free. This allowed the rider to rise out of the saddle when necessary to wield weapons more effectively. Sir Bertrandon de la Brocquiere, after returning from Jerusalem disguised as a Muslim, reported that: "their saddles are commonly very rich, but hollow, having pommels before and behind, with short stirrup-leathers and wide stirrups.... They sit as in an arm-chair, deep-sunk in them, their knees very high and with short stirrups, a position in which they cannot support the smallest blow from a lance without being unhorsed.... I suffered so much that when I dismounted, I could not remount without assistance, so sore were my hams; but after a little time this manner seemed even more convenient than ours."[44] Horsemanship in the Medieval Middle East was approaching the standard of modern horsemanship. Muslim military horsemanship represents a balanced accounting for the essentials of functional military riding: military utility, control and contact with the horse, comfort of the rider, and health and well-being of the horse.

Medieval Cavalry in Battle

Success in mounted warfare in Middle Ages required skilled warriors, trained mounts, and leaders who understood how to effectively use the rider and his mount and mitigate their vulnerabilities. Of these attributes, skilled leaders were the most important in battle.

Hattin, 1187

One of the largest, and the most decisive battles that matched the European knight against the Saracen cavalry of the Middle East was the battle at Hattin in 1187. This battle demonstrated the superiority of the latter. The victory also demonstrated the tactical superiority of the Islamic leader Saladin.[45]

Disunity among the Muslim states in the region characterized the initial years of crusader history in the Middle East. This began to change with the rise of the

Ayyubid caliphate in Damascus. The situation became critical for the Europeans in 1186 when Saladin, one of the most capable Islamic commanders in history, took over effective control of the Ayyubid caliphate.

War broke out between the Ayyubid Empire and the kingdom of Jerusalem in 1187 when a crusader force under Reynald of Chatillon captured a large Muslim caravan and refused to release the prisoners. Saladin responded by assembling his army and raiding against unprotected crusader lands. This raiding brought unity to the divided crusader leadership. Count Raymond of Tripoli swore homage to the King of Jerusalem, Guy of Lusignan, though personal animosity and distrust remained between them. King Guy directed that the Christian army assemble for battle with Saladin.

Saladin had assembled a diverse army representing virtually every corner of the Ayyubid Empire. Its central core was a professional, multipurpose cavalry force of about 12,000 who were equally capable of fighting with lance and with the composite bow. A host of auxiliaries and infantry of various types added another 28,000 troops to the army. When the crusader army assembled under King Guy at the end of June, it included approximately 1,200 knights and about 4,000 sergeants and other mounted combatants, including *turcopoles* (Turkish mounted archers). The bulk of the army consisted of a mixture of professional and levied infantry numbering between 15,000 and 18,000. Saladin's army outnumbered King Guy's three to two, and his mounted force outnumbered the Europeans two to one. The only advantage the crusaders' had was the close combat capability of their armored knights and sergeants.

On June 26, Saladin moved his army into the area known today as the Golan Heights. He organized his army into three battles. His nephew, and best senior officer, Taqi al Din, commanded the right wing of the army, Saladin himself commanded the center, and the commander of the left was a distinguished amir, Muzaffar al Din Gokbori. On June 27, Saladin sent raiding parties into the kingdom of Jerusalem to attack the area between Nazareth, Tiberius, and Mount Tabor. On July 1 Saladin moved his army toward the crusader army assembled at Sephorie, possibly to lure the crusaders into battle. The crusaders did not respond, and on July 2 Saladin laid siege to the crusader fortress at Tiberius while simultaneously positioning the bulk of his army, and most of his cavalry, on the hills between King Guy's army and the besieged garrison.

As Saladin positioned his army, King Guy held a council of his leaders to discuss their options. Count Raymond argued that the crusader position at Sephorie was strong and the army should remain on the defensive. If they moved to Tiberius they would be entering into a battle under conditions that Saladin had carefully created. The route from Sephorie to Tiberius was approximately 15 miles and contained no fodder for the horses, and more importantly, few sources of water. In the middle of the summer, the daytime temperatures would likely be over 100 degrees. In a move to Tiberius, all the advantages would be with Saladin. On July 2, King Guy agreed with Count Raymond that the crusader army would remain on the defensive, leaving Saladin the option of attacking or calling off his offensive.

Gerard de Ridefort, the leader of the Templar knights, argued that the crusaders had to be aggressive. He persuaded King Guy to change his mind. On the morning of July 3, Guy marched his army to the north of Saladin's position, past the village of Lubia, intending to continue south of the hill known as the Horns of Hattin, and then down a steep gorge to the town of Tiberius. Count Raymond of Tripoli led the forward battle; the king himself led the center formation; and Balian d'Ibelin commanded the rear battle. The cavalry forces marched in the center of each battle, with the infantry in moving formations around the cavalry. The formation intended to protect the valuable cavalry horses from attack by mounted archers. The crusader army was well on its way early in the morning to take advantage of the coolest part of the day. In a portent of things to come, the bulk of the cavalry horses refused to drink water either the night before or the morning of departure.

Upon hearing that the crusaders were on the move, Saladin rousted his army and prepared to intercept them. At ten in the morning of July 3, Guy's forces had traveled five miles and passed the last water source en route to Tiberius, but the army did not stop to drink. A crusader history of the period reported: "As soon as they had left the water behind, Saladin came before them and ordered his skirmishers to harass them. From morning until midday they rode at great cost up towards the valley called Le Barof, for the Turks kept engaging them and so impeded their progress."[46]

This harassing fire intensified as the crusaders continued to move, and Saladin was able to rotate more of his horse archers into position and fire into the Christian ranks. Mailed knights and sergeants were essentially immune to this harassing fire, but infantry without armor and the crusader horses, which were mostly unarmored, were not. By noon, repeated attacks had slowed the pace of the army to a crawl; many troops had used all their water, and the rear battle, consisting of the Templar and Hospitaller knights and the turcopoles, was falling behind the lead elements as the archers singled it out for more attacks.[47]

As Raymond's vanguard reached the point to turn south of the Horns of Hattin he learned that Guy had ordered a halt because the rear guard, a mile and a half back, was hard pressed. Raymond convinced King Guy to change the march plan: instead of descending to the lake south of the Horns of Hattin, the army should move northwest of the Horns and halt for the night at the village of Hittin only four miles ahead–where there was water. The march could then continue to Tiberius the next day. Guy agreed to this change of plans.

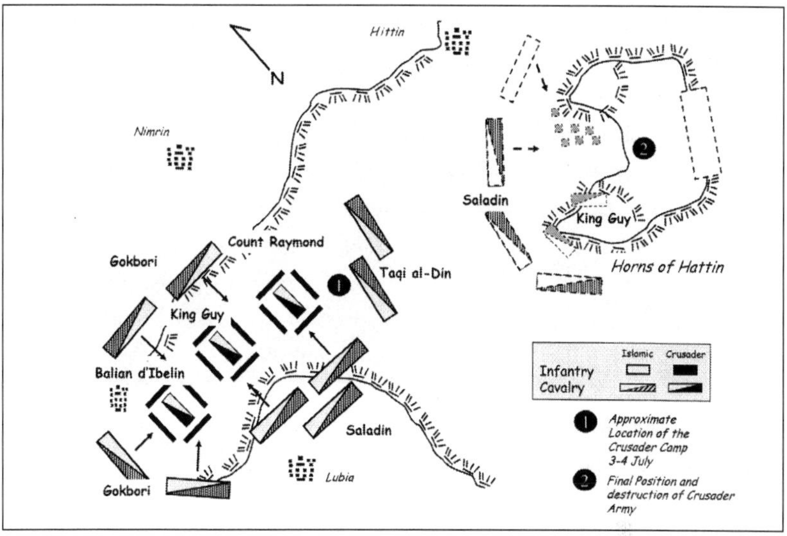

The battle of Hattin, 1187.

Saladin, positioned to command his army from the hills south of the crusaders' route, observed the enemy's change of direction. Taqi al-Din's more mobile cavalry easily moved ahead of Raymond's force, staying between the crusaders and the springs at Hittin and prohibiting a quick move to the watering point. Meanwhile, the rear battle had halted again to allow the Templar knights to counterattack and drive off the horse archers. This attempt failed. The crusaders, particularly the infantry, were suffering from the heat and the lack of water. At this point, King Guy took council of his leaders again and deliberated over two options: consolidate his army overnight in a camp without water and strike out for water in the morning, or immediately attack Saladin's forces in the hills near Lubia. Guy, on the advice of Count Raymond, made camp for the night.

The crusaders spent a miserable thirsty night surrounded by Saladin's forces: "Christians were in great discomfort. Great harm befell the host since there was not a man or a horse that had anything to drink that night. The day that they left their camp was a Friday, and the following day, the Saturday, was the feast of Saint Martin Calidus, towards August. All that night the Christians were stood to arms and suffered much through thirst."[48] Caravans of camels replenished Saladin's army with fresh arrows and water. The Muslims also spent the night collecting dry brush and piling it on the windward side of the valley, along the projected crusader line of march.

Early on the morning of July 4, the crusader army assembled for its march to the water at Hittin. Some of Guy's men deserted, carrying reports to Saladin of the crusaders' low morale. Soon after the march commenced Saladin ordered the center and left of his army to attack while the right flank remained on the defensive between the crusaders and Hittin.

Squadrons of horse archers closed in on the crusader formation, firing their arrows, and then wheeling away to be replaced by a fresh attack. The frustrated crusaders counterattacked. Raymond in the vanguard charged the forces of Taqi al-Din in front of Hittin. Balian d'Ibelin, the Templars, and probably the main battle under King Guy charged the main Muslim formations under Saladin and Gokbori. The crusaders drove Taqi al-Din's force back to the village of Hittin and the horse archers were temporarily push backed from the center and rear battles. But the crusaders lost many more horses to the archers and many knights were dismounted. Sometime during this period Saladin's army also ignited the collected bundles of dry brush. As the smoke of the fires intensified the crusaders' thirst, their infantry formations began to crumble.

The crusaders probably only advanced a mile before the Muslims renewed their assault. Again, the mounted archers executed devastating attacks on the perimeter of the crusader army. Countercharges by small groups of men-at-arms were less and less effective. The crusader formations began to disintegrate into formless gaggles of struggling infantry, disconnected from the remaining mounted men-at-arms. Count Raymond launched another desperate charge against Taqi al-Din's position at Hittin. This time the Muslim cavalry dispersed and allowed Raymond's knights to ride through the village and into the gorge descending to Lake Tiberius. The Muslim cavalry then reformed behind Raymond's force, cutting him off from the rest of the crusader army. Raymond had to choose: fight his way back up the gorge into what was an obvious deathtrap or disengage from the battle. He chose the latter course and took his knights, probably numbering less than a thousand, to Tyre.

Meanwhile, the rest of the crusader army drifted into a gap between Saladin's main force and that of Taqi al-Din and found itself on the slopes of the Horns of Hattin. The infantry, detached from the men-at-arms and King Guy, took refuge around the northern horn. The knights assembled both in the mountain's saddle and around the southern horn. Saladin now brought up his infantry and, in combination with his cavalry, closed in on the crusaders from all directions. The few mounted knights continued to countercharge, briefly threatening Saladin and his personal guard. However, as more horses and men were lost the crusaders were reduced to defending themselves. It was probably during one of these last charges that some mounted men-at-arms under Balian d'Ibelin broke through the Muslim lines and escaped. The destruction of the army was recorded several months later in a letter to the master of the Hospitallers:

> Therefore Saladin sent against us Techedin [Taki-Eddin] with twenty thousand chosen soldiers who rushed upon our army, and the battle raged very fiercely from the ninth hour to vespers. And, because of our sins, very many of ours were killed, the Christian people were conquered, the king was captured, and the holy cross and count Gabula and Milo of Colaterido and Onfred [Honfroy] the youth, and prince Reinald [Reginald] captured and killed. And Walter of Arsun and Hugo of Gibelen [Gibelin] and the lord of Botrono [Botron] and the lord of Marachele and a thousand others of the best, captured and killed, so that not more than two hundred of the horsemen and soldiers escaped."[49]

One by one the banners of the crusaders fell. And as Saladin observed Guy's tent collapse at the center of crusader resistance, all hope was lost. The exhausted Christians surrendered.

The crusader casualties were significant, probably around 17,000 killed or captured. However, about 3,000 soldiers, mostly mounted men-at-arms, escaped. The battle resulted in the effective destruction of the only Christian army indigenous to the region. In the future, expeditionary crusader armies would arrive in the region from Europe, but after Hattin the permanent European population of the crusader states was never again able to field its own army. Following the battle, Saladin systematically captured most of the inland crusader cities and fortresses. In fact, many surrendered without a fight having lost most of their garrisons at Hattin. Jerusalem, the symbol of the European presence in the Holy Land, surrendered after a 19-day siege. The garrison, under Balian d'Ibelin, was spared.

The battle of Hattin, poor generalship aside, demonstrated the limited tactical flexibility of the European heavy cavalry when faced with an opposing cavalry that was truly mobile. European cavalry were most effective in close combat. They only had a mobility advantage over infantry. Faced with the superior speed and maneuverability of the general purpose cavalry of the Muslim armies, they were incapable of closing with the enemy on favorable terms. At the operational level, the entire Muslim army could be maneuvered into or out of battle depending on the situation. At the tactical level their greater mobility allowed them to choose not only when and where to attack, but also how. Fundamentally, Hattin illustrated the superiority of the Islamic military system–centered on general purpose cavalry and tactical mobility–over the European military system centered on heavy cavalry and close combat.

Crécy, 1346

Moving forward 159 years, the battle of Crécy demonstrated another aspect of cavalry warfare that developed over the course of the Middle Ages: the difficulty of successfully conducting a mounted charge against disciplined infantry supported by effective missile weapons.[50] The battle occurred during the Hundred Years War. In 1346 King Edward III of England landed an invasion force on the Cotentin Peninsula in Normandy and on July 12 began a march toward Paris. The objective of Edward's invasion of Normandy is not clear. Edward himself was very secretive and never clearly articulated exactly what he hoped to achieve. Edouard Perroy, an expert in the history of the Hundred Years War, asserts that Edward III's actions throughout the first part of the campaign suggest he was not seriously pursuing the crown of France.[51]

The Crécy campaign began like a large-scale chevauchée. Following their landing, the English moved rapidly (but systematically) through Normandy, plundering and looting as they went. By July 26 the English had marched more than 80 miles in nine days and taken Carentan, St. Lo, and the port of Caen. The English fleet, paralleling the army's movement, linked up with the army in Caen. On July 31 the advance resumed, marching on a line that would take it to the banks of the Seine River–midway between Paris and Rouen, the capital of Normandy.

As the English advanced, King Philip had moved his army from Paris to Rouen. In Rouen the two armies were 40 miles apart. The French army controlled the major crossing point of the Seine River, which at this location was 300 yards wide. However, the English reconnaissance identified the French forces at Rouen, and they quickly turned upriver toward Paris. The two armies marched on parallel courses: the French army destroyed or set guards at every Seine River crossing between Rouen and Paris; the English army burned and pillaged a 30-mile stretch of land on the south side of the river. By August 14, English raiders were south of Paris, and the smoke from burning settlements could be seen from the city. Paris was in a panic and Philip was preparing his army to defend the city. Edward had his carpenters repaired the bridge at Poissy and then crossed over to the north side of the river on August 15. Clearly, Edward's objective was to get north of the Somme River and link up with the Flemish army moving south from Ypres.

Philip sent his army in pursuit. The immediate objective of both armies was the same: the bridges across the Somme River. The English made for Airaines while the French moved on a parallel course to Amiens. The French cavalry made good time. They arrived at Amiens on April 20, having traveled 75 miles in three days. The infantry was moving up rapidly behind them. The English arrived at Airaines on August 21. On the 22nd they found that all the bridges between Abbeville and Amiens either destroyed or strongly defended. They decided to ford the river at Blanchetaque, west of Abbeville. This ford could only be used at low tide, so on the morning of August 24 the English waited on the banks of the Somme for the tide to

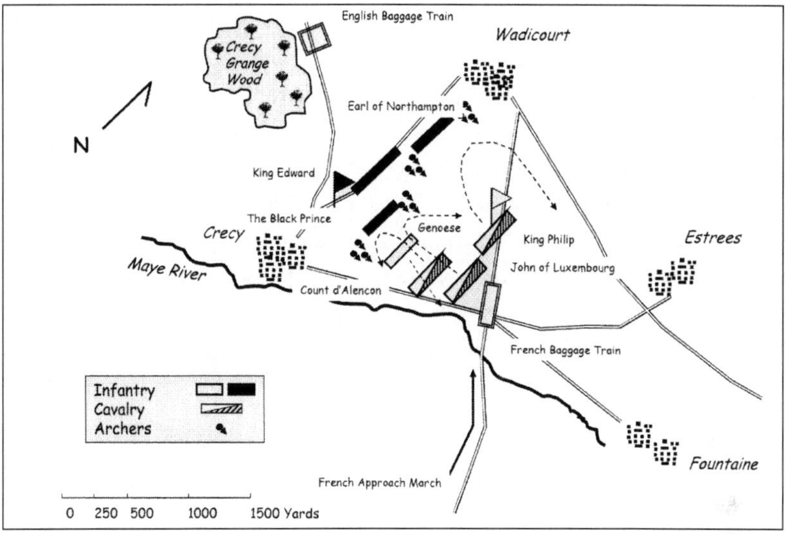

The battle of Crécy, 1346.

go out. A brief skirmish occurred as the English crossed, but the crossing was complete before a major French force could arrive at the scene.

After the crossing at Blanchetaque, English morale soared. Many horses had been worn out by the strenuous march—350 miles in six weeks—and knights saddled farm horses stolen from the ravaged French countryside. The boots of the infantry were also in tatters. Still, the successful crossing of the Somme, and the decisive routing of the French defenders, was seen as a sign of divine support for their campaign. Not all the news was good however; soon after crossing the river Edward discovered that the Flemish army he was hoping to link up with had withdrawn to Flanders. Edward concluded that he had no alternative but to fight Philip. King Edward's focus then became finding a suitable place to do battle.

He chose a low ridge between the villages of Crécy and Wadicourt. On August 25, Edward moved his army into the Crécy Wood. The next morning, he positioned his army along the ridge. The entire force was dismounted, and horses were placed with the baggage train north of the army's position. The main defense rested on two battles of men-at-arms. Edward, Prince of Wales, 16 years old and newly knighted, commanded the right of the line; he was supported in command by the Earls of Warwick and Oxford. The veteran Earl of Northampton commanded the left of the English line. King Edward placed his main battle in reserve, in the center of the position. Edward personally took up a place in the loft of a windmill, behind the battle of the Black Prince, from which he had an unobstructed view of both armies.

The English position was unusual because the entire force was dismounted. The English, in their battles with the Scots, had come to respect the defensive power of a disciplined line of infantry. They did not attempt to create a formal shield wall, but the effect of the 5,000 dismounted men at arms was formidable. The archers covered the flanks of the two forward battles. They assembled in triangular formations slightly forward of the main battle line, and once the enemy had closed on the men-at-arms, the archers could continue to fire inward–into the exposed flanks of the attackers. Trip holes were dug one foot square and one foot deep to protect the archers and the infantry line from cavalry attack. This was the extent of defensive preparations.

The English army spent the daytime hours of August 26 waiting for the French. Reviewing the troops, Edward rode the battle line slowly on a white palfrey and talked encouragingly to his soldiers. The soldiers were then released for the noon meal at the baggage train. There, they were advised to stand ready to return to their position once the French were sighted.

At 6:00 p.m. the army held evening prayers. Soon after, when lookouts spotted the vanguard of Philip's army, the English were called to battle positions. The French scouts soon spotted the English army arrayed on the ridge. Philip was surprised by their presence. The French intelligence system had not been aware of the English army's position, despite the fact that the English had been near Crécy for more than 24 hours. The French king ordered the army to halt and called a quick council of war. Opinions differed greatly. After much deliberation, the king sided with those who advised waiting till morning to give battle. The French army was strung out in a long column toward Abbeville, which it had left that morning.

King Philip's decision to halt the army was one of the last tactically informed decisions made by the French during the battle. Knights in the vanguard either ignored the halt order or never received it. They could see the English army arrayed for battle; honor dictated that they destroy the enemy. They also knew they outnumbered their foe, especially in terms of men-at-arms. Anxious for glory, the army moved forward, ignoring the king's orders. Realizing that his commands were not being obeyed King Philip changed his orders and permitted an attack.

The French army moved directly into the attack from the march. The army moved in columns across the Mayre River with units then wheeling left to strike west into the English position. This caused the bulk of the French attack to fall on the right of the English line commanded by the 16-year-old Prince of Wales. His force consisted of about 2,000 archers, 1,000 Welsh spearmen, and 800 men-at-arms.[52]

Attacking from the march was a difficult task even for a well-trained and well-drilled army. It was an almost impossible task for Philip's army that had no experience in drill, little discipline, and only a rudimentary command and control system. Confusion and frustration immediately plagued the army as the leaders tried to establish order before the attack commenced. Units crossed paths, and trailing formations literally ran into the lead formations trying to form before attacking. The horses would have marched unarmored, and it is unlikely that there was time to retrieve armor from the baggage train. It is also unlikely that there was time for many knights to change horses, thus leaving many knights to charge on mounts that were fatigued and not their best-trained war horses. The French commanders probably had about three hours of daylight to ensure victory–this was not even enough time to move the entire French army to the field.

The French battle plan was relatively simple. They would soften the English position with a barrage of bolts from the contingent of Genovese mercenary crossbowmen. The French would then follow with a decisive charge with the heavy cavalry to close with and destroy the line of English men-at-arms. However, this simple concept was beyond the abilities of the French to execute.

After some delay, the Genovese, one of the few well-commanded French units, managed to get into position and move forward. These men were professionals and, unlike the French cavalry, operated in distinct units and under firm command of their officers. But the situation they marched into was not one suited for success. Because of the haste in organizing the attack, they moved forward without their protective *pavise* shields. These shields were a critical piece of equipment as they were used to protect the crossbowmen during the reloading process. They also moved forward with no supply of quarrels, other than those carried on their person. Nonetheless, the Genovese advanced in good order and managed, in a series of short marches, to position themselves about 150 yards from the Prince of Wales. The two sides opened fire simultaneously.[53]

If each army fired at the maximum rate for the first minute of combat, the 2,000 English archers in the English battle would have released 20,000 to 24,000 arrows (at a rate of fire of 10 to 12 shots per minute) while the 6,000 Genovese would have fired approximately 12,000 bolts (at a rate of fire of 2 shots per minute). Sometime shortly after the volleys began, the Genovese, having taken severe casualties, broke contact with the English. The English vollies likely caused twice the number of casualties as the Genovese. In addition, shortly before the battle began, a short but severe rainstorm had swept the battlefield. The English archers removed their bow strings to keep them dry. This was impossible with the crossbow. It's likely that a significant number of French bolts fell well short of their target because the wet strings of the crossbows had lost some of their power. At least one Medieval source indicates that this was the case. Given the volume of fire coming from the English, the Genovese must have realized the futility of continuing the failed assault. The retreat of the Genovese professionals under these adverse conditions was a reasonable command decision.[54]

The Genovese withdrawal ended the French infantry's contribution to the battle. The 12,000 mounted French men-at-arms would carry out the remainder of the fight. The last act of the retreating Genovese was to become entangled in the mounted battle of Charles II Count of Alençon. The French cavalry were positioned closely behind the crossbowmen and were anxious to execute a charge. The two units had never worked with each other, and the French cavalry refused to open ranks for the retreating Genovese. The result was a stalemate in which the French cavalry were unable to advance with any speed or cohesion. This collision took place within range of the English archers who continued to rain arrows on both groups. The chain mail armor of the men-at-arms provided only limited protection against the arrows, although their shields proved somewhat more effective. The unarmored horses suffered much more than the riders. Count Alençon gave the order to ride down the Genovese crying, "Away with these faint-hearted rabble!" But his order did little to prevent the hopeless entangling of the two forces. The initial cavalry charge against the English started in a disrupted state and never recovered.[55] Alençon's charge dissolved into a mass of confused and dying infantry, rearing wounded horses, unhorsed and wounded men-at-arms, and general chaos–before it ever reached the English battle line. Any men-at-arms that extracted themselves from the confusion became solitary targets for the forward ranks of archers. Those who did reach the English battle line were easily dispatched.

As Alençon's charge failed, the second battle of the French army moved forward. The blind Bohemian king, John of Luxembourg, commanded the second battle. John's reputation as a warrior was respected on both sides, and his followers were veterans known for their loyalty to their king. In addition to the inherent difficulties all Medieval armies had executing a coherent charge against a line of infantry, King John's battle had to negotiate a battlefield strewn with the debris of two previous failed attacks. At this relatively early point in the battle the field across which King John was to charge would have been littered with thousands of dead and wounded Genovese, men-at-arms, and horses. In addition, the sun was setting behind the English battle line, casting long shadows and making it difficult to see the English lines. Horses have particularly poor night vision, and they have difficulty distinguishing shadows from holes or solid objects. Under these conditions, the horses would have been hypersensitive and much more prone to shying, bolting, or refusing to go forward. The French cavalry horses were already fatigued before they charged; they had been on the move since early morning, and the leading elements had had an 18-mile march en route to the battlefield. The French cavalry may also have been plagued with many foundered horses because of several days of hard riding. Foundered horses would have been challenged just to keep up on the march and would have been totally incapable of charging.[56]

The blind King John led the charge with his reins tied to those of his escort. His directive to his escort was simple: "Sirs, ye are my men, my companions and friends in this journey: I require you bring me so far forward, that I may strike one stroke with my sword." The Bohemian contingent likely advanced at the trot, moving between 8 and 10 miles an hour, trying for cohesion and control rather than great speed. Still, given the clutter of the battlefield they could not have maintained a tight stirrup-to-stirrup formation. At about 250 yards the missile attack from the English archers began. Using both direct fire from the first rank and high-angle fire from the rear ranks, the 2,000 English bowmen would have released another 24,000 arrows in the one minute it took King John's force to cross the deadly ground in front of the English battle line.[57] Casualties were significant on the flanks of the charge, and the effect of the archery attack naturally compressed the center of the formation as the horses and riders on the flanks shied away.

Just before hitting the English battle line the cavalry encountered the trip holes. The holes surprised the French, and a few horses must have fallen. This would have slowed the charge even further. When the charge closed on the English it would not have had the momentum to crash through the battle line. Instead, the men-at-arms, mounted and dismounted, would have immediately become engulfed in a melee as the mounted force tried to penetrate the line. The dismounted men-at-arms, horsemen themselves, would have had little psychological fear of the horses, but the size, strength, and quickness of the horses still gave the mounted force an advantage. Offsetting this French advantage were the English longbowmen, who continued to pour fire into the flanks and rear of the French force.

The struggle between the forces of the English right flank under the Prince of Wales and King John of Luxembourg's battle was the hardest fought of the evening and the closest the French came to achieving success. At one point the French penetrated to the young prince's standard and knocked the prince off his feet. His advisers sent a messenger to King Edward requesting reinforcements. Edward, positioned in the windmill to the rear of the right flank, was undoubtedly aware that what little success the French were having was temporary and local. The left flank English battle had hardly been engaged, and the English reserve was uncommitted. The king's response to the request for reinforcements was to let the prince "win his spurs; for if God be pleased, I will this journey be his and the honour thereof, and to them that be about him." Though fighting valiantly, the second French charge was eventually destroyed and the English battle line remained firm. The bodies of King John and his escort were found the next day in a group, their dead horses still harnessed together.[58]

Though the French would launch as many as 13 separate cavalry charges at the English battle line, none came as close to achieving a penetration as the second charge. The records of the battle do not indicate any orders or actions taken by King Philip to organize or control his army after the attack began, although toward the end of the evening, he personally led several attacks and reportedly had as many as three horses killed from under him. As French units arrived on the battlefield, their tactical commanders, with little or no guidance, launched them in an uncoordinated manner on the closest English force. Because the Prince of Wale's position was closest, most of the French attacks fell on the English right flank. Each French charge was more difficult to assemble and execute as darkness fell, and horse and human casualties turned the field in front of the English position into a huge obstacle. The French cavalry had to coax their mounts forward at a walk to avoid tripping over the bodies that littered the field. Walking forward increased the exposure time of the French to the rain of arrows. When the advancing French cavalry arrived before the English men-at-arms they did so in small groups that were relatively easy to deal with: the English men-at-arms swarmed around the outnumbered French horsemen, pulled them from their mounts, and quickly put them to the sword. Any small groups of French cavalry that did reach the English line were not supported; the English could quickly re-form and close any gaps created.

Some reports have the battle continuing until well after sunset. If so, action was very limited. Large-scale cavalry operations would have been increasingly difficult as daylight faded–and totally impossible after darkness. All reports indicate that the French cavalry at Crécy did not retreat but rather dissolved. Individual men-at-arms and small contingents just drifted off the battlefield in the darkness. At some point, King Philip and his retinue left the field. The English army slept in its battle positions. No pursuit was attempted.

In the morning a heavy fog covered the field. When it lifted the English were able to identify more than 1,500 French nobles lying in the field before them. Some short skirmishes occurred that day as French levied infantry, unaware of the previous day's results, wandered into the battle area, and were routed by mounted English men-at-arms. Total French casualties may have numbered as high as 10,000. English casualties were few–probably in the range of 100 to 300 killed.

The battle of Crécy is often heralded as the demonstration of the tactical superiority of the longbow and the supremacy of firepower over heavy cavalry. In future engagements, the French dismounted their cavalry for battle and added more archers to their armies. However, the charge of the French cavalry at Crécy could not have been more mismanaged. Though the French cavalry charged in absolutely the worst conditions the battlefield losses were still not as significant as one might suppose. Assuming that the total number of men-at-arms killed was twice that of the nobles identified by the English, one can infer that the total losses amounted to 3,000 men-at-arms. That would mean that about 25 percent of the cavalry force died. That was not an unusually high number, especially among an elite component of the army. If one assumes horse casualties were twice rider casualties, the French may have had a force of 6,000 cavalry available even at the end of the day. This force could have threatened Edward the next day. But the cavalry was not available because of the haphazard organization of the French army and King Philip's total lack of leadership.

Early fourteenth century drawing of twelfth or thirteenth century knight. This drawing accurately depicts the heavy lance, the great helm, full mail suit, shield, and highly restrictive war saddle. Note the feet forward riding seat. The horse's caparison intentionally prevents observing the horse armor underneath. (Illustration from *The Manesse Codex*, a book produced between 1305 and 1340)

The original French plan to delay the battle for a day would undoubtedly have greatly effected its course. Even attacking when they did, had the French focused concerted cavalry attacks against the English archers, they would have drastically changed the tactical situation. Eliminating the archers would have removed the source of the devastating fire, increased the cohesion and shock effect of the French cavalry charges, and might have opened a vulnerable flank to attack. Such an attack had a high probability for success. At Crécy, the ground conditions and terrain supported a cavalry attack. The English archers, though protected by trip holes, were not surrounded by stakes (as they would be at Agincourt) and were in exposed positions. The trip holes would have been a nuisance but not an insurmountable obstacle to the French cavalry. At Bannockburn in 1314, when English archers opened flank fire against the Scottish infantry, the reserve cavalry of Robert the Bruce, "who well knew that archers were dangerous and their shot hard and right grievous," ordered forward his cavalry reserve. The reserve of 500 men-at-arms successfully charged and rode down the English archers of King Edward II, turning the tide of battle in favor of the Scots. One French knight who was in the midst of the English archer formation at Crécy easily cut his way completely through the formation unscathed; he was not brought down until he rode back to the French lines. The French failure to attack the archers is attributable to a chivalric focus on the English men-at-arms, cultural disdain for common infantry, and a lack of appreciation for the effects of the longbow.[59]

The English use of trip holes at Crécy was not innovative. For centuries infantry had attempted to protect itself from cavalry by the use of obstacles. These obstacles included trip holes, ditches, caltrops, and stakes. Caltrops, small pointed iron objects shaped symmetrically so that no matter how it was thrown one small spike always pointed straight up, were one of the first antihorse obstacles. One of earliest reported uses of caltrops was at Guagamela in 331 BC. They were part of the Greek as well as Roman army equipment. The Scottish army under Robert the Bruce used caltrops as well as trip holes at Bannockburn to attempt to canalize the English cavalry in 1314. At Agincourt the English archers pounded sharpened stakes into ground around their positions to protect against mounted attack. Numerous disadvantages are associated with these antihorse obstacles. First, they are only useful if a commander determines that he will fight a purely defensive battle. Then, they require exact positioning in order to block the attack. In the case of caltrops, though usually only the size of a fist, the defender had to use an immense number of them to achieve an effective size and density. Creating an antihorse obstacle was extremely time-consuming and labor intensive. Finally, the effects of the obstacle were at best temporary. All obstacles could be by passed or breached. They could slow or canalize, but not stop the enemy. Cavalry, encountering the rare effective obstacle, simply rode around it or retreated. For these reasons, obstacles such as caltrops, stakes, ditches, or holes had only limited tactical effects on cavalry, and no impact on the role of the war horse in battle. Commanders only considered obstacles in special circumstances. Later, in the modern era, industrialization permitted the use of immense obstacles which did have a major impact on the employment of cavalry.

The other important aspect of Crécy was the effectiveness of the English dismounted men-at-arms. Though outnumbered, they held their position with relative ease against repeated cavalry attacks. Disciplined infantry stopped the French cavalry. More than the rise of the longbow, Crécy marks the return of disciplined infantry to the battlefield.

The Medieval period was a time of fundamental change. Europe began this period with a military system that had regressed in the years since the fall of the Roman Empire. At the end of the Middle Ages, Europe was poised to begin a series of social and military revolutions that would continue for 500 years. A close study of the military issues and events of the Middle Ages reveals that cavalry was not the dominant force on the battlefield that popular history claims. Warfare in the Medieval period was dominated by fortifications. Open battle was rare, and large bodies of disciplined infantry were even more uncommon. Though cavalry had a role to play it was chiefly in the execution of the chevauchée–the raid. In those highly mobile operations cavalry were integral to success.

In the occassional open-field battle, cavalry had a significant but overrated role. The lack of disciplined infantry artificially inflated the role of cavalry. The veteran professionals of the period probably did not understand the reason cavalry appeared to be so dominant. The English armies of the Hundred Years War demonstrated that dismounted men-at-arms were one solution to the deficit of disciplined infantry and were one of the main reasons that the mounted heavy cavalry lost its dominant role in battle. The longbow, too, was effective in a role supporting infantry or cavalry against enemy mounted forces.

The English victories in the Hundred Years War were more the result of generalship and tactics than of technology. English leaders knew the key to victory was the careful use of terrain and the integration of infantry, missile weapons, and cavalry. French ineptitude was the major cause of the defeat at Crécy, and later at Poitiers (1356), and Agincourt (1415). Defeats such as that of the French cavalry by Flemish pikemen at Courtrai (1302) represent the triumph of French folly rather than the superiority of Flemish infantry.[60]

The Crusades represented a fascinating clash of cultures and military systems. These wars demonstrated the superiority of the Middle Eastern military system over the European system. This was primarily because of the superiority of Middle Eastern cavalry, who were far better organized and better horsemen. As Ann Hyland observed, "horsemanship in Europe did not make significant advancement until after the close of the Medieval period and the rise of the sixteenth-century Italian masters."[61] That being said, it is interesting to ponder how the multipurpose cavalry of Saladin, ably led and featuring the composite bow, might have matched up with the English combined men-at-arms and longbow army of Edward III and Henry V.

The battles of the Medieval period represent early and imperfect experiments in combined arms warfare. This type of warfare would eventually evolve to consist of three elements: missile weapons to provide standoff and wear down the enemy at long range; infantry to hold or take ground; and cavalry to provide rapid maneuver and shock. The perfection of these experiments would require greater military professionalism, which would develop in the early modern era that followed the Middle Ages.

Chapter Five

STEPPE WARRIORS

By nature they are good at riding and archery. Therefore they took possession of the world through this advantage of bows and horses.

–ANNALS OF THE YUAN DYNASTY

The composite bow was an important weapon to mounted warriors of many of the great ancient empires: the Egyptians, the Assyrians, the Persians, and the Islamic armies of the Middle Ages. However, these great armies were merely borrowing this weapon from its inventors and greatest practitioners: the horse warriors of the central and east Asian steppe. The most important manifestation of the horse-rider weapons system in the history of warfare was the composite bow wielded by a skillful archer and mounted on the versatile and virtually indestructible steppe horse.

The tribes of the steppe survived because they were the masters of the horse and composite bow. A long line of ferocious nomadic tribes, beginning with the Scythians and the Sarmatians of the first millennia BC and ending with the last of the Mongol Khans in the sixteenth century, built their armies around this weapons system. Tactically, they were unmatched by any other mounted forces. For 2,500 years the horse-archer armies of the steppe were virtually undefeatable. Before the invention of gunpowder, no weapons system could stand against the steppe horse archer.

The Eurasian steppe is a sea of grassland that extends 5,000 miles from Manchuria to Hungary. In the north, deep forests border the steppe, and in the south, deserts and mountains edge the grasslands. It is divided into western and eastern subregions. The western steppe begins on the Hungarian plain and extends east to the Pamirs, the western Tien Shan, and the Altai mountains in the area of modern Tajikistan. The eastern steppe has a northern and southern band on either side of the Tien Shan in modern Kyrgyzstan, which join in Mongolia. The eastern steppe has more deserts, much colder winters, and is at a higher elevation than the west. The harshness of the eastern steppe accounts for the generally westward migration of steppe people over time.[1] The mountains are not a major obstacle to movement. The steppe was the perfect environment to encourage the development of riding and the early relationship between man and horse.

Over the centuries there were four reasons for the excellence of the steppe horse-archer armies. The first was the composite bow used by the skilled archer. The second reason was the unique steppe horse. Together they formed the horse-archer weapons system. The third component of success was a simple but highly effective military system. Finally, the steppe armies achieved success through the inspired leadership of excellent commanders who were bold and demonstrated a thorough knowledge not only of their own capabilities and limitations but also those of their enemies.

The Steppe Horse Archer

A variety of pieces and materials make up the composite bow.[2] Its opposite is the self-bow, a bow made up of a single stave of wood. The exact origin of the composite bow is impossible to determine, but evidence indicates it originated on the steppe around 1500 BC. In order to maneuver the bow across the horses' neck, the bows used by steppe archers were much shorter than those used by standing archers such as the Egyptians. Bowyers began construction of the bow by gluing several pieces of wood or bamboo together to form a lightweight core. Steaming the core on a form gave it the correct basic shape: a curve away from the archer. Once he formed the core, the bowyer shaped boiled horn and glued it to the belly (the side toward the archer) using fish or hide glue. He allowed it to dry after tightly wrapping the bone to the wood. After two months or more, sinew strips taken from the hamstrings or back tendons of a cow or deer were dried, crushed, mixed with glue, and applied to the back of the bow (facing away from the archer). The bow was then set to cure for as long as a year. Once the glues had set, a protective material, commonly birch bark or leather, covered the entire bow to protect the horn and sinew from the elements.

The completed bow dramatically curved away from the archer. However, when strung the curve was reversed and the stresses resulting from stringing the bow gave it its power. The Huns further enhanced the curve of the bow by adding bone or wood ears set into the ends at an angle from the curved limb. These ears acted as a lever when the bow was drawn causing the limbs to bend further, maximizing the draw, and thus further increasing the power of the bow.

The arrows used for the bow were in some ways more important than the bow. A good archer could compensate for the problems of a less-than-quality bow, but there was no way to compensate for arrows that did not fly true. Archers made arrows from reed, cane, or some other wood. Reed arrows were lighter and so had a longer range but were likely to break upon impact and not be reusable. Although archers preferred an arrow length matched to the archer, the sheer volume of arrows dispensed in battle required the issue of a standardized size. The heads of the arrows consisted of a large variety of styles. Early arrowheads were made of bone; later they were made of metal.

Steppe archers used both bow and arrow quivers. The Scythians used a combination quiver that the Greeks called a *gorytos*, which stored the bow and had a pocket on the outside for arrows. Most of the steppe tribes used separate bow and arrow quivers. Bow quivers carried the strung bow in a protective case. The archer usually slung the quiver over his shoulder or fixed it to his belt. Half of the bow protruded from the case allowing quick access. Arrow quivers were also important. There were two main designs of arrow quivers: a tube shape and an hourglass shape. The hourglass-shape quiver accommodated the fletching of arrows carried point up for easier arrowhead selection. Depending on the type of quiver, an archer could carry between 30 and 150 arrows. Marco Polo reported that the Mongolian archer carried a quiver with 60 arrows. Thirty of the arrows were light arrows designed to pierce armor, and 30 were heavy broadhead arrows for use at close range.[3]

The warrior had to pay careful attention when stringing the bow. The archer carefully adjusted tension to achieve the optimum power while at the same time not too tight that it might compromise the integrity of the string. The archer made the strings from sinew, horsehair, and various vines. Use of different strings depended on climate conditions; for example, horsehair strings were best for extreme cold. Archers always carried spare bowstrings.

The composite bow had a maximum effective range of approximately 175 yards but had an accurate killing range of 50 to 60 yards. Archers trained not only to shoot directly at the target but also to fire at a high angle. Launching the arrows at a 45-degree angle at a designated area or dense target resulted in the arrows descending on the target almost vertically. Trained archers maintained a sustained rate of fire of 12 arrows per minute for area fire while a charging archer could loose five arrows in ten seconds while moving at a gallop. In the gallop the archer stood and balanced in his stirrups, steered with his knees, and timed his shot at the point in the canter or gallop when all four of the horses' feet were off the ground. The preferred gait for firing on the move was the gallop. At a gallop the horse lengthens and lowers his body and head, giving the archer a clearer field of fire; the stride of the horse is smoother; and the horse has a greater tendency to move straight ahead without rein guidance.[4]

The steppe warriors almost universally fired their arrows using the "Mongolian draw." This difficult technique was unique to the steppe and drew the arrow using only the thumb. They fired the arrow off the right side of the bow. The hand was turned perpendicular to the string and the thumb locked around the string from left to right (for a right-handed archer). The index finger then covered the thumb locking the thumb in place. The horse archer then drew the string to his ear while

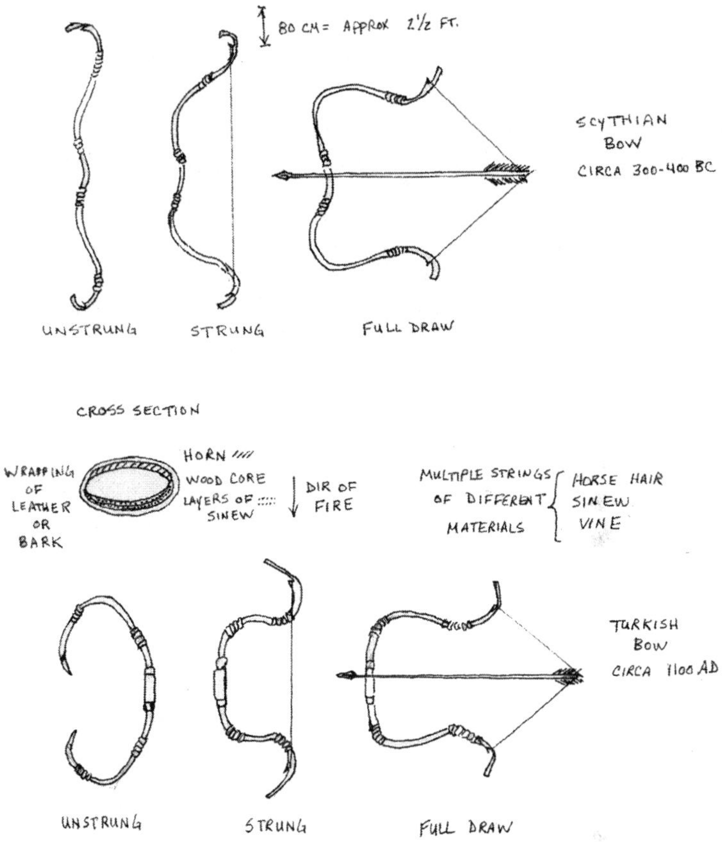

The composite bow of the steppe warrior. A Scythian bow of third century BC is pictured at top, and a more powerful Turkish bow from the Middle Ages is at bottom. (*Author*)

extending his left arm and the bow body toward the target. The thumb draw eliminated some of the finger pinch associated with the finger draw on a short bow, and it allowed greater security of the cocked arrow while riding.[5] Releasing the thumb discharged the arrow. The archer wore a ring on his right thumb which made the release smoother and more comfortable.

Some historians believe the steppe warrior was also his own bowyer, making and maintaining his own bows. Others agree with historian Otto Maenchen-Helfen that composite bow making in general was so complex a craft, and the Hunish war bow in particular was so perfectly made that professional bowyers must have been used.[6] However the bow was a central feature of both war and life on the steppe. Therefore, it is reasonable to assume that all steppe warriors were intimately familiar with the bow-making process, were capable of making their own bows, and with the possible exception of the superbly organized Mongol army made their own bows whenever possible.

Though a highly effective weapon, especially as part of the mounted archer system, the composite bow did have limitations. The crossbow and the dismounted archer could outrange the horse archer. In addition, chain mail, shields, and even the padded undergarment, the gambesons, were effective protection from the horse-archer attack at some ranges. Thus, the composite bow was a weapon that a well-trained and well-led adversary could overcome. Still, its rate of fire, accuracy, power, and most important, the fact that it could be employed from a moving horse made the composite bow an important weapon until well after the arrival of gunpowder. Steppe archers from the Crimea employed the weapon with good effect well into the seventeenth century.[7]

In the early steppe armies, before the establishment of the Mongol Empire, there were no major class distinctions. Every man in the tribe was a warrior, a horseman, and an archer. He learned his skills informally from his family and clan. Leaders such as Attila and Genghis Khan gained their following partly through their prowess in basic warrior skills. The individual steppe warrior led a hard life that toughened him to hard campaigning and gave him excellent fieldcraft skills. Life on the steppe inured him to heat and cold and he had incredible eyesight. Mongol horsemen could to distinguish a rider from an animal at a range of four miles across the steppe.[8]

In the early steppe armies the horse archer equipped himself. His service was an obligation to his family, clan, and tribe. In most steppe armies soldiers received no pay but did receive a portion of all loot and booty. Steppe tribes divided booty according to strict rules. He brought to his service his string of horses and two or three bows. Personal equipment of the steppe warrior was not usually equal in quality with that of his opponent. Horse archers did not formally wear armor. Veteran steppe cavalrymen armored themselves over time with captured equipment. The standard dress was soft leather boots and a quilted tunic. A lasso, short sword, and dagger made up the individual archer's general equipment.[9]

The Steppe Horse and Horsemanship

Horses were central to the economy and culture of the steppe tribes. The horse was valued above all other possessions, and booty and tribute usually included a large component of horses. When the Mongols established the Yuan dynasty in China the bulk of the art produced by the royal artisans centered around the subject of horses.

A mounted competitor and reenactor, Lukas Novotny, at the International Horse Archery Festival in 2004, riding at a full gallop a moment after releasing his shot. The rider stands in his stirrups and guides the horse with his knees and body position. This type of riding, even more so than other military riding, has to be instinctive to permit the total concentration of the archer on the shot. (*International Horse Archery Festival*)

All of the steppe tribes from the Scythians to the Mongols ate horsemeat. They also all drank mare's milk and used it to make cheese. The tribes used horsehide for clothing, tenting, and equipment, and horsehair for bow strings. Steppe leaders recognized the importance of the horse. Genghis Khan issued strict orders on the humane treatment of the army's horses. He prohibited leading horses with a bit in their mouth. The Mongols never destroyed battle horses but rather put them to pasture when they were no longer useful. War horses were never used for food. When a warrior died, his favorite war horse was killed and buried with him so that their spirits could ride together. Riders exchanged ridden horses every few hours, especially during rapid movement. The Mongol army segregated horse herds by color. White horses were sacred and fit only for princes.[10]

Horses

The tribes of the western steppe at the time of the Roman Empire, the Scythians and the Sarmatians, had mixed central Asian horses with the type 1 ponies of the Germanic tribes of central Europe, producing a smaller horse than might have been found further east. The Romans described the horses of the Scythians as misshapen, with short legs and big heads. To the Romans, steppe horses were too short to ride.[11] In addition, during this period wild horses still existed in the western steppe. The wild horses of Europe, known as Tarpans or Eurasian wild horses, were direct descendants of prehistoric horses and were not genetically part of the *Equus caballus* line, the domestic horse, but rather a distinct species, *Equus ferus.* These horses existed in the wild in Europe into the nineteenth century but ultimately went extinct around 1875. Many of the northern European pony types, such as the Polish Konik pony, show strong influences of breeding with Tarpans. Modern scientific methods of reverse breeding using horses that have obvious strong genetic links to Tarpans have resulted in a modern Tarpan breed that is believed to be very close to the original species.[12] It is probable that the horse herds of the western steppe tribes contained animals that were a product of type 1 Celtic ponies, type 3 Central Asian horses, and Tarpans. The resulting type of horse was extremely rugged, ugly (by Roman standards), and relatively small–13 to 14 hands high.

This small horse of the western steppe continued to dominate the horse herds of the region as the Hunish tribes arrived in the fourth and fifth centuries. Vegetius, in his veterinary work *Mulomedicina,* described the Hun horses as hardy creatures, accustomed to cold and frost, and long living. They had "great hooked heads, protruding eyes, narrow nostrils, broad jaws, strong and stiff necks, manes hanging below their knees, overlarge ribs, curved backs, bushy tails, cannon bones of great strength, small pasterns, wide-spreading hooves, hollow loins; their bodies are angular, with no fat on the rump or the muscles of the back, their stature leaning to length rather than to height, belly drawn, and bones huge." According to Vegetius, they were thin and beautiful in their ugliness. He also stated that they were quiet and sensible, and bore wounds well.[13]

The early steppe tribes of Mongolia had a much less diverse genetic pool of horses in their herds. The wild Mongolian horse, also known as the Przewalski horse, was the primary source for the early Mongolian horse herds. The Przewalski horses are the eastern subspecies of the wild horse species *Equus ferus.* The efforts of zoologists and naturalists in the early twentieth century saved the Przewalski horse from extinction after they were the rediscovered by the Russian explorer Colonel Nikolai Przewalski in 1881. The failure to save the Tarpan in the decades before Przewalski's discovery contributed to the desire to save the last of the ancient wild horses. "Przewalski's horse is similar to the domestic horse though it has a smaller, more robust build, an upright mane, and a low-set tail. The most common colors are sandy tan, dun, and reddish bay. The horses have a dorsal stripe, a shoulder stripe, barring in their legs, and lighter coloring on their muzzles and bellies." The Przewalski horse is small, averaging between 12 and 14 hands. These horses, once captured and domesticated by the Mongolian tribes, eventually mixed with the domestic horses owned by the Mongols. The wild horse can breed successfully with the domestic horse breeds, but after one generation the specific chromosome characteristic of the wild horse (66 chromosomes) is lost in the offspring in favor of the characteristics of the domestic horse (64 chromosomes).[14] Still, the resulting domestic horse, the Mongolian horse, had many of the physical characteristics of the Przewalski horse including its stamina and endurance.

The Wild Mongolian Horse or Przewalski horse, the eastern subspecies of the wild horse *Equus ferus*, is still carefully managed in its original state in Mongolian. The average height of Przwalski horse is 13.1 hands. (*Author*)

A top priority of the Mongols was improving the breeding of their mounts. After capturing Beijing in 1215, the Mongols used the royal horse herds to improve the stock of the Mongol cavalry. The best of the Chinese imperial horses were the Ferghana horses which the Chinese captured from Turkish steppe tribes living in what is modern Kyrgyzstan. The Ferghana horses were as tall as 16 hands, significantly larger than the Mongolian horses. These royal horses were likely related to the central Asian horse type. With the successful conquest of Persia and penetration deep in into the Middle East, Ogodei Khan requested that "tall horses with long necks of western breed" be sent back to Mongolia as gifts. During the Mongols' campaigns against the Khwarazm Empire, they came into possession of thousands of horses of this type, which were integrated into the existing army horse herds. Based on archaeological findings, the horses used in campaigns in the thirteenth century were probably on average a hand taller than the usual Mongol horse today, putting them in the 15-hand range, with some being 16 hands.[15]

Regardless of the original horse herd composition, the geographic range of steppe tribes and their native interest in quality horses resulted in the creation of a diverse herd. Still, the steppe army horse types shared some general characteristics that were absolutely essential to mounted warfare as waged by steppe tribesmen. The horse had to be an easy keeper, that is, hardy and able to subsist on a wide variety of low-quality feed. Early Mongol mounts existed just on grazing but later, after the conquest of China, the Mongol army made provisions for providing mounts with both fodder and grain. The horses also had to have exceptionally durable feet.[16] Horseshoes were never in general use by steppe tribes. The logistics of horseshoes would have been unmanageable for a steppe army.

Steppe horses were extremely obedient. Neither the Mongols nor the Huns used spurs; both tribes, instead, made use of whips to urge their horses to speed. Mongol horses were trained to follow their assigned rider in file on the march. This eliminated the need for horse attendants and massive horse herds. Riders trained their horses to respond to calls and whistles. The horses were not tied together while marching. The horses were physically tough; they had to be able to withstand a wide range of temperatures, particularly extreme cold, since winter was the steppe warrior's preferred campaign season. An important characteristic of the steppe horse was its ability to find grass even in winter. The thirteenth-century papal emissary to the Mongol Khan, Giovanni di Plano Carpini, mentioned this trait: "When we arrived there [Kiev], we consulted about our route with a millenarious [Mongol officer] and other nobles who were there. They told us that if we led the horses we had into Tartary, they would not know how to dig grass from beneath the snow when it was deep, as Tartar horses do, and it would not be possible to find anything else for them to eat because the Tartars have neither straw nor hay nor fodder, and they would all die. So, we talked among ourselves and told the two boys who looked after them to send them away."[17]

Because of the large numbers of horses and their importance, steppe tribes marked their horses with brands to indicate the family, clan, or tribe that owned them. The brands could either be cuts on the ears, or marks made on the shoulders or hindquarters with a hot iron. The Sarmatians were the first to mark their horses; the Alans and Mongols also used horse marks. Since the practice was well established in other steppe tribes researchers believe that the Huns marked their horses also.[18]

The evidence indicates that the primary Hun war horses were geldings. Geldings were also preferred in the Mongol army because the army prized discipline in both horse and rider. Mares were included in the herd because of their milk. Discipline in the Mongol army was codified in the *Yasa*, which also addressed issues of horse management: horse herds and breeding were centrally controlled; all colts except for the absolute best were gelded; horses were broken at the age of two, but not considered ready for campaign until they were five; and stallions were not used on campaign because they were too difficult to control. To enforce and oversee the management of horses, Genghis Khan established a supervisor of geldings and supervisor of horse herds. These positions were appointed from among the senior army leadership.[19]

Horsemanship

The steppe tribesmen were perhaps the most gifted horsemen that the world has known. Sidonius described horsemanship among the Huns: "Scarce had the infant learnt to stand without his mother's aid when a horse takes him on his back, You would think that the limbs of man and horse were born together, so firmly does the rider always stick to the horse; any other folk is carried on horseback, this folk lives there." All the steppe tribes shared this skill, which was integral to both their survival and their military success. The Mongols placed their children on horses at the age of three and armed them with bows by the time they were five. Their primary horsemanship instructor was their mother.[20]

The concept of the saddle originated with the steppe tribes, and the steppe produced the first framed saddles. Contemporary chroniclers specifically describe a pyre of horse saddles that Attila intended to set afire when the Romans surrounded him in 451. The archeological evidence in nomadic grave sites of the fourth and fifth centuries AD indicates that the Hun's saddle had a straight vertical pommel and a somewhat higher cantle that was inclined to the rear. The Huns probably did not have stirrups because the Germanic tribesmen as well as the Romans with whom they fought would have copied this innovation. Stirrups, which appeared around the fifth or sixth century on the steppe, were made of wood or iron and were round. The Alans, a steppe tribe that appeared in the west after the Huns, probably brought the stirrup to the attention of Europeans in the sixth and seventh centuries. Mongol saddles were made of wood and leather. They had a very high flat pommel, probably as an aid for archery, and an equally high cantle. The saddle provided a secure seat and had significant gullet that gave good wither clearance. The stirrup straps were centered, putting the rider in a balanced position. A thick felt pad was laid between the wood and leather saddle and the horse.[21]

The steppe archer rode with a short stirrup. The French traveler Beauplan commented on Crimean tartar horsemanship in the seventeenth century: "They are very skillful and dangerous when mounted, but they are badly seated because they have their legs folded up and ride very short; they are mounted on horse like a monkey on a greyhound."[22] Europeans did not understand the balanced seat of the steppe horseman in the seventeenth century any better than they had in the Middle Ages.

The Mongol cavalry preferred a snaffle bit, but the bit they used was very thin making it more severe than most snaffles. An unusual feature of the Mongol bridle was that a noseband was connected to the cheek pieces and included a chin strap. This is similar to a modern drop noseband bridle, which keeps the horse's mouth closed, thus preventing the horse from avoiding the bit. The Mongols valued control of their horses. Control was necessary to train the horses to execute the intricate tactics of the horse-archer formations. The steppe horse was not a naturally agile horse. It tended to move with its weight on the forehand and had a weak hindquarters, which made it less able to turn quickly and accelerate. The Mongols compensated for this conformation flaw by training on the circle; this taught the horse to carry itself in a more balanced manner and strengthened its hindquarters. This training produced a horse that impressed Marco Polo: "Their horses are so well trained they can turn as quickly as a dog."[23]

Steppe warriors could literally live in the saddle. The Eastern Roman historian Zosimus, writing in the beginning of the sixth century AD, said that they "live and sleep on their horses." The Mongol cavalry carried their rations with them on the horse. They poured mare's milk into leather pouches where it curdled into cheese. They soaked horsemeat in saltwater and carried it under the saddle as jerky. One European observer erroneously reported that a testament to the ferocity and barbarity of Mongol troops was that they ate raw horseflesh cut from the horses. The observer likely observed the troops cutting strips of jerky from underneath their saddles. In extreme situations Mongol cavalrymen could subsist by periodically drinking the blood of their horses. They would make small cuts and drain blood for this purpose from the horse's neck.[24]

Steppe Warriors: The Early Tribes to the Huns

The first of the great steppe tribes were the Scythians. They inhabited the region north of the Black Sea and east to the Caspian Sea from about 700 BC to 100 BC. In the 600 years of their existence the Scythians laid the foundations for warfare on horseback and the mounted archer armies. The Scythians were one of the first mounted forces that made use the composite bow. The Scythians rode bareback and used a snaffle bit. Scythian burial excavations have revealed horse remains in the 15 hands range and are similar to the modern Akhal-Teke breed. Scythian cavalry included both mounted archers and lance-armed and laminar-armored heavy cavalry. In their encounters with the Assyrians and especially the Persians, the Scythians demonstrated the characteristic steppe warrior capability of withdrawing and avoiding combat until the conditions were most favorable. The Scythian king Idanthyrsus replied to a challenge to battle from Darius the king of Persia by saying, "If you want to know why I will not fight, I will tell you: in our country there are no towns and no cultivated land; fear of losing which, or seeing it ravaged, might indeed provoke us to a hasty battle."[25] In two years of campaigning Darius was unable to bring a sizable Scythian force to battle and ultimately withdrew from the steppe in frustration.

Like all the nomadic steppe tribes, their forte was raiding and their targets were the border empires of the northern Middle East including the Assyrians and the Urartu. The Scythians participated in the destruction of both of these kingdoms. The Scythians raided as far south as Egypt. They also traded with the same people with whom they fought, and it was through the Scythian contacts that the concept of

Mongol hunters with their Mongolian horses (top) on the eastern steppe in the 1920s. The Mongolian horse typically stands 12.2 hands and at one time often were bred to Przewalski horses. Horse equipment, particularly the Mongolian saddle, and the horses themselves are representative of the equipment and mounts of the Mongolian armies. Note the very high straight pommel on the saddle which was an aid to horse archery. (*Cavalry Journal* [U.S.]) The modern Mongolian horse is similar in size and proportion to those used in the thirteenth century. Note the saddle details and the brand on the thigh. (*Timothy May*)

fighting from horseback was introduced into the Middle East. Between 514 and 512 BC the Scythians repelled an invasion by the Persian king Darius and in the 490s the Scythians allied with Sparta against the Persians. The Persians, Greeks, and Macedonians never defeated the Scythians. In fact, they held their own and outlasted the eras of all three of these important regional powers. However, in another characteristic of steppe tribes, the land of the Scythians was ultimately inherited not by a sedentary power, but rather by another steppe tribe, the Sarmatians, migrating west. The Sarmatians who had moved into the area north of the Black Sea in the late fifth century BC coexisted for a time with the Scythians. The strength of the Sarmatians grew as the Scythians declined in influence and importance. In the third century BC the Scythians withdrew into Crimea where the Bosphoran Kingdom defeated and absorbed them in the second century.

By the first century AD the confederation of subtribes that made up the Sarmatians extended from the east coast of the Caspian Sea to the Danube where they abutted the eastern edge of the Roman Empire. For the next two centuries, the Romans and the Sarmatians skirmished along the Danube. The Sarmatians were unable to defeat the disciplined legions of Rome and their leaders continuously sought accommodation with Rome. By the second century, the Romans permitted some tribes to migrate into the interior of the empire. Numerous groups of Sarmatians were absorbed into the Roman army, mostly as cavalry alae. The records indicate a significant Sarmatian cavalry presence among the Roman garrisons in Britain.

As the Sarmatians were absorbed into the Roman Empire their place in the western steppe was taken by the Germanic Goths who were not pastoralists.[26] However, the Goths' period of ascendancy on the western steppe was relatively short. In the fourth century a new and uniquely fierce migrating steppe people known as the Huns quickly and violently forced the Goths across the Danube into the protection of the Roman Empire. Thus by the time the Goths and the Romans fought the battle of Adrianople in 378 AD, the Huns had already established themselves as the predominant tribe in the western steppe from the Danube east along the Black Sea to the Caucasus Mountains, having conquered the regions of the both the Alans and the Goths. In the late fourth century the Huns came in direct conflict with the Romans.

The initial Hun raids originated in the Caucasus Mountains and penetrating into the Roman Middle East: Anatolia, Armenia, and even as far as Syria. Raiders also crossed the Danube into Thrace. The Roman military was in disarray, still suffered the disruption caused by the defeat at Adrianople, and could not mount an effective response before the Huns successfully withdrew to the steppe with the profits of their raiding.

Neither the Germanic tribesman nor the Romans could match Hun horsemanship. The Roman historian Ammianus Marcellinus writing in the late fourth century describes Hunish warriors as "almost glued to their horses, which are hardy, its true, but ugly, and sometimes they sit on them woman-fashion, and thus perform their ordinary tasks. And when deliberations are called for on weighty matters, they all consult for a common objective in that fashion [mounted]." The Huns combined steppe riding skills with the typical tactics of the mounted archer as described by Zosimus: "they wrought immense slaughter by wheeling, charging, retreating in good time, and firing arrows from their horses."[27] Ammianus Marcellinus wrote in 392 a description of Hun tactics based on the accounts of the defeated Goths:

> When provoked they sometimes fight singly but they enter the battle in tactical formation, while their medley of voices makes a savage noise. And as they are lightly equipped for swift motion, and unexpected in action, they purposely divide suddenly in scattered bands and attack, rushing about in disorder here and there, dealing terrific slaughter; and because of their extraordinary rapidity of movement, they cannot be discerned when they break into a rampart or pillage an enemy's camp. And on this account you would not hesitate to call them the most terrible of all warriors, because they fight from a distance with missiles having sharp bone, instead of their usual points, jointed to shafts with wonderful skill; then they gallop over the intervening spaces and fight hand to hand with swords regardless of their own lives; and while the enemy are guarding against wounds from sword thrusts, they throw strips of cloth plaited into nooses over their opponents and so entangle them that they fetter their limbs and take from them the power of riding or walking.[28]

While Hun raiding died down in the first years of the fifth century a mass migration of German tribes broached the Roman border along the Rhine River. The expansion of the Huns into the barbarian territories east of the Rhine including the Hungarian plain caused this migration. The German tribes, including Goths and Franks, were shepherded into the Western Roman Empire in a process that eventually would break down the political integrity of that part of the empire. In 408 AD the Huns launched a large raid into Thrace in the Eastern Roman Empire.[29] Paying off the Hun leadership stopped that raid, but that set the precedent of the Romans paying tribute to the Huns along their border in exchange for peace, but it was a policy that proved of limited effectiveness.

During the late fourth and early fifth centuries the Huns were far from a unified political entity. The various subtribes had a great deal of independence, and thus their relationship with the Romans varied considerably. There were instances of the Huns raiding Roman holdings as well as instances of Huns providing mercenary forces to Roman commanders for military operations against Germanic enemies. The Romans also persuaded Hunish subtribes to fight independent of direct Roman control against Rome's enemies. This relationship speaks to the growing weakness of Rome as well as to the lack of unity among the Huns.[30]

Because of their small numbers, the Huns could not completely overcome their steppe rivals or consistently challenge the Roman military. The individual Hun subtribes totaled only about 5,000 members and were only able to mount forces of about

1,200 warriors. This was likely the size of the standard mounted Hun force whether it was raiding Roman holdings or serving as a mercenary force under Roman command.[31] Only the lure of exceptional loot or the influence of charismatic leaders could unite subtribes for military operations. This phenomenon explains why, during some periods, there is no record of large-scale Hun military activity. Absent a driving cohesive factor the Hun subtribes lost much of their military ambition.

The united tribes, however, were a formidable military force. Three factors combined to create the Huns' military prowess. The first two were the traditional capabilities of bow and horsemanship that they shared with the Scythians and the Sarmatians before them.. With their exceptional equestrian skills and marksmanship, the Huns advanced the state of horse archery. Their composite bow itself was innovative, with its flexible ears on the tips and its asymmetrical design which enabled the Hun to wield a considerably larger bow than other horse archers. The Hun bow was between 55 and 62 inches in length. The archer drew the arrow at a point about a third the way from the base of the bow. This allowed the bow to still clear the neck of the horse. These modifications gave greater power to the bow and did not affect its accuracy.[32]

What made the Huns special, and what has become to some degree their historical legacy, is the psychological affect they had on their enemies. All of the contemporary observers of the Huns remarked on their fierce and startling appearance. Ammianus described them as "so prodigiously ugly and bent that they might be taken for two-legged animals or the figures crudely carved from stumps, which are seen on the parapets of bridges." Saint Jerome, writing at the beginning of the fifth century, succinctly stated the psychological impact of the Huns, observing that "The Roman army is terrified by the sight of them."[33] This psychological advantage probably mitigated the fact that Hun horsemen wore little or no armor protection. This lack of armor did not discourage them from closing with the armored cavalry of Rome.

The most famous Hun leader, who flourished when their military power was at its height, was Attila. Attila came to power in 434 AD at the death of his uncle Rua. For the first few years he shared power with his brother Bleda. In 445 Attila eliminated Bleda and consolidated all the Hun tribes under his personal control. Attila pursued different policies with the western and eastern empires. From 445 to 451 he maintained relatively friendly relations with the western empire and in fact provided Huns to serve under Roman command. At the same time he followed a belligerent policy with the eastern empire. He first raided the eastern empire in 440, taking advantage of a war between the eastern empire and the Persians, to capture and destroy numerous cities along the Danube. In 443 the Eastern Romans agreed to provide an annual tribute of 2100 pounds of gold as well as other concessions in exchange for peace. In 447 Attila again invaded the empire and created a swath of destruction that led to the walls of Constantinople. The Huns captured or destroyed more than 70 cities and fortresses. The Eastern army confronted Attila, and he destroyed it in battle. In a peace treaty signed in 448, Attila doubled the gold tribute and insisted that the Romans move the boundaries of the eastern empire well south of the traditional Danube frontier.

With the eastern empire cowed, Attila turned his attention to the western empire. In early January 451, Attila moved his forces, numbering 10,000 troops, across the Rhine into Gaul. Less than half of the force, however, were cavalry, the rest being Germanic allies who were mostly infantry. Still, the horse herd supporting the campaign numbered between 50,000 and 60,000 horses.[34] His stated objective was Toulouse, the capital of the Visigoths, but in reality he intended to destroy as many of the Western Roman cities as possible, and extracting favorable concessions from Valentinian III, the Western Emperor. By April, Attila's squadrons were ranging as far west as Belgium, and on April 7 the fortress city of Metz fell to the Huns. The Huns then moved toward Orleans, whose defenses successful rebuffed the Hun attack in June. Meanwhile, a Roman army under Senator Flavius Aëtius had come up from Italy and linked up with the Visigoth army under King Theodoric, and this combined force moved to intercept Attila. The two armies met toward the end of June somewhere in the modern French province of Champagne.

The allied army formed a battle line with the best troops on the flanks: the Visigoths on the left flank and the Romans on the right flank. Less reliable tribal forces held the center of the allied line. Attila deployed the Huns with the main Hun force in the center and the wings held by allied tribes. The two forces battled throughout the day and into the night. Finally, the Romans forced the Huns to retreat to the safety of their baggage wagon laager. The Visigoths proposed to lay siege to the wagons and ensure the complete destruction of Attila and his force, but the Roman leader, Aëtius, pointed out that the Visigoth's king, Theodoric, died in the battle and therefore their new king needed to return home to ensure the legitimacy of his reign. With the departure of the Visigoths, Attila was able to successfully extract the remainder of his force back across the Rhine.[35]

The defeat of his army did not discourage Attila, and he planned an even more aggressive campaign the next year. This campaign took him over the Alps in the spring of 452 and into the heart of Italy. Attila's return to the offensive caught the Romans by surprise. There was no army to oppose him, and through the summer Attila captured and destroyed dozens of Italian cities including Milan. The road to Rome was open and the city undefended. The Western Roman Empire's only hope to end the rampage of the steppe warriors was negotiation. A delegation of distinguished citizens, including Pope Leo, met with Attila and induced him to end the campaign. An important factor in Attila's decision was that Italy had just suffered a period of famine, and disease was rampant throughout the region.[36]

Attila returned to the Hungarian plain to plan his next action. The new Eastern Roman emperor Maximus had refused to pay tribute, and Attila planned to punish the eastern empire and reestablish Hun dominance. As the Hun army assembled in 453 for the new campaign Attila took a new wife. On the morning after his wedding his lieutenants found him dead in his bed. The forthcoming campaign was canceled, the territories were divided among his sons, of which there were many, and this transition set the stage for the ruin of Hun dominance. Within months of Attila's passing his sons began warring with each other, individual subtribes asserted their independence, and conquered allies such as the Ostrogoths successfully rebelled. Some Hun subtribes were absorbed into the Roman Empire as cavalry formations. In a relatively short period, the Huns lost their tribal and cultural identity including their language. Little evidence remains in the modern world of the 50 years during which the Huns were the premier and most feared military power in Europe.[37]

Although Attila and the Huns had little long-term impact on the course of European history other than to move along the dissolution of the Western Roman Empire, the Huns demonstrated the superiority of a quick-moving cavalry army based on the horse archer. The military importance of the horse-archer army would not diminish over the next several hundred years. When it next appeared in European history the Mongols coupled it with an efficient and effective command system to create arguably the most powerful army seen in the history of warfare.

The Mongols

By the thirteenth century, the mounted archer and the deadly composite bow was an old weapons system, however, it was in the 1200s that the history of this weapons system intersected with the history of an army that would bring the military horse and rider to its full potential. The Mongol armies of the thirteenth century, with the mounted archer as their primary combat system, achieved a level of world domination never equaled. Over a period of fewer than 200 years, they executed a series of campaigns which brought most of the known world under their rule.

In their initial campaigns orchestrated by the great Genghis Khan, the Mongol army was almost a pure cavalry army. Certainly one of the purest horse armies ever fielded. Over time, they developed other capabilities including considerable skill in siege craft, which was necessary to capture fortified cities. They also built large and capable fleets. In most cases conquered adversaries-turned-allies built, manned, and often commanded the siege equipment, infantry contingents, and fleets. The core of the Mongol armies throughout the period of their empire remained the horse archers and their steppe horses.

At the time of the birth of Temuchin (c. 1162)–who would later rename himself Genghis Khan, what is now modern Mongolia was inhabited by five tribes: the Mongol and Tatar in the east, the Kerait tribe in the center, the Merkits to the north, and the Naimans in the west. Despite speaking different languages, the Mongol and Tatar tribes lived the same pastoral nomadic life and freely intermarried. The Tartars were probably the most important of the tribes because the Chinese supported them. Medieval Europeans referred to all the eastern steppe tribes as "Tartars."[38]

Temuchin was born into the family of a minor clan chieftain. Tartars murdered his father and created an animosity that would eventually result in the destruction of their tribe. With their chief dead, the followers of Temuchin's father abandoned their chief's family and Temuchin struggled to survive. As he came into young adulthood, his natural leadership and martial abilities attracted a personal following sufficient to establish his own clan within the Mongol tribe. This group of close followers became the nucleus around which Temuchin ultimately built his army and they provided many of the generals, such as Subotai, who later commanded their far-flung expeditions. Temuchin shrewdly allied himself with the Kerait tribe, and used them to further increase his power until he eventually was able to claim leadership of the Mongols. From that point on, he systematically waged war on, and defeated, all of the tribes in Mongolia. His policy was not to destroy (though the fate of the Tartars was an exception) but rather to assimilate the other tribes under his leadership. Manpower was too precious not to make use of it whenever possible. By 1206 he had succeeded in unifying by force the eastern steppe tribes under his leadership and at a great *quriltai* he was acclaimed Genghis Khan (universal leader).[39] Genghis provided an organizational ability and vision, that combined with the proven horse archer weapons system, permitted the Mongol army to successfully conduct military operations on a scale never before attempted and never again equaled.

Genghis Khan's objective was China. The purpose of his other campaigns was to shape strategic conditions to permit the best Mongol forces to focus on the conquest of China. Genghis Khan envisioned the conquest of China in five operational phases. The first phase was a campaign to secure the approaches into northern China. This required the conquest of the land of the Xixia (1205–10) who could threaten any force attacking China from the north. The second phase was a reconnaissance in force of the northern Chinese Empire, the Jin. This took the form of a large-scale mounted raid and then a campaign that secured the northern holdings of the Jin (1211–15). The third phase of the Chinese campaign was securing the rear or southwestern border of the Mongol Empire through the campaign against the Khwarazm Empire in Persia (1219–25). The fourth phase was the complete conquest of the Jin (1230–34). The last phase was the conquest of the southern Chinese Empire, the Song (1254–79). Genghis Khan personally supervised the first three phases but died as the armies prepared for the final offensive against the Jin. It was in the last two phases of the conquest of China that the Mongol armies matured into a comprehensive military machine capable of sophisticated siege and naval operations while retaining its core competency of mounted combat in open battle.

China was the great prize designated by Genghis Khan, but the Mongol armies were numerous and competent enough to pursue campaigns that expanded the empire into areas remote from China. As Genghis's heirs, Ogedei Khan and Kublai Khan, supervised operations in China, other Mongol leaders led armies into Europe as far as Hungary and the Adriatic (1237–42), and into the Middle East as far as Syria (1251–60). After China was conquered, it became a base for expansion into Southeast Asia as far as modern day Indonesia. Conquering Korea was very difficult and required a series of invasions between 1216 and 1273. Japan was invaded twice (1274–81) and saved due to the intervention of a typhoon that destroyed much of the Mongol invasion fleet.[40]

The Mongol Army

At its core the Mongol army was a cavalry army in which every warrior was mounted. Soldiers were extremely disciplined, and well trained. The Mongol leaders held commanders personally responsible for the equipment and training of their men. John of Piano Carpini, a friar, observed the Mongols and wrote: "These men are more obedient to their masters than any other men in the world, be they religious or secular."[41] The army had a superb command and control system and the ability to conduct planning on the strategic level. Most importantly, the army had a unique and unmatched logistics capability which gave it strategic mobility.

A major training task conducted by the army was the annual hunt. That event involved the entire army, and all units that were not on active campaign in the distant regions of the empire replicated the event wherever they were. The hunt began with the army deployed in a single line by unit with the troopers literally stirrup to stirrup. When the entire army assembled, 100,000 cavalrymen stretched in a single line for more than 60 miles. The line moved out at a controlled pace driving the game before it. Gradually, under the control of their officers, the units on the wings would advance ahead of the center. Ultimately, after moving for days or weeks and covering hundred of miles, the wings would gradually converge to complete a circle and the army would then drive the game to the center. The hunt caught all manner of ani-

Mongolian soldiers reenact the advance of a Mongol jaghun unit. An arban or unit of ten comprises each file, marked by a banner. (*Timothy May*)

mals from rabbits to bears. The soldiers did not allow any game to escape and killed anything that attempted to break out of the trap. The hunt tested all of the soldiers' weapons skills. Once the circle closed a mass killing concluded the hunt and provided meat and hides to take care of the army through the coming winter.

The hunt served to provision the army and tested and trained all of the army's critical combat skills. It exercised the army command and control at every level as commanders kept the various far-flung elements of the hunt coordinated. Unit positioning and movement had to be tightly controlled. Officers provided constant tactical command and detailed supervision of their formations. Individual weapons skills were extremely important as the trapped larger game attacked the mounted troops. Hunting was a skill used to train warriors in many cultures, but none used it on the scale of the Mongols nor used it to train the type of synchronized movement which was one of the unique characteristics of the Mongol armies.

Mongol armies were bigger than the average European and Middle Eastern armies. This was due to the mobilization of the entire society and flexible logistics. All adult males below the age of 60 were liable for military service. The Mongol army organized on a simple decimal system. The smallest group was the squad of 10 men led by the captain, the *arban*. Each man swore allegiance to the arban, who was personally loyal to the leader of the 100 men of the *jaghun*. This leader in turn owed his loyalty to the *mingghan*, the leader of a 1,000-man organization which fit similarly within the *tumen* of 10,000 horsemen. This system, like feudalism, emphasized personal loyalty, but it was also a meritocracy where promotion and advancement were based on ability. Though large, the size of Mongol armies was usually overestimated in contemporary accounts. In part, the large number of remounts that accompanied the army on campaign contributed to the impression of the large size of the army. Typically, a steppe warrior had 5 to 6 remounts. Thus, a typical Mongol tumen, included roughly 50,000 war horses. The Mongols also intentionally encouraged the inflation of their numbers, even going to the extent of mounting dummies on remount horses led in trail behind a single cavalryman. Two relatively reliable sources place the strength of the Mongol force at the quriltai of 1206 at 105,000 men, and the strength at the time of the death of Genghis at 129,000. These numbers seem reasonable because they are sufficient to execute the operations which were conducted by the Mongols, and they were logistically supportable given that a 100,000-man army would have been supported by more than one million horses.[42] Still, considering the scope of Mongol operations, the standing army was not large. When it met enemies in battle the Mongols were often outnumbered and defeated their adversaries with skill and not size.

Several tumen combined to form each of the three components of the fighting army organization: the left wing, the right wing, and the center. During the conquest of the Jin the right wing of Genghis's army numbered 38,000, the left wing 62,000, and the center 29,000.[43] Size of the wings was adjusted based on the tactical situation and the mission by transferring tumen between the army components. Wings were capable of being detached from the main body and operating as separate field armies. The tumen was also totally self-sustaining and capable of independent action such as an advance reconnaissance and raids. The independence of the tumen permitted the army to move on multiple axis. This type of organizational flexibility would not be matched in Europe until Napoleon introduced the corps system at the end of the eighteenth century.

The organization of the army transcended tribal lines. Genghis Khan intentionally assigned individuals of different tribes to the 1,000-man unit. This had the effect of completely destroying the clan and tribal structure leaving no alternative to the individual but to transfer his loyalty to his unit and to the universal khan. Exceptions were made for the original loyal clans and tribes which aided Genghis in establishing his hegemony over the tribes, but even these trusted tribes were not allowed to organize in any unit larger than a thousand.[44]

The army came to include infantry and special troops who were auxiliaries. These troops were not Mongols but were impressed into the army for special purposes from conquered territories. Generally they were not critically important to operations with the exception of siege experts who were recruited from China and Persia. The two primary pieces of equipment they used were a light and a heavy catapult. These two pieces of equipment gave the Mongols the ability to capture cities. Both eventually evolved into the simpler trebuchet designs. The light catapult was

Model of a Mongolian light cavalry archer, left. The horse archer was the mainstay of the army and was used for reconnaissance, raiding, and to support the heavy cavalry in the attack. He is unarmored except for his thick winter coat specifically designed to enable him to campaign in the arctic conditions of the steppe winter. His primary weapon is his composite bow. Model of a Mongolian heavy cavalryman, right. This heavy cavalryman is armored with a lamellar armor halberk, made of iron scales and an iron helmet. Though the heavy cavalry were armed and skilled with the composite bow, they were designed for close combat with sword and lance. (*Author*)

designed to be disassembled and carried on pack horses. It was assembled and manned by a crew of 40. The heavy siege equipment had to be either pulled behind oxen or built on site. If the defenses did not warrant heavy siege equipment it was not brought on campaign. The light siege equipment followed all Mongol armies as part of an artillery train. Even in open battle mobile light catapults played a role hurling smoke bombs designed to conceal unit movements and add confusion to the battlefield. If the enemy defended in dense formations the artillery could be used to pound designated positions to create a weak point for attack.[45]

A Mongol army on the move was a large enterprise. A 10,000-man tumen was supported by 40,000 noncombatants, and as many as 600,000 animals of all types. A typical Mongol army on the move consumed eight square miles of grassland a day. The march schedule typically was organized into a morning march, afternoon grazing of animals, and evening rest. In this manner the army could sustain a movement rate of 14 miles a day. For many reasons, the army logistics system worked better if the army and its support structure continued to move. Grazing requirements prevented the army from remaining in one place very long.[46]

Although the horse archer was the symbol of the Mongol Army, heavy cavalry delivered the decisive attack. Mongol armies included a large number of heavy cavalry, typically up to 40 percent of the force. Heavy cavalry wore lamellar armor with either iron or hard leather scales. A cuirass of this type weighed approximately 20 pounds. Heavy cavalry were armed with a 12-foot lance which had a hook on it designed to pull adversaries off their mounts. The horses of the heavy cavalry were likewise heavily armored with laminate armor including a chamfron, peytral, crinet, and crupper. The heavy cavalry followed the horse archers in an attack and were also an effective counterattack force.[47]

Mongol Army Strategy and Tactics

Sometimes planning for Mongol operations occurred years in advance. Planning gave very careful consideration to logistics. A reconnaissance in force often preceded the campaign to test the enemy capabilities as well as determine the impact of terrain on operations. River crossing requirements and the grazing potential of the area of operations were of particular concern to Mongol leaders. Mongol leaders understood the concept of strategic political objectives and formally pronounced the campaign objectives so that subordinate commanders could use them to provide direction and coherence to the army on campaign. Mongol leaders told operational commanders what to achieve but not how to achieve it.[48]

The need for the army to graze its animals required subunits to march in a widely dispersed formation, but the units were able to assemble quickly for battle. This required a sophisticated means for communicating at the tactical, operational, and strategic levels. During battle, command and control was exercised by officers who used flags, drums, signal arrows (which whistled as they flew), and lanterns. At the operational level, couriers maintained contact between various Mongol units ensuring that column commanders understood where friendly forces were located so that they could synchronize actions even though the units were out of direct contact with each other. The couriers primarily carried messages and reports but also could send signals using a simple semaphore system.[49]

At the strategic level, a corps of elite imperial couriers carried official messages between field armies and the khan. Hundreds of post stations positioned at 30-mile intervals supported these couriers. The post stations provided logistics support for the system including remounts, had provisions for riders, included fresh riders, and had a small garrison of soldiers for protection. This system, know as the *Yam*, was

Mongolian horse archers pursuing enemies from a thirteenth-century album. Note the compound bows. (*Bildarchiv Preussischer Kulturbesitz*)

very similar to the American Pony Express mail service developed 700 years later. As the army moved in the field, commanders established new courier stations expanding the network. A message could travel up to 120 miles a day in this system. A special rider was dedicated to important messages while routine messages used relays of riders.[50]

The Mongol armies were extremely mobile–able to move twice as fast as their enemies. This mobility, combined with their ability to synchronize the movement of multiple columns, allowed them to always have the initiative. The Mongols rarely were attacked; they were usually the attacker. When battle was not imminent, the average movement was 14 miles a day. A Mongol army could cover 40 miles a day and up to 60 miles in a day if unusual conditions required it. In 1221 Genghis Khan moved his army 130 miles in two days. In 1241, Subotai moved his army 180 miles in three days through snow.[51]

A contemporary European observer Robert of Spolato commented on the tactical proficiency of the army: "There is no people in the world who know so well how to overcome an adversary in the open by skill in warfare." The army maneuvered and moved based on the concept of "reconnaissance pull." Mounted scout units ranged 35 to 70 miles ahead of the main body. They also scouted to the flanks and rear. The scouts were the eyes and ears of the commander as he sought information. They also provided a highly effective security screen that prevented the enemy from gaining information about the Mongol army and prevented surprise from any direction. Using this strategy, scouts and their reports "pulled" the army in the direction of the enemy. The scouts then carefully managed handover of the battle to the main body. As the main body approached, the scouting force would begin to skirmish with the enemy, distracting and fixing them in place. The main body came on line well to the rear and began to move its wings forward to envelop the enemy. The scouts maintained constant communication with the army leaders during the approach to battle. The scouts permitted the main body to maneuver to achieve an advantageous position before it ever came into physical or even visual contact with the enemy.[52]

Once in contact, the Mongol force approached the enemy in five parallel lines facing the enemy. Scout detachments, deployed in a thin line of skirmishers, advanced well forward and to the flanks of the main lines. The troops in each line aligned tightly stirrup to stirrup. The first two lines consisted of heavy cavalry while horse archers made up the following three lines. As much as 200 yards separated the lines themselves. As the formation approached maximum bow range, the heavy cavalry created gaps in their formation permitting the first line of horse archers to pass to the front and charge. As the first line of horse archers passed through, the heavy cavalry closed ranks behind them and charged. The rear ranks of horse archers may have halted at this point. The lead rank of horse archers, turned obliquely across the front of the enemy formation firing rapidly as they moved. The rear ranks of archers elevated their bows and fired indirectly into the enemy formation over the heads of the charging archers and the heavy cavalry. As the lead rank of horse archers turned away from the enemy formation the heavy cavalry charge with its lances and armored horses crashed into the now disrupted enemy formation.

The heavy cavalry charge was the decisive point in the attack. The archers set the conditions for success. As Di Plano Carpioni noted, the purpose of the archer was to wear down the enemy: "only when the men and horses are worn down by arrows, do they come to close quarters." The attack speed was described as a "wolf lope" but probably was a slow controlled canter. During the approach the Mongols maintained silence throughout the formation. As the unit broke into the gallop for the culmination of the attack, a great kettledrum that accompanied the commander beat the tempo of the attack and the attacking cavalry gave a war yell. The shout and drum, coming after the silent approach, was calculated to create terror in the enemy formation.[53]

The ability of the Mongol cavalry to attack was facilitated by one of its most effective tactics: the feigned retreat. This tactic was a favorite of horse-archer armies. It took advantage of the horse archer's tactical mobility and firepower. It also indicated a sophisticated understanding of the psychology of combat. The horse-archer attack was designed to infuriate as well as damage the adversary. The archers played upon the inability of many enemies to return fire and timed their retreat to take advantage of the enemy's desire to close with them in hand-to-hand combat. The feigned withdraw caused the enemy to break from their tight defensive formation and expose themselves as they pursued the retreating horse men. This set the enemy up for a surprise cavalry charge as well as ambush by concealed archer attacks from the flanks. The feigned retreat caused the enemy cavalry to exhaust their horses making them vulnerable to countercharge by rested Mongol cavalry.

The Mongol army followed a campaign cycle that was unusual for most horse-powered armies. The preferred campaign season, unlike European armies, was the winter.[54] The Mongols did not like the spring season because swollen rivers and heavy rains inhibited their mobility. The summer season was used to build their logistics base, train, and most important, get their horses fit. Campaigning began with the first hard freeze. In winter the rivers were frozen, so instead of being obstacles to operational-level mobility, they could be crossed easily or could be used as highways along which the steppe horse armies could move rapidly. While the weather confined other armies in their bases, the ability of the Mongol horses to forage grass from under the snow allowed them to stay in the field. The goal of Mongol campaigns was to achieve the campaign objective by spring. Another characteristic of the Mongol campaigns was operational and strategic vision and patience. No other armies before, and few since, could match the Mongol armies ability to visual a campaign conducted over several years in pursuit of a strategic objective. Additionally, the Mongol leaders were also able to visualize how several simultaneous campaigns, each covering great expanses of space and time, fit together to achieve strategic ends.

Steppe Cavalry at War: The Invasion of Europe

Analyzing individual battles does much to increase our understanding of how the employment of horses and riders led to victory. However, analyzing the Mongol army in battle does not completely demonstrate how and why the Mongol cavalry conquered the world. To understand the capability of the Mongol cavalry requires an analysis of the cavalry army on a complete campaign. The Mongol army was one of the first to wage war on the scale of campaigns rather than battles. One of the most important and effective campaigns executed by the Mongols was the invasion of Europe conducted between 1237 and 1242.

The Reconnaissance

The idea for a campaign to the west was conceived by the great Mongol general Subotai who approached Genghis Khan at the conclusion of the Khwarizmian campaign and suggested that he and General Jebe be permitted to conduct a long reconnaissance of the region west of the Caspian Sea to investigate the reports of "narrow-faced men with light hair and blue eyes." The Khan gave his permission for the 30,000-man force to embark on the mission with the condition that it return to Mongolia within three years.[55]

The reconnaissance force consisted of three tumen, two under the command of Subotai, and the other under the command of Jebe: a total of about 30,000 men. The entire force was under Subotai's command. The force spent the summer of 1220 in northern Persia south of the Caspian Sea and then marched north in the winter of 1220–21. For two years the Mongols moved steadily across the steppe, noting the conditions of the land and people, establishing an intelligence network, and defeating several European and tribal armies despite being outnumbered. In late 1223 Subotai's and Jebe's forces rejoined the main army of Genghis Khan near the Aral Sea. The "men with light hair and blue eyes"–Russians–were mystified by the force that had assaulted them. One Russian commented, "We do not know where these evil Tartars came from nor where they went."[56]

This Mongol reconnaissance was one of the greatest cavalry raids of all time. Subotai's force traveled more than 5,500 miles over three years and fought a dozen successful battles against superior numbers. Most important, they brought back the information that there existed a steppe corridor from central Asia to the doorstep of Europe sufficient to sustain the invasion of a large cavalry army. Additionally, Subotai left behind a network of spies and messengers that continued to update the Mongols on the political and military events of the region.

The Conquest of Russia

Based on the information provided by Subotai and his intelligence network, the Mongols put together an extensive plan for the invasion of Europe. The invasion plan envisioned seizing all of Europe from the Urals to the Atlantic. The first phase was to conquer all the land to the end of the steppe. In subsequent phases, the army would move on its own schedule in a systematic conquest of Europe, one region at a time. The conquest of China would be the model. The plan required an army of 150,000 men and would take between 16 and 18 years to complete. The new Khan, Ogedei, appointed a grandson of Genghis, Batu Khan, to command the expedition. Subotai would be second in command and the chief planner.[57]

The offensive into Europe was only one of several operations undertaken simultaneously by the Mongols, but it was the primary task in the summer of 1236. The Mongols assembled several units of Chinese and Persian engineers to operate siege equipment. The core of the army was 50,000 veteran Mongol horsemen. Conquered central Asian steppe tribes supplied another 50,000 or more troops. Because they shared the basic horse and archery skills necessary to be part of the Mongol military system, the incorporation of these tribes into the army was relatively easy. Just as the original eastern steppe tribes were broken up to form tumen, the Mongols distributed the central Asian tribesmen among new mingghan and tumen, all officered by veteran Mongols. The army spent the summer of 1236 training and fattening their horses for the coming winter campaign.

In the fall of 1236 Subotai led a small contingent of the army to systematically conquer the land of the Bulgars and other unconquered steppe tribes east of the Volga River.[58] In the early winter of 1237 the main army under Batu Khan crossed the Volga River and moved northwest. The plan was to capture the northern Russian principalities first. This would eliminate any flank threat to the main thrust west across the steppe. The campaign to subdue northern Russia relied on speed to defeat the disunited Russian princes before they understood the threat and could unite in defense.

The first to fall were the Russian cities of the Riazan principality. The Mongols captured the towns of Riazan, Pronsk, and Kolomna in a matter of weeks. In all cases the Mongol attacks were ruthless. The Russians built their northern cities within a wooden palisade that was hardly a challenge to the Chinese and Persian engineers. They assembled the light catapults from their pack horses and easily breached the walls. Then Mongol cavalry rode through the breach shooting and slaying without regard to age or gender. They put the entire citizenry of the pillaged towns to the sword as part an intentional strategy of creating terror among the population. The only survivors were those deliberately spared and allowed to escape in order to spread the word of the approaching invaders.

The destruction of the cities of Riazan demonstrated to the Grand Duke of Suzdalia, the most powerful of the northern princes, the danger approaching, but this knowledge did nothing to slow the Mongol advance. In February 1238 Moscow fell to the invaders, followed in early March by the capital city of Vladimir where the royal family of Suzdalia died along with all the other city inhabitants. The army then split into two formations. Half of the army under Batu Khan proceeded northwest with the objective of capturing northern Russia's most prosperous city, Novgorod. The other half of the army, under Subotai, moved north to destroy the last remaining Russian army under the Grand Duke. Batu's advance continued to be irresistible as the towns of Dmitrov, Tyer, and Torzhok all fell to the Mongols. However, Torzhok took two weeks to capture, and at the completion of the siege the spring thaw came and turned the 60 miles between Batu and Novgorod into a marshy mass of swollen rivers and muddy fields. Meanwhile Subotai surrounded and destroyed the army of the Grand Duke. With the changing season Batu called a temporary halt to the campaign, and the Mongol army moved south.

In the summer of 1238, Batu Khan's army established itself in the Don River basin in what is today western Ukraine. There the army received new horses and recruits for the losses it suffered. The army rested and trained on the banks of the Don for 18 months, regaining its strength and planning the second phase of the conquest of Russia. The Mongols began the 1240 campaign by marching west into the Russian provinces of Pereiaslav and Chernigov. Following the east bank of the Dnieper River north, the Mongols sacked the province capitals of Pereiaslav and Chernigov before turning their attention to Kiev, the cultural and religious center of Russia. In November 1240, the Mongols attacked Kiev, breaching its one wooden gate and gaining entry into the city. Once inside the city the battle was over. The Mongols proceeded street by street, methodically killing the citizens and burning the wooden buildings to the ground, and plundered the accumulated relics of the Russian church. Kiev was the final Russian stronghold, and after destroying the city the Mongols advanced west, virtually unopposed, to the borders of Hungary.

The Conquest of Poland and Hungary

The conquest of western Russia was the opening move in a very complex plan to conquer Hungary, the most powerful kingdom in Eastern Europe. The future conquest of central Europe would make use of Hungary as the main operational base. Batu Khan had an army of about 100,000 at his disposal for the operation. The plan for Hungary called for a major diversionary attack into Poland to prevent forces moving from Poland to reinforce King Bela IV of Hungary, while the main army crossed the Carpathian Mountains in three widely separated march columns. The columns would then unite at point to be designated east of the Danube River.

The diversionary attack into Poland consisted of two tumen under the command of the princes Baidar and Kadan. They moved out in the middle of the winter of 1240–41 and struck the Polish city of Lublin in February. Lublin fell with little resistance. The Mongols then crossed the frozen Vistula River and captured the city of Sandomir. By late February, the Mongols had still not encountered a major Polish army, and the princes were concerned about successfully accomplishing their mission of preventing Polish reinforcement of Hungary. To increase their ability to locate the Polish army the two commanders decided on the bold move of dividing their relatively small force in half. Kadan and his tumen of 10,000 men struck north while Baidar and his similar size force continued west toward Cracow.

At Cracow the Mongols feigned retreat and lured the army of Vladimir, the Palatine of Sandomir and Cracow, out from the city walls. Eleven miles from the city the Mongols turned on the Poles and destroyed them in a hail of arrows. Hearing the news of the defeat, the citizens of Cracow abandoned the city and, on March 24, 1241,

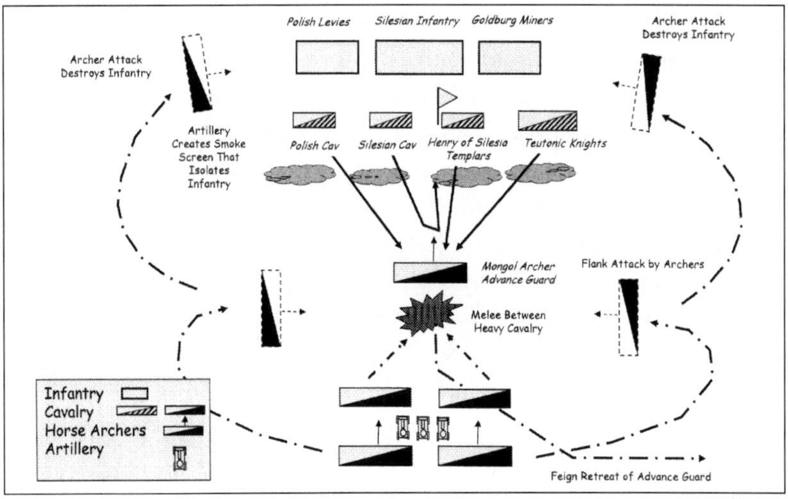

The battle of Leignitz, 1241.

the Mongols arrived and pillaged and burned it. Baidar and Kadan continued their advances, destroying villages and towns as they marched. Ultimately the two tumen linked up at Breslau. There they prepared for a siege when scouts reported that a large Polish army was near. Breaking off the siege the Mongols raced to meet the army of Henry of Silesia.

Henry of Silesia assembled an army of 25,000 at the town of Liegnitz with the intent of going to the aid of the king of Hungary. Duke Henry's army was an assorted collection of peasant levies and men-at-arms. His best troops were the knights of his own retinue as well as a sizable contingent of Teutonic knights under their Prussian *landmeister*, Poppo von Osterna. In addition there were small contingents of Templar and Hospitaller knights. Backing up the mounted men-at-arms were contingents of infantry levies from Poland, Silesia, and German gold miners from Silesia. The European levies were poorly armed with field tools. In size the Europeans had a slight advantage, but that was the only advantage they had.

The Mongol army attacked with a mingghan advance guard of 1,000 archers. Henry deployed with his cavalry in front, backed up by his infantry levies. As the Mongol advance guard moved forward Henry ordered his Silesian cavalry to charge and disperse the archers. Several volleys of arrows met the advancing Silesians forcing them to retreat. Henry then ordered the Polish cavalry and the Teutonic knights forward. These units closed with the archers and began to push them back. Henry then committed his last mounted force, his personal guard and the Templars. As they rode forward the Mongol advance guard retreated.

The retreat of the Mongol advance guard was a carefully timed maneuver. As the European cavalry pursued the retreating archers, the Mongol heavy cavalry moved forward and countercharged the advancing Europeans. Mongol catapults fired smoke pots behind the European cavalry creating a haze that separated the battle from the infantry levies to the rear. Also, fresh mingghans of archers moved to both flanks and poured a devastating fire into the flanks of the attacking European cavalry. Attacked from three sides the European cavalry suffered tremendous casualties and broke and ran from the battlefield pursued by the Mongols. The Mongol archers then advanced through the smoke and attacked the almost defenseless infantry. Showers of arrows systematically destroyed the hapless formations. Henry tried to escape the battlefield, but archers rode him down and killed him and his attendants. There were few survivors of Henry's army.

Ironically, unknown to Henry but tracked by Mongol scouts, a 50,000-man strong European army under Wenceslas of Bohemia was less then a day's march away and moving to join Henry. The Mongol commanders were aware of the intentions of Wenceslas and executed their attack knowing that if they delayed the combined European armies would be too strong for them to confront. After the battle, in the face of Wenceslas's large army, the Mongol force broke apart into small contingents and continued to raid throughout the month of April to ensure that Wenceslas did not move to the aid of Hungary. In May, with their mission a success, they retreated to the Danube and rejoined the main Mongol army.

As Baidar and Kadan caused chaos in Poland, the three columns of the main army completed their crossing of the Carpathians. The main army, 70,000 strong, advanced toward the city of Pest on the east bank of the Danube River. The Mongol army remained within sight of Pest until word came that the northern diversion was successful and no reinforcements would be arriving in Hungary. With that knowledge, Batu Khan began to withdraw his army east toward the Sajo River. The withdrawal to the Sajo River was a carefully thought-out and planned maneuver designed to place the Hungarian army in a position where it could be destroyed.

Upon arriving at the river the Mongols crossed on a single bridge, moved an additional ten miles, and then encamped in wooded hills. The Hungarian army followed the retreating Mongols to the river crossing. King Bela ordered a strong reconnaissance force across the bridge, and they reported that the far side of the river was clear of any sign of the Mongols. The bulk of King Bela's 100,000-man army made camp on the west side of the river inside a fortified wagon laager.

During the night the Mongol army came out of its hidden positions and Batu Khan led a force of 40,000 back to the Sajo River crossing. As the Hungarian army woke up on the morning of April 11, 1241, the Mongols attacked the force on the east bank of the river. The small Hungarian security force on the east bank repulsed the initial attack against the bridge. This bought time for the Hungarians to form a battle line on the west bank and withdraw their force from the east bank. The Hungarians easily repulsed several Mongol attacks across the narrow span. Batu then brought up seven catapults that fired into the massed ranks of the defenders on the west bank. Taking advantage of the confusion caused by the artillery fire, the Mongols forced the crossing of the bridge and established a foothold on the west bank. The Mongols slowly expanded their foothold while repelling repeated counterattacks by the Hungarian army. Mongol casualties were heavy, nonetheless Batu began to thin his ranks in order to lengthen his line and encircle the Hungarians. This was a risky maneuver as the Mongol line was already hard pressed to hold its position.

The Hungarians were on the verge of victory. However, before they could organize a last concerted attack on Batu, 30,000 horsemen under General Subotai appeared in their rear. Subotai had marched out of the Mongol camp late the night before and moved south along the river, built a makeshift bridge, crossed the river, and then marched against the Hungarian rear. Poor security on the part of the Hungarian scouts allowed the Mongols to execute this complex maneuver completely undetected. With the arrival of Subotai's force the Hungarians retreated into the protection of their wagon laager.

As the Hungarians sheltered into their laager the Mongols brought forward their catapults and began to bombard the Hungarian position. Subotai's force completed the encirclement of the position but intentionally left one break in the Mongol lines that offered an escape. As the Mongol bombardment continued several Hungarian horsemen broke from the defensive position and were allowed to make their escape through the opening in the Mongol lines. This encouraged the bulk of the Hungarian army to give up the defensive position and attempt to retreat. When this occurred the Mongols sprang their trap. Archers had flanked the apparent escape route and created a gauntlet of arrows along the corridor. The Mongols positioned heavy cavalry to ride down any who survived the archers. The Hungarian army was destroyed as it retreated. Bodies littered the road west to a distance of 30 miles. Conservative estimates were that 60,000 men perished in the Mongol trap, though King Bela escaped and survived. The defeat at the Sajo River destroyed the last effective European army between Batu Khan and central Europe. The Mongols advanced to Pest and burned the city but did not cross the Danube. Batu Khan had determined to consolidate his position in Eastern Hungary during the summer of 1241. Continuing the campaign would await the winter freeze of 1241–42.

The campaign began anew with the first freeze in November 1241. During the summer of 1241 the Mongols had refit their army and received horses and men from the east. The Europeans, in contrast, had done little to prepare additional defenses and forces to oppose the expected Mongol advance. A war was raging between the Pope and the Holy Roman Emperor, King Frederick II of Austria. Neither side would put aside their internal squabble to prepare for the Mongol threat. In fact, Frederick took advantage of the defeat of Hungary to occupy several western Hungarian provinces. The Mongol intelligence system was totally aware of this disarray, and Batu Khan and Subotai were prepared to take full advantage of it.

The initial Mongol operations seized a base of operations on the west bank of the Danube by seizing the cities of Buda and Gran. With these bases in their possession the Mongols launched a reconnaissance in force toward Vienna. Additionally, they dispatched a tumen south into the Balkans in search of King Bela. The reconnaissance into Austria advanced without encountering any significant field army. The Mongols bypassed several garrisons as the reconnaissance was more interested in information than capturing territory. It advanced as far as the suburbs of Vienna before it returned to the west bank of the Danube and ended that winter's operations. The army spent the spring and summer of 1242 preparing to resume the campaign the following winter. However, in September word arrived that the supreme Khan, Ogedei, had died in December 1241 and the royal family was required to assemble in Mongolia for the election of a new Khan. This news ended the Mongol plans to attack into central Europe. Instead, the winter of 1242–43 was spent advancing east back into the heart of the steppe as Batu Khan and members of the royal family on the campagin began their long trip to Asia. Europe was spared invasion, and the Mongol army would never return.

Eventually Batu Khan would return to the western steppe. His conquest of eastern Europe had made him fabulously rich and able to establish a separate regional khanate that became known as the Golden Horde. The units recruited from the defeated central steppe tribes proved to be very loyal, and the Mongol officers who commanded them preferred to remain in Europe rather than return to Mongolia. For 200 years the Golden Horde's horse-archer armies would roam from their base between the Don and Volga Rivers raiding and exacting tribute from the Russian princes.

Modern historians have speculated on the probable outcome of a return of the Mongol cavalry to Europe. Most conclude that the results would have been devastating to Europe.[59] One of the characteristics of the Mongol army was its sophisticated and capable intelligence service. This, combined with the strategic vision of commanders such as Subotai, gave the Mongols an unrivaled ability to accurately visualize operations on a grand scale. The Mongol commanders almost certainly understood that attacking beyond the western steppe of Hungary was an operation that had significant strategic risk. Central Europe would have severely tested the Mongol way of war. Without the immense steppe to sustain the horse herds, the logistics of the army would have been strained. Heavily forested terrain would have constrained the mobility of the horse formations and worked to the advantage of Europeans. Numerous rivers that did not usually freeze in the winter would also have been a further obstacle to mobility. Magyar raids into Germany in the tenth century led to the fortification of the German frontier in Bavaria. This was an effective tactic against raiding.[60] As demonstrated in the Middle East, the Europeans excelled at fortification. Unlike the wood palisades of Russia, the numerous stone fortified cities of central Europe would have posed a major challenge to the Mongols, which in turn would have further stressed their logistics system. Certainly, it was within the capability of the Mongol armies to achieve a conquest of Europe, and Subotai had considered a campaign lasting as long as 18 years. Their ability to conquer China demonstrated that no task was beyond them. However, they also understood, as the challenges of fighting in Korea demonstrated, that some victories came at a disproportionate cost. Ultimately, the new Khan decided not to renew the campaign.

The global Mongol Empire ended with the death of Kublai Khan in 1294. In the fourteenth century the sons and grandsons of the khan continued to rule their inherited regions with increasing autonomy and regional distinction. From the fourteenth century on, each of the individual kingdoms would follow its own history, no longer united by a single leader and global vision.

The steppe armies reached their zenith in organization and in operational and tactical ability under Genghis Khan, his family, and generals. The Mongols' talent for organizing, training, and using their horses set them apart from all their contemporaries and from all future armies. The Mongol army was a modern one in every sense except technology. The mobility of the sturdy steppe horse enabled the Mongols to pursue their strategies and their modern concept of operational maneuver. Their horses and horsemanship, as much as their tactics and weapons, made them the master of every enemy that they met. Not until the age of mechanized armies would any army match both their prowess and their intellectual grasp of the art of war.

Chapter Six

EARLY MODERN CAVALRY

The duty of the cavalry on a day of action is to attack, as soon as ordered, in the manner that I have prescribed.
–FREDERICK THE GREAT, *Instructions to His Generals*

Between 1500 and 1800, Europe underwent a profound period of military and political transition. Europe, which had remained relatively isolated as a civilization during the Middle Ages, reached out to discover new worlds and establish political and economic ties around the globe. Armies applied science to warfare and became professional, marking the beginning of modern military forces. The most significant change in warfare was the introduction of gunpowder. In 1494, the French king Charles VIII fielded the first modern army as defined by historian Michael Howard. The army had three distinct components, cavalry, infantry, and artillery; commanders could arrange these components in various tactical combinations; and a centralized treasury paid the soldiers.[1] Man's relationship with the horse also changed fundamentally during this period. Breeding, long recognized as a means of improving the quality of horses, became a science: more exact, documented, and specialized. Riding too, became a scientific pursuit of techniques and methods designed to achieve the optimum relationship between horse and rider. Cavalry, which kept pace with the advancing technology and evolving military organizations, remained a decisive force on the battlefield.

The sixteenth century marked a distinct break from warfare of the Middle Ages. Armies during this period increasingly relied on mercenary professionals for both their numbers and for professional technical expertise.[2] Armies included deadly disciplined infantry formations of pike phalanxes pushing against one another and capable of destroying heavy cavalry formations. The Thirty Years War (1618–48) brought back the concept of decisive battle, though sieges continued to be critically important. Infantry formations included muskets along with pikes, artillery was a major factor on the battlefield, and cavalry experimented with the mounted employment of carbines and pistols. In the seventeenth century national and state battalions and regiments, still serving for pay, but united by bonds of language, culture, and loyalty slowly replaced mercenary formations. During the English Civil War (1642–46) cavalry was an important, if not the most important, battle arm, but it struggled to find the balance between shock action and firepower. In the wars of the late seventeenth and the eighteenth centuries–the French Wars (1667–1714), The Great Northern War (1700–1721) and the Seven Years' War (1755–63)–true cavalry units, companies, squadrons, and regiments manned by paid national professionals took the field. Cavalry tactics became bolder and more decisive despite great leaps in infantry and artillery weaponry. The dominating theme of the early modern period was adaptation of the war horse, cavalry tactics, and horsemanship to the quickly changing military technology.

Infantry and Artillery Developments

Central to the changes of the early modern period was the development of gunpowder weapons which slowly but decisively changed the nature of warfare. By the middle of the sixteenth century, cannon had achieved a very traditional looking form which did not change significantly for the next 300 years. The gunners of the American Civil War armies would have been familiar with their capabilities and operation. Though still most effective as a siege weapon, field cannon in the sixteenth century were common, made from bronze, and fired a ball of 12 to 15 pounds.[3] Their major limitation was mobility. They could not quickly reposition once in place on the battlefield. Commanders planned and executed cavalry maneuvers around the positioning of the enemy's field cannon.

The invention and evolution of firearms also greatly changed the nature of the battlefield. The first hand-held firearms were inaccurate, awkward to handle, and slow to fire. The harquebus of the early sixteenth century took several minutes to reload and was accurate only up to 100 yards. As the musket replaced the harquebus, infantry fire became more lethal. In the mid-sixteenth century the heavy matchlock musket became the primary infantry firearm. In 1591, Humprey Barwick stated that a lead musket ball could penetrate the best armor at 200 yards, regular armor at 400 yards, and kill an armored man at 600 yards. The early seventeenth-century matchlock musket took two minutes to reload. Volley fire by ranks could mitigate the problem of rate of fire; the problem of accuracy was more difficult to solve. Aimed fire was still only somewhat accurate between 100 and 200 yards.[4] The only way to compensate for lack of accuracy was to increase the number of weapons firing. A long linear formation was ideal to maximize firepower of the musket but was vulnerable to a cavalry attack. A box formation, with integrated guns and pikes, could hold off cavalry but was slow to maneuver and had difficulty achieving maximum effects with the firearms. Eventually, infantry battle lines became a checkerboard of square pike formations and rectangular musket formations. The problem of infantry command became one of managing formations in the heat of combat to achieve maximum effects without creating vulnerabilities. Infantry firepower continued to increase as infantry converted from the matchlock musket to the flintlock musket around the end of the seventeenth century. The flintlock was a more reliable firing system and increased the rate of fire of well-drilled infantry to about three rounds per minute.

The introduction of the bayonet simplified the tactical problem of managing formations. The conversion from pikes to bayonets began in the 1680s and was largely complete by 1705.[5] Bayonets were effective protection against slow-moving cavalry attacks. The adoption of the bayonet drastically increased the number of firearms on the battlefield and improved the versatility of the infantry formation. It also made the command of infantry easier as it removed the requirement to carefully coordinate pike and musket positions.

Sixteenth-Century Renaissance Cavalry

The aristocracy of Europe were the leaders of military reform and innovation. Reform progressed rapidly with little opposition because it did not challenge the social structure of society. The military reforms of the sixteenth century included the transition of the aristocracy from feudal mounted warriors to the new positions of authority as the officers commanding the infantry, artillery, and the still important cavalry formations. This change occurred gradually over the course of the sixteenth century, but the major powers of Europe effectively implemented the change by the end of the century. The chivalric ideal of the horse-mounted cavalryman and individual glory had a strong allure within the military culture, but the quest for victory was even stronger.

Use of the heavy lance had not changed since Medieval times. The sword was the secondary weapon and came into play after the cavalryman discarded the lance in battle. The pistol-armed *reiter* cavalry at first challenged and then ultimately replaced the traditional lance-armed cavalry. By the end of the sixteenth century, the lance had all but disappeared from the battlefield though manuals such as John Cruso's *Militarie Instructions for the Cavallrie*, published in 1632, still considered the lancer to be an important cavalry type.

Full plate armor was the norm for sixteenth-century cavalry and was very effective protection against lance, sword, or bow. It was also effective against the relatively light harquebus bullet. To deal with bullets, armor plates were reinforced and made thicker at the most vulnerable points, particularly the chest. It became common to "proof" the ability of the armor to protect against bullets by testing each piece with a shot into the chest plate. The resulting dimple in the chest armor remained on the finished armor as the armorer's mark attesting to the quality of his work. Even this armor, as effective as it was, did not overly encumber the mounted warrior. Fully armored cavalrymen could mount their horses without aid, and could twist and turn in the saddle with no problem. Heavier specialized tournament armor was much more cumbersome.[6]

True cavalry emerged over the course of the sixteenth century, as the heavily armored mounted men-at-arms–originally dominated by the nobility–became part of a military branch of service. This change took place at the same time that the concept of battlefield formations evolved into the idea of permanent military units. The mounted arm evolved from groups of mostly noble men-at-arms who were individual warriors to systematically organized tactical units made up of soldiers and horses.[7] The difference between the two was the shift from the individual to the organization.

Light Cavalry

Many of the more mundane tasks of campaigning–scouting, securing key points, running messages, and protecting the army from surprise–were suited to cavalry but not suited to the armored heavy cavalry. The sixteenth century saw the increasing use of light cavalry to do these important tasks. The term *light* referred specifically to the fact that riders wore little armor and the horses of the light cavalry were smaller. The light cavalry excelled at tactical tasks that required speed, great mobility, and only a limited amount of combat capability. Light cavalry also were adept at quick attacks against vulnerable supply trains, marching infantry, and artillery formations.[8] Many of the best light cavalry came from eastern Europe. By the end of the seventeenth century most armies applied the Hungarian name *hussars* to the light cavalry even if they had no connection to Hungary. The term *hussar* derives from the Hungarian word *huzz*, which means 20, reflecting the fifteenth-century practice of recruiting every twentieth man for the mounted militia.[9]

The Reiters

A new type of heavy cavalryman appeared in Germany in the 1540s: the *reiters*, also called cuirassiers. The German historian Hans Delbruck considers the reiters the fathers of the modern cavalry just as the Swiss pikemen were the fathers of modern infantry. Reiters wore the traditional plate armor of the heavy cavalryman and their task was to defeat opposing bodies of infantry and heavy cavalry. However, their primary weapon was not the heavy lance but rather a wheellock pistol, which was small enough to handle in one hand and fire from horseback. The *reiters* also carried a sword and a dagger, and sometimes a harquebus or musket. Each pistol was good for one shot. Pistols had a limited range of about 10 or 15 feet. The reiters trained to aim at the hip of the rider or at the shoulder or head of the horse. Though the pistol was somewhat unreliable, it was much easier to use with minimum training than the lance. Further, the horse could be smaller and required less training. A mounted pistoleer and his mount could be trained in three months.[10] The reiters served for pay and fought for whatever side could afford them. The mercenary aspect of their organization, and the use of the pistol, broke all connection between early modern cavalry operations and Medieval chivalry. Individual combat and glory were not part of the reiter ethos.[11]

Sixteenth-Century Cavalry Tactics

The tactical employment of the reiters utilized a maneuver called the *caracole*. In this maneuver, the reiters formed in a fairly narrow but very deep formation just out of effective range of the targeted enemy. They then advanced at a trot in a column composed of a series of lines to within point-blank range of the enemy. The first line then wheeled to the left, fired their pistols, and rode to the rear of the column as the next rank took their place and fired. A perfectly executed operation allowed time for the reiter to reload before moving forward to repeat the process. This tactic was particularly effective against pure pike infantry formations. The French captain Blaise de Montluc described the effect of the reiter caracole as "seeing nothing but fire and steel." Though the pistol-armed reiter was not a chivalric figure, practicality won out, and by the end of the sixteenth century he replaced most lance-armed heavy cavalry. The caracole was less effective against infantry formations that contained musketeers. Musket fire could devastate the relatively slow caracole formation before it could get within pistol range. Still, the caracole remained an important tactic well into the Thirty Years War (1618–1648).[12]

Organizing cavalry was the subject of much debate and experimentation during the sixteenth century. One issue was whether it was best to have several relatively small units, 30 to 100 horsemen, formed in one or two ranks over a wide area, or to have a square or rectangular formation that was as many as 17 horsemen deep and as many as 100 horsemen across. The smaller unit brought more men into contact with the enemy. However, without numbers behind pushing the forward ranks forward, the horsemen would tend to avoid direct confrontation with the enemy. Additionally, the wider formation was difficult to control and required a higher quality of horsemanship to maintain. A large part of a commander's concern in the sixteenth century was cavalrymen who avoided close combat. Tavannes pointed out that this was a major issue that argued for a deep formation. He encouraged commanders to consid-

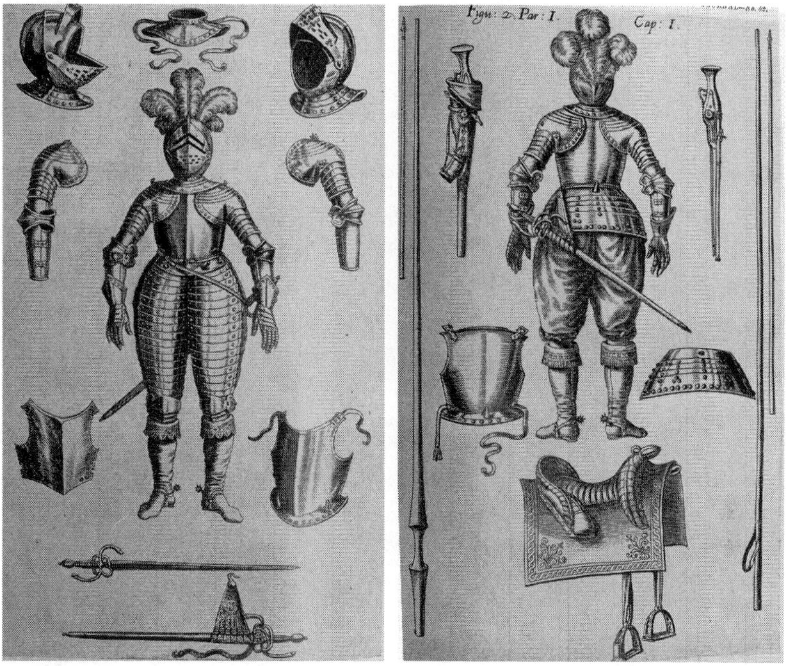

These diagrams from John Cruso's *Militarie Instructions for the Cavallrie*, published in 1632, depict the full armor and weapons of the reiter or cuirassier. It was not significantly different from that of the medieval knight. The wheellock pistol, upper right, became the important cavalry weapon in the late sixteenth and early seventeenth centuries. (*Cavalry Journal* [British])

er walking or trotting into the attack because it was more difficult for cowards to duck out of the formation when it was moving slow. He noted that a captain who covered 15 paces at the gallop might find himself arriving at his target completely alone.[13]

The attitude of the mercenary cavalry argued for the use of the deeper formation. The deep formation also facilitated the execution of the caracole maneuver. The caracole maneuver was a difficult operation that took extensive training to execute properly. The historical legacy of the caracole was not its tactical effectiveness, but rather the drill training required to execute the maneuver effectively in combat. The number of hours spent practicing the caracole served to instill in the European horse, for the first time, the concepts of discipline, responsiveness to command, and unit cohesion that was absent from Medieval cavalry. It also highlighted the importance of individual horsemanship. Thus, the caracole, though it may have had only marginal value on the battlefield, was a superb training tool and was central to the transition of bodies of mounted warriors into cavalry units.[14] Over time, the deep squadron gave way to the wider shallower formation. This was possible because of better training and horsemanship within the formation.

Seventeenth-Century Cavalry

During the seventeenth century, the reforms of the previous century continued to be refined and developed as cavalry adjusted to further technological advances in infantry weapons and cannon. By the end of the seventeenth century, cavalry was facing an even more lethal battlefield made up of massed flintlock muskets and light mobile cannon. The major developments in cavalry were demonstrated in the Thirty Years War, the English Civil War, and the French Wars at the end of the century.

Seventeenth-Century Cavalry Tactics

Cavalry avoided attacking the pike and musket infantry formations directly. Basic cavalry tactics positioned cavalry on the wings to fight a "cavalry battle" against their mounted opponents. If this was successful they then threatened the enemy infantry rear and flanks, or waited patiently for a break in the discipline of the enemy infantry formation to allow a frontal attack. Cavalry tactics in general resembled somewhat the classic cavalry tactics of the Romans and Macedonians.

The accepted cavalry tactic at the beginning of the seventeenth century was the caracole; but during the Thirty Years War, cavalry leaders modified it to be more practical. The cavalry moved forward in two ranks at the trot to within pistol range of the enemy, halted, and the first rank fired a volley. The horseman returned the pistol to the holster and then fired a second pistol. At that point the front rank countermarched to reload while the second moved into position and fired its volleys. Cavalry completely abandoned the classic caracole well before the end of the Thirty Years War.[15]

During the Thirty Years War the cavalry did not normally engage in close combat. Gustavus Adolphus is given credit by some historians with bringing cavalry back to a position of importance on the battlefield by reintroducing the charge with cold steel. His orders to his cavalry were described by German political and military theorist Bogislaus Philip von Chemnitz writing in the early 1640s: "Only the first or at most the first two ranks, when near enough to see the whites of the enemy's eyes, were to give fire, then to reach for their swords; the last rank however was to attack without shooting but with swords drawn, and to keep both pistols (or in the front ranks, one) in reserve for the melee."[16] The attack with saber returned as the essential tactic of Gustav's cavalry, but it was a trend that had already become evident among German cavalry before the arrival of the Swedes.

The Swedish cavalry, though competent and aggressive, could not stand up to the charge of the German Imperial cuirassiers. The body armor of the cuirassiers gave them great protection in a sword-on-sword melee. Their armor allowed cuirassiers to close with sword-armed cavalry and use their pistols at point-blank range. On several occasions, Imperial cavalry rode completely through Swedish cavalry. Recognizing this weakness, Chemnitz relates that Gustav advised his cavalry that it was pointless to try fight the German cuirassiers on even terms. Instead they "need only give the horse a deep thrust with the sword, twist broadly with it and rip open the wound; in this way horse and man would be quickly bowled over, and beaten just the same."[17]

The French view remained as expressed to the king by D'Aurignac, a student of the great Marshall Turenne, in 1663: "It is the cavalry that ordinarily wins battles." Though the French had officially adopted the tactics of the German reiters, pistol attacks were unpopular with many commanders. Some French commanders felt forced to use the caracole by the decrease in riding skills among their cavalrymen and because of the inability of the lance to make an impression on disciplined infantry with pikes. French king Henry IV was an advocate of a return to close combat as the cavalry's preferred method of fighting. By the beginning of the seventeenth century the French cavalry were firing an initial volley of pistol fire and then closing in with the sword. A formation of about five or six ranks replaced the deep caracole formation. Later in the century, under the influence of Gustavus Adolphus's example, minor changes in tactics occurred, including reducing the formation depth to three ranks where it remained until the end of the century.[18]

Seventeenth-Century Cavalry Weapons and Armor

Over the course of the seventeenth century, cavalry organizations gradually became simpler as the understanding of cavalry capabilities increased. Near the start of the century, John Cruso identified five types of cavalry, most by the type of weapon that they employed: cuirassier, lancer, harquebusier, dragoon, and carabinier.[19] These were the types of cavalry found in most armies of the Thirty Years War. During that war, the types of cavalry continued to be refined. Imperial cavalry divided into four main types: cuirassiers, harquebusiers, dragoons, and Croats (light cavalry). By the end of the century, most armies had adopted three or four types of cavalry: cuirassiers, line cavalry, dragoons, and light cavalry (going by a variety of names including light dragoons, hussars, and Croats).

The harquebusier was named after his principle weapon, the harquebus. They usually wore only a breast and back plate and performed a variety of mounted duties. Additional weapons included a saber and pistols. His role in battle was to support the cuirassiers with fire and protect their flanks.[20] Typically, harquebusiers rode small horses. The intent was that they use their harquebus from horseback though they rarely did. Over time, they adopted similar weapons and armor as cuirassiers, and the two types were often indistinguishable. The harquebus was the first successful firearm. A slow-burning wick lowered into and igniting a pan of powder fired the weapon. Designed as an infantry weapon, it was adapted for use by mounted forces by shortening the barrel. The carbine was a similar weapon to the harquebus but designed specifically for use by mounted forces. The length of the weapons was the same. The difference between the carbine and the harquebus for mounted service was the bore. The carbine had a bore that was similar in size to a pistol bore. Thus, the bullet size for the carbine size was the same as the pistol: 24 to the pound.[21] Armies discarded the harquebus weapon with the fielding of the flintlock firing mechanism after the English Civil War.

For most of the seventeenth century firepower was a major concern of cavalry. Toward this end, building on the model of the reiters, pistols were regular equipment for all cavalry. At the beginning of the century the wheellock pistol was still the standard cavalry pistol. Around 1639 the flintlock pistol began to replace the wheellock. The advantages of the flintlock pistol were a slightly greater range, more reliable firing mechanism, and greater ease of loading. The barrel length of the flintlock pistol, at 14 inches, was shorter than the standard wheellock making it easier to handle.[22]

Through the century the sword and the pistol vied to be the primary arm of the cavalry. German cavalry relied on the pistol. The French cavalry began the century practicing the caracole, then after the Thirty Years War they emphasized the sword. By the end of the century, however, the French had returned to an emphasis on the pistol as their preferred close combat weapon. The French cavalry sword of the late seventeenth century was a straight blade made for thrusting rather than slashing. After the Dutch wars at the end of the century, they traded their straight swords for curved sabers that were better for slashing. Most cavalry of the seventeenth century used a straight sword with the exception of light cavalry, which typically adopted a curved blade saber.[23]

At the beginning of the seventeenth century, although the completely armored cuirassier was the ideal, the reality was that many wore only breast and back plates, and open-faced helmets. The partly armored cuirassiers were called "half-cuirassiers." They carried a sword and two pistols. By the end of the century the idea of the cuirassier and the half-cuirassier merged, and the cuirassier wore only the breast and back plate. This armor, called the cuirass, remained the defining equipment of the heavy cavalry until the twentieth century.

At the beginning of the seventeenth century, the preference was for cavalry to wear armor, and many, like the reiters, were equipped in full plate armor. Mounted harquebusiers wore only the breast and back plate armor, and dragoons did not wear armor at all. Through the seventeenth century the trend was for cavalrymen in the field to lighten their armor load despite regulations which required more armor. French cavalry began shedding their armor during the Thirty Years War. In 1638, Louis XIII had to order officers to wear their armor under threat of losing their noble rank. In 1675, Louis XIV had to issue a similar order demanding that all cavalry officers wear their cuirasses.[24] The cuirass during this period weighed about 30 pounds or more. In comparison, a full set of Medieval plate armor weighed as little as 45 pounds. The difference was the thickness necessary for the cuirass to be able to stop musket fire. By the middle of the century, most cavalrymen abandoned armor except for in the heavy cavalry who wore a minimum armor set consisting of an open face helmet and a cuirass.

British Royal cavalry after the restoration of the monarchy under Charles II. These troopers represent the typical mid-seventeenth Century cavalryman. The breast and back plate is the only remaining piece of armor. No helmets were worn. The cavalryman was equipped with a mixture of arms which includes pistols, carbine, and sword. ("A Royal Progress, 1660," by Harry Payne, *Cavalry Journal* [British])

One of the most interesting developments in cavalry armor was the introduction of the buff coat. These coats appeared sometime after 1610 and by the end of the Thirty Years War were in wide use on all sides. The buff coat developed from the padded doublet worn under full armor. They were made from thick cow or elk hide. They were somewhat effective against saber slashes and many considered them no less effective against firearms than armor.[25] In England and elsewhere the buff coat disappeared as cloth uniforms appeared in the last quarter of the seventeenth century.

The English Civil War also saw the development of a another unique piece of armor known as the bridle gauntlet. The bridle gauntlet covered the left hand and arm only, and was designed to protect against an enemy saber slash at the arm or bridle itself, because a successful blow could destroy the rider's ability to control his horse.

National Cavalry

At the beginning of the seventeenth century Sweden fielded one of the first truly national cavalry forces. Swedish farmers received an exemption from taxes for providing a fully equipped cavalry trooper with horse to Gustavus Adolphus's army.

Swedish cavalry fought for king and country, and their nationalistic bond made them more cohesive than mercenary units. Each Swedish cavalry regiment consisted of two 175-man squadrons. At their largest in 1631, they organized in five regional regiments of eight companies of 125 horses each. This gave Sweden a cavalry force of 5,000 men.[26]

Gustavus Adolphus ignored the specialized types of cavalry. He took the pistols and saber of the cuirassiers, and the light armor of the harquebusiers, and combined them into a new general purpose cavalry. This new cavalry was not light cavalry but rather a standardized form of the half-cuirassier. They were able to charge in the main battle as well as perform scouting and other campaign duties. They could do neither mission as well as specialized heavy and light cavalry but were more cost effective in the long term due to their versatility.[27] In many ways this change harkened back to the general purpose cavalry of the Romans as well as the general utility of Medieval Middle Eastern and Mongol cavalry. Over the period of the seventeenth century, other nations copied this form of general purpose cavalry, and it was sometimes referred to simply as "horse."

The other important national cavalry of the seventeenth century were the French. By the late seventeenth century most French cavalry also became a general purpose type, called *cavalerie legere*. They were almost identical to the cuirassier heavy cavalry except that they did not wear armor. They were the regular battle cavalry of the French army and the most numerous of the cavalry types. Their primary weapons were the pistol and the sword. In the last part of the century the French also added a company of *caribiniers* to each cavalry regiment. Their purpose was to move forward of the cavalry companies and use their carbines to prevent harassment of the main companies by infantry or light cavalry as they maneuvered. The French included dragoons as part of their mounted force throughout the century. The term *dragoon*, originated with the French who initially armed mounted infantry with a type of blunderbuss firearm called a *dragon*. The French establishment did not include permanent light cavalry units until 1692.[28]

The basic organization of the French cavalry was the company which could vary widely in size. In 1610 French companies numbered 100 troopers. Over the century they fluctuated in size, usually numbering between 45 and 70, but by the end of the century they hit their lowest authorized strength of 20 men. In the early seventeenth century all companies were separate organizations. In 1635, Louis XIII ordered the formation of the first 12 regiments of cavalry, one of carabiniers, and six regiments of dragoons. Initially, each regiment was composed of two squadrons, and each squadron of two companies. Like the number of troopers in a company, the number of regiments fluctuated greatly. At one point there were 170 regiments on active service while at other times virtually none. In 1671 they formed a relatively permanent structure of 99 regiments. Regiments consisted of either 8 or 12 companies organized into two or three squadrons. The squadron became the main tactical unit replacing the company.[29]

Eighteenth-Century Cavalry

During the eighteenth century cavalry continued to be an important and even battle winning component of the European armies. Although the proportion of cavalry compared to the size of the army decreased in some armies, others maintained very large cavalry forces throughout the century. In 1720 the Russian regular army's 36,000 cavalry were 38 percent of the force. Twenty years later in 1740, Frederick the Great inherited a Prussian army in which 17,000 cavalrymen made up 43 percent of the force. Where numbers of cavalry decreased it was because cavalry cost three times more than infantry to maintain. An examination of numbers and individual battles indicates that though many historians and even generals of the period believed that "Firearms and not cold steel now decide battles," this was in fact an inaccurate overgeneralization.[30] Throughout the eighteenth century, cavalry remained an extremely critical component of the army and often was the battle-winning arm.

Eighteenth-Century Cavalry Weapons and Armor

The debate over cavalry armor and specifically the cuirass continued into the eighteenth century. Some nations had abandoned it early in the eighteenth century only to have it return to use a hundred years later. In some armies it was part of the regulation uniform but ignored by the army in the field. Some armies wore the entire front and back plate while others just wore the front plate. By the middle of the eighteenth century it was generally no longer in use except by the heavy cavalry cuirassiers and officers. By mid-century all other cavalry were wearing long cloth coats of varied colors according to function and nation, with distinguishing linings and facings.[31]

Some cavalry continued to wear other elements of armor, notably helmets, in the first years of the eighteenth century. However, helmets eventually went away except for ceremonial purposes in all but a few heavy cavalry regiments. The common military headgear was the tricorner hat which was an impractical piece of equipment for cavalry purposes but was the standard for both infantry and cavalry until the last decade of the century. The heavy cavalry wore a metal insert inside the hat to help protect against sword blows. Thigh-high boots, often rolled down to give double protection at the knee, were the standard footwear of the cavalry.

Arms remained essentially unchanged from the end of the seventeenth century although, as in the previous period, there were variations based on regiment, specific year, nationality, and type of cavalry organization. The basic equipment was a straight sword, two flintlock pistols in pommel-mounted holsters, and sometimes a carbine slung over the shoulder. Dragoons all carried either a carbine or a shortened dragoon musket. Dragoons wore a carbine belt over the left shoulder with a clip that attached to a ring on the weapon allowing them to carry the weapon easily off their right hip while mounted. Another belt over the opposite shoulder supported a cartridge box for the carbine.

Types of Cavalry

Through the eighteenth century, varieties of cavalry, though functioning under numerous national titles, divided into four functional groups: heavy cavalry, horse, dragoons, and light cavalry. Various countries may have eliminated or combined one or more of these functional groups. For example, the British service combined heavy cavalry, horse, and dragoon functions into one standard cavalry type, though different traditional unit designations remained to confuse the issue. The Austrians and Prussians organized only heavy cavalry (cuirassiers), dragoons, and light cavalry (hussars). The French organization included all four groups. In addition, the mounted forces of most nations included the household cavalry of the various monarchs as a fifth group. These elite units were usually equipped as either heavy cavalry or horse, but riders were often physically larger, always better paid, and had higher quality equipment and mounts than the cavalry of the regular army.

The Regiment

A critical aspect of cavalry organizations which predates the eighteenth century but became fully developed during that period was the regiment. In the eighteenth century, the regiment became the basic standard military organization in all nations, replacing the smaller company, which had been the basic organization. A colonel commanded the regiment and was responsible for its training, equipping, and performance in combat. He was of noble birth, either was appointed to his position by the monarch or purchased it, and ran the regiment as a business within the guidance of the army regulations and his chain of command. The professional qualities of colonels varied widely from country to country. Some were absolute professional soldiers while others were absentee property owners, and the regiment's lieutenant colonel actually ran the day-to-day activities of the regiment. The colonel of the regiment could also be absent because he was promoted to general officer or higher rank, in which case he often did not give up his colonelcy.

All cavalry, regardless of nation or type, followed a similar organizational structure. The regiment was the largest permanent organization. Colonels assisted by a lieutenant colonel, and sometimes a major, commanded regiments. Regiments were made up of companies. The numbers and size of companies in the regiment varied widely. Typically, a regiment might have 6 to 12 companies. Captains, assisted by lieutenants, a quartermaster, and sergeants and corporals, commanded companies. Regiments on a war footing might number approximately a thousand men. Company size varied typically between 40 and 70 troopers. Each company had one or two trumpeters who were the primary means of conveying orders, particularly in battle. A nonpermanent organization that saw great service in combat was the squadron. The squadron was an ad hoc unit organized to meet the requirements of a particular battle or campaign. It could consist of two to four companies commanded by the senior company commander, or a major or lieutenant colonel of the regiment. The differences between squadrons and companies became blurred as individual nations diverged in using the term. In the British service the term squadron was used instead of company.[32]

Heavy Cavalry and Horse

The heavy cavalry differed from the regular army horse in their armor and in some cases the size of their mounts. The heavy cavalry were the preferred unit for the decisive charge in battle. They were usually better paid and were more senior in terms of the history of the regiment, therefore less likely to deactivate in peacetime. The cuirass was the distinguishing equipment of heavy cavalry. In the armies that had them, the regular horse regiments were the mainstay of the cavalry forces but were subject to frequent deactivation when peace prevailed. Because of this, many of the more junior regular cavalry regiments were not up to the training standard of the heavy cavalry or the most senior of the horse regiments. Both heavy and regular cavalry carried a straight sword and a brace of pistols. An indication of the increasing versatility of all cavalry over the course of the eighteenth century was that in the Austrian service, by the middle of the century, all horsemen, including cuirassiers, carried carbines.[33]

Dragoons

Dragoons, though technically mounted infantry, by the eighteenth century had evolved into general purpose cavalry suited to a variety of duties and capable of functioning across the spectrum of cavalry requirements from charging as heavy cavalry to scouting as light cavalry. The status of dragoons varied considerably from army to army. In the Russian service dragoons made up the bulk of the mounted force–25 of

30 regiments in 1711. The Russian dragoons as well as the French dragoons were the equal of, or superior to, the line cavalry in prestige. In British service the opposite was true. Dragoons, officers and troopers, received less pay than cavalry. Although total numbers were constantly changing, in French service the number of cavalry and the number of dragoons were approximately equal. In British service between 1707 and 1714 there were 11 cavalry against 18 dragoon regiments, although in British service there was little difference between the two types of units and their employment. In most armies, a dragoon regiment was slightly larger than a regiment of horse. A Russian dragoon regiment in 1712 numbered 1,328 men while at the same time a cavalry regiment counted 1,100 men.[34]

Light Cavalry

Light cavalry became an even more important part of the cavalry arm in the eighteenth century. They continued to specialize in independent operations away from the main body. Missions such as raids, reconnaissance, rear and advance guard, and foraging were most common. In the Russian service hussars of the regular army shared these special light cavalry missions with Cossack auxiliaries. In the British service light dragoon regiments performed the role of light cavalry.

By the time of the Seven Years' War, reform of the Prussian cavalry had produced quality hussars who could hold their own even with the Austrian-Hungarian regiments, who were the premier light cavalry in the first half of the eighteenth century. Prussian hussars also benefited by their greater integration into the main army, which permitted them to work effectively with horse artillery and other types of cavalry in the main battle. The Prussian light horse, though not the battle-winning arm that the cuirassiers were, were recognized as the place where future senior leaders learned independence, audacity, and good judgment.

Eighteenth-Century Cavalry Tactics and Training

Basic cavalry drill developed in the late seventeenth century remained unchanged throughout the eighteenth century. The four basic movements remained facing, doubling, countermarching, and wheeling. The emphasis on linear formations remained the standard. The test of the cavalry commander was his skill using the basic movements in the correct combination and the correct time and place, in order to put his unit in the most advantageous position to execute the attack.

At the end of the seventeenth century, the French cavalry were the best trained and commanded cavalry in Europe. However, this changed quickly in the eighteenth century. By the end of the century the French cavalry were possibly the worst in the Europe. The French reliance on pistol fire, and charging at the trot in three ranks

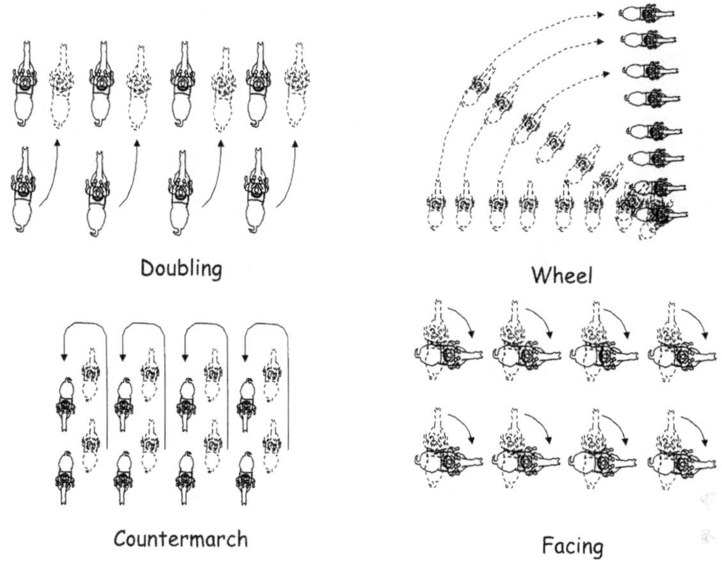

Common cavalry drill movements. (*Author*)

became increasingly ineffective as the century progressed. Their horsemanship also got worse: at any pace above the trot they lost all coherence in their formation and turned into a mob. They were notoriously ill disciplined, and this caused their poor performance at the battle of Dettingen in 1743. Tactical failure was not uncommon: French cavalry charges at Fontenoy (1745) were stopped before they could reach the British lines, and at Minden (1759) advancing British infantry drove back French cavalry.[35]

British cavalry were aggressive, but they too charged at the trot. Unlike the French, the British cavalry preferred the saber as their primary weapon. Marlborough issued his cavalry only three rounds of pistol ammunition to be used for personal protection on foraging expeditions. He developed the tactic of maintaining a large cavalry reserve, and at Blenheim he employed his reserve at a critical point to win the battle. This tactic was copied by other generals and became common.[36]

Until 1742, Prussian cavalry were among the least effective in Europe. They were viewed as a show force of large men on large horses–unable to move with any speed. Following the battle of Mollwitz in 1741, Frederick the Great and Friedrich von Seydlitz set about remodeling the Prussian horse in order to create an effective shock weapon. By 1745, they had created a proficient force trained to charge at the full gallop knee to knee. Speed became the priority of the Prussian cavalry and leaders reduced equipment and arms to the bare minimum in order to increase speed. By the end of the Seven Years' War, Prussian cavalry were capable of executing complex maneuvers across rough terrain at a full gallop. The ability of Prussian cavalry to close on an infantry formation at a full gallop negated much of the effectiveness of the bayonet. Much of the early success of the bayonet was based on cavalry closing at a trot. The slow-paced charge allowed sufficient time for the infantry to volley fire against the approaching cavalry, and melee with the mounted force. The speed and power of cavalry at the gallop against bayonet-equipped infantry physically and psychologically intimidated the best infantry and easily destroyed troops arrayed in a line formation.[37]

The Prussian cavalry were a major battle-winning arm of the Prussian army. The charge of the Bayreuth "Death's Head" Dragoons won the battle of Hohenfriedburg in 1745, the cavalry played a large role at Lobositz in 1756, and Seydlitz's two charges destroyed the combined French and German armies at Rossbach. The Prussian cavalry typically formed in battle with three types of cavalry grouped with cuirassiers forward and dragoons aligned behind the cuirassiers in support; hussars positioned themselves on the flanks of the other cavalry to guard against a surprise. The dragoons' mission was to be flexible; and depending on how the charge of the cuirassiers went, they would move forward to support the charge or they were prepared to move to the flanks to support the hussars. The Prussian cuirassiers initially charged in three ranks with the purpose of the third rank to fill gaps that developed in the first. Experience indicated that at a gallop the middle rank was hard to maintain, and so the Prussian switched to a two-rank attack formation. Frederick the Great changed the practice of charging in small squadron-size formations to charging in massed regiments. This tactic had been avoided because of the vulnerability of large blocks of cavalry to artillery and musketry, but Frederick relied on speed, timing, and supporting firepower to permit his cavalry to close with the enemy. Supporting firepower was provided by new light artillery, called appropriately horse artillery, which was pulled by six or eight horses and was integral to all cavalry formations including the hussars. Horse artillery was trained to unlimber and go into action quickly to provide close support for attacking cavalry. Horse artillery was rapidly copied by all the armies of Europe.[38]

Basic cavalry operations as expressed in the eighteenth-century Prussian army were simple. Cavalry's role in the battle was to first charge the opposing horse as described by Prussian General of Hussars Emanuel von Warnery: "[The] whole attack will be very much facilitated by the operation of the cavalry, engaging or defeating that of the enemy; should they succeed in obliging the enemy's cavalry to retire, and leave the flank of their infantry uncovered, or, as it is called, in the air; the affair is completed by the attack of the infantry, assisted by a few squadron of the reserve, falling upon that unprotected wing, as it happened towards the conclusion of the battle of Prague, which was decided in our favor."[39]

Warnery then provided a detailed description of the conduct of the charge itself:

> At the first sound of the trumpet the whole begin to move forward, first and second line, and the reserve: The attacking wing perfectly dressed in line, marches on at a walk; at the second sound, which ought to be doubled, the whole begin to trot, (which the second line, and the reserve, continue to do till after the charge is finished), at the third sound, which is tripled, at about 150 or 200 paces from the enemy, the first lines begins to gallop, and when they approach with 70 or at most 80 yards of the enemy, the trumpets found gay and lively fanfares or flourishes of the trumpet, then the troopers prick with both spurs, and push forward at full speed, without however entirely slackening the bridle, as all the horses cannot gallop with equal velocity; but when within about 20 paces, they must force their gallop as much as possible, to give the full impulse of the charge, or as the king of Prussia used to call it, the grand coup de collier; the rear ranks must then also press forward with all their weight and speed, as if they would force forward their front ranks or file leaders; this is called furnishing the shock.
>
> The troopers of the front raise their swords to the height of their faces, the arm extended in tierce, the point against the eyes of the his enemy, and the hand a little turned, that the branch of guard of the sword may cover his own; they must raise themselves a little in the stirrups, the body forward, and aim to place a thrust with the point against the man or the horse opposed to him; in a word, he must do his best, either by thrusting or cutting, to disable the enemy; thus the shock or charge is soon finished.
>
> The charge being successful, and the enemy's line broken, the word halt must be given, and the appel, or call, sounded.[40]

Warnery's description, based on his extensive experience, represents the ideal envisioned by Frederick when he reformed the Prussian cavalry in the early 1740s. Warnery also emphasizes the control, particularly at the end of the charge, necessary to achieve mass at the point of attack and retain the cavalry for subsequent action immediately after the successful execution of the charge. In concept, this use of cavalry remained consistent with the employment of cavalry by Alexander the Great.

Horses and Horsemanship

During the early modern period systematic breeding programs for military horses emerged in Europe. In the sixteenth and seventeenth centuries the most important of these programs were the royal horse breeds which capitalized on the reputation of the Spanish horses established in the Middle Ages. These breeds included the Friesian, Lusitano, and Lipizzaner. The most important of the "royal" breeds emerging in the sixteenth century was the Spanish Andalusian.

Spanish horses had been esteemed for their quality since Roman times. The introduction of Barb and Arabian influences after the Islamic invasion only improved the quality of the indigenous Spanish horse. In the Middle Ages, central Europeans used Spanish stallions as a means of improving the quality of their horses. The Andalusian breed emerged in the fifteenth and the sixteenth centuries as the best representation of the Spanish horse. The purity of the Andalusian breed owes a great debt to the Carthusian monks of Spain who established studs and carefully managed the breeding program despite political instability and war.[41]

In the sixteenth and seventeenth century Andalusians were used to start other royal breeds. The Friesians of north Holland were a product of Andalusians bred with indigenous north European forest ponies. The Lipizzaner, the classic high school equitation horse of Austria, are descendants of Andalusians imported by the Austrian court in the late sixteenth century, inspiring the name of Vienna's famous Spanish Riding School. The Lusitano breed of Portugal is very similar to the Andalusian, the primary difference being slightly less Arab and Barb influence. In conformation and size the two breeds are very similar. Careful examination of the illustrations of sixteenth- and seventeenth-century equitation manuals clearly show horses that resemble the modern royal breeds were the preferred horse for military use. The seventeenth century marked the shift from the Medieval preference for stallions to the calmer, more easily controlled geldings, though some stallions were still found in the formations.[42] It is likely that the increased requirement for ordered formations contributed to this change. By the eighteenth century, geldings had become the universally preferred military mount.

A very good representative of the best of the seventeenth-century cavalry mounts was Streiff, the mount of King Gustavus Adolphus of Sweden. One of his German cavalry colonels, Johann Streiff von Lauenstein, presented Streiff to the king in 1631. The colonel purchased the horse for 1,000 Imperial thalers. At the time the average cost of a good war horse was 100 thalers–Streiff was therefore a very expensive mount. Streiff was Adolphus's mount when he was killed at the battle of Lützen in 1632. The horse returned on his own to the Swedish lines severely wounded. The army recovered the king's tack and pistols from the horse who died of his wounds while being transported back to Sweden. Streiff's body was mounted and placed on display at the Swedish army museum. From his preserved remains, it is possible to get a very accurate picture of the seventeenth-century cavalry mount.

Streiff was a heavily muscled bay (deep brown colored with black mane, tail, and lower legs) standing about 15.2 hands. He was a stallion with a small, refined head, thick neck, and well-developed chest and hindquarters. The horse had many of the characteristics of Spanish type royal horse.[43]

The growing scale and the almost continuous nature of warfare in the sixteenth and seventeenth centuries were conditions under which breeding horses specifically for military use became very profitable. Though the horse did not wear armor, the equipment of the rider still remained substantial. Pistols, cartridges, carbine, and the 30 or more pound cuirass of the heavy cavalry replaced the armor of the knight. In addition, unlike Medieval knights, the emerging cavalry regiments did not allow for additional horses or pack animals to help carry the trooper's equipment. Thus, overcoats, blankets, food, and cookware added to the combat load of the war horse. This reinforced the requirement for large horses. The Spanish horses, traditionally the best military mounts in Europe, were not up to the size required of the heavy cavalry. However, larger horses were not a simple answer to the need because tactical requirements mandated that military mounts have the athleticism of the Spanish horses including the ability to train in the high school manner. Horsemen in Germany began to breed a horse specifically for these requirements. Three areas of Germany produced large but athletic horses ideal for military purposes: Schleswig-Holstein, Hanover, and Westphalia.

The most important of the three regions in the early modern period was the German province of Schleswig-Holstein. This area had been breeding what in modern times are known as warm-blooded horses, since the thirteenth century when the count of Holstein and Storman, Gerhard I, granted grazing rights to land around the cloister to the monastery at Uetersen. A warm-blooded horse is a horse breed that combines the sprit, endurance, and athleticism of a hot-blooded breed (an Arab or Andalusian, for example), with the size and calm disposition of a coldblood (a draft horse type such as the Percheron). The resulting horse is large, athletic, with great endurance, but relatively calm and trainable. The warmblood makes an ideal military mount. The Uetersen monastery produced just such a horse that became known as the Holsteiner, the oldest of Germany's many warmblood breeds. The International Museum of the Horse's modern description of the breed is indicative of why the Holsteiner became one of the premier cavalry mounts of the eighteenth century: "Traditionally, the Holsteiner has been bay with a preference for no or few white markings. It is a well balanced horse, maturing between 16 and 17 hands with round, generous strides and a natural, elastic movement. A lovely head with large, kind eyes is carried on a nicely arched neck, rising upward out of its withers, producing elegance, lightness and self-carriage. Their temperament is relaxed and willing, with good character and an eagerness for work."[44]

An indication of the popularity of the Holsteiner and the extent of the breeding program were the 10,000 horses exported from the region in 1797. Prussian army expert, historian Christopher Duffy, described the Holsteiner in Prussian service: "The mount par excellence of the cuirassiers and dragoons was the powerful native horse of north Germany, and in particular the long-winded Holstein animal–a rather lighter creature than the breed of the same name in the nineteenth century. It was the endurance of the Holstein horse which enabled the twenty-six Prussian squadrons at Soor in 1745 to charge across a ravine, then up the steep slopes of the Austrian position on the Graner Koppe and so on to the valleys beyond."[45]

The Holsteiner was also highly sought after by other armies including the Austrians. Austrian cuirassiers required large horses: regulations stipulated a horse at least 15.2 hands tall. Light cavalry horses had to be at least 14.2 hands. Regulations required the horse to be dark colored: blacks and bays were preferred. Fox colored and gray horses were not accepted. The Austrians relied on private breeders to meet these requirements.

Austria did not have an indigenous war horse breeding program, and peasants were incapable of breeding horses suitable to cavalry work. Therefore, it relied heavily on imports to meet its cavalry needs. The army hired contractors to find and purchase horses. Imported horses from the German areas of Hanover, Westphalia, and Holstein provided most Austrian heavy cavalry mounts, while Hungary, Poland, and the Ukraine provided the dragoon and hussar horses. Contractors delivered horses to specified central points, where senior cavalry officers inspected them. Contractors usually delivered the remounts in February or March, out of shape, underfed, and only green broke (broke to basic riding but no specialized skills). Once accepted the horses were shipped to the regiments for assignment to riders and training. During wartime there was only time for minimal training of the annual levy of new mounts before the spring/summer military campaign season began.[46] Thus as battles took their toll on experienced horses, cavalry performance on the battlefield declined proportionate to the number of replacement horses in the ranks.

An early exception to the high standard of horses in European armies was the army of Gustavus Adolphus. When the Swedish army arrived in Europe in the early seventeenth century, their European contemporaries considered them grossly undermounted. The Swedes were mounted on ponies indigenous to Scandinavia that stood on average 14 hands tall for officers, and 11 to 13 hands high for the average trooper. A prominent Catholic commander in the Thirty Years War, Johann Tserclaes, Count of Tilly, pointed out to his men that the Swedes were "so badly mounted that your baggage boys have better horses than them." After the battle of Breitenfeld the Swedes gradually transitioned to larger continental mounts. To per-

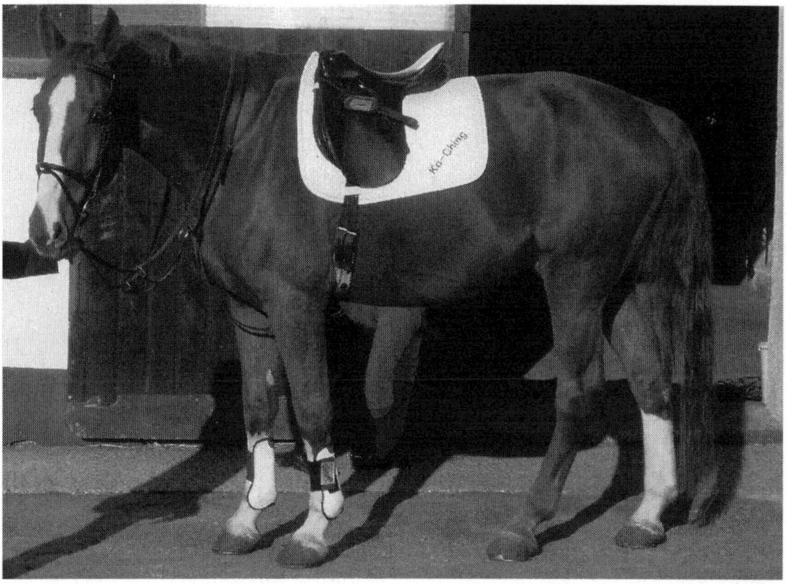

Prussian and Austrian cavalry were reliable consumers of horses and galvanized the German horse breeding programs in the early eighteenth century. Pictured here is the German Westphalian warmblood, Ka-Ching, 16.2 hands tall and representative of the powerful but athletic horses bred specifically for the Austrian and Prussian heavy cavalry. (*Author*)

manently improve the quality of the Swedish cavalry mounts the Royal Stud at Flyinge began to cross native horses with Spanish, Friesian, Arab, and Barb horses. The result was a superb warmblood horse, known today as the Swedish Warmblood.[47] These excellent horses were the mounts of King Charles XII's expert Swedish cavalry that was critical to the early Swedish successes against Poland and Russian in the Great Northern War, 1700 to 1721.

In England, civil war threw breeding programs into chaos. After the civil war and the restoration of the monarchy, King Charles II, facilitated by a stable domestic political situation, focused on rebuilding the quality of domestic horses. By the end of the seventeenth century, King William III, an acknowledged horse master, had imported heavy coldblood stallions from Holland and Flanders to increase the size of the English army horses. William was a keen student of breeding, and his goal was to mate the stallions with the lighter English and Irish horses of the army. The result was that the British heavy cavalry rode large dark, often black horses, and were some of the best-mounted troops in Europe during Marlborough's campaigns.[48]

Horsemanship

Prior to the early modern period most knowledge of horsemanship was a function of local tradition and experience. Some pictorial evidence exists that suggests that Medieval horse training in some cases was very sophisticated.[49] Unfortunately, the knowledge developed during the Middle Ages was not captured in writing and is therefore difficult to document. The increased interest in a scientific approach to training, combined with the ability to publish manuals, facilitated the acceptance of standardized training procedures beginning in the sixteenth century.

In the sixteenth century, there were literally dozens of books written on equitation. Most came out of Italy, the center of progressive renaissance thought. The first and most famous of these was the 1550 work of Federic Grisone of Naples, *Gli Ordini di Cavalcaree*.[50] Grisone focused on high school equitation. The purpose of classic high school equitation was to showcase the horse and rider and was specifically a means for the aristocratic class to simultaneously demonstrate their mastery of the horse and to add to the pomp and circumstance of a noble presentation. It was art and not practical riding. The main thrust of classical riding was to get the horse to "collect" himself. This required that the horse bring his rear legs close underneath his body where they became the primary source of power. This is not the natural way of the horse. Horses in the wild tend to put their weight and derive their power from their front legs. This is called being "on the forehand." Thus, one of the basic goals of classical equitation was to retrain the horse from its natural way of moving.

The earliest trainers and writers justified many of the most advanced movements of classical equitation on their practical military application. This claim remains (as it is often repeated in modern times) false. Unfortunately, though appearing to have the potential to be quite effective when demonstrated in the riding hall, the high school movements were completely impractical on the battlefield. Russian World War I cavalryman and internationally recognized trainer Vladimir Littauer observed, "I, myself, as an ex-cavalryman who participated in cavalry charges during the First World War and heard many on-the-spot accounts of others, can assure you that the success of any attack does not depend on refinements of equitation." Even the English sixteenth-century horseman who translated Grisone's work in 1560, Thomas Blundeville, commented that in the midst of battle who would want a horse that "falls a-hopping and dancing up and down in one place?"[51] The lack of practical application of advanced high school equitation did not prevent it from becoming the standard for equine training among cavalrymen across Europe because it provided a systematic and scientific methodology of producing fundamentally competent horse and rider combinations.

Classical equitation became the military standard for Continental Europe in the seventeenth century, but, ironically, as practitioners perfected the techniques of high school equitation in the eighteenth century, military riding began to deemphasize its usefulness. The successful employment of cavalry by two great battlefield commanders, the English duke of Marlborough and the Prussian king Frederick the Great, caused a reevaluation of cavalry training techniques. The cavalry forces of both commanders specifically rejected the most advanced high school traditions perfected over the previous 200 years. The riding tradition of the hunt field was the strongest influence on the English cavalry, while the Prussian king deliberately broke with the European classical riding tradition in order to establish the capability for boldness and speed within his cavalry force.

The English nobility never adopted high school equitation either as a training methodology or as a social characteristic of the English aristocracy. Young English gentlemen, rather than schooling in the riding hall, met the expectations of society in the hunt field. Riding to hounds was a favorite pastime of the English nobility: hunting stressed the ability of the horse and rider to ride cross-country. The privatization of land after the English Civil War resulted in an abundance of walls, hedges, ditches, and fences dividing the country. The task of the hunter was to ride cross-country at speed and deal with obstacles. This introduced jumping as a riding requirement. The English introduced a new riding position adapted to their sport. This early hunt seat placed the riders back far to the rear against the cantle and his feet forward of the pommel in a shorter stirrup than was prescribed for classical riding. Long hours in the saddle argued for the comfort of this seat, and its security during the negotiation of obstacles was also important. It was, however, not a comfortable seat for the horse.

The hunt seat was primarily used for the canter or gallop, but during a day's hunt the trot was the most common gait. A new technique developed to make this potentially bone-jarring gait manageable–the act of "posting" or rising in the trot. The term posting likely originates with English post chaise (carriage) riders in the mid-eighteenth century, who favored the new technique. The rising trot required the rider to lean slightly forward and rise slightly out of the saddle with the weight and balance going into the stirrups as the horse trotted. The trot has two beats per stride and a moment of midair suspension. The rider timed his rise from the saddle in rhythm with the horse such that the rider rose as the horses back moved up and the rider came down lightly into the saddle as the horse's back moved down. The rising trot allowed the horse and rider to move at a rapid trotting pace for long periods without undue fatigue because the technique was very comfortable for both.[52] The hunting riding style passed to the English cavalry through the aristocratic officer corps and reflected in the cavalry tactics of Rupert, Cromwell, and Marlborough. Hunting strongly influenced the riding techniques of the British cavalry into the twentieth century.

Friedrich Wilhelm Baron von Seydlitz was the key to the successful reform of Prussian cavalry. Von Seydlitz was a school-trained classical rider who combined that discipline with bold cross-country riding at the gallop. The combination of aggressiveness and horsemanship made Prussian cavalry the dominant mounted force of the mid-eighteenth century. (*Cavalry Journal* [British])

In 1741 the new Prussian king, Frederick, disgusted by the performance of Prussian cavalry at the battle of Mollwitz, determined to transform his cavalry into a lean bold force that could charge aggressively under even the most difficult conditions. Frederick was blessed in his endeavor by having one of the eighteenth-century's premier cavalry leaders under his command: Friedrich Wilhelm Baron von Seydlitz. Seydlitz believed in the methodical training of fundamentals. First, he exercised his men on foot, then on a wooden horse, and then when they mounted a live animal he demanded "they must ride without stirrups until they have faultless posture." The Prussian cavalry had no written riding manual but informally required two years to train a competent trooper.[53] Seydlitz was personally a bold and gifted horseman. At an early age he trained to lift a hat from the ground with his saber, shoot a hat in the air with his pistol, and ride at a gallop between the revolving sails of a windmill. As a commander, he began every day by riding from his home and jumping a water trough and his closed front gate on his way to his headquarters. He demanded the same exercise of his staff and also encouraged hunting.

Seydlitz was also a master of high school classical riding. On one occasion, he gained wide acclaim by executing three difficult *capriole* movements while on parade in honor of the king. He required all of his officers to train in classical riding with the regimental riding master. Seydlitz's influence in the Prussian army was twofold. First, he greatly increased the basic horsemanship of the army through his emphasis on formal classical riding fundamentals. Second, he instilled in the cavalry the boldness and discipline that, combined with sound horsemanship, facilitated complex maneuvers cross-country and charging at the gallop. These two contributions identified the two major aspects of horsemanship that became the standard of all cavalry into the twentieth century: sound fundamentals combined with bold cross-country riding.

Cavalry training was complex. Training in individual horsemanship skills so that the rider and horse could cope with anticipated battlefield situations was the first priority. After completing basic horsemanship, troopers then trained to fire and load their pistols and carbine from the saddle. Regiments maintained a dedicated training cadre to supervise training of horsemanship and weapons. All training included both horse and rider. Once the training cadre certified the soldier, he could participate in unit training. The Prussians were unique because all of their cavalry types, light cavalry hussars to heavy cavalry cuirassiers, received the same basic individual and unit training and thus had the capability of performing a variety of functions on the battlefield.[54] The smoke and noise of firearms was a new part of the battlefield environment. Systematic training enabled war horses to perform in the new conditions of battle. Cruso's seventeenth-century manual described how to train the horse for the terrifying action of firing pistols and harquebuses from the horse's back:

> When he is at his oats (at a good distance from him) a little powder may be fired, and so near to him by degrees. So may a pistol be fired some distance off, and so nearer: in like manner a drumme or trumpet may be used. The groom may sometimes dresse him in armor, and he may be sued (now and then) to eat his oats from the drumme head. It will be very usefull sometime to cause a musketier to stand at a convenient distance, and both of you give fire upon the other, and thereupon to ride up close to him: also to ride him against a compleat armour, so set upon a stake, that he may overthrow it, and trample it under his feet: that so (and by such means) your horse (finding that he receiveth no hurt) may become bold to approach any object.[55]

All armies used similar techniques, and they remained a basic part of remount training into the last years of the cavalry in the twentieth century.

Horse Equipment

During the 300 years of the early modern period the standard bit for controlling the horse remained the curb bit; however, saddle design went through profound changes. At the beginning of the period the saddle did not vary much from that observed in the Medieval period. By the end of the period, the saddle and most other equipment had taken a shape and function that would remain essentially unchanged until the last of the great cavalry formations disbanded in the twentieth century.

In the sixteenth century the combat saddle had both a high pommel and cantle. The cantle wrapped around the hips of the rider locking him into place. The pommel was high and extended down the forward part of the saddle to provide protection to the groin area as well as the thighs. Both of these facets of the saddle could be armored. Some sixteenth-century saddles included a horn on the pommel similar to a modern western saddle horn but its purpose was as a handhold. The rider's thighs were wedged between pads in front and back locking his leg in place. The rearward pads were inclined to the front to push the rider's thigh forward thus providing support in the accepted forward leg position.[56] The saddle varied little from a Medieval war saddle.

The seventeenth century saw a move to greater practicality and the move away from an armored rider and the lance-influenced saddle design. In the first half of the century, designs lowered the pommel and the cantle, and the cantle no longer had the stringent high wrap-around style. The padded rolls were still in place and continued to push the rider's leg forward. It was during this period that one of the leading classic riding instructors, the duke of Newcastle, began to advocate a more balanced riding position. This, combined with the increased cross-country riding in England resulted in dramatic saddle design changes beginning in the second half of the seventeenth century.

By the last quarter of the seventeenth century French riding master Francois Robichon de la Guérinière instigated a redesign of the classic school saddle that was reflected in military saddle design. He flattened the pommel to allow the rider to ride closer to the horse's center of balance and removed the forward and the rear leg roll in the saddle, allowing the leg to hang naturally underneath the rider, closer to the horse. In addition, the stirrup leather attachment was moved to the center of the saddle. These changes permitted the rider to sit in the center of the saddle and allow his legs to be "perpendicular as when he stands upon the ground." With more leg in closer contact with the horse, control using the leg aid was easier. Having the leg closer to the horse also eliminated the need for the exceptionally long Medieval spurs.[57]

By the early eighteenth century, two thoroughly modern types of saddle designs developed. One was a very deep curved seat which sloped gracefully down from the rounded pommel and then up to the cantle. The other was a very flat seat in which the pommel and the cantle rose almost vertically from the seat. Both types had a wooden frame built on a pair of short padded wooden side bars which lifted the saddle off direct contact with the horse's spine. Saddles included a leather flap that laid between the leg and the girth, and some designs included a sweat flap between the girth and the horse's body. Buckles under the saddle flap attached the girth to the saddle. A folded wool blanket placed under the saddle prevented rubbing against the horse. Adjusting the folding of the blanket ensured the proper fit of the saddle to the horse's body. The need to attach pistol holsters, coats, water bottles, and a variety of other essential field gear required additional buckles and fasteners placed about the pommel and cantle. In the last quarter of the eighteenth century a leather-lined cloth or sheepskin covering called a shabraque covered the saddle. The shabraque protected the saddle from the elements and added additional comfort to the seat. Usually the shabraque displayed intricately designed regimental or royal markings. By the middle of the eighteenth century both types of saddle seats were in use in all the European armies, and all were very modern looking. In fact, the British army saddle used at the end of the eighteenth century was not significantly different in its essential design from the Universal Pattern (UP) saddle model 1912 issued to British troopers in the First World War. British army ceremonial mounted units continue to use this model saddle today.[58]

Early Modern Cavalry in Battle

The capabilities and employment of cavalry evolved greatly over the early modern period of warfare. A study of how two great captains of the period, Gustavus Adolphus and Frederick the Great, integrated cavalry into battle, reveals how commanders used the capabilities of the war horse and rider to influence battle.

Lützen, 1632

King Gustavus Adolphus landed in Germany with his Swedish Army in 1630 and won a string of victories culminating at Breitenfeld in 1631.[59] He built a reputation as an unbeatable tactician, and Protestant forces flocked to his banner. In the spring of 1632, he launched a new campaign determined to follow up his successes of the previous year. His goal was to knock the Hapsburg Empire's ally, Bavaria, out of the war. However, the campaign did not go well as the Imperial resistance under their accomplished commander, Albrecht Eusebius von Wallenstein, was much more significant than anticipated. The two armies met and fought an inconclusive battle at Alte Feste in September 1632 then broke contact and maneuvered for advantage. Neither side had good intelligence of either their opponent's size or intentions.

In early November, Wallenstein concentrated his forces in Saxony, well north of the Swedish army which was still operating in Bavaria. His goal was to eliminate Saxony from the Protestant coalition and to cut the Swedish direct line of communications to north Germany. In response Gustav march his army north, covering over 375 miles in 17 days. Throughout November, the two armies maneuvered and skirmished in Saxony. Finally Wallenstein came to the incorrect conclusion that Adolphus did not want to give battle and that the Swedes were preparing to go into winter quarters. The Imperial army then made preparations to do the same. Capitalizing on Wallenstein's inaccurate analysis, on November 15 Adolphus moved his army toward Lützen with the intent of catching the Imperial army scattered in its winter cantonments. The plan was to engage the scattered Imperial forces piecemeal and defeat them through sheer weight of numbers. As he marched to Lützen, a small Imperial group commanded by Rudolf Freiherr von Colloredo intercepted Adolphus's army at the Rippach River. The small Imperial force had no hope of stopping the Swedish army, but they fought an inspired delaying action while dispatching messengers to sound the alarm to the rest of the Imperial forces. Adolphus's intent was to push on and destroy the Imperial army the next day. The lost time at the crossing, however, allowed Wallenstein to take steps to assemble the Imperial army, completely changing the tactical situation.

All through the night and into the morning of November 16 the Imperial army alerted units and put them on the road to Lützen. At about 5:00 a.m. the Swedish army awoke and began the short march to Lützen. At about 8:30 a.m. Imperial forces spotted the Swedes, and by 9:00 a.m. the Swedish army knew they were confronting a tired but mostly assembled Imperial army on the outskirts of the town. The only major Imperial force not assembled at Lützen was Feldmarschal Gottfried Heinrich Graf zu Pappenheim's corps. This 6,000-man force was stilling moving to join Wallenstein when the battle began.

The armies that met at Lützen were not the heavy cavalry dominated armies of Medieval times, but rather balanced forces consisting of infantry, artillery, and cavalry forces. The Swedish army numbered 20,000 of which 6,000 were cavalry, 30 percent of the force. The Swedish cavalry, like the army, was a composite force that consisted of both Swedish and Germany forces. The best cavalry were the Swedish regiments. The Swedish cavalry were not heavily armored and relied on the sword as their attack weapon. The allied German cavalry were of different types. The most important were cuirassiers who wore plate armor and fought with their pistols. The Imperial army numbered 13,500 of which 5,000 were cavalry of different types, a total of 37 percent of the force. Pappenheim's force was another 6,000 men of which half were cavalry. The Imperial cavalry were of three types: cuirassiers, mounted harquebusiers, and Croatian light cavalry. The cuirassiers were the most important and capable. They occupied all the most forward positions. The harquebusiers could be of value except most of them were inexperienced. The Croatian light cavalry were capable scouts and raiders but not capable of contributing to the main battle.

In the fog of the early morning, the Swedish army could observe the Imperial army deployed in a battle line along the Lützen to Leipzig road. The right of the Imperial line anchored on a mud-brick wall that surrounded the town of Lützen. Musketeers deployed within the mud wall were able to fire through loopholes in the wall. Within 200 yards of the wall, next to three large windmills, the Imperials positioned the main Imperial artillery battery of 13 large-caliber guns. The center of the battle line consisted of five large formations of pikes and muskets. The left flank of the infantry anchored their position on a seven-gun artillery battery located near the

Swedish King Gustavus Adolphus leads a prayer before the battle of Lützen. The king is unarmored, wearing only a thick buff coat. Behind him most of his officers and cavalry wear the heavy cavalry armor described by Cruso. Adolphus could not wear heavy armor due to previous war wounds. (*Author*)

road ditch. The Imperial cavalry echeloned to the right and left rear of the main infantry formations in positions to protect the flanks. The second battle line, positioned about 200 yards to the rear, consisted of two infantry pike formations and several additional squadrons of cavalry. In front of the main Imperial positions, musketeers deployed as skirmishers in the ditches that ran on both sides of the Leipzig road. In addition, Croatian light cavalry deployed across the front of the army and on both flanks. The most vulnerable portion of the Imperial position was the open left flank where no natural obstacle existed to aid the defenders. The flank had a heavy cavalry presence but no infantry. To compensate for this weakness Wallenstein created a mock infantry position using baggage drivers and camp followers.

The Swedish army deployed slowly because of the fog and because of difficulty crossing the Flossgraben stream that lay between them and the Imperials. By midmorning, they formed about 700 yards south of the Imperial army in two battle lines though not all of their artillery was in position. The first battle line consisted of an infantry center with four pike and musket brigades. The right flank infantry brigade was the Swedish brigade and to its right were deployed six squadrons of Swedish cavalry with supporting companies of musketeers. On the left flank of the army were six squadrons of the German cavalry supported by musketeers. The second battle line was virtually identical to the first. Four infantry brigades made up the center while cavalry squadrons occupied both wings. The major difference between the first and second battle lines was that the second line cavalry were less numerous and were not supported by musketeers.

The battle began at around 10:00 a.m. with an artillery duel between the two sides. Infantry and cavalry formations stood their ground and endured the fire. During the artillery exchange Gustavus moved three squadrons of cavalry from his second rank far out to his right flank to guard against a flanking attack. Also during this period, Wallenstein had the town of Lützen put to the torch in order to deny its use to the enemy. Smoke from the burning buildings was blown directly across the battlefield replacing the morning fog, obscuring the entire area. At 11:00 a.m., Gustavus ordered the first battle forward to attack.

The Swedish battle line stepped off as a unit to attack: a single line one-and-a-half miles long. The reserve line followed but remained 500 to 600 yards back. As the army advanced smoke enveloped it, and the battle dissolved into three separate attacks: right wing, center, and left wing.

The right wing attack was made by six regiments of Gustavus's elite Swedish cavalry supported by five 200-man companies of musketeers. The Swedes advanced with regiments on line, each regiment ranked three horses deep. Gustavus advanced with the right wing cavalry and could identify the Croatian light cavalry to his front and behind them the Imperial cuirassiers. He gave orders accordingly: "As for those fellowes [the Croatian light cavalry] I care not for them, but charge me those blacke fellowes soundly: for they are the men that will undoe us."[60] As the Swedish cavalry line approached the Leipzig road they found that the ditches on either side, in addition to filled with enemy musketeers, were also impassable to the horses. Therefore, the squadrons turned east, away from the main battle area looking for a place to cross. The Croat light cavalry dispersed without engaging the Swedes. The accompanying Swedish musketeers took on the task of capturing the ditches and the Leipzig road.

The six squadrons of Swedish cavalry managed to find a place to cross the road. The smoke on the battlefield made observation difficult, and the right wing front line commander, Överste Torsten Stålhandske, led the three lead squadrons in an attack against the mock position of baggage drivers. The other three squadrons turned toward the Imperial cavalry and met in a confusion of charge, countercharge, and melee in the midst of the smoke. Rittmeister Octavio Piccolomini, commanding one of the Imperial cuirassier squadrons, claimed that the successful stand of the Imperial cavalry on the left was largely due to "the blessed Madonna and their cuirasses of proof."[61] It was during this action that Gustavus, traveling with one of the trail squadrons and not wearing any armor, was killed. The Imperial cuirassiers repulsed the Swedish cavalry attack.

As the Imperials beat back the three squadrons from the immediate left flank of the Imperial army, Stålhandske assembled the other three squadron for a much deeper attack on the flank. After scattering the fake baggage wagon position, he was in a

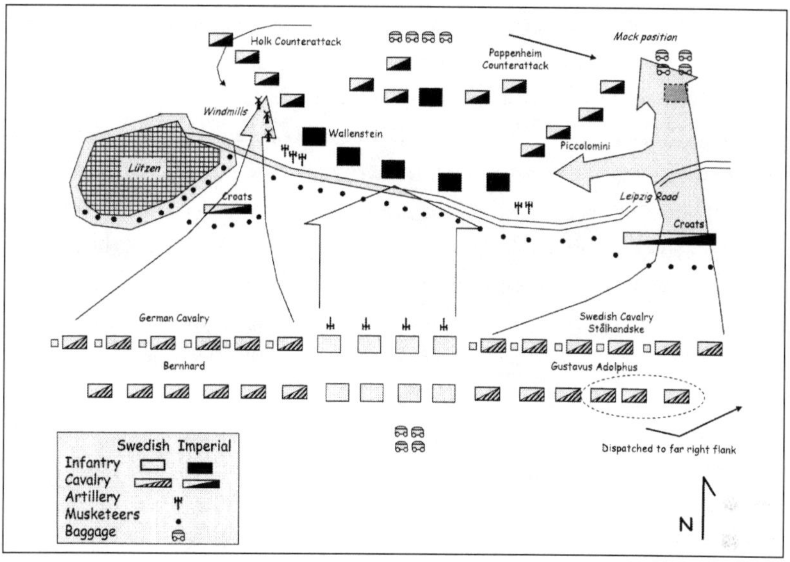

The battle of Lützen, November 16, 1632.

good position to circle behind and attack the Imperial rear. At this point, about noon, most of the cavalry component of Pappenheim's corps arrived–several squadrons, totaling 2,000 horses, led by Pappenheim himself. Immediately Pappenheim led a countercharge against Stålhandske's Swedes. He also dispatched his Croatian light cavalry on a wide-flanking movement to attempt to get around the Swedish flank. Both attacks failed. Swedish musketeers and regimental guns that had caught up with Stålhandske's cavalry defeated Pappenheim's main attack. The three Protestant squadrons of the second line sent to secure the far right flank just before the battle began thwarting the Croatians flanking effort. Though unsuccessful in pushing the Swedes back, the attacks fixed the Swedish attack and stabilized the situation on the Imperial left wing. Stålhandske later moved his force back across the Leipzig road when word came of Gustavus's death.

On the Swedish left flank, the allied German cavalry, commanded by Duke Bernhard of Sachsen-Weimar, advanced in good order to the Leipzig road. Neither the Croatian light cavalry or the musketeers in the road ditch gave them any problems. They then trotted forward into the four squadrons of the Imperial right wing cavalry. The Imperial cuirassiers had determined to meet the Protestant charge at the halt. As the two forces closed, the Germans put the steel of their swords against the aimed pistol fire of the Imperials. A fierce melee then resulted with the Protestant cavalry having to deal with the Imperial cavalry as well as musketeers firing at their rear and flank from the mud-brick city wall of Lützen. One Imperial squadron of mounted harquebusiers routed, but the Imperial cuirassiers stood firm. Eventually, the Protestant cavalry broke off the attack and moved back across the road to reform. Both sides suffered heavy casualties.

Bernhard reformed his squadrons and brought forth several squadrons of the left wing second line. He then renewed his attack. Bernhard's reinforced cavalry had the advantage of numbers and began to push back the Imperial cuirassiers and to overlap the right flank of the Imperial line. However, before the completion of the decisive flanking movement, Heinrich Holk, Wallenstein's second in command and most-trusted subordinate, arrived with Pappenheim's cavalry who he had rallied. He led a countercharge into the left flank of Bernhard's cavalry and began to push them back. This was a pistol charge executed at the trot. Holk's countercharge had the advantage of numbers, a flank position, and the energy of fresh horses and troopers. This attack pushed Bernhard's cavalry back across the Leipzig road for the second time.

By 3:00 p.m. the Imperials had successfully survived cavalry attacks on both flanks. In the center, the Imperial artillery and infantry had also held firm against the enemy musket and pike brigades. The Imperial artillery, in particular the windmill battery, had devastated the attacking infantry formations. The battle paused as the Swedish and allied German commanders reformed and prepared for a final assault.

When the new assault came, about 3:30 p.m., it consisted of the fresh brigades of the Swedish second line that had not been committed in the earlier attacks. The battle renewed in the manner of the previous fighting. The two cavalry forces fought on the wings to attempt to clear the enemy's horse from the field. Neither was successful. Piccolomini, emerging as the leader of the left wing Imperial cavalry, had six horses shot out from under him and was wounded five times. His cuirassier squadron made 10 separate charges and suffered 200 killed or wounded of the 500 who started the battle. On the Swedish side, Bernhard's German squadron had attacked 15 times and barely mounted 50 troopers of the 500 who started the battle. Though the Imperial line was never broken, the weight of the Protestant attack slowly pushed it back. Finally, as dark closed in on the battlefield, the protestant infantry captured the Imperial windmill battery that had been the mainstay of the defense. With that triumph, fighting gradually diminished and then ended. Both sides were emotionally and physically exhausted. In the dark, the Swedes withdrew back across the Leipzig road. In the darkness Pappenheim's infantry arrived as reinforcements, and the Imperial commanders argued for an attack at first light. Wallenstein vetoed the option and ordered his army to withdraw. The next morning the Swedish army was in possession of the battlefield.

Although generally thought of as a Protestant victory, Lützen was a curious battle in which bought sides could and did argue for the right of claiming victory. The reality was that at the tactical level the battle was a draw. Swedish losses were about 1,500 dead and another 3,500 wounded. Imperial casualties were about 3,000 total dead and wounded. A the operational level the Swedish army achieved its objective of pushing Wallenstein out of Saxony, and, having lost all its artillery, Wallenstein's army was no longer a viable combat force. Strategically, the battle's major consequence was the loss of Gustavus Adolphus, the Protestant's most brilliant commander and the focus of political unity for Protestant forces.

The battle demonstrated some important points about seventeenth-century cavalry warfare. First, in line with ancient cavalry operations, the battle showed that without cavalry success on the flanks, battle devolved into an infantry slugfest which was both costly, and often, as in this case, indecisive. The inability of the Swedish army to overcome the Imperials despite its numerical superiority, and arguably the tactical superiority of its infantry and artillery, was largely due to the performance of the Imperial cavalry. Including Pappenheim's cavalry, the Imperial cavalry actually outnumbered the Swedes 7,000 to 5,000. The late arrival of the Pappenheim as well as limited effectiveness of the light cavalry components prevented the Imperials from taking the offensive, but their numbers still allowed them to retain control of both flanks throughout the battle–even if just barely. Neither cavalry force appeared to be able to create an offensive capability that was decisive. Numbers are part of the reason. Another reason was the employment of cavalry in small squadrons with little mass. The average squadron size was about 300 men while the largest was 500. The largest concentration of cavalry strength was the charges by Bernhard and Pappenheim, but Bernhard's force only numbered about 1,500 men and Pappenheim's about a thousand. Neither had a significant numerical advantage over their opponent. Another reason for the lack of decisive results is that the cavalry maneuvered at the trot and relied extensively on pistols. This eliminated much of the shock value of a charge. Still, without a doubt the outcome of Lützen was directly attributable to the outcome of cavalry battle. It is easy to envision that success by the Swedish cavalry on either flank would have resulted in a catastrophe on the scale of the ancient battle of Cannae. The survival of the Imperial army is directly attributable to the successful defense of the flanks by the Imperial horse squadrons.

Rossbach, 1757

By 1756 Frederick the Great of Prussia had built a substantial military force based on the foundation that his father had given him. That force had been tested in two wars, the First Silesian War (1740–42), and the Second Silesian War (1744–45), and in both instances had bested the respected forces of Austria. In 1756, the Austrians built a coalition to assist them regaining their dominant position in central Europe.

Frederick was aware of the negotiations going on between Austria, France, a coalition of German principalities, Sweden, and Russia. Frederick's only allies were Great Britain and Hanover.[62] Frederick determined not to allow the alliance gathering against to him to gain the initiative and he opened the war in 1756 with a preemptive invasion of Saxony.

In the spring of 1757 Frederick was again on the march. As Frederick operated in Bohemia, allied armies marched against Prussia from every direction. Faced with multiple threats, Frederick had no choice but to break his army into pieces, each tasked with defending and delaying the enemy while the king looked for an opportunity to attack. The best opportunity for success was in Saxony where the armies of Soubise and Saxe-Hildburghausen were advancing. These two armies were operating together but were not under a single command. In addition, Saxe-Hildburghausen's army was a composite force made up of single regiments, some newly formed and barely trained, from a variety of different German principalities. This front offered the greatest chance for operational success, and in the early fall of 1757 Frederick moved the army under his command into northern Saxony.

The army of French general Prince de Soubise consisted of about 25,500 men of which 5,500 were cavalry, 22 percent of the force. The cavalry forces were mostly good quality cavalry of the line. Observers saw "well set up men on large, powerful horses. . . . [They] formed a regiment which lived up to the reputation of the French for having a fine-looking cavalry. We have to admit that the mounted arm of the French is in an incomparably better state than that of their infantry."[63] Their appearances aside, the French cavalry tactically still practiced much the same techniques as they had at end of the seventeenth century. Although the regulations of 1755 emphasized shock action, neither troops, horses, or officers had assimilated the new emphasis. Pistols and charging at the trot was still standard. The German army under Saxe-Hildburghausen was much smaller, totaling 10,800 men, of which about 30 percent, 3,300, were cavalry. Some of Saxe-Hildburghausen's regiments were high quality, notably the Austrian cuirassier and hussar regiments, but most of the German state units were not of the same quality as the French and Austrians. Some of the cavalrymen in the German regiments had never been on a horse before beginning the campaign. These units were barely able to march as a group and were completely incapable of complex maneuvers. Still, in total, the two allied armies numbered almost 40,000 combatants, and though not of the highest quality, they had a significant numerical advantage over the Prussians.

Frederick assembled his army in Saxony by bringing in a variety of dispersed detachments. His army organized into three infantry components, the left and right wings, and the second line, and a cavalry component. The infantry numbered 16,000 while the cavalry counted 4,500, 22 percent of the force. The cavalry consisted of five cuirassier regiments, two dragoon regiments, and two regiments of hussars. Though outnumbered, Frederick's troops were all superbly trained veterans. Both the cavalry and the infantry were the finest in the world at that time.

On November 5, 1757, the two armies faced each other across two-and-half miles of open rolling terrain. The allies were in their camp south of the town of Mücheln arrayed on line facing east with the German force in the south and the French to the north. The Prussians were also in a camp, between the town of Bedra in the north and Rossbach in the south. Frederick set up his headquarters in Rossbach. Both sides were considering attacking. Frederick had reconnoitered the allied camp and discovered that it was a well-prepared defensive position. He believed his outnumbered army could succeed, but he was in no hurry to attack because he recognized that any attack against the strong defensive position would incur heavy casualties. Saxe-Hildburghausen, though commanding the smaller force, was the senior of the two allied commanders and was also considering attacking. Though he was in a good defensive position, he was concerned that his line of communication to Freyberg, his logistics base, was exposed. He also knew that he outnumbered Frederick and recognized that the exposed left flank of the Prussian force was vulnerable. He convinced the reluctant General Soubise, who had secretly received orders from the French government to begin to disengage from the front, to support his action.

Saxe-Hildburghausen's plan was simple, aggressive, and tactically sound. He proposed to deploy a screening force in front of his positions, then turn the allied army from its position on line into two columns and march the army south and then east on to the flank of the Prussians. Then it would be a simple matter of halting the army in column, facing to the left (north) and being in the perfect position on line to assault the Prussian left flank. Unfortunately, though a sound plan, the quality of the troops available, as well as the dysfunctional command structure, made it difficult to execute.

The allies determined that the French contingent would lead the army. This required the French to swing behind the Germans and move south. The German contingent would then fall in behind. Once given the order it took the French army three hours to break camp and begin the march. Once they were clear to the south the Germans followed. Neither army was very good at march discipline, and the two march columns got confused and eventually became four. As the armies reached their southern turning point and swung east, further confusion of march units resulted in the formation of a fifth column. Saxe-Hildburghausen rode forward with an advance guard consisting of most of the allied cavalry. Soubise marched with the lead elements of the French army. This left the German regiments further back in the column under their own command.

As the marching armies cleared the town of Zeuchfeld, about 1:00 p.m., Soubise called a halt. He was not enthusiastic about continuing the maneuver and argued for reforming the army in place where it was. The new position covered the road to Freyberg and threatened the Prussian flank. Saxe-Hildburghausen was disgusted with this view. He had reports that the Prussians were retreating and argued for speed in the march to trap the Prussians before they escaped the flanking maneuver. French officers supported Saxe-Hildburghausen and the march continued. Saxe-Hildburghausen continued to move with the advance guard two miles ahead of the marching main body.

As the allies maneuvered, Frederick was enjoying lunch with his generals in Rossbach. His scouts had reported the breaking of the allied camp, but Frederick was sure that the allies were retreating along their line of communications. He did not feel a need to hurry to follow them though he gave orders for a detachment to prepare to do that. As the allies reached Zeuchfeld, observers in Rossbach could see the marching allied infantry turning east. Frederick berated the officer who brought the report. Despite the king's opinion, General Seydlitz, chief of the Prussian cavalry, sent word for the cavalry to prepare to move. Seeing the cavalry saddling and mounting, the Prussian artillery also prepared to move–all without orders from the king. Soon, after a third messenger arrived indicating that the allied infantry were now on the flank of the Prussian line, the king was finally convinced that the enemy was maneuvering for battle. He immediately dispatched Seydlitz to intercept the allies with the Prussian cavalry. Seydlitz held a quick conference with his commanders, most of whom were senior to him, and famously remarked "Gentlemen, I obey the king, and you obey me!"[64] He then led the waiting mounted regiments east out of the Prussian camp.

The allies had stolen a march on the Prussians, and by the time the Prussians were aware of the threat, the allies were almost ready to spring a trap. In these circumstances most eighteenth-century armies would have focused on extracting themselves from the predicament. However, no army in the eighteenth century was as responsive to its commander's orders as the Prussians, and few commanders were as bold as Frederick. Rather than break camp and extricate his army from the trap that Saxe-Hildburghausen was setting up, Frederick determined to reverse the trap.

It was about 2:30 p.m. when Seydlitz's cavalry galloped to the east behind the mass of Janus hill. The hill screened his movement from the marching allies. After a move of about three miles, he wheeled his regiments into line and brought them up to the crest of the eastern edge of the ridge. Simultaneously, the Prussian artillery occupied the top of Janus hill facing south where they could see the allied advance guard of cavalry moving east in column formation. Saxe-Hildburghausen could see Prussian hussars to his left flank but assumed they were screening the Prussian retreat that he thought was happening.

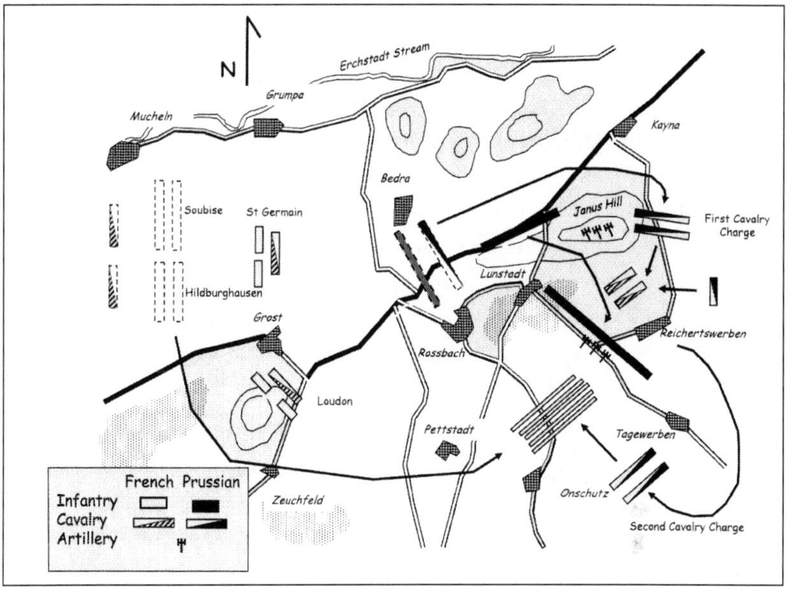

The battle of Rossbach, November 5, 1757.

Seydlitz calmly formed his seven regiments of 3,300 troopers into two lines. Each regiment formed in two ranks of horsemen. Two cuirassier and one dragoon regiment, 1,500 troops, made up the first line, while the second line consisted of three cuirassier regiments and one dragoon regiment totaling 1,800 men. Seydlitz, ever intolerant of poor horsemanship, observed a captain of one of the cuirassier regiments who was unable to control his horse and was disturbing the ranks. He ordered the captain out of the formation.

The first indication that the allies had of the Prussian threat was the artillery fire into their flank from Janus hill about 3:15 p.m. The allied generals perceived the artillery as covering fire for the Prussian retreat and the allied advance guard continued to move east without changing from their column formation. About the same time, Austrian hussars ranging ahead of the advance guard sent back word that a large force of Prussians was maneuvering against them. Saxe-Hildburghausen's response to the hussar report was "How can that possibly be.... You hussars are useless! A waste of the rations the Empress gives you!"[65]

At 3:30 p.m. the Prussian artillery ceased fire, and at that moment over the crest of the ridge in front of the allied advance guard trotted the first line of Seydlitz's cavalry. The commander of the Austrian hussars commented "the enemy cavalry came trotting over the hill, closed up so tightly that there was no interval between squadrons."[66] As the Prussians came on at a trot, Seydlitz, at their head, threw his long-stemmed Dutch pipe in the air to signal the charge. The Prussian cavalry then moved to the gallop with drawn sabers and swept down on the surprised allies.

The allied commanders instantly recognized that the Prussian cavalry attack was a major attack and not a covering move. The lead elements of Austrian cavalry quickly moved from their column formation into line to receive the charge. Supported by Austrian hussars and dragoons, they were partly formed when they met the Prussian first line. This bought time for the German cavalry to advance into the melee and for forward French cavalry to spur forward in support the Austrians. Soubise, to the rear, understood the importance of the cavalry confrontation and led forward additional French cavalry and called for the cavalry reserve. The quick allied reaction checked the initial charge of Seydlitz's first line. However, as the Prussian and allied cavalry traded sword blows and pistol fire, the Prussian First Hussar Regiment, 1,000 strong, charged. The hussars, who had maneuvered to the southeast, charged into the right rear of the allied cavalry reinforcements as they came up. This attack threw the arriving allied cavalry into confusion. At this point the second and stronger line of Prussian heavy cavalry surged into the battle at a gallop. The melee swirled for perhaps 20 or 30 minutes as several German regiments disintegrated under the Prussian attack, and the others tried vainly to retain their cohesion. Both allied commanders, Soubise and Saxe-Hildburghausen were in the midst of the action, fighting for their lives. Soubise sustained a saber cut to his ear while Saxe-Hildburghausen took a bruising blow across his shoulders from the flat of a Prussian hussar's saber. Neither was in a position to command the army.

The allied cavalry outnumbered the Prussians almost two to one, but the Prussians had training, discipline, and the shock and momentum of a surprise attack executed at the gallop. The Prussians also launched their attack in mass while the allied cavalry were committed to the fight as individual regiments. Psychologically, the Prussians had a huge advantage, and as the less well trained German regiments broke the psychological advantage increased. Once the two cavalry forces made contact individual combat dominated. Each individual cavalryman had the capability to fight or flee–each cavalryman had to make that judgment for himself. For the Prussian cavalrymen there was no question of their psychological state: they had supreme confidence in their training, their leaders, and their plan–they fought. For the individual allied cavalry the decision was not as clear. The quick disintegration of the German cavalry, the disciplined advance of the Prussians, their enemy's ability to maneuver with cohesion at the gallop, and the surprise of it all cracked the will of the allied cavalry. The horses took their attitude from their riders. Increasingly the allied horses sensed panic. Within a half hour the entire allied force was broken and streaming to the rear.

The destruction of the allied advance guard and cavalry was only the opening move of the battle. As the Prussian cavalry were setting the tone for the battle, the Prussian infantry were demonstrating the value of the precision drill for which they were world famous. They had broken camp formed on line behind the western edge of the Janus hill, and as the cavalry drove the allied advance guard from the field, they marched over the western portion of the hill. They then pivoted on the town of Lunstadt and conducted a massive wheel to put themselves on line astride the advance of the main body of the allied army.

As the enemy cavalry fled from the field the Prussian cavalry did not pursue. Instead, Seydlitz recalled his cavalry and moved them to the south of the town of Tagewerben where they were reformed into their original two battle lines out of sight, but no more than a thousand yards from the flank of the advancing allied infantry columns. The allied infantry knew that a disaster had occurred to the advance guard and the cavalry from the stream of refugees flooding past their columns. However, leaderless, they were not in a position to understand the scope of the disaster, the enemy maneuvers, or to make any grand change in their disposition. They literally marched into a trap even more dangerous than the one sprung on the allied cavalry. As the Prussian infantry line took its position it brought the French infantry, still moving in column, under devastating musket and artillery fire. One by one, the infantry regiments tried to form lines while under Prussian fire. The French infantry in front took the brunt of the Prussian fire and slowly gave ground. The German infantry coming up from the rear moved forward on the French right and was partly successful in coming on line. The Prussian cavalry then emerged at a gallop from the low ground to the right of the allied line of advance and hit both of these formations in the flank . Already weakened by the fire of the Prussian infantry, the surprise flank attack of Seydlitz's cavalry crumbled the formations of the allied infantry. Whole battalions turned and ran, and other battalions further to rear fled without even coming in contact with the Prussians. The complete destruction of the army was only avoided because far to the rear the covering forces of Generals St. Germain and Loudon, tasked with keeping watch on the Prussian camp, were uncommitted and in good order. They were able to reposition and check the Prussian cavalry and allow some time for the broken formations to flee. By 4:45 p.m. the Prussians had swept the allied army from the battlefield. The battle had lasted from the opening salvo of artillery to the route of the infantry, about 90 minutes. Frederick's infantry were only in battle for about 15 minutes of that time, and only seven battalions of infantry (out of 27) engaged in the fight. Saxe-Hildburghausen later reported to the Austrian emperor that "it was a stroke of utmost good fortune . . . that night fell, otherwise, by God, nobody would have escaped."[67]

The strategic, operational, and tactical losses to the allies at Rossbach were immense. At the strategic level the Prussian victory threw the French government, never enthusiastic about operations against Prussia, into chaos. The Prussian people and Prussia's alley, Hanover, were heartened. At the operational level, it eliminated the western threat to Prussia, allowing Prussian forces to redeploy to the east and southeast. This created the ability to mass forces against the Austrians and win decisively at the battle of Leuthen one month later. The remnants of the two allied armies retreated in different directions and were no longer a threat. Together the total allied losses from all causes including prisoners was about 10,000. Virtually all the artillery was lost, and over 10,000 muskets were thrown into the Saale River. Most of the survivors were unarmed, and most of the surviving cavalry were without horses. In comparison, Frederick's forces suffered less than 200 killed.

The cavalry action at Rossbach was the most successful employment of cavalry of the early modern period, and one of the most successful uses of cavalry since the days of Hannibal and Alexander. A variety of factors combined to make the success at Rossbach possible. Terrain and the actions of the enemy were major factors. Janus hill was critical in the action because it allowed to the Prussians to maneuver out of sight of the enemy commanders and then achieve surprise once they were in position. In addition, the flank march of the allied army placed it in a very vulnerable position. However, these two factors would have been for nothing if the Prussian cavalry was not able to maneuver with speed and precision to take advantage of them. This maneuvering was only possible because of the training, and in particular the horsemanship training, the quality of the Prussian Holsteiner horses, and the visionary leadership of Frederick and Seydlitz.

Training, discipline, and horsemanship were also factors which permitted the Prussian cavalry to win in the close combat of the charge. The speed of charge gave them both a physical and a psychological advantage over their opponents. Speed negated any role of defending cavalry pistol fire. If the French and Austrian cavalry used their pistols at all they were so ineffective that there is no historical mention of it. The discipline which permitted them to regroup and charge again against the infantry ensured the complete destruction of the enemy armies. The training program of the Prussians, which required every cavalry type to train in the basic maneuvers of the arm, permitted the dragoons, and even the hussars, to contribute to the decisive combat of the battle. No other hussars could have charged with the effect that the Prussian had, and this was directly a result of the unique Prussian training requirements. Rossbach became the icon of cavalry success to all cavalrymen of every nation. It inspired cavalryman and generals for generations. For the next 150 years every cavalry general dreamed of repeating Rossbach with themselves in the role of Seydlitz.

Charge of Seydlitz's cuirassiers at Rossbach, 1757. This charge represented the culmination of Frederick's reform of Prussian cavalry units that had the horsemanship to both precisely control their mounts in order to maintain the integrity of their formation, and the ability to gallop aggressively across country. This combination permitted the Prussians cavalry to make two distinct charges against different enemy formations and decisively win the battle. (*Cavalry Journal* [British])

The period 1500 to 1800 is generally perceived as the time when the role of cavalry in battle was eclipsed by the increased capabilities of infantry and artillery. This perception is not just overstated, it is demonstratively false. Just as the perception that Medieval cavalry dominated the Medieval battlefield is an inaccurate generalization, the idea that the pike and then the bayonet and musket greatly reduced the role of cavalry on the battlefield is incorrect. If anything, cavalry, operating as one of the three essential combat arms, became increasingly decisive throughout the early modern period.

For a short time pikes successfully challenged the dominance of the heavily armored cavalry, but the introduction of effective firearms was a threat to both the armored cavalryman and the pike infantryman. Eventually firearms and the bayonet eliminated the pike completely from military inventories. Firearms, though making the battle more lethal, did not preclude the use of cavalry. Firepower was a double-edged sword. Cavalry had to be conscious that a well-timed musket volley could destroy an entire regiment. Conversely, musket and artillery fire could create opportunities for decisive cavalry action. Thus, though the battlefield was more lethal, what affected cavalry operations most was the increased complexity of the battlefield. Precise maneuvers, speed, boldness, and timing were more important than ever in achieving effects with cavalry. The margin of error separating cavalry success and failure got smaller.

Cavalry formations in the closing decades of the eighteenth century were much more capable than they were at any previous time. Better individual horsemanship and bigger, faster, and more athletic horses gave cavalry unprecedented mobility and speed; better and more lethal weapons, including firearms and horse artillery, made cavalry more dangerous; and superbly trained formations enabled cavalry to maneuver with precision across all kinds of terrain. When conditions presented themselves on the battlefield, eighteenth-century commanders had lethal and responsive cavalry that could launch battle-winning strikes.

Chapter Seven

ALL THE EMPEROR'S HORSES

Without cavalry battles are without result.–NAPOLEON

The Napoleonic period, 1796-1815, marked a revolution in the politics of Europe and in the history of warfare. The French Revolution introduced the concept of *levee en masse,* which mobilized the entire population of the nation for war. Nations conducted warfare on a scale never before imagined. Warfare practiced by huge armies of conscripts, and prosecuted with all the power of a fully mobilized nation, replaced the controlled, limited warfare of professional armies as practiced by Frederick and Marlborough. Nations aspiring to continental domination replaced the limited objectives of kings and princes. Consequently, the cavalry forces fielded in the Napoleonic period were immense and drew upon the entire horse population of Europe.

THE FRENCH REVOLUTION AND THE NAPOLEONIC WARS

The French Revolution eliminated the French monarchy, the French aristocracy, and other institutions associated with the political and social power of those two sectors of society. One of the most important of these was the army. The army was closely associated with monarchial power and personal loyalty to the royal family. Army officers were largely members of the aristocracy. Therefore, as part of the sweeping elimination of the monarchy, the army's connections to prerevolutionary political institutions had to be broken. In order to create a reliable army loyal to the revolution, the French army had to be completely rebuilt.

Sweeping reform on the scale required by the revolution demanded dramatic change. During the first years of the republic, Royalists either quit the army, were removed, or in drastic cases, were executed. Within a few years, the leadership of the French army at every level was new and, though inexperienced, were largely chosen based on merit. Every able-bodied man was required to respond to the call to the colors. This allowed the French to field armies of extraordinary size. The French army also cut itself loose from depot logistics, traveling with key supplies instead, which dramatically increasing its operational range. The French adopted a new tactical system that, without totally abandoning the infantry line, emphasized columns that moved quickly in the assault to engage the enemy in close combat. Napoleon also introduced a new concept of combined arms warfare, creating the division composed of infantry, artillery, and cavalry as the basic fighting unit, and the corps as an army subunit capable of totally independent sustained operations. As these changes matured and developed in the French army, Napoleon's forces became almost unstoppable on the European battlefield. French success forced the other European powers to adapt and copy the French techniques or be defeated.

Napoleonic Cavalry

The cavalry arm reached the highest point of its popular and professional acclaim during the Napoleonic period. Although the proportion of cavalry forces in the overall force during this period declined, this was relative to the much larger conscript armies. Actually, the size of cavalry forces increased dramatically: Austria maintained a force of over 40,000 cavalry through the entire 25-year period–in 1809, the Austrian cavalry consisted of 44,940 men and 42,791 horses. The total allied cavalry in the 1813 campaign numbered approximately 100,000 men and horses.[1] In 1788, the French cavalry numbered 62 regiments organized into 210 squadrons with a total strength of 37,782 men. By 1794, the French cavalry force had grown to an astonishing 96,000 men.

Organization

The basic cavalry organizations, companies, squadrons, and regiments did not change in the Napoleonic period. However, Napoleon added important organizations above the regimental level. He created cavalry brigade, division and corps organizations above the existing companies, squadrons, and regiments. As occurred in the eighteenth century, the exact composition of any organization from company to corps depended entirely on the specific time and country. Size of a particular unit also varied over the course of a campaign. In general authorized regimental strength throughout the period varied between 800 to 1500 men. Average regimental battle strength was about 500 men in Europe, and 300 to 400 men in the Peninsula after 1809.[2]

The most important national cavalry of the era were the French because Napoleon's army was central to all of the major military actions of the period. In addition, because of its extraordinary early successes, the other powers of Europe copied many of the techniques and practices of the French cavalry. French cavalry reached their optimum level of performance and organization in the years 1805–7. During this time, the Cavalry Reserve alone made up more than 10 percent of the total French army, and each army corps had a full division of well-trained and capable light cavalry. After this period, the army and the cavalry force divided between the northern army in central Europe and the army in Spain. In addition, campaign casualties after 1807 rapidly eroded the quality of French cavalry leadership, troops, and horses.

Had the French cavalry been well trained and equipped, it would easily have been the most powerful cavalry force Europe had ever seen. Unfortunately, the new French Republic did not have the management expertise to maintain such a large cavalry force. By 1796, replacement of horses could not keep up with the numbers that were dying from starvation in their stalls. Part of the reason for the administrative breakdown within the French cavalry was growing too large too fast. Another part of the reason was poor leadership. General Berruyer, inspector general of the cavalry in the armies in Italy, described the state of the French cavalry of that time: "The mounted regiments are in a deplorable state. The great familiarity which exists between superiors and subordinates and the crass ignorance of senior officers who, scarcely knowing how to sign their names, cannot read let alone understand the military regulations which they should be applying, has utterly destroyed discipline. I have seen regiments deficient in everything, whose horses have not been groomed for a year because there are no implements do it with. . . . The cavalry which France possesses at this moment is useless."[3] This was the low point of the French cavalry. Over the coming years, the French cavalry would rapidly improve coincident with the rise to power of Napoleon.

In the early years of Napoleon's reign cavalry were organized into five primary types: cuirassiers, carabiniers (both heavy cavalry), dragoons (medium cavalry), and hussars and chasseurs (both light cavalry). Later, lancers were added as a new type of medium cavalry. A separate component of the cavalry arm were those units of the Imperial Guard which operated only under Napoleon's personal command.

The cuirassier became the elite of the cavalry. They received special pay and recruited their men and horses carefully for their size (in order to handle the armor). Napoleon usually commanded them personally and excused them from the mundane mounted duties such as scouting or operating outposts that were standard for all other types of cavalry. They earned a fearful reputation among the allied armies. For years after the battle of Austerlitz, the Spanish general Palafox made raising the alarm of "French cuirassiers" an act punishable by death because of the panic it could cause.[4]

There were only two regiments of carabiniers in the army, and they were usually brigaded together. They were the best and most disciplined horsemen in the

French cavalry forces. They had begun their history in the Royal army in 1679, when every cavalry company had two snipers armed with rifled carbines. The French eventually consolidated the snipers, first into companies and then ultimately into two special regiments of carabiniers. They were the royal favorite of the regular cavalry, and always served on the right of the cavalry line–the place of honor. They functioned as heavy cavalry in the Napoleonic period and eventually were equipped for that role, ending the period wearing cuirasses and helmets, and without their carbines.[5]

The lowest priority cavalry formations were the green-clad dragoons. By the Napoleonic period dragoons had evolved from mounted infantry into a medium cavalry force that rarely dismounted. However, due primarily to a lack of sufficient horses, a provisional dragoon division began the 1805 campaign dismounted and responsible for guarding the army's baggage train. By the end of the campaign captured horses provided mounts. Napoleon was never impressed with his dragoons and often criticized their poor horsemanship. In 1808, he transferred 24 of the 30 regiments of dragoons to Spain where they were the main cavalry component of the French army there. They did not return to service in the north until the invasion of France and the situation turned desperate in 1814.[6]

The most numerous cavalry type were the light cavalry, and the most numerous of these were the *Chasseurs a Cheval.* The chasseurs were a new type of unit that only began to appear within the French cavalry organization in the last part of the eighteenth century. They were organized and equipped identically as the hussars, but since they did not wear the lavish uniforms of the hussars, they were considerably cheaper to raise and maintain. Both units had identical missions of scouting, screening, raiding, and pursuing broken enemies. The cavalry division of the infantry corps, the individual cavalry regiment in the infantry division, as well as the light cavalry component of the Cavalry Reserve were all chasseurs or hussars. Light cavalry were the most numerous of all types in all armies–double the number of all other types combined. All light cavalry, by the Napoleonic period, had acquired the ability to charge as part of the main battle. Russian Cossacks, who did not have the required discipline and formal training, were the only important light cavalry incapable of participating in the main battle.[7]

One of Napoleon's first acts as he consolidated his position as head of state was to form the Consular Guard, consisting of infantry, cavalry, and artillery units. Eventually it reached corps strength and became the French Imperial Guard. Its mounted branch consisted of two major components, the *Grenadiers a Cheval*, or Horse Grenadiers, which recruited the best men from the heavy cavalry and dragoon regiments, and the *Chasseurs a Cheval*, which chose the best men of the hussars and chasseurs. The Chasseurs a Cheval provided Napoleon's personal bodyguard.[8]

Napoleon's most innovative organizational concept was the arrangement of the cavalry above regimental level. He created cavalry brigades, consisting of two regiments (later as many as four regiments), and cavalry divisions, consisting of two or three brigades. Divisions of cavalry organized into cavalry corps. Cavalry divisions contained their own organic horse artillery batteries. At its highest level, Napoleon's cavalry was broken into two very large categories: the Grande Armée Cavalry Reserve formed in 1804 and the cavalry of the army's infantry corps. Marshal Joachim Murat commanded the former for most of the Napoleonic period. At a minimum, the Cavalry Reserve consisted of the cavalry of the Imperial Guard as well as two cuirassier divisions (8 regiments) and the brigade of carabiniers. The Cavalry Reserve frequently organized into multiple corps as well as the Guard Cavalry.

The cavalry of the army's infantry corps usually consisted of a division of cavalry for each corps—either light cavalry or occasionally dragoons—and single regiments of cavalry within each of the infantry divisions. This organization of corps and division cavalry achieved several purposes. First, because they were permanent commands, command and control of large numbers of cavalry was not an issue. Commanders could quickly mass large cavalry formations for decisive action. A French army corps using only its own cavalry could, if it desired, mass almost 4,000 cavalrymen for a particular decisive action (by consolidating the 4 regiments of its cavalry division with the individual cavalry regiments of each of its four infantry divisions). Corps cavalry gave corps commanders the ability to operate independent of the main army. Not only did this facilitate the independence of the corps, but it also prevented the piecemeal employment of the army reserve cavalry in support of subordinate units. This allowed the army commander, usually Napoleon, to save his most elite cavalry for use at the decisive time and place in the battle in a grand cavalry charge.

French cavalry, as the chief protagonist of the era, was foremost in importance among the cavalry forces of Europe. However, the allied armies also fielded large and capable cavalry forces. The large Austrian cavalry contained very competent individual regiments, but problems at the higher levels of command prevented them from being as effective in battle as they might have been. The Austrians recognized this characteristic in their own forces and in their 1806 regulations claimed that good officers with poor troops were superior to good troops with poor officers. The British cavalry establishment went through a variety of organizational redesignations during the Napoleonic period. In 1809 it consisted of three regiments of household cavalry; seven regiments of dragoon guards (heavy cavalry); six regiments of dragoons (variously considered heavy or medium cavalry); and more than 20 regiments of light dragoons (light cavalry). Though on paper the British had a very large cavalry force (an authorized strength more than 35,000), most of the British army remained in garrisons in England during the Napoleonic period. For example, in 1809 only 5 of 16 heavy regiments were on foreign service.[9]

Cavalry Weapons and Armor

In the French cavalry equipment was notable by its absence. In the early republic years French cavalry was notoriously short of all types of equipment. The Colonel of 13th Chasseurs noted his regiment was short 337 carbines, 340 pistols, 150 sabers, 143 coats, 143 pairs of trousers, and 280 cloaks. In 1793, a French hussar unit charged in combat without saddles or sabers, using batons as weapons. The equipment shortages persisted until the very end of the Empire. In 1814, orders directed dragoons to give their muskets to the infantry, and the 1st Chasseurs had only 202 sabers for 234 troopers. Sometimes there was virtually no equipment for new recruits.[10] This was a function of the requirement to equip armies of unprecedented size without the manufacturing capability of the industrial revolution, which had not yet had a major impact in Europe.

Pistols were still a part of all cavalry equipment but no longer played any important role in the charge or melee. The medium and light cavalry units carried carbines, and these units varied in the emphasis they placed on the weapon. The French probably put the most value on carbine fire and in several cases tried to break up enemy cavalry charges with it. However, weapons shortages frequently caused the French cavalry to give up their carbines to hastily raised infantry units. In some countries cavalry troops thought so little of carbines that they discarded the weapons in the field to save on weight.[11]

The main weapons of all cavalry were the sword and saber. The difference between the saber and the sword was the curve of the blade. The employment of the weapons was fundamentally different. The sword, with its straight blade, was a thrusting weapon, while the curved blade of the saber was designed for slashing. Most heavy cavalry carried swords. The intent was that they would engage as part of the charge, and their first blow would be a thrust that carried both the weight of the horse and rider behind it. The saber was the weapon of the light cavalry. The curve of the saber added momentum to the slash and allowed a greater impact of the blade in less of an arc. For lancers the saber was a backup weapon. Most casualties inflicted by cavalry were from behind: either when the enemy was routed (most common) or when the cavalry fell upon an exposed flank or rear of a formation.[12]

Both edged weapons had drawbacks. The saber was preferred in melee combat, but it was difficult to execute a fatal blow. It was not uncommon for cavalrymen to suffer dozens of saber wounds in a single battle with none being fatal. The sword,

Austrian cavalry hussar, left, in 1800 in the distinctive uniform of the Hungarian tribesmen. The hussar uniform remained in military fashion until World War I. Polish Lancer and Chasseur of the French Imperial Guard, 1815, right. The Polish lancers fought for the French in the name of Polish independence. Their success brought the lance back as a viable cavalry weapon. (*Cavalry Journal* [British])

when used to pierce, was lethal. However, cavalry complained that it was not very effective in melee combat. Napoleonic cavalry leaders split in their advocacy of one weapon over the other. French leader General de Brack favored the sword: "It is the points alone that kill; the others serve only to wound. Thrust! Thrust! As often as you can: you will overthrow all whom you touch, and demoralize those who escape your attack, and you will add to those advantages that of always being able to parry and never uncovered."[13]

In contrast, the 1796 British *Rules and Regulations for Sword Exercise of Cavalry* advised that the slash was the most effective attack against other cavalry. Although the overall melee effectiveness of the sword was debated, its thrust was without a doubt the deadlier attack. After an engagement with French cavalry, British dragoon officer Captain Bragge of the 3rd Dragoons observed: "Scarcely one Frenchman died

British 2nd Dragoons (Scots Greys) heavy cavalry of the Union Cavalry Brigade, 1815. Superbly mounted and aggressive cross-country riders, the British cavalry charge was a formidable force. Note the shabraque which covers the saddle and displays the royal cipher of King George III and the regimental number. (*Cavalry Journal* [British])

of his wounds although dreadfully chopped, whereas 12 English Dragoons were killed on the spot and others dangerously wounded by thrusts. If our men had used their swords so, three times the number of French would have been killed."[14]

The lance made a comeback in the Napoleonic period but was a difficult weapon to master–much more difficult than the sword. Lances ranged in length from 12 to 14 feet in Russian, Austrian, and Prussian forces, to about 9 feet in length in the French cavalry. Poorly trained lancers stabbed their own horses, their neighbor's horses, or ran their lances into the ground. However, the lance had the major advantage of being able to reach beyond the infantry bayonet and therefore was an excellent weapon to use to break an infantry square. A British sergeant remarked, "Of all descriptions of cavalry, certainly the lancers seem the most formidable to infantry."[15] Bayonets were useless against lancers.

In Eastern Europe, the lance had remained a prime cavalry weapon, particularly in the hands of Polish cavalry. One of the first and most respected leaders of Polish cavalry was a Lithuanian nobleman named Hulan. His cavalry unit was known by the name of its leader–the Hulan corps. Very quickly, the German enemies of the Poles began to refer to all lance-armed cavalry as Hulans, from which the term *uhlan* is derived. In German and Austrian armies, uhlans became the accepted designation of lance-armed cavalry. When Napoleon conquered Prussian controlled Poland, Polish lancers rallied around the French tricolor. They saw the French conquest of Austria and Prussia, and war with Russia, as promising a new era of Polish independence. The elite Polish Lancers became one of the most famous formations in the French cavalry. In the Polish system, followed by most French lancers, only the first rank of the formation used a lance. The second carried carbines.[16]

The Napoleonic period saw the return of the cuirass and the helmet as standard equipment in the heavy cavalry. By the end of the eighteenth century, the Austrians

Elite French Cuirassier heavy cavalry, 1815. Napoleon reintroduced the cuirass as well as the helmet for heavy cavalry. In this illustration a bearskin covers the saddle. (*Cavalry Journal* [British])

had abandoned the back plate of the cuirass, and the British and French heavy cavalry had abandoned the cuirass entirely. Napoleon brought back the cuirass. The French cuirass was a formidable piece of armor. Initially, specifications required that it be musket proof. This proved difficult to achieve, but eventually the French adopted a design that could provide long-range protection against musket fire, and was impenetrable by pistol, sword, or lance. In the opinion of some cavalry leaders, however, the primary effect of the cuirass was that it raised a unit's morale.[17] Napoleon also brought back helmets to replace the tricorner hat. Helmets soon became a favorite piece of cavalry equipment in the period. They were very effective at deflecting a saber slash at the head. They were also effective in protecting troopers from rain and a fall from a horse, and they were relatively comfortable. British light dragoons were unhappy when they converted to hussars and lost this valuable and practical piece of equipment.

Tactics

Cavalry was always important and often decisive in Napoleonic battle. On the tactical battlefield, cavalry remained an integral part of battle as the adroit coordination of the combined arms continued to be the key to success. As Napoleon observed: "Infantry, cavalry, and artillery are nothing without each other."[18] Cavalry was not confined to the wings and did not have as its primary role the defeat of an opponent's cavalry. Armies were too large and too capable to be defeated quickly by successfully overthrowing an entire flank, and an army's flank could not simply be turned by defeating the enemy's cavalry. All commanders formed reserves, and it required the cumulative effects of a series of tactical successes to win a battle.

Napoleon pioneered the new way of employing cavalry. Rather than using cavalry in the tradition of Frederick and Gustavus against the enemy's flanks to clear the enemy horse, he formed a large cavalry reserve in the tradition of Marlborough and then launched it at a decisive point, usually occupied by infantry. A massive artillery bombardment softened up the target before the charge.[19] Napoleon's maximums are very clear in terms of his views of cavalry.

> Charges of cavalry are equally useful at the beginning, the middle, and the end of a battle. They should be made always, if possible, on the flanks of the infantry, especially when this last is engaged in front.
>
> Artillery is more essential to cavalry than to infantry, because cavalry has no fire for its defence, but depends upon the saber. It is to remedy this deficiency that recourse has been had to horse-artillery. Cavalry, therefore, should never be without cannon, whether when attacking, rallying, or in position.[20]

As the distinguished Napoleonic historian David Chandler remarked, "The use of 'shock action' by cavalry, whether heavy cuirassiers, intermediate dragoons, or light hussars and lancers, in co-ordination with infantry and guns was a fundamental condition of Napoleonic tactics and indeed of most of his opponents."[21]

The basics of successful cavalry tactics were preserving a reserve, maintaining proper formation, guarding against flank attacks, and reconnoitering the ground. Cavalry was the most complex of the arms of the Napoleonic period. Small numbers of cavalry, employed correctly, could change the course of a battle. The key to the successful employment of cavalry in battle was understanding the complex interaction of men, conditions, and–equally as important–horses. Because of these intangible factors, historian Rory Muir accurately describes its characteristics as a battlefield tool: "Cavalry was a powerful but fragile weapon which needed an extraordinary mixture of caution and daring in its use."[22]

The Cavalry Charge

The mounted charge continued to be the tactical operation that justified cavalry's presence on the battlefield. Charges generally followed the Prussian model. Organized into five stages: walk, trot, within 150 to 200 paces canter, within 70 to 80 paces full gallop, and within 20 paces the charge *á la sauvage*, an extreme uncontrolled gallop. One of the products of the slow acceleration from walk to trot, trot to canter, canter to gallop was a steady process of mentally preparing the charging cavalry. The intent was that in the last phase of the charge engaged the rider and the horse emotionally so that they were impervious to the shock of contact with the enemy. The charge was the tactic used against other cavalry, infantry, and artillery. Captain Louis Edward Nolan observed, "The success of a cavalry attack depends not so much on the description of the cavalry or horse employed, as on the determination of the men." Nolan was describing the fact that the success of a cavalry charge was most dependent on psychological factors. Napoleonic cavalry did not use pistols in the charge at all. Historian Rory Muir put it more bluntly: "Cavalry's main weapon was fear." There were two aspects of a successful charge: first was the morale and spirit of the charging cavalry and second was deftness of the cavalry commander's timing. The relative size of the forces was not overly important. There were numerous cases of light cavalry defeating medium cavalry, medium cavalry defeating heavy cavalry, and smaller bodies of cavalry forces defeating larger bodies of infantry or cavalry.[23]

Timing was everything in cavalry operations, and the difference between success and failure was often a matter of minutes or seconds. Ideally, as Napoleon indicated, cavalry operated as part of a combined arms team, and the attack of cavalry had a much greater chance of success if supported by infantry or artillery. At the battle of Borodino the Cavalry Reserve's great charge was supported by 100 guns of horse artillery that could move with the cavalry and position rapidly in support.[24] Attacking without support of the other arms, though occasionally successful, was a gamble that could cost the cavalry high casualties as it did at the battle of Eylau in 1809 and at Waterloo in 1815.

Speed was another essential ingredient of the charge. Once within the effective range of the infantry musket, cavalry had to move at the gallop to reduce their exposure to fire. In addition, the gallop not only positively effected the morale of the cavalry but also adversely effected the morale of the enemy–especially infantry and artillery. Hundreds of horses moving in a tight formation at the gallop were a very imposing sight and could literally make the ground shake under the feet of the infantry and artillerymen. The advantage of speed in cavalry combat required cavalry to immediately countercharge when opposing cavalry attacked. Austrian cavalry regulations prohibited receiving a charge at the halt. The British usually countercharged when attacked. The French still occasionally relied on carbine fire to receive an opposing cavalry attack. In 1812 the 16th Chasseurs used this tactic against Russian Cossacks. Instead of countercharging, they fired a volley of carbine fire at the Cossacks at a range of 30 paces. It had little effect, and the Chasseurs suffered severely as a result.[25] A drawback with achieving speed was that it made control difficult and required well-trained horses and riders.

For action, cavalry typically operated in a line formation of two or three ranks–most armies used two. For maneuver, cavalry moved in column. A key cavalry training task was to move rapidly from column to line. A new formation that evolved in the Napoleonic era was a modified line called *echelon.* In this formation, a line of cavalry was broken into squadron segments and then arranged in echelon to the rear by squadron. Typically, anywhere from 150 to 300 meters separated the squadrons in echelon.[26] This formation was used for the charge. The echelon had several advantages. First, it dispersed the cavalry formation in depth without decreasing the total front of the formation. This greatly increased a defending infantry formation's fire control problem. If the entire infantry formation fired on the first squadron of the echelon, the other squadrons were out of range but would be on the infantry before they could reload. It also confused the infantry as to the point of the attack. Echeloned squadrons could incline and reinforce the point of attack of the lead echelon, they could attack other points, or they could attack across the entire front. Additionally, the following echelons could break off a charge before they got within effective range if the commander judged by the results of the first echelon that the charge would be unsuccessful.

The problems of commanding the charge remained significant and were expressed by French cavalry commander A. J. Rocca in his 1828 *Memoirs of the War in Spain*: "When a regiment or squadron of cavalry charges, either in line or column, the exact order in which it commenced to gallop cannot long be preserved; for the horses incite each other, and their ardour increases, till he who is best mounted finds himself foremost, and the line of battle is broken." Commanders relied on bugles, personal presence and example, and preplanned orders to facilitate control of the cavalry when it charged. The problem was as much a training problem as it was a tactical problem. British Captain William Tomkinson noted, "In England I never saw nor heard of cavalry taught to charge, disperse, and reform, which of all things, before an enemy, is most essential."[27] Battle taught cavalrymen these hard lessons–if the cavalryman survived long enough. Veteran cavalry were likely to understand the dangers of not controlling the charge and the necessity to quickly rally. However, for many of the major campaigns, most of the allied and French cavalry were far from veterans.

British cavalry were notorious for losing control while charging. Even when they were successful, as they were at Waterloo, they took severe casualties because their commanders could not control them. This led to Wellington's famous analysis "I consider our cavalry so inferior to the French from want of order, that although I considered one of our squadrons a match for two French, yet I did not care to see four British opposed to four French, and still more so as the numbers increased, and order (of course) became more necessary. They could gallop, but could not preserve their order." British cavalry were prone to overpursuing after the charge and then enduring a subsequent cavalry countercharge. This habit of British cavalry frustrated Wellington: "Our officers of cavalry have acquired a trick of galloping at everything. They never consider the situation, never think of maneuvering before an enemy, and never keep back or provide for a reserve. All cavalry should charge in two lines, and at least one-third should be ordered beforehand to pull up and reform, as the charge has been delivered, and the enemy been broken."[28]

The Infantry Square

Ultimately the goal of cavalry was to defeat or contribute to the defeat of the enemy's infantry. The Napoleonic armies were predominantly infantry armies, and the defeat of a Napoleonic army required the defeat of the infantry. Infantry used the same basic formations as cavalry: the line and the column. The infantry line was used to facilitate infantry firepower, and the column was used to maneuver and for the quick bayonet attack. The problem with the basic infantry formations was that they were vulnerable to cavalry attacking at the gallop. Infantry were always concerned about the location and intention of cavalry. Austrian infantry commanders had a great fear of the charge. This fear was so great that they insisted that each maneuvering infantry formation have a body of cavalry to protect it from enemy cavalry. This had the effect of parceling out the Austrian cavalry strength and preventing it from forming a massed reserve for decisive employment.[29] It was the formation of the infantry square that provided a means by which infantry could protect itself from a cavalry charge.

The bayonet wall of the square, with the infantry formed in three ranks, presented about seven bayonets in a 36-inch space, which was equal to that filled by a single cavalryman. The concept of the square assumed that no horse would willingly impale itself on such a wall of bayonets. However, the horse did not perceive bayonets. What the horse perceived was a three-rank-deep wall of men that formed an obstacle, but the horse could sense the rider's fear. The rider's fear of the square was more likely to cause the horse to balk during the attack than the horse's own perceptions. Also, the bayonet was not the infantry square's most important protection against cavalry. The real key to an effective square was firepower. Infantry firepower, when delivered in a timely and sustained manner, could break the back of a cavalry charge. The other key to the square's success was that the formation of a square was equally strong in all directions and did not have any flank or rear vulnerable to cavalry attack.

Cavalry approaching at a trot would have almost no chance of success against a square because attacking at the trot greatly diminished the physical and psychological power of the mounted formation, and the infantry commanders had a much easier time judging distances and effectively directing the fire of their defensive volleys. The French cavalry charges at Waterloo advanced at the trot. A British observer at Waterloo described the charges coming at a trot uphill through mud and artillery fire as "visits." The effectiveness of British fire devastated the French cavalry. A French lieutenant reported, "They showered us with musket balls, seven of which hit my horse."[30] Cavalry trotting against a square was destined to fail.

Another problem that Napoleonic cavalry had when dealing with the square was the training of the horse. A horse could be trained to crash through such an obstacle just as a horse could be trained to walk through shoulder high grass, or to jump a fence. However, there is no record of such training occurring. [31] There is no record of formally training horses to charge a square. Even worse is the record of feigned charges against squares. In these feints, the cavalry rode down on the infantry square, and then the riders intentionally halted and wheeled away or veered around the square. After doing this once, the horse, with its phenomenal memory, remembered that action. A single false charge could wipe out months of training and taught the participating horses to avoid close combat with the square. Over the course of a campaign, unless commanders were very conscious of the training of their horses–and most were not–veteran horses, rather than better trained, could become less responsive in combat because they had inadvertently been taught to avoid the enemy.

Given the effectiveness of the square, the obvious question is why cavalry attacked it at all. The answer is that the square was only effective when it had time to form, discipline held, and command was competent. These perfect conditions were necessary because the cavalry charge put the infantrymen in the square under severe psychological stress. British Captain Tomkinson explains the view from within the square: "It is an awful thing for infantry to see a body of cavalry riding at them at a full gallop. The men in the square frequently begin to shuffle, and so create some unsteadiness. This causes them to neglect their fire. The cavalry seeing them waver, have an inducement for riding close up, and in all probability succeed in getting into the square, when it is all over."[32]

Military thinkers believed correctly that the power of the cavalry was the horse and that the average infantryman was more afraid of the horse than the rider. The stress of battle and fear could cause the infantry to make any one of a variety of mistakes: officers ordering fire before the horses got close enough for the fire to be effective; officers ordering fire too late; individual infantryman firing without orders and setting off spontaneous fire, ruining the fire plan of the square; positioning on or near terrain allowing the cavalry to get close to the square undetected or protected from fire; positioning on terrain causing gaps or holes in the square; forming a square where it was subject to artillery or infantry fire; and individuals flinching and running from their position and causing gaps or spreading panic.

The infantry square was a formation that was incapable of offensive action and extremely vulnerable to artillery and infantry attack. Infantry forced to form square took significant risk. If cavalry could force infantry into a square and then bring infantry or artillery in support, the infantry could be defeated even if the cavalry charge was unsuccessful or perhaps never executed at all. Because of this, good infantry commanders resisted forming a square until the last minute. This increased the chance that the square was incompletely formed or incorrectly positioned, and increased the chance of cavalry success.

Observing the battlefield and having its pulse were keys to the successful employment of cavalry, particularly against infantry who, properly handled, had formations and firepower that were capable of stopping a cavalry charge. Successful tactical employment of cavalry required experience, training, and tactical acumen. The cavalry commander had to instantly recognize windows of vulnerability and then attack to take advantage of them. The Germans would later call the tactical intuition of the commander, so important to cavalry's tactical success, *fingerspitzengefühl*–literally, "fingertip feel." This intangible understanding of the dynamics of battle was required in order to recognize and grasp the complex and diverse factors of combat that were absolutely critical to the successful employment of cavalry on the battlefield.

Horses and Horsemanship

The cavalry forces of the Napoleonic period were of unprecedented size. A phenomenal number of horses, certainly the vast majority of the horse population of central Europe, were directly or indirectly involved in the Napoleonic Wars. At the same time, the nature of the battlefield required horses of exceptional quality. They had to have the stamina to endure marches from one end of the continent to the other, and they had to be big, fast, and obedient to achieve success on the battlefield. A large number became casualties. Horse losses were an evitable cost of war. Napoleon's view was "if such great objects may be obtained as the destruction of a whole hostile army, the State can afford to lose a few hundred horses from exhaustion."[33] Napoleon estimated that he had three or four horses killed for every trooper lost, and he didn't consider disease and nonbattle injuries. Just the first phase of the 1807 campaign in Poland cost the French cavalry 16,000 horses.[34] The nature of war and the tempo of operations put a premium on finding, procuring, and training quality remounts.

Horses

The Napoleonic Wars stressed the remount systems of all of the European powers to their limits. Some of them broke down and ceased to function. The Austrians and Prussians continued to run the same type of remount systems that they had operated throughout the eighteenth century. The confiscation of the entire military horse populations by the French in accordance with surrender terms stressed both the Austrian and Prussian remount programs. French cuirassiers reached the peak of their effectiveness in 1807 when they acquired the best of Prussia's big warmbloods.[35]

French Remounts

The French remount program was the most directly effected by the 20 years of war of the Napoleonic period. The French horse breeding system suffered from the revolution, several invasions, and ultimately defeat. War completely wiped out some of the developing French horse breeds. During the revolution, the royal stud farms were disbanded and 1,116 stallions were sold off. From that point forward, the army purchased its horses on the open market. A shortage in horses drove the cost of each animal higher, making the equipping of cavalry much more expensive than it should have been. It did not help that the republic authorized an unrealistically large cavalry arm. Battle losses only added to the problem, and the military wastage of horses throughout Europe was immense.

Napoleon tried unsuccessfully to reestablish a state remount system, but the main source of French cavalry horses as they prepared for the campaign of 1812 were war prizes and levies. Ultimately, the French assembled 42,000 new horses for the invasion of Russia.[36] This was sufficient to bring the cavalry horse population up to strength, but just barely–units did not have excess horses. The campaign began with the crossing of the Nieman River on June 23, 1812. Napoleon and his allies had a total cavalry force of 80,000 mounts. The cavalry began to experience problems immediately. Forage was so scarce that troopers took straw from mattresses to feed their mounts. Within eight days of the opening of the campaign the army had 8,000 horses die, mostly from lack of care. The Cavalry Reserve itself mustered 40,000 men and horses; three months later, on September 26, the total was 11,434. Marshall Murat, the Cavalry Reserve commander, described the situation as grim and wondered, "What will become of the army this winter."[37]

Fighting several battles along the way, French forces entered Moscow on September 14, 1812. They remained in the city for four weeks waiting for the Czar to surrender. With winter coming on, Napoleon decided to withdraw. On October 19 the French army pulled out of Moscow and began one of the longest and most desperate retreats in military history. The struggle out of Russia became a fight against distance, weather, and starvation more than a fight against the Russian army. In one fortnight in mid-November, the cold was so intense that 30,000 horses died. The only positive aspect of their death was that they provided meat for the starving army. When the French finally crossed into Poland in November 1812, the cavalry force was nearly destroyed. Typical of the cavalry losses were those of the 7th Hussars, who began the campaign with 1,100 mounted troopers and ended the campaign with 120 men and 20 horses. In total, French cavalry lost all but 1,500 horses.[38]

The 1812 losses, forced the French to conduct the campaign of 1813 chronically short of horses, and with cavalry units that were an odd combination of seasoned veterans and untrained recruits. The horse shortage continued into 1814. The depot at Versailles reported that it had only 6,284 horses for 9,786 recruits.[39] The campaign of 1812 had broken the back of the French cavalry, and it was impossible for the French cavalry to recover from the debacle. When Napoleon returned to power briefly in 1815 veterans flocked to his colors. However, no matter how many veterans he gathered, it was not possible to mount them on the quality horses necessary to conduct the type of operational maneuver and shock attacks that were the hallmarks of his earlier campaigns. Those horses simply did not exist.

The British Thoroughbred

In sharp contrast to the French, the British remount system provided quality mounts to the cavalry throughout the Napoleonic period. The British cavalry remount program operated solely on the purchase system. The main source of horses was professional breeders who were large landowners or prosperous farmers. Because the British army kept a very small permanent military establishment during peacetime, there was no profit in breeding purely for army needs. What was available to purchase as remounts were the standard commercial breeds. The best of the British breeds were bred for sport.

Breeding for sport was a tradition of the English royalty. Charles II (1660–85) went to great efforts to import Barb, Turk, and Arab mares to breed as racehorses. He managed to put together a stable known as "the king's mares" that greatly influenced the creation of the British racehorse on the dam's side.[40] On the stallion's side the English racehorse was the product of three great Asian stallions: the Byerley Turk, captured by Colonel Robert Byerley at the siege of Buda (modern-day Budapest) in 1688 from a Turkish officer; the Darley Arabian, bought by Thomas Darley in Aleppo Syria in 1704; and the Godolphin Arabian, which came to the earl of Godolphin by way of the king of Tunis and the king of France in 1729. The offspring of these three stallions established the beginning of the English Thoroughbred breed. The stallions provided speed and spirit to the breed, while the mares provided size and strength. Although the late-eighteenth-century Thoroughbred was slightly smaller than the modern example, by the Napoleonic period the basic breed characteristics as described by the International Museum of the Horse were set:

> The Thoroughbred stands a little over 16 hands on average and its appearance reveals its Arabian ancestry. A refined head with widely spaced, intelligent eyes sits on a neck which is somewhat longer and lighter than in other breeds. The withers are high and well defined, leading to an evenly curved back. The shoulder is deep, well-muscled and extremely sloped while the heart girth is deep and relatively narrow. The legs are clean and long with pronounced ten-

> dons and move smoothly in unison through one plane. The bone structure of the upper hind leg makes room for long, strong muscling. The thighbone is long and the angle it makes with the hipbone is wide. The powerful muscling of the hip and thigh continues to the gaskin that is set low. Coat colors in Thoroughbreds may be bay, dark bay, chestnut, black or gray; roans are seen only rarely. White markings are frequently seen on both the face and legs.[41]

Today, all modern Thoroughbreds can trace their linage back to the three great stallions that founded the breed and imparted the characteristics that made the Thoroughbred one of the most important breeds in history.

In the late eighteenth century, fox hunting became a popular sport in England. The horse markets responded to the needs of the sport and developed a hunter-type horse. This horse, the hunter, was not a particular breed, but rather was a horse that had the attributes to make a good fox-hunting mount. Fox hunting required a horse that was fast to keep up with hounds, had endurance to hunt extended distances for an entire day, and was nimble so that it could carry itself well cross-country and jump obstacles when necessary. The Thoroughbred so closely matched the requirements of fox hunting, that the hunter-type horses were often pure Thoroughbred or strongly influenced by Thoroughbreds. The army officer class were avid hunters, and beginning in 1780s, Thoroughbred and Thoroughbred-type hunters became the preferred type selected by the army. This preference continued through the end of the horse cavalry in the twentieth century. Many of the breeders of these great cavalry mounts were located in Ireland, and for the remaining history of the British cavalry a large portion of the remounts were Irish hunters.

The Thoroughbred is a very spirited horse. Some British cavalrymen believed that their horses contributed to the command problems that the British cavalry had controlling the charge. One writer in the *Royal Military Chronicle* described the problem in 1811:"in every charge the British horses run away with their riders; and that, after the first effort has been made, it is a work of much time and difficulty to bring them again into regular line." The solution recommended was more and better horsemanship training, and training cavalry remounts in the classic high school manner. But in general British cavalry was satisfied with the superior power their mounts gave them in the charge.[42]

Horse Equipment

Horse equipment evolved during the Napoleonic period into basic designs which would not vary significantly until the end of horse cavalry. Two pieces of equipment which represent the state of the art of horse equipment of the period are the English universal pattern (UP) saddle and the double bridle.

The Thoroughbred "hunter type" horse which became the preferred British cavalry mount in the last part of the eighteenth century and would remain so through the history of the British horse cavalry. (U.S. Cavalry School, *The Rasp*, 1914)

Saddles

In most countries, Napoleonic period cavalry saddles were of a modern design that, with a few notable exceptions, would not change in its basic features for the rest of the history of the horse cavalry. The British universal pattern saddle used at Waterloo was similar in all major respects to that used 40 years later in the Crimea, and 100 years later in World War I. It was a good saddle, comfortable for the horse and rider, allowed air to circulate, and distributed the weight of rider and equipment evenly. It was also easy to repair with simple tools and materials. Finally, it was easily adaptable to different size and shapes of horses simply by adding strips of felt to the sidebars or varying the thickness of the folded saddle blanket.[43]

Prior to the late eighteenth century, there was no uniformity of equipment within the British cavalry. Regimental commanders individually contracted for equipment of their preferred design. A regimental commander could make a profit operating his regiment and some commanders skimped on equipment, while others were lavishly furnished. This began to change at the end of the century. In 1796 the Board of General Officers decided on a standard pattern for heavy cavalry saddles. In 1805 they decided on a different standard for light cavalry. The regimental commander still made the actual purchase. The British saddle had to be suitable for operations on a global scale. It also had to be adaptable to all types of terrain, weather, and different types of horses.[44]

In 1791 Frederick, the duke of York, visited Prussia to study the Prussian military. His brother, the prince of Wales, asked that he arrange to send examples of Prussian horse equipment to England. The duke sent two complete sets. One was a cuirassier heavy cavalry set and one was a hussar set. The heavy cavalry saddle UP model of 1796 was virtually a direct copy of the Prussian cuirassier saddle acquired by the duke of York. The major difference between the two was that the British model had brass edging to protect the cantle of the saddle.[45]

Like the heavy cavalry saddle, the British based their light cavalry saddle on the Prussian model acquired by the duke of York. The Prussians copied their hussar saddle design directly from their adversaries, the Austrian light cavalry. The saddle design had been used by the Hungarian cavalry since about the fifteenth century and in the eighteenth century was adapted for use by all Austrian cavalry. The design not only spread to Prussian and Britain but was also used during the Napoleonic period by France, and in 1812 was adopted by the American army.[46] The hussar saddle would remain the standard British light cavalry saddle until after the Crimean War.

The hussar saddle was a relatively simple design. A high pommel and cantle connected two beech wood sideboards. Iron gullets reinforced the pommel and cantle. A rawhide seat ran from cantle to the pommel, tied to the sideboards by rawhide bindings. The seat rode well off the horse's back. Two slotted extensions called spoons sat in the center of the pommel and cantle. Burs and fans were extensions of the sidebar forward of the pommel and cantle, respectively. These provided stations for the attachment of equipment in front of and behind the saddle seat. A padded leather cover hooked to the spoons on the pommel and cantle and draped over the wood and rawhide tree of the saddle.[47]

French light cavalry used a design similar to the other European hussar saddles. French medium and heavy cavalry saddle design was hard on horses and was made worse by shoddy construction. Because they had no metal bands to reinforce the forks and keep them in position the saddles broke down and put weight directly on the horses' spine. Improper fit and poor construction caused back sores on horses. By 1811 saddles were being constructed with wood so green that they did not hold shape, warped, and became loose. When Napoleon inspected the equipment of the elite Polish lancers of the Imperial Guard he found 60 broken saddlebows.

The Double Bridle

The double bridle first appeared at the very end of the seventeenth century and the equitation writings of the duke of Newcastle referred to the new equipment. Eighteenth-century high school master Guérinière also mentioned it. Beginning in the mid-eighteenth century–about the time of the Seven Years' War–European cavalry began to convert from a curb bit bridle to a double bridle, which included a curb bit, and a snaffle bit called a bridoon. The double bridle required a separate set of reins and separate check pieces for each bit. The curb bit was a standard curb bit and fixed to the horse in the normal manner. The bridoon had smaller rings than a standard snaffle and positioned above the curb bit and curb chain. A rider could identify the bridoon reins because they were slightly wider than the curb reins.[48] It is unclear exactly what drove the conversion of cavalry bridles from the standard curb bridle to the double bridle. It may have been the influence of high school training on cavalry officers, who insisted that the bridle be used by their troopers. Regardless of the reason, by the Napoleonic period it was in general use throughout Europe and remained, in various configurations, the accepted military bit and bridle combination through the twentieth century.

Early military manuals do not explain the intent of the double bridle. Guérinière writing in the 1731 indicates that the bridoon's primary practical purpose was as a backup feature "in case of an accident, when the reins have broken, for example, or have been cut in combat, one may thus resort to the bridoon."[49] Though expert horseman advocated the routine use of both bits, its is doubtful that this was practiced in the field during the Napoleonic period because, given the relatively low level of horsemanship, the average trooper did not require nor had the skill to exploit the subtle capabilities of the double bridle. Most of the depictions of eighteenth- and even nineteenth-century cavalrymen show troopers riding exclusively on the curb, with the bridoon reins slack and draped over the pommel of the saddle. The use of the double bridle today is primarily traditional rather than functional.[50] It is likely that the average cavalryman of the Napoleonic period used the bridoon bit as a backup set of reins and bit, as Guérinière suggested.

Horseshoes

Horseshoeing was a standard part of all cavalry routine maintenance operations. In the Napoleonic period campaigns were long and covered hundreds of miles. Poor shoeing or failing to consider the impact of shoeing had a considerable effect on operations. In the British cavalry, each regiment had a farrier major who was a sergeant and each company had a company farrier. The farrier sergeant worked directly for the regimental veterinarian and supervised the work of the company farriers. He was also responsible for the maintenance and movement in the field of the farrier carts.[51]

The terrain in the Spanish campaign, for example, was extremely tough on horse's feet. Horseshoes were an important aspect of maintaining the horse's serviceability in the rocky terrain of the region. Horseshoes lasted only 15 days instead of the usual 25. Initially the British cavalry suffered from a shortage of horseshoes. During the Corunna campaign, the 7th Hussars lost 560 horses due to lameness caused by a lack of shoes. The British did not evacuate hundreds of horses that survived the campaign because of lameness. Sadly, the required shoes were in the theater of operations, but the supply system could not get them to the front. Subsequently, British cavalrymen were required to carry a full set of shoes and nails as part of their standard kit on campaign.[52]

Horsemanship

Military horsemanship took a definite turn for the worse during the Napoleonic period due to the large size of the armies, the high number of casualties, and the constant warfare. These conditions created a huge demand for cavalry troopers, which placed a great stress on training programs. In most countries abbreviated riding programs taught the trooper the basics before he joined his unit. In some cases, particularly in France in the last few years of Napoleon's reign, cavalrymen often went to their regiments, and even into combat, almost unable to ride.

A French cavalry expert opined that it took three or four years to properly train a cavalryman for combat whereas an infantryman could be trained in six weeks. This amount of time to train cavalry riders was never available to the French during the entire period from the revolution to Waterloo. Instead, troops got a very quick introduction to the basics. French cavalry training was limited to teaching the trooper to stop, turn by pulling on the reins, drive the horse forward by kicking, and once the horse was going in the right general direction to let the reins "float."[53] During short times of peace, the French were able to put recruits through more horsemanship courses. but he quality of horsemanship declined steadily. A French cavalry commander reported to the army chief of staff in 1813, "I must inform Your Highness that my division of light cavalry and cuirassiers are greatly reduced through horses having to be sent to the rear, or dying of fatigue. . . . One reason for the grave number of horses' injuries is the exhausting marches which we have been making for some time, but mostly it is the fault of soldiers in the newly joined detachments, the majority of whom are first put on horseback at the moment when they set out from France." General Delort reported the status of his new cuirassier division: "No-one but a madman would expect me to charge with such cavalry."[54] There is little doubt that the abysmal horsemanship of the French cavalry in the last years of the Empire were a factor in the defeats suffered in 1814 and 1815.

Britain had very good horses, but the general state of horsemanship was not impressive. The best-known British horseman of the late eighteenth century was Henry, the earl of Pembroke, colonel of the Royal Horse Guards, and his evaluation of the equitation skills of British cavalry was that they were "a disgrace to themselves and the animals they ride." The earl was an accomplished classical rider but believed that high school riding skills had no role to play in training cavalry troopers except possibly selected remount trainers. He insisted that units teach soldiers and horses to jump. In his work *Military Equitation* (1778) the earl gave the first instructions on how to jump a horse over an obstacle. Though the British military seat was very classical, the light cavalry were encouraged to ride in a shorter stirrup than heavy cavalry were.[55] Light cavalry adopted a seat that was closer to the hunt seat of the period than the classic seat.

Horsemanship had a major impact on how cavalry preformed in battle. The level of horsemanship forced commanders to make a decision between speed and good order. Ideally, commanders wanted both, but this was only possible with exceptionally well-trained horsemen and well-conditioned horses such as those possessed by Seydlitz at Rossbach. Lacking either or both, commanders adjusted their tactics. The French rarely galloped anywhere. France's senior cavalry commander, Marshal Murat, was perfectly satisfied if his cavalry could walk on the march and trot in the presence of the enemy.[56]

In contrast, British cavalry were eager to gallop into combat–much to Wellington's disgust. The discrepancy between the mediocre performance of British cavalry in battle and the quality of their horses was explained by the French cavalry commander General Excelmann who told a British officer, "Your horses are the finest in the world and your men ride better than any continental soldier. With such material the English cavalry ought to have done more.... The great deficiency is in your officers who seem to be impressed by the conviction that they can dash or ride over everything, as if the art of war were precisely the same as the art of fox-hunting."[57]

Perhaps the finest horsemen of the Napoleonic period were the Russian Cossacks who consistently frustrated the French cavalry. French cavalry commander General Morand commented

> These rude horsemen keep their horses close between their legs; their feet rest in broad stirrups, which support them when they use their arms. They spring from a state of rest to the full gallop, and at that gallop they make a dead halt: their horses second their skill and seem only part of themselves; these men are always on the alert, they move with extraordinary rapidity, have few wants and are full of warlike ardour."[58]

The French were never able to solve the problem of Cossack cavalry. The failure of the French 1812 campaign is in many ways attributable to the French cavalry's inability to match the Cossacks ability to operate effectively in severe winter conditions. This capability was no accident, but rather a characteristic of the Cossacks inherited from the Mongol horsemen of the Golden Horde from whom they were descendant.

Horse Management

Recruits were not only trained in horsemanship, but also horse management. Horse management was the routine management of all aspects of the horse's care to ensure that he was fit and healthy. Grooming and stable cleaning were important aspects of horse management. By British regulations, troopers were supposed to groom horses and cleaned stables three times a day. Watering, with clean and cool water, also occurred three times a day. British cavalry horses were nag-tailed, or docked. This made British cavalry readily distinguishable on the battlefield but was not sound horse mastership; without its tail, the horse was more vulnerable to flies and other insects and therefore to disease.[59]

Despite extensive regulations on the subject, and officers and NCOs who should have known better, the management of horses in both the British and French armies was far from adequate. Historian Sir Charles Oman's evaluation of British horse mastership could apply equally well to either army: "In countless places, in diaries no less than dispatches, we find the complaint that the trooper of 1810 was, when not well looked after by his officers, a bad horse-master—careless as to feeding his mount and still more so as to saddle-galls and such like." Oman notes that the only exception was the German hussars of the king's German legion who were "far more conscientious and considerate to their beasts."[60]

The French cavalry was notorious for neglecting their mounts. After the 1806 campaign, when the French cavalry were at their highest state of training and competence, a surprise inspection of 40 men from the 26th Dragoons revealed that half the horses had sore backs. To make matters worse, the regimental veterinarian accompanied this detachment. Men would attempt to shirk duty by intentionally injuring their horse. A favorite trick was to put stones or even tacks under the saddle to cause back sores and thus eliminate horse and rider from duty. In the last campaigns, the French may have lost more horses before battle than in battle. Probably one of the most graphic condemnations of the French cavalry was the saying that one could notice the approach of a French mounted unit by the smell of the infected sores of its neglected horses.[61]

Overloading horses was a constant concern. Both troops and commanders were guilty of this infraction. Commanders wanted to add equipment, arms, and ammunition. Troopers wanted to add personal comfort items as well as booty. The average weight of a troop horse was about 1,000 pounds. A horse can carry 25 percent of its own weight for extended periods without any problems. This meant the average troop horse could carry about 250 pounds of rider and equipment. One experiment done by British light dragoons in 1775 indicated that the basic load of equipment and soldier came to a total of 316 pounds—a full 66 pounds more than a horse should have to carry. Overloading horses eventually resulted in leg injuries and lameness. Some equipment, mostly tentage and blankets, could be carried on baggage carts, but there were only two carts authorized per squadron.

Wellington described the Spanish theater as "the grave of Horses." Most of the horse casualties were due to nonbattle injuries and disease. To help reduce horse losses every regiment was assigned a veterinarian. In the British cavalry, the regimental veterinary surgeon was the officer primarily tasked with all things related to the health and well-being of the horses. He supervised the regimental farrier major as well as the company farriers. His duties included a daily horse sick call where all sick horses paraded for him, and after which he visited all the horses that were too sick to attend parade. On Sundays, he held another parade that included all sick and lame horses as well as all horses shod by the farriers during the previous week. The veterinarian was responsible for inspecting all pastures considered for use by the regiment, and also for the stockage of shoes in the farrier's stores.[62]

To some cavalrymen, and to many noncavalrymen, the horse was a piece of war equipment. The army cared for and used horses like any other weapon, and discarded them when they were no longer useful. However, to the best soldiers and leaders, the horse was more than a weapon, it was a partner and comrade that, when well trained and treated, responded with faithful service that could save lives and win battles. Horses were not just a piece of army equipment, and even the military bureaucracy recognized this fact, which is why through the long history of the war horse, armies always gave them individual names.

The Napoleonic period is the first period where a large portion of the riders were literate. Because of this, it is the first period where the personal relationship between the military horse and the soldier was recorded. In almost all armies of the period, horses were individually assigned to riders, and the two would often remain a team until they were separated by death or wounds. The shared experiences of hardship, danger, and often wounds over a long period of time created strong bonds between war horses and their riders. Private Melet of the dragoons of the French Imperial Guard rode the same horse, Cadet, from 1806 to 1815. They parted only when Melet was wounded and Cadet killed at Waterloo. British dragoon Captain William Tomkinson's personal mount, Bob, took him through four years of campaigning in Spain. Bob was wounded once by a French bayonet, and was much neglected when Tomkinson was wounded and absent, but recovered and was shipped with Tomkinson back to England in 1813. Bob was returned to Tomkinson's family home and did not join him on the Waterloo campaign. He lived for many years and became his master's favorite hunt horse.[63]

The memory of their wartime companions stayed with both the horse and rider even after the fighting ended. French sergeant Reynier ended his career with the 4th Chasseurs and managed to start another career with the gendarmerie. Months after leaving the army, he heard a horse whinny as he passed through the city of Fontenay and he immediately recognized his older charger, Hants. Tears ran down the veteran's face as he stroked the muzzle of his comrade. Reynier and Hants had together sustained 36 wounds at Waterloo alone.[64]

Napoleonic Cavalry in Battle

An examination of Napoleonic cavalry in battle demonstrates how important horsemen were to victory. Cavalry was a battle-winning arm. The psychological aspects surrounding the all-important timing of cavalry action was absolutely critical. Practical issues of horses and horsemanship were also important to the performance of cavalry in battle and on campaign. Waterloo, the decisive battle of the Napoleonic wars, demonstrated all the capabilities and limitations of cavalry. The outcome of the battle was determined by the opponents skill at employing their cavalry.

Waterloo, 1815

Napoleon returned from exile on March 1, 1815 and quickly regained the loyalty of the French army. The French king Louis XVIII fled to Belgium. The allies mobilized armies to move against France as quickly as possible. Napoleon's plan was to inflict a quick and decisive defeat on an allied army, and then use the fact of that defeat as an advantage in negotiations with the other European powers. There were several allied armies in the field, but the two most dangerous were the Anglo-Dutch army under the duke of Wellington and the Prussian army under Gebhard Blücher. Individually, Napoleon's main French army of over 100,000 outnumbered either of the two allied armies by themselves. However, if the allies combined they would have the numerical advantage. Thus, it was critical to Napoleon's plan to keep the two armies separated.[65]

Napoleon marched north and divided his army into three components. Marshal Michel Ney commanded the left wing while Marshal Emmanuel Grouchy commanded the right wing. The largest component of the army was the reserve which Napoleon commanded himself. The campaign began on June 15, when Napoleon's troops crossed the Sambre River and attacked the forward positions of the Prussians.

On June 16 two battles were fought which set up the final confrontation of the armies at Waterloo two days later. The first battle was fought a Quatre Bras where Napoleon's left wing under Marshal Ney collided with the advance elements of Wellington's army. The French initially outnumbered the British, but Ney failed to attack aggressively. This allowed the British time to reinforce so that when Ney attacked in the afternoon, the two sides were evenly matched and he failed to make any progress. Meanwhile, the reserve and the right wing of the French army met the Prussians to the east of Quatre Bras at Ligny. Napoleon decisively defeated the Prussians, who lost more than 20,000 men and retreated. Blücher, commanding the Prussians, had his horse killed and was trapped under him. During his absence, with the battle lost, his chief of staff General August von Gneisenau ordered the army to retreat. However, instead of retreating east as expected, the Prussians retreated north to Wavre. This kept the Prussians within supporting distance of Wellington. This serendipitous move would ultimately decide the outcome of the battle of Waterloo.

As the Prussians retreated north on June 17, Napoleon dispatched Marshal Grouchy with the 30,000 men of the right wing to pursue them, and, most importantly, prevent them from marching to join Wellington. The Prussian retreat exposed Wellington's left flank, and so he too retreated north, moving to a defensive position he had previously reconnoitered fixed upon the ridgeline known as Mont St. Jean. Napoleon, with the reserve and the left wing under Ney, marched in pursuit of Wellington and encamped across the valley from Mont St. Jean on the evening of June 17. The Prussians were located 8 miles to the east at Wavre. A heavy rain drenched all three armies and thoroughly soaked the ground on the night of June 17.

When the French army reformed under Napoleon in March 1815, it only had 16,000 horses on the cavalry rolls. The army acquired horses quickly to bring the cavalry back up to a fighting strength. The regiments received 4,000 horses from the French gendarmerie to equip the heavy cavalry, farms using borrowed cavalry mounts provided another 5,000, and the army purchased 5,700. Though the men who made up the French cavalry in 1815 were almost exclusively veterans, most the horses upon which they were mounted were of marginal quality. British cavalry, in contact with French lancers after Quatre Bras, commented on the small size of the French horses. Napoleon found it much easier to rally experienced soldiers to his flag than acquire experienced remounts.

The French reconstituted the Cavalry Reserve for the Waterloo campaign, and it consisted of four corps: one light cavalry corps, one dragoon corps, and two heavy cavalry corps. The heavy cavalry corps were the IV Cavalry Corps consisting of eight regiments of cuirassiers, about 2,800 horsemen, and the III Cavalry Corps consisting of two regiments of dragoons, four regiments of cuirassiers, and the two elite regiments of the Carabinier brigade, numbering more than 3,500 troopers. Two batteries of horse artillery supported each of the corps.

Though veterans, the ranks of the French cavalry were riddled with distrust between those who returned to the colors to fight for Napoleon and those who had continued service under the king and then returned to Napoleon. This caused considerable indiscipline among the ranks. Many officers who had stayed in service for the king after Napoleon's initial abdication could not be sure their orders would be followed.

Leadership problems extended to key positions in the cavalry formations. Marshal Grouchy was initially to command the Cavalry Reserve but subsequently was assigned to command one of the army wings and was not replaced. Therefore, there was no overall Cavalry Reserve commander during the Waterloo campaign. Compounding the problem, General Kellermann took command of the III Cavalry Corps only 10 days before the battle.

Wellington's army consisted of approximately 60,000 troops of which about 20,000 were British. The remaining were a mixture of Dutch, Belgium, and Hanoverians. The cavalry component was approximately 14,000 of which approximately 6,000 were British.[66] Of the British cavalry, the light dragoons were mostly veterans of Spain, while most of the heavy cavalry had little or no previous experience. The British heavy cavalry formed two brigades. General Lord Edward Somerset commanded the Guards Cavalry Brigade consisting of the 1st and 2nd Regiments of the Life Guards, the Royal Horse Guards (the Blues), and the 1st (King's) Dragoon Guards, numbering 1,090 troopers. General Sir William Ponsonby led the Union Brigade with the 1st (Royal) Dragoons, 2nd (Scots Greys) Dragoons, and 6th (Inniskilling) Dragoons, totaling 1,181 men and horses.

Wellington was an expert at the defensive battle and deployed his forces using techniques that he had perfected during his operations in Spain. His defensive line was anchored on three strong points along a line running west to east: the Hougoumont complex of buildings and orchards on his right, western, flank; the center of the line included the farm of La Haye Sainte; and the left, eastern, flank was anchored on the village of Papelotte. The allies fortified all of these building complexes and occupied them with infantry. These three positions were all on the forward slopes of the Mont St. Jean ridge. The main Brussels road ran south to north through the center of the position just to the east of La Haye Sainte. At the top of the ridge was a hedge-lined road than ran its entire length from east to west. Wellington positioned the bulk of his artillery forward of these hedges. Most of the infantry and all of the allied cavalry were positioned to the rear of the road and hedges and on the northern, reverse slope, of the Mont St. Jean ridge. The allied cavalry deployed in reserve to the rear of the allied infantry. On the left flank north of Papelotte were four cavalry brigades: two British light brigades and two Hanoverian brigades. In the center were the two British heavy brigades backed up by three Dutch-Belgium heavy brigades. On the right flank behind Hougoumont were three light brigades made up of British and King's German Legion (KGL) hussars and light dragoons.

As Napoleon contemplated the Allied position he had few good options for attack. The hedges at the top of the ridge prevented good observation of the road and the troops along the crest and behind the ridge. Thus, he did not have good information on the disposition of the allied battle line, nor was he able to see and anticipate any allied maneuvering because the Mont St. Jean ridge masked allied movement from sight. In addition, time was an important factor. Napoleon knew that Blücher's Prussian army was somewhere to his right. He hoped that Grouchy could fix the Prussians, but he expected that eventually the Prussians would arrive to support Wellington. He had to defeat Wellington before that happened. Given this constraint, Napoleon could not maneuver Wellington out of his defensive position but had to accept battle on the terrain that Wellington chose. Further, he knew that any attack against the allied strong points would be very time-consuming and thus ruled out an attack at the flanks. This left him two options, a frontal attack against the allied center west of the Brussels road or a frontal attack against the allied center east of the Brussels road. Both attack avenues would be subject to enfilading fire from the allied strong points. Further complicating the planning was the fact that it had begun to rain the previous afternoon and had rained most of the night. The ground was soft and muddy, and this greatly effected the maneuver of men, horses, and artillery.

Napoleon's force organized into five major components: three infantry corps, I, II, and VI Corps; the Imperial Guard; and the Cavalry Reserve. General Honoré Reille's II Corps deployed on the left and Jean-Baptiste Drouet, Count d'Erlon's I Corps on the right. Napoleon chose to launch a diversionary attack at Hougoumont with the II Corps to indicate an effort to take Wellington's right flank. The intent was to draw reserves from the allied center. Once the center was weakened, I Corps would launch the main French attack east of the Brussels road between La Haye Sainte and Papelotte. Napoleon gave himself great flexibility by keeping a large reserve consisting of the Imperial Guard, Lobau's VI Corps, and the Cavalry Reserve.

The battle began at about 10:00 a.m. when the French infantry attacked Hougoumont. This diversionary attack soon developed into a major action. The French eventually committed almost all of the II Corps–15,000 infantry–but it had little effect on the allied dispositions and thus the diversion failed in its primary objective.

Napoleon delayed the main French attack until about 11:30 a.m. because of the difficulty of positioning heavy artillery over the soft ground. It began with a bombardment of the allied positions by the French massed artillery. This bombardment was unsuccessful because few of the allied positions were visible and the soft ground absorbed many of the cannon balls. At about 1:30 p.m. the Infantry of the French center, the four divisions of d'Erlon's I Corps, 18,000 infantry, attacked between La Haye Sainte and Papelotte. The left flank division surrounded La Haye Sainte, the right flank division captured Papelotte, and the center two divisions achieved the top of the ridge where they gained the ridge-top road and slowly began to push back the British infantry positioned there.

At this point two French cuirassier regiments (1st and 4th) of the IV Cavalry Corps' 1st Brigade, 13th Cavalry Division, commanded by General Baron Dubois, moved forward on d'Erlon's left flank and charged over the ridge. The timing of the French cavalry attack was perfect but did not account for the sunken road at the crest of the ridge. Just as the French cavalry hit their stride, they hit the road. The left regiment was unable to stop, and horses and riders tumbled into the road. The debacle at the road threw the entire regiment into confusion and destroyed the charge before it met the enemy. The right flank regiment was able to halt before the road and scramble across it. However, by the time they gained the far side all order was lost. It was then that they and d'Erlon's lead infantry spotted advancing British cavalry.

At this point the allied left center was in danger of collapsing. To reestablish the center Henry William Paget, the earl of Uxbridge and commander of the allied cavalry, ordered the two British heavy brigades to charge d'Erlon's infantry. The British cavalry attacked with Somerset's Guards Brigade on the right in two lines. The first line consisted of, from right to left, the 1st Life Guards, the King's Dragoon Guards, and the 2nd Life Guards. The second line was the Horse Guards. The Guards Brigade hit the French cuirassiers. The disorganized French were in no position to receive a cavalry charge. After a fierce but short melee the French cavalry broke and scattered to the rear. The British regiments carried on into the flank of d'Erlon's Corps already engaged by the Union Brigade.

The French infantry were organized in wide columns and not prepared for a cavalry attack. The British cavalry attacked with Somerset's Guards Brigade on the west side of the road and Ponsonby's Union brigade on the east side of the road. The plan was for the Union Brigade to attack with the 1st (Royal) Dragoons on the right and the 6th (Inniskilling) Dragoons on the left in the first line. The 2nd (Scots Greys) Dragoons would follow in the second line. However, as the charge developed the Scots Greys came on line with the other two regiments, and the Union brigade effectively charged with all three regiments in the first line and no reserve. As the British cavalry came up, several of the French battalions were able to get off volleys of musket fire but they were uncoordinated and not effective enough to deter the British cavalry. The three heavy cavalry regiments hit the center two French divisions. French Colonel Duthilt, fighting in the front ranks of the French infantry described the attack from the infantry perspective:

> Just as I was pushing one of my men back into the ranks I saw him fall at my feet from a sabre slash., I turned round instantly to see English cavalry forcing

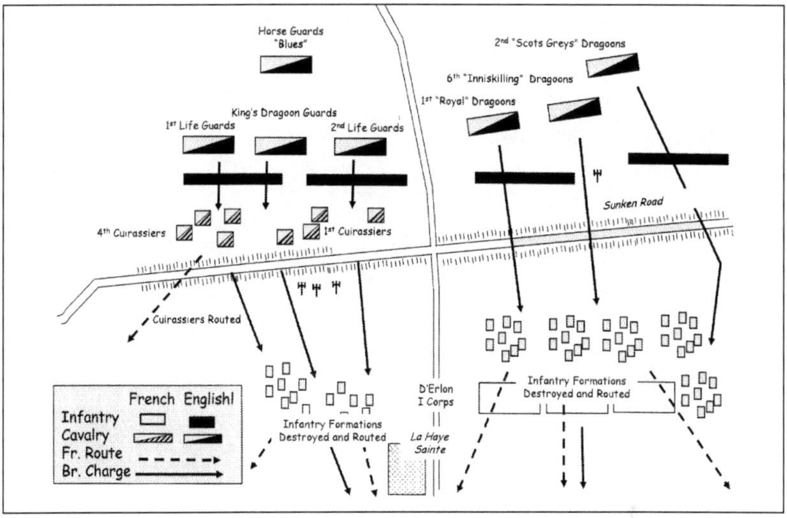

The battle of Waterloo, 1815, the charge of the British Heavy brigades.

> their way into our midst and hacking us to pieces. Just as it is difficult, if not impossible, for the best cavalry to break into infantry who are formed into squares and who defend themselves with coolness and daring, so its is true that once the ranks have been penetrated, then resistance is useless and nothing remains for the cavalry to do but to slaughter at almost no risk to themselves. This is what happened, in vain our poor fellows stood up and stretched out their arms; they could not reach far enough to bayonet these cavalrymen mounted on powerful horses, and the few shots fired in the chaotic melee were just as fatal to our own men as to the English. And so we found ourselves defenceless against a relentless enemy who, in the intoxication of battle, sabred even our drummers and fifers without mercy.[67]

In minutes the French battalion columns were destroyed and infantrymen were being sabered and run down as they fled the southern slope of the Mont St. Jean. The ferocity of the British attack became legend. Six-foot-four-inch tall Scots Greys Sergeant Charles Ewart described how he captured the eagle of the French 45th Regiment.

> It was in the charge I took the eagle from the enemy. He and I had a hard contest for it; he made a thrust at me groin, I parried it off and cut him down through the head. After this a lancer came at me; I threw the lance off by my right side, and cut him through the chin upwards through the teeth. Next a foot soldier fired at me, and then charged me with his bayonet, which I also had

> the good luck to parry, and then I cut him down through the head; thus ended the contest. As I was about to follow my regiment, the general said, "My brave fellow, take that to the rear; you have done enough till you get quit of it." I took the eagle to the ridge and afterwards to Brussels.[68]

The Union brigades' 1,100 horseman forced almost 10,000 infantry off the crest of the Mont St. Jean. British infantry followed closely behind the heavy cavalry and recaptured La Haye Sainte and Papelotte. In total the charge of the two heavy brigades, slightly more than 2,000 cavalrymen, completely routed the entire French II Corps of 18,000 men and the two cuirassier regiments. The exact number of casualties inflicted on the French was impossible to determine, but fully 3,000 prisoners were taken and the French corps temporarily ceased to exist as a fighting unit.

Had the charge of the heavy brigades ended at that point, it would have been the most successful cavalry action in the history of the British army. However, it did not. As the French infantry scattered, the six regiments found themselves at the base of the shallow valley south of Mont St. Jean. Barely 300 yards in front of them, and totally exposed, was Napoleon's grand artillery battery composed of some 70 guns. Without a thought to the disorganization that existed among the regiments, the larger tactical situation, or the possible danger of a countercharge, the heavy brigades continued the attack south, up the opposite slope of the valley, against the French guns.

The British cavalry, led by their officers, ignored the recall trumpets and continued the charge against Napoleon's grand battery. They achieved the artillery position with little trouble and then proceeded to saber the gunners, cut the traces of the horses, and in general wreaked havoc among the French. Napoleon, positioned only 300 yards south of the artillery, witnessed all the action. The cavalry put between 12 and 40 guns permanently out of action.

As the British cavalry finished their action on the battery position, they became aware that the valley behind them, their route back to their own positions, was filling with French cavalry. Two regiments of lancers and two regiments of cuirassiers had finally responded to the British threat and were rapidly closing a trap behind the heavy brigades. The British were totally disorganized, squadrons of the various regiments were intermingled, and their horses were exhausted. Under these conditions, they were no match for the French. The only British regiment with some organization left was the Royal Horse Guards of the Guards brigade. The 200 troopers of the Horse Guards were the supporting line of the Guards brigade charge and were in a position to engage the French cavalry. With the help of the Horse Guards, much of Somerset's heavy brigade was able to escape back to the British lines. The Union Brigade was not as fortunate. Because the Scots Greys became intermingled with the

Initial Charge of the British Guards Brigade at Waterloo. Three regiments of the brigade drove off French cuirassiers before plunging into and routing the French I Infantry Corps. This charge destroyed the most serious French attack of the day. (*Cavalry Journal* [British])

first line, no support existed for the Union Brigade. Thus the French cavalry caught the entire brigade disorganized and on tired horses. Knee-deep mud further inhibited the British retreat. The retreat of the Union brigade was every man for himself, and many did not make it. French lancers, on fresh horses, easily rode down the retreating British, and their 9-foot lances were the ideal weapon to attack the backs of the fleeing British. The complete destruction of the Union Brigade was only averted by the charge of General John Vandeleur's light cavalry brigade (the 11th, 12th, and 16th Light Dragoons), which forced the French cavalry to break off their pursuit of the Union Brigade.

The two British heavy brigades suffered severe casualties during their charge. The bulk of the losses came during the retreat from the French artillery position. Three of seven regimental commanders were killed, as was Ponsonby. In the Scots Greys only 8 of 23 officers were not killed or wounded. The Union Brigade suffered 525 killed, wounded, or missing out of 1,181 engaged. The Guards Brigade suffered 533 casualties out of 1,226 engaged. Though both brigades eventually reformed and remained in reserve for the rest of the battle, having suffered 44 percent casualties, they were unable to play an important role. Lord Uxbridge, the British cavalry commander, admitted that the major fault of the attack was that he placed himself at the head of the charge and thus lost control. Subsequently he stated that he should have positioned himself with the second line so that he could control their commitment and effect the tempo of the attack. The overaggressiveness of the Scots Greys also cost the Union Brigade the support they needed to disengage after the charge. Still, despite the disorganization and the casualties suffered as a result, the charge of the British heavy brigades had accomplished a great deal. d'Erlon's attack was the French's best opportunity for success at Waterloo. The repulse of the French I Corps severely complicated the tactical situation for Napoleon and left him in a disadvantageous position with only a limited number of options for the further conduct of the battle.

As Count d'Erlon's attack failed at the crest of Mont St. Jean, word came that the Blücher Prussians were approaching the French right flank. Grouchy, despite having two of Napoleon's five infantry corps, and almost two complete cavalry corps, had failed to fix Blücher in position. With the arrival of Blücher at Waterloo, the numerical advantage shifted to the allies. This forced Napoleon to dispatch Lobau's VI Corps from his reserve to meet the threat in the east. This left Napoleon with only the two heavy cavalry corps and the Imperial Guard in reserve.

The retreat of the British cavalry left the two armies facing each other across the small valley south of Mont St. Jean in almost the same positions from which the battle had begun. Except now the battlefield was confused by smoke, mud, thousands of dead and wounded bodies, and the flotsam of riderless horses and limping retreating soldiers. In this confused pause, Marshal Ney, Napoleon's tactical commander at Waterloo, perceived what he thought was the retreat of the British army. In reality what he saw was wounded and stragglers moving to the rear. Given this false impression, Ney made the first of several bad decisions and decided that the time had come to commit the cavalry reserve. Around 4:00 p.m. Ney gave orders for a brigade of cuirassiers from the IV Cavalry Corps to advance.

The French cavalry reserve arrayed with the III Cavalry Corps to the rear of the left of the line and the IV Cavalry Corps to the right of the Brussels road to the rear of I Corps. The Guard cavalry positioned with regiments behind the two cavalry corps. When Ney ordered one of IV Corps' brigades forward General Baron Jacques Delort, the 14th Cavalry Division commander, protested the order. Delort pointed out that the British infantry were in a good position and unshaken. In response Ney, whose judgment seemed to have abandoned him, ordered not only the original brigade forward but the entire corps "Forward for the sake of France!" Thus, with reluctance, the Corps Commander, General Edouard Milhaud ordered the almost 3,000 troopers of the IV Cavalry Corps to attack.

The grand spectacle of the French cavalry attacking up the slope of Mont St. Jean was inspiring. Michel Ordener, commander of the 1st Cuirassiers saw "Our four superb lines were practically fresh; they moved simultaneously to cries of Vive l'Empereur! . . . Marshal Ney was at our head." However, the spectacle lost its grandeur upon closer inspection. Troopers fought to keep their horses aligned as they struggled over ground strewn with the debris of battle and churned into a quagmire by the previous trampling of tens of thousands of men and horses. In some places the mud came to the horses' knees. British dragoon Sergeant George Farmer described the ground conditions after the rainfall had soaked the fields: "Every few steps you took, you sank to your knees, and your foot, when you dragged it to the surface again, came loaded with some twenty pounds of clay."[69] In such conditions the mud sucked the shoes off the horse's feet, and any stumble resulted in a down horse and rider. Managing a trot uphill was a major accomplishment. The French lines began coming apart and units intermingled before the cavalry formations were halfway up the slope. By the time the cavalry reached the crest of the hill they had covered a mile of ground, and many of the horses were already blown. Still, they had not yet reached the enemy positions.

As the mass of French cavalry crested the ridge the allied artillery positioned there blasted them at close range. The artillery, firing a double shot of round shot and canister, tore huge wholes in the lead formations. They were impossible to miss. The artillerymen then dashed to the safety of the British squares or hid under their guns, which provided cover from both horse and saber.

Reeling from the blast of artillery, the French cavalry next confronted a checkerboard of infantry squares arrayed across the reverse slope of the ridge. The mass of cavalrymen surged toward the squares and flowed around them moving at a steady trot. There was no impact on the squares, which methodically began to take down huge swathes of riders and horses with musket volleys at point-blank range. At this point the helpless French cavalry faced short sharp charges from the numerous allied light cavalry brigades stationed in support of the infantry squares. Allied infantry literally surrounded the disorganized French cavalry who were taking musket fire from all directions. Under these conditions what was left of unit cohesion disintegrated. The French were easy victims for the allied light cavalry, which stayed under good command and forced the French off the ridge without pursuing them.

The French cavalry fell back to the base of the hill and reformed. Under the courageous command of the French officers, the regiments reassembled and attacked again. The previous sequence of events was repeated. The carnage was even greater as many of the French horses could barely walk and the French riders were literally helpless as they absorbed the fire from the allied infantry and artillery. The bodies of French horses formed ramparts around the British squares further impeding the French attack. Once again the countercharge of the allied cavalry easily pushed the French off the ridge.

After two charges, the IV Cavalry Corps and its eight regiments of cuirassiers was shattered. At this point Marshal Ney determined to launch General

Kellermann's III Cavalry Corps into the same death trap that had destroyed Milhaud's corps. Marshal Ney was reinforcing failure–a violation of basic tactical principles. Kellermann's corps moved off to the attack between Hougoumont and La Haye Saint. The Imperial Guard cavalry, positioned behind the III Corps, also moved into the attack with the cuirassiers.

Kellermann's charge was a repeat of that of Milhaud's. The French cavalry arrived at the British positions exhausted and disordered and then were butchered by allied musket and cannon fire. Kellermann's squadrons reformed and attacked five times. Despite Kellermann's efforts to hold back the Carabinier Brigade as a reserve, Marshal Ney committed all of remaining mounted formations to the attack, and they were all equally unsuccessful and suffered horrendous casualties. Many of the regiments were totally broken in the cavalry attacks while others only survived as handfuls of men and horses gathered around a few officers.

The failure of the French cavalry attack wasted the French cavalry, and it also wasted valuable time. The attacks had been a reprieve to the allied center because during the cavalry attacks the French artillery had been unable to fire. The artillery had been doing steady damage to the allied infantry all afternoon, and the infantry actually welcomed the French cavalry attacks because they were much less damaging than the artillery fire. As the hapless cavalry attacked the Mont St. Jean positions, the Prussian army arrived and steadily pushed back the French right flank. This forced Napoleon to move major portions of his Imperial Guard infantry to the right flank to prevent a total disaster from occurring. Thus, by the time the French cavalry failure became apparent, much of the Imperial Guard infantry reserve was committed to the right flank. The critical point in the battle had come, and the French reserve had dwindled to the battalions of the Old Guard–the most distinguished veterans of the Imperial Guard. When these elite troops were pushed up the bloody ridge late in the day and then decimated by allied artillery and musket fire, the battle was lost. A few battalions and squadrons of Imperial Guard infantry and cavalry bought enough time for Napoleon to flee, but the destruction of the Old Guard broke the back of the remaining French infantry formations who crumbled as Wellington ordered a general advance of the allied line and the Prussians enveloped the French right flank. Waterloo was a battle that was Napoleon's to win until the final hours when the ally's numbers and persistence overcame the valor of French arms.

The cavalry actions were critical to both the allied victory and the French defeat. The perfect timing and aggressiveness of the charge of the British heavy brigades during the early afternoon saved the allied center. The decisive defeat of d'Erlon's corps by the two British brigades totally upset the French plan and changed the dynamics of the battle. It destroyed the French of infantry in the center, the sector that

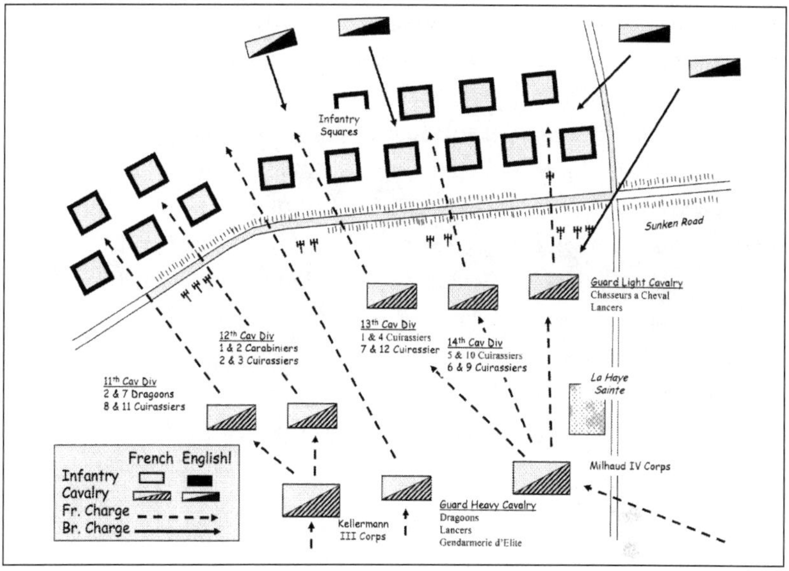

The battle of Waterloo, 1815, the charge of the French Cavalry reserve.

Napoleon had chosen as the main effort. Ney's attempt to continue to attack the allied center with cavalry alone was a demonstration of total tactical incompetence. The ground and the deployment of forces all worked against the prosecution of an effective attack. Most important, there was no chance of creating the psychological conditions required for really effective cavalry action. The failed French cavalry attacks by almost 10,000 horsemen, contrasted with the success of 2,000 British cavalry, demonstrated that numbers alone were only a small element in the complex mixture that included psychology, speed, surprise, aggressiveness, and mass necessary for success. Of the two primary French commanders, Ney and Napoleon, neither developed a feel for the pulse of battle at Waterloo necessary to accurately recognize the window of opportunity when the decisive cavalry charge could win the day. Ney violated Napoleon's own maximums for the use of cavalry by employing them in frontal attacks against unbroken infantry and without close infantry or artillery support.

Cavalry reached the height of its influence on battle during the period of the Napoleonic wars. Commanders understood that employment of cavalry at the proper moment could achieve decisive battle-winning results. Because of this, and despite the considerable investment of time and expense, the total numbers of cavalry during the Napoleonic period were huge.

Although cavalry was a battle-winning arm, success required that an expert employ it. Inattention to basic horse mastership could have devastating impacts on a campaign. More important, successful employment of cavalry required an intuitive understanding of the complex material and psychological effects of battle. Timing was key to cavalry's success and required a professional understanding of movement rates, terrain effects, and horsemanship, as well as a feel for the morale of both the friendly and enemy forces. Austrian cavalry, though highly competent throughout the Napoleonic period, rarely had significant battlefield success because the Austrians lacked commanders who could employ the well-trained cavalry effectively. Commanders such as Kellermann of France and Uxbridge of England were worth dozens of regiments in combat.

The French army was the premier army of the period against which all others were measured. Its cavalry served as a similar yardstick. The French army historian John Etling paraphrased Archduke Charles of Austria's accurate summary of the quality of French cavalry: "The French cavalry was, on the whole, poorly mounted and poorly equipped; its men were awkward horsemen. Yet it outclassed its opponent simply because, when the order ran and the trumpets clarioned 'Charge!' it put in its spurs and charged all out, charged home!"[70] This critique is generally accurate but overstates French horsemanship, which was rarely well developed enough to charge at the gallop. Still, the archduke does capture the essence of cavalry in the Napoleonic period. What was most important about cavalry in combat was that it could win battles if properly employed. The Napoleonic era was the last era in which cavalry could make such a general claim of importance.

Chapter Eight

INDUSTRIAL WAR AND CAVALRY

There is many a war-horse who is more entitled to immortality than the man who rides him.–General Robert E. Lee

Professional military men only slowly recognized the changes in warfare that followed the Napoleonic period. A relatively long peace followed the 1815 Congress of Vienna and the Treaty of Paris. Armies studied the slowly emerging new technologies, but few had an immediate major military impact. These technologies included the railroad–the first rail lines opened in England in 1825, the telegraph–first successfully set up and used in 1844, and the steam engine adapted to ocean shipping in 1818. Two of the most significant purely military developments were the rifled musket, which first went into service in the early 1850s, and the breechloading rifle, which was issued to troops in Prussia in the early 1840s. After midcentury, several small-scale European conflicts hinted at the changing nature of war: the Crimean War (1853–56), the Italian wars of independence (1848–49; 1859), the wars of German unification (1864; 1866), and the Franco-Prussian War (1870–71), but none of them were long enough or large enough to truly demonstrate how significantly warfare had changed. The American Civil War (1861–65) demonstrated the full impact of new technologies on the conduct of war at all levels, tactical through strategic. Unfortunately, except for a few observers, European armies ignored the American Civil War. However, that ignorance does not distract from the Civil War's importance as a benchmark in military history.

The American Civil War

The American Civil War was the first war where the *levee en masse* and nationalism of the Napoleonic period combined with the science of the industrial revolution. The physical scope and dimensions of this war rivaled anything fought on the European continent including the Napoleonic wars themselves. The two adversaries fielded armies numbering more than a million combatants, and the theater of operations was of continental dimensions. Despite the size of the war, the fact that it was thousands of miles from Europe, had mostly regional and domestic implications, and was fought by armies that were raised through a combination of volunteers and conscription, caused many European military professionals to dismiss it as unworthy of serious study. Additionally, within a year Europeans had their own war, the Austro-Prussian War of 1866 to study. Thus, Europeans did not seriously study many unique aspects of Civil War operations which indicated future trends, including those relating to cavalry.

The Rifle Musket

Among the important new technologies that effected tactical warfare in the American Civil War was the rifle musket. The rifle musket entered service in a variety of armies in the 1850s. Though hailed as a major leap forward in technology, superficially it did not appear to be much different from the smooth bore musket. The drill and loading procedures for the rifle musket were very similar to those of the smooth bore. The rate of fire of the two weapons was not radically different. The dramatic difference was the range of the weapon. The French issued one of the first rifle muskets, the Minié rifle, to elite French infantry units in 1846. It had a range beyond 1000 yards and was effectively accurate out to at least 600 yards. By 1857, the French army was converting all smooth bore muskets to the new Minié design. The British adopted the Enfield rifled musket in 1853. It was effective out to 900 yards. The United States followed with a knockoff of the Enfield design called the Springfield rifle in the late 1850s.[1] Many military thinkers believed that the new rifle would completely change the tactics of warfare.

Cavalry in the American Civil War

Cavalry was an important part of both the Northern and Southern forces in the American Civil War. In many ways, the relative performance of the opposing cavalry was a microcosm of the general conduct of the war. At the beginning of the war, Union cavalry was neglected, poorly trained, and hardly a combat force worth mentioning. Southern cavalry, on the other hand, was the pride of the army, well led, and an important part of the Southern war machine. Just as 1863 marked a changing point in the war in general, it also was a watershed in the relative performance of the cavalry forces. Union cavalry were reorganized, found new leadership, received the latest equipment, and individually were more competent horsemen. At the same time, the strains of resource shortages and leadership lapses began to tell on the Southern cavalry.

Organization

Though the Union army possessed a regular army cavalry force of six regiments when the war began, these units were widely scattered and in no position to provide a basis for building a robust cavalry force. Resources to organize a Union volunteer cavalry forces, however, were not lacking. At the end of the first year of the war, on December 31, 1861, the cavalry strength of the Union army was 4,744 regulars and 54,654 volunteers. By the last year of the war, in February 1865, the total strength of the Union cavalry arm was 160,237 men of which 105,434 were present and fit for duty. The size of the cavalry forces in the Civil War rivaled any force seen in Europe.[2]

A Union cavalry regiment organized into 12 companies. Two companies, commanded by the senior company commander, constituted a squadron. Two squadrons made up a battalion commanded by a major. A colonel, assisted by a lieutenant colonel, commanded the three battalions of the Union regiment. At the beginning of the war, the Union army assigned cavalry by individual regiments, and sometimes even companies, to infantry divisions and corps. This dispersed organization prevented the Northern cavalry from making significant contributions to battle early in the war. In 1863, the Army of the Potomac formed its own cavalry corps, bringing the cavalry regiments together into brigades (of four regiments) and divisions (of two or three brigades) where they could operate in mass. By the summer of 1863, Union cavalry in the east, organized into a large cavalry corps, was very capable of independent operations. From 1863 on, cavalry on cavalry combat, mounted and dismounted, became much more common, and Union cavalry quickly demonstrated its superiority in these deliberate engagements.[3]

Southern cavalry typically, though there were many exceptions, organized in a 10-company regiment. The regiment included only three field grade officers and did not break down easily into squadrons. Thus, company grade officers and the company organization was the most important and cohesive. This resulted in a more decentralized approach to operations in Southern regiments.[4]

Weapons and Equipment

Because the cavalry forces of the Union and of the South were primarily volunteer forces, there was little inherent tradition operating on the forces. If there was any uniquely American mounted military tradition, it was a tradition of the mounted rifleman and dragoon. Because they were free of preconceptions of cavalry, American cavalry were more flexible in terms of incorporating new weapons and tactics into the force than cavalry forces in Europe.

Though the Union forces, including the cavalry, were lavishly equipped, the Union did not master the ability to get the right weapons into the hands of the right troopers until well into the war. The ability to equip the Union cavalry with the proper weapons in the numbers required was achieved in 1863 and was one of the reasons that the effectiveness of Union cavalry increased dramatically in that year. It cost between $500,000 and $600,000 to equip a single Union cavalry regiment.[5] The fact that the Union was able to field well over a hundred regiments demonstrates the abundant resources ultimately available once the North fully mobilized its industrial capability and organized its administration. It also demonstrates the investment Union leaders were willing to make in a robust cavalry force.

Southern cavalry, from the start, operated at a major equipment disadvantage. Southern cavalry came to war with a variety of personal weapons including muskets, double-barreled shotguns, pistols, fowling pieces, carbines, and sabers. Efforts to manufacture pistols, carbines, and sabers in the South were generally unsuccessful. Southern-produced weapons were inferior to Northern products and were often dangerous to the trooper. In mid-1864, a Southern commander commented, "nearly all my men were armed with captured arms." The government first discouraged this practice but eventually embraced it to the point that Southern munitions factories made ammunition for Union weapons.[6] A mixture of weapons within Southern cavalry regiments was the norm–some captured from the enemy, some government issued, and some brought from home. This resulted in huge, almost insurmountable problems of ammunition resupply.

Two weapons appeared during the American Civil War that made a mark on American cavalry and differentiated it from European cavalry until the end of the century. The two weapons were the revolver and the carbine. The revolver became a standard piece of individual equipment in the Civil War cavalry forces. In Union forces it supplemented the saber, while in the case of the Southern cavalry, it ended up replacing the saber in most cases. The carbine became the standard dismounted weapon of Civil War Union cavalry, and in some leaders minds, it also came to represent the cavalry's primary role in battle.

The pistol had been a standard arm of American cavalry since the formation of the first regular dragoon regiment in 1833. Samuel Colt developed the most effective version of the revolving cylinder pistol–the revolver. In 1854, the Colt .36-caliber model 1851 navy revolver replaced the single-shot 1842 pistol in the American army. The U.S. cavalry discarded the saddle holster, and troopers carried the weapon in a holster on their belt. By the time of the Civil War, the model 1860 Colt army .44-caliber revolver was the most popular pistol with the troopers. The army issued over 145,000 Colt army revolvers during the war. They also issued 130,000 of the popular Remington .44-caliber army revolvers.[7]

Revolvers were exceptionally easy to use while mounted, and it was relatively easy to switch between sword and pistol. The acceptance of the pistol by the

American cavalry resulted in a tactic known as the "pistol charge" in which cavalry attacked with drawn pistols. The tactic became a unique characteristic of American cavalry never copied by Europeans. In a charge, the pistol was a simple and effective way to engage the enemy. It took almost no training to get an individual to be competent with the revolver. At Murfreesboro, Tennessee, the Southern cavalry brigade of the Army of Tennessee, under General John A. Wharton, charged Union cavalry relying almost exclusively on pistols. In minutes, the 2,000 Southern troopers routed the Union force.[8] Some Southern cavalry, Texas cavalry in particular, relied almost exclusively on the revolver for their combat power. Many, especially rank-and-file Southern cavalrymen, considered the revolver far superior to the saber. The major shortcoming of the revolver was the difficulty of reloading while riding. It was a paper-wrapped cartridge weapon, the six cartridges, along with percussion caps, required careful loading into the revolver cylinder. The complicated loading system prevented reloading the weapon while riding. The Remington pistols had an advantage over the Colts because extra cylinders could be preloaded and the entire cylinder exchanged fairly easily while mounted. However, since the cylinder contained six shots, reloading was not a major drawback. Another disadvantage of the revolvers was their expense. A pistol cost the army from $14 to $20.

A Union cavalryman armed with a saber and a French LeFaucheux revolver. American cavalry fully embraced the revolver as an important cavalry weapon and continued to make pistols standard issue until cavalry disbanded in the twentieth century. Interestingly, European cavalry never adopted the pistol as a standard weapon. (*Charles G. Worman*)

The Union cavalry were armed with the Model 1860 light cavalry saber. By the end of the war, the Union had a very powerful affection for the saber and respected its effectiveness in the melee. Most Northern officers were adamant that the weapon gave the Northern cavalry a decisive superiority over the South in the cavalry melee. Southern cavalrymen were not fond of sabers. They considered it a terror weapon. Former regular army Southern commanders such as Stuart disagreed with this sen-

Two of the most important breechloading carbines of the American Civil War were the Sharps (top) and the Spencer (below). The Spencer with its seven-shot magazine was the first successful repeating firearm manufactured in quantity. Both carbines were readily adopted by cavalry and proved particularly effective during dismounted action. (*John Kuhl*)

timent but were unable to override the prejudice of their troops.[9] Sabers, regardless of the weapon's actual effectiveness, had a psychological effect, particularly if one side had them and the other did not.

Though commanders on both sides of the conflict disagreed on the various merits of the pistol and the saber, there was almost no disagreement on the effectiveness of the new breechloading carbines. The breechloading carbine became the Civil War cavalryman's most important weapon, particularly among the Union cavalry. The Union cavalry issued a variety of carbines–in total 32 different types.[10] However, two types had the greatest success and became standard issue in the North: the Sharps and the Spencer. Modern firing tests demonstrated that the Sharps carbine was extremely accurate at 100 yards and effective out to 200 yards. The Spencer, less accurate than the Sharps, was only highly accurate at 50 yards and effective to about 100 yards.[11]

The simplest, most reliable, and the most available carbine in the early years of the war were the various models of the Sharps breechloading carbine. By 1865, the Sharps Company had delivered 77,330 carbines to the government. The Sharps used paper cartridges and still required manually emplacing a percussion cap to ignite the cartridge. The carbine was a .52-caliber weapon; it weighed 7 3/4 pounds and was 39 inches long.[12]

The most numerous and popular of the Civil War carbines was the Spencer seven-shot repeater. General James H. Wilson, a successful of Union cavalry leader and advocate of repeating arms, said that with the Spencer carbine "Green regiments, that you couldn't have driven into a fight with the old arms, became invincible." The basis of the Spencer design was a spring tension seven-round tube magazine. This magazine inserted into the butt of the weapon. When the trigger guard of the weapon was levered, it ejected the spent round in the chamber and opened the breech, allowing the spring to push a fresh round into the chamber. Closing the lever sealed the chamber. After cocking the hammer manually, the carbine was ready to fire. The Spencer fired a .52-caliber metallic cartridge and did not require percussion caps. A Spencer carbine-armed trooper could maintain a sustained rate of fire of 14 or 15 aimed shots per minute. In an emergency, a trooper could fire the seven rounds in the magazine in 10 seconds or less, but at that rate of fire the barrel would get too hot to hold. It was a heavier weapon than the Sharps, weighing 8 1/4 pounds empty and was the standard carbine length of 39 inches. The government purchased 95,181 Spencers, and it became the most popular weapon of the Union cavalry by the end of the war.[13]

Carbines of any sort were rare among Southern cavalry throughout the war. Many Southern leaders felt that the double-barrel shotgun was a suitable solution to the problem of insufficient carbines for the cavalry. Cavalry leader Nathan Bedford Forrest believed the shotgun was the "best gun" for cavalry. The Southern Secretary of War, J.P. Benjamin, stated the double-barreled shotgun was an acceptable cavalry weapon and that sabers were not necessary: "after a month or two sabers are universally discarded as useless, men not being thoroughly trained to the use of that arm."[14]

Both the North and the South experimented with lances. The 6th Pennsylvania cavalry equipped with the weapon in the spring of 1862 and were known as "Rush's Lancers." However, the weapon required too much skill, was unsuited to carrying through wooded terrain, and was too specialized for great utility. By May 1863, the lances were retired. The Southern cavalry also experimented with lances. The attraction of the lance to the South was the ease and lack of expense associated with its manufacture. The 5th Virginia Cavalry received lances as a trial but quickly found the weapon to be unmanageable.[15]

Tactics

American cavalry contributed to operations in three ways. The first was through the traditional role of reconnaissance and security duties. The second way was through contributions to the main battle both in a mounted and dismounted role. The final contribution of cavalry was through independent cavalry operations–cavalry raids–that caused disruption in the enemy's rear areas.

The Cavalry Charge

The general view of the charge in the American Civil War is that both sides rarely used the tactic. However, most analysis of the Civil War overstates the dearth of cavalry charges and misunderstands the reasons why the charge was not a more common tactic on Civil War battlefields. In the early years of the war, many leaders, including cavalry officers, reached the conclusion that the cavalry charge was an impractical tactic. An article in the *Scientific American* magazine in January 1862 criticized the expense and uselessness of the cavalry and called on the army to "get rid of this arm of service."[16] The basis of this analysis was the theoretical capability of the rifle musket and ignored both the actual capability of the rifle and the real-world dynamics of the cavalry charge.

As discussed in previous chapters, the cavalry charge was largely a psychological event. Under actual combat conditions the rifle musket's performance, though much better than the smooth bore musket, was not sufficient to stop a well-conducted cavalry charge. The immense psychological effect of a cavalry attack, plus the normal stresses of combat, effected the concentration necessary to aim the rifle musket for long-range accuracy. Even more detrimental to accurate fire was the speed of the cavalry charge. The speed of the cavalry once the charge began caused the range to the target to change rapidly and made accurate range estimation almost impossible. Accurate range estimation was essential for the rifle musket to hit the target. Thus, musket fire at anything but short range was problematic. At short range, 300 to 400 yards, cavalry at the gallop would be into the infantry line in less than a minute. Under these conditions, most infantry officers, faced with a cavalry attack, would choose to hold their fire for one effective volley once the cavalry got within extremely short range, probably less than 200 yards, when the trajectory of the round was not significant. Thus, despite its more effective long-range capability, infantry formations would likely only get to fire one, at most two, good volleys at charging cavalry. Thus, the dynamics of the cavalry charge were essentially unchanged between the Napoleonic period and the American Civil War.[17]

The fact remains, however, that American cavalry in the Civil War charged less often as part of the main battle than European cavalry did in previous conflicts. The reasons for this lie in circumstances other than the effectiveness of the rifle musket. Cavalry early in the war could not execute cavalry charges because of heavily wooded and fenced terrain, because of how it was organized, and because of its training. Later in the war, terrain was still a major inhibitor, but as training and organization improved, infantry developed the tactic of hasty fortification, which became an obstacle to cavalry attack.

The horsemanship of Civil War cavalry made executing the charge a risky venture regardless of the battlefield conditions. Trooper Henry R. Payne, of the 1st New Jersey Cavalry, described a saber charge he witnessed which ended in disaster.

> Pressing upon one another, strained to the utmost of their speed, the horses catch an infection of fear which rouses them to frenzy. The men, losing their places in the ranks, and all power of formation or hope of combined resistance, rush madly for some point of safety upon which it may be possible to rally. Each check in front makes the mass behind more dense and desperate, until horses and men are overthrown and ridden over, trampled on by others as helpless as themselves to rescue or to spare. The speed grows momentarily greater. Splashing through the pools of mud, breaking down fences, darting under trees, with clang of sabers and din of hoofs, officers wild with shame and rage, shouting themselves hoarse with unavailing curses, and the bullets of the enemy whistling shrilly overhead, the mingled mass sweeps on, until utter exhaustion stops them.[18]

The Union cavalrymen of the Civil War focused on mastering the basics of drill and were unable and uninterested in learning the advanced intricacies of the various tactics manuals available.[19] By the end of the war as horsemanship and drill improved, small-scale cavalry charges became more common, but the massed cavalry charge–a maneuver that challenged the best European professionals–was still not possible.

Southern individual horsemanship was superior to that found in the Union cavalry, at least in the first years of the war, but Confederate cavalry were even worse at drill than Union cavalry. Southern cavalry, though it operated in brigade and division strength, rarely trained or drilled at any level higher than regiment. This lack of training reduced the cavalry's ability to execute massed mounted operations effectively, especially charges. Austrian Cavalry officer Fitzgerald Ross observed Southern cavalry and stated that there was no time to train the cavalry in drill and use of the saber. He felt the terrain, forested and with many fences, precluded large-scale cavalry battle maneuver. He also believed that since Southern cavalrymen provided their own horse, they were overly protective of their mounts.[20]

Dismounted Cavalry

An unanticipated change in warfare was the importance of dismounted cavalry action. During the war, though not designated as dragoons, the American dragoon tradition was very much in evidence. Dismounted action by cavalry occurred on a scale never before seen in the history of mounted forces. Union cavalry, because of their training and weapons, were far superior to Southern cavalry once on the ground. Typically, three of every four cavalrymen would dismount and go into action with their carbines, while the fourth soldier held the horses. If the action needed more dismounts, tying the horses together in groups of 15 to 20 released additional men for the fight. A Union cavalryman, Frederick Whittaker, estimated that a unit could dismount and be in action in less than two minutes.[21] After 1863, the Union cavalry's ability to operate equally well, mounted or dismounted, made it an impressive highly mobile multifunctional combat force. Union cavalry were willing to dismount and storm fortified positions with their carbines. Southern cavalry, due to their lack of emphasis on dismounted drill and inferior weapons, were not very effective in a dismounted role.

The Cavalry Raid

Throughout the Civil War, bought sides used cavalry forces to attack deep into enemy rear areas. These raids served numerous operational and strategic purposes. They destroyed logistics capability and diverted resources away from the main battle areas. Raids provided a diversion that covered the movement of the main body of the army. At the strategic level, bold cavalry raids attracted public attention and were effective at raising friendly military and civilian morale while depressing the morale of the enemy. Raids were, however, risky operations, and more raids resulted in marginal gains or significant losses than noteworthy successes.

Horses and Horsemanship

At the time of the Civil War, scientific and controlled horse breeding did not exist on a large scale in the United States. Horses were judged in terms of very broad types. Neither army of the war had a particular type preference. Formal horsemanship also did not exist to any appreciable extent in the United States. Though the lack of a breeding program did not greatly inhibit the quality of horses or operations during the war, the general ignorance of the science and art of horse management and riding did–especially in the North.

Horses

In 1860, the horse population of the United States was the largest in the world. The census of 1860 counted 4,504,852 horses in the country and significantly most of them were concentrated in states and territories that remained under Union control. The United States was also rich in acreage for forage. Three-fourths to four-fifths of the cultivated acreage in New England and upper New York grew hay. The challenge was tapping into these abundant resources in an efficient manner. Late in 1861, the government set up a network of purchasing stations across the country, to which large and

Dismounted action with breech-loading repeating carbines was a decisive cavalry tactic developed during the American Civil War but ignored by European powers. Reenactors from the 2nd U.S. Cavalry represent Buford's cavalry force at an annual Gettysburg event. (*2nd U.S. Cavalry Reenactors*)

small horse dealers brought their horses for inspection by army officers and civilian employees. The horses were purchased for a set price that fluctuated between $150 and $185. The horse was the most expensive piece of cavalry equipment–pay for a Union cavalry private was $13 a month., while a new Spencer repeating carbine cost $25.[22]

In the first two years of the war, 1861 and 1862, the Army remount purchase system provided 284,000 remounts for a cavalry force of 60,000 troopers. The Army horse standards were clear: six years old, no less than 950 pounds, and no less than 15 hands tall. However, purchase agents often ignored these standards to the detriment of the mounted units. Corruption riddled the remount system. In one lot of 400 horses sold to the quartermaster in St. Louis in late 1861, five died within hours of the sale, and 300 others were smaller than the standard, lame, blind, or sick. A 1st New York Cavalry veteran observed, "in no other branch of the service has there been so much fraud, so much corruption, so much utter worthlessness." The establishment of the Cavalry Bureau in the fall of 1863, which among other duties oversaw the remount purchasing system, finally gained control of the problem of corruption.[23]

Horse Equipment

The horse equipment issued to the Union cavalry was generally of good quality and very functional. The bit used to control the horse was a curb bit. American cavalry would not adopt the double bridle, common in Europe, until the end of the century.

The McClellan saddle was very functional and remained the U.S. standard military saddle until the end of the horse cavalry era. It was used by the south whenever it could be captured from the enemy. (*2nd U.S. Cavalry Reenactors*)

The use of curb bits on horses not used to the bit, and with inexperienced riders, made the training of horses and riders difficult as most of the horses reacted adversely to the severe bit.[24] However, the requirements of military riding permitted no alternative.

Union cavalry used a saddle that was different from anything used in Europe. Its design was developed by Captain George B. McClellan (later to be Commander of the Army of the Potomac), and he claimed that it combined features of the Hungarian saddle he observed during his travels in Europe and features of a Mexican saddletree. Randy Steffen, an expert on American cavalry equipment, opined that McClellan's inspiration was really of domestic origin. Regardless of its inspiration, the unique "McClellan saddle," in different model forms, adopted in 1859 remained the standard U.S. cavalry saddle, and a unique characteristic of American cavalry, until the end of the horse era.

The saddle consisted of two wood sideboards connected by high wooden pommel and cantle arches. Rawhide covered the wood to strengthen it. Although generally considered a good saddle, the saddle's rawhide seat cracked after repeatedly getting wet and then drying. These cracks formed sharp hard raised edges on the seat that made the saddle extremely uncomfortable and often unserviceable. The Civil War model saddle also included side skirts riveted to the sidebars. Subsequent models, beginning in 1874, covered the tree with leather eliminating the cracking issue, and removed the side skirts based on recommendations from the field. The most distinguishing feature of the American McClellan saddle was that it did not have a covered seat between the sidebars. Instead, the sidebars were wide to support the weight of the trooper, and an open slot ran the length of the saddle between the cantle and pommel. Though the initial impression was that this would cause discomfort to the rider, in fact, no weight was born directly down the center of the saddle and the saddle with the slot in the center was not uncomfortable. Another uniquely American feature of the saddle was the use of leather hooded wooden stirrups, designed to protect the legs in thick underbrush, instead of the open iron stirrups common among European saddle designs.[25]

Union Cavalry reenactor on patrol. He rides the 1859 McClellan saddle, curb bit bridle, and is armed with a carbine and the light cavalry saber. It was often common practice to wear a halter with lead attached under the bridle as is the case here. This facilitated holding the horse during dismounted action without pulling on the bit with the reins. (*First Maine Cavalry Inc.*)

American Horsemanship

American cavalry prior to the American Civil War rode in a deep military seat as outlined in a manual titled *A System of Tactics, Adapted to the Organization of Dragoon Regiments*, published in 1841. This manual was almost a direct translation of the French *Regulations* of 1829. The emphasis of this manual was on the free movement of the horse and basic equitation. Collection of the horse and classical high school equitation was not a part of American cavalry training. The American military seat was similar to that practiced by European cavalry of the period. Unlike most European cavalry, however, American cavalry did not post to the trot.[26]

Southern cavalry did not have as large a training challenge because each trooper had to provide his own horse and therefore knew the basics of riding. A British observer, Lord Wolsley, commented that the Southern cavalrymen he observed "rode well, in which particular they present a striking contrast to the Northern cavalry, who can scarcely sit their horses, even when trotting. . . . Every man in the South rides from childhood."[27]

The Union army built "Camps of Instruction" to organize, train, and equip recruits. At these camps the army issued uniforms, weapons, and horses. Officers formed individual recruits and companies of recruits into regiments. Noncommissioned officers taught the recruit how to care for the horse and tack, dismounted drill, how to ride, and finally mounted drill. Trained instructors were always in short supply and the NCOs who supervised the training were often only a day ahead of the recruit learning the task.[28] The collective low level of training of both horses and riders was demonstrated by a mounted review by the 7th Indiana Cavalry for the state governor in the fall of 1861. What occurred, as related by the unit historian, happened numerous times in many regiments throughout the Union cavalry in the first years of the war:

> The horses having been but recently drawn, had never been exercised in drill. Some of them had never been backed. . . . The men were as green as the horses. Some of them never having been on a horse's back, did not know how to mount. Those who had wild steeds, had great difficulty in maintaining their positions in the saddle, and some in attempting to mount suddenly found themselves on the ground. However, after great effort, the horses were sufficiently quieted, so as to stand in reasonable proximity to each other. The hour having arrived for the review, the companies were marched to the parade ground, and the regiment, after long and patient effort, formed in a reasonably straight line. Governor Morton and his Staff, accompanied by Colonel Shanks, took their positions in front of the regiment. Colonel Shanks, in genuine military style, gave the command "Draw Sabres." The men obeyed the order. The sabres in being drawn made a great rattling and clatter, and waved over the horse's heads, the sight and sound of which greatly frightened them. This was more than they could bear. Some of them reared and plunged, depositing their riders on the ground; others darted over the commons, their riders hatless, holding on with both hands to the horses' manes, or the pommels of their saddles, presenting pictures not in keeping with accomplished equestrianism. . . . So ended the first grand review of the regiment.[29]

President Lincoln witnessed the sorry state of the cavalry himself at a presentation of colors to the 2nd New York Cavalry when an infantry unit set off the regiment's horses, which went "kicking, plunging and falling over the field, to the great amusement of the crowd."[30] It took two years before the Union cavalry developed even a general mediocre level of horsemanship.

Good horse management was just as important if not more, as good riding skills. Effective horse management was the exception among Union forces rather than the rule. The best units were the six experienced regular cavalry regiments, and the 3rd Indiana Cavalry–the only volunteer unit in which the troopers supplied their own horses. In the early years of the war, ignorance at all levels of command led to the negligent if not cruel treatment of Union army horses. Plentiful remounts contributed to the general lack of emphasis on horse care. Horses were overworked, poorly shod, ungroomed, and often underfed and unwatered. Throughout the war hundreds of thousands of horses were lost due to neglect or mistreatment.[31]

American Cavalry In Battle: the Gettysburg Campaign

Cavalry in the Gettysburg campaign represents most, if not all, of the major characteristics of cavalry employment in the American Civil War. In the summer of 1863 General Robert E. Lee, commander of the Army of Northern Virginia, determined that he could only change the strategic situation by embarking on a bold offensive into Union territory. His intent was to move his army into Pennsylvania and bring the war home to the Union's civilian population.[32]

Lee's first problem in the campaign was to get his army on the move and into Pennsylvania without alerting the Army of the Potomac. This required that he march his army unobserved. Lee assigned the task of preventing the Union army from observing the march of Lee's corps into Pennsylvania to his cavalry under the command of General Stuart. General Alfred Pleasonton and the Army of Potomac Cavalry Corps had the task of ensuring that the Northern army was aware of Lee's location at all times. Thus, from the initial opening of the campaign, the relative performance of the two cavalry corps was critical to the success of their armies.

Lee's army was initially positioned around Culpeper, Virginia, south of Brandy Station. Hooker positioned the Union army near Fredericksburg between Lee and Washington, D. C. Lee began moving his army on June 10, the day after the inconclusive cavalry battle at Brandy Station. The II Corps, under General Richard Ewell, was the first to move. This move was completely undetected by Union cavalry. The Confederate plan called for the army to move northwest into the Shenandoah Valley, and then north across the Potomac River, through Maryland, and into Pennsylvania. On June 14, two of Ewell's divisions captured Winchester and cleared Union forces from the valley. The next day, June 15, Ewell's lead division, led by the corps' attached cavalry brigade under General Albert Jenkins, crossed the Potomac into Maryland.

General Hooker realized almost immediately that Lee was moving but did not know where or for what purpose. On June 17, Hooker gave specific orders to General Pleasonton to move the Union Cavalry Corps across the Blue Ridge Mountains and into the Shenandoah Valley to locate Lee's army: "[The] commanding general relies upon you with your cavalry force to give him information of where the enemy is, his force and his movements. You have sufficient cavalry force to do this. Drive in . . . [his] pickets, if necessary, and get us information. It is better that we should lose men than to be without knowledge of the enemy, as we now seem to be . . . the general directs that you leave nothing undone to give him the fullest information."[33] On that same day, Stuart's cavalry began to occupy blocking positions in the towns and villages approaching the gaps across the Blue Ridge. Stuart's mission was to prevent the Union cavalry from observing into the valley. Pleasonton's cavalry would have to fight through Stuart to get the information Hooker needed.

Over the four days, June 17 to 21, Pleasonton's two divisions, numbering over 6,500 troopers, and Stuart's five brigades of cavalry fought a running battle all along the approaches to the Blue Ridge. Pleasonton's two divisions were commanded by General John Buford (1st Division) and General David Gregg (2nd Division). Stuart's cavalry division consisted of six brigades named after their brigade commanders: Wade Hampton, Fitzhugh Lee, Albert Jenkins, John Chambliss, Beverly Robertson, and William E. Jones.

The first encounter took place on the afternoon of June 17, at the town of Aldie, between Judson Kilpatrick's Brigade of Gregg's Division, and Fitzhugh Lee's Brigade temporary commanded by Colonel Thomas Munford. Advancing Union cavalry came upon Southern pickets and immediately charged and drove them through the town. With the town in the possession of Kilpatrick's force, the Federals realized that Munford's five regiments outnumbered their four regiments. Munford's troopers set up a position west of the town that controlled the road leading from it. They then charged with two regiments and drove back Kilpatrick's right flank regiment, the 1st Massachusetts. Kilpatrick ordered the 4th New York Cavalry to countercharge but the unit routed before the charge had barely begun and streamed to the rear. To restore the situation, Kilpatrick borrowed the 1st Maine Cavalry from J. Irwin Gregg's brigade, which was following his, and led them in a countercharge. Kilpatrick's horse was shot out from under him, but the 1st Maine pushed the two Confederate regiments back and reestablished the position. Kilpatrick then took the offensive and led the 1st Maine and the 1st Massachusetts in a charge against the Confederate left. However, the Southern cavalry prepared for the attack by hiding sharpshooters in a ditch just off the turnpike that the Union cavalry charged down. The sharpshooters waited until most of the lead regiment, the 1st Massachusetts, passed and then rose up and raked the rear and flank of the regiment with point-blank rifle fire. The rifle fire decimated the regiment, causing 167 casualties in the 300-man unit. However, the 1st Maine was far enough back to avoid the fire and proceeded to capture the Confederate position and most of the sharpshooters.

The 1st Maine then took over the attack, supported by the 2nd New York Cavalry, and advanced another half mile to find the Confederate reserves dismounted and protected by a stone wall. The two regiments charged the wall and, while sustaining heavy casualties, drove the Confederates off. Darkness ended the battle, and the Union cavalry retained control of the town. However, the Southern brigade had not been defeated and had merely withdrawn to a new position. Casualties on both sides were heavy.

This action typifies the push of Pleasonton's corps to the Blue Ridge. The cavalry fighting was mounted and dismounted, charge and countercharge, and in the small towns, street to street. As the towns exchanged hands several times, the bodies of horses and riders piled up in the streets. A trooper from Maine recounted, "The road where we charged was literally covered with blood and to see the dead piled up was perfectly horrid."[34] Finally, on the evening of June 21, Buford's cavalry secured a ridge where they could look over the top of Confederate forces holding Ashby's gap, and into the valley beyond. Buford's scouts could see the camp fires of Longstreet and Hill's corps far away in the valley and, with this knowledge, accomplished the mission. Buford reported the information, and with it Hooker deduced that Lee's army was moving to invade the North.

Having accomplished his mission, Pleasonton disengaged his cavalry in order to refit. Since Brandy Station on June 10, the corps had been in almost continuous combat and had sustained over 1,700 casualties. He assumed that with the Southern army moving north through the Shenandoah, Stuart's cavalry could not leave the defensive positions in the Blue Ridge, but Stuart had other plans. On June 23, Stuart got General Lee's approval to conduct a raid into Pennsylvania separate from the army's offensive. He proposed moving his cavalry to the other side of Hooker's army and then crossing the Potomac and raiding through Maryland and into Pennsylvania, where he would link up with Lee again. The advantages of the raid were numerous: It would confuse the enemy as to the intentions of Lee; it could harass Hooker's rear and flanks; provide exact intelligence about the enemy movements; reduce the logistics burden on the Southern army's march route; and it would secure for the army much needed supplies. Neither commander mentioned the fact that the raid would place the entire Union army between Lee and his cavalry support as his army made the dangerous and decisive invasion of the North. Lee agreed to the proposal, and on June 25, Stuart began his movement first east and then north. He left two of his five brigades behind to cover Lee's march through the valley.

With the Southern forces on the move, Hooker kept his army in place. Finally on June 25, after a pause of six days, Hooker started the Army of the Potomac north across the Potomac with General John Reynolds Corps leading and Reynolds in command of the advance units. On the same day, A. P. Hill's Confederate corps completed crossing the river and Longstreet, the last major element of Lee's army, began to cross further upstream. Neither cavalry force was in contact with the enemy.

Pleasonton's cavalry corps covered the army's crossing of the Potomac with Buford's division protecting the northern side and Gregg's division protecting the south side. Stuart's cavalry encountered the Union II Corps as it moved north, but the report never reached Lee, and Stuart bypassed the Federals and continued to move east to get around Hooker's army.

On June 26, both armies completed moving north of the Potomac. On June 27, Hooker and General in Chief of the Army, General Henry Halleck, argued over the disposition of the Union garrison at Harpers Ferry. In anger Hooker offered to resign his command, and Halleck and President Lincoln, unhappy with Hooker's lack of aggressiveness, accepted. On June 28, the president appointed General George Meade as the new army commander. Because of this major command change in the middle of the campaign, the Union Army paused around Frederick, Maryland, for the day. As part of the shake-up, Meade gave Pleasonton permission to reorganize the cavalry corps and attached a new division under General Stahel to the corps, bringing the corps to a strength of 12,700 troopers–four times the strength of Stuart's force. Pleasonton, in turn, immediately relieved Stahel and both of his brigade commanders. Judson Kilpatrick, a Pleasonton protégé, became the new commander of the 3rd Division.

While the Union army focused on reorganizing its command, Stuart moved his cavalry across the Potomac behind the Federal army. On June 28 he was marching north between the Army of the Potomac and Washington, D.C., and stumbled across a huge Union supply wagon train in Rockville, Maryland. The Confederate cavalry swooped down on the hapless teamsters and captured 125 loaded supply wagons. Several wagons escaped back to Washington, and in chasing them, Stuart's troopers came to within four miles of the almost defenseless capital. His troopers could see the unfinished dome of the capital building. There may have been an opportunity for a raid on Washington, but those were not Stuart's orders and he resumed his march north, now slowed by the huge wagon train in his possession.

While the rest of the army rested, the Union cavalry moved out on June 28 with the mission of locating Lee's army. It was Meade's intention to find Lee's army and fight it. The Army of the Potomac marched north with Buford's 1st Division screening the left flank and reconnoitering to the west and northwest; Kilpatrick's 3rd Division moved forward of main body of the army, and Gregg's 2nd Division was responsible for the right flank and the rear.

The pace of operations to this point had been rapid. In keeping pace with Lee's army, the Army of the Potomac had moved more often, further, and faster than it had at any point prior in the war. The cavalry of both armies were almost continuously in the field, and fatigue was a factor. A Pennsylvanian cavalryman described the strain of operations:

> [The men] had previously been in the saddle on an average for twenty hours out of the twenty-four for three days, without sleep and with scarcely anything to eat for man or horse. The intense heat at times was almost unbearable, the dust almost impenetrable. Horses by the scores fell from exhaustion along the road.... Officers and men, begrimed past recognition, trampled along on foot, leading their worn-out horses to save their strength.... Dismounted cavalrymen, who horses had fallen dead or dying, struggled along, some carrying their saddles and bridles in hopes of being able to beg, borrow, buy or help themselves to fresh mounts, others without anything but their arms.[35]

Still, morale of both cavalry forces was high. The Southern cavalry were enthusiastic about being on the offensive in enemy territory; and the Union troopers were encouraged by the friendly civilian population.

By the evening of June 29, Buford's division had crossed into Pennsylvania while the bulk of the Army of the Potomac was poised on the Maryland border ready to cross into the Pennsylvania the next day. Buford bivouacked for the night at Fairfield, ten miles southwest of Gettysburg.

Gregg's 2nd Division moved east of the army on June 28 to locate Stuart's cavalry. Gregg's division moved down the rail line of the Baltimore and Ohio line expecting to find Stuart's force destroying track. Not locating the enemy, but knowing they were close, the division turned north on June 29 and continued to follow the trail toward Winchester. After an all-night march, they arrived at Westminster, Maryland, at dawn on June 30, in time to catch stragglers from Stuart's force, but having missed the main body by a few hours. The pursuit continued throughout the day, finally the command stopped at Manchester, Maryland, on the night of the thirtieth for much needed rest, about 3 miles south of the Pennsylvania border. Gregg's division crossed into Pennsylvania early on the morning of July 1, about 20 miles southwest of Gettysburg.

Moving in the center of the cavalry fan, Kilpatrick's 3rd Division had the mission of locating the northern Confederate forces, reported to be in the vicinity of York, Pennsylvania. In the late evening of June 29, Kilpatrick's troopers stopped at Littlestown, Pennsylvania, just across the border from Maryland. On June 30, the division continued to Hanover with a portion of George Custer's Michigan brigade in the lead. Reaching Hanover early in the morning the division paused briefly, dispatched reconnaissance patrols into the surrounding countryside, and then continued north. After most of the division had passed out of the town, patrols discovered Southern cavalry east of the town. Skirmishing between patrols quickly developed into a full-scale battle, and Confederate cavalry attempted to enter the town.

Stuart's scouts had made contact with the Union forces on June 28, and he realized that he was well south of the Union army positions. What Stuart didn't know was the location of Lee's main body; he didn't realize that Lee didn't know where he was, and also that the two brigades that he had left on the Blue Ridge had not moved north with Lee. So, while the Union cavalry corps of seven brigades spread out reconnoitering forward and to the flanks of the Union army, only Jenkins's single cavalry brigade attached to Ewell's corps supported Lee's entire army. The information he had was enough for Stuart to understand that he needed to link up with Ewell's corps near York as soon as possible, but his movement toward Ewell put him on a collision course with Kilpatrick's division. It was Stuart's advance guard that ran into the tail of Kilpatrick's column in Hanover on the morning of June 30.

The initial action at Hanover developed in a manner similar to the cavalry fights two weeks previously along the Blue Ridge. The Confederate advance guard, the 2nd North Carolina Cavalry, charged and routed the Union 18th Pennsylvania Cavalry. The Union brigade commander, Elon J. Farnsworth, immediately counterattacked leading a charge of the 5th New York that pushed the Southerners out of the town. Both Stuart and Kilpatrick moved their troops to the scene of the action as quickly as they could. Farnsworth's brigade ultimately occupied the northwestern and western approaches to the town, while Custer's Michigan brigade defended the southern approaches. Stuart positioned his three brigades from left to right, Lee, Chambliss, and Hampton. Both sides exchanged artillery and carbine fire throughout the day. Custer personally led several dismounted attacks against Lee's brigade, and, though they caused problems, both were eventually repulsed. Stuart, as he realized the strength of the Union position and worried about Gregg's division who might come up on his rear, determined to wait for darkness, break contact, bypass Hanover, and continue to York. As soon as darkness descended, Stuart moved his command off to the east, and Kilpatrick was content to not pursue.

As Kilpatrick engaged Stuart, Buford's 1st Division advanced to Gettysburg. As he moved northeast from Fairfield on the morning of the thirtieth he encountered two infantry regiments of Heth's division of A. P. Hill's corps. Buford decided to avoid decisive engagement, skirmished with the infantry as he bypassed them, and continued his movement to Gettysburg. He understood that contact with infantry indicated that the main body of Lee's army was nearby. En route to Gettysburg he met with Reynolds at his headquarters in Emmitsburg and briefed him on his assessment of the situation. By the evening of the thirtieth Buford's division was in Gettysburg. Buford's assessment was that the road network that met at Gettysburg would attract Southern forces from almost all points of the compass. Reading reports from scouts, and considering his contact with Heth's regiments that morning, Buford concluded that the greatest danger was to the west. He therefore deployed his two brigades oriented to the northwest along both sides of the Chambersburg Pike. He determined to hold Gettysburg until ordered to withdraw or relieved by Reynolds' infantry. William Gamble's brigade deployed on the south side of the road and Thomas Devin's brigade on the north. His third brigade, Merritt's brigade, had been detached with the division supply train the previous day and was not at Gettysburg.

As Buford occupied his positions in Gettysburg on the evening of June 30, Confederate brigade commander General James J. Pettigrew, whose regiments had skirmished with Buford that afternoon, reported that veteran Union cavalry held Gettysburg. Pettigrew's superiors, both Heth and A. P. Hill, discounted the reports. The Southern commanders, with no cavalry of their own to confirm the reports, determined that the Army of the Potomac was far to their south. They decided that the cavalry Pettigrew encountered had to be Pennsylvania mounted militia. General Lee also disagreed with Pettigrew's report. He was certain that if Union cavalry were so far north in force he would have received a report from Stuart. Therefore, early in the morning of July 1 Heth led his entire division toward Gettysburg, with both Hill's and Lee's permission, to obtain supplies from Federal warehouses located near the town. Hill prepared his other divisions to join Heth, as Lee sent orders to Ewell to also begin movement to Gettysburg. Lee had decided that Gettysburg was a good location to concentrate his forces before striking against the Army of the Potomac.

Buford had prepared a strong picket line of skirmishers along Herr Ridge, about 1,000 yards forward of his main positions on McPherson's Ridge. At about 5:00 a.m. Buford's skirmishes on Herr Ridge began to exchange fire with the skirmishers of General James Archer's brigade, leading Heth's division. The Confederate skirmishers, who initially assumed Union infantry opposed them, could not penetrate Buford's strong picket line. Once they realized it was cavalry, they assumed by the volume of fire that the cavalry were using repeating carbines. In fact, most of Buford's men were firing single-shot Sharps carbines, though the flank companies of Gamble's brigade had recently received Spencer repeaters. In the face of the cavalry firepower, Heth deployed his division. It took two hours to form the division for battle and then attack. The cavalry held their position until the infantry charged. Then, as the infantry moved forward with a shout, the skirmish line retreated off Herr Ridge covered by horse artillery and carbine fire from the main positions on McPherson's Ridge.

General Reynolds had moved his infantry divisions to within five miles of Gettysburg the previous night. At 8:00 a.m., he rode forward to Gettysburg and was greeted with the sounds of battle. At 10:00 a.m., he reached Buford's command post on Seminary Ridge to the rear of McPherson's Ridge. From that vantage point,

Reynolds could see cavalry troopers kneeling behind fences and laying prone, firing their carbines. Buford assured Reynolds that he could hold until Reynolds' I Corps arrived to take over the battle. Reynolds launched messengers to hurry the I Corps, as well as the following IX Corps, and to inform Meade that the battle was joined.

At about 10:15 a.m. the battle began to reach a crisis point. Devin's brigade began to run out of ammunition, and lead elements of Ewell's Corps that was marching toward Gettysburg on Lee's order from the north threatened his northern flank. Gamble's front began to crack under the weight of two attacking infantry brigades and their supporting artillery. However, Heth's push came too late. As Gamble's troopers gave way, the infantry of the 1st Division of I Corps, moving at the double-quick, formed on Seminary Ridge to their rear in support. The infantry opened ranks and Gamble's weary troopers turned the battle over to the infantry.

North of the Chambersburg Pike, Devin's brigade continued to hold its position. As infantry formed behind them, the cavalrymen replenished their ammunition. Around 11:00 a.m. the combined efforts of the brigades of Hill's corps and Ewell's corps gradually pushed the cavalry back. Devin's troopers retired in good order, moving back to successive lines by squadron and regiment. Devin delayed back for two hours before turning his portion of the fight over to the infantry of General Howard's IX Corps around 1:00 p.m.

The arrival of the infantry did not end the battle for Buford's troops. The commanders integrated the two cavalry brigades into the infantry fire lines. The Confederate attack gained even greater momentum and forced the Union infantry back through the town of Gettysburg on to the heights of Cemetery Hill. Reformed on the new position, and reinforced by artillery, the Union troops held their position. Once on Cemetery Hill, General Hancock, now commanding the battle, ordered Buford to feign a charge against the Confederate left (eastern) flank. Buford assigned this mission to Gamble's brigade, and the 8th Illinois Cavalry, supported by the rest of the brigade, executed the charge to the east of Cemetery Hill. The cavalry charge caused the advancing Confederate infantry to halt and form squares. The Union troopers, mounted and dismounted, then poured withering pistol and carbine fire into the infantry squares. With the Confederates temporarily checked, Buford's cavalry broke contact. This gave General Hancock time to reinforce his line atop the hill. With darkness coming, the senior Southern Commander on the scene, General Ewell, called off further attacks.

Far southeast of the battlefield, Stuart, after his encounter with Kilpatrick at Hanover, marched through the night of the thirtieth to arrive at York on July 1. There he learned that Ewell had left the day before, marching southwest under Lee's orders toward Gettysburg. Instead of following Ewell, Stuart proceeded northwest to

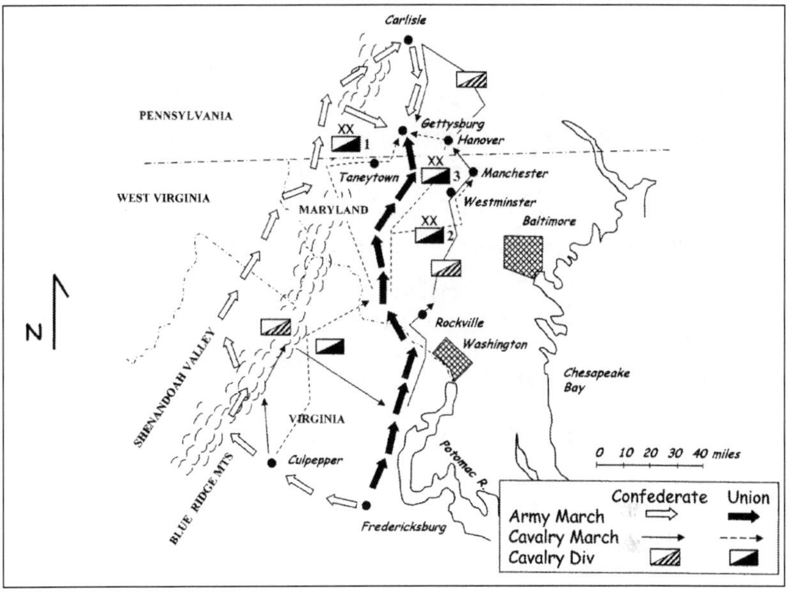

The battle of Gettysburg, July 1863.

Carlisle. Arriving at Carlisle late in the day, Stuart found it occupied by Pennsylvania militia. Avoiding decisive engagement, he shelled the town and burned the cavalry school barracks located there. Early in the morning of July 2, Stuart turned his command south and began to march to Gettysburg. The encounter with Kilpatrick and the detour to Carlisle had cost him a day's march.

Kilpatrick spent July 1 searching for Stuart north of Hanover. On July 2, he received orders to move his command to Gettysburg. As he approached Gettysburg, his troopers ran into Stuart again, about two miles east of the northern edge of the battlefield. Kilpatrick interpreted Stuart's presence as an attempt to turn the eastern flank of the Union army. Stuart assumed Kilpatrick's division was attempting to do the same to Lee's army. The two antagonists charged and countercharged each other. Kilpatrick reported that the "enemy was driven from this point with great loss." Stuart reported that Hampton's brigade compelled "the enemy to leave the field and abandon his purpose."[36] Both sides disengaged and held their initial positions through the night. During the afternoon, Gregg's division arrived to support Kilpatrick.

On July 3, as the two infantry armies battled for the Union positions south of Gettysburg, the Union cavalry was arrayed with both Gregg's and Kilpatrick's divisions guarding the right flank. Orders sent Buford's brigade to Westminster to guard the army trains. In the afternoon, Kilpatrick, with Farnsworth's brigade, shifted to the Union southern flank where it joined Merritt's reserve brigade. Jenkins' brigade, meanwhile, reinforced Stuart who continued to maintain his position on the Confederate left flank opposite Gregg.

The sounds of main battle drifted to the cavalry positions as General Pickett led three divisions in the infamous desperate charge against the center of the Union line. Timed to coincide with Pickett's charge, Stuart also took the offensive, sending Jenkins' brigade forward as dismounted skirmishers in an attempt to push through Gregg and into the Union rear area. Armed with rifle muskets, they could out range the Union carbines, but each of Jenkins' troopers only had ten rounds of ammunition. Gregg responded with his own dismounted skirmishers. At that point, orders came from Kilpatrick for Custer's brigade to join him in the south. Gregg, realizing that without Custer he would be outnumbered and his was the only command between Stuart and the Union rear, countermanded the orders.

The Union and Confederate skirmishers met in a furious exchange of gunfire, beginning the engagement called the battle of East Cavalry Field. As feared by Stuart, Jenkins' men ran out of ammunition. Backed by accurate horse artillery fire from Union batteries, Gregg's skirmishers forced Jenkins to withdraw. Stuart responded by ordering three regiments of Chambliss and Hampton's brigades into a mounted charge against Gregg's skirmishers which routed them. Gregg then ordered Custer's brigade to countercharge. Captain Miller of the 3rd Pennsylvania Cavalry described the action:

> The 1st Michigan, drawn up in close column of squadrons near Pennington's battery, was ordered by Gregg to charge. Custer . . . placed himself at its head, and off they dashed. As the two columns approached each other, the pace of each increased, when suddenly a crash . . . betokened the crisis. So sudden and violent was the collision that many of the horses were turned end over end and crushed their riders beneath them. The clashing of sabers, the firing of pistols, the demands for surrender, and cries of the combatants, filled the air.[37]

The Union cavalry were outnumbered perhaps two to one as the melee proceeded. Stationed on the Union right (east) flank and facing west was an uncommitted squadron of the 3rd Pennsylvania. Their orders were to hold their position and protect the flank. Against orders, they spurred into the attack against the exposed left flank of the Southern cavalry. Other uncommitted squadrons spontaneously attacked the Confederate right flank. Seeing the enemy waver, Custer shouted, "Come on you Wolverines!" as he led his Michigan brigade into the midst of the Southern horsemen. This broke the Southern attack. Hampton, himself wounded, led his men back to their starting position pursued by the fire of Union horse artillery. The aggressive action of Gregg's division supported by Custer's brigade stopped Stuart's attack with 20 regiments. Though neither side retreated, the Union cavalry successful defended the army flank, kept Meade's rear area secure, and denied Stuart an opportunity to redeem his absence from the army.

The standoff on the Union right flank ended the important cavalry actions of the Gettysburg campaign. The totality of the campaign demonstrated the importance, the lethality, mobility, and tactical flexibility of well-led cavalry armed with the new breechloading carbines. The various actions proved that the speed of mounted cavalry, combined with the firepower of dismounted cavalry, could provide a decisive advantage to a commander in battle. The success of the cavalry in its security and reconnaissance roles was the key factor allowing the Union army to get into a good position for the battle and denying information to the Confederate army. The actions demonstrated that the mounted charge remained an important tactical capability. The Gettysburg campaign also demonstrated the danger of the cavalry raid. Raids had a physiological impact but otherwise could be a waste of valuable resources. Any serious study of the Gettysburg campaign by military professionals at the time would have revealed that cavalry, rather than relegated to second status by technology, remained a critical component of warfare. However, the role cavalry played and its tactical employment had evolved considerably. Unfortunately, few European professionals were willing to look seriously at the operational lessons of American cavalry.

European Cavalry in the Nineteenth Century

After a long period of international peace after the Napoleonic experience, the Crimean War, 1854–56, marked a new period of renewed European warfare. The Italian War of 1859, the wars of German unification, the Austro-Prussian War of 1866, and most important, Franco-Prussian War of 1870 applied the emerging technologies of the nineteenth century to warfare. In addition, Prussia demonstrated the powerful effects of a brilliant general staff system. Still, the traditional political system of Europe contained the wars of the late nineteenth century sufficiently to mask many of the implications of the new technologies on the battlefield. The wars hinted at the type of destruction and the impact on tactics inherent in the new technologies, but they were sufficiently short in duration that the significance of those hints was not widely recognized.

Of the combat arms, cavalry changed the least after the Napoleonic period. Almost none of the lessons of the American Civil War cavalry experience had an impact on European cavalry. The Franco-Prussian War, in which the Prussians quickly defeated the French army, reputed to be the best in Europe, demonstrated to some professionals that there were serious problems with employing cavalry on a battlefield where infantry and artillery were equipped with rapid firing, breechloading rifled weapons. The cavalry casualties, particularly on the French side, were appalling, and worse, the cavalry action usually achieved nothing. Breach-loading rifles and artillery systematically destroyed cavalry brigades and divisions that bravely charged infantry and artillery positions.[38] Still, there was just enough cavalry success using traditional methods for the role of cavalry and its place in battle to remain largely unchanged through the end of the century.

Organization

By the middle of the nineteenth century, European cavalry still organized much as it had during the Napoleonic period. Small changes did occur, the most important of which was a steady blurring of distinctions between the cavalry types. In most European armies, each cavalry regiment within the army had a distinctive uniform style and color. Cavalry on parade still presented a dazzling array of military dress; however, the distinctions were increasingly superficial. During the Franco-Prussian War, both French and German cavalry retained their distinctive types and functions. After the war, the trend to a general purpose cavalry accelerated. By the end of the century, the unit titles and distinctive uniforms were mostly honorific as the armies standardized actual organization, training, and equipping of cavalry.

Prussian cavalry was organized within the structure of the infantry-dominated army. Each infantry division had a cavalry regiment, each corps a regiment or brigade, and each army a division or a cavalry corps. Cavalry units did not operate separate from the higher infantry organization. The Prussians did not form a cavalry reserve, or cavalry corps capable of independent operations. The Prussians divided their cavalry into line and guard cavalry. By the time of mobilization for the Franco-Prussian War, the cavalry forces of Prussia had an authorized strength of 41,400. As the Prussians went to war with France their forces included the cavalry of allied German states, adding an additional 13,800 cavalryman to the Prussian force.[39]

Throughout the nineteenth century, the French maintained a very robust cavalry arm. In 1855, it consisted of 51 regiments and an authorized strength of 61,200 troopers. French cavalry organization changed little between 1859 and 1870. In contrast to the Prussians, who did not maintain an independent cavalry force, the French army, in addition to assigning a cavalry division to each corps, maintained a separate cavalry reserve in the Napoleonic tradition, consisting of 3 cavalry divisions–a total of 12 regiments with 7,200 men.[40]

General-purpose cavalry was in place in most European armies by the end of the century, although the traditional names such as cuirassier, dragoon, and hussar continued to designate individual regiments. In some countries, larger horses and riders wearing cuirasses continued to distinguish heavy cavalry, but in other respects these units were identical to other cavalry.[41] Lancers were one of the only cavalry types to retain its identity in many European armies.

Weapons and Equipment

The equipment of European cavalry did not change significantly throughout the nineteenth century. Though the Prussians fielded the breechloading rifle in the 1840s, cavalry forces were not very interested in new weapons. In the Crimean War, cavalry operated essentially as it had in the Napoleonic period. It was not until after the Franco-Prussian War that European cavalry began to change in ways similar to that of American cavalry at the end of the American Civil War.

The lance remained in service with all European cavalry throughout the nineteenth century and continued in service in many armies until the end of horse cavalry. In fact, the lance was a more common weapon among cavalry forces in the nineteenth century than it had been since the Middle Ages. The British added their first lancers after the Napoleonic period. All German cavalry, regardless of type, had lances by the end of the century, as well as swords and carbines. In France, both dragoons and lancers carried lances.

The premier cavalry weapon in Europe throughout the nineteenth century was the saber. The only challenge to the saber for dominance, until the end of the century, came from the lance. The arguments between saber and lance advocates revolved around the utility of the lance against infantry, the superiority of the saber in cavalry versus cavalry action, and the difficulty of training troops to use the lance effectively. These were the same arguments that plagued Napoleon's cavalrymen. Lancers perfected their technique through a popular cavalry sport called "tent-pegging," which required the mounted lancer to lift tent pegs from the ground with the point of the lance. British cavalry on colonial service also practiced their lance skill hunting wild pigs.[42]

The breechloading carbine came slowly to European cavalry, not because the technology was unavailable but because cavalry leaders were uninterested in and did not see much use for an improved carbine as a cavalry weapon. Prussian cavalry only received a breechloading carbine in 1860s. The British army bought 6,000 of the first Sharps carbines between 1856 and 1858, but only the five royal regiments serving in India received the weapon. The British cavalry went through at least three more issues of different carbines before the end of the century, finally settling on the magazine-loaded Lee-Metford carbine in 1896. This carbine was the first British cavalry weapon to use the new smokeless powder.[43] By 1885, most European cavalry carried both a sword and an effective breechloading carbine. Despite having breechloading carbines, there was little interest in using the carbines in combat or in fighting dismounted. This only started to change at the very end of the century, after the British experience in South Africa.

Though they were readily available beginning in the 1850s, revolvers, like breechloading carbines, were a weapon that European cavalry mostly ignored. Pistol use steadily declined, and most cavalry forces abandoned the saddle holster pistols in the late Napoleonic period or soon thereafter. In the British Cavalry, only NCOs, officers, and buglers had revolvers. However, this did not happen until the 1890s. Most of the other European nations, the Germans and Russians among them, followed the British example and issued pistols only to selected individuals.[44] The neglect of the tactical possibilities inherent in the pistol reflected the pervasive conservatism of European cavalry.

Cuirasses remained in service through the Franco-Prussian War. During the war, French cavalry credited their cuirasses with substantially reducing the casualties of the cuirassier regiments, even when their charges were total failures, because the French cuirass was capable of stopping all but point-blank fire from Prussian breechloading rifles.[45] However, by the 1880s, new rifles were easily able to penetrate cuirasses, and by 1885, few of the major European powers issued cuirasses except for ceremonial purposes.

Tactics

Following the pattern of equipment, European tactical employment of cavalry did not substantially change during the nineteenth century. The charge remained the central focus of European cavalry doctrine, organization, and training through the end of the century. The charge remained central to European tactics largely due to the well-publicized successes of a few major charges including the charge of both the British heavy and light brigades at Balaclava in the Crimean war, as well as the perceived success of both French and Prussian cavalry executing charges during operations around Vionville during the Franco-Prussian War.

The most famous successful charge of the Franco-Prussian War was by Major General Friedrich Wilhelm von Bredow's 12th Cavalry Brigade, of the Prussian 5th Cavalry Division on August 16, 1870, during the battle of Mars-la-Tour. The Prussians charged against an infantry and artillery position that was wreaking havoc on the Prussian infantry on the left flank of the Prussian III Corps. The brigade, consisting of one regiment each of cuirassiers, uhlans, and dragoons, used the smoke of the battlefield and rolling terrain to maneuver to within a few hundred yards of the French lines before bursting forth at a gallop. They quickly got into the French gun line, routed the infantry, and put two French batteries out of action, temporarily relieving pressure on the Prussian infantry.[46] French cuirassiers countercharged and drove the Prussians back. Major Count von Schmettow, commanding the 7th Cuirassiers, described the charge:

> We penetrated into the first battery, of which but two guns succeeded in firing. The battery commander and all the men were cut down. Conscious of the prime necessity of overthrowing as many of the enemy as possible between the wood and chaussee, the regiment, under a flanking infantry fire from the wood, threw itself upon a second battery and an infantry column. Whatever of this battery did not reach the shelter of its infantry was cut down... the regiment cut down and stabbed everything within reach... two squadrons of hostile cuirassiers suddenly assailed the regiment in the rear, which now had every avenue of escape cut off except on the right. In selecting this route we retreated pell-mell with the French cuirassiers, who attacked with little energy, and some of whom accompanied us on their runaway horses to the rear of our infantry, where they were cut down.[47]

The French viewed the countercharge as an equally successful cavalry operation. Von Bredow's brigade's casualties were 397 men and 403 horses–about 45 percent of the roughly 900 men committed to the attack.[48]

Later that same day, the French threatened the III Corps' left flank again. Again, Prussian cavalry came forward and prevented French exploitation. This time the opposing forces met near Rezonville. As happened earlier in the day, the French cavalry counterattacked. What ensued was a massive cavalry battle involving three French cavalry divisions, and the 5th and 6th Cavalry Divisions of the German 2nd Army. In total, more than 5,000 cavalry eventually joined in a huge melee. In the dust and confusion, both commands completely lost control of their units, and the fight became individual on individual. The melee included dragoons, hussars, lancers, and chasseurs. Prussian dragoons, mounted on powerful warmbloods, literally bowled over French light cavalry whose horses were hundreds of pounds lighter. The French lancers, dressed in blue, were mistaken for Prussian dragoons and almost destroyed by French dragoons determined to give no quarter, and who thought shouts that the lancers were French were merely a Prussian ruse. Finally, the commands of both sides trumpeted a rally call, and the troopers disengaged. The French remained masters of the field and claimed a victory, but from the perspective of the operational commander, the charge of the Prussian divisions had saved the Prussian left flank and was therefore a success.[49]

The successful cavalry attacks during the Franco-Prussian War were the exceptions. Typically, cavalry gained time for infantry units to regroup or reposition by charging against well-formed infantry, and without supporting friendly infantry and artillery. Commanders ordered these hasty charges without proper reconnaissance of the ground and usually without sufficient numbers. Under these conditions cavalry was rarely successful. Such a situation resulted in the destruction of the cavalry divisions of the French I Corps at Wörth early in the war.

On August 6, 1870, the French I Corps was desperately trying to hold its defensive positions on the edge of the Vosages Mountains. The German 3rd Army was attempting to turn both of the French flanks. In a last effort to stop the Germans, the French cavalry reserves were committed to the battle. First was the 2nd Cavalry Division of the army reserve under General Bonnemains. It attacked on the corps' left flank, and within minutes rifle fire decimated all four of its regiments before they ever made contact with the Prussian infantry sheltering in hop fields and woods. Casualties in all the regiments were extensive. The losses of the 2nd Cuirassiers were representative: they lost their colonel, five officers, 129 men, and 170 horses killed in the charge. An equal number were wounded, and 80 horses died of wounds within the next few days.[50] With total casualties about 50 percent, the division was combat ineffective.

That same day, at the other end of the I Corps front, the 3rd Brigade of the corps' cavalry division, under General Michel, attacked the village of Morsbronn to facilitate the withdrawal of infantry and prevent the right flank of the corps from being turned. The 8th Cuirassiers led the charge of three regiments. Two command volleys of infantry rifle fire met the charging cavalry. The fire immediately took down two thirds of the horses and scattered the survivors of the lead regiment. The casualties of the first line formed a wall of dead and wounded horses and dismounted riders that destroyed the cohesion of the formations of the 9th Cuirassiers and the 7th Lancers who were following. Those two regiments went out of control and rode into the village of Morsbronn where obstacles in the streets trapped them and Prussian infantry firing from windows shot them down. The Prussians killed or captured the bulk of the two regiments.[51]

In a single day most of the I Corps cavalry—seven elite cavalry regiments—were destroyed. It is doubtful that the French troopers caused a single casualty among the defending Prussian infantry. The fate of the I Corps cavalry was not an isolated event. Ten days later on August 16, in the action near Vionville, German infantry and artillery destroyed the elite French Guards Cuirassiers Regiment and a regiment of lancers under similar circumstances. Infantry volleys "reduced each splendid unit in turn to a line of kicking, bloodstained heaps, while survivors galloped wildly over the battlefield until rounded up or hunted back to their own lines by German hussars and dragoons."[52]

Possibly the most hopeless cavalry charge of the war was that of the French reserve cavalry 1st Division, under the command of General Jean Auguste

Melee between French and Prussian Cuirassiers at Rezonville in 1870. The great engagement at Rezonville involved more than 5,000 cavalry in what was to be the last massive cavalry against cavalry combat in history. ("Rezonville" by French artist Aime Morot)

Margueritte at Sedan on September 1, 1870. The Prussians invited numerous dignitaries to watch the destruction of the French army from an observation point on a hill overlooking the battlefield and witnessed the charge. Among the observers were King William of Prussia, the Prussian prime minister Otto von Bismarck, and chief of staff of the Prussian army von Molke. The American general Philip Sheridan was another witness to the destruction of the seven cavalry regiments by German artillery and rifle fire. Sheridan, a cavalry veteran of some of the most intense fighting of the Civil War, said that he had never seen any attack so desperate, useless, and sanguinary. The German newspapers reported on the hopeless bravery of the French cavalry:

> Suddenly the French cavalry appeared on the scene; it was their last hope, and their attack was intended to take the batteries that were causing them such loss in flank, and also to charge our infantry, who had to withstand the onslaught of cuirassiers, hussars, and chasseurs d'Afrique, the latter mounted on splendid barbs. At several points they endeavoured to break our line and thus open a road for their infantry, but their efforts were repulsed by a cool and well directed fire, which laid the majority low. Let us give credit to our valiant adversaries, who rushed to death to save, if possible, the rest of their army.[53]

After the first charge failed, the commander of the 2nd Brigade was asked if his men could try again. General de Gallifet replied cheerfully, "As often as you like, *mon general*, so long as there's one of us left." The French division attacked three times and only succeeded in overrunning the Prussian skirmishers. French cavalry casualties in men and horses averaged 50 percent in the regiments. Three general officers of the division were killed. A legend associated with this charge claims that as the decimated ranks of the division were repulsed for the final time, Prussian officers ordered a cease-fire and saluted the retreating French–allowing them to reach the safety of their lines unmolested.[54]

Although these types of catastrophic cavalry charges occurred throughout the Franco-Prussian War and were typical of cavalry versus infantry actions, the few successful charges we noted and the fact that the war was of such short duration made it difficult to determine whether the cavalry charge against rapid-firing breechloading weapons was viable or not.

The rifle musket, because it did not have a significantly greater rate of fire than the smooth bore musket, did not fundamentally change the dynamics of the cavalry charge. However, the new generation of breechloading rifles, fielded immediately after the American Civil War, had a major impact on the dynamics of cavalry tactics. breechloading rifles, the American Springfield, the French Chassepot, and the Prussian Dreyse needle-gun all had significantly simpler, and therefore faster, reloading procedures than the musket. The ease and speed of loading gave the infantryman time to aim accurately; it allowed him to seek cover, fire from behind rocks, and while prone. Most important, it gave the infantryman confidence in the lethality of the individual rifleman. This began to change the fragile psychological dynamics of the cavalry charge. The thundering hoofs of the mass cavalry attack could not as easily intimidate a rifleman who knew that he could fire three or more aimed shots before the cavalry got to his position. This realization was the key to the demise of the cavalry charge as an effective tactic on the battlefield. Infantry no longer relied on the square for protection: rifle fire was protection enough. The destruction of the French cavalry during the Franco-Prussian War plainly made this point for any analyst who cared to see it.

Though large cavalry formations, up to corps size, were organized, and adequate breechloading carbines were developed and issued, most European cavalry ignored the potential combat power of the carbine.[55] European cavalry did not operate independently like American cavalry did, nor did it operate dismounted in any great numbers.

European Horses and Horsemanship

Through the nineteenth century, European cavalry officers closely scrutinized the horse and its equipment searching for ways to improve capabilities. European countries refined horse breeding and institutionalized and more carefully regulated their remount services. Equipment design improved to increase its utility and improve the comfort of horse and rider. Armies established centers of equestrian excellence that studied the art and science of riding and passed that knowledge to the regiments to improve their tactical capabilities.

Horses

During the nineteenth century, the horses of Prussia and after 1870, Germany, became the premier cavalry mounts of Europe. By the end of the nineteenth century, Germany had a horse population of over 4 million, of which more than 3 million horses were in Prussia alone. The German cavalry annually took in 9,000 carefully selected remounts from this population. The preferred remount came from Eastern Prussia, the horse breed that today is known as the Trakehner. During the nineteenth century, and until the end of World War II, warmbloods from East Prussia were known as "East Prussians," and only those that came from the royal stud were known as Trakehners. The breed traces its origins to Fredrick Wilhelm I, the king of Prussia and the father of Frederick the Great, who established the stud at Trakehnen in East Prussia in 1732, specifically to develop a Prussian royal breed and provide remounts for the cavalry. The Prussians chose the Thoroughbred as one of the foundations of the breed because of Fredrick Wilhelm I and Frederick the Great's admiration for them. Even though the Prussian cavalry at the time were mounted on very fine Holsteiners, Frederick the Great and his entourage were always recognizable because their personal mounts were imported English Thoroughbreds. Initially, they established the breed by using small local mares known as Schwaike matched with English Thoroughbred and Arabian stallions. Once the breed was established, it was strictly controlled and the only authorized outside breeding was to carefully selected Thoroughbred or Arabian stallions, a practice continued to the present day. The Arab and Thoroughbred were specifically selected to ensure that the breed could meet the needs of the cavalry for fast and maneuverable high-performance horses.[56] The modern description of the horse according to the American Trakehner Association is not much different from the horse as it would have appeared on the battlefields of 1866–70:

> The observer should immediately be aware of a striking, elegant presence. The combination of size, bone, and substance, with a classic breediness, produces this unmistakable Trakehner type, a type clearly distinguishable from all other warmbloods due to its refinement. The charm and nobility are evident in the refined head, often slightly concave in profile, with its broad forehead, smallish muzzle, large, kind, wide set eyes, and solid jawbone. The throatlatch is clean and fine and the long, graceful neck is set into the shoulder at just the right angle to provide maximum balance. The ideal Trakehner has a large, solid body, standing in a rectangular frame–compared to the square frame of,

> for example, the Thoroughbred–with a deep, sloping shoulder that allows for tremendous freedom of movement. The legs should be straight and the movement true and square. A back of medium length flows into large and powerful hindquarters with broad, solid hocks carried well under the animal as it travels. A deep barrel provides the necessary lung capacity and is closely coupled to a long, sloping croup. It is the combination of the thrust from the quarters, the swinging back and the freedom of the shoulder that produces the Trakehner's famous floating trot, the trot that eats up the ground, is supremely comfortable, and is so light and springy that it actually looks as if the horse does not quite touch the ground as it strides.[57]

The Germans distributed cavalry horses among cavalry units by size: heavy cavalry horses were 16 hands or larger; light cavalry horses were between 15.2 to 16 hands. The Germans operated a very efficient remount system as a special department of the War Ministry. A major general, who was the inspector general of remounts, ran the department. An American evaluator, cavalry Lieutenant Jonathan Boniface, considered that it produced "superior cavalry horses, and it may be taken as the best system in existence." Lieutenant Boniface described the details of how the system was organized and operated:

> Horses are, in times of peace, purchased at from three to four years old by commissions consisting of cavalry officers and veterinarians under the orders of the Remount Department of the War Ministry. This commission begins its work in May of each year and continues until September. The number purchased is always 5 per cent over and above the number required, in order to make allowances for losses and those proving unfit for service. In the Bavarian and Saxony systems, the remounts were sent directly to the regiments after purchase, but in the Prussian system, they were distributed to four remount depots, where they were kept for a year, during which time they have an opportunity to develop. At the end of this time all remounts fit for the cavalry service are sent to their regiments. At the head of each remount depot is a civil official, the administrator, who is selected for his good judgment in regard to horses, his own good horsemanship, and his ability as an agriculturist. Under him is an accountant, with an inspector over each of the farms, from one to four under the administrator's charge. There are from one to three veterinary surgeons at each depot, and one forage-master for each farm. The grooms are hired civilians, and the remainder of the employees are old soldiers. The stables on these remount farms are mere closed sheds, in which the horses are never tied up, but are allowed free access at all times to the paddocks adjoining

An outstanding Trakehner stallion, Morgenstrahl, foaled in 1896, at the Trakehnen Stud in East Prussia. (*Cavalry Journal* [British], No. 14 [April 1909])

> their stables. They are neither marked in any way except by a numbered ticket, nor shod and receive only ten minutes' grooming a day. . . . The training of the remounts at the remount depots receives the greatest attention. The greatest care is taken from the very beginning not to spoil their dispositions and to gradually accustom them to military duties. The first few weeks they are merely ridden around among the old horses to make them feel at home in their new surroundings and to accustom them to having the weight of a rider on their back. They are then gradually taught to allow their teachers to handle them on all parts of their bodies, and the greatest patience is exercised to give them confidence in their riders. Later on much attention is paid to jumping, and the remounts are taught first to go over the obstacle led alongside an old horse, and afterwards by themselves.[58]

This remount system supplied the cavalry in peacetime. In order to prepare for war, the German government conducted a census of all horses in the country every 10 years. They identified horses for cavalry, artillery, and draft service in the event of war. Upon mobilization, the government levied the German states for a designated number of horses of the various types. The government then purchased them at a set fee. By the end of the nineteenth century, upon mobilization, Germany could mount a cavalry force of over 100,000 trained cavalrymen and horses.

In the nineteenth century, France focused on redeveloping its horse breeds devastated by the Napoleonic wars. By 1870, the system was still not able to provide sufficient quality mounts for the large cavalry force, and France was forced to meet some of its 15,000 annual remount requirement through foreign purchases. The French bought large numbers of horses in the United States but found them to be unsatisfactory. France's most successful imports were a smaller lighter horse from its North African colonies, and first represented by the mounts of the French Chasseurs d'Afrique–French light cavalry recruited in the French North African colonies of Tunisia, Algeria, and Morocco. Thus, the French cavalry were mounted on smaller horses than many of the other European forces. The French cavalry horse had a strong Barb influence, and the average light cavalry horse was 14.2 hands tall. The horses were purchased at three and half years old and then trained at one of the remount depots, St. Cyr, the Paris War School, or Saumur, for a year before being released to the regiments at four and a half years old.[59] The French were not very successful developing a domestic breed to meet the needs of the heavy cavalry.

Horse Equipment

Throughout the nineteenth century, cavalry horse equipment did not change significantly. The double bridle was the standard military bridle. Saddles were refined to better accommodate the changing equipment of the troopers, the comfort of horse and rider, and last, to reduce weight.

The German army saddle of 1885 had most of the characteristics of a modern sport saddle; however, it was specifically designed with the needs of campaigning in mind. It came in five different sizes, selected to match the horse. The smallest size was only used in service in South Africa. The tree was wood with side boards covered with wool stuffed cloth. It had a webbed seat with a leather cover. Both pommel and cantle were wood, reinforced with metal strips. The saddle included side skirts that covered the girth strap and buckles, and slotted for the stirrup leathers that attached under the skirt to the tree. The side skirts also included forward knee rolls that positioned the rider's leg and provide support. The saddle disassembled without any tools for cleaning, repair, and maintenance. The ease with which the saddle disassembled also facilitated replacing worn or broken parts rather than repairing them. Parts were interchangeable between saddles of the same size.[60]

By the end of the nineteenth century, all cavalry armies recognized that the total weight carried by the horse was a significant operational issue. In 1888, Major General Rosenberg, Inspector General of the German Cavalry wrote, "Cavalry carrying more than 15 stone 10 lb. (220 lb.) are fit for nothing. Weight ruins horses." Both American and British cavalry leaders agreed with Rosenberg. Yet average horse loads were considerably heavier in most of the world's cavalry forces. Since, for optimum performance, a horse should not carry more than one fifth of its weight, and that the average cavalry horse during this time weighed about 1,100 pounds, the horses should not have been carrying more than 220 pounds. Only the U.S. cavalry, with its very light McClellan saddle, and the Belgian cavalry met this requirement. All other European cavalry overloaded their horses, some by as much as 60 pounds, and thus were asking for the horses to break down on a lengthy campaign.[61]

Horsemanship

European horsemanship changed after the Napoleonic wars. Through the Napoleonic period, beginning in the late eighteenth century, the general trend in cavalry riding was toward a more rough-and-ready style. After the Napoleonic wars Europe, as a reaction to the liberal expressions of the French Revolution, reverted to its conservative roots–including in the riding arena. The most successful cavalry through the Napoleonic period were Frederick's cuirassiers under Seydlitz, who combined the discipline and technique of classical high school ménage riding with a daring and aggressiveness that embraced cross-country riding at speed. Subsequent cavalry rarely achieved the combination of aggressiveness and discipline that the Prussian formations had, but that was the goal. During the Napoleonic period, the British aggressive style seemed to be superior to the French preference for control when the numbers were equal. After Waterloo, however, the trend was reversed. Cavalry forces in most of the world's armies began to put greater and greater emphasis on classical riding form and control. Even the Russians, with their superb but undisciplined horsemen–the Cossacks–joined the classical riding trend that some historians blame for the poor performance of Russian cavalry in the Russo-Turkish War (1828–29).[62]

Military equitation in the mid-nineteenth century broke into two schools, both originating in France. The first was that of Francois Baucher who was a classical high school advocate. The second school adhered to the principles of Comte Antoine Cartier d'Aure, who emphasized cross-country riding, hunting, and the steeplechase. The renewed emphasis on a scientific approach to horsemanship was represented by prestige of the great cavalry schools of Europe. The most famous was the French cavalry school at Saumur. Upon the return of the monarchy, Louis XVIII reestablished the cavalry school in 1814 but moved the new school from Versailles to Saumur, the home of the cavalry regiment for which he was honorary colonel. The instructors came from two sources: officers serving in cavalry regiments and civilian experts from Versailles. Over time the school added a veterinary program. In 1852, D'Aure added a cross-country obstacle course to the facilities, establishing a training tech-

High school equitation at the French Cavalry School at Saumur. Two officers execute the courbette. The great cavalry schools developed the art and science of equitation to its highest form. (*Cavalry Journal* [British]).

nique that eventually became a standard against which all cavalry horses and riders were measured. The key to the success of the school was the *Cadre Noir* (the "black cadre" on account of their uniform color), a select group of expert cavalry officers who were devoted to instruction and developing the rider and horse to their greatest potential. By the end of the nineteenth century the school offered a balanced approach to equitation that took the best of the D'Aure and Baucher and seamlessly integrated them into courses of instruction for cavalry officers, remount sergeants, and riding instructors.[63]

Saumur set a standard of excellent horsemanship copied in all cavalry forces throughout Europe as well as places like the U.S. Cavalry School at Fort Riley, Kansas. Most European countries formed their own schools and attempted to impart both the skill of cross-country riding, with the finesse and discipline of classical high school riding. It was accepted that effective cavalry needed a horse and rider that was versed in a variety of types of riding so that the two, horse and rider, could adapt to the widest variety of conditions on the battlefield.

The nineteenth century was a period of contradictions. It saw great change but also conservative inflexibility in cavalry forces. The cavalry of Sheridan and Wilson, operating in the closing months of the American Civil War, represented a major departure from the specialized forms of cavalry that were the legacy of the Napoleonic period. Armed with revolvers, carbines, and sabers, the cavalry became equally adapt at mounted and dismounted actions and were able to switch seamlessly between shock action and firepower attack, and between offense and defense. Cavalry raids and other independent actions demonstrated the mobility advantage of cavalry, which in a war of maneuver could have decisive operational and strategic effects. Mobility and the new firepower capability were a powerful combination.

European ignorance of the lessons of the American Civil War prevented European cavalry from developing to its full potential. They remained tied to the infantry and its speed and made no serious effort to develop a firepower capability. An analysis of operations in France in 1870 would have revealed numerous instances where independent cavalry operations or dismounted cavalry actions might have had decisive effects. The cavalry of Europe ignored hints regarding the need for change resulting from the 1870 war and, later, British operations in South Africa. European cavalry did, however, continue advances in horse breeding and horsemanship. Nevertheless, the most important characteristic of European cavalry in the nineteenth century was its conservatism, which produced a narrow approach to operations without due consideration of new technologies and tactics. Because of this inflexibility, European cavalry entered the modern era with large and well-trained traditional cavalry forces that had not changed significantly since Napoleon. When the intensity of World War I revealed the shortfalls that had existed for decades, it was too late.

Chapter Nine

MOUNTED GUERRILLA WARFARE

My horse, be swift in flight,
Even like a bird.
My horse, be swift in flight.
Bear me now to safety,
Far from the enemy's arrows,
With streamers and ribbons red.
–A Dakota Warrior Song

At the same time nineteenth-century European powers were measuring their military might against each other on the continent, they were also using their military power to expand their global influence. The age of imperialism was at its height. The quest for greater influence and wealth also occurred in the United States. Where the Europeans expanded overseas in places like India, Africa, and Asia, the United States expanded into its sparsely inhabited western territories. Existing populations resisted the European and American aggressive extension of influence and political control. This resistance was ruthlessly suppressed using military power. In the first half of the century, native populations were rarely successful in putting up more than a token resistance to the modern military forces empowering expansion. However, as indigenous populations gained access to new weapons, their military capability increased enormously. Two instances where the existing populations were most successful in their resistance, though ultimately failing, were in the American West and in British South Africa. In both cases weapons technology was not the only reason for the success of the natives. The other major reason was the horse. Both American Indians and the original Dutch settlers of South Africa, the Boers, took advantage of their horses and their superior horsemanship to achieve a mobility advantage over their adversaries. Horses were central to the military power of both societies. The mobility that the horse gave American Indians and the Boer farmers was a major component in the stubbornness of their resistance against two of the nineteenth-century's most formidable powers. Ultimately, the resistance to British and American expansion failed because both modern armies developed tactics and strategies, also largely based on mounted forces, which overcame the ability of the less sophisticated military forces to resist.

The Plains Indian Wars

Warfare between the European settlers of North America and American Indians began in the seventeenth century, soon after the first colonies were established, and continued intermittently almost to the twentieth century. The Europeans had the advantages of weapons, organization, and numbers, and these advantages ensured European victory. In the decades before the American Civil War, the heirs of the European settlers, the Americans, came into contact with the American Indians of the western plains. Warfare began on a small scale when the United States acquired significant western territory after the war with Mexico. The year after the Civil War, 100,000 settlers passed through the city of St. Louis immigrating west. Between 1860 and 1870, a million Americans poured into the western territories of the United States.[1] Many of the Indians west of the Mississippi were determined to resist this migration. These Indians had several advantages over their brethren east of the Mississippi River. They lived in an area that was vast, largely unexplored, and except for the Indian tribes, uninhabited. The Indians were also blessed with horses, whose mobility permitted them to take advantage of the terrain and space of the American plains. The Plains Indians were highly mobile nomads who used their mobility to strike swiftly and avoid pursuit. With these characteristics working in their favor, they were able to wage effective military operations against the United States.

The U.S. army had several advantages that made victory a foregone conclusion. They had some advantages in weaponry over the Indians. This was mostly in terms of availability, ammunition and supply, and in some specific special weapons capability such as artillery. Other technologies gave the U.S. army a superiority over the Indians. Trains, telegraphs, and steamships provided operational advantages to the American army in its battles and campaigns. Most important, the army had the benefits of organization, political cohesion, and an almost unlimited depth of resources including people. These advantages helped to overcome the tyranny of distance on the plains, small budgets, and the fieldcraft and military skill of the Indians.

In simplest terms, the Great Plains of the United States extend from the Missouri River at Kansas City, west to the base of the Rocky Mountains. They also straddle the north-south length of the United States from its southern border in Texas and New Mexico, to its northern border in Montana and North Dakota. The area is generally rolling grasslands broken by small ranges of hills and canyons in places such as the Black Hills of South Dakota. Forests exist in the extreme north, and in the west along the base of the Rocky Mountains. Desert conditions exist in the extreme southwest. The last of the independent American Indian tribes flourished in this harsh and isolated land in the nineteenth century. Their presence slightly overlapped the exact geographic dimensions of the area, extending north into Canada, south into Mexico, and west into Arizona, Nevada, Idaho, and Oregon. It was in this area that the Indian tribes of the plains made their final stand against the advance of the U.S. government.

The Plains Indian Wars were a series of wars fought by the U.S. army almost continuously from 1866 to 1890 against different tribes across the width and breadth of the western plains. The major wars of the plains included Red Cloud's War (Montana, 1866–68); the Tonto Basin War (Arizona, 1872–73); the Red River War (Oklahoma 1874–75); the Centennial Campaign, also called the Great Sioux War (Montana and Wyoming, 1876–77); the Nez Perce War (Montana, 1877); the Victorio War (New Mexico 1879–80); the pursuit of Geronimo (New Mexico, 1881–86); and the Ghost Dance War (South Dakota 1890–91). These wars were only the highlights of continuous small-scale patrolling, policing, raiding, and engagements which kept the 10 regular regiments of U.S. cavalry in a constant state of operations throughout the period. The wars also indicate the geographic scope of the Plains Indian Wars. Cavalry regiments were continuously on the move to concentrate in the areas of greatest hostilities.

The Plains Indians

In 1866 the U.S. government estimated that there were 270,000 American Indians in the West, divided into 125 distinct groups. By 1866, however, only the most powerful tribes were in a position to oppose the policies of the U.S. government. The 11 most powerful hostile tribes numbered fewer than 100,000 people. However, significant unity did not exist among the tribes, and they had little sense of corporate Indian identity.

Organization

The largest sense of collective identification that the Indian recognized was the tribe. The major tribes with whom the Americans were concerned were the Blackfoot, Crow, Sioux, Arapaho, Cheyenne, Comanche, Kiowa, Apache, Iowa, Wichita, Pawnee, Nez Perce, Bannock, and Ute. Some of the tribes shared the same language group but were otherwise not connected. The tribes subdivided into bands. The bands shared language and culture and occupied the same geographic area. For example, the Blackfoot consisted of three distinct bands or subtribes, the Piegan, Blood, and Blackfoot proper. Together they ranged over a territory of 120,000 square miles. Similarly the Sioux organized into at least seven different bands of which the most warlike were the Oglala and Hunkpapa. During most of the year, hundreds of miles might separate the bands, but in winter they tended to concentrate to within a few miles if not into a single large winter camp. Bands tended to self-identify as independent units and did not feel in any way bound by agreements or treaties made by another band of the same tribe.[2]

The bands were informal democracies. They selected leaders by popular consent based on proven wisdom and warrior skills. Popular consent expressed through councils limited their power. Multiple leaders could exist simultaneously, each responsible for an area of proven expertise such as camps, hunting, and the most prestigious—war. Leaders of exceptional ability and charisma could have influence beyond their band to the tribe in general.[3]

Initially southern Plains Indians copied the equipment of their equestrian models, the Spanish, including horse armor (made from leather rather than metal), and lances. The horse armor did not flourish among the Plains Indians, but other aspects of Spanish influence did. The lance became an important weapon among the Indians. It was most prevalent among the southern tribes, notably the Comanche. Indians did not throw the lance, but rather used it as a shock weapon wielded from horseback and couched under the arm. The lance was a very powerful symbolic weapon among the Indians because the warrior had to engage in close combat to use it. Thus, only the most notable warriors choose it, and carrying a lance was associated with great prestige. Comanche warriors used a lance six or seven feet in length with a head made from chipped stone in an open leaf shape. Later, metal heads replaced the stone. Particularly prized as lance heads were blades from cavalry swords. Captured cavalry swords were highly prized symbolic weapons among the Indians.[4]

Though the lance was associated with the greatest prestige, the weapon of choice among the Plains Indians was the bow. Plains Indians carried a short, generally three to four feet, bow which they fired with equal ability from horseback or on foot. U.S. Colonel Henry B. Carrington determined that the Indian's arrow "is shot with more precision than the pistol ball, and its blade is not, like a bullet, to be deflected by tendon, cartilage, or bone." Design of the bow varied in its specifics from tribe to tribe across the plains, but usually the Indian bow was a single stave weapon. Compound bows were not unknown but required a skilled craftsman and were therefore rare. The Nez Perce were known for their compound bows and used them as an important trading commodity with other tribes. Some tribes strengthened the bow with a sinew backing, while the best bows, in the steppe fashion, also used bone. Although some contemporary accounts give a range for the native bow as much as 500 yards, the weapon was probably effective at 100 yards or less. Although lacking the range of firearms, its rate of fire and accuracy ensured that it was the most popular and most effective weapon in the Indian arsenal until the advent of metallic cartridge repeating rifles. Even after good firearms were available to the Indians, they never completely replaced the bow.[5]

By the time of the Indian campaigns many of the Plains Indians warriors carried high-quality firearms. The archeological evidence discovered on the Little Bighorn battlefield gives a good indication of the sophisticated and modern armament of the Indians in 1876. That evidence indicated that the Indians present on the battlefield used a minimum of 29 different types of firearms. Cartridge evidence on the battlefield shows that at least 62 Indians used .44-caliber Henry repeating rifles. The second and third most prevalent Indian rifles indicated by the archeological evidence were 27 .50-caliber Sharps breechloading rifles, and seven .44-caliber Winchester 1873 repeating rifles.[6] Estimates are that at the Little Bighorn battle, one in every three Indians carried a firearm. The rest used the traditional bow. This evidence indicates that in terms of individual firearms the Indians were at least as well armed as the cavalry, and under some circumstances better armed. At close ranges, the repeating rifles of the Indians would have been able to generate significantly more firepower than the single-shot carbines of the cavalry.

Tactics

Indian culture focused on the individual warrior. This focus is reflected in the tactics the Indians employed. Bands of warriors went to war based on mutual consent. A chief led the war band but did not give orders. Warfare was about individual bravery and skill. Man for man, the Indian warrior totally outclassed his opponent in the American army. However, the emphasis on individual bravery and skill represented a corresponding weakness in unit discipline and team work. Thus, in a conventional open battle, the army could defeat Indian war parties with trained and disciplined troops operating together under their officers' orders. However, the conventional open battle was a situation that the Indians avoided. Well organized and prepared soldiers caused the Indians to disperse and retreat. The Indians used tactics designed to take advantage of their superior fieldcraft and mobility. Warriors lured soldiers into ambushes by retreating. Raids hit isolated outposts and patrols and relied on surprise, shock, and speed for effect. The Indians then avoided pursuit using superior horsemanship, speed, and dispersal.

An important weakness in the Indian's method of warfare was the lack of any overall strategic direction. Because of a lack of overall Indian unity, and large ignorance of events beyond the local region, the American Indian fought a skillful tactical war designed to defeat local enemies. However, there was no operational or strategic direction to the tactical conflict. Thus, the greatest Indian victories, such as the victory over Custer at the Little Bighorn in 1876 had only temporary local effects.

Horses and Horsemanship

The Plains Indians' horses were the basis of their military power. But, unlike the horse cultures of the steppe, the Indians adapted their culture to the horse very late in their history. In fact, the horse was a European product that the natives of North America procured from the earliest European colonists. A testament to the adaptability of the Plains Indians was the speed with which they integrated the horse into tribal society and used it to improve all aspects of their life.

Horses

Horses had been absent from North America for 45 million years before the Spanish explorers reintroduced them in the sixteenth century. Hernán Cortés brought the first horses to mainland North American in 1519. By the middle of the sixteenth century there were tens of thousands of horses in Mexico. By 1600, most Indians in northern Mexico had horses, acquired through stealing Spanish stock. The first Indians west of the Mississippi and north of the Rio Grande Rivers to culturally adopt horses were the Navaho of modern New Mexico. In 1683 an Apache-Navaho shaman-priest named Popé led an Indian uprising that destroyed Spanish power in New Mexico. The Indians captured a large part of the Spanish horse herd, which numbered at least several hundred. The Indian trading system then introduced the horses into the Great Plains. By 1685, Indians in east Texas had horses originally taken from the Spanish in New Mexico.[7]

The first mounted combat on the plains may have occurred in a 1694 battle in modern Nebraska, between Navaho equestrians, whose mounts descended from the Spanish, and Pawnee horsemen, who got their horses from the French. By 1700, Comanche, riding out of Wyoming, were raiding Apache and Navaho villages in New Mexico, armed with guns provided by the French. The period between 1750 and 1800 saw the birth of American Indian horse culture on the western plains. The domain of the Plains Indian tribes was an area of 3 million square miles; approximately 75 percent of the present continental United States. Within a 50-year period virtually all of the western plains tribal cultures transformed from sedentary hunter gatherers into nomadic horsemen.[8]

As the horse was arriving on the plains, so were additional tribes. With the establishment of the United States, midwestern tribes came under increasing pressure to move west. As they migrated, tribes such as the Sioux, leaving Minnesota, traded their canoes for horses.[9] At the same time the horse was being absorbed into Plains Indian life, firearms were arriving. The migration of the eastern tribes, who began using firearms prior to the beginning of the eighteenth century, accelerated the adoption of firearms by the Plains Indians . By the end of the eighteenth century, the

Indian mounted warrior, armed with bow and musket, was the dominant military and cultural force west of the Mississippi River.

Sources of horses for the newly mounted tribes coming from the east included trading with the southern tribes, breeding their own horses, trading with French and English traders (despite prohibitive laws), and war booty. Another source of horses was feral horse herds which existed on the northern plains. Wild horse herds, escapees from Indian, French, and Spanish ownership, existed in large numbers throughout the plains. Captain Zebulon Pike, exploring the Colorado plains for the U.S. government described an encounter with one of these herds in 1806:

> Upon using my glass to observe the adjacent territory, I observed on the prairie a herd of horses. Dr. Robinson and Baroney accompanied me to go and view them: when within a quarter of a mile they discovered us, and came immediately up near us, making the earth tremble under them: this brought to my recollection a charge of cavalry. They stopped and gave us an opportunity to view them; among them were some very beautiful bays, blacks and grays and indeed of all colors. We fired at a black horse, with an idea of creasing him, but did not succeed; they flourished around and returned again to see us, when we returned to camp.[10]

One estimate is that by the middle of the nineteenth century, within the Comanche territory on the southern Great Plains, there were as many as 2 million wild mustangs.[11] The wild mustangs of the West may have been part of the seed population of some tribal horse herds, but once tribes acquired horses, their horse herds were mostly self-sustaining.

The abundant supply of horses ensured that there was no distinguishable Indian horse type. However, some tribes were very particular about the quality of their horses. A tribe that demonstrated a conscious concern about improving and sustaining the quality of the tribe's horses were the Nez Perce of eastern Washington, Oregon, and Idaho. The Nez Perce were the only major Indian tribe that carefully managed and selectively bred their horse herds. The Nez Perce bred for speed, surefootedness, and color. They divided their herds into solid color horses and spotted horses. The spotted horses of the Nez Perce eventually became the Appaloosa, and the modern breed represents some of the best features of the American Indian horse type.

In 1855 the Nez Perce agreed to a treaty with the U.S. government that granted the tribe a 1,000,000 acre reservation. In 1877 the U.S. government arbitrarily reduced the reservation to less than 200,000 acres in order to permit gold mining. Parts of the tribe resisted the new treaty, and in the ensuing tensions warriors engaged in a short sharp battle with a company from the 1st Cavalry Regiment at

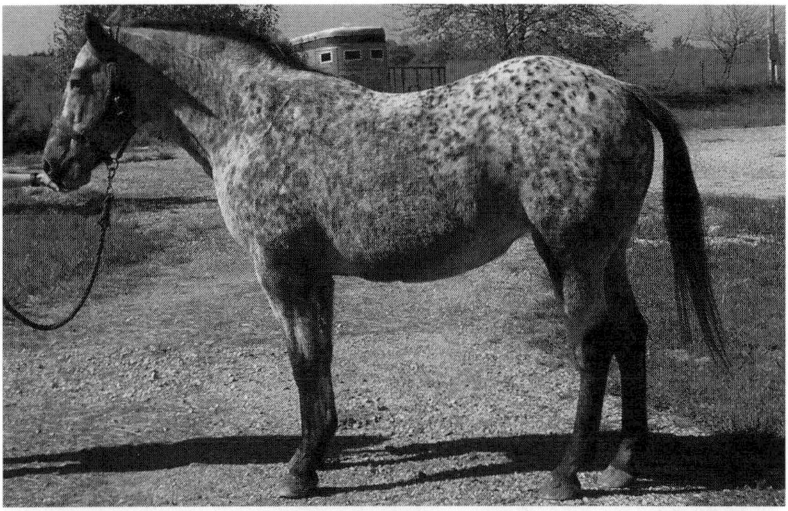

Appaloosa Horses. These two appaloosa horses show the diversity of coloring which the breed can demonstrate. The top horse, Topeka, is a light gray with brown leopard pattern spots, and the bottom, Dodger, is a dark bay with a white blanket and spots on the blanket. (*Author*)

White Bird Canyon. There, an outnumbered and dismounted force of 60 to 70 warriors routed the mounted cavalrymen–killing 34 in exchange for 3 wounded. This battle began a running campaign of pursuit and escape, as Chief Joseph of the Nez Perce led the 800 people of the hostile bands on a 1,700-mile and three-month march to safety. The bands brought their entire population, and most of their possessions with them. Among their possessions was a pony herd of over 2,500 horses. The army mobilized several columns in pursuit of the Indians. Fighting numerous small battles, and consistently defeating small army contingents, the Nez Perce were within 40 miles of their goal, the Canadian border, when they were surprised on September 30, 1877, by a combined mounted infantry and cavalry force led by Colonel Nelson Miles. With a battalion of mounted 5th Infantry in support, a cavalry squadron of the 7th Cavalry charged the Indian camp while another squadron of the 2nd Cavalry, accompanied by Sioux and Cheyenne scouts, attacked the pony herd.

The attack quickly captured the pony herd, but accurate Indian rifle fire hit the 7th Cavalry hard and stopped their attack. The 5th Infantry moved up to support, and together the two units pushed the Indian skirmishers back toward their camp. The Indians understood how to fight the army, and Indian marksmen singled out officers and NCOs in the attacking force. The marksmen killed every officer but one and all three company first sergeants in the 7th Cavalry squadron. In the midst of the fight a snowstorm dumped five inches of snow on the combatants making maneuver difficult. The battle evolved into a stalemate. Without their horses, the Indians lost their mobility and couldn't break contact. On the fifth day of the standoff, Chief Joseph of the Nez Perce surrendered about 100 warriors and 300 noncombatants of the tribe. During the previous night, about 300 people escaped the camp and ultimately made it to Canada. Chief Joseph's Nez Perce suffered about 120 dead during their flight, about half of them women and children. The army lost about 180 killed and another 150 wounded over the three months. The trek, though only partly successful, demonstrated the mobility and fighting abilities of well-led Indians.[12]

After the surrender, the army confiscated the Nez Perce horse herd. About 1,000 of the original 3,000 horses fell into the army's hands. These were the best Indian horses in the country–the result of several generations of careful breeding. The army understood that Indian military power was more a function of the horse than any other factor. The army killed many of these horses to deny them to the Indians, and dispersed the remaining horses as war booty. This largely destroyed this carefully nurtured native American breed. However, when the Nez Perce left the northwest they left behind stock from their herds that they didn't have time to gather, or that were too young or old to make the trek. Sixty years later, in 1938, an Oregon farmer, Claude Thompson, established the Appaloosa Horse Club to gather, register, and reestablish the spotted horse breed by bringing together the scattered remnants of the Nez Perce horses. The name *Appaloosa* derives from the name of the Palouse tribe located near the Palouse River in Washington State. Like the Nez Perce, the Palouse were also known for their spotted horses. Although the coat pattern is the main characteristic of the breed, there are four major physical characteristics: coat pattern, mottled skin, white sclera, and striped hooves. A sparse mane and tail as well as the strength of their hoof horn are also characteristics of the Appaloosa. The modern Appaloosa is the third most popular breed in the United States. Appaloosas normally range between 14 and 15.2 hands tall, are very athletic, and have a superbly calm disposition. As might be expected of a breed descended from Indian ponies, the Appaloosa excels in competitive endurance riding.[13]

Horsemanship

To the Plains Indians, riding was a fundamental of life. Plains Indians taught their youth to ride at a very early age. The Blackfoot claimed that five-year-olds could ride on their own. Learning to ride was a well-thought-out systematic process. Instructors led kids using a woman's saddle on a gentle horse; they progressed to riding faster, bareback, using reins; and then, eventually, body position to control their mount. The trader Francois Larocque reported in 1805 that six- and seven-year-old Blackfoot were accomplished riders. Among the Indians, only the Apache wore spurs. However, all tribes used some type of whip or quirt as an aid in communicating with their horses.[14]

Army lieutenant colonel George Custer considered Indian horsemanship the best in the world. Dr. W. A. Bell, a traveler in western Kansas in the 1860s, wrote that "the Buffalo Indians are probably the finest horsemen in the world. Accustomed from their childhood to chase the buffalo, they lived half their time in the saddle." Army Captain William Clark reported that among the Indians "The Comanches and Utes are considered by many Indians the best horsemen, and the Nez Perce and Cayuses as having the best or fastest ponies. The Southern Indians perform more daring and difficult feats on horseback, and are more expert in the use of the lasso than the Northern."

Horse Equipment

Contrary to a popular conception, Indians did not normally ride bareback but used hand-crafted saddles. In 1719, explorer Claude Charles Du Tisne found Wichitas in Oklahoma mounted using "saddles and bridles similar to those of the Spaniards." In 1880 a Sioux raider explained to army Lieutenant Hunter Liggett of the 5th Infantry (Mounted), that despite stealing more than 150 horses, they needed saddles more than anything else. Indian warriors used a simple pad saddle, while women used a wooden saddle with a high wooden pommel and cantle extended from wooden sidebars. The seat was wood or rawhide fastened between the cantle and pommel and suspended above the horse. Thus, like all modern saddles, the Indian framed saddle transferred the rider's weight to the sidebars and not directly onto the spine of the horse. Some saddles had horns attached to the pommel and the cantle. These served as fastenings for equipment. The parts of the saddle–pommel, cantle, seat, and side boards–were attached to each other with wet rawhide thongs laced through holes bored in the wood. Straps connected the side boards to a cinch holding the saddle to the horse. A woven blanket protected the horse from the saddle tree, while a buffalo or bear skin covered the saddle and gave some comfort to the rider. They used cruppers and breast collars with both designs of saddles. These attachments as well as the saddles themselves were often highly decorated with beads. The women's framed saddles were much more elaborately decorated then the more utilitarian pad saddle.[15]

Warriors used the pad saddle exclusively, and it was the common saddle for the hunt and war parties. Its design was simple and functional. Two hourglass shaped pieces of hide were sewn together and the interior filled with deer hair. The seat of the saddle was reinforced with an additional leather pad to which was sewn a cinch strap as well as stirrup straps. The entire assembly weighted approximately three pounds. The saddle could have additional straps sewn on that enabled the Indians to rotate their body onto the side of the horse in order to use the horse's body for protection during raids. The pad saddle was probably derived from a Mexican pack saddle while the woman's frame saddle was a unique plains design.[16]

Both type of saddles used stirrups. Craftsmen made the stirrups from wood. On the framed saddle, stirrup leathers attached to slots in the side boards. In the latter part of the eighteenth century and into the nineteenth century, Indians traded for items such as metal buckles and rings which were highly prized additions to the indigenous saddles.[17]

Despite the functionality of crafted saddles, the Indian saddles could not match the well-made leather and wood saddles produced by American and Mexican craftsmen. By the middle of the nineteenth century, one of the mounted Indian's most prized possessions, after his horse and his weapons, was a Mexican or American stock saddle. Hundreds of McClellan saddles also came into the possession of various tribes through war booty and theft. Once the saddles came into the possession of the Indians, they were decorated according to the tribe and personal preference with beads, bone, and colored cloth. Indians cut away excess leather. Thus, they modified the manufactured saddle to match the traditional regalia of the mounted warrior.

Indians fashioned simple bridles and reins using rope. The simplest bit was a rope run through the horse's mouth and fastened under his chin. This then had additional ropes tied to it to make reins and a bridle. When they could acquire one, Indians used Mexican or American curb bits, attached to a native-made bridle. By the late nineteenth-century, Indian craftsmen made very serviceable leather bridles and reins, and used trading post bits.[18]

American Cavalry in the West

The only serious opponents of the Plains Indians were the mounted forces of the U.S. army. These forces were organized, equipped, and trained similarly to the Union cavalry forces of the American Civil War. Most of the cavalry officers and many of the senior enlisted men were veterans of that conflict and therefore were experienced and competent professionals. Thus, it would seem a relatively straightforward operation for the professional veterans of the American army to impose the will of the U.S. government on a relatively small group of disorganized native tribes. However, operations against the Indians stressed every aspect of the army and required resolute perseverance on the part of the army leadership to see the various campaigns through to their successful completion. Many diverse factors worked against the quick success of the American army. These included resources, training, political and public interference, and terrain. Victory required patience, learning and applying new tactical lessons, and using strategic principles gleaned from the Civil War.

Organization

After the Civil War the army increased the number of active regular army cavalry regiments from 6 to 10. The 9th and 10th cavalry regiments were designated to be filled by black troops. These all-black regiments, led by white officers, proved to be two of the most reliable of the regular regiments with very high reenlistment and low desertion rates. The Indians recognized the fighting capability of the black troopers and nicknamed the 9th and 10th Cavalry "Buffalo Soldiers."

The cavalry strength of the army during the Plains Indian Wars never changed from the original 10 cavalry regiments of the regular army. With an average strength of 500 to 600 troopers in each regiment, the army's cavalry strength to meet the requirements of Indian campaigning was never more than about 6,000 mounted troopers. If they could have unified, the Indians had the potential to greatly outnumber the mounted forces of the army. Even given the independence of the tribes, 6,000 troopers were hard pressed to meet the requirements of campaigning, patrolling, and providing security in an area of operations of 2.5 million square miles against as many as 100,000 hostile Indians, including possibly more than 20,000 warriors. To partly compensate for the insufficient numbers of the mounted forces, some commanders mounted portions of infantry regiments on captured Indian horses to increase the mounted capability–the most effective of these was Colonel Nelson Miles's 5th Infantry Regiment (Mounted).

A regular army cavalry regiment of the Plains Indian Wars period was similar to the cavalry regiment of the Civil War. It consisted of either 10 or 12 companies. The companies were rarely all stationed together but, rather, stationed at small forts garrisoned by individual companies or a battalion of three to five companies. Forts were built as needed to meet the Indian threat. In 1886 a cavalry company was authorized 64 privates. In 1876, after the Custer disaster, Congress increased the size of the company to 100 privates. Company assigned strength varied considerably. All soldiers were volunteers for five years of military service, but despite their volunteer status, desertion rates were very high. In 1878, at least one frontier company reported an assigned strength of only 16 men.[19] Troop strength greatly constrained the tactical and operational choices of commanders.

Weapons and Equipment

Standard cavalry equipment during most of the Plains Indian Wars was adapted from that of the Civil War. Much of it was surplus Civil War equipment. Horse equipment remained generally unchanged, though in 1874 the cavalry adopted a new, lighter, and simpler version of the McClellan saddle.

American cavalry remained armed with the saber, revolver, and carbine of the Civil War. They completely embraced the concept of dismounted fighting, and therefore the trooper, if he carried a saber in the field, attached it to the saddle. Often commanders left the sabers behind on campaign. Immediately after the Civil War, cavalry carried one of the two popular proven carbines of the Civil War: the Spencer repeating carbine or the Sharps single-shot. In 1873, after a board evaluated over 100 models, the cavalry converted to a new standard Springfield carbine. The single-shot Springfield carbine fired a .45-caliber metallic cartridge and would remain the standard army carbine until just before the Spanish American War. The primary attribute of the Springfield was its accuracy. Immediately after the Civil War, all pistols were still the Colt or Remington cap-and-ball types. However, in 1872 the army approved the new Colt .45-caliber army model revolver firing metallic cartridges. In 1873 the army bought 13,000 of the single-action "Peacemaker" six-shooters as the standard cavalry sidearm. It continued to buy the revolver at the rate of about 1,000 a year until 1891.[20]

The army had significant problems with uniforms on the frontier. Temperature ranges were extreme. Summer temperatures all across plains, but especially in the southern regions, easily topped 100°F for weeks on end. At the other end of the spectrum were the almost arctic winter conditions on the northern plains from November to February. Weather conditions on the plains were volatile and could change dramatically. Storms, both rain and snow, were sudden and violent. Issue clothing, much of it Civil War surplus, was totally inadequate. In response, soldiers discarded much of their issue and substituted subdued civilian hats, shirts, and coats. One of the exceptions to the inadequate Civil War surplus was winter equipment.

American cavalry on the frontier frequently campaigned in the dead of extremely cold winters. To protect troopers under these conditions the army issued ankle-length buffalo fur coats and muskrat hats, facemasks, fur mittens, and fur boots.[21] The winter issue proved to be effective and popular and contributed to the cavalry's ability to conduct tactical operations in extreme cold.

Tactics

Warfare on the western plains was an operational challenge. The tactical problem was not defeating the enemy–once the cavalry got into the fight with the Indian their unit cohesion and tactical discipline usually could win the day. The tactical problem was finding and fixing the Indians so that they had to fight and couldn't escape battle. The Indians had no desire to fight unless conditions were of their choosing; in other circumstances they would use their usually superior mobility to break contact and flee.

The first problem that American cavalry had to surmount was the tremendous distances that characterized the theater of operations. To help find Indian groups the army employed civilian and Indian scouts. The Army Reorganization Act of 1866 authorized the army to formally enlist up to 1,000 Indians to act as scouts, and these scouts became a standard arm of the army. Tribes who were either neutral or enemies of the Indians subject to a particular army campaign provided the scouts. The field-craft of scouts gave the army the ability to track large hostile bands of Indians as well as smaller war parties. The more aggressive and mobile the enemy was, the more important the scouts became in the campaign. General August Kautz estimated one company of scouts was worth six companies of regular cavalry.[22] Scouts gave the army a superb intelligence capability that understood the culture of the enemy, knew the terrain intimately, were expert trackers, and could question and interrogate non-combatants that might have military information.

To mitigate the effects of distance, army commanders carefully studied march techniques. The cavalry had to be able to march long distances, relatively quickly, and without destroying their horses. Colonel Wesley Merritt, writing in 1888, maintained that a well-managed mounted unit could sustain a march rate of 25 miles a day, marching six days a week, throughout the term of a campaign. According to Merritt, the beginning of a well-ordered march was completely controlled by six bugle calls. The first two were "reveille," troops awakened and dressed; and "stables," troops moved immediately to their horses to groom and feed them. After these actions were completed, soldiers themselves breakfasted. When the supervising commander observed that the troops had finished eating, he ordered the bugler to sound the final four commands: "general," soldiers packed their personal equipment;

"boots and saddles," horses were saddled and packed, and troops moved to formation; "mount," troopers mounted their horses; and "forward," troops moved out on the march by fours. Merritt was insistent that no command be given before the previous action was complete. He asserted that it was better to begin late than to begin a march with unprepared horses or troopers. Company size and larger units always marched in a column of fours. If the unit had multiple companies, then companies maintained some distance between them, to lessen the effects of dust.

At the end of the first hour of the march, the column halted for 10 to 15 minutes to adjust tack. At this point soldiers or horses with health problems went to the rear to join the support train and ambulances. Once the march commenced again, it stopped every hour for five minutes. At the second halt the command did not rest but rather proceeded forward dismounted leading the horses for 20 minutes. The troopers then remounted and proceeded forward at the trot for 20 minutes. The last 20 minutes of the second hour were completed at the walk. This pattern–lead, trot, walk–was repeated with slight variations for the remaining three hours of the march. Commanders injected short gallops into the march to allow the horses to stretch. In this manner the first hour of the march covered about 4 miles of terrain, and the remaining four hours covered an additional 20 miles or more. The goal of the command was to cover 25 miles in less than 6 hours marching time.

Merritt insisted that discipline was the key to successful marching without injury to horses or men. He advised commanders to "arrest an officer or confine a trooper who willfully neglects attention to the smallest details of the march so necessary to the endurance of the men and horses." Thus, a mounted unit could cover 150 miles a week and 600 miles over the course of a month without detriment to its men and horses. Merritt went on to relate that well-conditioned cavalry could march at a rate of 50 miles a day for three to five days in an emergency. One of the most successful forced marches during the Indian campaigns occurred in 1879 when a squadron of the 5th Cavalry marched to the relief of a besieged unit, covering 170 miles in 65.5 hours. This unit sustained a march speed of over 62 miles per day. This march was particularly noteworthy because no horses were lost, no horses were injured, and the command was totally fit for service when it arrived.[23]

Using the method described by Colonel Merritt, the army formed mobile columns to pursue the Indians. Multiple columns limited the Indian's maneuver options and attempted to trap the mobile tribes and bands in a position where they had to fight. Scouts assisted the columns to locate the enemy, and commanders played a constant game of attempting to determine the Indian's intentions. Columns could only be successful if they could anticipate the Indians actions and gain a marching advantage on them. The telegraph, railroad, steamships, and couriers allowed

U.S. cavalry on winter campaign supported by Indian scouts. The U.S. cavalry's ability to campaign in severe winter weather negated much of the Indian's superior mobility. (*Frederick Remington*)

department, division, and column commanders to remain in touch with each other and coordinate. Columns were somewhat successful, but as the pursuit of the Nez Perce indicated, they were time-consuming, costly, and did not always produce decisive results.

The army used another tactic based on the strategic lessons of the Civil War. The Civil War taught the army that the most decisive form of warfare was total war. In total war military forces attacked the enemy's entire society. General William T. Sherman was the army's most successful Civil War practitioner of total war, and he employed this same strategic approach against the Indians. The army realized that pursuing the Indians with mobile columns was pitting the army against the Indian's greatest strength–their mobility on horseback. The entire tribe, not just the warriors, was mobile. A village could pack up and move with only hours notice. In this contest of mobility the army's conventional organization, mediocre horsemanship, and logistics requirements put them at a disadvantage. The space of the West worked in favor of the Indians. The army determined to overcome the Indians mobility advantage by campaigning in the winter.

In the winter the Indians had to occupy permanent encampments. This was necessary to ensure adequate forage for the large pony herds. Additionally, moving in the extreme cold of the northern plains winter, though possible, was slow and hazardous. The army determined to take advantage of this vulnerability through large-scale winter campaigns. The focus of the campaigns was not on battling the warriors, but on raiding the villages and capturing the families and pony herds. The army then moved the families under guard to reservations and destroyed or sold the pony herds.

The intent was, under the cover of winter, deprive the Indian warriors of their support and mobility. If the Indian warriors stood to defend their villages and herds, army commanders considered that so much the better.

Once locating the winter camps, commanders had the option of executing a mounted charge. This was usually only practical if the Indians were surprised. Most often, the cavalry dismounted and advanced in skirmish order with the men dispersed using cover, and every fourth man in the rear holding the horses. In most cases, the cavalry's longer range Springfield carbines and disciplined deployment gave them the advantage over the Indians.

The combination of summer pursuits and winter attacks on the camps was brutally effective. Over the period of the conflicts, the army systematically shifted units throughout the West and reduced the hostile tribes one by one. In many cases it took several years, but ultimately the American cavalry forced even the most warlike and independent tribes and bands to acknowledge that the group's only chance for survival was on the army's terms on the reservations. Thus, between 1866 and 1890 the U.S. cavalry, while suffering numerous tactical setbacks, prevailed in establishing the uncontested dominance of the American government over the western territories.

Horses and Horsemanship

Though the American cavalry was dramatically reduced in size after the Civil War, the war left the force with an experienced cadre of leaders. These leaders ensured that the American cavalry were well-mounted, competent riders and understood how to manage the care and health of their horses.

Horses

The army quartermaster purchased cavalry horses. Purchasing officers did not consider formal breeding in the selection of remounts. Their most important criteria was health and stamina. The purchasing officers understood well the rigors of campaigning to which the horses would be subject. Cavalryman Frederick C. Kurz of the 8th Cavalry at Fort Clark, Texas, described his troop's horses in 1885 as "a mixture of Mexican Bronco and American, but [they] made pretty good mounts and stood hard riding after being broken in." Englishman Archibald Forbes described American cavalry horses of the Indian wars period as "stout, hard, active, and wiry, accustomed to endure hardship and to graze and stand quiet when picketed."[24]

The best known of the American cavalry horses, and one of the best known horses in American history, was Comanche, the mount of Captain Myles W. Keogh, commander of Company I, 7th Cavalry. Comanche's fame resulted from the horse being the only recovered survivor of Custer's command after its destruction at the Little

Comanche, a survivor of the Little Big Horn battle. Comanche was of unknown origin but was a typical American cavalry remount of the late nineteenth century. The horse was a bay gelding and stood about 15.1 hands tall. After the battle he remained with the regiment but only served for ceremonies. (*Cavalry Journal* [U.S.], 317)

Bighorn battle.[25] Comanche was severely wounded in the battle, was nursed back to health by the surviving members of the regiment, and became their mascot, carefully maintained for the rest of his life. Because of his notoriety, Comanche's life was better documented than any other cavalry remount, perhaps in history. Though an officer's mount, Comanche came to the 7th Cavalry as a regular government-purchased remount in 1868 and thus is representative of the remounts supplied to the cavalry during the plains wars period.

The history of Comanche before he became a remount is obscure. Comanche was a gelding who stood between 15 and 15.2 hands. He was a bay with a short white sock on his left rear foot, white patches in the saddle area, and a small white star on his forehead. He weighed about 950 pounds. He was not an overly large horse but fit very well within the average range of cavalry remounts.[26]

Comanche entered army service in St. Louis, Missouri, where the army quartermaster purchased him for $90 on April 3, 1868. The army then moved him for training to Fort Leavenworth, Kansas. After he completed basic training, together with a group of 40 remounts, the army assigned Comanche to the 7th Cavalry, stationed at Fort Riley, Kansas. Captain Tom Custer, in charge of retrieving that particular groups of remounts, reported that they "were in good condition. . . . Most of them were looking well and I regard them as a choice lot of horses."[27] Comanche was probably six years old when he arrived in the regiment. The horse came to the attention of Captain Keogh who, since officers provided their own mounts, bought him from the government as his personal mount.

At the Battle of the Little Bighorn in 1876, Comanche was one of the veteran horses: 14 years old with 8 years service in the field. Some historians report that at this point in his career Comanche had already been wounded in battle on three separate occasions. Unlike Comanche, many of the regiment's other horses were new and unaccustomed to hard campaigning. In addition, the horses of the regiment entered the battle tired, and many were close to exhaustion–Custer had a reputation for pushing his men and horses hard. The regiment had been riding for weeks prior to the battle. In the 33 hours before the battle the Custer and Reno battalions had covered over 60 miles. On the day of the battle, at least four troopers dropped out of formation because their mounts were too exhausted to continue. Elwood Nye, a twentieth-century American horse cavalryman and veterinarian, and in the 1930s one of the army's experts on long-distance cavalry marching, came to the definitive conclusion that Custer began the Battle of the Little Bighorn on exhausted horses.[28] Certainly there were many circumstances and mistakes that led to the Custer disaster, exhausted horses was one of them and may explain why Custer's men were incapable of escaping by simply riding away.

Two days after the battle, General Terry's command rescued the surviving battalions of Custer's command. As the army forces surveyed the battlefield where Custer's battalion had been wiped out, they counted 210 dead soldiers. Hundreds of dead horses also littered the field. As burial parties worked, soldiers discovered a wounded cavalry horse in the riverbed of the Little Bighorn River. Several soldiers disregarded the animal because of its wounds, but Lieutenant Henry Nowlan recognized the horse, Comanche, as Captain Keogh's mount and organized efforts to save the animal. Reports vary regarding the extent of Comanche's injuries. He was wounded at least twice, probably more; an official description of him done some years later noted 12 scars caused by wounds. Comanche was nursed back to health, and in 1878 the colonel of the regiment posted a special order declaring that Comanche would never be ridden and would march with the regiment on all parades. In addition, "his kind treatment and comfort should be a matter of special pride and solicitude on the part of the 7th Cavalry, to the end that his life may be prolonged to the utmost limit."[29] Comanche lived a long life, dying in his troop stables in 1891 at the age of 29 years. Comanche's remains were mounted and remain on display at the University of Kansas Museum of Natural History.

Horsemanship

Upon entering service, cavalry recruits received initial training at Jefferson Barracks, Missouri. In the years after the Civil War, training occurred in the regiments, but in later years a recruit might spend several months receiving basic training at the barracks. In the 1880s, cavalry recruits received basic equitation, with and without saddles as part of their entry training.[30] Horsemanship was important but exceptional skill was not required. The American cavalryman on the plains was at best a workman-like horseman, as were his superiors.

Though high-quality formal horsemanship was not a characteristic of American cavalry, a great deal of emphasis was placed on horse care. On the plains, often hundreds of miles from nearest town or ranch, it was obvious to all cavalrymen, soldier to commander, that the trooper's life might depend on his horse. The Civil War luxury of quickly acquiring remounts did not exist in the army of the West. Thus, units and officers prided themselves on the health and stamina of their mounts. The professional cavalry of the Indian Wars, when compared to the volunteer cavalry of the Civil War, though perhaps not greatly superior riders, were much better horse masters. This was a function of more experience, better leadership, and operational necessity.

Though from a strategic perspective the outcome of the Plains Indian Wars were inevitable, the wars themselves were hard fought actions in which both sides displayed at times brilliance, and at other times tactical shortcomings. The wars pitted two very competent, but very different, mounted forces against each other. Though the American cavalry were backed by extraordinary strategic resources, the operational and tactical odds were much more even than is generally appreciated. The Indians excelled in horsemanship and the tactical battle. Their knowledge of the terrain and fieldcraft were without peer. The American cavalry were well led, well equipped, and persistent, but limited in size to a few long-serving and often undermanned regiments resourced by a very meager military budget. The American leadership understood the nature of the wars better than the Indian leadership and pursued tactics and strategies which attacked the Indian's greatest vulnerabilities. The length of the conflict is a testament to the determination and skill of both the army and native horsemen.

The Boer War

At the end of the American Civil War, many observers concluded that the war indicated that cavalry continued to have an important role in warfare despite new weapons, tactics, and technology. The importance of horses and cavalry in the

American campaigns against the Indians reinforced the Civil War conclusions, and hinted that under some conditions mounted forces were absolutely decisive. The employment of cavalry in the European wars of the late nineteenth century left a more ambiguous legacy. European thinking was that cavalry was still important, but in a traditional way. Events in South Africa at the end of the century demonstrated that the American cavalry experience was not an isolated event, and that the mounted rifleman was a modern evolution of the cavalry arm that could not be ignored.

The Boer Wars contested the right to independence of the Boers, the original Dutch settlers of South Africa, from British rule. The first Boer War occurred 1880–81 and was a relatively brief military affair during which the British were decisively defeated on several occasions and, as a result, granted the Boers independence in two regions of South Africa: the Transvaal and the Orange Free State. In the late 1890s British speculators used their influence with the British government to obtain British government interference in the internal affairs of the two independent Boer governments, ostensibly to protect the rights of *uitlanders*. Uitlanders were British citizens living and working in the two African states. The Boers, rather than await British intervention, opened hostilities in October 1899. The war divided into three phases. In phase one, the Boers decisively defeated British offensive operations against the Orange Free State and the Transvaal. In phase two, an extremely large British army, commanded by Field Marshal Frederick Sleigh Roberts, Lord Roberts of Kandahar, systematically captured all of the major Boer cities. At the conclusion of this phase, Roberts declared victory and returned to England, turning over mopping-up operations to his chief of staff, General Horatio Herbert Kitchener, Lord Kitchener of Khartoum. Kitchener's mopping-up operation turned out to be anything but, as the Boers launched the third phase of the war—the guerrilla war phase. This phase began in June 1900 and continued until the two sides negotiated a peace in May 1902.

Inept British command, poor tactics, and inadequate troops and organization characterized the first phase of the war. The Boers began this first phase with offensive operations beginning on October 11, 1899. As part of these operations, they forced several large British contingents to retreat into defended towns where the Boers besieged them. In these early operations, the British were still employing linear infantry tactics, often with the troops marching almost shoulder to shoulder.[31] Overwhelming numbers, more cavalry, and the beginnings of an understanding by the British command of the importance of mobility and speed all contributed to the success of British conventional operations in the second phase of the war. The handling of the British mounted forces as well as the addition of well-trained mounted Australian and New Zealand colonial units to the fight permitted the British to gain

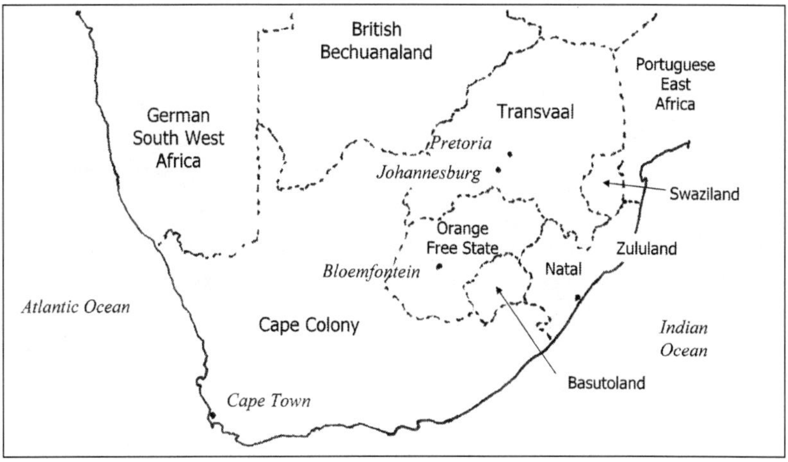

Map of the Boer War area of operations.

the upper hand in conventional operations. This resulted in several British victories, and the successful British campaign to capture Bloemfontein, the capital of the Orange Free State, and Pretoria, the capital of the Transvaal.

After Kitchener replaced Roberts, the new commander quickly realized that the war was far from over. The Boer governments were still active and at large, and the best Boer field forces and commanders were still in the field. Boer raids began to take a toll on isolated columns and detachments until Kitchener put the army back on a complete war alert. He then devised tactics to fix the Boer field forces and destroy them. The war became a war of mobility. The Boer forces kept on the move constantly, living off the population and captured British supplies. The British put out expeditionary columns who coordinated their movement in order to trap the Boer field forces. Though always containing a mounted contingent, the British columns could not match the Boer's speed because wagon trains and infantry slowed them down. Boer forces were completely mounted and operated throughout the occupied territories as well as in the Cape Colony and Natal. By placing their forces on alert however, the British greatly reduced the number of successful ambushes and raids. The British were unable to pin down the elusive Boers, but the Boers found it difficult to make decisive strikes. The Afrikaner populations of Natal and the Cape Colony, though willing to support the Boer raiders, were unwilling to rise in rebellion. Thus, through the rest of 1900 and into 1901 the war was a stalemate.

In 1901 Kitchener began to change his strategy. Recognizing that the Boers' mobility was due to their ability to support themselves through the local population, the British began a policy of population relocation and farm burning. The British forcibly removed the Boer families from their homesteads and relocated them into some of the world's first "concentration camps." In many ways, as the British government took responsibility for the families, Boer field forces found themselves with greater operational flexibility.

The concentration program was not a success, but the British continued their efforts to limit the Boers' mobility. The second effort, which was somewhat successful, was the blockhouse strategy. This began as a tactic to protect railroad lines and other fixed positions. The British then expanded the program by turning the rail lines into fortified barriers to movement. Prefabricated block houses were positioned along the lines, in some places as close as every 200 yards, and manned with infantry. The intent of cordoning the wide open spaces was to limit the mobility of the Boers. It became impossible for a Boer unit to cross a rail line without a battle. The British then began to extend the system: first to key river fords and mountain passes, and then along lines to further segment the terrain. This program was expensive and extremely manpower intensive. Vigorously administering the strategy required increasing the size of British field forces to 250,000 in late 1901. Eventually the blockhouse lines accounted for 3,700 miles of territory and were manned by 66,000 infantry. Though the system could not stop the Boers, it significantly limited their mobility options at the operational level.

A final tactic the British employed was improving their intelligence system. Employing Boers as scouts greatly enhanced British intelligence efforts. These scouts knew the terrain, knew how the commandos operated, and could match the Boers' mobility and horsemanship. Mobile columns continued to operate, and more and more of the British forces were mounted. British mounted forces now consisted of regular cavalry, Afrikaners, other colonial troops from New Zealand, Australia, and Canada, large numbers of mounted infantry (MI), and Imperial Yeomanry (reserves) from England. The columns continued to operate, moving men and horses by rail and then dismounting from the trains at strategic locations.

The new blockhouse lines, the vast number of troops, the war weariness of the Boer people, and the increasing effectiveness of the mounted columns began to take a toll on the Boers. The British had several significant successes including capturing the entire Free State government and all of its records. However, the elaborate British system was not capable of stopping the Boers entirely. Boer forces achieved several notable successes into 1902, including the destruction of one of the most capable British columns and its commander Colonel G. E. Benson in October 1901; and the destruction of a major column under General Methuen and the capture of the general and 600 of his troops in March 1902.

The Boers

The Boer states did not have standing armies. Instead, they organized the citizenry into militia units called commandos which mobilized in times of emergency. The Boer states provided only weapons and ammunition. But, despite a lack of professional military training and experience, the commandos preformed superbly against one of the most professional armies of the nineteenth century.

Organization and Equipment

The Boers began the war by mobilizing a field strength of 50,000 troops. The Boers organized their forces in regional burgher commandos of mounted riflemen. Commandos varied in size from as small as 60 from the most isolated rural areas, to as many as 3,000. The average command size was 300 to 400 men. The commando subdivided into field-cornets of 150 to 200 men. These were further divided into corporalships of about 25 men each. The members of the units elected all leaders from the commando to the corporalship.

Each Boer brought his own horse, personal equipment, and rifle upon mobilization. Boers were not paid. The most common rifle among the Boers was the German 7-mm M1895 Mauser. The Boer states bought 40,000 of these weapons as well as large stocks of ammunition before the war. They then sold the weapons to citizens at a nominal fee or issued them to the commandos as they formed upon mobilization in 1899. The Mauser was an extremely effective magazine-fed bolt-action rifle. The Mauser ammunition used smokeless powder and had a maximum range of 2,000 yards. A good marksman, and the average Boer was an excellent marksman, was very effective with it, using open sights, at 700 to 800 yards. The Mauser had a five-round magazine which was loaded from clips. The clips made reloading extremely quick. The Boers carried the five-round clips in a 12-pouch ammunition bandolier, making the basic load of the Boer mounted rifleman 60 rounds.[32] Virtually all photos show the typical Boer rifleman with his bandolier worn over the shoulder; often he wore two bandoliers.

The Boers wore no uniforms but generally fought in utilitarian earth tone farm clothes. Almost all wore wide-brimmed hats. These hats were common among all forces on both sides except the British regulars. The British regulars began to adopt wide-brimmed slouch hats in 1901. Both sides followed the custom of turning up one side of the hat brim.

Tactics

The Boers fought the first phase of the war conventionally. They had their own artillery and employed it in conventional warfare with the British. The Boer experi-

Boer Commandos armed with a variety of weapons including Mausers (back row) and captured British Lee-Enfield rifles (front row). Slouch hats and bandoleers of ammunition were the most uniform aspects of the Boers' appearance. (*Author*)

ence in this phase was that they were more than able to defend against the British, but that they did not have an ability to overcome prepared British defenses. After the initial maneuvers of the war, the Boers found themselves unable to sustain large-scale offensive operations.

In the second phase of the war the Boers found that improved British leadership, the large number of British reinforcements, and increasing numbers of British mounted units made even a conventional defense impossible. The British cavalry cut off Boer defensive positions, subjected them to intense artillery fire, and then assaulted the position with disciplined British infantry. Under these circumstances, the Boers were able to inflict significant casualties on the British but could not stop the British assaults. Thus, in the second phase of the war the Boers were systematically defeated in their defensive positions.

The Boers abandoned conventional operations in the third phase of the war. They determined to fight a war designed to cause as much damage to the British military and its interests as possible, while avoiding decisive defeat. The strategic goal in this portion of the war was to make the war so militarily and politically costly that the British would negotiate for an end on terms favorable to the Boers.

For this phase of the war, the Boer military forces broke up into commandos and prosecuted a war of raids and ambushes. Military operations divided into two types. The first type was operations against the British forces occupying the Transvaal and the Orange Free State. The Boers considered these strategic defensive operations designed to make the occupation as costly as possible. The second type of operations were strategic offensive operations into the British Cape and Natal colonies. These operations demonstrated the continued offensive capability of the Boers and attempted to rally the colonial populations to the Boer cause.

In practice, the two types of operations were similar. The Boer commandos attacked the British rail-based logistics system. They also ambushed isolated British patrols and outposts. The key to success was to inflict damage without sustaining losses themselves. Thus, the Boer attacks were sudden, swift, and included a detailed plan to elude pursuit and escape. In frustration, Kitchener described how the Boers fought in the third phase of the war: "Divided up into small parties of three to four hundred men, they are scattered all over the country without plans . . . and on the approach of our troops they disperse, to reassemble in the same neighbourhood when our men pass on. In this way they continue an obstinate resistance without retaining anything or defending the smallest portion of this vast country."[33] The key to the successful Boer tactics was the mobility provided by the horse. All Boer combatants were mounted and were excellent riders.

Horses and Horsemanship

For the first two years of the war the Boers were well mounted on their own Afrikaner horses. This was a type horse that was brought to South Africa by the Boer settlers and bred indigenously by them. Though relatively small, its chief advantage was its adaptation to the environment, its hardiness, and the fact that it was an "easy keeper," able to sustain itself on the available forage. After a successful action against a British force, Boer Francis Reitz described his horses and his evaluation of the British cavalry horses which he took as booty:

> My brother brought my roan and his own two riding-horses down the ravine, and we took two more horses from the English lines, where many stood picketed. Searching out saddles and wallets to match, we loaded our caravan with spoil. . . . We were refitted from head to heel, we carried a Lee-Metford rifle apiece, in lieu of our discarded Mausers, and above all we were well found in horse-flesh. My gentle loyal old roan was as flourishing as ever, and I had a fine little chestnut pony, which I had chosen in preference to the large but less reliable chargers in the English camp. I gave the other horses away in order to reduce our stable to manageable proportions; my brother had the two horses which he had brought with him from the North. One was a toll-free chestnut and the other was the strangest horse I have ever known. . . . Well-mounted as we were, my brother and I felt that we could ride anywhere and be ready for anything.[34]

Reitz's own riding horses eventually gave out, after 10 months of hard campaigning his roan was severely foundered. Still, the loyal horse gave him one last gallop into action in a famous raid on a squadron of the 17th Lancers. There he reequipped himself with "a cavalry-tunic, riding-breeches . . . a sporting Lee-Metford, full bandoliers and a superb mount, a little grey Arab. . . . [He] also selected a strong riding-mule in preference to another horse, for experience during the past fortnight had taught me that a good mule for long marches and a light nimble pony for use in action, were the ideal combination." Reitz's red roan of which he was quite proud "was so exhausted that when I tried to lead her away she could scarcely put one foot before the other, so I unsaddled her, throwing the saddle aside . . . removing the bridle and halter, I turned her loose in the hope that some neighbouring farmer would look after her, for she too had shown the mettle of her Free State pasture, and the marvellous endurance of the South African horse."[35]

The effect of the British tactics was hard on men and horses, and both died from exposure and exhaustion. Normally, horses are very tolerant of weather conditions, but in an underfed and fatigued state, the horses succumbed to the sometimes dramatic changes of weather. Reitz reported that in one night, freezing rain and cold killed 60 of slightly more than 200 horses. The solution to losing Boer horses was capturing British mounts. The same mounts that Reitz and his companions ignored early in the war became valuable prizes worth fighting for in the last months of the war.[36]

The Boers were natural horsemen, and their horsemanship gave them a tactical advantage over pursuing British mounted forces, many of whom never rode until after their arrival in theater. British officers who underestimated Boer horsemanship did so to their detriment. In the fall of 1901, the British were sure that their columns had trapped the raiding commando of Boer General Jan Smuts.[37] The British had relentlessly pursued the commando for days and kept it continuously on the move for 40 hours. The Boer riders and horses were exhausted. The British, using trains to quickly move mounted forces ahead of the Boers, finally trapped them on a plateau. Taking their time, the British carefully positioned machine guns to cover all the exits off the escarpment but refrained from attacking. They left the Boers no choice but to surrender or risk a suicidal charge against the machine guns. The Boers chose neither option. The British left an almost vertical precipice unguarded. Under the cover of darkness, Smuts led his 200 men and horses over the edge, sliding and falling down the slope but staying in the saddle, and then riding out of the trap. Reitz described the experience:

> We now began to descend what was probably the nearest approach to the vertical attempted by any mounted force during the war. I doubt whether we could have accomplished it by day, but horses are more tractable and surer-footed in the dark, so we pulled them over the edge and went slithering down. At times whole batches of men and horses came glissading past, knocking against all in their course, but luckily the surface was free of rock, and covered with a thick matting of grass which served to break the impact, and after a terrible scramble we got down without serious damage. For the time being we had shaken free of the enemy once more.[38]

The horsemanship of the Boers gave Boer commanders tactical options that they would otherwise not have had and was a decisive factor in the Boer's ability to continue to execute successful mounted operations against a numerically superior enemy into the last months of the war.

British Cavalry

Elements of 21 regular British cavalry regiments served in the war.[39] At the war's height, almost a third of the 250,000 British troops in South Africa were mounted. The regular establishment, however, did not come anywhere near meeting the mounted requirements of the war. In order to field the almost 80,000 mounted troops it needed, the British army relied on three additional sources: colonial forces, mounted infantry, and yeomanry.

The British colonies provided the war's colonial forces. The four primary colonial forces were African, Australian, New Zealand, and Canadian. Eventually, the English colonies provided two-fifths of the mounted troops used in the war, the largest contingents coming from South Africa, followed by Australia.

Probably the most distinguished colonial unit of the war was the Imperial Light Horse (ILH). The unit members were uitlanders, mostly from Transvaal. The two founders were the South African-born Aubrey Wools-Sampson and the Australian Walter Karri Davies. Both men were advocates of uitlander rights. They began their unit by recruiting 500 picked men from the more than 5,000 who applied. They selected the initial squadron based on knowledge of the veldt, horsemanship, and marksmanship. The Natal colonial government sponsored the unit, and the British government sanctioned it for service at a standard rate for colonial troops. It immediately became one of the elite units of the war, eventually growing to a regimental strength of 1,200, and ultimately formed a second regiment. Commanders specifically asked for the ILH, and it fought in many of the important battles in the first year of the war. After the war, it became the premier unit of the South African colony, and its descendant remains a part of the national army of South Africa.[40]

Australia offered units for service before the war began. Each of the Australian colonial states raised units. They would eventually number more than 16,000 troops. Though small in number, the Australian contingent contributed capability out of proportion to its total numbers. This was because most of the Australian contingent was mounted and made up almost 20 percent of the total mounted force. In addition, the Australian mounted forces came from a similar climate as found in South Africa and could match the Boers in horsemanship and fieldcraft. Thus, the quality of the Australian force was exceptional and ideally suited to the war. As the war progressed the British authorized independent companies from the same colonial state to unite in battalion size contingents under a major. These units were approximately 400 to 600 men strong. In 1901 Australia became a sovereign nation, and the subsequent mounted units provided to serve in the Boer War were designated Australian Commonwealth Light Horse. A Boer described the abilities of the Australians:

> For the first time in the war, we were fighting men who used our own tactics against us. They were Australian volunteers and though small in number we could not take their position. They were the only troops who could scout our lines at night and kill our sentries while killing and capturing our scouts. Our men admitted that the Australians were more formidable opponents and far more dangerous than any other British troops.[41]

Though not skilled in the art of conventional combat, the Australian contingent, and other colonial forces, gave the British mounted forces the fieldcraft, marksmanship, and horsemanship skills that were essential to successful antiguerrilla warfare.

Yeomanry units were volunteers from the British home guard. They were not mobilized for the war but individual volunteers were taken into service and formed into units specifically for deployment to South Africa. These units were poorly trained and notorious for their poor horsemanship and horse mastership. The final type of unit formed for the war were the mounted infantry. These units formed by mounting battalions of regular infantry regiments. Though poor riders, they were a valuable tactical tool once they arrived at the place of battle and dismounted.

Weapons and Equipment

The British cavalry began the war armed and equipped in typical nineteenth-century European fashion: swords and carbines for all cavalry, plus lances for those regiments. During the war the issue carbine became the Lee-Enfield six-round magazine carbine, which was 40 inches long and weighed 7.5 pounds. The cavalry sword was the Model 1890 pattern, now in keeping with the trend to field utility, painted drab. Another new innovation was the new sword scabbard was fitted with frogs and not carried on the trooper's person. Instead it fitted into a holder that buckled to the saddle on the near side below the cantle. A bandolier of five ten-round pouches carried ammunition for the carbine.[42] Yeomanry units were equipped similar to the regular cavalry.

Unlike cavalry, colonial units as well as mounted infantry only carried rifles and bayonets. In October 1900, the cavalry began to reequip to better meet the needs of the war. First they turned in their swords and lances. The only exception was that the regular cavalry regiments of General French's cavalry division retained their swords. Carbines were also turned in. Cavalry armed with carbines had a maximum range of 1,200 yards but an effective range of only about 200 to 300 yards. They needed rifles

Australian Bushmen. The most effective solution to the unorthodox tactics of the Boers was colonial cavalry. These troopers are armed with older Martini-Henry lever-action rifles rather than the newer Enfields. (*Author*)

to duel with the Boers. As replacements, the army issued all cavalry units the infantry pattern Lee-Enfield .303-caliber rifle with bayonet. This permitted the cavalry to match volleys with the Boer riflemen armed with Mausers. The Lee-Enfield, like the Mauser, was a bolt-action magazine-fed rifle. It had twice the magazine capacity of the Mauser, 10 rounds, but each round had to be loaded individually, thus making it slower to reload. Mounted troops carried the rifle slung over the shoulder. Arming cavalry with the rifle required retraining of cavalry in dismounted tactics and shooting. By June 1901 the reequipping process was complete.

Tactics

During phase one of the war, British cavalry were used primarily as auxiliaries and rarely played an important part in operations. In the second phase of the war, under Lord Roberts, British cavalry operations began to improve considerably. Part of the reason was the formation of a cavalry division under the able leadership of Major General John French. This division, using the speed and mobility inherent in a mounted organization, was the key to the successful offensive that eventually captured Pretoria in 1900. The most decisive action, which began the string of tactical success that marked the offensive, was the relief of the British garrison at Kimberly by French's division. French's cavalrymen then defeated and captured Boer General Conje 'Cone's large commando of 4,105 men at Paardeberg on February 27, 1900.

In the third phase of the war, the mounted forces played the all-important role of pursuing the raiding Boer commandos, while infantry units provided security of static positions and manned the growing lines of blockhouses. The tactics intended to keep unrelenting pressure on the Boer commandos, trap them between the pursuing columns and a static infantry force or a natural terrain feature, and then destroy them. Many of the columns that pursued the Boer commandos were all-arms columns that had no hope of finding the fast-moving Boers. The best column commanders formed all mounted subunits that detached from the main column. The best of these pursuit units, and the ones that were most successful, adopted the field manners of the Boers.

Colonel Harry Scobell's force represented mounted pursuit units at their best. Scobell lived like his men and insisted that subordinates keep horse loads to a minimum. In Scobell's column food was a luxury, and the troopers ate well only when they captured Boer stores. Pack mules carrying three days of food for a six-day expedition provided the column's logistics support. He did not permit wagons. He led a mixed force consisting of 1,100 men and horses of the 9th Lancers, the Cape Mounted Rifles (a colonial unit), and British yeomen. On the night of September 5–6, 1901, in the midst of pouring rain, he led his men on a night march. Following the lead of Afrikaner scouts, they planned to attack the laager of a 100-man Boer commando. The commando had taken shelter for the night in a sheep shed on an abandoned farm. In the darkness, the British cavalry surrounded the position and waited until dawn. However, they didn't realize the Boers were in the shed and not the stone house that was also on the property. Just as the sky was beginning to pale, the Boers in the sheep shed surprised a squadron of mounted lancers approaching the farmhouse. The exchange of fire took down the first rank of lancers, but then the massed fire of the surrounding British tore into the shed. The Boers, surrounded and hopelessly outnumbered, surrendered as quickly as they could. The British suffered 10 killed, mostly among the lancers. The Boers lost 13 dead, 46 wounded, and 107 captured. None escaped. The British later executed the eight leaders of the commando.[43] This small sharp success by Scobell's force represents the characteristics of British mounted antiguerrilla columns at their best: good reconnaissance and intelligence, stealthy movement and surprise, hard riding and speed, and overwhelming combat power.

Only the best British mounted units could match Scobell's capability. Rarely were the British regular cavalry or yeomen a central part of the best mobile columns, though their performance improved dramatically over the course of the war. The colonial units were the best suited for mobile operations. New tactics, colonial support, and improved performance by the British regulars gave the British a relatively effective mounted force by the end of the war. As one Boer described the British mounted forces: "the enemy has adopted our methods of fighting. . . . He is making night raids all over the country, and practicing our own stratagems upon us."[44]

The tempo and scope of British mounted actions in the Boer War was tremendous. The area of operations was half the size of Europe. Men and horses were pushed to their limits. The British tactic of continuous pressure by multiple mounted columns, though effective, strained British resources of men and horses. These tactics, combined with a general lack of knowledge of horse care on the part of many British mounted units, contributed to a phenomenal loss of horses during the course of the war.

British cavalry in an ambush. The cavalry carbine carried by the first British cavalry was inadequate for fighting Boers armed with Mauser rifles. The British cavalry had a hard adjustment from conventional tactics to the unconventional hit-and-run guerrilla tactics practiced by the Boers. (*"Ambush" by Harry Payne; Author*)

Horses and Horsemanship

The type of horse preferred for cavalry operations changed drastically over the course of the British experience in South Africa. Many characteristics of previous British cavalry operations, however, remained unchanged. The British remount system proved itself as efficient as ever. Unfortunately, British horse management in the field was also as derelict as it had ever been.

Horses

At the beginning of the war, the British standard for cavalry horses remained what it had been for over a century: a relatively large horse, over 15.2 hands tall, and of the Thoroughbred hunter type. By the end of the war, the preferred type had changed dramatically. In the summer of 1901 the army ordered purchasing officers in the United States not to buy any more cavalry horses and to only buy cobs. Cobs were a short stocky horse type, generally in the 14 hands range that the army saw as the ideal mount for the mounted infantry. However, their endurance and their ability to stand up to the poor diet and strains of campaigning caused their migration from the army into the cavalry ranks. As their reputation grew, Kitchener reduced the preferred size of cobs from 14.3 to 14.1 hands.[45]

To meet the needs of the mounted forces, the army imported horses and cobs from all over the world. There was little unanimity of opinion among British mounted leaders regarding the quality of the numerous types of horses brought to South Africa. Imported Russian cobs stood up to the conditions of the theater well, but some cavalrymen thought them too slow for effective operations. Others thought they were the best of the imported horses. Few regarded Hungarian, Australian, and Argentine imports very favorably. English horses were too big and required too much care. Indian Walers were a quality remount. But, for every knowledgeable opinion, there was an equally knowledgeable opposite view. This was a function of the different officers seeing different groups of remounts under different conditions and after different transport experiences.[46]

The South African horse was the horse that received the highest praise from British cavalry leaders. This horse had the advantage of going into service without undergoing the hardships of travel and acclimation. The South African horse had considerable Arab and Thoroughbred influence. An officer of the Rimington Scouts, a colonial unit, described some of the qualities which made the South African horse a favorite:

> The South African pony, wretched little brute as he looks. [He] will triple and amble on, week after week and month after month, with a heavy man on his back, and nothing to eat but the pickings of sour, dried-up veld grass and an occasional handful of Indian corn. . . . All the imported breeds will gradually languish and fade away and drop and die, worn down by the unremitting work and the bad, insufficient food; but your ragged little South African will still amble on, still hump himself, or make an occasional hearty meal off the straw coverings of a case of whisky bottles. With an action that gives the least possible exertion; with the digestion of an ostrich and the eye of a prairie dog for any stray morsel of food; with an extraordinary capacity for taking rest in snatches and recouping himself by a roll whenever you take his saddle off.[47]

Perhaps no war in history saw a wastage of horses on the scale as those that suffered and died in service to the British army in South Africa. Where the American Civil War saw perhaps as many as 50 percent of the animals in service die, in the Boer war British army horses suffered a fatality rate of almost 70 percent–350,000 of 500,000 perished. British commanders in the field blamed the remount system for British horse losses. In fact, when the British government did a detailed investigation of the British remount system after the war, they discovered that the very small remount service responded extremely well to the totally unanticipated and extraordinary demands placed upon it. By January 1902, the British remount system was able to supply 14,000 horses and 2,000 mules a month to South Africa.[48] Some knowledgeable contemporaries determined that Major General Thurman, the Inspector General of cavalry who oversaw the remount system, was most responsible for the military success on the battlefield. Perhaps the only somewhat legitimate critique of the remount system was that, like the Union system in the American Civil War, it was so efficient providing remounts that the system encouraged units in the field to neglect the mounts they had.

The British cavalry, because of its preference for its own horses and its extended colonial service, was experienced with moving horses by ship. In the early months of the Boer War, a new system was designed for horse accommodation aboard ships. With the new system, the losses during transit averaged 3.5 percent. The greatest losses averaged 9.23 percent on horses coming from Britain. This was attributed to the requirement to only ship from specific home ports, and to the rough seas in the home waters. The lowest percent lost was 2.65 percent of horses crossing the Atlantic from the United States and South America. Overall, sea travel only accounted for 3.7 percent of all horse losses.[49]

The British ability to meet the massive requirements for horses in South Africa was a success enabled by foreign purchases. The largest overseas purchases were made in the United States. At its height, the British army was shipping more than 6,000 horses a month out of the port of New Orleans. The British set up a very elaborate remount purchase system in the United States headquartered in Kansas City. It included a 7,000 acre ranch in Missouri used to classify horses and check them for disease and soundness. Another massive operation was set up at New Orleans, where horses rested for four days before loading on ships. Horses traveled up to 3,000 miles to the port of embarkation from all over North America. This travel was on special fast horse trains, which usually moved 300 to 400 horses per train. These dedicated and efficient rail accommodations were not available anywhere else in the world. By American law, horses were required to be periodically unloaded, exercised, watered, and fed.[50] The efficient American transport system resulted in few losses before embarkation.

With a plentiful supply of serviceable horses, and an efficient system for getting them to the theater of war, the cause of horse losses was traced to the theater of operations where efficient operations broke down. There, the holding depots were notoriously undermanned, which prevented the depots from breaking and training horses, and even from exercising them. Units in the theater were also chronically short of farriers. A cavalry regiment was authorized three farrier sergeants and 18 shoeing-smiths. In the first five months of the war the entire theater remount department had a total of two shoeing-smiths. The organization of the army's veterinary services also proved to be defective. Veterinarians were withdrawn from regiments in 1887 and consolidated in the army veterinary corps. However, the corps was not organized to segregate and hospitalize sick horses. This left sick horses in the units or depots where they infected other horses. The one veterinary hospital in theater was used to hold healthy remounts for issue, instead of quarantining and servicing sick horses.[51]

Intentionally poor ration allocations resulted in the near starvation of thousands of horses that later succumbed to disease. British commanders, despite veterinary advice to the contrary, mandated a near-starvation ration for unit horses. This was because of a poor appreciation of the type of horses that the troops had, and the working conditions of the horse. Financial and transport constraints also limited the ration. Mounted commanders argued that a smaller number of horses well fed would have made a more effective mounted force than more horses who were starving. The short rations available, sometimes no hay for weeks at a time, also motivated commanders to ask for small cobs instead of full-size cavalry horses.[52]

Horsemanship and Horse Management

The difficulties faced by the remounts caused by the circumstances of war and administration were severe. However, upon arrival in the units many horses faced their greatest challenges. The basic requirements of mounted operations–horsemanship and horse management–were lacking in many British units. Even the cavalry units, though they knew how to ride, were terrible at taking care of their horses. One of the reasons was unprofessional and detached leadership. The historian of the 12th Lancers wrote, "It has been contended that the British cavalry officer talked more and knew less about horses than anyone else on earth."[53]

The horsemanship of British cavalry was sufficient not to effect operations. Most colonial cavalrymen were first-rate riders. However, the tales of the horsemanship of the mounted rifle units and the yeomanry were reminiscent of the Union Civil War cavalry experience. An anonymous yeoman reported: "We got a draft of men and it was a pantomime when they got their horses (rough horses off the veldt). The air was full of arms and legs and saddlery. When the dust cleared there were men lying in all directions and they lost thirty horses, saddles and all!"[54]

Horse mastership was an area where the regular British mounted force was also grossly deficient. Here, even the regular cavalry were deficient, though again the colonial units were considered very capable. Marquess Anglesey, premier historian of the British cavalry, notes that, "a cursory look at most of the continental cavalry of the time and at the native cavalry of India is enough to show that their horse mastership was greatly superior to that of the British regulars. It was universally agreed, too, that the men of the British artillery, both field and horse, were generally good horse masters–infinitely better than the cavalry or mounted infantry." This trait of the

British cavalry had not changed since the Napoleonic era. Throughout the regular and yeomanry cavalry forces there was a cultural stigma associated with dismounting and resting the horse's back. British cavalry felt that dismounting reduced them to status of infantry. Yeomanry would sit on their horses for a half hour during halts unless directly ordered to dismount.[55]

Off-loading horses from ship. This horse is being off-loaded from a cargo vessel to a lighter. Through the nineteenth century the British army became expert at transporting horses by sea. They also developed a global horse purchasing system. Typically, the British army expected to lose about 3% of the horses they transported across oceans to disease or accident. (*Cavalry Journal* [British])

The veterinary surgeon of the 6th Dragoons kept very detailed records of the horses assigned during the regiment's wartime service. The regiment lost 3,750 horses during the war, while the unit traveled 6,116 miles. The regiment lost a horse for every three and a half miles traveled. As if to make a bad situation worse, it wasn't just horses that were lost. Some British cavalry did not even remove the tack when a horse became unserviceable on campaign. The yeomanry units were the worst. One yeoman cavalry unit was issued 610 horses, and after a short 14-mile march to their cantonment, lost 40 to the hospital and had to destroy another 35. They also left the 75 sets of saddles with the dead and disabled horses.[56]

The number of horses lost in the Boer War was in many ways unprecedented, especially since the British could not claim, with 21 professional regiments in service, that their cavalry were complete novices. The horse losses, however, did not represent some particular under-appreciation of animals by the British. Rather, the horse losses represented the overall gross inefficiency of the late-nineteenth-century British army in staff procedures and organization in the field. The British army that deployed to South Africa was administratively unable to deal with the massive resources assembled to prosecute the war. Not only were horse casualties excessive, but the British lost 13,589 men to disease while only losing 8,600 to combat. Even more depressing, over 20,000 Boer women and children, under British care in the concentration camp system, died from diseases related to malnourishment and unsanitary conditions. Thus, the appalling record of horse care in the British mounted forces reflected the general incompetence of the British army in planning and executing the staff operations necessary for large-scale operations.

The British mounted operations in the Boer War were ultimately successful, when combined with other tactics, in bringing the Boers to the negotiating table. The Boers ceased hostilities on terms well short of their political objective of independence. On the other hand, the Boer combatants and politicians returned to pretty much the antebellum status quo despite more than two years of very intense fighting, and huge costs in lives and resources to the home government. Boer combatants were not prosecuted after the war. The reason for this was that the Boers were successful in making the war too costly for the British government to sustain indefinitely. At the end of the war 250,000 British troops, including an 80,000-man mounted force, were required to prosecute the war against 20,000 Boer commandos. The British could not match the Boers tactically without a very large field army, and the British government was unwilling to sustain such a large force in the field indefinitely. The Boers' military successes, directly attributable to their superior employment of mounted forces, allowed Boer politicians to obtain acceptable conditions for ending the conflict through negotiation.

Occurring on opposite sides of the globe, and involving completely different cultures, the American Plains Indian Wars and the Boer War offer interesting similarities, as well as important contrasts in the use of mounted forces. The terrain, size of the area of operations, and general nature of the conflict were in many ways similar. The most striking similarity was the importance of the horse and mounted forces in both conflicts. Superior horsemanship and horse mastership were major factors that enabled a small unconventional mounted force to wage an effective guerrilla campaign against a much better resourced conventional army.

Both wars also demonstrated that a highly mobile enemy could only be effectively opposed by a force of near or equal mobility. In both cases the infantry and artillery arms functioned in a wholly supportive role. Almost exclusively, mounted forces prosecuted the decisive actions of the wars. The mounted operations in the American West and South Africa demonstrated that mounted forces could be employed very effectively in unconventional warfare–if they were versatile and were capable of mounted and dismounted combat. Both conflicts demonstrated, as the American Civil War portended, that the future of cavalry was tied to the mounted rifleman: an effective combat system characterized by tactical lethality, and tactical and operational mobility.

In both wars, conventional troops were at a disadvantage because they could not match the enemy in fieldcraft. Both conventional armies overcame this disadvantage in similar ways. The U.S. army enlisted Indian scouts; the British army recruited Boers and also augmented their regular cavalry with colonial cavalry that matched up well against the Boer's fieldcraft and horsemanship.

The wars also demonstrated some markedly different approaches to the military problem of highly mobile hostile guerrillas. The U.S. army effectively opposed the Indians with a relatively small cavalry force that it was able to concentrate systematically on individual enemy forces, thus achieving local superiority. The British approach was to employ large numbers of professionals and an even larger number of volunteer forces. Neither force could match the mobility of its foes, but the Americans, with a solid cadre of experienced professional leaders, were ultimately able to negate the mobility advantage of the Indian to the point that over time it was not decisive. One significant difference in these two approaches was in the length of the war. The British conflict was shorter than the American's, but the results were less decisive. The Americans were able to sustain a longer war by employing a small professional force, which required fewer resources, cost less, and attracted less public scrutiny and debate.

The Americans also demonstrated that a professional mounted force could achieve remarkable mobility without the huge loss of horses that characterized British operations. The soundness of American horses on campaign was mainly attributed to superior leadership, recognition that the horse was a valuable asset, and–in the case of the American West–an irreplaceable commodity. American troopers were not more knowledgeable than the British, but American leaders placed more emphasis on horse management and closely supervised horse care. At the rate of horse wastage in the Boer War, an American cavalry regiment would have been completely dismounted after the first three weeks of an Indian campaign. Horse wastage on the scale of the Boer War, although almost equaled in the American Civil War, would have been operationally disastrous given the conditions and the resources available during the Plains Indian Wars.

Finally, both the Plains Indian Wars and the Boer War demonstrated that the marriage of firepower and mobility was the most important military characteristic of cavalry. Combining magazine rifles and horses allowed cavalry to quickly move long distances and be militarily significant when they arrived. Shock tactics, though not without a place in the evolving modern role of cavalry, could not overcome a prepared infantryman, while cavalry firepower married to rapid maneuver could do so.

Unfortunately, much of what was–or could have been–learned from the American and British experiences was largely ignored by the large cavalry forces of the world. Many countries continued to pursue organizations, doctrine, and tactics more reminiscent of a Napoleonic battlefield than a modern one. The British cavalry, however, learned from their experience and came away from the war with a sound appreciation for horsemanship, horse mastership, and marksmanship. They would use the experience gained in the Boer War to field the most capable and successful mounted force in World War I.

Chapter Ten

THE LAST CHARGE

Do they remember? Well, they are only horses! The troopship and Egypt's sands lie between them and the paddocks they knew. Perhaps when they stand dozing with slack head-ropes, vagrant pictures flit through their minds. Who can tell? These are the veterans.

–Frank Dalby Davison, *The Wells of Beersheba: A Light Horse Legend*

Cavalry forces entering the twentieth century did not know they were approaching the end of an era. World War I would be a rude awakening. Cavalry had incredible difficulty operating against enemies entrenched behind wire and equipped with machine guns, rifles, and artillery support. In addition, motorized transportation made its first appearance on the battlefield in World War I and hinted at technology that could match or exceed the mobility of horsepower. Still, on the eastern front, and in the Middle East, cavalry had some notable successes. In addition, though wheeled and tracked transport made its debut, it did not demonstrate a capability for replacing cavalry. Thus, in many ways cavalry was no more obsolete at the end of World War I than infantry, which also proved unable to operate against the new incredibly powerful defensive systems. During the interwar years, between World Wars I and II the pace of technological advance increased. Motorized and mechanized technologies increased dramatically, and armies and cavalry forces around the world studied them closely. By the beginning of World War II, most countries were seriously considering abandoning their cavalry arms. The opening campaigns of the war–Poland in 1939, and the defeat of France in 1940–convinced several armies that the time to end the 3,000-year relationship between man and war horse had come. But large formations of war horses and riders took the field one last time in a conflict that also included jet aircraft and nuclear weapons.

Cavalry in World War I

Cavalry on World War I's western front was important during the initial war of maneuver, as the Germans and French launched their offensives. However, neither cavalry force demonstrated an ability to take advantage of the horse's mobility. Timidity existed in the French and German cavalry, which may have been a reflection of their clearly subordinate role in operations, as well as a lack of confidence in their troops, tactics, and weapons. Both high commands also shared some blame for not understanding the potential and capabilities of their cavalry forces. Neither force trained or equipped its cavalry to fight dismounted.

In contrast to the Germans and French, the cavalry division of the British Expeditionary Force (BEF) was a well-trained, well-led, experienced professional force. Soldiers were accustomed to dismounted action and were expert marksman. Most of the middle- and senior-grade officers were veterans of the Boer War and prepared units, troopers, and horses well for rigorous campaigning. The British employed their cavalry with confidence and decisiveness. Despite their small size, they made a solid contribution to the success of the BEF: blunting the German offensive at its most critical point. In encounters with enemy cavalry, they consistently bested their German counterparts despite fighting outnumbered.

The maneuver phase of the war was over by October 1914. From that point on, the impact of mounted forces on the western front was negligible. The Germans transferred most of the major German cavalry formations to the eastern front. British cavalry were eventually withdrawn from the trenches and formed into a cavalry corps that became part of the BEF reserve for the remainder of the war. French cavalry, like the British, were withdrawn from the front line. The British used their mounted units as a highly mobile reserve which would ride to a threatened portion of the front and then dismount and fight as infantry. The British transferred two complete cavalry divisions to Palestine and converted some regiments into machine-gun troops. However, they retained three divisions in France until the end of the war. The French dismounted some cavalry regiments and used them as infantry. The remaining mounted units served as a reserve.

The eastern front was a much different war than the war in the west. Though cavalry used many of the same tactics, the front was much larger, and the consequent greater dispersal of the troops made for more opportunities for maneuver. Cavalry, both German and Russian, played an important role on the eastern front. Its reconnaissance and security capabilities were in constant demand to find the enemy and follow him. In defense, cavalry provided vital security for infantry forces as they retreated to new positions. Cavalry was used on the flanks to prevent attacking armies from being surprised in these vulnerable areas, and to ensure the enemy did not infiltrate around defending forces.

Conditions in the Middle Eastern theater also offered opportunities for maneuver solutions to the tactical problems that faced the combatants. However, for the first two years of the war, it was a low-priority theater, and both sides were content to remain on the defensive. This changed with the arrival of British General Sir

Edmund Allenby, a cavalryman. His solution to the stalemate on the Mediterranean coast was to take advantage of the mobility advantage he had in the Desert Mounted Corps's four cavalry divisions. With these forces he broke the deadlock with a daring cavalry attack on Beersheba in October 1917. This successful attack broke the Turkish line and contributed to the quick capture of Jerusalem. In the summer of 1918 Allenby resumed the offensive, once again led by his cavalry divisions, and destroyed three Turkish armies and occupied Damascus. The success of Allenby's cavalry-led offensive prompted Turkey's withdrawal from the war.

Organization

In the opening months of the war the total cavalry forces in the field, counting all the combatants, was over a half a million horses and men. To fight World War I Russia fielded perhaps the largest cavalry force ever assembled. The peacetime strength of Russian cavalry was impressive: 106 regiments manned by over 100,000 troops. The peacetime strength of the Russian army was approximately 1.4 million troops, thus the cavalry, for all its size, was less than 10 percent of the force. Upon mobilization, more than 140 additional Cossack regiments activated, bringing the strength of Russian cavalry to approximately 250,000 men and horses.[1]

At the beginning of World War I a standard Russian cavalry division had four regiments of different types: one regiment each of uhlans, dragoons, hussars, and cossacks. The regiments were identical except for their uniforms, which still reflected the traditional cavalry type. A Russian cavalry regiment consisted of six squadrons. Each squadron had two companies and totaled 150 men and horses. The six squadrons gave the regiment a total strength of 900 men, and with supporting troops, the total was over 1,000. Two regiments made up a brigade, and two brigades a division. Horse artillery and other attachments gave a Russian cavalry division a strength of over 5,000 men and horses. Each cavalry division included a machine-gun section of eight Maxim machine guns.[2]

The French organized for war in the tradition of previous conflicts. They moved into the first combat operations in brightly colored uniforms and shining metal helmets.[3] Their organization did not differ much from the organization of French cavalry in the Napoleonic period or in the Franco-Prussian War. The French divided cavalry into four types: cuirassiers, dragoons, hussars, and chasseurs. Only the cuirassiers had an appreciable functional difference, remaining as heavy cavalry and prepared to execute the classic cavalry charge. All the others were general purpose cavalry.

There was a total of 93 regiments in the French cavalry arm. This gave France a total cavalry strength of approximately 75,000. Seven of the 10 cavalry divisions supported the five French field armies. Three divisions, including the heavy division with the bulk of the cuirassiers, made up a general headquarters (GHQ) cavalry reserve. As the war continued, conditions forced France to begin to dismount its cavalry. Ultimately four of the 10 divisions dismounted. A national shortage of horses influenced this decision as well as tactical considerations.[4] The balance of the remaining cavalry divisions formed a second cavalry corps used as a reserve.

At the beginning of World War I, German cavalry also organized much as it had in the Franco-Prussian War: broadly divided into cavalry to support infantry divisions and independent cavalry divisions. Usually one cavalry regiment was assigned to each infantry division. The German army formed 4 cavalry corps in the opening stages of the operations on the western front. At the beginning of operations the four cavalry corps operated under the command of supreme headquarters and were in effect separate cavalry organizations. But, by the middle of August 1914, the high command subordinated each to an army headquarters. In total, the Germans formed 11 cavalry divisions, each with 3 brigades of 2 regiments each, for a total of 6 regiments in a division.[5] At its height, the German cavalry forces numbered about 126,000 men. As the war progressed, the need for infantry to man the trenches also drove the Germans to dismount large numbers of cavalry. In August 1916, the Germans converted one-third of their regiments, 53 of 157, to dismounted cavalry regiments.[6]

Cossacks

Much of the cavalry strength of Russia as it entered World War I was in the form of Cossack cavalry. The Cossacks were a unique military culture that had no equivalent in any other country. Cossacks had been a central feature of Russian cavalry since the seventeenth century, and an important part of Russian society since the reign of the great sixteenth-century and Muscovite Prince, Ivan the Terrible.

The word *Cossack* (*Kazak*) derived from the Turkish work *Quazak* meaning "adventurer."[7] The Cossacks descended from people who lived in the great expanses of the steppe east of the more civilized agricultural and urban communities of northern Russia and the western Ukraine. The original inhabitants of this no-man's-land were roving bands of Mongols who had lost their association with the Mongol khans. These nomads subsisted by raiding Mongols, Turks, as well as Europeans. Although originally primarily Asian, the Cossack ranks were swelled by immigration from European Russia. The only requirements for new members to join the Cossacks was that the new comer be able to ride and perform military service. Over time, the Cossacks also became Christian, and new members had to embrace the Russian Orthodox faith.

A Cossack from the Caucasus Mountains. He wears the traditional papakha hat, an army tunic, loose pants, and no spurs. The saddles are the traditional Cossack saddle with a thick pillow seat. The horses are of the small mountain type, characteristic of the Kuban and Terek hosts. (*Cavalry Journal* [British])

Most of western Europe was ignorant of the Cossacks until their exploits during Napoleon's 1812 Russian campaign made them legends. The regular French cavalry, especially inexperienced recruits, were terrified of them. At the great allied victory parade in London in 1814, the Russian Cossack participants were the most popular of the visiting allied contingents.[8]

The Cossacks organized into geographic groups called hosts, which in turn were organized in a military manner. An *ataman*, who was also a general officer of the Russian army, led the host. In the years leading up to World War I, all Cossack males served in the Russian military for 4 years, followed by 20 years in the reserves. They served only in their own units and under their own officers. Each Cossack brought all his own kit to military service, including his horse. The rifle and ammunition were the only items issued to him by the government.[9] At the time of World War I, there were 11 hosts: Don, Ural, Terek, Kuban, Orenburg, Astrakhan, Siberian, Transbaikalian, Amur, Semiretshensk, and Ussuri.[10] When the Cossack reserves mobilized for World War I, virtually every male Cossack up to age 45 entered military service.

In the Russian cavalry of World War I, the most numerous of the Cossack hosts were the Don Cossacks: 58 of 160 cavalry regiments were from the Don Cossack host, while 100 of the 172 separate squadrons were also Don Cossacks. The second most numerous were the Kuban Cossacks, making up 33 regiments and 30 squadrons. The Kuban Cossacks were originally from the Ukraine but over time had immigrated to the eastern Black Sea region and settled around the Kuban River. They were the Russian bulwark against invasion from the Caucasus Mountains. The Kuban and Terek hosts adopted many of the traditions of the people of the Caucasus, and the czar authorized them to wear the traditional *papakha*, *cherkesska*, and *burka* instead of imperial uniforms. The *papakha* was a sheepskin hat of any natural color. The *cherkesska* was a long woolen belted coat with the slashed cartridge loops sewn into the breast. The *burka* was a thick black woolen cape worn instead of the army winter greatcoat. Other Cossack cavalry wore the standard army uniform but could be distinguished by blue pants with a pant stripe and shoulder board color designating the host.[11]

In 1905 and 1906 the government used Cossack cavalry units, mostly Don Cossacks, to put down civil unrest in many of the major Russian urban centers. To this point, the Cossacks had a generally positive image among the Russian peasants and public. After 1905, they became increasingly associated with the oppressiveness of the regime. The Czar's personal escort, the *Konvoi*–made up of Cossacks always wearing traditional cherkesska, reinforced the image of the Cossacks as a repressive tool of the regime.

The Cossacks had an international reputation as ferocious fighters, and their physical appearance matched that image. British General Knox described the Cossacks he saw while observing the Russian front lines: "I saw a squadron of Ural Cossacks in Sandomir–big, red-bearded, wild looking men, nearly all with a waterproof coat over their military great-coat. I don't wonder that the Austrians are frightened by them." Though greatly respected by civilians, the enemy, and allies, by the time of World War I, many in the Russian cavalry believed that the Cossacks had lost their special military prowess because the Russians had succeeded in civilizing them. Most Russian cavalry leaders considered the line Russian cavalry superior to Cossack cavalry, but this may have reflected a prejudice within the army against the Cossacks' special status.[12]

Weapons and Equipment

The general armament of cavalry in World War I was lance, saber, and rifle. However, there were many exceptions. Among cavalrymen, debates on the utility of the lance continued, and in many organizations, cavalrymen questioned the utility of the saber. Additionally, carbines saw their last days as a cavalry weapon; during the war rifles replaced carbines in those armies that had not made the change before the war.

Russian cavalry in World War I carried a saber, rifle, and lance. The cavalrymen understood that the lance was a throwaway weapon. All Russian cavalry units had the lance and were very proficient in its use. In the charge, only the first rank would carry the lance. Just like lance-armed cavalry centuries before, after the initial contact, the cavalryman discarded the lance and switched to the saber. British General Knox ascribed the unwillingness of Austrian cavalry to meet Russian cavalry in a melee due to the former's not being armed with a lance. "Every trooper in the Russian cavalry would now carry a lance if it were allowed. The German lance is a few inches shorter, a discovery which pleased the Russians." Like the Russians, all German cavalry carried lances. The German lance was hollow cast steel and 10 and a half feet long. In the French cavalry, the cuirassiers were the only cavalry not armed with a lance.[13] In the British cavalry the lancer regiments carried lances, but other cavalry did not.

Austrian cavalry trooper 1914. The helmet, saber, blue coat, and red britches are indicative of the traditional view of cavalry favored by the Austrians. The horse is a heavy German warmblood type (*Cavalry Journal* [U.S.])

French cavalry, including cuirassiers, carried an 8mm carbine with a three round magazine. Cuirassiers carried the weapon in a bucket in the near side of the saddle while all other cavalry types carried it by the sling across the back.[14] The weapon, a carbine version of the French Lebel rifle accepted into service in 1886, was inferior to the standard cavalry arms of all the other combatants. The weapon was not very accurate, had a slow rate of fire, and because of its tube magazine, occasionally set off a round in the magazine. The poor quality of the French carbine reflected the French disinterest in dismounted fighting.

The German cavalry had the 1898 pattern Mauser short rifle, which was the same weapon as the 1898 rifle but 5 1/2 inches shorter. The German cavalry's rifle was a quality weapon whose main weakness was the lack of training the cavalry trooper had in its use. Both the British and the Russians cavalry also carried very serviceable rifles. The British had the .303-caliber Lee-Enfield bolt-action rifle. It was a solid weapon with a respectable 10-round internal magazine. Because of the Boer War, marksmanship and dismounted tactics received great emphasis in the British cavalry before the war. The Russians used a cavalry rifle that was a lighter and slightly shorter version of the standard infantry rifle the M91/10 Mosin-Nagant. The Russians modified their sword scabbards with loops to attach the rifle bayonet to the outside.

At the beginning of the war, the sword was a standard weapon of all cavalry. Russian cavalry were great believers in the sword, particularly the Cossacks. The Cossacks used a unique traditional saber called a *shashka*. It was slightly curved, razor sharp, and uniquely had no guard around the handgrip. It was a deadly and feared weapon. Russian cavalry Captain Littaeur related the story of a 4-man Cossack patrol encountering a 12-man German cavalry patrol, which they engaged with their shashkas. Within minutes, 11 Germans were dispatched, all with the deadly shashka. Cossack commander Captain Tikhotsky described the awful damaged the *shashka* could cause when he examined an Austrian battery overrun by a charge of Cossack cavalry: "I was awed at the result of the saber slashes: some bodies lay headless, others had been sliced in half from shoulder to waist, the victims' innards lying bloodless. Like some ghastly anatomical exhibits." The Kuban Cossacks, who executed that particular attack, disdained lances and learned to wield the shashka from early youth.[15]

Most of the cavalry forces had discarded the colorful trappings of the Napoleonic era or adapted them to the drab uniform requirements of the modern battlefield as the war went on. The French cuirassiers, however, chose to retain the cuirass as a piece of equipment. They were the only cavalry still using the ancient armor in the twentieth century. It weighed about 15 pounds and provided no useful protection against modern small arms.[16] They designed canvas covers for the cuirass and for their polished helmets to keep them from being too conspicuous. The only explanation for the continued use of this impractical piece of equipment was the positive psychological effect of the traditional heavy cavalry kit on the cuirassiers who the French army still expected to charge in massed formations.

Tactics

Cavalry leaders debated operations in the years before the war, and one of the most important works on cavalry tactics was German Lieutenant General Frederick von Bernhardi's *Cavalry in Future Wars*, published in English in 1909. Bernhardi saw the necessity of a complete reevaluation of continental cavalry based on changes in warfare. He maintained that cavalry had to be able to operate independently. Bernhardi, a student of both the American Civil War and the Boer War, recognized that cavalry firepower was a critical factor in its future success.[17]

In Britain, a debate raged over the cavalry lessons of the Boer War. Both sides used excerpts of Bernhardi's book for support. One side of the debate maintained that the traditional cavalry role of massed shock action was still not only valid but central to cavalry's contribution on the battlefield. Two books written by Erskine Childers, *War and the Arme Blanche* published in 1910 and *German Influence on British Cavalry* published in 1911, both explored in detail the cavalry lessons of the Boer War for the British service and represented the essence of arguments that countered the cavalry traditionalists. Childers' view complimented Bernhardi and made the unequivocal point that the future of cavalry was associated with firepower: "Far from being weakened, Cavalry, if properly equipped and trained, have potentialities immensely greater than the Cavalry of 1870, because they now possess–in our country at any rate–the weapon [the rifle] which, united with the horse, qualifies them to tackle any other arm on their own terms."[18] Though writing very convincingly, neither

Bernhardi nor Childers had a major impact on the cavalry forces of the period outside Britain.

During World War I, no army created a truly independent cavalry force. Both the French and the Russians showed an interest in independent cavalry action, but creating such a force was a lower priority than supporting the infantry formations. The Russians simply did not have enough cavalry to create a separate cavalry force. The French formed the GHQ cavalry reserve whose primary purpose was employment as a decisive shock force. Though organized well for its shock role, its organization, equipment, and training did not permit operating independent of the infantry. The French envisioned the GHQ cavalry winning the tactical battle with a decisive charge. Its actual employment in the war was more as a reaction force to cover the flanks or gaps in the infantry line. The British eventually formed a cavalry corps that, like the French, functioned during the war as a reserve. In the Palestine theater the British Desert Mounted Corps (DMC) was probably the closest organization in the war to a pure mounted cavalry force capable of independent action, though it, like all cavalry corps in the war, was tied closely to the maneuver plan of the infantry. The DMC, however, was capable of breaking from the infantry and executing independent pursuit operations as it demonstrated in the last months of the war.

Though the various cavalry forces were alike in that they supported the infantry, they differed in their tactical techniques. The experience of the Franco-Prussian War was still the greatest influence in France and Germany, and those two countries, along with the Austrians, represented a traditional approach to cavalry. The French were determined to influence the tactical battle with a large cavalry reserve executing the massed charge in the Napoleonic tradition. The French "Regulations for the Service of Armies in Campaign" stated, "Mounted attack with *Arme Blanche* (saber or lance), which alone gives rapid and decisive results, is the principal mode of action of cavalry. Dismounted combat is employed when the situation or terrain momentarily prevent attaining the mission by mounted action." The Germans had a similar view. After the war, the German inspector general of cavalry stated, "Before the war, the importance of dismounted combat had not been given its just value. . . . Going into the war with the idea of mounted combat, with troopers of three years service knowing how to use their lances, the cavalry was poorly prepared for combat by fire. The advice of General von Bernhardi had not been listened to sufficiently."[19]

Units below regimental level most effectively executed cavalry charges. A determined charge by one small body of horseman against another often decided cavalry patrol actions. However, charging in formations regimental size or larger became increasingly problematic as the war went on. Large cavalry charges were impossible on the western front after October 1914. On the eastern front there was always some possibility of a charge, with the understanding that the larger the force the greater the difficulty in execution. Infantry and artillery firepower was an important defense against the charge, but not the only one. Wire was a major problem. A few simple strands of wire, not even barbed wire, were sufficient to stop a galloping regiment cold. For a charge of any significant body of horseman to have a chance of success they had to have clear ground. British Captain Francis Grenfell described a charge by the 9th Lancers in 1914 that encountered wire: "we simply galloped about, like rabbits in front of a line of guns. Men and horses falling in all directions. Most of one's time was spent in dodging the horses."[20] Cavalry had no hope charging against entrenched infantry supported by deliberate barbed wire obstacles.

Another major obstacle to the success of the charge was the loss of the psychological advantage. With quick-firing rifles, machineguns, and pistols, dismounted troops were much less likely to break than in previous eras. The dismounted soldier was very confident in the ability of his weapons to bring down a horse and rider, especially at close range. In a cavalry charge by Cossacks against an Austrian artillery battery, the Austrian gunners fought the Cossacks to the last man with pistols and rifles rather than run away or cower under their guns. No nineteenth-century gun crew would have ever considered standing and fighting against saber-wielding Cossacks. The psychological aspect of the charge was critical, and as the new confidence of dismounted troops diminished the fear of a charge, the chances of a successful charge were greatly reduced.

In contrast to the Germans, French, and Austrians, the British and Russians had developed a very capable dismounted capability in their cavalry forces without diminishing their ability to attack mounted. These two cavalry forces made important contributions from the beginning of the war by dismounting and employing the firepower of the rifleman. A captured German baron said to a Sergeant Hanna of the 15th Hussars, "the British shooting was marvelous and dreadful to watch, the men being wiped out by it."[21] The Russians and British also did not hesitate to attack dismounted when their officers recognized the conditions did not support the mounted charge. The French, Austrians, Germans, and other cavalry armies eventually recognized the importance of dismounted action and adapted.

Horses and Horsemanship

Despite the fact that close to 2 million horses saw service as cavalry mounts in World War I, the quality of the mounts was superb. This was a function of the professionalism of cavalry leaders, the efficient organization of remount and other support activities, and the proliferation of well-organized and scientific training systems. Many of the mounts seen in previous conflicts were present in great numbers on the European battlefields: American grade, French Barbs, British hunters, and German warmbloods. British regiments arriving from South Africa rode Afrikaner ponies.[22] Several new breeds and types got wide attention for the first time on the continent and in the Middle East and were impressive in their ability to handle the physical and psychological stresses of combat. Among these were the various breeds of the Cossacks and the sturdy horses of Australia.

Horses

In the early twentieth century the remount systems in Europe were exceptionally well organized. In Russia, government stallions stood for stud, which cost a civilian peasant or farmer 3 rubles. Four years later the army would buy the progeny back for as much as 400 rubles. From there the horse went to a reserve regiment where it was broken and trained for a year. Officers had their choice of government horses, which they purchased from the reserve training unit for 450 rubles. All officers had two mounts, one private and one issued. The army named all horses bought in a given year with names beginning with the same letter. By regulation, the horses served for 8 years and then went to public auction for sale. However, leaders ignored this regulation to get rid of troublesome mounts and to keep on steady, strong horses even when they exceeded the maximum age. Captain Littauer relates that when his squadron went to war it had four horses that were 20 years old. The Russian cavalry was an extremely well-mounted force. All of the horses were Russian bred. Most were three-quarters Thoroughbred or had a strong Thoroughbred influence. Russia's horse population according to a 1900 census was 22 million head. From these, the cavalry had the pick of the best. The army rated only about one percent as cavalry material. The Don horse was one of the most popular and numerous of the breeds in the cavalry.[23]

At the time of World War I, the mount of the Cossacks differed depending on the host. The most numerous host, the Don Cossacks, rode an exceptional cavalry mount bred on the steppes of the Trans-Don region. The horse was the result of crossing Mongolian ponies with Arabs stolen from the Turks. This original Don horse was the mount of the Cossacks of the Napoleonic period. The Russian general Ivan Krasnov described the breed as "small, thin, light, hot-tempered with a strong back and firm hoof, rarely sick, impervious to cold and wet and eating almost anything."[24] In the nineteenth century, the breeders mixed considerable Thoroughbred blood into the breed. The result was a horse that was relatively fast and bigger but still was very hardy, and had remarkable endurance. Krasnov believed that these new Trans-Don horses, bred specifically for the Russian cavalry, were inferior to the original steppe breed. However, the Don horse as described by the French war correspondent Dick de Lonely, on campaign with the Russian army in 1877, measured up to military requirements quite well:

> He represents the ideal of the war horse: frugal to an amazing degree, he lives contented with a handful of oats or barley, and when no other fodder is available, he will munch on the thatch of the peasant huts. He sleeps in mud and snow and the next day will put in the longest march with no complaint. Slower than the thoroughbred, he surpasses him in endurance and hardiness . . . and what a charming animal (15–16 hands) with his lean body, expressive head and intelligent eyes. He loves his master and will follow him like a dog. When his master rides another, he sulks and shows his jealousy. Grateful, he responds to each caress and falls in with the mood of his owner. In combat he takes part with unrestrained rage: mane flowing, with bloodshot nostrils, he kicks and bites the enemy's horses with the greatest furor. No one in our European world can imagine the Cossack's attachment to his horse: how often have I witnessed hardened warriors crying like children when their horses fell to enemy bullets![25]

The communists carefully nurtured the Don horse associated with the Russian cavalry and the Cossacks after the 1917 revolution in order to staff the regiments of the Red Cavalry of the Soviet Union. They evacuated the breed east of the Ural Mountains during World War II to protect it from the German invasion, and it is still an important riding breed in Russia today.

The Cossacks of the Caucasus, the Kuban, and the Terek hosts, rode horses of the Kabarda and Karabakh breeds. The two breeds are closely related. The Kabarda is common in the north Caucasus Mountains of modern Russia. The breed numbers today are very small. The Karabakh is the national horse of Azerbaijan. Both breeds are small high-quality mountain horses, in the 14 hands range, with a strong Arabian influence. They made excellent cavalry horses, but because pasture was not plentiful in the Caucasus Mountains there was always a problem finding enough of them to mount the Cossack regiments. Cossacks of the east (Ural, Orenbourg, Ussuri, Siberian, Seven Rivers, Amur, and Trans-Baikal) rode smaller and more primitive horses. In the extreme east the Trans-Baikal Cossacks rode the Mongolian horse that hadn't changed since the time of Genghis Khan.[26]

The Don and Siberian horses were not exclusive to Cossack regiments; the regiments of the regular cavalry rode them as well. War correspondent Stanley Washburn reported on Russian horses in general and the horses of a regular cavalry lancer regiment in particular during the summer of 1915:

> I have never seen mounts in finer condition, and I believe there is no army on any of the fronts where this is more typical than in the Russian. On this trip I

The Russian Don horse, top, mounted by a Russian dragoon officer in 1914. Bred on the steppes north of the Black Sea, and deriving his name from the Cossacks and the River basin where the horse originated, the Don horse was a superb medium-size cavalry mount. (*Cavalry Journal* [British])

> have been in at least fifteen or twenty cavalry units, and, with one exception, I have not seen anywhere horses in bad shape; the exception had been working overtime for months without chance to rest or replace their mounts. . . . I had a good chance to note the condition of both men and mounts, which were excellent. The latter were Siberian ponies, which make, I think, about the best possible horses for war that one can find. They are tough, strong, live on almost anything, and can stand almost any extremes of cold or heat without being a bit the worse for it. These troops have had, I suppose, as hard work as any cavalry in the Russian Army, yet the ponies were as fat as butter and looked as contented as kittens. The Russians everywhere I have seen them are devoted to their horses.[27]

The steppe and mountain breeds of the Russian cavalry had direct connections to the horses which the best of the steppe horseman rode for centuries. In World War I they demonstrated that the steppe horses remained war horses of the first order.

The Australians were another force well mounted on horses which were unfamiliar to most European armies. The horse of the Australian light horsemen was the New South Wales horse, or "waler" for short. The waler was descended from the original horses brought to the Australian New South Wales colony from the Cape colony with the first fleet in 1788. Over the first half century of the colony various breeds were combined with the original Cape horses to meet the saddle horse requirements of the colony where primitive conditions and long distances demanded a strong horse, able to subsist simply, and capable of sustained work. Breeding for these characteristics produced the waler type horse. The quality of the horse's military attributes attracted the attention of British remount officers, who began purchasing walers in the 1840s for British cavalry units in India. A steady remount trade developed which confirmed and encouraged the characteristics of the waler. During the Boer War, the waler type became the standard of Australia's own mounted forces.

During World War I, Australia exported over 160,000 walers to serve with the Australian Imperial Forces and 19 other nations. The appearance of walers in World War I reflected their diverse origin. The Australian official history of the war described the not-always-attractive Australian horses in the Middle East and why they made excellent cavalry mounts:

> The horses of a light horse regiment were not uniform. They included every kind of animal; large sturdy ponies, crossbreds from draught Clydesdale mares, three-quarter thoroughbreds, and many qualified for the racing stud-books. As a consequence of such mixed breeding, they frequently offended the horse-lovers eye by their faulty parts. But one quality they all possessed which made them superior to the horses from other lands: they were all, or nearly all, got by thoroughbred sires. This quality, reflected throughout in their spirit and their stamina, was their distinguishing characteristic. During sustained operations, on very short rations of pure grain and no water over periods which extended up to seventy hours–when horses of baser breeds lost their courage and then their strength–the waler, though famished and wasted, continued alert and brave and dependable. The vital spark of the thoroughbred never failed to respond. As long as these horses had strength to stand they carried their great twenty-stone loads jauntily and proudly.[28]

Lieutenant Colonel R. M. P. Preston, British cavalryman, described the performance of the walers in the history, *The Desert Mounted Corps*. Preston concluded that "there is no doubt that these hardy Australian horses make the finest cavalry mounts in the world." The walers had a special relationship with their riders. The light horsemen took a national pride in the quality of their mounts and developed strong bonds with them. Many of the mounts were the personal horses of the troopers, sold to the government upon enlistment, and then reissued to the trooper. Few other combatants in World War I were as isolated from their homeland as were the Australians.

Australian Light Horseman, bottom, and his Waler. The Waler was a type that represented the working stock horses of Australia. The horse pictured here served throughout the campaign in Sinai and Palestine, 1916-1918. The saddle is the universal pattern (UP) Model 1912. (*Australian War Museum*)

Many of the men were gone from Australia for four years.[29] This isolation brought the troopers even closer to the walers who represented a link to home.

The story of the Australian walers had a chilling ending. In February 1919, as the Australian forces were preparing to sail for home, the order was given to destroy all horses over eight years old. The expense of shipping and the extensive quarantine requirements necessary to prevent any exotic diseases entering Australia prompted the order. Worse, the command ordered the younger animals sold on the open market in Egypt. The thought of selling the younger horses for local use caused a near riot within the Australian regiments. The troopers preferred to give their mounts a quick and humane death rather than condemn them to a life likely full of pain and abuse which the troopers knew to be typical of working horses in Egypt.

Eventually, the Australian command changed the order so that the best mounts went to the British cavalry remount detachments set up to support British forces in the Middle East. To honor their remaining mounts the Australian Mounted Division held a final race day. Then, the bulk of the horses were led out to the olive groves outside Tripoli where they were fed a last bag of grain before special squads of marksmen put them down.[30]

Horsemanship

Horse equipment changed little during World War I. The standard army saddles developed in America, Britain, and Germany in the nineteenth century proved to be functional and offered little room for improvement in the twentieth century. Russian army tack resembled standard European models with the exception of the Cossack units. The Cossack riding gear, as did many aspects of Cossack service, continued to adhere to the traditions established on the steppe. Thus, the Cossacks rode in a traditional Cossack saddle rather than a government issue one. Captain Tikhotsky of the 1st Kuban Cossacks described the saddle and the horsemanship of his men: "The Cossacks rode on their own kind of saddle consisting of a light wooden frame covered by a soft leather pillow. At the trot, canter and gallop the riders stood in the stirrups, bodies leaning forward–the seat similar to the modern form of equitation called the Forward Seat."[31]

The Russian regular cavalry rode in the traditional European style and were equipped comparable to their European counterparts. However, during the second year of the war they dramatically departed from a thousand years of military riding tradition. In 1915, the Russian cavalry abandoned the curb bit, and after that point all Russian cavalry rode only in the snaffle bit. Captain Littauer stated that the "experiences of war proved them [the curb bit] to be not only unnecessary but even a handicap in cross-country riding, and they were sent to our wagon transport. From then on we rode on snaffles."[32] The Russian cavalry did not experience any great impact in changing the horse bit since their own Cossacks had always only ridden with just the snaffle. The snaffle remained the Soviet cavalry standard bit through World War II.

The institutionalized training systems of Europe's cavalry produced uniformly competent horsemen. Most of the cavalry of the period trained in the manège tradition. The various approved cavalry seats varied only in the details. The military stirrup was not as long as it had been in midcentury–causing a moderate and natural bend at the knee. "[The] flat of the thighs and inside of the knees lightly pressed against the saddle, legs from the knees downward slightly behind the perpendicular, toes a natural angle, heels forced downwards and pressure of the stirrup iron on the sole of the boot." The position of leg was slightly forward of the hips.[33]

Though the manège form, including a long stirrup, was still the predominant accepted riding style among the cavalry forces of World War I, things began to change just before the war started. One of the most important innovations in horsemanship since Xenophon came about just before World War I and influenced all military riding during the interwar years and continues to be the largest influence on sport riding into the twenty-first century. This was the advent of the forward seat. In its early days it was often referred to as the Caprilli or Italian seat, after its inventor, Italian cavalry Captain Federico Caprilli, an instructor at the cavalry school at Pinerolo, from 1903 to 1907. Caprilli developed the forward seat while scientifically improving the ability of cavalry horses to go cross-country and over obstacles. His

Italian Captain Federico Caprilli. Caprilli demonstrates his new forward riding and jumping style over a brick wall. His new riding technique revolutionized riding but did not have a major impact until after World War I. (*Cavalry Journal* [U.S.])

conclusions and methods rocked the horse world because they were the opposite of the "scientific" methods taught by the classic riders for hundreds of years.

A horse's center of gravity at the halt is a vertical line through its withers, while the rider's center of gravity is through his body sitting in the saddle behind the withers. Much of riding theory is concerned with bringing these two different centers of gravity into harmony, permitting the horse to be balanced while carrying a rider. Classical riding's solution to the problem of the different centers of gravity was to keep the centers of gravity as close as possible by bringing the horse into balance as he moved. As discussed previously, this was termed collection. A horse's natural movement put the center gravity even further forward of the withers as he picked up speed and his head and body extended. Classical riding tried to control this by collecting the horse–bringing the horse's head back using the bit, and by bring the horse's hind legs under him. Thus, as the horse picked up speed the rider helped the horse maintain his balance by keeping it collected, thus keeping his and his rider's centers of gravity as close together as possible.

Caprilli recognized the problem exactly as the classical riders did but completely rejected their solution. Caprilli believed that the way to balance the horse was not to collect the horse by bringing the horse to the position of the rider, but rather, to move the rider to the horse's center of gravity. This required shifting the rider forward, closer to the horse's withers, and, at high speed, out over the horse's neck. At slow gaits, merely shortening the stirrup and moving the ankle position back under the hip had the effect of slightly inclining the upper body of the rider forward over the withers. As speed increased, the rider extended the reins and allowed the horse's head to naturally extend. The rider did not lengthen the reins, instead the reins were extended by moving the hands forward causing the rider's upper body to lean further out over the horse's withers, and raising the rider's rear out of the saddle. The rider then balanced himself through his legs pressing down into the stirrups. Caprilli reasoned that by allowing the horse to run naturally cross-country, allowing him to use his neck to balance, the horse was less likely to stumble and could more easily negotiate obstacles.

Though a relatively simple system, the new technique was strongly opposed by traditionalists, including the prestigious French cavalry school at Saumur. However, as Caprilli enthusiasts easily dominated the international horseshow competitions, the new riding style began to attract serious attention. The British and Italian cavalry embraced the system prior to World War I, with corresponding improvements in the quality of troop riding. A large portion of the Russian army was already using the Caprilli system but didn't realize it. The Caprilli riding method was largely a scientific explanation of the short stirrup style of the Middle Eastern and Asian horsemen of the steppe. The Cossacks were already, unknowingly, using the system. After the war its merits for jumping horses and for cross-country riding received almost universal acceptance. Most postwar cavalry forces adopted the forward seat, after modifying it for their own situations, while still retaining elements of classical riding form and technique. This occurred in the United States, where the American cavalry's most outstanding horseman of the 1920s and 30s, Colonel Harry D. Chamberlin, toned down the Italian's extremely forward position of the rider, to a more secure but still forward position known in the United States as the balanced or military seat.[34]

In many of the World War I cavalry formations horsemanship was not only good but was exceptional. The Russian Cossacks, despite a very unorthodox style, were exceptional horsemen and capable of extraordinary gymnastic feats while riding at a full gallop. Cossacks wore no spurs. A short whip, called a *nagaika*, typically stuffed in the boot when not used, aided control of the horse. The Russian army made no attempt to train the Cossacks to ride in a European cavalry manner. The army also did not attempt to interfere with Cossack horse training.[35]

The Russians were not the only cavalry who incorporated natural horsemen into their forces. The Australian light horsemen were also, for the most part, exceptional horsemen who the army made little attempt to train. They were "not mere riders of educated horses, but men who had from their school-days undertaken, as a matter of honor and pride or of necessity, the breaking and backing of bush-bred colts and the riding of any horse that came their way. Their horsemanship came next to, if not sometimes before, their religion."[36] The quality of the light horse regiments was largely due to channeling the talent of the troopers rather than disciplining them to the army's ways.

Horse Mastership

Horse mastership in most of the armies was well developed. Again, this was a product of the increasingly professional and scientific approach to horse care evident in all of the armies, and the influence of formal cavalry schools. Veterinary services in all the army's were much more robust and capable. The British cavalry had taken the lessons of the Boer War to heart, and horse care became the foundation of the British cavalryman's duties. The travesties of the Boer War were not repeated. The French were an exception and continued to exhibit some of the same bad habits that had been characteristic of French cavalry since the Napoleonic period. French cavalry continued to considered dismounting an undignified act for a cavalryman. The French were astounded to see columns of British cavalry walking their horses. British observers commented on French cavalry who remained mounted even when halted for hours. "At times, they [the French cavalry] remained weeks without unsaddling. They had difficulty in watering their horses as often as was necessary. No later than the last of October [1914], the best commands had lost 2/3 of their horses, of which half were lost from overriding." Simple horse care habits such as feeding and watering during breaks, or loosening a girth, were not emphasized in the French cavalry.[37] Still, the type of wholesale wastage of horses due to neglect that was common in the Boer War and the American Civil War did not occur in World War I.

Cavalry in Battle: Megiddo and the Palestine Campaign of 1918

Though not representative of the employment of all war horses and riders in World War I, the dramatic success of the Desert Mounted Corps in the Palestine campaign was a demonstration of the potential that existed in mounted units during the war. It was also history's last decisive use of large mounted formations in battle.[38]

At the beginning of the war, British strategy in the Middle East was defensive and focused on protecting the Suez Canal. After the failure of the British amphibious operation at Gallipoli, the troops were evacuated to Egypt. This increased troop strength in Egypt gave the British forces sufficient capacity to consider offensive operations to remove the Turkish threat to the canal. The British decided to methodically move their defensive line across the Sinai Desert. Despite Turkish opposition, by January 1917 the British had established a solid defensive line well away from the canal.

With the canal well protected, the British determined that by attacking the enemy's alliance and knocking out the weakest member, Turkey, Germany's other allies, Bulgaria and Austria, might also collapse. In support of the new strategy, the British determined to launch an offensive into Palestine in the spring of 1917, with the ultimate campaign goal of knocking Turkey out of the war. In the fall of 1917 the new British commander, General Sir Edmund Allenby, former commander of the BEF cavalry division, and later the British cavalry corps in France, organized an offensive that resulted in the capture of Jerusalem on December 9, 1917. The key to the success of the offensive was a bold mounted effort by the Desert Mounted Corps

(DMC), led by the Australian Mounted Division (AMD) and the famous charge at Beersheba by the light horsemen. Requirements in France delayed continued offensive operations, but in September 1918, sufficient troops returned to the Middle East from France for Allenby to again attack.

A large number of troops from the Indian army reinforced Allenby's Egyptian Expeditionary Force (EEF) during the summer. These troops, combined with Australian, New Zealand, French, South African, and yeomanry units, gave the army a very non-British character. The EEF consisted of three corps. The XX and XXI Corps were infantry corps and included two and five infantry division respectively. The two infantry corps contained about 56,000 troops. The premier unit of the EEF was the DMC. Australian Lieutenant General Sir Harry G. Chauvel commanded this corps. It consisted of 4th and 5th Cavalry Divisions, as well as the Australian Mounted Division. In addition to the DMC, Allenby also had the Chaytor Force under command of Major General Chaytor. Chaytor Force was a task force built around the combined Australian and New Zealand Mounted Division, detached from the DMC and reinforced with royal artillery and an Indian infantry brigade.

The DMC was one of the most powerful mounted forces assembled in the war. The two cavalry divisions organized similarly. Each consisted of three brigades and each brigade had three regiments. For the most part, in each brigade, one regiment was British yeomanry cavalry, and two regiments were Indian cavalry. One of the two Indian regiments was usually lancers, though some of the cavalry regiments also equipped themselves with lances. The AMD consisted of three light horse brigades each with three light horse regiments. The light horse brigades of the Australian division, since their famous charge with bayonets at Beersheba in October 1917, had swords. A light horse regiment consisted of a headquarters and three squadrons, with a total number of men and horses at 522. In total the DMC consisted of approximately 10,000 horsemen, plus supporting machine guns, artillery, and light armored car units. The Australian New Zealand Division added another 3,500 mounted troops to the total in the EEF.

Allenby aligned his force with XXI Corps on the left, on the coastal plain, and the XX Corps north of Jerusalem. The Chaytor Force was positioned on the extreme right of the line near Jericho on the west bank of the Jordan River and oriented east in the direction of Amman. The DMC was in reserve, positioned on the coast, in the vicinity of Jaffa, close behind XXI Corps.

The Turks opposed Allenby's EEF with the Yilderim Army Group composed of five infantry corps organized into three armies. In total the three armies fielded about 32,000 infantry and 3,000 mounted troops. The Turkish left flank was anchored on the Dead Sea and then curved north and west across the Jordan river, through the mountains about 10 miles north of Jerusalem, and then to the sea about 10 miles north of Jaffa. The 4th Army had responsibility for the east bank of the Jordan including Amman. The 7th Army positioned in the center of the line and held the west bank of the Jordan north of Jerusalem. The 8th Army was responsible for the coastal plain.

Allenby's plan was the reverse of the concept which he had used to break the Turkish lines at Gaza. There, the main effort had been in the interior, at Beersheba, while a feint went against Gaza on the coast. In 1918, Allenby planned a feint up the Jordan valley, while the main effort occurred on the coast, north of Jaffa. The key to deceiving the Turks, commanded by German General Otto Liman von Sanders, was the mounted force. Allenby understood that the Turks would deduce the location of the main effort by the position of the DMC. This was the motivation for detaching the Australian and New Zealand Division from the DMC, and creating the Chaytor Force. This force, positioned on the extreme right of the line, showed the Turks a large cavalry presence in the east. With its Indian infantry, it gave the impression of a cavalry force positioned behind the infantry. Allenby's men built dummy horse lines using wooden horses and blankets, and drug sleds through the sand to raise dust clouds to reinforce the impression that the entire DMC was in the east. The deception plan worked superbly, and the Turks believed the EEF positioned the DMC on the extreme right of the line in the Jordan valley.

As the deception plan worked on the eastern flank, Allenby massed his forces in the west. The XXI Corps consisted of five divisions, about 36,000 troops, to achieve a breakthrough of the Turkish lines on a 15-mile front. The XX Corps, with only two divisions, covered a 45-mile front north of Jerusalem. Behind the XXI Corps were the 10,000 horsemen of the DMC. Their job was to follow through the gap created by XXI Corps, destroy the rear areas of the Turkish 8th Army, and then swing east through the rear of the 7th Army, and trap that army between XX Corps, XXI Corps, and the Jordan River. Once the Jordan valley was secured, the final phase of the operation was designed to destroy the 4th Turkish Army located east of the river, as it tried to flee north through the desert.

During the night of September 18-19, 1918, the XX Corps launched a diversionary attack up the Jordan valley. Just after midnight the Royal Air Force attacked the headquarters of the 8th and 7th Armies, as well as the main switchboards connecting them to the Yilderim Army Group headquarters. At 4:30 a.m., XXI Corps began its preliminary artillery bombardment, firing at one point, over 1,000 shells a minute. The bombardment, which was unprecedented in the Palestine theater of operations, shattered the Turkish lines as well as the Turkish supporting artillery positions. The British infantry followed quickly behind the artillery and overwhelmed the stunned Turkish infantry. Within a couple of hours, the Turkish XXII Corps defending the coast, was wiped out. The British infantry divisions then wheeled right and formed a solid shoulder behind which the DMC quickly moved north.

The DMC units reached their assigned objectives behind the infantry screen. The AMD sent its 5th Light Horse Brigade (LHB) on the corps right flank to cut the lateral road and rail connection between 8th and 7th Armies. The 4th Cavalry Division moved in the middle of the encircling arc to capture the Musmus Pass through the Samarian hills, and then the rail and communications center at Afula. The 5th Cavalry Division moved on the outside of the arc, advanced to Nazareth to capture the Yilderim Army Group headquarters. The AMD, minus the 5th LHB, moved behind the 4th Cavalry Division as the reserve.

The 5th Cavalry Division moved 45 miles in less than 24 hours, through disorganized light resistance, but terrain that was so rough that at some points the lead brigade had to dismount and lead the horses. The speed of the move caused a number of horses to founder, and they had to be put down. At dawn on September 20, the lead brigade charged into Nazareth. A stiff fight erupted for the town as the 13th Cavalry Brigade tried to simultaneously secure the town, prevent the Yilderim headquarters from escaping, and prevent reinforcements from the south coming into the town. The mission was too big for one brigade to handle, but the 14th Cavalry Brigade to its south was heavily engaged and too encumbered with 1,200 prisoners to assist. The 13th Cavalry Brigade was finally forced to retire from the town center and contented itself with guarding the approaches into the town. The Yilderim commander, General Sanders, managed to escape the town in the confusion of the battle. The 13th Cavalry Brigade commander was relieved for mishandling the battle around Nazareth.

The 4th Cavalry Division, with the 10th Cavalry Brigade leading, had about 25 miles to travel to achieve the south end of its first objective, the Musmus Pass. By 9:00 p.m., the 2nd Lancers of the Brigade had secured the south end of the pass, but the brigade did not reinforce them The commander of the 10th Cavalry Brigade disobeyed the division order to move to the pass at 10:00 p.m. and instead watered his horses. When he finally got moving, the brigade got lost in the dark twice. The division commander was so frustrated with the confusion and slow movement that he relieved the brigade commander from command. As the 10th Cavalry Brigade wandered lost in the dark, the 12th Cavalry Brigade secured the north end of the pass, taking the 2nd Lancers under brigade control. At 5:30 a.m., the 2nd Lancers emerged from the pass and attacked the rail center at Afula. By 8:00 a.m., the 4th Cavalry Division had captured Afula and linked up with the 5th Cavalry Division there, having traveled 37 miles and having fought several strong engagements in the previous 24 hours. The division concentrated its brigades at Afula and then resumed the

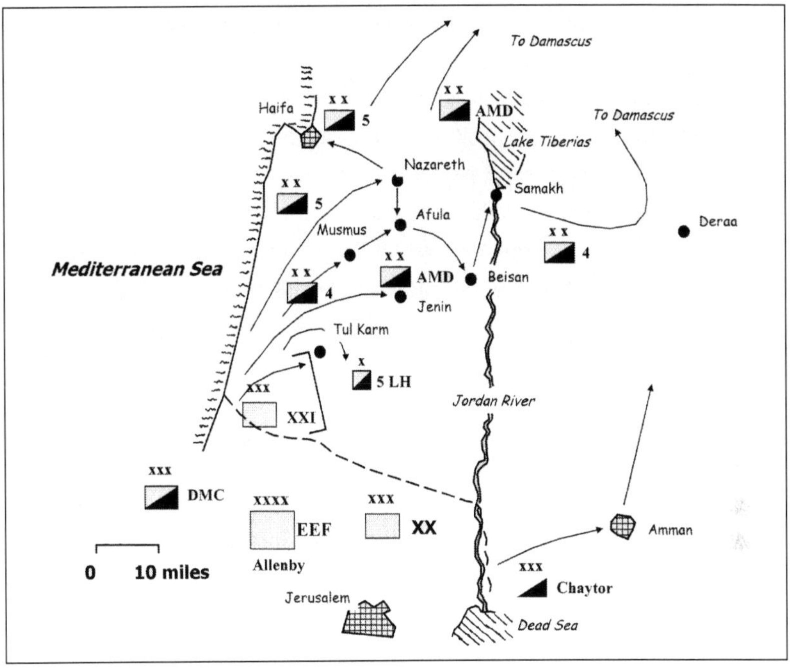

The Area of Operations of the Egyptian Expeditionary Force (EEF) offensive to seize Damascus, September 1918.

attack at 1:00 p.m. Five hours later it had seized its next objective, the town of Beisan. At Beisan the division rested its horses after 34 hours of marching and fighting, over a distance of 70 miles. That night, a night march by the 19th Lancers covered 20 more miles and secured the division's final objective, the railroad bridge over the Jordan at Jisr el Majami, on the morning of September 21. The 19th Lancers had traveled 90 miles in 46 hours.

As the two cavalry's divisions moved rapidly north and east, the AMD followed. The detached 5th LHB successfully isolated the Turks in Tul Karm and took over 1,000 prisoners. The 4th LHB was detached to secure the Corps headquarters and the 5th Cavalry Division trains from straggling Turkish elements. The remaining brigade, the 3rd LHB, and the division were ordered to intercept Turkish troops retreating north from Jenin. The lead regiment, moving as quickly as it could, covered 11 miles in 70 minutes and came on Jenin from the north in the early evening of September 19. There it surprised a defending German and Turkish force and took 1,200 prisoners. Over the rest of the night the brigade took over 8,000 prisoners as broken Turkish units streamed back to the town and fell into the hands of the light horsemen.

Three days after the offensive began, the DMC completely controlled the area from the west bank of the Jordan to the sea. The Turkish 8th Army was all but destroyed and the escape routes north for the 7th Army were all occupied. The DMC took about 15,000 prisoners. Allenby determined at this point that he would pursue the enemy to Damascus and that he would need the port of Haifa to logistically support the continuation of the campaign. In addition, aerial reconnaissance indicated that the remnants of the 7th Army were fleeing across the Jordan to the east. On September 23, Chauvel ordered the 5th Cavalry Division to seize Haifa as well as Acre 12 miles to the north. Rapid mounted action and bold cavalry charges took both towns. The 4th Cavalry Division moved south on the 23rd overrunning Turkish infantry guarding the various crossings across the Jordan River and taking an additional 9,000 prisoners. On September 24, five days after the offensive began, the 4th Cavalry Division made contact with XX Corps completing the encirclement and destruction of the Turkish 8th and 7th Armies. The next day, a charge of the 4th LHB at Samakh, south of Lake Tiberias, destroyed the last Turkish forces and reinforcing Germans.

While the DMC was in action on the west bank of the Jordan, the Chaytor Force crossed the river and began to move east. On September 25 the Australian and New Zealand Mounted Division captured Amman and 2,500 prisoners. With the capture of Amman, the Turkish 4th Army began a retreat to Damascus which quickly turned into a route. The pursuit was turned over to the DMC which dispatched the 5th Cavalry Division and the AMD west of Lake Tiberias toward Damascus, and the 4th Cavalry Division east to Deraa and from there to Damascus. By September 29, the AMD and the 5th Cavalry Division were intercepting and capturing 4th Army units being pushed toward Damascus and beyond by the 4th Cavalry Division. On 1 October 1918, the AMD entered Damascus followed quickly by the 5th Cavalry Division, and the Arab army with T. E. Lawrence. Several thousand more troops surrendered as the city was occupied. From Damascus, the 5th Cavalry Division continued the pursuit of the remaining Turks north through Hama to the ancient city of Aleppo which was captured on October 26.

On October 31, Turkey's Grand Vizier requested an armistice. In 38 days of fighting, the EEF had advanced 350 miles, destroyed three Turkish armies, captured more than 100,000 prisoners, and caused an untold number of casualties. Its losses had been 782 killed and 4,179 wounded. Many of the mounted units had traveled more than 500 miles. The 5th Cavalry Division had covered about 550 miles and lost, in the process, about 21 percent of its horses. The DMC had accounted for about 80,000 prisoners and its total casualties were 649. One historian captured the irony of the location of the final actions of the campaign: "The greatest exploit in history of horsed cavalry and possibly their last success on a large scale, had ended," as Wavell put it, "within a short distance of the battlefield of Issus (333 BC), where Alexander the Great first showed how battles could be won by bold and well-handled horsemen."[39]

The EEF's successful Palestine campaign was the result of careful planning and bold execution. Combined and coordinated use of artillery, infantry, the RAF, and cavalry were all essential aspects of the plan. However, what transformed the battle from a successful penetration of the 8th Turkish army's front into a great battle of annihilation that ended in the total destruction of three armies was the adroit and bold use of cavalry. Allenby and Chauvel pushed their cavalry hard but never lost control of them. They stressed the endurance of men and horses without exceeding them. They were ruthless in punishing subordinates who did not do the same with their men and horses. The professional competence of the two cavalry generals, Allenby and Chauvel, in handling the DMC, combined with the excellent tactical skills of the English, Indian, Australian, and New Zealand regiments, was the reason a tactical success was transformed into a strategic war-winning victory.

World War I ended with mounted forces in an ambiguous position. The employment of cavalry on the war's most decisive front, the western front, had been a complete failure. The one opportunity for maneuver, for both sides, was in the opening months of the war, and neither cavalry force (French or German) was able to achieve on its own or enable its army to obtain the type of decisive success which may have been possible before the trenches were dug. On the eastern front, cavalry had played an important role, but the chaos and confusion that transpired when the Russian revolution interrupted operations prevented any serious evaluation of lessons learned from that experience. Finally, the astounding success of mounted forces in Palestine precluded a complete disregard for the arm in the postwar world.

The development of the cavalry horse neared it final form in the years before and during World War I. Horse mastership, remount systems, and veterinary services all combined to produce the healthiest most capable cavalry mounts in the history of warfare. The quality and types of horses would not significantly change in preparation for World War II. The introduction of the forward seat created a riding style that was completely modern. The cavalry horses of the World War I era represented the bulk of the important modern breeds that remain the top riding horses into the twenty-first century.

Cavalry in World War II

There was no immediate drawdown in the cavalry arm of the world's armies after World War I. Cavalry had shown some limitations in the war, particular when opposed by prepared infantry, but the difficulty overcoming deliberate defenses, represented by trench warfare, was a military problem that was not exclusively associated with cavalry. Infantry and the new awkward tank forces, both suffered horrendous casualties attacking trench positions during the war. None of the armies in World War I discovered a definitive solution to the military problem of the trenches; without which it was not possible to determine whether the horse cavalry's time was over.

The gradual demise of horse cavalry began in the early 1930s, not as recognition of the vulnerability of horses to modern weapons, but rather as a recognition that automotive technology was advancing to the point of being able to provide operational and tactical mobility, including cross-country, equal or superior to the horse. In the 1930s many armies concluded that vehicles could provide the mobility needed for a quick victory through maneuver. Not surprisingly, the leading industrial country in the world, the United States, led the way in automotive technology and also in replacing the horse with other more efficient forms of transportation. At first, many believed that motorcycles could replicate the horse's mobility. However, the U.S. army, after a few years of experimentation, determined that the motorcycle was too unstable, accident prone, and maintenance intensive for large-scale use. In the American army, the vehicle that ultimately displaced the horse by demonstrating a cross-country mobility that was comparable to that of the horse, and with an overall speed and mobility that was much superior, was the jeep.

Most European powers followed a similar mechanization process. However, nowhere was it as rapid, complete, and as effective as the motorization and mechanization of the U.S. army. All other armies entered World War II, and fought the war, with some type of horse component in the supply and services role as well as the combat role. The two most important cavalry forces that survived with a horse-mounted combat capability into World War II were those of the German and Russian armies.

Organization

Though only the Germans and Russians fielded large cavalry forces during World War II, numerous other nations had small contingents of cavalry including Japan, China, Italy, Romania, and Hungary. However, the large formations of Germans and Russians were the most significant and the only ones that had an impact on major operations.

The American jeep in action. The jeep's small size, incredible cross-country mobility, simplicity of operation and maintenance, and relatively low cost made it the ideal replacement for the horse. (*Cavalry Journal* [U.S.])

German Cavalry

After World War I, German cavalry reorganized as a component of the Reichswehr, the army of the Weimar Republic. The Treaty of Versailles limited the Germans to an army of 100,000 men. The army organized into 10 divisions of which 3 were Kavallerie Divisions. The Reichswehr had 18 reiter regiments manned by a total of 16,400 men. In relative size, the mounted component of the Reichswehr was substantial.[40]

The German military expanded greatly after the rise of Hitler in 1933. However, this increase in size did not portend an increase in the size of the cavalry. The Nazis focused on mechanizing the German army. Through the middle and late 1930s they converted most cavalry regiments to motorized or mechanized regiments. The Germans realized that motorization promised superior mobility to the horse. Still, in 1939, on the eve of war, the German mounted forces consisted of 13 kavallerie regiments whose main mission was to support the infantry divisions with reconnaissance, and the 1st Cavalry Brigade, whose two reiter regiments were capable of independent mounted action.[41]

After the invasion of Poland in September 1939, the 1st Cavalry Brigade expanded to division size. The new 1st Cavalry Division had 3 heavy regiments (reiters), of 6 squadrons each, and a light (kavallerie) regiment of 3 squadrons. In addition, the division had a bicycle battalion, a light artillery regiment, an engineer battalion, an antitank company, and a signal battalion. The 1st Cavalry Division participated in the invasion of France in 1940 and in the initial stages of Operation Barbarossa in 1941. The division had about 4,500 cavalry troops and included 17,000 horses in its various units. It was converted into the 24th Panzer Division in Russia during the winter of 1941–42.[42]

The German infantry organization had a significant number of horsemen. The reconnaissance battalion of each infantry division divided into 3 squadrons: a horse squadron, a bicycle squadron, and a heavy motorized squadron that included armored cars and antitank guns. In addition, each German infantry regiment had a horse platoon in the regimental headquarters that carried out a variety of duties including reconnaissance and security. Thirty-one riders manned this unit.[43] These infantry horsemen were the only army mounted forces from the end of 1941 until early 1943. At that point a young German captain, Rittmeister Georg von Boeselager, with the aid of the Army Group Center commander, Generalfieldmarschall Günther von Kluge, began the process of reestablishing large army cavalry units.

Boeselager was a highly decorated veteran of the 1940 campaign in France. He had commanded the horse squadron of the 6th Reconnaissance Battalion and was a winner of the Knight's Cross. He proposed forming a regimental-size mounted unit to operate behind German lines against enemy partisans. Replacement soldiers, some with riding experience, some not, volunteer Cossacks, cavalry officers, and an assorted mixture of horses assembled to form the unit. In February 1943, Reiterverband (Mounted Unit) Boeselager was operational. Its capabilities were quickly recognized and its organization and missions expanded. By the end of March 1943, success caused the Germans to expand the unit and give it new and more difficult missions. By April 1943, the unit organized into a regiment of 5,000 troopers and mounts. Meanwhile, army groups North and South copied the concept and also created independent mounted regiments. In 1944, Boeselager's unit expanded again and reorganized as the 3rd Cavalry Brigade with 2 regiments. In the summer of 1944, together with the 4th Cavalry Brigade (formed from the North and South army groups regiments), and the 1st Hungarian Cavalry Division, the unit joined the 1st Cavalry Corps, known as the Harteneck Cavalry Corps. The Germans expanded both brigades into the 3rd and 4th cavalry divisions in early 1945. The corps probably averaged a total strength of about 15,000 to 20,000 horses and riders. The 3rd Cavalry Division alone had a reported strength of 11,333 men in February 1945. The corps fought together for the balance of the war in East Prussia and Hungary, and surrendered to the British and Americans in 1945.[44]

In addition to the army cavalry units, the German military organized two special cavalry forces that are worth mentioning. The first of these were the cavalry units of the Waffen SS. Waffen SS cavalry began as a mounted component of the SS Totenkopf security forces–SS Totenkopf Reiterstandarte (SS Deaths-Head horse regiment) specifically for operations in Poland. The SS cavalry units organized and equipped like those of the army. By the time of the invasion of the Russia, the regiment reorganized and expanded into an SS cavalry brigade with two SS cavalry regiments. By March 1942, the brigade's casualties were so high that the command withdrew it from the front and reorganized it with a third regiment added. In August 1943, the brigade added a fourth regiment and in October 1943 it became the 8th SS Cavalry Division. At its greatest strength, it numbered about 15,000 men. In March 1944, the division received the honorary title "Florien Geyer," after a sixteenth-century German hero. In the spring of 1944, the Germans raised a second SS Cavalry Division from ethnic German volunteers. The unit was designated the 22nd SS Cavalry Division and eventually reached a strength of three regiments built around a cadre of Florien Geyer veterans. The Soviets destroyed both cavalry divisions in the siege of Budapest in early 1945.[45]

The other special German cavalry force worth noting were the Cossacks in German service. After World War I, most of the Cossack hosts participated in the Russian Revolution on the White Russian side. As a result, after the victory of the communists, the Cossack communities were persecuted and their leaders executed or imprisoned. The communists destroyed the traditional special autonomy that the Cossacks had enjoyed in Russian society. Thus, as the German army invaded Russia, many Cossacks viewed the arrival of the Germans as liberation from communist rule. Though most Russians in the lands invaded by the Germans were anti-communists, German racial prejudice and ill-conceived policies prevented the Germans from tapping into this large potential resource. The Cossacks were an exception because the German army was familiar with their fighting abilities and anticommunism. The Cossacks had retained enough community identity, leadership, and internal organization that they were able to use the German presence to pursue their own agenda against the Soviets.

The Cossack movement was spontaneous and always ahead of the sometimes grudging German support. In the winter of 1942, as the Soviet counterattack burst around Stalingrad, it did so into the midst of the newly liberated Cossack lands around the Don River and in the Caucasus Mountains. The Germans, in their desperation, turned to the Cossacks, who were waiting for the opportunity to fight the communists again. German cavalry Colonel Helmuth von Pannwitz formed a cavalry group from Don Cossacks in November 1942, known as the Pannwitz Mounted Force. In August 1943, two other large Cossack contingents joined Pannwitz's command to form a three regiment Cossack division. The Division eventually expanded to six regiments in two brigades, and then the second brigade became the basis of a second Cossack division. In the last months of 1944, the two Cossack divisions came under von Pannwitz's control in the new XV Cossack Cavalry Corps. The unit's main area of operations was in Yugoslavia, where they fought Tito's partisans and then Soviet forces. The Cossack Cavalry Corps surrendered to British forces in Austria in May 1945. At the time of the surrender the total strength of the Corps was between 12,000 and 15,000 men. The British, betraying promises made to the German and Cossack officers of the corps, forcibly turned the Cossacks, their German officers, and their families who had followed the soldiers out of Russia over to the Soviet Army. Most of the Cossack men were sent to slave labor camps in Siberia. The officers were executed.[46] Numerous other small detachments of Cossacks served with German units as auxiliaries. Many of these escaped repatriation to the Soviet Union.

Soviet Cavalry

The German army, at its height in the last year of the war, fielded three active cavalry corps with a total of six divisions. The likely strength of the German cavalry at its height in the final months of the war was probably about 45,000. In contrast, Soviet cavalry on the eastern front numbered at least 200,000 men after mobilization in 1941, and well over 100,000 at war's end. The Red Army cavalry, though probably not as able horsemen as their Czarist predecessors, accrued a very commendable record over the course of World War II, and represented the last great employment of large mounted military forces.

The Red Army began the war with a large cavalry force. The cavalry at the beginning of the war consisted of four cavalry corps, and 13 cavalry divisions, totaling 80,000 men. The standard cavalry corps consisted of two divisions and a signal squadron. Each division contained four cavalry regiments each with five cavalry and one machine-gun squadron. The division also included a light tank regiment, artillery, antiaircraft, antitank, and reconnaissance battalions, engineer and signal squadrons, and chemical, supply and transport units.[47]

In the opening month of the attack into Russia, the Germans destroyed one complete cavalry corps and severely damaged another. The Russians lost more than 50 percent of the cavalry strength opposing the Germans. However, this did not discourage the Soviets regarding the importance of horse cavalry, because during the same period, the Germans destroyed over 10,000 of the Soviet's 23,000 tanks. Thus, the cavalry losses were not unique. Throughout 1942 the strength of the cavalry corps increased as equipment and units became available. The average corps structure increased to three cavalry divisions. In February 1943, the army again added tanks to the cavalry division structure, this time in form of the powerful T-34 tank. In 1943, the cavalry corps structure achieved its largest and most powerful form. Each corps included three divisions. By late 1943, a typical Soviet cavalry corps had more than 21,000 men and 18,000 horses.[48]

Soviet cavalry was heavily engaged in combat against front-line German forces throughout the war. Casualties among the cavalry from German aircraft and artillery were particularly high among the horses. In order to keep the cavalry corps as capable as possible, the Soviets, beginning in 1942, steadily reduced the number of cavalry units while maintaining the strength of the remaining units. In July 1942, the forces consisted of 12 corps and 42 divisions; in February 1943 it was 10 corps and 30 divisions; and in December 1943 it was 8 corps and 26 divisions. The importance of mounted cavalry operations did not decrease with the decreasing size of the force.[49]

Equipment

German cavalry in World War II gave up all pretense of being a shock weapon. They discarded sabers in all mounted units by the time of the invasion of Russia in 1941. German cavalry relied on dismounted action and the rifle and light machine gun for its firepower. The only exceptions to this were the Cossack forces which retained their traditional shashka sabers and did not hesitate to employ them at every opportunity. At the beginning of the war cavalry troopers were equipped with the latest version of the bolt-action Mauser–the Kar98k. By 1941, most cavalry units added the 9-mm MP-40 machine pistol (submachine gun). In the last year of the war, many cavalrymen had the 7.92mm MP-44, one of the first modern assault rifles. Armed with automatic weapons, cavalry's dismounted firepower increased significantly. Soviet cavalry arms, like German cavalry, included the rifle, submachine gun, and assault rifle by the end of the war. Soviet cavalry, however, retained the saber as an important piece of equipment throughout the war.

Tactics

The growth of German Cavalry during World War II was inversely proportional to Germany's war fortunes. The Germans had early on made a decision that motorization was a more effective means of battlefield mobility. However, the German industrial base could not meet the motorized requirements of the army. The Germans brought cavalry back into their force structure in order to compensate for a lack of automotive capability as the war progressed. American army intelligence concluded at the end of the war that: "The marked growth of independent cavalry toward the end of the war is not to be interpreted as signifying a basic change in German military theory. The new units were required primarily to protect communication lines in the Balkans, where they operated in small independent groups, or to cover the flanks of armies during large-scale withdrawals on the eastern front. In both cases, the use of cavalry was largely dictated by lack of motor transport. In late 1943 and early 1944 German military requirements began seriously to exceed production capacities."[50]

Terrain and weather were also important reasons why the Germans brought back cavalry formations. After a year of operating in Russia, many German commanders realized that the German assumptions regarding the utility of cavalry were based largely on conditions in Western Europe. In Russia, the lack of roads, terrible extremes of weather, dense forests and marshes, and the vast distances all stressed the numbers, mechanical reliability, and the cross-country capability of German motorized and mechanized forces. These conditions of the theater had much less effect on horse cavalry.

After 1942, antipartisan activities became the major focus of German mounted forces. Cavalry's mobility gave it the speed required to have an advantage, or against mounted partisans, match the enemy, as the partisans sought to retreat after attacking. Soviet partisans used deep forests, marshes, and mountains as sanctuaries from which to raid the extended German supply lines. Cavalry had two missions in regards to this threat. Mobile cavalry patrols escorted convoys and patrolled rail lines. More effective were cavalry strike forces, pursuing the partisans into their sanctuaries, destroying the bases, and keeping the partisans focused on survival rather than attack. In these missions, the German cavalry operated in a similar manner as U.S. cavalry pursuing Indian bands, or the British tracking Boer commandos.

In 1944, as the Soviet forces began to press against the frontiers of Germany and her allies, the role of German cavalry began to change again. Germany used the cavalry forces as fire brigades, moving as a mobile reserve to blunt Soviet penetrations of the line. In addition, they had the very difficult task of screening and covering the retreat of German forces. Cavalry, with their superior mobility, fought dismounted, as the infantry behind them marched to new defensive positions. The horsemen then quickly mounted and retreated, usually as Soviet tanks crushed the positions that they had just held. Using forests and rough terrain impassible to motorized forces, the cavalry raced ahead of the advancing tanks, so as to pass behind the new friendly infantry lines before the next battle began.

In their role as a quick reaction and covering force, the German cavalry fought hundreds of short sharp nameless engagements, usually against desperate odds. Polish historian Janusz Piekalkiewicz, described the 4th Kuban Cossack Regiment executing this type of small unit action in March 1945, fighting as a rear guard for German forces retreating through Yugoslavia:

> A green flare gave the signal for the cavalry to mount and ride off. On the road ahead, the first mines exploded. The hollow thunder of hundreds of horses' hoofs drowned even the shots which were crackling through the night air. The Cossacks galloped off into the darkness. "Za parva-za Kuban!" resounded the Cossack's battle cry. One squadron got caught up in an entanglement of barbed

German cavalry during the initial invasion of Russia. The saddle is the Model 1925 army saddle. (*Cavalry Journal* [U.S.])

> wire, but the other squadron, yelling "Hurrah!" as it forged ahead, reached a Soviet gun emplacement without hindrance. The Cossacks turned the captured guns around and fired on the enemy.[51]

These types of limited counterattacks allowed German infantry units to retreat with fewer casualties and caused the Soviet advance to slow and proceed more cautiously.

The German view of cavalry, for the most part, was that it was an important supplementary force that had some utility for reconnaissance, security, and antipartisan activities, which helped enable the decisive main action of tanks and infantry. As the war progressed, the Germans grudgingly formed large cavalry units to compensate for the lack of motorized equipment but without changing their basic view that cavalry was an auxiliary arm.

The Soviets had a completely different operational view of the role of cavalry. Based on the successes and failures of operations in 1941 and 1942, the Soviets determined that the most important role for cavalry was as a deep strike force. Cavalry, working with mechanized and tank formations, was organized and employed to exploit the penetration of the enemy's defense. Unlike every other modern army in World War II, when faced with the question of "horse or motor" the Soviet answer was "horse *and* motor."[52] Over the course of the war, the tactical details of cavalry employment changed, but the basic concept for the use of cavalry did not.

The Soviet tactic was to obliterate a narrow section of the front with an intensive artillery barrage followed by a massive integrated tank and infantry attack. The tank and infantry attack then penetrated the German first-, second-, and third-tier defenses. Once they achieved the penetration, and only then, were the mobile forces committed. The mobile forces, tank corps and cavalry-mechanized corps, then streamed through the gap. Supported closely by the air force, the cavalry and armor attacked to operational depth destroying command and control capability, overrunning logistics facilities, and isolating large sections of the front, preventing the enemy's retreat.[53]

Cavalry had several roles when fighting together with armor. First, cavalry provided a mobile mounted infantry capability that could quickly dismount to support the tanks. The tanks protected the cavalry from enemy armor while the cavalry protected the armor from enemy infantry attack, especially those soldiers armed with the effective *Panzerfaust* antitank weapon. Second, cavalry ensured that terrain conditions did not provide sanctuaries from tanks in which the enemy could organize a retreat. Finally, unlike motorized infantry, cavalry armed with sabers contributed to the shock value of the mobile troops. Tanks moving in mass through the rear areas terrorized German troops. Saber-wielding cavalry had a similar psychological effect as German rear area troops and facilities were ridden down by charging horsemen. The mounted cavalry forces also had an all weather, all terrain, advantage over armor units which allowed breakthrough operations to be conducted or to continue in terrain and weather conditions which would have stopped a purely armored spearhead. The different logistics requirements of horses and tanks also gave the penetration forces flexibility: when fuel was low the advance continued with cavalry; and when the horses were tired the advance continued with tanks.[54] In the Soviet doctrine for mobile warfare horse cavalry was an integral and important capability in the prosecution of decisive offensive operations.

The Soviets demonstrated the deep penetration capability of Soviet cavalry early in the war with General P. I. Belov's cavalry corps, which participated in the Soviet counterattack around Moscow in the winter of 1941–42. After playing an instrumental role in halting the German offensive just 14 miles short of Moscow, Belov's 1st Corps of Cavalry Guards counterattacked with other Soviet forces on January 9, 1942. The cavalry corps penetrated through the German lines with the mission of cutting the German road to Smolensk. The entire corps stayed isolated in the German rear, attacking German columns and facilities, and using deep forests for cover until May 1942. Paratroop battalions reinforced the cavalry, and supplies were brought in and wounded evacuated by air. The German 4th Army, whose communications and logistics was paralyzed by these troops, did not have enough mobile armored forces to pursue them through forests, deep snow, and subzero arctic winter conditions. The

Germans had no horse units. At one time, in the spring of 1942, the German army in Russia faced a total of six Soviet cavalry divisions operating in its rear. The effort required to minimize the impact of these forces had serious detrimental effects on the German's ability to defend at the front, and to prepare to renew offensive operations in the spring.[55]

Soviet Cavalry Charge. The Soviets understood well the important psychological effect of the cavalry charge and thus the saber was not only issued throughout World War II but used. (*Cavalry Journal* [U.S.])

Horses and Horsemanship

Horses and horsemanship had reached their modern form before World War II. The challenge of the war was to provide enough trained horses and riders to meet the large requirements of operations on the eastern front. As the war ended, an additional challenge was to save some of the most valuable breeds from being lost in the whirlwind of destruction that characterized the last year of the war.

Horses

Germany maintained about 1,100,000 horses in military service throughout the war,. The bulk of these horses were in the supply and transport service, or in the field artillery. The well-organized German remount system continued to produce quality warmblood horses for the German army until the last year of the war. The German horses, being very finely bred, were stressed by the extremely difficult physical conditions of the eastern front. The logistics system on the eastern front was fragile and strained by partisan attacks, distance, and terrain and weather conditions. Horses starved along with the men, especially in the winter months when the horses could not forage on the countryside. Still, over the course of the war, the German horses adapted, survived, and continued to provide valuable service. After the war a German cavalry general described the perfect breed for operations in Russia as "a highly bred horse, small and sturdy, with short legs and broad ribs." This, however, was not a description of the finely bred warmbloods, which were the most common horses in the German remount system. Instead it more closely described the mounts of the Red Army cavalry.[56]

The Soviet cavalry mounts, though suffering through roughly the same conditions as the German horses, fared much better. Soviet cavalry mounts were broadly of two different types. The foremost was the Don horse type described previously. The Budenny breed augmented the Don breed. The Budenny was similar to the Don, and developed from the Don by introducing more Thoroughbred blood into the breed. The Soviets developed the Budenny on State stud farms in the Don River region in the 1920s and 30s. They named the breed for Marshall S. M. Budenny, a hero of the Soviet cavalry forces during the revolution. However, many of the cavalry's best horses were lost in the massive defeats that occurred in the opening months of the war. As the Germans advanced, the state stud farms evacuated to the east, and they could not meet all the army's remount requirements. To continue to mount the large Soviet cavalry force required drawing on other sources for horses. Mongolia provided 6 million horses as a gift to the Soviet war effort in World War II.[57] These small Mongolian mounts were physically perfect for the harsh conditions of warfare on the eastern front. The Mongolian horses were augmented by a variety of other ponies bred for the harsh conditions of the steppe. The Germans called the generic ponies found on the steppe Panje ponies. The Panje was a type of small steppe horse that in modern breeds is represented by the Carpathian pony of eastern Europe and the Konik pony of Poland. These small ponies were perfect for draft work on the eastern front, and when remounts were scarce they were employed as saddle horses. Both sides made extensive use of Panje ponies, though the Germans did not use them as a cavalry mount to any large extent. Soviet cavalry did use the robust ponies. The small horses, especially when shod for conditions, were particularly mobile in winter months. This capability was similar to the winter campaign ability of the mounted Mongols using similar horses in the same geographic area 600 years earlier.

Horsemanship

The horsemanship of German units and their allies was excellent, especially among allies such as the Cossacks and the Hungarians. Prewar Reichswehr cavalry were also exceptionally well trained horsemen. Troopers and NCOs who had 12 years of service typically had more than 3,000 hours of training time in the saddle. The Cossacks serving with the Germans were excellent horsemen, but their traditional style of riding was not perfectly suited to the German cavalry way of doing things. After the war General Major Burkhard Mueller-Hillebrand described the Cossacks riding style: "The Cossacks were natural horsemen, to whom the German school of riding is completely foreign. They are accustomed to riding over rough ground, and usually travel at a fast trot or a Cossack gallop, a gait that frequently caused injury to the legs of German horses. The Cossack is extremely interested in the welfare of his horse, and

Soviet Cossack Cavalry. Though the Soviets had "Cossack" units as part of their cavalry forces, these units were mostly honorary titles. For propaganda purposes the Soviets equipped conscripts in Cossack designated units in traditional Cossack dress. Note the use of spurs in the photo. (*Cavalry Journal* [U.S.])

makes it his inseparable companion. But while he gives it plenty of forage, he does not appreciate the value of grooming."[58] Fortunately, General Pannwitz, commanding the Cossacks, understood that for the Cossacks to be effective they could not be molded to the German army system.

Soviet cavalry horsemanship and horse mastership was generally fair but was a constant training challenge as the cavalry had to quickly integrate large numbers of replacements to make up for losses. In 1936, the Soviet Union designated some of its line cavalry regiments and divisions as Cossack units and uniformed them in a variation of traditional Cossack dress. These units were Cossack in name only. The designation of Cossack units was an effort to link the Soviet regime to Russian history, to falsely portray the integration of Cossacks into the Soviet military and society, and for propaganda purposes both domestically and internationally. During the war the Soviets widely published the success of "Cossack" divisions and corps for propaganda purposes.

During World War II Soviet cavalry regiments were manned by conscripts from all over the Soviet Union. They were melded together into squadrons and regiments by a small group of professional cavalrymen of the prewar Soviet army. All units, including the new Cossack units, used standard army equipment. Unlike the authentic Cossacks in German service, Soviet Cossacks, like all Soviet cavalrymen, wore spurs. Soviet Cossack cavalry were issued government shashka swords with the traditional hilts without a guard. On parade some also wore the traditional *cherkesska* and *burka*. Pictures showing Soviet Cossack cavalry in traditional garb were often staged. Another item that became general issue for all Soviet cavalry, including non-Cossack units, was a Cossack style sheepskin hat called a *kubanka*.[59] Unfortunately, though they could be dressed as Cossacks, and called Cossacks, the Red Army cavalry could not ride like Cossacks. Lieutenant Yakushin described his first experience with a horse when he arrived in the 24th Guards Cavalry Regiment as a replacement.

> The duty NCO offered me a selection of dragoon saddles. I pointed my finger at the first one I saw, and as I did not yet know how to saddle a horse, ordered him to do it for me. Then, as I had no clue how to mount a horse using stirrups, I left the stables and started looking for a suitable elevation from which I could lower myself onto my new steed. After several attempts, I dragged my horse into a ditch and mounted it. I was lucky this operation took place in complete darkness and that no one saw me: otherwise, my reputation in the regiment would have been lost for a long time–if not for good–and I would have become an eternal object of fun.[60]

Yakushin's experience is representative of many if not most Soviet replacement cavalrymen. However, Soviet cavalrymen learned by experience and quickly became knowledgeable working horsemen, if not experts.

Saving the Breeds

World War II was extremely hard on horses. Like all previous wars, horses, because of their size and their inability to take cover quickly, suffered casualties at rates significantly higher than their riders. Because of the massive scale of total war, several famous horse breeds were almost completely wiped out. It was only to through the intercession of knowledgeable and dedicated horsemen that some of these breeds were saved from complete extinction. The German Trakehner breed is one of those that was almost lost in the closing months of the war.

In the fall of 1944, the Soviets launched an offensive into East Prussia which threatened the Trakehner stud farm and the precious breeding stock of mares and stallions. The Nazi district leader prohibited the people and horses from evacuating. Finally, as the Russians closed in, an evacuation in the dead of winter was permitted. Eventually, 2 central stud stallions, 28 mares, and six foals were evacuated to Holstein where they remained under German control within the British occupation zone at the end of the war. The private breeders, without government resources, had a more difficult time evacuating and saving their horses. Prized East Prussian warmbloods were harnessed to wagons loaded with families and personal possessions. Using frozen back roads and trails, fighting freezing weather and dwindling rations, the horses and owners struggled to the west. Some were killed in Russian air attacks on

A motion picture still showing part of the Lipizzaner herd rescued from probable destruction during World War II. (*2nd Cavalry Group*)

the convoys of refugees, while others were overtaken by advancing Soviet ground forces who often pillaged the refugees and butchered the horses. Still others died of the cold and exposure. Some of the refugees stopped in central Germany. These were caught up in the Russian occupation as the Russian offensive swept to the Elbe River in the spring. About 1500 purebred broodmares arrived in areas that became part of West Germany. Over half of these survivors, however, were lost in the chaotic conditions immediately after the war. Fortunately, about 700 registered mares and 60 stallions survived to rebuild the Trakehner breed in West Germany after the war.[61]

Another famous rescue was that of the Spanish Riding School's Lipizzaner brood mares. These irreplaceable horses were rescued through the efforts of one of the American cavalry's top horsemen, Colonel Charles Hancock "Hank" Reed, who commanded the American 2nd Cavalry Group (Mechanized) during World War II. Reed's group was closing on the Czechoslovakian border in the last weeks of the war when it captured a German intelligence unit. In conversations with the German unit commander, a Luftwaffe general and horse enthusiast, Reed learned about the location of a German remount depot at Hostau, across the German frontier in Czechoslovakia. A few nights later, German army veterinarian, Captain Lessing, arrived at Reed's headquarters to request American protection of the horse herd at Hostau. The Germans were concerned that the valuable horses would be slaughtered by advancing Russian troops. Reed understood that to protect the horses they would have to be evacuated to Germany, because Czechoslovakia was designated to be occupied by the Soviets. Reed had strict orders not to advance into Czechoslovakia. Nonetheless, Colonel Reed agreed to provide protection and to evacuate the horses. He then sent a message to his higher headquarters, the 3rd U.S. Army under General George Patton, informing them of his intended action. Patton was also a horseman and had shared horse cavalry assignments with Reed, and he approved the mission.

Reed launched an attack into Czechoslovakia and secured the surrender of the horse herd. The American also liberated about 400 allied prisoners of war. According to Colonel Reed, the horse herd "consisted of about 300 Lipizzaners, the Piber [Austrian] Breeding Herd plus the Royal Lipizzaner Stud from [Hungary]–well mixed together. Over one-hundred of the best Arabs in Europe, about two-hundred Thoroughbred and trotting bred race horses collected from all of Europe–finally about 600 Cossack breeding horses–Don and Urals." Once the herd was prepared to move, Reed organized an evacuation using the Cossacks in the German service, the German officers, and an American armored cavalry escort. They moved the horse herd into Germany where they fell under American control. Colonel Reed was willing to undertake the Lipizzaner rescue because he thought it could be accomplished with no casualties, and because he completely understood the traditions and history invested in the Lipizzaner mares. The Austrian mares were returned to the Spanish Riding School, thus preserving hundreds of years of horsemanship history. The remainder of the herd became the property of the U.S. army. Eventually the U.S. army remount system shipped some of the Hungarian Lipizzaners to the United States. Later they were sold by the army and perpetuated the Lipizzaner breed in the United States.[62]

The two world wars proved to be the last to feature major military operations conducted by horse-mounted forces. The history of cavalry in those wars validated much of the previous understanding of the value of mounted military units. It also demonstrated that the practical use of large-scale horse-mounted forces had come to an end.

Cavalry operations in the world wars, despite their diminishing importance, continued to demonstrate that a calvary force's success in battle was most dependent on the psychological factors among the attackers and defenders. It was no accident that cavalry leaders talked about the "moral" superiority of one cavalry force over another. Once one side achieved that psychological advantage, tactical success usually followed. Thus, under the right circumstances, even in World War II, cavalry forces could execute successful charges. The success of the DMC in the closing weeks of World War I was possible because once the confidence of the defending Turks was shattered, the speed and shock of the subsequent cavalry operations prevented them from reestablishing the coherence of their formations. One of the values of Soviet cavalry in World War II was the alarm that the cry "Cossacks!" spread through the German army. It didn't matter that Soviet cavalry were not real Cossacks.

The world wars also demonstrated why the conditions for instilling fear on the part of cavalry became rarer. The increasing capability of small arms, rifles, and machine guns, and the accompanying confidence in these weapons, made infantry more certain of their ability to defeat a cavalry charge. This realization, combined with the lethality of the modern small arms, made the prospects of a successful cavalry charge executed against prepared infantry almost impossible. Thus, though Soviet cavalry might spread terror through the rear areas of the German army, German infantry had no real fear of cavalry.

Probably the most important factor in the demise of large cavalry formations was the advance in automotive technology. Firepower did not make cavalry obsolete on the battlefield, but the ability of vehicles to match the cross-country mobility of cavalry did. When this technology was matched with the industrial capability to build hundreds of thousands of motor vehicles relatively cheaply, the major military characteristic of the horse, its mobility, was superseded. The combination of automotive technology, armor, and cannon in the form of battle tanks created the first weapons system able to match both the mobility of the horse and the shock effect of the cavalry charge. In the years after World War II, automotive technology and industrial capacity continued to increase to such an extent that the last of the large horse cavalry formations, those of the Soviet Union's Red Army, disbanded in the mid-1950s.

EPILOGUE

At the end of World War II, after more than 3,000 years of usefulness, large-scale horse formations became obsolete–replaced by modern transportation and weaponry. The Western allies never reconstructed the horse formations that they abandoned during the war, while the horse units of the Axis powers were destroyed. Only the Russians retained a large cavalry force, which remained in the Soviet military well into the 1950s, until it too was dismantled. What is amazing is not that the horse disappeared from military history, but that it lasted so long and then disappeared so swiftly. At the end of World War II several million horses were still in military service all over the world, and riding was an essential skill for all professional officers. Within a generation the number of horses in military service could be counted in the thousands, and riding skills became almost unknown in modern armies.

Technological development–more specifically the speed of that development–brought about this dramatic change. For thousands of years technology had evolved slowly and predictably, in a linear fashion. Beginning in the nineteenth century, the Industrial Revolution spurred advances in science and manufacturing at an unprecedented rate. Technological change rapidly diminished the capability of the war horse to the point it could no longer make a unique contribution to military operations.

Before World War II, two characteristics of the horse made it an important military asset. The first was its mobility. Horses could move large bodies of troops 25 to 30 miles a day for extended periods of time and transport troops even faster in an emergency. Armies could maneuver at speeds and over distances that allowed them to achieve regional and even continental-scale effects. The Mongol armies were accomplished at leveraging the operational and strategic mobility of the horse. Operational mobility was the key to Alexander the Great's pursuit of Darius after Gaugamela in 331 BC and the U.S. cavalry's pursuit of the Nez Perce Indians in 1877. The mobility of the horse also had tactical benefits. Cavalry forces, moving at many times the speed of dismounted troops, were able to act and react quickly and could change the course of a tactical situation in minutes, as the Goth cavalry did at Adrianople in 378 AD.

The second major characteristic of the horse was its shock effect. The size and speed of horses, particularly when massed, allowed for the psychological dominance of one side over the other. This was the essence of the well-executed cavalry charge. Often physical contact was not necessary. Most cavalry charges were won or lost before the two sides came together. The earthshaking thunder of hooves, the dust, the noise, and the sheer mass of legions of massive animals advancing at speeds of up to 40 miles per hour was enough to destroy the will to fight of all but the most disciplined troops. The charge of Cossacks in 1944 used essentially the same techniques and sought the same effects as the charge of Medieval knights a thousand years earlier.

The horse itself, through its mobility and mass, was a significant asset in battle. Horse and rider together added a third dimension to mounted operations–firepower. Saladin's army at Hattin, the Mongol forces of Genghis Khan, Buford's cavalry division at Gettysburg, and Chauvel's Desert Mounted Corps all put these aspects together. Whether the firepower was the composite bow or the breechloading repeating carbine did not matter. Horses and riders could move quickly anywhere on the battlefield, indeed anywhere in the theater of operations, could ride down and terrify troops, and could stand off and destroy the enemy with handheld weapons, and when combined with the best commanders it was a weapons system that could win wars and conquer continents.

By the middle of the twentieth century automotive technologies equaled or surpassed the horse's tactical mobility and greatly exceeded its operational and strategic mobility. Accurate, rapid-firing, easy-to-use small arms gave an infantry soldier the confidence to withstand a cavalry charge, which negated the horse's psychological effects. And automotive technology combined with armored protection and modern small arms and cannons produced a superior mobile firing platform. When these elements were brought together during World War II military mounted forces were eliminated almost overnight.

Though horse cavalry continued to exist in military forces that were not international powers, neither the horses nor their riders were pitted against technologies that exceeded the abilities of the horse. Many countries in the developing parts of the world retained horse-mounted forces into the 1980s and 1990s. Such forces most commonly were used against partisans and guerrillas in countries where few roads existed and where the surrounding countryside–grasslands, mountains, jungles, or swamps–severely constrained the use of vehicles. Militaries like that of Rhodesia in the early 1980s made use of horse-mounted units such as Greys Scouts to track and attack antigovernment guerrillas. In Latin America several armies used mounted forces in to the 1990s to pursue outlaws, drug runners, and insurgents. The horsemanship and horse mastery in these military forces, benefiting from the latest techniques of veterinary science and horse training were superb. Through these forces, the history of the military horse and rider continued to the doorstep of the twenty-first century.

War horse and rider stepped into the twenty-first century in the fall of 2001, when the United States deployed Special Operations Forces to Afghanistan. The United States emplaced a Special Forces Operational Detachment A (ODA) with the Northern Alliance, a rebel force opposing the rule of the Taliban regime, which was allied with the Al-Qaeda terrorist organization. The army's Special Forces, with almost no intelligence regarding the rebels they were going to team up with, were inserted deep into the mountains of northern Afghanistan by MH-47E Chinook helicopter. Just after sunrise on October 19, 2001, the high-technology aircraft released its cargo of commandos into the one of the last remaining bastions of steppe horse culture in the world. Here, the horse was still an important military tool.

The first indication that the ODA team leader, Captain Mike Nash (a pseudonym), had that his mission was going to be challenging in ways the American army had not experienced in 60 years, was the arrival of their ally, General Dostum, at the linkup point:

> About 20 horsemen came galloping up. They were armed to the teeth, looking pretty rough. . . . [They had] your typical Soviet small arms–light machine guns, AK-47s, RPGs [rocket-propelled grenades]. And they come galloping up on horseback. And about 10 minutes behind them, another 30 horsemen arrived with General Dostum. This was his main body of his personal body guards, coming there to meet us. . . . This was our first chapter in the Wild, Wild West events that we would participate in every day. [Dostum] jumped off his horse. He shook our hands. Thanked us for coming. Led us into his little base camp.[1]

American intelligence was unaware that Dostum's force was a horse-mounted unit. This was the ODA's first introduction to the horse culture of Afghanistan. It was a culture that had links to the Persian armies of Darius and Xerxes, when the land was called Bactria. It had been conquered by Alexander the Great's companions and had provided horses and men for Genghis Kahn's army as it marched into Persia and on to the Euphrates valley. The southern steppe, just to the north of the area of operations, is where scientists believe the first contact between horse and man occurred and where the concept of the war horse and rider originated.

Captain Nash and his team were to work with General Dostum's army to help them defeat the Taliban. Dostum's army consisted of 2,000 horsemen armed with modern small arms. The enemy was equipped with relatively modern tanks and artillery. Captain Nash would support Dostum by using laser guidance systems to

Modern horse mounted operations. U.S. Special Forces operating with mounted forces of the Afghanistan Northern Alliance in the fall of 2001. (*Department of Defense*)

direct precision bombing attacks by the U.S. Air Force. Nash's team were experts in hi-tech warfare. But they were not experts in the manner in which Dostum's army traveled–exclusively by horse. Many of the ODA's 12 highly trained commandos had never been on a horse.

Fortunately, Captain Nash was one of the few U.S. army officers who was also an experienced horseman. He had grown up on a cattle farm in Kansas and been a rodeo rider in college. He had a solid working knowledge of horsemanship and was able to ensure that his team's inexperienced riders were at least safe. Nash noted that the Afghan mounts were "tough little mountain ponies, like American mustangs from out West." As they were all stallions, there was constant biting and kicking going on among the horses and they were not easy to manage, even for experienced riders. The saddles were small and tight, and the stirrups were short and barely big enough for the American's heavy-soled combat boots. The Afghans used a simple broken snaffle bit to control the horse, which meant riders had to develop a feel for the task, and the traditional short stirrup style of the steppe was not easy for a novice to use. Nash's instructions to his men were simple: "Keep your feet light in the stirrups. . . . If anyone is thrown by his mount and has a foot caught in the stirrup and the horse doesn't stop immediately, the nearest man has to the shoot the horse dead. . . . You'll be killed if you're dragged on this rocky ground."[2] Nash was also smart enough to understand the problems associated with overburdening the horses. Packhorses and donkeys were used to carry the team's rucksacks and heavy equipment. One of his first acts was to request quality saddles for his men–either U.S. army–style McClellan saddles or lightweight Australian endurance saddles. He knew that with 70 pounds of equipment per man, the saddles had to be lightweight. He specifically requested that the army *not* provide him with the popular American stock saddle, which can weigh as much as 40 pounds.

Over a three-week period, Captain Nash and his team helped General Dostum and his horsemen fight their way through the Balkh Valley and into the strategically important city of Mazar-e-Sharif. The Afghans were extremely protective of the Americans, surrounding them with special guard details. The U.S. soldiers' primary task was to direct air power against Taliban positions. They did this with GPS, laser range finders, and digital satellite radios. After the enemy's bunkers and tanks were destroyed, the Afghan fighters would then charge the positions on horseback. Nash described a typical attack: "Once they closed with the Taliban, their technique can best be described as the swarm. They were at the gallop, firing their assault weapons, not accurately, but it was scaring the hell out of the Taliban. And they would simply ride down any Taliban that attempted to resist against them or refused to surrender. And we had a front row seat to this every day."[3]

As the enemy was pushed back, Nash and his men kept pace, often spending 12 hours a day in the saddle. In mid-November General Dostum's forces occupied Mazar-e-Sharif and the terrain changed so that the ODA could continue to support the Afghans while operating out of vehicles. To the American public, this largely ended the brief return of the military horse. In reality the Afghans continued, as they do to this day, to rely on horse-mounted forces when resources, terrain, and weather require it.

The war in Afghanistan is indicative of the likely future requirements for military horses: isolated situations, probably of short duration, in undeveloped environments. And their occurrence will be unpredictable. The U.S. army was unprepared for the need for commandos to have horsemanship skills. Some other modern armies would be better prepared to employ horses for military purposes. The German, Austrian, and Swiss armies all maintain a military horse capability to support the operations of their mountain forces. An example is the German army's *Gebirgstragtierwesen* (mountain animal transport unit) 230. The unit is equipped with mules and Haflinger mountain horses. Their mission is general transportation support to mountain troops under terrain and weather conditions that preclude wheel or air support. They also use the Halflingers for mounted reconnaissance in mountains or deep forest terrain. The unit has been used to support peacekeeping missions in the Balkans.[4] The Austrian mountain troops perform a similar role and also use mules and Haflingers to execute their missions. The mountain horse support units of the Swiss army use Freiburger Swiss mountain horses. The Swiss force is unique because it is a reserve force. The horses, more than 500 of them, are issued to individual soldiers who are paid a stipend to support the horse. The horse is stabled privately by the soldier, and it is his so long as the horse remains fit, meets army care requirements, and is present for duty at reserve training.[5]

The modern military uses of the horse are limited in scope, but the impact of military horsemanship is still strongly in evidence in the modern horse community. One of the most direct influences is on urban mounted police techniques. Police horses are used for patrolling and riot control. The training techniques for police horses are quite similar to the techniques used to train cavalry remounts. Horses must be acclimatized to the diverse and frightening sights and sounds of a busy city. For riot control, police remounts are trained to remain under control amid the stress and confusion of masses of people even when assaulted by sign-waving, bottle-throwing protesters. War horses faced similar distractions in the middle of a melee. A police horse must also be willing to move, often at a canter, against a crowd of rioters. This action, and its associated training, is similar to a small-scale charge. The effect that the police are trying to achieve is the same as a cavalry charge: to psychologically shock the crowd into a panic—effectively dispersing it. The intimidating size, speed, and combined mass of the police horses can disperse a crowd without physically coming in contact with it. The great psychological advantages that horses give the police in controlling large crowds make it an ideal nonlethal law enforcement tool.

Austrian *Gebirgsjäger* (mountain troops) on a training patrol with their Haflinger tragtier (pack animals). (*Austrian Ministry of Defense*).

Perhaps the most publicly visible legacy of the military horse is in the world of horse sports. The major international horse sports are the three Olympic horse disciplines: dressage, show jumping, and eventing. Today's professional civilian equestrians and their expensive carefully bred and trained horses are essentially measuring and testing themselves against the standards set for the war horse and his rider over the course of 3,000 years of military history. The formal salute to the judge that begins the competition is a direct link to the military roots of horse sports. Dressage's relationship to the military is through the extensive use made by mounted forces of high school dressage training techniques. The European military seat of the eighteenth and nineteenth centuries and the standard military double bridle are still integral to modern dressage. Show jumping as a sport began as a military entertainment and competition among officers. Modern jumping techniques are directly the result of the military experiments of the Italian Captain Federico Caprilli. The equestrian sport most directly connected to the military is eventing. Eventing, still known in many European countries as "the military," was specifically designed to compare and test cavalry chargers in the late nineteenth century. Its components, show jumping, dressage, and a grueling distance course followed by a cross-country

Cavalry Remount Champion: "Jenny Camp," winning the Silver Medal at the Berlin Olympics, 1936. (Rau, Gustav. *Die Reitkunst der Welt and Olympischen Spielen 1936, 1937*)

obstacle course, were all designed to ensure that the winner was the best all-round war horse. All three of these sports, when they were incorporated into the modern Olympics in 1912, were originally only open to competitors who were serving military officers. This did not change until after World War II, and not until 1952 did significant numbers of civilian equestrians compete in the Olympic horse events.

The Olympic equestrian events represent the ultimate athletic test of the horse and rider. In the 1930s an American horse named Jenny Camp was a typical American remount horse without a distinguished lineage, bred only for army service at the Front Royal, Virginia, remount depot. Jenny Camp was 15.3 hands tall, and a bay three-quarters Thoroughbred. At the Fort Riley, Kansas, cavalry school, she was being used to train cavalry officers, and it was thought she might make a fine polo pony. Purely by accident the officers discovered that the horse was a very proficient jumper, and she was included in the mounts that the U.S. cavalry was preparing for the Olympics. She was 6 years old at her first Olympic appearance in Los Angeles in 1932, and 10 when she appeared in the 1936 games in Berlin. Jenny Camp, by most measures a typical remount, won two silver medals and one gold medal in the Olympics–one of only three horses in the history of the games to win medals in consecutive games. Had it not been for a lucky accident, this superb horse might have been issued to any private on a dusty army post in the American Southwest. Jenny Camp illustrates the top-quality horses that a well-run army remount system could routinely produce in the last decades of the horse-mounted cavalry. The science of breeding superb horses, the science that produced the world's most famous horse breeds, Trakehners, Dons, and Andalusians for military service, is another part of the legacy of the war horse.

One other visible reminder of the pageantry of the war horse and rider is the dozens of governments that maintain horse ceremonial units. Usually these units are uniformed and equipped as the famous national regiments of the eighteenth and nineteenth centuries. The most famous of these is the British Household Cavalry, which is manned by serving soldiers of the modern British army. These ceremonial units may not be perfect historical replicas of the original uniforms, but they nonetheless capture the grandeur and spirit associated with the war horse that made the cavalry the most popular branch of the military. And they convey an aura of martial majesty embodied in the war horse that no piece of modern military equipment can match.

Now and again a concerned citizen or horse enthusiast writes a letter to a newspaper, a legislator, or an army general suggesting that there is still a viable military use for the horse. This is true, as suggested by the horses of the European mountain troops. But the time of large-scale military use of the horse is over. All horse lovers should understand that probably the most fortunate thing that has happened to horses in the history of our relationship with the animal is that the horse finally is obsolete as a military weapon. The horse's military role exposed these magnificent animals to the best of mankind, represented by superlative horsemen like the Prussian general von Seydlitz and compassionate and dedicated horse peoples such as the Cossacks, and put the horse at the very center of many of the great moments in human history. It also exposed the horse to all the horrors of mankind's most wasteful, painful, and often purposeless endeavor–warfare. The plight of war horses in combat was even worse than the soldier's: they had no choice and no understanding of their situation, yet suffered and died in the thousands because of their selfless and faithful service.

APPENDIX

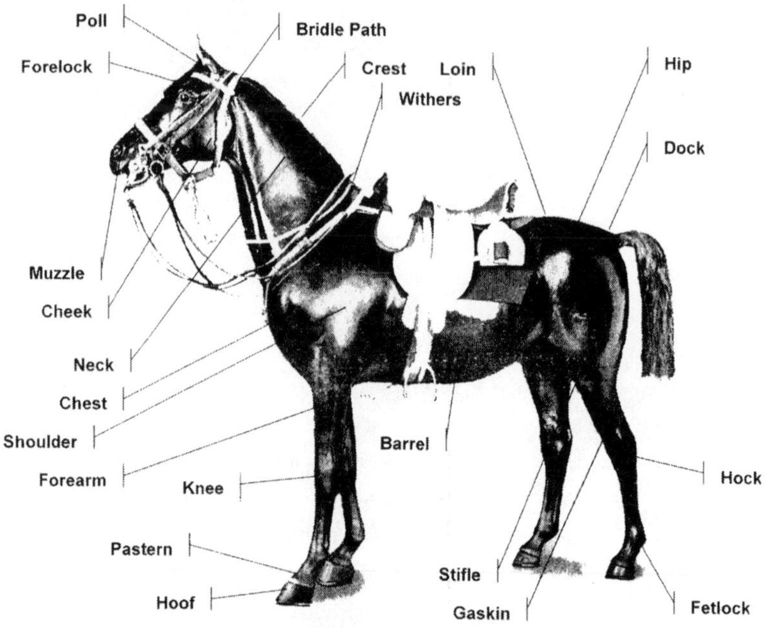

A 1920s British cavalry mount with the major body parts of the horse identified. (*Author*).

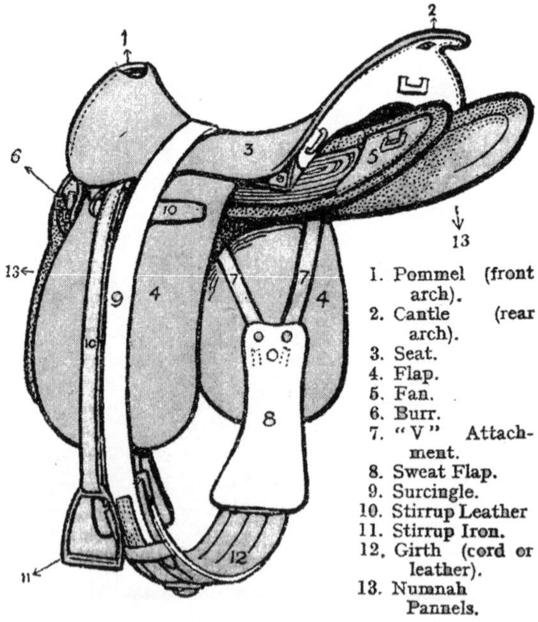

Standard named parts of the saddle. This illustration is the British Model 1912 Universal Pattern Saddle. (*Manual of Horsemastership, Equitation, and Driving*, 1929)

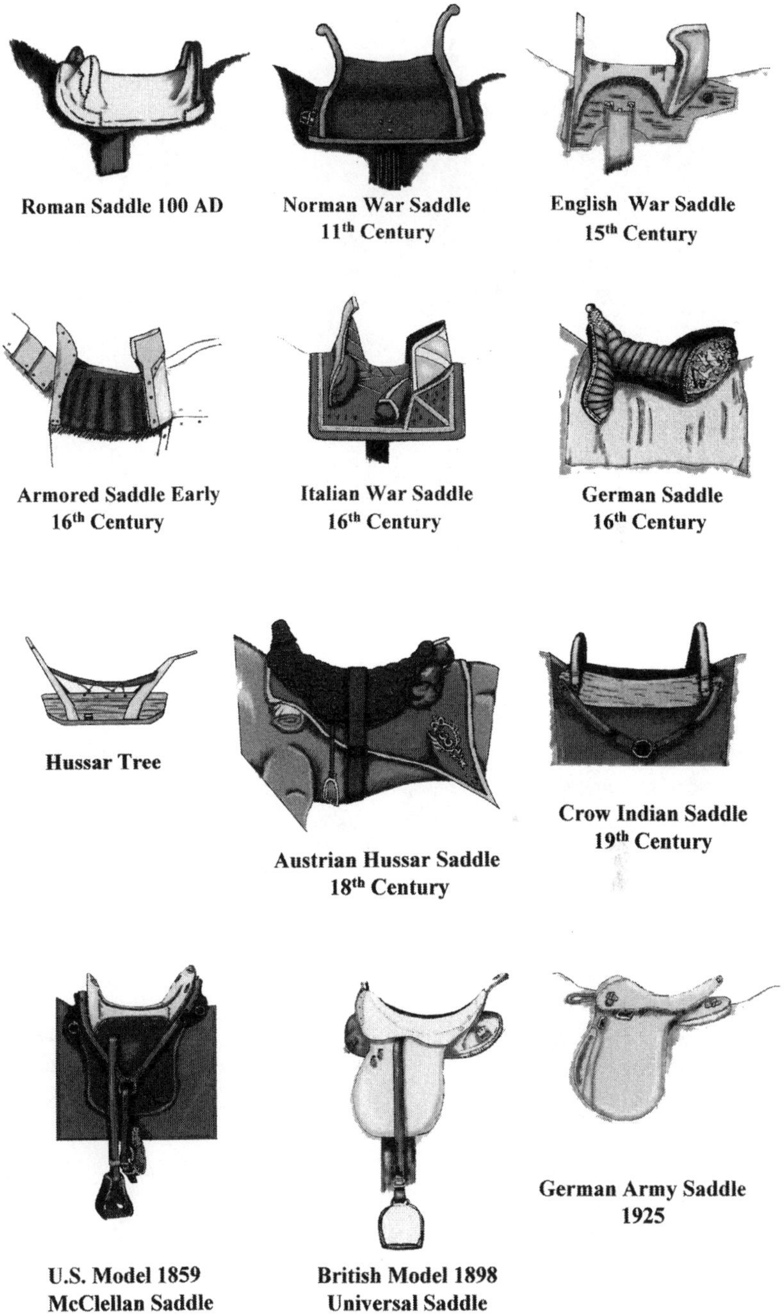

Development of the military saddle beginning with one of the first frame saddles, the Roman four horn saddle, and ending with one of the last saddle designs, the 1925 German field saddle. (*Author*)

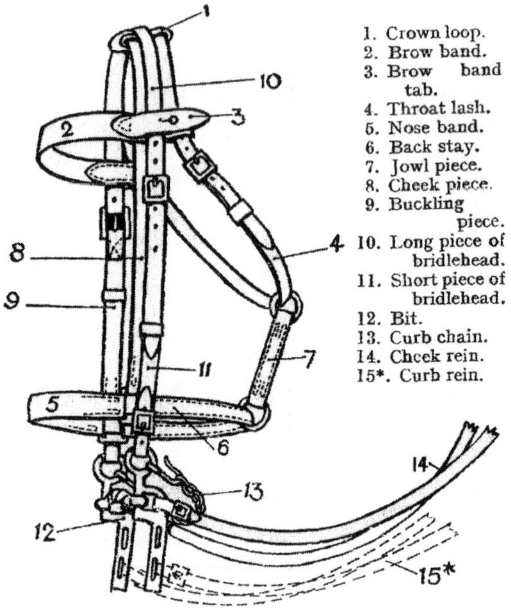

British standard issue bit and bridle of the 1920s. This is a Pelham bit which is a combination snaffle and curb. Unlike traditional bit and bradoon combinations, the Pelham is a single bit with several rein attachment points. Attaching reins at the mouth caused the bit to act like a snaffle. Attaching reins at the end of the shank caused the bit to act like a curb. Using two sets of reins on the bit gave the rider the ability to use the bit in the same manner as the double bridle. (*Manual of Horsemanstership, Equitation, and Driving, 1929.*)

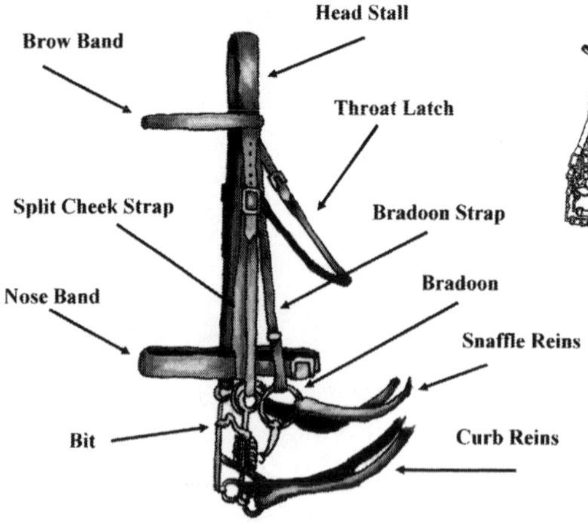

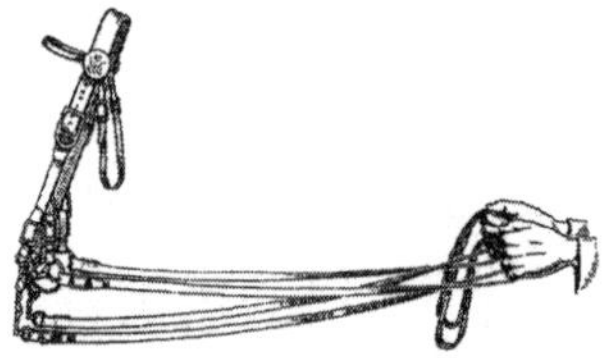

The U.S. Army manner of holding double reins. (*ROTC Manual Cavalry Basic, 1942*)

NOTES

Chapter 1: The Ancients

1. The discussion of the family Equidae and how it is scientifically classified is extracted from Clutton-Brock, *Horse Power*, 17–25.
2. Ibid., 24.
3. Anthony Dent, "The Predomestic Horse," in *Encyclopedia of the Horse*, 14. Types of horse are not universally agreed on, although Dent's four types are generally accepted. Other authors add additional types to the list, see, for example, Dossenbach and Dossenbach, *The Noble Horse*, 30–31.
4. Dossenbach and Dossenbach, *The Noble Horse*, 103, put the time period between 3000 and 2000 BC, but the earlier date is probably more accurate according to Clutton-Brock, 56.
5. In "Domestication and the Early Horse People," *Encyclopedia of the Horse*, 16–17, Dent discusses the diversity of possible original domestication of the horse and the virtual impossibility of determining conclusively a single point of origin as well as the impossibility of determining which geographic area and specific tribe or group was first. He does postulate that the type 2 Norse horse may have been the first domesticated by northern hunters already familiar with domesticated reindeer somewhere in north-central or eastern Asia.
6. Clutton-Brock, *Horse Power*, 56.
7. David Anthony, "The Opening of the Eurasian Steppe at 2000 BC," in *The Bronze Age*.
8. Clutton-Brock, *Horse Power*, 68.
9. All the consulted sources agree that Ur provides the first evidence of use of horses as part of an organized military establishment, Clutton-Brock, *Horse Power*, 69; Anglim et al., *Fighting Techniques*, 80–81; and Keegan, *History of Warfare*, 157.
10. Clutton-Brock, *Horse Power*, 71–72.
11. Anglim et al., *Fighting Techniques*, 81.
12. Keegan, *History of Warfare*, 155.
13. This discussion of Kikkuli is taken from *Legacy of the Horse*, "The First Horses." The other source that gives a small amount of background on Ann Hyland's research is "Kikkuli Method of Horse Training," *Splitters Creek*. Ann Hyland in *The Horse in the Ancient World*, 39, also addresses this particular aspect of the Kikkuli texts. She provides a detailed discussion of exactly what the equivalent distances are for a "danna" and an "iku." Her conclusion is that a "danna" equals 1,640 yards and an "iku" equals approximately 15 yards .
14. Cotterell, *Chariot*, 50.
15. *Legacy of the Horse*, "The First Horses."
16. This description of the heavy chariot is a distinction made by Mark Healy in his study of the Egyptian army in *New Kingdom*, 21–22, and various color plates.
17. Short discussion of horse armor found in Healy, *New Kingdom*, 62.
18. Anglim et al., *Fighting Techniques*, 81.
19. Colin Walters, "Late Roman and Byzantine Egypt," in *Penguin Encyclopedia of Ancient Civilizations*, 57.
20. Anglim et al., *Fighting Techniques*, 81–85.
21. Healy, *New Kingdom*, 23–24.

22. Mark Healy in *Qadesh*, puts the date as 1300; other sources put it as 1275 BC. In addition the city name is variously spelled "Qadesh" and "Kadesh." The *Penguin Encyclopedia of Ancient Civilizations*, 30, spells the name "Kadesh" and puts the date of the battle as 1286 BC.
23. Some of the controversial details are omitted because they do not add to an understanding of chariot warfare. In addition to Healy's well-thought-out description of events, Anthony J. Spalinger also does an in-depth analysis of the battle in *War in Ancient Egypt*, 209–34. Spalinger's conclusions do not all coincide with those of Healy. In many cases the evidence appears to make either interpretation equally plausible, although as an academic work Spalinger's is more complete in citing the sources for his conclusions.
24. Several articles in the *Penguin Encyclopedia of Ancient Civilizations* contributed to this discussion of the Sea People: Colin Walters, "Ancient Egypt," 22–44; N. K. Sanders, "The Sea Peoples," 44–46; and O. R. Gurney, "The Hittites," 111–17.
25. Clutton-Brock, *Horse Power*, 66.
26. The advance in horsemanship and equipment is easily discerned by visually examining the cavalry depicted in the relief drawings found in the ruins of the Assyrian Empire and displayed in a variety of sources including Healy, *Ancient Assyrians*, 11, 24; Anglim et al., *Fighting Techniques*, 94–95; and A. K. Grayson, "Assyria," in *Penguin Encyclopedia of Ancient Civilizations*, 107.
27. Grayson, "Assyria," in *Penguin Encyclopedia of Ancient Civilizations*, 105.

Chapter 2: Cavalry Armies

1. Summarized from T. Cuyler Young Jr., "Persia," in *Penguin Encyclopedia of Ancient Civilizations*, 147–52. Cyrus the Great and his son are also referred to in some texts as Kyros the Great and Kambyses; see De Souza, "Greek Persian Wars," in De Souza, Heckel, and Llewellyn-Jones, *Greeks at War*, 27.
2. Gaebel, *Cavalry Operations*, 74.
3. Warry, *Alexander*, 33, 53.
4. Hanson, *Western Way of War*, 27–32.
5. Hyland, *Horse in the Ancient World*, 27–28, 120–21.
6. Hyland describes the Assyrian system in this regard; ibid., 96.
7. Ibid., 120–22.
8. The Caspian head is short and fine with large eyes, a small muzzle, and large nostrils placed low. There is a pronounced development of the forehead; the ears are very short; the neck slim and graceful, well attached to sloping shoulders; withers are pronounced; back straight; and the tail is set high on a rather level croup. The legs are slim and dense, strong bone and no feathering at the fetlock. The hooves are extremely strong and oval shaped—more like those of the ass than the horse. The overall impression of the Caspian is that of a very small, well-proportioned horse. Subsequent studies confirmed the visual picture osteologically; the Caspian is a horse, not a pony. Xenophon, *Persian Expedition*, 201; Horse height is measured in hands, where one hand equals 10 cm (4 in); E. Webster, "Caspian Horse Today;" "Caspian," *Breeds of Livestock*.
9. Joyce Covington, secretary and treasurer, Caspian Horse Society of the Americas, interview by the author, October 29, 2005.

10. "Fossil and Frozen Horses from Prehistoric Times: The Pazyryk Horses" www.turanian-horse.org
11. The Akhal-Teke should be longer than it is tall, with a rectangular silhouette. The back is long, but strong, with a level top-line. Withers are prominent and attached to a well set in shoulder. Shoulders should be nicely sloped and extremely free moving. The hip angle is wide and gives the appearance of strength. Tail set is low. When viewed from the front, the chest is narrow, although the heart girth is deep. The skin of the Akhal-Teke is very thin, with their coat and hair being quite fine. Often the breed shows a sparse mane and tail, little or no forelock, and the absence of feathering on the fetlocks. Any color is acceptable, as is any combination of white markings. The characteristic "metallic gleam" is a desirable feature. Overall, the Akhal-Teke should give the impression of lithe athleticism without excessive musculature. Akhal-Teke Association of America, "Breed Standard."
12. Herodotus, *History of Herodotus*, bk. 7; Ibid., bk. 9.
13. Bosworth, *Conquest and Empire*, 163; Hyland, *Horse in the Ancient World*, 30.
14. Xenophon, *Art of Horsemanship*, 53, 58.
15. Spence, *Cavalry of Classical Greece*, 165.
16. The size of Xerxes' army is the subject of much analysis by historians. These figures are based on a variety of estimates as discussed in Connolly, *Greece and Rome at War*, 12, and De Souza et al., *Greeks at War*, 49.
17. These numbers are according to Herodotus as reported in Connolly, *Greece and Rome at War*, 30.
18. Gaebel, *Cavalry Operations*, 79.
19. Connolly, *Greece and Rome at War*, 29; summarized from a variety of accounts including Connolly, *Greece and Rome at War*, 30–35; De Souza et al., *Greeks at War*, 76–78, and Gaebel, *Cavalry Operations*, 74–80.
20. Worley, *Hippeis*, 29–30; Spence, *Cavalry of Classical Greece*, 25.
21. Worley, *Hippeis*, 29.
22. Laffin, *Brassey's Battles*, 417–18.
23. Spence, *Cavalry of Classical Greece*, 167.
24. A lot of the source discussion debates the equipment of the Greek cavalry. This issue is highly problematic because of the length of the time period discussed, the cultural differences and preferences of the individual different Greek states, a definite lack of comprehensive evidence, and the constantly changing nature of warfare during the Peloponnesian Wars period. This subject is addressed in Gaebel, *Cavalry Operations*, 29, Worley, *Hippeis*, 36–48, and Spence, *Cavalry of Classical Greece*, 49–65. Worley in particular relies on pottery art relics for most of his opinions on pre-Persian Wars cavalry. His analysis in this area tends to overemphasize the role of cavalry in the Mycenaean and early Archaic periods based purely on the recovered pottery depictions (900–500 BC).
25. Worley, *Hippeis*, 154.
26. Ibid., 153–54; Gaebel, *Cavalry Operations*, 148–49.
27. Spence, *Cavalry of Classical Greece*, 26.
28. Plutarch, "Plutarch's Parallel Lives: Alexander" in *Fall of the Roman Republic*; Arrian, *Campaigns of Alexander*, 282–83. In the introduction, Hamilton notes that Plutarch refers to many ancient sources who report that Bucephalas was killed in battle, and Arrian also refers to "the blow which killed his beloved horse Bucephalas," 274.

29. Connolly, *Greece and Rome at War*, 72–73.
30. Worley, *Hippeis*, 156; Connolly, *Greece and Rome at War*, 70–73.
31. Markle, "Macedonian Arms," 87–111; Gaebel, *Cavalry Operations*, 168–71.
32. Worley, *Hippeis*, 155, and Gaebel, *Cavalry Operations*, 161.
33. Worley, *Hippeis*, 155–56. Connolly's discussion of cavalry organization matches Worley's, but he adds that only seven squadrons plus the royal squadron participated in the invasion of Asia, 71.
34. Arrian, *Campaigns of Alexander*, 73.
35. Plutarch, "Plutarch's Parallel Lives: Alexander."
36. Gaebel, *Cavalry Operations*, 162n6n11.
37. Ibid., 154, and Worley, *Hippeis*, 159.
38. Arrian, *Campaigns of Alexander*, 71, and Warry, *Alexander 334-323 BC*, 19; Macedonian numbers here vary slightly depending on the source. I have rounded the numbers and compromised some between sources. The numbers provided by the Greek historian Diodorus are 12,000 Macedonian infantry, 7,000 allies, and 5,000 mercenaries. For cavalry the numbers were 1,800 Macedonian, 1,800 Thessalians, and 600 from the rest of Greece. Diodorus quoted in Waldemar Heckel, "The Wars of Alexander the Great, 336–323," in De Souza et al., *Greeks at War*, 27.
39. Arrian, *Campaigns of Alexander*, 71-75.
40. Ibid., 120–21.
41. Warry, *Alexander 334–323 BC*, 52–54.
42. Bosworth, *Conquest and Empire*, 78; Warry, *Alexander 334–323 BC*, 59.
43. The bulk of the Gaugamela description is derived from Arrian, *Campaigns of Alexander*, 164–72, Bosworth, *Conquest and Empire*, 81–85, and Warry, *Alexander 334–323 BC*, 53–66.
44. Arrian, *Campaigns of Alexander*, 171–72.

Chapter 3: The Romans

1. Goldsworthy, *Roman Warfare*, 49.
2. Dixon and Southern, *Roman Cavalry*, 21.
3. Connolly, *Greece and Rome*, 134.
4. Goldsworthy, *Complete Roman Army*, 27; McCall, *Cavalry of the Roman Republic*, 147–49; Connolly, *Greece and Rome*, 133–34.
5. Ibid.
6. Ibid., 47.
7. Cheesman, *Auxilia*, 31–32; Vegetius, *Roman Military*, 89.
8. Goldsworthy, *Roman Warfare*, 107; G. Webster, *Roman Imperial Army*, 145; Goldsworthy, *Complete Roman Army*, 56–58; Cheesman, *Auxilia*, 21.
9. Cheesman, *Auxilia*, 60–62.
10. Goldsworthy, *Roman Warfare*, 126–27; G. Webster, *Roman Imperial Army*, 282; Goldsworthy, *Roman Warfare*, 133.
11. Dixon and Southern, *Roman Cavalry*, 27–30, quoting Josephus, the Jewish historian of the Jewish revolt in his work *The Jewish War*. In *Greece and Rome at War*, 217–18, Connolly reaches the same conclusion as Dixon and Southern.
12. Suetonius, "The Lives of the Caesars," LVII; Plutarch, *Fall of the Roman Republic*, 261; Suetonius, "The Lives of the Caesars," LXI.

13. Anglim et al., *Fighting Techniques*, 107. Ann Hyland, *Equus*, 116, comments that experiments with the Roman saddle indicate that leather leggings are absolutely essential for a secure seat; Dixon and Southern, *Roman Cavalry*, 35-53, and Connolly, *Tiberius Claudius Maximus*, 29.
14. G. Webster, *Roman Imperial Army*, 151–52; Cheesman, *Auxilia*, 58, 69; Connolly attributes the beginning of fully armored Roman heavy cavalry to Hadrian after meeting Sarmatian heavy cavalry along the Danube in the second half of the first century, *Greece and Rome at War*, 235.
15. Dixon and Southern, *Roman Cavalry*, 49, 61–62, 66–67. Intricate metal eye protection is well illustrated in Connolly, *Tiberius Claudius Maximus*, 22–23.
16. Goldsworthy, *Roman Warfare*, 182; Elton, *Warfare in Roman Europe*, 103; Goldsworthy, *Roman Warfare*, 202; Simon MacDowall makes this point explicitly in *Late Roman Cavalryman*, 3.
17. Goldsworthy, *Roman Warfare*, 167; MacDowall, *Late Roman Cavalryman*, 4.
18. Ibid., 5–7; Ibid., 59; Roger Tomlin, "The Mobile Army," in Connolly, *Greece and Rome at War*, 257.
19. Goldsworthy, *Roman Warfare*, 201.
20. Hyland, *Equus*, 24.
21. Ibid., 11, 4.
22. Ibid., 20–21.
23. The description of the construction, analysis, and testing of the four-horned saddle is from Connolly and van Driel-Murray, "Roman Cavalry Saddle," 33–50.
24. When doing lateral work from the horse's back the value of the rigid horns becomes even more apparent. They enable very sharp, rapid turns to be executed during which the front horns lock the rider in very effectively. When using a weapon, as for instance if the *spatha* is employed from the right over the horse's neck and delivered in a downwards cut to the left of the animal's shoulder, the natural tendency would be for the weight of the torso and weapon arm, plus the poundage of thrust, to disrupt the rider's equilibrium. By locking the right thigh hard under the right horn the rider can maintain his seat, if not with ease, with greater sense of security than when riding on a soft or bareback. Hyland, *Equus*, 134.
25. Ibid., 134.
26. Ibid., 135.
27. Hyland, *Equus*, 50, Dixon and Southern, *Roman Cavalry*, 181–205; Vegetius, *Roman Military*, 57, 63, 69.
28. Hyland, *Equus*, 139.
29. Dixon and Southern, *Roman Cavalry*, 229–33.
30. Goldsworthy, *Roman Warfare*, 79–80.
31. "Strabo: The Geography," bk. 3, chap. 4.
32. Wilcox and Treviño, *Barbarians against Rome*, 73–74.
33. Caesar, *Ancient History, Archaeology, and Biblical Studies*, bk. 4, chap. 33.
34. "Strabo: The Geography," bk. 4, chap. 4; Caesar, *Ancient History, Archaeology, and Biblical Studies*, bk. 4, chap. 2; Robert Browning, "The Later Roman Empire," in *Penguin Encyclopedia of Ancient Civilizations*, 266–67.
35. Goldsworthy, *Roman Warfare*, 139; E. J. Keall, "After Alexander," in *Penguin Encyclopedia of Ancient Civilizations*, 157.

36. Farrokh, *Sassanian Elite Cavalry*, 7, 3-5.
37. Keall, "After Alexander," in *Penguin Encyclopedia of Ancient Civilizations*, 159.
38. Ibid., 159–61.
39. Farrokh, *Sassanian Elite Cavalry*, 16–17.
40. Ibid., 7–16.
41. Ibid., 29–31.
42. Ibid., 19.
43. Vegetius, *Roman Military*, 112; Caesar, *Ancient History, Archaeology, and Biblical Studies*, bk. 2, chap. 8; Goldsworthy, *Roman Warfare*, 126.
44. Connolly, *Greece and Rome at War*, 134; Caesar, *Ancient History, Archaeology, and Biblical Studies*, bk. 8, chap. 17.
45. Goldsworthy, *Roman Warfare*, 55–56.
46. Vegetius, *Roman Military*, 132.
47. Ibid., 79.
48. This account of the battle of Carrhae is a summary of the account by Plutarch, *Fall of the Roman Republic*, 137–55.
49. Goldsworthy, *Roman Army at War*, 64–68.
50. Anglim et al., *Fighting Techniques*, 116.
51. Farrokh, *Sassanian Elite Cavalry*, 44–45.
52. Ibid., 47–50.
53. The account of Adrianople is based on Simon MacDowall's comprehensive work on the subject, *Adrianople*.
54. Ammianus quoted in MacDowall, *Adrianople*, 80.

Chapter 4: The Knight and His Mount

1. Oman, *Art of War*, xii.
2. John Gillingham, "An Age of Expansion, 1020-1204," in *Medieval Warfare: A History*, 59. Gillingham points to gold at the primary motivation of Norman expansion, ibid., 61.
3. Gillingham, "An Age of Expansion" in *Medieval Warfare: A History*, 71–73; Edbury, "Warfare in the Latin East," in ibid., 107; Gillingham, "An Age of Expansion," in ibid., 78.
4. Andrew Ayton, "Arms, Armour, and Horses," in *Medieval Warfare: A History*, 196.
5. Gravett, *Norman Knight*, 28–29.
6. This thesis is convincingly articulated by Stephen Morillo, "The 'Age of Cavalry' Revisited," in *Circle of War*. Morillo's thesis is that primarily social and political causes more accurately describe the relative rise and fall of cavalry and infantry capabilities as opposed to technological changes. Specifically, he argues against the stirrup as the explanation for the rise of cavalry dominance in the Middle Ages. The importance of the stirrup is expanded later in a subsequent section of this chapter. For a complete discussion of historiography of the stirrup debate see Sloan, "Stirrup Controversy."
7. Crosbie-Weston, "Charlemagne," in *Cavalry*, 49; France, *Western Warfare*, 60–61; Oakeshott, *Knight in Battle*, 20; Christopher Allmand, "New Weapons, New Tactics, 1300–1500," *Cambridge Illustrated History of Warfare*, 100.
8. Allmand, "New Weapons, New Tactics, 1300-1500," *Cambridge Illustrated History of Warfare*, 99. Allmand is very specific that he is counting men-at-arms as cavalry, regardless of how they are ultimately employed in battle.

9. Oakeshott, *Knight in Battle*, 16.
10. Delbruck, *Medieval Warfare*, 510–11.
11. Ibid., 294–95; Rothero, *Armies of Crécy*, 18–19; Davis, *Medieval Warhorse*, 24.
12. Eric Maclagan, "The Bayeux Tapestry," *Battle of Hastings*, 33–44; Davis, *Medieval Warhorse*, 16–17; Bachrach, "Caballus et Caballarius."
13. Gravett, *World of the Medieval Knight*, 30; Ibid., 44–45; Davis, *Medieval Warhorse*, 23–24; Prestwich, *Armies and Warfare*, 27; Arnold, *Renaissance at War*, 110.
14. Prestwich, *Armies and Warfare*, 27.
15. Gravett, *Norman Knight*, 11, 33, 50–52. Nicolle, *French Medieval Armies*, 25, 42; Based on English tomb effigies of the twelfth and thirteenth centuries illustrated in Wise, *Armies of the Crusades*, 7; Verbruggen, *Art of Warfare*, 23–24.
16. Gravett, *World of the Medieval Knight*, 20–21, Prestwich, *Armies and Warfare*, 18–22.
17. Ibid., 24–23.
18. Oakeshott, *Knight in Battle*, 81.
19. Gravett, *World of the Medieval Knight*, 17; Oakeshott, *Knight in Battle*, 101.
20. Rabanus Maurus's interpretation of Vegetius quoted in Bachrach, "On Roman Ramparts," 66; Verbruggen, *Art of Warfare*, 27.
21. Ibid., 39.
22. Verbruggen, *Art of Warfare*, 25–26.
23. Davis, *Medieval Warhorse*, 34–37.
24. Hanson, *Carnage and Culture*, 141; Hyland, *Medieval Warhorse*, 92–93. Based on the Medieval poetry of Wolfram von Eschenbach.
25. Davis, *Medieval Warhorse*, 40–41.
26. Hyland, *Medieval Warhorse*, 86; Chenevix Trench, *History of Horsemanship*, 72; These estimates are based on the skeletal remains evidence recorded by D. James Rackham, "Appendix: Skeletal Evidence of Medieval Horses from London Sites," in *Medieval Horse*, 169–70 chart 128.
27. Chenevix Trench, *History of Horsemanship*, 73; Seward, *Hundred Years War*, 26; Davis, *Medieval Warhorse*, 18; Hyland, *Medieval Warhorse*, 93.
28. Oakeshott, *A Knight and His Horse*, 10–12; Davis, *Medieval Warhorse*, 67.
29. *Cavalry*, 48; Vernam, *Man on Horseback*, 63–65. De Camp, "Before Stirrups," 159–60, puts the date of the first definite mention in writing to Emperor Maurice's *Strategikon* sometime between 582 and 602. His time line is a mounting loop with the Scythians around 100 BC, and then the rigid stirrup invented by the Sarmatians in the same period.
30. Hyland, *Medieval Warhorse*, 7, makes this point based on the saddles depicted in the St. Gallen Psalter, c. 890–924, illustrated in Davis, *Medieval Warhorse*, 13; Hyland, *Medieval Warhorse*, 7-8; Verbruggen, *Art of Warfare*, 25; This description is primarily based on the excellent Italian war saddle and detailed armor plates depicted by Pyhrr, LaRocca, and Breiding in *Armored Horse in Europe*, 60–71.
31. Vernam, *Man on Horseback*, 71.
32. John Clark, "Horseshoes," in *Medieval Horse*, 75–81.
33. Dirk H. Breiding, "Horse Armor in Medieval and Renaissance Europe: An Overview," in Pyhrr et al., *Armored Horse in Europe 1480-1620*, 8–14; Gravett, *World of the Medieval Knight*, 35.
34. Hyland, *Medieval Warhorse*, 86; Davis, *Medieval Warhorse*, 37.

35. Rothero, *Armies of Crécy*, 319.
36. This general description is based on Nicolle, *Saracen Faris*, 31, on a survey of the variety of mounted types discussed and illustrated in *Saracen Faris*, 33–44, and in Nicolle, *Saladin*, 25–32.
37. Nicolle, *Saracen Faris*, 8, 11.
38. Nicolle, *Mamluks*, 9–10.
39. Hyland, *Medieval Warhorse*, 91; Nicolle, *Saracen Faris*, 23; Davis, *Medieval Warhorse*, 37.
40. A wide variety of references to horses attributed to Muhammad are recorded in various *hadeeth* (assembled comments attributed to Muhammad). According to Malik's Muwatta, bk. 21, no. 21.19.47: "Yahya related to me from Malik from Yahya ibn Said that the Messenger of Allah, may Allah bless him and grant him peace, was seen wiping the face of his horse with his cloak. He was questioned about it and said, `I was reproached in the night about horses.' i.e., not taking care of them." Found in the *USC-MSA Hadith Database*; Dossenbach and Dossenbach, *Noble Horse*, 132.
41. Davis, *Medieval Warhorse*, 37.
42. "Arabian," *Breeds of Livestock*.
43. Nicolle, *Saracen Faris*, 54; This analysis of the Islamic Medieval cavalry saddle is based on exploded diagrams of two saddles in Nicolle, *Saracen Faris*, 41–42.
44. Nicolle, *Saracen Faris*, 10; Based on the illustrations and commentary in G. Smith, *Medieval Muslim Horsemanship*, 10–11; Sir Bertrandon quoted in Chenevix Trench, *History of Horsemanship*, 80.
45. The primary reference for the description of the battle of Hattin, except as noted, is Nicolle, *Hattin (1187)*. Nicolle's account agrees in all important respects with Fuller's in *Decisive Battles*.
46. Nicolle, *Hattin (1187)*.
47. Fuller, *Decisive Battles*, 426.
48. Nicolle, *Hattin (1187)*.
49. Munro, *Letters of the Crusades*.
50. This summary of the battle of Crécy is based on descriptions of the campaign and battle in Nicolle, *Crécy;* Burne, *Crécy War*; and Fuller, *Decisive Battles*, except as otherwise noted.
51. Perroy, *Hundred Years War*, 69–71.
52. Froissart, *Chronicles*, 84.
53. Nicolle, "Failure of an Elite."
54. Rate of fire for the longbow is put at 12 arrows per minute. Andrew Ayton, "Arms, Armor, and Horses," in *Medieval Warfare: A History*, 203–4, also quoting Prince Louis Napoleon in Boutell, *Arms and Armour*, 135. Verbruggen, *Art of Warfare*, 119, puts the rate of fire of the longbow at 10 to 12 shots per minute and the crossbow at 2. Both Delbruck, *Medieval Warfare*, 386, and Verbruggen, *Art of Warfare*, 119, agree that the crossbow had greater penetrating power, though Verbruggen suggests it depends on what model crossbow is being compared; Oman, *History of the Art of War*, 2:142; Estimates of Genovese strength vary from 2,000 to 6,000. If the strength of the Genovese was closer to 2,000, then the archer's fire dominance would have been completely devastating. These calculations are based on the archers thought to be present with the battle of the Black Prince. It is possible that archers from the reserve battle may have moved forward to participate in the opening exchange of fire, and that some or all of the archers of the Earl of Northampton's battle may

have also been in range depending on the frontal deployment of the Genovese. In either case the situation of the Genovese becomes exponentially more difficult.

55. Oman, *History of the Art of War*, 2:142; Some chroniclers mention English cannon at Crécy, and most accounts give them credit for physiological effects during this phase of the battle. Oman does not think they were present, *History of the Art of War*, 2:142. It is doubtful, if they were present, that they had any material effect on the battle.

56. Perroy, *Hundred Years War*, 119. Founder is a condition known as laminitis in which the laminate inside the hoof becomes inflamed and softens. This permits the cannon bone in the hoof to rotate down changing drastically the angle of the bone alignment within the hoof. The horse will become very lame and any weight on the hoof is painful. Foundered horses require extensive rehabilitation and often cannot be saved. It can be caused by a wide variety of conditions including overeating or any significant change in diet, heat stress, and overwork. If founder was having an effect on the French cavalry it would probably have been caused by hard riding and summer heat.

57. Froissart, *Chronicles*, 89; Verbruggen states the speed of cavalry movement as 250 yards per minute at the trot and twice that at the gallop, 187.

58. Froissart, *Chronicles*, 92. .

59. Some historians believe that the archers may have deployed in line along the front of the English position and then retreated behind the men-at-arms on the approach of the cavalry. This would have protected the archers from the potential of a cavalry attack but would have significantly reduced their influence on the close fight between men-at-arms since their fire would have been masked by the English men-at-arms; The chronicle of Lanercost quoted in Oman, *History of the Art of War*, 2:95; Armstrong, *Bannockburn*, 68-69; Oman, *History of the Art of War*, 2:144; This analysis is largely supported by Bennett, "Development of Battle Tactics."

60. Norman Housley, "European Warfare, c. 1200-1320," in *Medieval Warfare: A History*, 114.

61. Hyland, *Medieval Warhorse*, 8.

Chapter 5: Steppe Warriors

1. Karasulas, *Mounted Archers*, 5–6.

2. The primary source for the discussion of the composite bow and horse archery is Karasulas, *Mounted Archers*, 18–28.

3. Turnbull, *Mongol Warrior*, 47.

4. The maximum range at which the weapon could have militarily significant effects was 175 yards. Gabriel, *Genghis Khan's Greatest General*, 34, puts the maximum range at 300 yards but whether he considers that effective is not clear, 35; Hyland, *Medieval Warhorse*, 134.

5. Finger pinch is the distortion of the bow string caused by the grip of the fingers on the string. A thumb draw, because it only has one grip on the string, distorts the string less than a Mediterranean draw where three fingers grip the string.

6. Karasulas, *Mounted Archers*, 26; Maenchen-Helfen, *World of the Huns*, 226.

7. Hildinger, *Warriors of the Steppe*, 100, 106; Morgan, *Mongols*, 91.

8. Turnbull, *Mongol Warrior*, 9; Gabriel, *Genghis Khan's Greatest General*, 30.

9. Turnbull, *Mongol Warrior*, 11, 15. In the later period of the Mongol Empire individual soldiers did receive pay; Gabriel, *Genghis Khan's Greatest General*, 25, 31; Chambers, *Devil's Horsemen*, 56.

10. Gabriel, *Genghis Khan's Greatest General*, 36; Chambers, *Devil's Horsemen*, 58; Chambers, *Devil's Horsemen*, 59.
11. Maenchen-Helfen, *World of the Huns*, 203–4.
12. Bell, Davis, and McBane, *Horse and Pony Breeds*, 176; "Tarpan," *Breeds of Livestock*.
13. Maenchen-Helfen, *World of the Huns*, 204.
14. Hyland, *Medieval Warhorse*, 125; "Przewalski," *Breeds of Livestock*; Bell et al., *Horse and Pony Breeds*, 214. There is a great deal of controversy regarding the scientific classification of the Tarpan and Przewalski horse. Some scientists believe that they are a distinct species from domestic horse because of blood mark and chromosome differences. Other scientists believe that they should be considered a subspecies within the domestic horse species. There is no scientific consensus on the issue.
15. Hyland, *Medieval Warhorse*, 126–27; Chambers, *Devil's Horsemen*, 57.
16. Hyland, *Medieval Warhorse*, 126; Hildinger, *Warriors of the Steppe*, 20.
17. Maenchen-Helfen, *World of the Huns*, 206; Gabriel, *Genghis Khan's Greatest General*, 36; Hildinger, *Warriors of the Steppe*, 16.
18. Maenchen-Helfen, *World of the Huns*, 211–13.
19. Ibid., 214; Hyland, *Medieval Warhorse*, 128–30.
20. Quoted in Maenchen-Helfen, *World of the Huns*, 206; Gabriel, *Genghis Khan's Greatest General*, 30.
21. Maenchen-Helfen, *World of the Huns*, 209, 207; Turnbull, *Mongol Warrior*, 17; Hyland, *Medieval Warhorse*, 131.
22. Hildinger, *Warriors of the Steppe*, 19–20.
23. Quoted in Hyland, *Medieval Warhorse*, 133.
24. Quoted in Thompson, *Huns*, 57; Gabriel, *Genghis Khan's Greatest General*, 30.
25. This summary of Scythian history is from Cernenko, *Scythians*; Hildinger, *Warriors of the Steppe*, 38.
26. A detailed account of Sarmatian history and military organization is in Brzezinski and Mielczarek, *Sarmatians*.
27. Maenchen-Helfen, *World of the Huns*, 209; Thompson, *Huns*, 57; Quoted in Thompson, *Huns*, 287.
28. Quoted in Maenchen-Helfen, *World of the Huns*, 201–2.
29. Thompson, *Huns*, 30–33.
30. Ibid., 36–40.
31. Ibid., 53–54.
32. Karasulas, *Mounted Archers*, 26,
33. Both quotes in Thompson, *Huns*, 56–57.
34. Maenchen-Helfen, *World of the Huns*, 213
35. Thompson, *Huns*, 148–156.
36. Ibid., 156–63.
37. Ibid., 163–75.
38. Morgan, *Mongols*, 55–57.
39. Ibid., 60–61.
40. The summary of Muslim conquests is based on the description outlined in Turnbull, *Genghis Khan*.
41. Ibid., 12.

42. Ibid., 10; Turnbull, *Mongol Warrior*, 11–12; Gabriel, *Genghis Khan's Greatest General*, 26; Turnbull, *Mongol Warrior*, 11. The exact number of horses maintained by the individual warrior varies greatly depending on author and sources. All agree that a significant number of remounts were part of the standard equipment. The minimum number cited was three horses per archer and the maximum number is 18 reported by Marco Polo. Hyland, *Medieval Warhorse*, 125; Gabriel, *Genghis Khan's Greatest General*, 36; Chambers, *Devil's Horsemen*, 58; Morgan, *Mongols*, 87. Consider that the Mongol's adversaries consistently put the numbers of individual Mongol field forces as from 200,000 to 800,000. Armies of such size would have required multiple millions of war horses not to mention the logistics requirements.
43. Ibid., 89; Turnbull, *Mongol Warrior*, 12.
44. Morgan, *Mongols*, 89.
45. Chambers, *Devil's Horsemen*, 63.
46. Ibid., 26, 42, 29.
47. Turnbull, *Mongol Warrior*, 13, 48; Gabriel, *Genghis Khan's Greatest General*, 28, 32.
48. Gabriel, *Genghis Khan's Greatest General*, 43.
49. Ibid., 43.
50. Turnbull, *Mongol Warrior*, 17; Chambers, *Devil's Horsemen*, 61–62.
51. Chambers, *Devil's Horsemen*, 65; Gabriel, *Genghis Khan's Greatest General*, 43, 30; Hildinger, *Warriors of the Steppe*, 17.
52. Turnbull, *Mongol Warrior*, 45-46.
53. Gabriel, *Genghis Khan's Greatest General*, 44–45; Chambers, *Devil's Horsemen*, 62–63.
54. Hildinger, *Warriors of the Steppe*, 71.
55. This description of the reconnaissance phase of the operation is taken from Gabriel, *Genghis Khan's Greatest General*, 89–103, except as noted.
56. Chambers, *Devil's Horsemen*, 32.
57. The descriptions of the remaining aspects of operations in Europe are derived from Chambers, *Devil's Horsemen*, 70–113, except as noted.
58. Gabriel, *Genghis Khan's Greatest General*, 106
59. Chambers, *Devil's Horsemen*, 112.
60. Hildinger, *Warriors of the Steppe*, 87.

Chapter 6: Early Modern Cavalry

1. Howard, *War in European History*, 20.
2. Ibid., 26–27.
3. Arnold, *Renaissance at War*, 34–37.
4. G. Parker, *Military Revolution*, 17, 18. Arnold, *Renaissance at War*, 94–96.
5. J. Black, *European Warfare*, 38–39.
6. Arnold, *Renaissance at War*, 109
7. Ibid., 106, 117.
8. Ibid., 111–12; Delbruck, *Dawn of Modern Warfare*, 117.
9. Chandler, *Art of Warfare*, 38; Brzezinski, *Army of Gustavus Adolphus*, 24.
10. Arnold, *Renaissance at War*, 112, refers to the pistol armed *reiter* cavalry as heavy cavalry because of their armor. Delbruck, *Dawn of Modern Warfare*, 125, calls them cuirassiers and

considers them light cavalry because their horses are not armored. The difference in view is relative to being compared to Medieval cavalry or to contemporary sixteenth-century cavalry; Delbruck, *Dawn of Modern Warfare*, 121–23, 135; Arnold, *Renaissance at War*, 112–15; Blackmore, *British Military Firearms*, 24.

11. Ibid., 124.
12. Arnold, *Renaissance at War*, 112–16; Delbruck, *Dawn of Modern Warfare*, 124.
13. Ibid., 128, 129.
14. Ibid., 124.
15. Tincey, *Ironsides*, 17.
16. Chenevix Trench, *History of Horsemanship*, 143; Brzezinski, *Army of Gustavus Adolphus*, 23; Childs, *Warfare in the Seventeenth Century*, 49.
17. Brzezinski, *Army of Gustavus Adolphus*, 6; Chemnitz quoted in Brzezinski, *Army of Gustavus Adolphus*, 33.
18. Lynn, *Giant*, 489, 497–99.
19. Cruso, *Militarie Instructions*, 28–29.
20. Brzezinski, *Army of Gustavus Adolphus*, 3–4.
21. Cruso, *Militarie Instructions*, 30; Tincey, *Soldiers*, 24; Blackmore, *British Military Firearms*.
22. Tincey, *Soldiers*, 14; Blackmore, *British Military Firearms*, 36.
23. Lynn, *Giant*, 490.
24. Cruso, *Militarie Instructions*, 28–31; Lynn, *Giant*, 490.
25. Tincey, *Soldiers*, 15, 19.
26. Childs, *Warfare in the Seventeenth Century*, 47.
27. Brzezinski, *Army of Gustavus Adolphus*, 4–5.
28. Lynn, *Giant*, 490-500.
29. Ibid., 492–94.
30. Chandler, *Art of Warfare*, 28-29, 31.
31. Ibid., 33–34.
32. Ibid., 43–47.
33. Duffy, *Instrument of War*, 256.
34. Ibid., 36–37; Cooper, *British Regular Cavalry*, 48; Konstam, *Peter the Great's Army*, 10.
35. Chandler, *Art of Warfare*, 52–53; Childs, *Armies and Warfare*, 129; J. Black, *European Warfare*, 50–51.
36. Childs, *Armies and Warfare*, 129; Cooper, *British Regular Cavalry*, 62–64; Chandler, *Art of Warfare*, 53–54;
37. Childs, *Armies and Warfare*, 128.
38. Ibid., 128–29.
39. Warnery, *Remarks on Cavalry*, 45.
40. Ibid., 46–47.
41. The breed was carefully nurtured at the small Monastery of Cartuja. In the nineteenth century the monks protected the breed from confiscation by the invading French army, later the monks, relatively isolated in their monasteries, protected the breed from epidemics that killed off large portions of Spain's horse population. It would not be until the 1960s that the Spanish government permitted the export of Andalusians.
42. Chenevix Trench, *History of Horsemanship*, 145.

43. Brzezinski, *Army of Gustavus Adolphus*, 4; Brzezinski, *Lutzen*, 62–67; Bell et al., *Horse and Pony Breeds*, 124–125.
44. "Holsteiner," *Breeds of Livestock*
45. Ibid.; Duffy, *Army of Frederick the Great*, 95.
46. Duffy, *Instrument of War*, 259.
47. Brzezinski, *Army of Gustavus Adolphus*, 4, 5, 20; Bell et al., *Horse and Pony Breeds*, 144–45.
48. Cooper, *British Regular Cavalry*, 60.
49. Chenevix Trench, *History of Horsemanship*, 101.
50. Translated by Thomas Blundeville as *The Arte of Ryding* and published in 1560 as the first riding manual written in English.
51. V. Littauer, *Development of Modern Riding*, 84; Chenevix Trench, *History of Horsemanship*, 103.
52. Loch, *Dressage*, 90–91.
53. Duffy, *Army of Frederick the Great*, 104.
54. Childs, *Armies and Warfare*, 105–106.
55. Cruso, *Militarie Instructions*, 31.
56. Chenevix Trench, *History of Horsemanship*, 105–106.
57. Loch, *Dressage*, 71.
58. This discussion is based on a comparison of a variety of national saddle patterns from the seventeenth and eighteenth centuries illustrated in contemporary drawings and sketches in a variety of sources including Cavendish, *General System of Horsemanship*, illustration 13; Chappell, *British Cavalry Equipments*, 5, 13, 19, 23, 36, 39; Chenevix Trench, *History of Horsemanship*, 156; Duffy, *Instrument of War*, 254; Konstam, *Peter the Great's Army*, 13; Loch, *Dressage*, 52; D. Smith, *Prussian Army*, saddle furniture illustration, n.p.; Tincey, *Ironsides*, 15; Warner, *British Cavalry*, 54.
59. The battle description of Lützen is based largely on Brzezinski, *Lützen*.
60. Quoted in Brzezinski, *Lützen*, 54, from William Watts, the *Swedish Intelligencer*, pt. 3 (London, 1633).
61. Quoted in Brzezinski, *Lützen*, 59.
62. The description of the battle of Rossbach is based largely on the account in Duffy, *Prussia's Glory*, 7–91. This was supplemented by Hook, *Rossbach and Leuthen*, 7–40, and Citino, *German Way of War*, 72–82.
63. Duffy, *Prussia's Glory*, 22.
64. Ibid., 73.
65. Ibid., 76.
66. Ibid., 76–77.
67. Ibid., 84.

Chapter 7: All The Emperor's Horses

1. Haythornthwaite, *Austrian Army*, 3; D. Johnson, *French Cavalry*, 129–30.
2. English horses, affected by the heat and humidity and by the diet of the Spanish theater, began to get sick and die as soon as they were unloaded. Oman, *Wellington's Army*, 194; Muir, *Tactics*,105.
3. Elting, *Swords around a Throne*, 246; D. Johnson, *French Cavalry*, 16, 18, 26; the quotation is on 32.

4. Johnson, *French Cavalry*, 75; Elting, *Swords around a Throne*, 233.
5. Ibid., 234.
6. Ibid., 236–38; Muir, *Tactics*, 107.
7. Elting, 238–39; Muir, *Tactics*, 108.
8. D. Johnson, *French Cavalry*, 47.
9. Haythornthwaite, *Austrian Army*, 3; Fosten, *Wellington's Heavy Cavalry*, 6, 8.
10. D. Johnson, *French Cavalry*, 21, 23, 137.
11. Rothenberg, *Art of Warfare*, 73.
12. Muir, *Tactics*, 109.
13. De Brack, *Cavalry Outpost Duties* (1893), quoted in Nosworthy, *With Musket, Cannon, and Sword*, 287.
14. Bragge quoted in Nosworthy, *With Musket, Cannon, and Sword*, 288.
15. Rothenberg, *Art of Warfare*, 73; Quoted in Muir, *Tactics*, 110.
16. Nosworthy, *With Musket, Cannon, and Sword*, 296–97; Elting, *Swords around a Throne*, 243.
17. Nolan, *Cavalry*, 68–70.
18. Napoleon I, *Military Maxims*, 72.
19. Oman, *Wellington's Army*, 98.
20. Napoleon I, *Military Maxims*, 73.
21. Ibid., 193.
22. Muir, *Tactics*, 137.
23. Nosworthy, *With Musket, Cannon, and Sword*, 270; Nolan, *Cavalry*, 93–94, quoting an unnamed officer in Austrian service; Muir, *Tactics*, 134; Nosworthy, *With Musket, Cannon, and Sword*, 279.
24. Rothenberg, *Art of Warfare*, 142.
25. Muir, *Tactics*, 122–23; Haythornthwaite, *Austrian Army*, 7; D. Johnson, *French Cavalry*, 118.
26. Muir, *Tactics*, 111.
27. Quoted in Muir, *Tactics*, 117; Oman, *Wellington's Army*, 111.
28. Quoted in Muir, *Tactics*, 120. Oman, *Wellington's Army*, 104; From Wellington's dispatches cited in Oman, *Wellington's Army*, 106.
29. Haythornthwaite, *Austrian Army*, 8.
30. D. Johnson, *French Cavalry*, 155, 152.
31. Nosworthy, *With Musket, Cannon, and Sword*, 322, 313. The training concept would be to gradually expose the horses to the same conditions that the square presented, only the bayonets would not be dangerous. The horses would then have no fear of the square. Such training would take time and was not conducted during the Napoleonic period.
32. Tomkinson, *Diary of a Cavalry Officer*, 280.
33. Napoleon quoted in Bukhari, *Napoleon's Cavalry*, 75.
34. D. Johnson, *French Cavalry*, 77, 82.
35. Muir, *Tactics*, 106.
36. D. Johnson, *French Cavalry*, 115.
37. Bukhari, *Napoleon's Cavalry*, 76; Johnson, *French Cavalry*, 116–17; Quoted in Johnson, *French Cavalry*, 119.
38. Ibid., 120, 123, 125.

39. Ibid., 137,
40. G. Tylden, *Horses and Saddlery*, 8.
41. "Thoroughbred," *Horse Breeds of the World.*
42. Fletcher, *Galloping at Everything*, 31–32.
43. Chenevix Trench, *A History of Horsemanship*, 156–57.
44. Tylden, *Horses and Saddlery*, 116–17.
45. Ibid., 127–28.
46. Ibid., 131.
47. Ibid., 131–32.
48. Harris, *United States Pony Club Manual*, 435–36.
49. Robichon de la Guérinière, *Ecole de Cavalerie*, 13.
50. Interview with Sallie Spenard, U.S. Dressage Federation gold medal winner and Grand Prix level dressage competitor, 11 June 2006.
51. Fosten, *Wellington's Heavy Cavalry*, 12.
52. D. Johnson, *French Cavalry*, 129; Fletcher, *Galloping at Everything*, 18.
53. Muir, *Tactics*, 111; Chenevix Trench, *A History of Horsemanship*, 162.
54. Ibid., 128–29, 138.
55. Pembroke quoted in Chenevix Trench, *A History of Horsemanship*, 154, 158-59; Fosten, *Wellington's Heavy Cavalry*, 23;
56. Muir, *Tactics*, 114; Chenevix-Trench, *A History of Horsemanship*, 162.
57. Ibid., 159–60.
58. Quoted in Chenevix-Trench, *A History of Horsemanship*, 162.
59. Fosten, *Wellington's Heavy Cavalry*, 21; Fletcher, *Galloping at Everything*, 16.
60. Oman, *Wellington's Army*, 112.
61. Johnson, *French Cavalry*, 77–78; Elting, *Swords around a Throne*, 228–29; Rothenberg, *Art of Warfare*, 142–43.
62 Wellington quoted in Fletcher, *Galloping at Everything*, 13; Fosten, *Wellington's Heavy Cavalry*, 10; Fletcher, *Galloping at Everything*, 18.
63. Elting, *Swords around a Throne*, 228; Tomkinson, *Diary of a Cavalry Officer*, 272.
64. Johnson, *French Cavalry*, 160.
65. This description of the cavalry actions at Waterloo is based on the accounts contained in Fletcher, *Galloping at Everything*, 237–78; D. Smith, *Charge!* 222–41, 298–99; and Johnson, *Napoleon's Cavalry*, 131–44.
66. Fletcher, *Galloping at Everything*, 224.
67. Quoted in Fletcher, *Galloping at Everything*, 246.
68. Quoted in Fletcher, *Galloping at Everything*, 247.
69. Quoted in Johnson, *Napoleon's Cavalry*, 39; Farmer and Gleig, *Adventurers of a Light Dragoon*, 141–42.
70. Elting, *Swords around a Throne*

Chapter 8: Industrial War and Cavalry

1. Nosworthy, *Bloody Crucible of Courage*, 28–30.
2. Katcher, *Union Cavalryman*, 4; Longacre, *Lincoln's Cavalrymen*, 15–16.
3. Nosworthy, *Bloody Crucible of Courage*, 479.

4. Longacre, *Lee's Cavalrymen*, 49.
5. Starr, *From Fort Sumter to Gettysburg*, 125; Katcher, *Union Cavalryman*, 4.
6. Nosworthy, *Bloody Crucible of Courage*, 287; Longacre, *Lee's Cavalrymen*, 39.
7. Longacre, *Lincoln's Cavalrymen*, 42.
8. Nosworthy, *Bloody Crucible of Courage*, 476; Steffen, *The Horse Soldier*, 2:75.
9. Longacre, *Lincoln's Cavalrymen*, 43-44; Longacre, *Lee's Cavalrymen*, 41.
10. Ibid., 36; Steffen, *The Horse Soldier*, 2:75.
11. Katcher, *Union Cavalryman*, 22, 48. Katcher discusses tests conducted by *Guns and Ammo* magazine where Sharps carbines under controlled conditions were able to put shot groups into a 5-inch circle at 100 yards, and the Spencer could only place shot groups in a 7-inch circle consistently at 50 yards.
12. Quoted in Nosworthy, *Bloody Crucible of Courage*, 477-478.
13. Starr, *From Fort Sumter to Gettysburg*, 24; Longacre, *Lincoln's Cavalrymen*, 41; Bilby, *Revolution in Arms*, 73; Steffen, *The Horse Soldier*, 2:75–77, 84–85; McAulay, *Carbines of the Civil War*, 5–12.
14. Longacre, *Lee's Cavalrymen*, 38; Quoted in Nosworthy, *Bloody Crucible of Courage, 287.*
15. Longacre, *Lincoln's Cavalrymen*, 44–45; Longacre, *Lee's Cavalrymen*, 40.
16. Longacre, *Lincoln's Cavalrymen*, 8; Longacre, *Lee's Cavalrymen*, 47; quoted in Nosworthy, *Bloody Crucible of Courage*, 299.
17. The essentials of this argument are made in Nosworthy, *Bloody Crucible of Courage*, 305–7.
18. Longacre, *Lincoln's Cavalrymen*, 7-8.
19. Ibid., 11.
20. Longacre, *Lee's Cavalrymen*, 45; Nosworthy, *Bloody Crucible of Courage*, 286.
21. Ibid., 292–93.
22. Longacre, *Lincoln's Cavalrymen*, 46; Starr, *From Fort Sumter to Gettysburg*, 130; McAulay, *Carbines of the Civil War*, 8.
23. Longacre, *Lincoln's Cavalrymen*, 46
24. Starr, *From Fort Sumter to Gettysburg*, 141.
25. Ibid., 124; Steffen, *The Horse Soldier*, 2:60–61, 166–74; Carter, *U.S. Cavalry Horse*, 160–62; An overview of American military saddles from the Grimsley through the 1859 McClellan is in Steffen, *United States Military Saddles*, 33–73.
26. Ottevaere, *American Military Horsemanship*, 15.
27. Longacre, *Lee's Cavalrymen*, 30.
28. Katcher, *Union Cavalryman*, 11–12.
29. Quoted from the history of the Seventh Indiana in Starr, *From Fort Sumter to Gettysburg*, 138–39.
30. Starr, *From Fort Sumter to Gettysburg*, 142.
31. Longacre, *Lincoln's Cavalrymen*, 50.
32. This description of the Gettysburg campaign is a summary of actions described in Starr, *From Fort Sumter to Gettysburg*, 396–441; Coddington, *The Gettysburg Campaign*; Wittenberg, *Protecting the Flank*, 43–121; Longacre, *Cavalry at Gettysburg*.
33. Hooker's order to Pleasanton quoted in Starr, *From Fort Sumter to Gettysburg*, 397.
34. Longacre, *Cavalry at Gettysburg*, 182.
35. Quoted in Starr, *From Fort Sumter to Gettysburg*, 419.
36. Ibid., 430.

37. Quoted in Starr, *From Fort Sumter to Gettysburg*, 435.

38. Howard, *Franco-Prussian War*, 115–18.

39. Grbasic and Vuksic, *History of Cavalry*, 243–45; Brown, *Unit Organizations*, 46, 67–71.

40. Ibid., 8–11, 20, 55, 58.

41. Carter, *U.S. Cavalry Horse*, 159.

42. Anglesey, *History of the British Cavalry*, vol. 2, *1851–1871*, 416.

43. Ibid., 419; Anglesey, *History of the British Cavalry*, vol. 3, *1872–1898*, 401–3.

44. Ibid., 403; Carter, *U.S. Cavalry Horse*, 175, 189.

45. Bonie, "French Cavalry in 1870," 28.

46. Howard, *Franco-Prussian War*, 157.

47. Kachler, "German Cavalry," 170.

48. Bonie, "French Cavalry in 1870," 50–51; Kachler, "German Cavalry," 176. Kachler provides exact loss numbers. The total number of troops committed in the two regiments is based on the strength of a full regiment, 600 men in four 150-man squadrons, minus one squadron in each regiment, for a total of 450 men in each regiment. The assumption is that the units were near full strength.

49. Bonie, "French Cavalry in 1870," 55–60; Howard, *Franco-Prussian War*, 159–60.

50. Bonie, "French Cavalry in 1870," 24–25.

51. Ibid., 27–28.

52. Howard, *Franco-Prussian War*, 112, 155–156.

53. Bonie, "French Cavalry in 1870," 90–91.

54. Ibid., 86–91. Gallifet is quoted in Howard, *Franco-Prussian War*, 215–16.

55. Anglesey, *History of the British Cavalry*, vol. 2, *1851–1871*, 419–20.

56. Boniface, *Cavalry Horse and His Pack*, 39; Duffy, *Army of Frederick the Great*, 95; "Trakehner," *Horse Breeds of the World*; von Velsen-Zerweck and Schulte, *Trakehner*, 12.

57. Goodman, "The Trakehner Horse."

58. Boniface, *Cavalry Horse and His Pack*, 40–43.

59. Ibid., 44–45.

60. Carter, *U.S. Cavalry Horse*, 175–78.

61. Tylden, *Horses and Saddlery*, 46. Most of Tylden's records are based on Carter, *U.S. Cavalry Horse*, 159–205.

62. Chenevix Trench, *A History of Horsemanship*, 165.

63. D. Williams, *Great Riding Schools*, 54–76.

Chapter 9: Mounted Guerrilla Warfare

1. Utley, *Frontier Regulars*, 2.

2. Ibid., 4–5; Taylor, *The Warriors*, 20-23.

3. Ibid., 23. Utley, *Frontier Regulars*, 5–6.

4. Calloway, *One Vast Winter*, 280; Taylor, *The Warriors*, 54.

5. Harry B. Carrington, "The Indian Question," in *Eyewitnesses to the Indian Wars*, 107; Taylor, *The Warriors*, 50–53.

6. Fox, *Custer's Last Battle*, 77–79.

7. Calloway, *One Vast Winter*, 267–68; Howard, *Horse in American*, 46–49; Calloway, 268.

8. Howard, *Horse in American*, 84-85.

9. Ibid., 86–87.
10. Quoted in Howard, *Horse in American*, 88.
11. Calloway, *One Vast Winter*, 284.
12. The chase of the Nez Perce is largely summarized from the account in Utley, *Frontier Regulars*, 305–28.
13. General description of the Appaloosa and breed history is from "The Appaloosa," *Horse Breeds*.
14. Taylor, *The Warriors*, 33; Vernam, *Man on Horseback*, 232.
15. Calloway, *One Vast Winter*, 269; Hunter Liggett, "Scouting under Miles," in *Eyewitnesses to the Indian Wars*, 390; Vernam, *Man on Horseback*, 219–30.
16. Ibid., 227–28; Taylor, *The Warriors*, 33.
17. Vernam, *Man on Horseback*, 229–30.
18. Excellent examples of nineteenth century bits and bridles in Horse Capture, *A Song For the Horse Nation*, 34–36.
19. Rickey, *Forty Miles a Day*, 75, 48-49;Utley, *Frontier Regulars*, 327.
20. Utley, *Frontier Regulars*, 71–73.
21. Rickey, *Forty Miles a Day*, 223.
22. Dunlay, *Wolves for the Blue Soldiers*, 47, 169.
23. Wesley Merritt, "Marching Cavalry," in *Eyewitnesses to the Indian Wars*, 84–89.
24. Frederick C. Kurz, "Reminiscences of an Old 8th U.S. Cavalryman," in *Eyewitnesses to the Indian Wars*, 304; Forbes, "The United States Army," in *Eyewitnesses to the Indian Wars*, 13.
25. Numerous horses survived the battle and were taken away by the victorious Indians. The army shot others too wounded to recover when it arrived on the battlefield two days later. Comanche was the only surviving horse of Custer's battalion to continue service in the army.
26. Lawrence, *His Very Silence Speaks*, 45, 49.
27. Quoted in Ibid., 38.
28. Ibid., 65–71.
29. Ibid., 94–109.
30. Rickey, *Forty Miles a Day*, 33–34, 43.
31. Barthorp, *The Anglo-Boer Wars*, 51.
32. Knight, *Boer Commando*, 9; Reitz, *Commando*, 20–23
33. Kitchener quoted in Anglesey, *History of the British Cavalry*, 4: 215.
34. Reitz, *Commando*, 137–40.
35. Ibid., 231–32. Reitz and his companions did not become aware until many weeks later that it was British policy to execute any Boer captured wearing British uniforms. Although this was done by the Boers as a matter of supply, on several occasions British camps were surprised by Boer's because they mistook them for friendly troops.
36. Ibid., 223–25.
37. Jan Smuts would later serve as a British army Field Marshal in both World Wars and Prime Minister of South Africa.
38. Reitz, *Commando*, 219.
39. Anglesey, *History of the British Cavalry*, 4: 243
40. Ibid., 41.

41. John Brown, "The Boer's Worst Enemy," *Digger History*; "Boer War," *Digger History*.
42. Chappell, *British Cavalry Equipments*, 33–34, diagram E.
43. Pakenham, *The Boer War*, 559–61.
44. Anglesey, *History of the British Cavalry*, 4: 216, 246.
45. Anglesey, *History of the British Cavalry*, 4: 307.
46. Ibid., 344–48.
47. Ibid., 342.
48. Ibid., 287, 298.
49. Ibid., 301–3.
50. Ibid., 308–11.
51. Ibid., 331, 332, 334.
52. Ibid., 350.
53. Ibid., 357.
54. Ibid., 356.
55. Ibid., 357, 363.
56. Ibid., 276, 370.

Chapter 10: The Last Charge

1. The U.S. Cavalry School estimated that the total was over 700,000 cavalrymen serving in over 100 cavalry divisions, Cavalry Association, *Cavalry Combat*, 8–9; V. Littauer, *Russian Hussar*, 296; Wrangel puts the peacetime strength of the Russian cavalry at 112 regiments at 1,200 men per regiment for at total strength of 134,400, Wrangel, *The End of Chivalry*, 2.
2. V. Littauer, *Russian Hussar*, 33, 36, 295; Knox, *With the Russian Army*, xxvi.
3. Clayton, *Paths of Glory*, 32–33.
4. War Office, *Handbook of the French Army*, 233–34, 243; Summer, *The French Army*, 4; Grbasic and Vuksic, *Cavalry*, 265–67.
5. Prioux, *Cavalry*, 509; *German Army Handbook*, 62.
6. Nigel, *The German Army of World War I*, 22; *German Army Handbook*, 63, 64.
7. Wrangel, *The End of Chivalry*, 2.
8. Ure, *The Cossacks*, 12–20.
9. Wrangel, *The End of Chivalry*, 3.
10. Seaton, *The Horsemen of the Steppes*, 193, 208–9.
11. V. Littauer, *Russian Hussar*, 296; Seaton, *The Horsemen of the Steppes*, 207.
12. Knox, *With the Russian Army*, 103; Seaton, *The Horsemen of the Steppes*, 196.
13. V. Littauer, *Russian Hussar*, 110; Knox, *With the Russian Army*, 109; *German Army Handbook*, 64; War Office, *Handbook of the French Army*, 236.
14. Ibid., 236.
15. V. Littauer, *Russian Hussar*, 115; Wrangel, *The End of Chivalry*, 55–56.
16. War Office, *Handbook of the French Army*, 237.
17. Bernhardi, *Cavalry in Future Wars*, 7–18,
18. Childers, *German Influence on British Cavalry*, 15–36, 211-12.
19. Quoted in *Cavalry Combat*, 6; Prioux, *Cavalry*, 9, 517.
20. Anglesey, *History of the British Cavalry*, vol. 7, *The Curragh Incident*, 121–22.
21. Ibid., 199.

22. Ibid., 204.
23. V. Littauer, *Russian Hussar*, 63–65; Wrangel, *The End of Chivalry*, 11.
24. Seaton, *The Horsemen of the Steppes*, 202.
25. Wrangel, *The End of Chivalry*, 4.
26. Seaton, *The Horsemen of the Steppes*, 203; "Kabarda," *Breeds of Livestock*; "Karabakh," *Breeds of Livestock*; Wrangel, *The End of Chivalry*, 4–7.
27. Stanley Washburn, *The Russian Campaign*, 265–68.
28. Gullett, *The Australian Imperial Force*, 39.
29. Quoted in "The Australian Stock Horse or Waler" *Horse Breeds of the World*; Anglesey, *History of the British Cavalry*, vol. 5, *Egypt, Palestine, and Syria*, 4–11.
30. Starr and Sweeny, *Forward*, 153–55.
31. Wrangel, *The End of Chivalry*, 49; Mercy, *Prairie Traveler*, 37.
32. V. Littauer, *Russian Hussar*, 204; Wrangel, *The End of Chivalry*, 49.
33. War Office, *Manual of Horse Mastership*, 92–93; Carter, *U.S. Cavalry Horse*, 154.
34. This discussion of the impact of Caprilli is based on Chenevix Trench, *History of Horsemanship*, 248–71; Ottevaere, *American Military Horsemanship*, 59–66.
35. Seaton, *The Horsemen of the Steppes*, 203–4.
36. Gullett, *The Australian Imperial Force*, 31.
37. Prioux, *Cavalry*, 92; Anglesey, *History of the British Cavalry*, vol. 7, *The Curragh Incident*, 81–82.
38. This battle narrative is largely based on Gullett, *The Australian Imperial Force*, 677–792; Anglesey, *History of the British Cavalry*, vol. 5, *Egypt, Palestine, and Syria*, 253–340; and Perrett, *Migiddo 1918*.
39. Quoted in Anglesey, *History of the British Cavalry*, vol. 5, *Egypt, Palestine, and Syria*, 340.
40. Richter, *Kavallerie*, 11, 16.
41. Ibid., 15.
42. Ibid., 18–20.
43. U.S. Military Intelligence Service, "German Horse Cavalry and Transport," *Intelligence Bulletin*, March 1946.
44. Boeselager would eventually be awarded the Knights cross with swords and oak leaves, one of only 159 German soldiers to receive the highest order of the Knight's Cross. Boeselager was closely involved in the plot to assassinate Hitler but was not found out after the plot failed. He was killed in action on the eastern front leading his brigade in August 1944; Richter, *Kavallerie*, 29; Piekalkiewicz, *Cavalry of World War II*, 223, 229, 241.
45. Piekalkiewicz, *Cavalry of World War II*, 241–43; Fowler, *Axis Cavalry*, 20–22.
46. Piekalkiewicz, *Cavalry of World War II*, 223–24, 230, 242–43; Fowler, *Axis Cavalry*, 38–40; Huxley-Blythe, *Under the St. Andrew's Cross*, 135–66.
47. Glantz, *Colossus Reborn: The Red Army at War*, 238.
48. Ibid., 240.
49. Ibid., 241.
50. U.S. Military Intelligence Service, "German Horse Cavalry and Transport," *Intelligence Bulletin*, March 1946.
51. Piekalkiewicz, *Cavalry of World War II*, 235.
52. Kournakoff, *Russia's Fighting Forces*, 149.
53. Piekalkiewicz, *Cavalry of World War II*, 222.

54. Piekalkiewicz, *Cavalry of World War II*, 209

55. Ibid, 214.

56. A. Niessel, "Cavalry," in *The Red Army*, 341.

57. U.S. Military Intelligence Service, "German Horse Cavalry and Transport," *Intelligence Bulletin*, March 1946.

58. Burkhart Mueller-Hillebrand, "Horses in the German Army 1941–1945," in Johnson, *Horses of the German Army*, 13.

59. Hyland, *Medieval Horse*, 126.

60. Yakushin, *On the Roads of War*, 87.

61. Schulte and von Velsen-Zerweck, *The Trakehner*, 230.

62. Various interviews by the author with veterans of the U.S. 2nd Cavalry Association including Lieutenant Thomas Stuart, who negotiated the rescue effort with the Germans, and Hauptmann Lessing in September 1996, as well as Charles H. Reed, "The Rescue of the Lipizzans Horses, a Personal Account."

Epilogue

1. Public Broadcasting Service, "Interview."

2. Quoted in Briscoe et al., *Weapon of Choice*, 125.

3. Public Broadcasting Service, "Interview."

4. "Einsatz und Ausbildungszentrum für das Gebirgstragtierwesen 230," 2007.

5. Interview with Major Matthias F. Sartorius, Swiss Army, June 2006.

Bibliography

Adcock, F. *The Greek and Macedonian Art of War.* Berkeley: University of California, 1957.

Akhal-Teke Association of America. "Breed Standard." www.akhal-teke.org/standard.htm.

Anderson, J. K. *Ancient Greek Horsemanship.* Berkeley: University of California Press, 1961.

Anglesey, George Charles (7th Marquess of Anglesey). *A History of the British Cavalry, 1816 to 1919.* Vol. 2, *1851–1871.* London: Leo Cooper, 1975.

______. *A History of the British Cavalry, 1816 to 1919.* Vol. 3, *1872–1898.* London: Leo Cooper, 1983.

______. *A History of the British Cavalry, 1816 to 1919.* Vol. 4, *1899-1913.* London: Leo Cooper, 1986.

______. *A History of the British Cavalry, 1816 to 1919.* Vol. 5, *Egypt, Palestine, and Syria 1914–1918.* London: Leo Cooper, 1994.

______. *A History of the British Cavalry, 1816 to 1919.* Vol. 7, *The Curragh Incident and the Western Front, 1914.* London: Leo Cooper, 1997.

Anglim, Simon, Phyllis G. Jestice, Rob S. Rice, Scott Rusch, John Serrati. *Fighting Techniques of the Ancient World, 3000 BC to 500 AD: Equipment, Combat Skills, and Tactics.* New York: St. Martin's Press, 2003.

Armstrong, Pete. *Bannockburn, 1314: Robert Bruce's Great Victory.* Oxford: Osprey, 2002.

Arnold, Thomas. *The Renaissance at War.* New York: Collins Books, 2001.

Arrian. *The Campaigns of Alexander.* Trans. Aubrey De Selincourt. Notes and introd. by J. R. Hamiliton. New York: Dorset Press, 1971.

Ayton, Andrew. *Knights and Warhorses: Military Service and the English Aristocracy under Edward III.* Rochester, NY: Boydell Press, 1994.

Babcock, Conrad S. "A Century of March Regulations." *Cavalry Journal* (October 1925).

Bachrach, Bernard S. "Caballus et Caballarius." *De Re Militari: The Society for Medieval Military History* www.deremilitari.org/resources/articles/bachrach3.htm.

______. "On Roman Ramparts, 300–1300." In *The Cambridge Illustrated History of Warfare: The Triumph of the West.* Cambridge: Cambridge University Press, 1995.

Bancroft-Hunt, Norman. *The Indians of the Great Plains.* Norman: University of Oklahoma Press, 1985.

Barclay, C. N. *Battle 1066.* Princeton, NJ: D. Van Dostrand, 1966.

Barthorp, Michael. *The Anglo-Boer Wars: The British and the Afrikaners, 1815–1902.* London: Blandford, 1991.

Bartlett, Clive. *English Longbowman, 1330–1515.* Oxford: Osprey, 1995.

The Battle of Hastings: Sources and Interpretations. Ed. Stephen Morillo. Suffolk, UK: Boydell Press, 1996.

"The Battle of Hattin (1187)." *De Re Militari: The Society for Medieval Military History* www.deremilitari.org/resources/sources/ctit2.htm.

Becke, A. F. *Nery, 1914: The Adventure of the German 4th Cavalry Division on the 31st August and the 1st September.* East Essex, UK: Naval and Military Press, n.d.

Bell, Caroline, Caroline Davis, and Susan McBane. *Horse and Pony Breeds: The Complete Handbook.* New York: Barnes and Noble Books, 2004.

"Bell VC." *Digger History: The Unofficial History of the Australian and New Zealand Armed Forces.* http://www.diggerhistory.info/pages-vc/bell-vc.htm.

Belloc, Hilaire. *The Tactics and Strategy of the Great Duke of Marlborough.* Bristol, UK: Arrowsmith, 1933.

Bennett, Matthew. "Development of Battle Tactics in the Hundred Years War." *De Re Militari: The Society for Medieval Military History* www.deremilitari.org/resources/articles/bennett2.htm.

Bernhardi, Frederick von. Trans. Charles Goldman. *Cavalry in Future Wars.* London: John Murray, 1909.

Biddulph, John. *The Nineteenth and Their Times: Being an Account of the Four Cavalry Regiments in the British Army That Have Borne the Number Nineteen and of the Campaigns in Which They Served.* London: John Murray, 1899.

Bilby, Joseph G. *A Revolution in Arms: A History of the First Repeating Rifles.* Yardley, PA: Westholme, 2006.

Black, Jeremy. *European Warfare, 1660–1815.* New Haven: Yale University Press, 1994.

Black, Robert W. *Cavalry Raids of the Civil War.* Mechanicsburg, PA: Stackpole Books, 2004.

Blackmore, Howard L. *British Military Firearms, 1650–1850.* London: Herbert Jenkins, 1963.

Bloch, Marc. *Feudal Society.* Trans. L. A. Manyon. Chicago: University of Chicago Press, 1974.

Bonie, Jean Jacques. "The French Cavalry in 1870." In *Cavalry Studies from Two Great Wars.* Kansas City, MO: Hudson-Kimberly, 1896.

Boniface, Jonathan. *The Cavalry Horse and his Pack. Being the World's Most comprehensive Military Study of the Equestrian Travel and Horse Packing.* Longrider's Guild Press, 2005 (Originally published Kansas City Mo. Hudson-Kimberly, 1903).

Bosworth, A. B. *Conquest and Empire: The Reign of Alexander the Great.* Cambridge: Cambridge University Press, 1988.

Boutell, Charles. *Arms and Armour in Antiquity and the Middle Ages.* Trans. M. P. Lacombe. Combined Books, 1996. Originally published London: Reeves and Turner, 1907.

Breeds of Livestock. Department of Animal Science, Oklahoma State University.

www.ansi.okstate.edu/breeds/horses/

Briscoe, Charles H., Richard Kiper, James Schroder, and Kalev Sepp. *Weapon of Choice: U.S. Army Special Forces in Afghanistan.* Fort Leavenworth, Kansas: Combat Studies Institute Press, 2003.

The Bronze Age and Early Iron Age Peoples of Eastern Central Asia. Ed. Victor H. Mair. Vol. 1. Washington DC: Institute for the Study of Man, 1998.

The Brooke Hospital for Animals. www.thebrooke.org/htdocs/Home_49.php.

Brown, John. "The Boer's Worst Enemy." *Digger History: The Unofficial History of the Australian and New Zealand Armed Forces.* www.diggerhistory.info/pages-conflicts-periods/other/boers.htm. Originally published in *Military History Magazine,* October 2001.

Brown, J. W. *Unit Organizations and Orders of Battle of the Great Armies of Europe, 1853–1870.* Minneapolis: Absinthe Press, 1994.

Brzezinski, Richard. *The Army of Gustavus Adolphus (2): Cavalry.* Oxford: Osprey, 1993.

_______. *Lutzen, 1632: Climax of the Thirty Years War.* Oxford: Osprey, 2001.

Brzezinski, R., and M. Mielczarek. *The Sarmatians, 600 BC–AD 450.* Oxford: Osprey, 2002.

Bukhari, Emir. *Napoleon's Cavalry.* San Rafael, CA: Presidio Press, 1979.

Burne, Alfred H. *The Crécy War: A Military History of the Hundred Years War from 1337 to the Peace of Bretigny, 1360.* London: Eyre and Spottiswoode, 1955.

Caesar, Julius. "Julius Caesar's War Commentaries." http://mcadams.posc.mu.edu/txt/ah/Caesar/index.html. Originally published as *Caesar's Commentaries.* Trans. W. A. McDevitte and W. S. Bohn. New York: Harper and Brothers, 1869.

Calloway, Colin. *One Vast Winter Count: The Native American West before Lewis and Clark.* Omaha: University of Nebraska Press, 2003.

The Cambridge Illustrated History of Warfare. Ed. Geoffrey Parker. Cambridge: Cambridge University Press, 2000.

Camp, John McK. *Horses and Horsemanship in the Athenian Agora.* Athens: American School of Classical Studies at Athens, 1998.

Carter, William H. *The U.S. Cavalry Horse.* Guildford, CT: Lyons Press, 2003.

The Cavalry. Ed. James Lawford. New York: Crescent Books, 1976.

Cavendish, William. *A General System of Horsemanship.* North Pomfret, VT: Trafalgar Square Publishing, 2000. A facsimile of the 1743 edition with introduction by William Steinkraus and technical commentary by E. Schmit-Jensen.

Cernenko, E. V. *The Scythians, 700–300 BC.* Oxford: Osprey, 1983.

Chambers, James. *The Devil's Horsemen: The Mongol Invasion of Europe.* London: Weidenfeld and Nicolson, 1979.

Chandler, David. *The Art of Warfare in the Age of Marlborough.* New York: Hippocrene Books, 1976.

______. *Dictionary of the Napoleonic Wars.* New York: Simon and Schuster, 1993.

Chappell, Mike. *British Cavalry Equipments, 1800–1941.* Oxford: Osprey, 1983.

Cheesman, G. L. *The Auxilia of the Roman Imperial Army.* Chicago: Ares, 1975.

Chenevix-Trench, Charles. *A History of Horsemanship.* New York: Doubleday, 1970.

Childers, Erskin. *German Influence on British Cavalry.* London: Edward Arnold, 1911.

Childs, John. *Armies and Warfare in Europe, 1648–1789.* New York: Homes and Meier Publishers, 1984.

______. *Warfare in the Seventeenth Century.* Washington, DC: Smithsonian Books, 2001.

Chun, Clayton K S. *US Army in the Plains Indian Wars, 1865–91.* Oxford: Osprey, 2004.

Churchill, Winston S. *Marlborough: His Life and Times* Vol. 2. Chicago: University of Chicago Press, 2002.

Circle of War in the Middle Ages: Essays on Medieval Military and Naval History. Ed. Donald J. Kagay and L. J. Andrew Villalon. Suffolk, UK: Boydell Press, 1999.

Citino, Robert M. *The German Way of War: From the Thirty Years War to the Third Reich.* Lawrence: University Press of Kansas, 2005.

Clayton, Anthony. *Paths of Glory: The French Army 1914–1918.* London: Cassell Military, 2003.

Clutton-Brock, Juliet. *Horse Power: A History of the Horse and the Donkey in Human Societies.* Cambridge: Harvard University Press, 1992.

Coddington, Edwin B. *The Gettysburg Campaign: A Study in Command.* New York: Scribner's, 1968.

Connolly, Peter. *Greece and Rome at War.* London: Greenhill Books, 1981.

______. *Tiberius Claudius Maximus: The Cavalryman.* Oxford: Oxford University Press, 1997.

Connolly, Peter, and Carol van Driel-Murray. "The Roman Cavalry Saddle." *Britannia* 22 (1991): 33–50.

Cooper, Leonard. *British Regular Cavalry, 1644–1914.* London: Chapman and Hall, 1965.

Cottrell, Arthur. *Chariot: From Chariot to Tank, The Astounding Rise and Fall of the World's First War Machine.* New York: The Overlook Press, 2005.

Cruso, John. *Militarie Instructions for the Cavallrie.* Notes and commentary by Peter Young. Kineton, UK: Roundwood Press, 1975. Originally published 1632.

Curry, Anne. *Essential Histories: The Hundred Years' War, 1337–1453.* Oxford: Osprey, 2002.

Dahmus, Joseph. *Seven Decisive Battles of the Middle Ages.* Chicago: Nelson-Hall, 1983.

Davis, R. H. C. *The Medieval Warhorse: Origin, Development, and Redevelopment.* Thames and Hudson, 1989.

De Camp, L. Sprague. "Before Stirrups." *Isis* 51, no. 2 (June 1960): 159–60.

Delbruck, Hans. *The Dawn of Modern Warfare: History of the Art of War.* Vol. 4 in *History of the Art of War.* Trans. Walter J. Renfroe Jr. Lincoln: University of Nebraska

Press, 1990. Originally published as vol. 4 of *Geschichte der Kriegskunst im Rahmen der Politischen Geschichte* in Berlin, 1923.

______. *Medieval Warfare: History of the Art of War*. Vol. 3 in *History of the Art of War*. Trans. Walter J. Renfroe Jr. Lincoln: University of Nebraska Press, 1990. Originally published as vol. 3 of *Geschichte der Kriegskunst im Rahmen der Politischen Geschichte* in Berlin, 1923.

De Re Militari: The Society for Medieval Military History. www.deremilitari.org/.

De Souza, Philip, Waldemar Heckel, and Lloyd Llewellyn-Jones. *The Greeks at War: From Athens to Alexander*. Oxford: Osprey, 2004.

DiNardo, R. L. *Mechanized Juggernaut or Military Anachronism? Horses and the German Army of World War II*. New York: Greenwood Press, 1991.

Dixon, Karen R., and Pat Southern. *The Roman Cavalry: From the First to the Third Century AD*. New York: Barnes and Noble Books, 1992.

Dossenbach, Monique, and Hans Dossenbach. *The Noble Horse*. New York: Portland House, 1987.

Drews, Robert. *Early Riders: The Beginnings of Mounted Warfare in Asia and Europe*. New York: Routledge, 2004.

______. *The End of the Bronze Age: Changes in Warfare and the Catastrophe ca. 1200 BC*. Princeton: Princeton University Press, 1993.

Drummond, Garrett B. "Some Famous War-Horses of Famous Leaders." *Cavalry Journal* 31, no. 128 (July 1922): 253–54.

Duffy, Christopher. *The Army of Frederick the Great*. New York: Hippocrene Books, 1973.

______. *Instrument of War*. Vol. 1 of *The Austrian Army in the Seven Years War*. Grand Rapids, MI: Emperor's Press, 2000.

______. *Prussia's Glory: Rossbach and Leuthen, 1757*. Chicago: Emperor's Press, 2003.

Dunlay, Thomas W. *Wolves for the Blue Soldiers: Indian Scouts and Auxiliaries with the United States Army, 1860–90*. Omaha: University of Nebraska Press, 1982.

"Einsatz- und Ausbildungszentrum für das Gebirgstragtierwesen 230." *Bundeswehr*. 2007. http://www.deutschesheer.de

Ellis, John. *Cavalry: The History of Mounted Warfare*. New York: G. P. Putnam's Sons, 1978.

Elting, John R. *Swords around a Throne: Napoleon's Grande Armée*. New York: Free Press, 1988.

Elton, Hugh. *Warfare in Roman Europe, AD 350–425*. Oxford: Clarendon Press, 1996.

The Encyclopedia of the Horse. Ed. Elwyn Hartley Edwards. New York: Dorling Kindersley, 1994.

Eschenbach, Wolfram Von. *Parzival*. Trans. A. T. Hatto. London: Penguin Books, 1980.

Farmer, George, and George R. Gleig, *The Adventurers of a Light Dragoon in the Napoleonic Wars. A Cavalryman during the Peninsular and Waterloo Campaigns, in Captivity and at the Siege of Bhurtpore, India*. New York: Leonaur, 2006.

Farrokh, Keveh. *Sassanian Elite Cavalry, AD 224–642.* Oxford: Osprey, 2005.

Felber, Bill. *The Horse in War.* Philadelphia: Chelsea House, 2001.

Ferrill, Arther. *The Origins of War: From the Stone Age to Alexander the Great.* London: Thames and Hudson, 1985.

"Feudalism." *HighBeam Encyclopedia.* www.encyclopedia.com. From *The Columbia Encyclopedia.* 6th ed. New York: Columbia University Press, 2006. www.encyclopedia.com/html/section/feudalis_characteristicsofeuropeanfeudalism.asp.

Eyewitnesses to the Indian Wars, 1865–1890. Vol. 5 of *The Army and the Indian.* Ed. Peter Cozzens. Mechanicsburg, PA: Stackpole Books, 2005

Fletcher, Ian. *Galloping at Everything: The British Cavalry in the Peninsular War and at Waterloo, 1808–15: A Reappraisal.* Mechanicsburg, PA: Stackpole Books, 1999.

"Fossil and Frozen Horses from Prehistoric Times: The Pazyryk Horses." December 19, 1998. *The Turanian Horse Website.* www.turanianhorse.org/prehistoric.html.

Fosten, Bryan. *Wellington's Heavy Cavalry.* London: Osprey, 1982.

Fowler, Jeffrey T. *Axis Cavalry in World War II.* Oxford: Osprey, 2001.

France, John. *Western Warfare in the Age of the Crusades, 1000–1300.* Ithaca, NY: Cornell University Press, 1999.

Froissart, Jean. *Chronicles.* Ed. and trans. Geoffrey Brereton. London: Penguin Books, 1968.

Fuller, J. F. C. *The Decisive Battles of the Western World.* London: Eyre and Spottiswoode, 1954.

______. *From the Defeat of the Spanish Armada, 1588, to the Battle of Waterloo, 1815.* Vol. 2 of *A Military History of the Western World.* New York: Da Capo Press, 1955.

Gabriel, Richard A. *Genghis Khan's Greatest General, Subotai the Valiant.* Norman: University of Oklahoma Press, 2004.

Gabriel, Richard A., and Karen S. Metz. *From Sumer to Rome: The Military Capabilities of Ancient Armies.* New York: Greenwood Press, 1991.

Gaebel, Robert E. *Cavalry Operations in the Ancient Greek World.* Norman: University of Oklahoma Press, 2004.

"Die Gebirgstragtiere der Bundeswehr." *Bundeswehr.* 2007. http://www.bundeswehr.de

German Army Handbook, April 1918. Nash, David, Introduction. New York: Hippocrene Books, 1977. Originally published by War Office, London, 1918.

"German Horse Cavalry and Transport," *Intelligence Bulletin*, March 1946. *Lone Sentry. Photos, Articles, and Research on the European Theater in World War II.* 2003–6. www.lonesentry.com/.

Glantz, David M. *Colossus Reborn: The Red Army at War, 1941–1943.* Lawrence: University Press of Kansas, 2005.

Goeldner, Christian T. *The Thoroughbred Field Hunter.* New York: A. S. Barnes, 1977.

Goldsworthy, Adrian. *The Complete Roman Army.* London: Thames and Hudson, 2003.

______. *The Roman Army at War 100 BC–AD 200.* Oxford: Clarendon Press, 1996.

______. *Roman Warfare.* London: Cassell, 2000.

Gonzaga, Paulo Gaviao. *A History of the Horse: the Iberian Horse from Ice Age to Antiquity.* J. A. Allen, 2004.

Goodman, Patricia L. "The Trakehner Horse–A History." *American Trakehner Association* www.americantrakehner.com/The%20Breed/history.htm.

Gorlitz, Walter, and Cord Von Hobe. *Georg v. Boeselager, Ein Reiterleben.* Dusseldorf: Verlag Sankt Georg GMBH, 1957.

Gravett, Christopher. *Norman Knight: 950–1204.* Oxford: Osprey, 1993.

______. *The World of the Medieval Knight.* New York: Peter Bedrick Books, 1996.

Grbasic, Z., and V. Vuksic. *The History of Cavalry.* New York: Facts on File, 1989.

Gullett, H.S. *The Australian Imperial Force in Sinai and Palestine, 1914–1918.* Sydney, AU: Angus and Robertson, 1923.

Hamilton, Jill. *Marengo: The Myth of Napoleon's Horse.* London: Forth Estate, 2001.

Handbook of the French Army. London: Imperial War Museum Department of Printed Books, 1995 (Originally published by the War Office, 1914).

Hanson, Victor Davis. *Carnage and Culture.* New York: Anchor Books, 2001.

______. *The Western Way of War: Infantry Battle in Classical Greece.* Berkley: University of California Press, 1989.

Harris, Susan. *The United States Pony Club Manual of Horsemanship: Advanced Horsemanship, B, HA, A Levels.* New York: Howell Book House, 1996.

Haythornthwaite, Philip. *Austrian Army of the Napoleonic Wars (2): Cavalry.* Oxford: Osprey, 1986.

Healy, Mark. *The Ancient Assyrians.* Oxford: Osprey, 1991.

______. *Cannae, 216 BC.* Oxford: Osprey, 1994.

______. *New Kingdom Egypt.* Oxford: Osprey, 1992.

______. *Qadesh, 1300 BC: Clash of the Warrior Kings.* Oxford: Osprey, 1993.

Herodotus. *History of Herodotus.* Trans. George Ralinson. *The Internet Classics Archive.* http://classics.mit.edu/Herodotus/history.html.

Herzog, Chaim, and Mordechai Gichon. *Battles of the Bible.* London: Weidenfeld and Nicholson, 1978.

Hildinger, Erik. *Warriors of the Steppe: A Military History of Central Asia, 500 BC to 1700 AD.* Cambridge, MA: Da Capo Press, 1997.

Hoen, Max v., and Egon Fhr. v. Waldstätten. *Die letzte Reiterschlacht der Weltgeschichte (Jaroslawice 1914).* Zurich: Amalthea, 1929.

Holmes, George, ed. *The Oxford Illustrated History of Medieval Europe.* Oxford: Oxford University Press, 1988.

Holmberg, Tom. Review of *Marengo: The Myth of Napoleon's Horse* by Jill Hamilton. A Review." *The Napoleon Series.* http://www.napoleon-series.org/reviews/biographies/c_hamilton.html.

Hook, Adam. *Rossbach and Leuthen 1757: Prussia's Eagle Resurgent.* Oxford: Osprey, 2002.

Hooper, Frederick. *The Military Horse.* 1st American ed. South Brunswick, NJ: A. S. Barnes, 1976.

Horse Breeds of the World. International Museum of the Horse. www.imh.org/imh/bw/home2.html.

The Horses of Gettysburg. Vol. 4 of *Civil War Minutes.* DVD. Dir. Mark Bussler. Pittsburgh: Inecom Entertainment, 2006.

Howard, Michael. *The Franco-Prussian War.* New York: Collier Books, 1961.

______. *War in European History.* Oxford: Oxford University Press, 1976.

Howorth, Henry H. *History of the Mongols, 9th–19th Century.* New York: Burt Franklin 1960. Reprints of the 1876 edition.

Huxley-Blythe, Peter J. *Under the St. Andrew's Cross: Russian and Cossack Volunteers in World War II, 1941–1945.* Bayside, NY: Europa Books, 2003.

Hyland, Ann. *Equus: The Horse in the Roman World.* New Haven: Yale University Press, 1990.

______. *The Horse in the Ancient World.* Westport, CT: Praeger Publishers, 2003.

______. *The Medieval Warhorse, from Byzantium to the Crusades.* Gloucestershire, UK: Sutton 1994.

______. *Training the Roman Cavalry: From Arrian's Ars Tactica.* Gloucestershire, UK: Sutton, 1993.

______. *The Warhorse, 1250–1600.* Gloucestershire, UK: Sutton, 1998.

Johnson, David. *The French Cavalry.* London: Belmont Publishing, 1989.

______. *Napoleon's Cavalry and Its Leaders.* New York: Holmes and Meier, 1978.

Johnson, Paul. *Horses of the German Army in World War II.* Atglen, PA: Schiffer Military History, 2006.

Kachler. "The German Cavalry in the Battle of Vionville–Mars-La-Tour." In *Cavalry Studies from Two Great Wars.* Kansas City, MO: Hudson-Kimberly, 1896.

Kagay, Donald J,. and L. J. Andrew Villalon, eds. *The Circle of War in the Middle Ages: Essays on Medieval Military and Naval History.* Suffolk, UK: Boydell Press, 1999.

Karasulas, Antony. *Mounted Archers of the Steppe, 600 BC–AD 1300.* Oxford: Osprey, 2004.

Katcher, Philip. *Union Cavalryman, 1861–1865: Weapons, Armour, Tactics.* Oxford: Osprey, 1995.

Keegan, John. *A History of Warfare.* New York: Vintage, 1994.

"The Kikkuli Method of Horse Training." *Splitters Creek Arabian Sport Horse Stud.* www.users.bigpond.com/splitterscreek/kikkuli%20books.htm.

Knight, Ian. *The Boer Wars (2), 1898–1902.* Oxford: Osprey, 1997.

______. *Boer Commando, 1876–1902.* Oxford: Osprey, 2004.

Knox, Alfred. *With the Russian Army 1914–1917.* New York: E. P. Dutton, 1921.

Konstam, Angus. *Peter the Great's Army 2: Cavalry.* Oxford: Osprey, 1993.

Kournakoff, Sergei N. *Russian's Fighting Forces.* New York: Duell, Sloan and Pearce, 1942.

Laffin, John. *Brassey's Battles: 3,500 Years of Conflict, Campaigns, and Wars from A–Z.* London: Brassey's Defence Publishers, 1986.

Lawrence, Elizabeth Atwood. *His Very Silence Speaks: Comanche, the Horse Who Survived Custer's Last Stand.* Detroit, MI: Wayne State University Press, 1989.

Legacy of the Horse: 56 Million BC–450 AD. "The First Horses." *International Museum of the Horse.* www.imh.org/imh/exh1.html.

"Letters of the Crusades Written from the Holy Land." www.shsu.edu/~his_ncp/Cruslet.html. Originally published as "Letters of the Crusaders Written from the Holy Land," in *Translations and Reprints from the Original Sources of European History,* trans. and ed. Dana Carlton Munro. Vol. 1, no. 4. Philadelphia: Department of History of the University of Pennsylvania, 1900.

Littauer, M. A. *Selected Writings on Chariots and Other Early Vehicles, Riding, and Harness.* Leiden: Brill, 2002.

Littauer, Vladimir. *The Development of Modern Riding: The Story of Formal Riding from Renaissance Times to Present.* New York: Howel Book House, 1962.

______. Russian Hussar: *A Story of the Imperial Cavalry 1911–1920.* Shippensburg, PA: White Mane Publishing Co, 1993.

Livingston, Phil, and Ed Roberts. *War Horse: Mounting the Cavalry with America's Finest Horses.* Albany, TX: Bright Sky Press, 2003.

Loch, Sylvia. *Dressage: The Art of Classical Riding.* North Pomfret, VT: Trafalgar Square Publishing, 2001.

Longacre, Edward G. *The Cavalry at Gettysburg: A Tactical Study of Mounted Operations during the Civil War's Pivotal Campaign, 9 June–14 July 1863.* Lincoln: University of Nebraska Press, 1986.

______. *Lee's Cavalrymen: A History of the Mounted Forces of the Army of Northern Virginia, 1861–1865.* Mechanicsburg, PA: Stackpole Books, 2002.

______. *Lincoln's Cavalrymen: A History of the Mounted Forces of the Army of the Potomac, 1861–1865.* Mechanicsburg, PA: Stackpole Books, 2000.

Lynn, John A. *The French Wars, 1667–1714: The Sun King at War.* Oxford: Osprey, 2002.

______. *Giant of the Grand Siécle: The French Army, 1610–1715.* Cambridge: Cambridge University Press, 1997.

MacDowall, Simon. *Adrianople, AD 378: The Goths Crush Rome's Legions.* Oxford: Osprey, 2001.

______. *Late Roman Cavalryman, AD 236–656.* Oxford: Osprey, 1995.

Maenchen-Helfen, Otto. *The World of the Huns: Studies in Their History and Culture.* Ed. Max Knight. Berkeley: University of California Press, 1973.

Malm, Gerhard A. *Bits and Bridles: An Encyclopedia* Valley Falls, KS: Grasshopper

Publishers, 1996.

Manual of Horse Mastership, Equitation and Driving. London: His Majesty's Stationery Office, 1929.

Marbot, Jean-Baptiste de. *Colonel of Chasseurs: A French Cavalryman of the Napoleonic Wars in the Retreat from Moscow, Lutzen, Bautzen, Katzbach, Leipzig, Hanau, and Waterloo.* Vol. 3 of *The Life of the Real "Brigadier Gerard."* New York: Leonaur, 2006.

______. *The Young Hussar: A French Cavalryman of the Napoleonic Wars at Marengo, Austerlitz, Jen, Eylau, and Friedland.* Vol. 1 of *The Life of the Real "Brigadier Gerard."* New York: Leonaur, 2006.

Markle, M. M. "Macedonian Arms and Tactics under Alexander the Great." In *Macedonia and Greece in Late Classical and Early Hellenistic Times.* Papers presented at a symposium at the National Gallery of Art, 14–15 November 1980, Washington DC: National Gallery of Art, 1982.

May, Timothy. *The Mongol Art of War.* Yardley, PA: Westholme Publishing, 2007.

McAulay, John D. *Carbines of the Civil War, 1861–1865.* Union City, TN: Pioneer Press, 1981.

McCall, Jeremiah B. *The Cavalry of the Roman Republic: Cavalry Combat and Elite Reputations in the Middle and Late Republic.* London: Routledge, 2002.

The Medieval Horse and Its Equipment. Ed. John Clark. Woodbridge, UK: Boydell Press, 2004.

Medieval Warfare: A History. Ed. Maurice Keen. Oxford: Oxford University Press, 1999.

Menning, Bruce. *Bayonets before Bullets: The Imperial Russian Army 1861–1914.* Bloomington: Indiana University Press, 1992.

Mercy, Randolph Barnes. *The Prairie Traveler.* Williamstown, MA: Corner House, 1968 (Originally published 1854).

Morgan, David. *The Mongols.* Cambridge, MA: Blackwell, 1986.

Muir, Rory. *Tactics and the Experience of Battle in the Age of Napoleon.* New Haven: Yale University Press, 1998.

Napoleon I. *The Military Maxims of Napoleon.* Ed. David G. Chandler. New York: Macmillan, 1988.

The Napoleon Series, 1995–2005. Ed. Robert Burnham. www.napoleon-series.org/.

Nicolle, David. *The Age of Charlemagne.* Oxford: Osprey, 1984.

______. *Armies of the Muslim Conquest.* Oxford: Osprey, 1993.

______. *Arms and Armour of the Crusading Era, 1050–1350: Islam, Eastern Europe, and Asia.* London: Greenhill Books, 1988.

______. *Attila and the Nomad Hordes.* Oxford: Osprey, 1990.

______. *Crécy, 1346: Triumph of the Longbow.* Oxford: Osprey, 2000.

______. *The Crusades.* Oxford: Osprey, 2001.

______. "Failure of an Elite–The Genovese at Crécy." Osprey, 2004.

______. *French Medieval Armies, 1000–1300.* Oxford: Osprey, 1991.

______. *Hattin, 1187: Saladin's Greatest Victory.* Oxford: Osprey, 1993.

______. *The Mamluks, 1250–1517.* Oxford: Osprey, 1993.

______. *Poitiers, 1356: The Capture of a King.* Oxford: Osprey, 2004.

______. *Saladin and the Saracens.* Oxford: Osprey, 1986.

______. *Saracen Faris, AD 1050–1250.* Oxford: Osprey, 1994.

______. ed. *Companion to Medieval Arms and Armour.* Suffolk, UK: Boydell Press, 2002.

Nigel, Thomas. *The Germany Army of World War I* (2). Oxford: Osprey, 2004.

Nolan, L. E. *Cavalry: Its History and Tactics.* With a new introduction and further reading by Jon Coulston. Yardley, PA: Westholme Publishing, 2007. (Originally published in 1854.

Nosworthy, Brent. *The Bloody Crucible of Courage: Fighting Methods and Combat Experience of the Civil War.* New York: Carroll and Graf, 2003.

______. *With Musket, Cannon, and Sword: Battle Tactics of Napoleon and His Enemies.* New York: Sarpedon, 1996.

Oakeshott, Ewart. *A Knight and His Horse.* 2nd ed. Chester Springs, PA: Dufour Editions, 1995.

______. *A Knight in Battle.* 2nd ed. Chester Springs, PA: Dufour Editions, 1998.

Oman, C. W. C. *The Art of War in the Middle Ages, AD 378–1515.* Ed. John H. Beeler. Ithaca, NY: Cornell University Press, 1953. Originally published 1885.

______. *A History of the Art of War in the Middle Ages.* Vol. 2, *1278–1485 AD.* London: Greenhill Books, 1998. Originally published 1924.

______. *Wellington's Army, 1809–1814.* London: Greenhill Books, 2006.

Osborne, Rex. "Operations of the Mounted Troops of the Egyptian Expeditionary Force, (continued)." *The Cavalry Journal,* January 1923, 38–39.

Ottevaere, James A. *American Military Horsemanship: The Military Riding Seat of the United States Cavalry, 1792 through 1944.* Bloomington, IN: AuthorHouse, 2005.

Pakenham, Thomas. *The Boer War.* New York: Random House, 1979.

Parker, Geoffrey. *The Military Revolution: Military Innovation and the Rise of the West, 1500–1800.* Cambridge: Cambridge University Press, 1988.

______. *The Thirty Years War.* London: Routledge, 1984.

Parker, Phil. *Armies of the Macedonian and Punic Wars, 350 to 150 BC: Organization, Tactics, Dress, and Weapons.* Goring by Sea: War Games Research Group, 1976.

The Penguin Encyclopedia of Ancient Civilizations. Ed. Arthur Cotterell. New York: Penguin Books, 1980.

Perrett, Bryan. *1918: The Last Great Cavalry Victory.* Oxford: Osprey, 1999.

Perroy, Edouard. *The Hundred Years War.* Bloomington: Indiana University Press, 1962.

Piekalkiewicz, Janus. *The Cavalry of World War II.* New York: Stein and Day, 1980.

Plutarch. *Fall of the Roman Republic: Six Lives.* Trans. Rex Warner. New York: Penguin Books, 1972.

______. "Plutarch's Parallel Lives: Alexander." *About.com.* http://ancienthistory.about.com/library/bl/bl_text_plutarch_alexander.htm.

Pluvinel, Antoine de. *The Maneige Royal.* Trans. Hilda Nelson. London: J. A. Allen, 1989. Based on the edition published by Gottfried Muller in Braunschweig, Germany, in 1626.

Podhajsky, Alois. *The Complete Training of Horse and Rider in the Principles of Classical Horsemanship.* Trans. Eva Podhajsky and V. D. S. Williams. Hollywood, CA: Wilshire Book, 1967.

Prestwich, Michael. *Armies and Warfare in the Middle Ages: The English Experience.* New Haven: Yale University Press, 1996.

Prioux. Trans. W. B. Bradford. *Cavalry before, during, and after the World War. Lectures by Lt. Col. Prioux at the French War College, 1923–1924 Course.* Fort Riley, KS: Cavalry School, 1925.

Public Broadcasting Service. "Interview: U.S. Special Forces ODA 595," *Frontline: Campaign against Terror.* Public Broadcasting Service (PBS), 1995–2006,

Pyhrr, Stuart W., Donald J. LaRocca, and Dirk H. Breiding Dirk H. *The Armored Horse in Europe, 1480–1620.* New York: Metropolitan Museum of Art, 2005.

The Red Army: The Red Army 1918–1945; The Soviet Army 1946 to the Present. Ed. B. H. Liddell Hart. New York: Harcourt, Brace, 1956.

Reed, Charles H. "The Rescue of the Lipizzans, a Personal Account," November 4, 1970. *The History Center.* http://history.dragoons.org/modules.php?op=modload&name=News&file=article&sid=146.

Reitz, Deneys. *Commando: A Boer Journal of the Boer War.* London: Faber and Faber, 1929.

Richter, Klaus Christian. *Kavallerie der Wehrmacht.* Wolfersheim-Berstadt, Ger.: Podzun-Pallas, 1994

Rickey, Don. *Forty Miles a Day on Beans and Hay: The Enlisted Soldier Fighting the Indian Wars.* Norman: University of Oklahoma Press, 1972.

Robichon de la Guérinière, Francois. *Ecole de Cavalerie.* Part 2. Cleveland Heights, Ohio: Xenophon Press, 1992. A partial reprinting of the 1733 edition.

Rothenberg, Gunther E. *The Army of Francis Joseph.* West Lafayette, IN: Purdue University Press, 1976.

______. *The Art of Warfare in the Age of Napoleon.* London: B. T. Batsford, 1977.

The R.O.T.C. Manual, Cavalry: A Textbook for the Reserve Officers' Training Corps. 13th ed. Harrisburg, PA: Military Service Publishing, 1942.

Rothero, Christopher. *The Armies of Crécy and Poitiers.* Oxford: Osprey, 1981.

Schulte, Erhard, and Eberhard von Velsen-Zerweck. Trans. Christina Belton. *The Trakehner.* London: J. A. Allen, 1981.

Seaton, Albert. *The Horseman of the Steppes: The Story of the Cossacks.* New York: Barnes and Noble, 1985.

Seward, Desmond. *The Hundred Years War: The English in France, 1337–1453.* London:

Penguin Books, 1978.

Shaw, Ian. *Egyptian Warfare and Weapons.* London: Shire Publications, 1991.

Simmons, Sue, ed. *The Military Horse: The Equestrian Warrior through the Ages.* London, Marshall Cavendish, 1976.

Sloan, John. "The Stirrup Controversy." *Internet History Sourcebooks Project.* www.fordham.edu/halsall/med/sloan.html. This work was posted by John Sloan on discussion list mediev-l@ukanvm.cc.ukans.edu on October 5, 1994 as part of the thread "The Stirrup Controversy."

Smith, Digby. *Charge! Great Cavalry Charges of the Napoleonic Wars.* London: Greenhill Books, 2003.

______. *The Prussian Army–To 1815.* Atglen, PA: Schiffer Military History, 2004.

Smith, G. Rex. *Medieval Muslim Horsemanship: A Fourteenth-Century Arabic Cavalry Manual.* London: British Library Board, 1979.

A Song for the Horse Nation: Horses in Native American Cultures. Ed. Emil Her Many Horses and George P. Horse Capture. Washington D.C.: National Museum of the American Indian, Smithsonian Institute, 2006.

Spalinger, Anthony J. *War in Ancient Egypt.* Oxford: Blackwell Publishing, 2005.

Speidel, Michael P. *Riding for Caesar: The Roman Emperors' Horse Guards.* Cambridge: Harvard University Press, 1994.

Spence, I. G. *The Cavalry of Classical Greece: A Social and Military History with Particular Reference to Athens.* Oxford: Clarendon Press, 1993.

Spencer, Charles. *Battle for Europe: How the Duke of Marlborough Masterminded the Defeat of France at Blenheim.* Hoboken, NJ: John Wiley and Sons, 2004.

Starr, Joan and Christopher Sweeney. *Forward: The History of the 2nd/14th Light Horse (Queensland Mounted Infantry).* Queensland, Australia.: University of Queensland Press, 1989.

Starr, Stephen. *From Fort Sumter to Gettysburg, 1861–1863.* Vol. 1 of *The Union Cavalry in the Civil War.* Baton Rouge: Louisiana State University Press, 1979.

Steffen, Randy. *The Horse Soldier, 1776–1943. The United States Cavalryman–His Uniforms, Arms, Accoutrements, and Equipments.* Vol. 1, *The Revolution, the War of 1812, the Early Frontier, 1776–1850.* Vol. 2, *The Frontier, the Mexican War, the Civil War, the Indian Wars, 1851–1880.* Vol. 3, *The Last of the Indian Wars, the Spanish-American War, the Brink of the Great War, 1881–1916.* Vol. 4, *World War I, the Peacetime Army, World War II, 1917–1943.* Norman: University of Oklahoma Press, 1977–79.

______. *United States Military Saddles, 1812–1943.* Norman: University of Oklahoma Press, 1973.

"Strabo: The Geography." http://penelope.uchicago.edu/Thayer/E/Roman/Texts/Strabo/home.html.

Suetonius. "The Lives of the Caesars, the Deified Julius." *The Ancient History Sourcebook Project.* www.fordham.edu/halsall/ancient/suetonius-julius.html.

Sumner, Ian. *The French Army 1914–18.* Oxford: Osprey, 1995.

Taylor, Colin. *The Warriors of the Plains.* New York: Arco Publishing, 1975.

Thompson, E. A. *The Huns.* Oxford: Blackwell Publishing, 1999. Originally published as *A History of Attila and the Huns.* Oxford: Oxford University Press, 1948.

Tincey, John. *Blenheim 1704: The Duke of Marlborough's Masterpiece.* Oxford: Osprey, 2004.

______. *Ironsides: English Cavalry, 1588–1688.* Oxford: Osprey, 2002.

______. *Soldiers of the English Civil War (2): Cavalry.* Oxford: Osprey, 1999.

Tomkinson, William. *The Diary of a Cavalry Officer in the Peninsular and Waterloo Campaign, 1809–1815.* Ed. James Tomkinson. 2nd ed. London: Frederick Muller, 1971.

Turnbull, Stephen R. *The Book of the Medieval Knight.* New York: Arms and Armour Press, 1995.

______. *Genghis Khan and the Mongol Conquests, 1190–1400.* Oxford: Osprey, 2003.

______. *Mongol Warrior, 1200–1350.* Oxford: Osprey, 2003.

Tylden, G. *Horses and Saddlery: An Account of the Animals Used by the British and Commonwealth Armies from the Seventeenth Century to the Present Day with a Description of their Equipment.* London: J. A. Allen, 1980.

Ure, John. *The Cossacks: An Illustrated History.* New York: the Overlook Press, 1999.

U.S. Cavalry Association. *Cavalry Combat.* Harrisburg, PA: The Telegraph Press, 1937.

USC-MSA Hadith Database. www.usc.edu/dept/MSA/fundamentals/hadithsunnah/muwatta/021.mmt.html#021.21.19.47.

Utley, Robert M. *Frontier Regulars: The United States Army and the Indian, 1866–1890.* New York: Macmillan, 1973.

Vegetius. [Flavius Vegetius Renatus.] *Roman Military.* Trans. John Clarke. Philadelphia, PA: Pavilion Press, 2004.

von Velsen-Zerweck, Eberhard, and Erhard Schulte. *The Trakehner.* Trans. Christina Belton. London: J. A. Allen, 1981.

Verbruggen, J. F. *The Art of Warfare in Western Europe during the Middle Ages: From the Eight Century to 1340.* Trans. Sumner Willard and R. W. Southern. 2nd ed. Suffolk, UK: Boydell Press, 1997. Originally published as *Der Krijgskunst in West-Europa in de Middeleeuwen, IXe to begin XIV eeuw*, Brussels, 1954.

Vernam, Glenn R. *Man on Horseback.* New York: Harper and Row, 1964.

Wagner, Arthur L. Editor. *Cavalry Studies from Two Great Wars.* Kansas City, MO: Hudson-Kimberly Publishing, 1896.

Wallace, R. I. *The Australians at the Boer War.* Commonwealth of Australia: The Australian War Memorial and the Australian Government Publishing Service, 1976.

Walter, Gilbey. *Small Horses in Warfare.* Honolulu, HI: University Press of the Pacific, 2003.

Warner, Philip. *The British Cavalry.* London: J. M. Dent and Sons, 1984.

Warnery, Emanuel von. *Remarks on Cavalry.* Introd. by Brent Nosworthy. London: Constable, 1997. Originally published in Great Britain, 1798.

Warry, John. *Alexander, 334–323 BC: Conquest of the Persian Empire.* Oxford: Osprey, 1991.

Washburn, Stanley. *The Russian Campaign. April to August 1915, Being the Second Volume of "Field Notes from the Russian Front."* London: Andrew Melrose, 1917.

Webster, Elizabeth. "The Caspian Horse Today." *Equiworld.net.* www.equiworld.net/uk/horsecare/Breeds/caspian/.

Webster, Graham. *The Roman Imperial Army of the First and Second Centuries AD.* 3rd ed. Norman: University of Oklahoma Press, 1998.

Wilcox, Peter, and Rafael Treviño. *Barbarians against Rome: Rome's Celtic, Germanic, Spanish, and Gallic Enemies.* Oxford: Osprey, 2000.

Williams, Brenda. *Ancient Egyptian War and Weapons.* Heinemann Library, 2003.

Williams, Dorian. *Great Riding Schools of the World.* New York: Macmillan, 1975.

Wise, Terence. *Armies of the Crusades.* Oxford: Osprey, 1978.

Wittenberg, Eric J. *Protecting the Flank: The Battles of Brinkerhoff's Ridge and East Cavalry Field. Battle of Gettysburg: A History and Tour Guide. July 2–3, 1863.* Celina, OH: Ironclad, 2002.

Wittenberg, Eric J. *Rush's Lancers: The Sixth Pennsylvania Cavalry in the Civil War.* Yardley, PA: Westholme Publishing, 2007.

Worley, Leslie J. *Hippeis: The Cavalry of Ancient Greece.* Boulder, CO: Westview Press, 1994.

Wrangel, Alexis. *The End of Chivalry: The Last Great Cavalry Battles, 1914-1918.* New York : Hippocrene Books, 1982.

Wyeth, John Allan. *That Devil Forrest: Life of General Nathan Bedford Forrest.* Baton Rouge: Louisiana State University Press, 1998.

Wylly, H. C. "Opposing View of the Action of the French and German Cavalry in the Great War." *The Cavalry Journal,* January 1923, 71–74.

Xenophon. *The Art of Horsemanship.* Trans. M. H. Morgan. London: J. A. Allen, 1962.

______. *The Persian Expedition.* Trans. Rex Warner. Introd. and notes by George Cawkwell. New York: Penguin Books, 1972.

Yakushin, Ivan. *On the Roads of War: A Soviet Cavalryman on the Eastern Front.* South Yorkshire, UK: Pen and Sword Books, 2005.

Index

Acknowledgments

This book could not have been written without the help of many people. Important assistance came from the staff of the U.S. Army's Combined Arms Research Library (CARL) at Fort Leavenworth Kansas. Their help in accessing the library's collection of military history works and especially the special collection of rare texts and complete volumes of the British and American cavalry journals was essential to my research and photo choices. Several horse breeders who specialize in rare breeds gave me the benefit of pictures and their expertise regarding the unique breed characteristics. These include Jessica Eile-Keith of KaraKum Akhal-Tekes; Peter Klandermans of the Foundation for the Preservation and Protection of the Przewalski Horse; Victoria Tollman of Brough Hill Fell Ponies and Tachara Caspians; and Joyce Covington of the Caspian Horse Society of the Americas. Several individuals were important to obtaining the unique pictures that represent the military horse and rider through the centuries: Nigel Apperley provided the excellent depictions of the Roman cavalry; Jasper Oorthuys contributed the pictures of Roman gravesites; John Garretson of the International Horse Archer Festival made available the superb pictures representing the Mongol horse archers; and Jerry Todd of the 1st Maine and Mark Sopko of the 2nd U.S. Cavalry provided excellent photos of Civil War reenactor cavalry in action. Joyce DiMarco, holder of German national riding badge in bronze, and Sallie Spenard, U.S. Dressage Federation gold medal rider, provided technical expertise on a variety of horse subjects as well as riding styles and techniques. Finally, a great deal of the ideas and concepts discussed within this book were first broached at the online forum of the Society of the Military Horse. The Society represents probably the single most knowledgeable assembly of experts on all aspects of the military horse. Finally, my greatest appreciation is to Pat Holscher of the Society of the Military Horse. Pat was irreplaceable in his role as critical reader, commenter, and motivator.